The New Y...

Guide to

Restaurants in New York City 2002

William Grimes
Eric Asimov

[handwritten notes:]

htst
Petrossian
7th ave bet. 56/57 next to Carnegie Hall

- Enterprise aircraft carrier
X-1 Chuck yeager

Shelly's bet 6th & 7th on W57th
mac & cheese hamburgers
crabs
canyon chanaters in ceuly
lunch or dinner

good bugers — delfrisco's 50th & 6th steak house McGraw Hill building
- Toy Rus

The New York Times
New York, New York

Please send all comments to:

The New York Times Restaurant Guide
122 E. 42nd St., 14th Floor
New York, NY 10168

Published by:
The New York Times
229 W. 43rd St.
New York, NY 10036

Copyright © 2002 The New York Times Co.
All rights reserved

ISBN 1-930881-03-7
Printed in the United States of America
First Printing 2001
10 9 8 7 6 5 4 3 2 1

For the New York Times: Mitchel Levitas, Editorial Director, Book Development; Thomas K. Carley, President, News Services Division; Nancy Lee, Director of Business Development.

Prepared by Elizabeth Publishing: *General Editor:* John W. Wright. *Senior Editors:* Alan Joyce and Alice Finer. *Researchers:* James Garver, Johanna Stoberock, Arlene Jacks.

Design and Production: G&H SoHo, Hoboken, N.J.; Jim Harris, Gerry Burstein.

Cover Design: Barbara Chilenskas.

Distributed by St. Martin's Press

Preface

The reviews in this guide are derived, for the most part, from the original ones written by William Grimes and Eric Asimov for *The New York Times* over the last three years. A number of reviews written by Ruth Reichl remain but many of the most popular restaurants have been updated by Mr. Grimes and Mr. Asimov for this book. All of these are noted. Other reviews by Ms. Reichl have been updated in various sections of the newspaper and on the *Times* Web site, NYToday.com. All reviews designated "$25 & Under" were written by Mr. Asimov.

Using This Book

What the Stars Mean:

☆☆☆☆	Extraordinary
☆☆☆	Excellent
☆☆	Very Good
☆	Good

Price Range: The dollar signs that appear at the top of each review are based on the cost of a three-course dinner and a 15 percent tip (but *not* drinks).

$	$25 and under
$$	$25 to $40
$$$	$40 to $55
$$$$	$55 and over

$25 & Under: A restaurant where you can get a complete meal, exclusive of drinks and tip, for $25 or less; recently, as a concession to inflation, some restaurants have been included where only an appetizer and main course total $25.

Abbreviations: Meals: B = Breakfast, Br = Brunch, L = Lunch, D = Dinner. LN = Late Night (restaurants open till midnight or later). **Credit cards**: AE = American Express; DC = Diner's Club; D = Discover; MC = Master Card; V = Visa; "All major" means at least three of these cards are accepted.

Table of Contents

Preface   iii

The Best New Restaurants in New York   **1**
   William Grimes

  What the Stars Mean   3
   William Grimes

Brooklyn and Queens: Cross a Bridge, Taste the World   **6**
   Eric Asimov

Ten Personal Favorites   **9**
   William Grimes   9
   Eric Asimov   13

Quick Guide to the Best Restaurants   **15**
   selected by William Grimes & Ruth Reichl

Quick Guide to the Best Inexpensive Restaurants   **17**
   selected by Eric Asimov

Restaurants of New York, A to Z   **19**

A Guide to Restaurants by Neighborhood   **439**
   The West Side
      West 100's   439
      West 90's   439
      West 80's   439
      West 70's   440
      Lincoln Center — West 60's   440
      Theater District — West 50's   441
      Theater District — West 40's   442
      Garment Ctr./Madison Sq. Garden — West 30's   443
      Chelsea and Environs — West 20's   443
      Chelsea and Environs — West 14th–19th   444

   The East Side
      East 100's   444

East 90's	444
East 80's	444
East 70's	445
East 60's	446
East 55th–59th	446
East 50th–54th	447
East 45th–49th	447
East 40th–44th	448
East 30's	448
East 20's	448
East 14th–19th	449
East Village (Below 14th St.)	449
Lower East Side	451
West Village/Greenwich Village	451
Chinatown	453
SoHo/TriBeCa	453
Financial District	455
The Bronx	455
Brooklyn	455
Queens	456
Staten Island	457
A Guide to Restaurants by Cuisine	**458**
A Guide to Restaurants with Special Features	**467**

The Best New Restaurants in New York

William Grimes

The collapse of the World Trade Center towers dealt a crushing blow to New York City, and the restaurant industry shared in the general calamity. One effect was immediate and permanent: **Windows on the World**, along with the **Greatest Bar on Earth** and **Wild Blue**, went hurtling to the ground, taking with it 79 restaurant workers, and a long, glorious chapter in New York dining. Restaurants in the area, which included such top-rank establishments as **Tribeca Grill**, **Chanterelle**, **Bouley Bakery** and **Danube**, closed for weeks. Planned openings were put on indefinite hold. Others may never reopen, and some restaurants, although not physically affected, knew that a depressed tourism industry and soft local demand spelled deep trouble. They saw the writing on the wall and folded. These included highly regarded restaurants like **Peacock Alley**, **Virot**, and **Meigas**.

It had already been a year of highs and lows. The economy was shaky, with the Dow going up and down like a yo-yo. Dot-com layoffs swelled to a stampede. But for much of the year New York restaurants were slow to get the message that the flush times might be over. Every week seemed to bring at least two or three notable restaurant openings. In fact, it would be hard to come up with a year in living memory in which New Yorkers could choose from as many new high-quality restaurants as they could in 2001, the year of three-star marvels like **Town**, **Craft**, **Pico** and **Ilo**; of sleekly executed American bistros like **The Dining Room**, **City Eatery** and **Ouest**. And toward the end came the cherry on the cake, Daniel Boulud's super-bistro, **DB Bistro Moderne**.

At times it seemed as if every restaurant had a one-syllable name and a location in a spanking new hotel. Hotel dining, which used to be synonymous with stuffy French food served in a stuffy French room, somehow became hip, as boutique hotels like the Hudson, W Union Square, and the Chambers Hotel offered sharp, contemporary design and a youthful feel that attracted a young, stylish clientele. Sometimes, the restaurant did nothing more than strike a hip attitude, like the abysmal **Hudson Cafeteria** in the Hudson Hotel, or the murky **Chinois-erie** in the Giraffe Hotel, yet another restaurant hoping to offer the allure of a lounge and night club.

Often, though, the hotels found top-rank chefs and gave them a showcase, and the chefs responded. At **Ilo** in the Bryant Park Hotel, across from the New York Public Library, Rick Laakkonen created a distinctive menu, American with global touches, that incorporated exotic ingredients like gooseneck barnacles and tea twigs. No matter how strange his ideas seemed on paper, they revealed a crystalline logic on the plate. A little farther uptown, in the new Chambers Hotel, Geoffrey Zakarian brought his own elegant brand of modern American cooking to a dramatic interior designed by the ubiquitous David Rockwell. Downtown, in the new restaurant row along Park Avenue South, Todd English established an outpost of his **Olives** chain in the W Union Square Hotel. English, the Franco Zefirelli of chefs, made his name with a florid, overblown style of cooking he calls "inspired Mediterranean." Jonathan Eismann, who left New York for Miami several years ago to open the highly praised Pacific Time, returned home and found a cozy spot in a hotel on Thompson Street, where he continues his adventures in Pacific Rim cooking at **Thom**. And the great Daniel Boulud, in a playful mood at **DB Bistro Moderne** in the City Club Hotel, showed that brilliant cooking was not incompatible with a rollicking, casual bistro. Hotel dining, against all odds, became chic last year. Once upon a time, the dining room off the lobby was the place you avoided. Suddenly, it became the place you couldn't get into.

It was not necessary to go to a hotel for good food. Tom Colicchio, the longtime chef at Gramercy Tavern, raised the curtain on his much anticipated **Craft**, a high-risk experiment in the art of simplicity. Diners at Craft are asked to assemble their own dishes from lists of basic ingredients, making decisions about flavor and texture combinations that are normally made in the kitchen. Craft places unusual demands on diners. But it also delivers magnificent food, prepared with a minimum of fuss. Colicchio, in a way, asks his customers to return to first principles, and experience the primal pleasure of unadulterated flavors. Terrence Brennan, the chef and owner of Picholine, indulged his passion for cheese in **Artisanal**, a handsome brasserie that he renovated to accommodate a menu of more than 200 cheeses from all over the world, and an ambitious wine list with more than 100 wines by the glass. In TriBeCa, the much admired John Villa came up with a highly personal interpretation of Portuguese food at **Pico**, a lovely, sophisticated restaurant that did justice to one of Europe's least-known cuisines.

Trend spotters were frustrated. There was no sexy new cuisine, or undiscovered region, to shine the spotlight on. But there was a drift toward pure flavors, simpler ideas and more pared-down presentations. **Craft** expressed the new mood perfectly. After a year when every plate seemed to be swathed in foam, and every dish was put through the deconstructionist wringer, New York's chefs rediscovered the beauty of basics. At **Bayard's**, Eberhard Müller, the longtime chef at Lutèce, put the menu back on a wholesome path that reflected his love of garden-fresh ingredients, many of them grown on his own farm. Restaurants like **City Eatery**, on the Bowery, seemed to take special pleasure in stripping their food of unnecesary adornment. At the same time, a number of chefs opted for intimate restaurants where they could practice a more personal style of cooking. The smallest was **NL**, one of the quirkiest restaurants to open last year. Does the Netherlands have a cuisine? Probably not. But it does have sturdy, appealing national dishes, and what better place to present them than downtown Manhattan? It took more than three centuries, but the Dutch finally made a comeback on the island they once owned. Who would have thought? It was that kind of year.

By autumn, the warning signs were becoming more insistent. The restaurant business was starting to go soft, even at blue-chip institutions like Jean Georges and Nobu. Anticipating a tough winter, restaurants began offering bargains, bonuses and special deals. Places like the Tonic and Patroon tempered their menus and their prices. The taste for simplicity, it turned out, might be just what the economy ordered. But with dozens of new restaurants already green-lighted, it was too late to put on the brakes. New York diners, already overserved, were going to get more, more, and still more. But the balance of power was tilting in favor of the consumer.

For restaurant owners, the year of living gloriously was about to become the year of living nervously. And when the World Trade Center came crashing down, all bets were off. It says something about New York that one of the first things that Mayor Rudolph Giuliani urged stunned residents to do was something they did better, and with less urging, than the citizens of any other city in America. In the midst of tragedy, with the smoke still rising in columns from Lower Manhattan, Mr. Giuliani exhorted New Yorkers to show their defiance and their determination to move forward by the simple act of going out to eat.

What the Stars Mean

Tracking the ins and outs, the ebb and flow, made for a busy year. Time and again, it forced me to rethink the critic's place in the dining picture. Restaurant critics may have power, but they don't have much pedigree. The modern restaurant did not appear until the 1760's, and for the next couple of centuries, the critical function fell to passionate amateurs, like Alexander Dumas or Brillat-Savarin, or to eminent chefs like Escoffier. The amateurs celebrated the pleasures of the table and the palate. The chefs delved into questions of technique, or set forth their culinary philosophy in a series of lofty pronouncements. The Michelin Guide has rated restaurants for more than a century, but their assessments, although critical, do not count as criticism.

Even in the 20th century, the most famous writers on food were not critics, but essayists and journalists who traveled with a pen in one hand and a fork in the other. A.J. Liebling and M.F.K. Fisher, to pull just two eminent names from the air, did not subject themselves to the week-in, week-out drudgery of eating at one restaurant after another and then filing an appraisal. They floated like butterflies from flower to flower, randomly and whimsically. In passing, they made critical remarks. Their body of work constitutes criticism of a kind. But it is not restaurant criticism as journalists know it today.

It's only in the last 30 years or so that daily newspapers and magazines have hired full-time employees whose job is to eat out regularly and report on the experience. I happen to be one of this happy band, but I am constantly amazed at how little the public, not to mention chefs and restaurateurs, understand the job — why it exists in the first place, the role it plays, and the standards that are used to size up a restaurant.

So. A few words of explanation. Although restaurant critics seem like potentates, chefs tremble at their approach, restaurant owners live in fear of their poison pens — they are nothing more than hired appetites. As a designated eater, I wander from bistro to trattoria to steakhouse to oyster bar, empowered with a fat expense account, and bring back nuts-and-bolts consumer information. A restaurant opens, and readers want to know the answers to the kind of questions that journalists have asked since the first newspaper went to press: who, what, where, when, how? What sort of restaurant is this? Who is the chef? What's on the menu? When does it serve food and how much does it cost? What does it feel like to eat there? What does it look like? Finally, and most important, how good is it? Should I go there and spend my hard-earned cash, or eat elsewhere?

In other words, I gather information, organize it in the form of a review, and in the end, make a judgment about quality, which is expressed in the stars (or lack of them) attached to every review. A lot goes into this judgment. Probably about 80 percent of a rating depends on the food, but food is not everything. Service matters. So does décor. For example, I was taken with the cooking at **71 Clinton Fresh Food** when it opened. It was imaginative, well-executed, visually arresting. It was also noisy and cramped, as you might expect in a little Lower East Side storefront. I thought of 71 Clinton as three-star food in a one-star setting, and my two-star rating reflected that reaction. Great food and abusive service does not earn as high a rating as great food and great service. The same goes for great food served in dismal surroundings. It did not hurt that **Danube**, David Bouley's splendiferous showcase for the cuisine of Austria-Hungary, was one of the lushest, most romantic interiors New York has seen. The visuals matter. So does the atmosphere, the service and the wine list. But nothing can compensate for mediocre food. I was enchanted by the multimillion-dollar renovation that transformed Le Régence into **Arabelle** at the Plaza Athénée, but the elegant dining room did not get food to match. Arabelle received a lone star, and I can think of several more restaurants whose investment in eye-popping design was more or less wasted. All of them could take a lesson from **Wallsé**, **Blue Hill** or **Fleur de Sel**, little neighborhood restaurants with minimally pleasing décors and terrific kitchens.

Much eating, and internal debate, yields a rating. The system often frustrates readers, chefs and restaurant owners. Some are downright perplexed. What separates a two from a three? Are four stars reserved for French restaurants? Why can't the world's greatest pizza parlor earn four? Why should chefs who have spent years perfecting their craft, and owners who have invested millions of dollars, have to see their efforts graded like a school exam?

I too find the star system frustrating at times. It is annoying to me that readers and restaurant owners obsess about the stars when they should be looking at the description and the judgments behind the stars. At the same time, the stars are a consumer convenience, a distilled expression of the content of a review, and in the end, I don't think the star system is any more irrational or complicated than baseball's strike zone. I often express the stars in terms of the power of a restaurant to derail a conversation. Imagine walking into a restaurant with two friends after seeing a film. At a one-star restaurant, the trio will leave with a sense of well-being, but the food will not come up in conversation more than a couple of times. At a two-star restaurant the conversation is equally divided between film and food. At a three-star, the food has taken over the conversation almost entirely. At a four-star, there's no conversation at all, only moans of ecstasy, and silent prayers of thanks.

On a scale of zero to four, each star covers a broad band. A restaurant that barely squeaks into the one-star category — a pretty nice neighborhood bistro — is not the same as a one-star that flirts with two. Variations within each category are inevitable, given the number of stars and the absence of half stars. But the review itself should clear up any confusion.

About that pizza parlor. No, it's never going to get four stars, no matter how good the pizza. If this seems unfair, think of Olympic skating. A good triple axel will always score higher than a perfect double axel. In cooking, too, the level of ambition matters. A neighborhood cafe lives in a different culinary universe than **Union Pacific** or **Restaurant Daniel**, or, to take the most lavish, most ambitious restaurant of them all, the new **Alain Ducasse at the Essex House**. I am certain that Mr. Ducasse can toss a mean pizza. But his mind is on other things, and when I go to his restaurant, so is mine.

Brooklyn and Queens: Cross a Bridge, Taste the World

Eric Asimov

In the last few years diners in search of good values have been left with one indisputable sentiment: Thank goodness for Brooklyn and Queens.

As the inexorable real estate machine has largely ground to dust the notion of the inexpensive Manhattan restaurant, Brooklyn and Queens have leaped into the breach, offering a fascinating spectrum of cuisines that, if they aren't always exactly cheap, are certainly less expensive than in Manhattan. The attitude on the Manhattan side of the East River, at least, seems to be: Let's take out our Hawaiian shirts, put on our pith helmets, grab our flashlights and go exploring!

Those who live in Queens and Brooklyn might well ask of their Manhattan counterparts: What took you so long to notice us?

Partisans of Queens have a point. For years, Queens has been the great American doorway to immigrants from all over the world, who've settled in ever-changing neighborhoods, found jobs and, of course, opened restaurants. Queens is the most ethnically diverse county in the world, demographers say, and anybody interested in the fascinating mosaic of world cuisines will find them in restaurants literally blocks apart in Queens.

Astoria, for example, houses dozens of Greek restaurants; it's regularly been called the largest Greek neighborhood outside of Greece. You can still find some good Greek restaurants in Astoria, like **Syros** on Broadway, for excellent dips and spreads and superb grilled fish, or **Christos Hasapo-Taverna** on 23rd Avenue, for fine steaks and occasional specials, like roasted piglet and baby lamb.

But more and more, the best restaurants in Astoria are not Greek at all. Walk on Steinway Street between 25th and 28th Avenues, for example, and as you pass Middle Eastern bakeries, where the smell of sweet tobacco smoke emerges from countless hookahs, you'll find **Mombar** and **Kabab Café**, top-flight Egyptian restaurants. Walk another block toward 24th Avenue and you'll find **Ubol's Kitchen**, an excellent Thai restaurant. Over on 28th Avenue is **Churrascaria Girassol**, a tiny rodizio with some of the best Brazilian food in New York. And on 31st Street near Ditmars Boulevard is **Trattoria L'Incontro**, an impeccable Italian restaurant.

6

Prowl some other neighborhoods and the contrasts will be amazing. At the corner of 37th Avenue and 74th Street in Jackson Heights you'll feel as if you're in the middle of India, with wonderful selections before you like **Dimple**, a simple takeout shop with simple but wonderfully spiced vegetarian food from the Gujarat region, and **Delhi Palace**, for complex curries from the north.

Within a couple of blocks, though, the entire environment changes and you may feel you've entered South America, a continent of diverse cuisines, from the largely pre-Columbian Peruvian, which you can taste at **Inti Raymi** (86-14 37th Avenue), to the almost European steak-based dishes of Argentina at **La Portena** (74-25 37th Avenue) to say nothing of Colombian, Bolivian or Ecuadorian restaurants, which you can also find easily.

As far as Queens goes, the neighborhoods are just beginning. Flushing is an Asian food-lovers paradise, with fascinating regional Chinese cuisines along with Malaysian and Korean restaurants. The original and best **Joe's Shanghai**, where the soup dumpling craze began a few years ago, is in Flushing, as is **East Buffet and Restaurant**, a huge and fascinating Chinese food hall.

In Forest Hills and Rego Park is a growing eastern European population, whose specialties you can sample at restaurants like **Salut** on 108th Street, a kosher Uzbek that serves lagman, a soup overflowing with lamb and vegetables, along with warm housemade loaves of bread. And you can try some of New York's best pizza at **Nick's** on Ascan Avenue.

Corona, Jackson Heights and Woodside are filled with thriving tacquerias like **La Nueva Espiga** on 102nd Street and **La Lupe** on Greenpoint Avenue, and if you head toward Jamaica, you'll find many southern restaurants, including neighborhood institutions like **Carmichael's Diner** on Guy Brewer Boulevard, where you'll find salty, leathery country ham, a wonderful acquired taste.

The atmosphere in Brooklyn is completely different, especially in neighborhoods like Carroll Gardens, Boerum Hill, Park Slope and Williamsburg, where the immigrants have come largely from Manhattan. In the last few years, restaurateurs, too, have fled the high cost of doing business in Manhattan, and have sought out the warmer, more welcoming Brooklyn neighborhoods.

Park Slope is perhaps the hottest of all, and has drawn such Manhattan success stories as **Blue Ribbon**, which opened on Fifth Avenue, and Johannes Sanzin, a critically acclaimed chef who opened **Bistro St. Mark's** on St. Mark's Avenue, along with countless other smaller places like **Chip Shop**, a truly British fish-and-chippery, **Rose Water**, which serves New American dishes with a Middle Eastern accent, and **Convivium Osteria**, a romantic Mediterranean spot.

Smith Street continues to boom, with another wave of successes like **Smith Street Kitchen** and **Panino'teca 275** taking their places alongside of barely more established restaurants like **Saul** and the **Grocery**. And some restaurants are pioneering new territories, like Clinton Hill, where **Locanda Vini & Olii**, a marvelously passionate trattoria, opened in a restored apothecary.

As good as these restaurants are, it would be a shame to neglect neighborhoods outside of Manhattan's gravitational pull. Flatbush Avenue beyond Prospect Park is home to some wonderful Jamaican roti shops and jerk stands, like **Danny and Pepper**, which occupies one wall within a Korean fish market, and offers excellent jerk chicken, spicy, well-charred and subtly smoky.

In Sunset Park, one of New York's well-dispersed Mexican neighborhoods offers streets full of bakeries, groceries and taquerias like **Tequilita's** at 5213 Fourth Avenue, for fine pozole and tacos. Close by is a largely Chinese neighborhood, where you can find good Vietnamese restaurants as well, like **Gia Lam** on 5402 Eighth Avenue. Bay Ridge is full of old-style Italian restaurants, while in Brighton Beach and Bensonhurst you have to read Cyrillic to understand the signs in the restaurants.

Manhattanites, sadly, are a provincial lot and proud of it. "Oh, I never go above 14th Street," downtowners like to gloat, just as uptowners never cross 42nd. How fortunate are those visionary few, who know they need only cross a bridge to see and taste the world.

Ten Personal Favorites

William Grimes

When people find out that I am a restaurant critic, they have two questions. Why aren't you fat? And what's your favorite restaurant. I have an answer for the first one. (I come from a long line of thin people.) But the second is, by its nature, unanswerable. Serious eaters have no single favorite, just as serious readers cannot single out one author, and moviegoers could not possibly settle on the one film they'd take to a desert island. But critics most certainly do have favorites, plural. Some of them are great restaurants. Others suit a certain kind of mood, or satisfy a particular craving. Still others have an intangible appeal that keeps you coming back, even though, objectively, they are not in the top rank, or even the second rank. The list that follows contains restaurants that represent all of the above. They're the places I look forward to eating at the most, time after time after time. If only I could get the time. They are presented in no particular order.

Bouley Bakery   For me, this is the tops. The setting is intimate, with a sense of luxury that's not overblown. This is TriBeCa, after all. David Bouley, the chef and owner, is a fearsomely temperamental, idiosyncratic chef, with something of the mad scientist about him. His food is sublime: subtle, adventurous, exquisite. Years later, I'm still reeling from his Japanese yellowtail, braised to a melting tenderness, that came with a simple accompaniment of shiitake mushrooms and glazed scallions in an ethereal, perfumed ginger sauce. Bouley is American, but French refinement and finesse informs every dish he sends out of the kitchen. And the prices, tempered by the location, have always made this restaurant a bargain relative to Manhattan's other top spots.

Daniel   There comes a time, when nothing less than the big splurge will do. For me, Daniel is worth whipping out the checkbook for. This is haute all the way. The surroundings are sumptuous, the service a model of perfection, and the cooking a pure French dream. Boulud is a country boy from the Lyons area. His training is classical, but his roots are deep in the French countryside, and his cooking, pure and refined, has always had a hearty, rustic tinge to it. I still wait for the second coming of an earthy terrine of oxtail, foie gras and mushrooms that melted in my mouth and made me go weak in the knees. The wine list is a graduate course in great vintages, but you can find terrific regional wines at a bargain price too. The cheese cart is second to none, and the desserts are designed to ravish. Do the soigné Upper East Siders who patronize the place savor every bite and play it over in their minds when they leave? I don't think so. They come because Daniel is the right sort of place, frequented by the right sort of people. The very rich are different from you and me. They get the best and barely know it. But I do.

Solera   I know that when I sit down, a small dish of salty green manzanilla olives will appear in front of me, my cue to order an icy copita of manzanilla sherry. Solera has a courtly atmosphere, and a suave Spanish interior that makes pleasing use of decorative glazed tiles. The restaurant has been serious about Spanish food from the beginning, and even more serious about Spanish wines and sherries. It also organizes adventurous dinners based on specific regional cooking styles; or it might create a menu designed to be enjoyed with five different styles of sherry. This is the kind of restaurant that, when an unusual fish comes in, makes phone calls to its regulars so they can run over. Solera stays the same, but it's always changing, which keeps me coming back. It isn't cheap, but it delivers a very civilized dining experience.

Sushi Yasuda   On a dingy block east of Grand Central, Sushi Yasuda, with its celery-green facade, glows like some strange mineral. Inside, it has a serene, almost spiritual atmosphere, perfectly fitting for this purist's haven. The sushi here comes in a startling number of varieties, and although I never did manage to come on a day when anglerfish was available, I did have six kinds of mackerel, and tuna presented in seven degrees of fatness, right up to the nth degree of otoro, or belly tuna, which melts almost on the way to your mouth. Sushi is only half the story. Appetizers and side dishes are equal partners here. It might be steamed monkfish liver in a tart ponzu sauce, or a textural medley of six seaweeds, arranged like small tumbleweeds on a white rectangular plate. Maomichi Yasuda, the chef, began his career in Japan as an eel chef. That background is reflected in the profusion of eels available on the sushi menu, and in an appetizer that I think of as the greatest bar snack ever invented: deep-fried eel backbones. Don't think about it. Just eat.

Fleur de Sel   Every chef dreams of opening his own little place and serving the food he loves best. Cyril Renaud didn't just think about it, he did it. He quit La Caravelle, found a little spot in the Flatiron District, brought over his father from France to do the decorating, and opened the doors. The result is one of the most charming restaurants in the city, a tiny, out-of-the-way spot with barely 10 tables, and the chef's artwork on the walls, that flourishes for the oldest and best of reasons: the chef has talent, and he cares, because it's his show. Renaud knows in a quiet sort of way how to create excitement on the plate. It might be an unfamiliar ingredient, like kamut, the fat-kerneled ancient Egyptian grain related to wheat, which makes a chewy, nutty accompaniment to his lamb loin marinated in Dijon mustard and thyme. It might be an unexpected flavor combination, like rose water and apricots, the unlikely partnership in a purée, which seems to coax extra richness and depth from seared foie gras. Or it might be a particularly satisfying presentation, like a neat rosette of mussels on a circular bed of tiny chopped vegetables, dressed with mustard oil and surrounded by confetti-color dots of sauce. When couples want a romantic spot where love can bloom, I send them here.

Wallsé   Cyril Renaud isn't the only chef dreaming a little dream. Kurt Guttenbrunner just happens to dream in a different language. He's Austrian, and Wallsé, in the West Village, is his personal theater for homey food that might seem to be a tough sell. Figure-conscious New Yorkers fear weight, and Austrian cuisine would seem to be fear on a plate. But Wallsé, sunny and airy, delivers the goods in a very appealing, lightened-up way. Even the desserts are light. Is it possible that Austrian food can be elegant? Guttenbrunner makes you think so with appetizers like asparagus and chanterelles in a riesling sauce, or yellow pike, its skin seared to a thick crackle, with thick strips of lightly marinated green and yellow squash accented with lemon thyme. You can also go for the gusto with rostbraten and goulash. The real national genius lies in desserts. You will be puzzled at the word "quark" on the menu. It is a cheese, and it goes into the making of a heavenly dumpling that melts on the tongue like manna. It's served with roasted apricots stuffed with red currants. The Austrian wine list makes for fun exploring. As neighborhood restaurants go, this breaks new ground.

Grand Central Oyster Bar   For anyone who wants the taste, the sights, and the sounds of real New York, this is the place. Skip the restaurant, which is very expensive and not worth it. I always head for the low-slung counters where fast-moving waitresses throw down the knives and forks, get the order fast, and then bring it fast. For years, when work has frazzled me, I have crept over to Grand Central for a half-dozen oysters, an oyster pan roast and a bottle of Bass ale. The combination promotes mental healing. I look forward to the small basket of superb biscuits that appear as soon as you sit down, and the oversize paper menu crowded with the names of oysters harvested all over North America. Will it be Blue Points, Malpeques, Olympias or Bras d'Or from Canada? It's a tough call. The pan roast is easy. It's a creamy stew, with a slight peppery zing, thick with soaked bread and plump oysters. New Yorkers have been eating it forever, and I hope I will too.

Tea and Sympathy Frequent travel to England over the years has given me a taste for unreconstructed working-class English food. It's a weakness, and Tea and Sympathy caters to it. This is the place for a cholesterol-laden English breakfast, for scones with clotted cream and jam, for steak and kidney pie, and for desserts buried under Bird's custard. The place is cramped, and you usually have to wait for a table. It's worth it if you love pork pie, strong tea and sweet desserts. This is comfort food in its most primitive form, and there are days when I find its lure irresistible. The food is modestly priced, and now there's a Plan B for those days when there's no chance of getting a table. **A Salt and Battery**, next door, is run by the Tea and Sympathy people. It's a fish-and-chips shop that does it the right way. And where else can you get a deep-fried battered sausage, followed by a deep-fried battered Mars Bar for dessert?

Manducatis Manducatis looks like a corner saloon. You have to walk past the bar and deeper into the premises to see that it's a restaurant, and then you have to understand that the menu means nothing. Wave it away. Then consult with Vincenzo Cerbone, the owner, and ask him what his wife, Ida, is making in the kitchen. It's a safe bet that there will be an appetizer of pasta tossed with Marzano tomatoes and porcini mushrooms sauteed in garlic. Succulent baby pig is a frequent main course. Chicken on a bed of radicchio is another favorite. One time, Mr. Cerbone had come back from Italy with a jar of olives in olive oil. He spooned out about four olives and some golden oil onto a slice of grilled bread. I've never had a better appetizer. The wine list is impressive, the pricing unpredictable, the atmosphere Italian through and through. And it's in my neighborhood. I wish I could eat here once a week.

Sac's Pizza. On weekends, after I pick up dry cleaning, buy cat food, get the car washed and harvest tomatoes from the backyard, I'm hungry. Lately I've been hungry for something very specific: two slices of thin-crust pizza and a cold Dr. Pepper from a little place in the neighborhood that used to be no great shakes. It's called Sac's, and it serves food I think of as neighborhood Italian. Things like baked ziti and linguine with clam sauce. The main draw for me is the brick pizza oven, which for quite some time turned out mediocre pizza. Then, for reasons I don't understand, the pizza got good. The crust became extra thin and crackling crisp. The tomato sauce got concentrated, and it was applied generously. (I am always dispirited by the sight of a pizza worker spreading out sauce with the round end of a ladle until it is nearly transparent on the dough). The cheese is properly melted and chewy. I step into Sac's, luxuriate in the blast of air conditioning, and secure a place at the counter. In five minutes I'm looking at two fat slices, hot from the oven, and I proceed to gorge. The bill? Four dollars and fifty cents.

Eric Asimov

Contrary to popular belief, the restaurant reviewing business has a definite downside. I spend so much time seeking out new places that I rarely have time to go back to the places I love, much less ingratiate myself with the chefs and owners.

Ah, the joys of being a regular. Imagine returning again and again to a place where they know your name, where your table is always open and where they cater to your preferences. I can hear it all now: "The chef has a little something you might like," they tell me as they begin to shave truffles over a surprise offering of fresh pasta. Or, "We have one glass left of the Grands Echezeaux, and we've saved it for you."

Of course it's pure fantasy. Maybe familiarity can't help but breed contempt. But it's my fantasy, and these are the restaurants I would return to again and again, if I had the chance.

Al Di La is the mom-and-pop trattoria of my dreams, a little place where the Venetian cooking is gutsy and passionate, whether pasta or simple ingredients like calf's liver or tripe.

Anytime I need to remind myself how good a steak can be, I return to **Peter Luger**, where the porterhouse for two is the benchmark of beef. The rough-and-tumble beer-hall environment, the veteran waiters and the ritual slicing of the steak and pouring of the juices all combine to form the perfect milieu to savor Luger's porterhouse perfection.

For beef of a different cut, the garlic-scented, vinegary pastrami sandwich at **Katz's Deli** is unsurpassed. The Carnegie Deli comes close, but the hand-carving at Katz's makes a textural difference.

I love great barbecue, which would make me one unhappy New Yorker longing for trips to Texas, but for **Pearson's Texas Barbecue**, an unlikely little place hidden in the back of a sports bar in Jackson Heights, Queens. Let others gorge on ribs or pulled pork; the true aficionado knows that the barbecue cut of choice in Texas is brisket. Pearson's is superb, rosy in the middle, crisp on the exterior and gloriously smoky.

As long as I'm enjoying American regional fare, let me not forget the best fried chicken in New York, at **Charles's Southern-Style Kitchen**, a small takeout counter in Harlem.

Great sushi is a spoiler, making it awfully hard to consider ordinary sushi again, and the best sushi I've had in the last year was at **Jewel Bako**, a wonderful little spot in the East Village. The combination of congenial atmosphere, extraordinary fish and a well-chosen wine and sake list makes Jewel my dream sushi bar.

Great Chinese food is the birthright of all New Yorkers, and I can't think of anyplace where the Sichuan food is as consistently excellent as at **Grand Sichuan International**, from tea-smoked duck to sliced conch in wild pepper sauce. The long educational booklet handed out with the menu makes for entertaining and enlightening reading.

Friday lunch at **Montrachet** is like a secret club for those aware that the restaurant opens for lunch only that day. A bottle from the fabulous wine list along with one of the delicious French dishes is a perfect segue to the weekend. Alternatively, the $35 lunch at **Cello** is one of the best-kept secrets in town. Laurent Tourondel's French seafood menu is wonderful. And if I'm by myself, I love to sit down at the bar at **Union Square Cafe** for whatever the special of the day is, with a selection or two from the wonderful list of wines by the glass.

If I want to go all out, I think of **Jean Georges**. Jean-Georges Vongerichten has his ups and downs — occasionally his creations are overly academic — but when he is on, his bold artistry with flavors and textures is unsurpassed.

This list of restaurants, however wonderful, feels incomplete. I'm still looking for an Indian restaurant to make my own, as well as a Thai and a Jamaican. I want a Mexican place, too, and a Vietnamese and Middle Eastern, and many more. Just keep the light on for me.

Quick Guide to the Best Restaurants

☆☆☆☆ — Extraordinary

Bouley Bakery	Jean Georges	Lespinasse
Daniel	Le Bernardin	

☆☆☆ — Excellent

Alain Ducasse	Gramercy Tavern	Park Bistro
Aquavit	Honmura An	Patria
Atlas	Ilo	Patroon
AZ	Judson Grill	Peter Luger
Babbo	Kuruma Zushi	Picholine
Café Boulud	La Caravelle	Pico
Cello	La Côte Basque	San Domenico
Chanterelle	La Grenouille	Sushi Hatsu
Craft	Le Cirque 2000	Sushi Yasuda
Danube	March	Tabla
Felidia	Molyvos	Town
Fifty Seven Fifty	Montrachet	Union Pacific
Seven	Next Door Nobu	Veritas
The Four Seasons	Nobu	
Gotham Bar and Grill	Oceana	

☆☆ — Very Good

Ada	Campagna	Etats-Unis
Alison on Dominick	Canal House	F.illi Ponte
An American Place	Chelsea Bistro & Bar	Firebird
Annissa	Chez Josephine	Fleur de Sel
Aquagrill	Cho Dang Gol	Gabriel's
Arqua	Chicama	Grill Room
Artisanal	Christer's	Guastivino's
Aureole	Churrascaria	Hangawi
Balthazar	Plataforma	Heartbeat
Bambou	Cinque Terre	Hudson River Club
Bayard's	Circus	Icon
Beacon	City Eatery	I Coppi
Beppe	City Hall	Il Valentino
Bice	D'Artagnan	Inagiku
Blue Hill	DB Bistro	I Trulli
Blue Ribbon Sushi	Destinée	Joe's Shanghai
Bolo	The Dining Room	L'Actuel
Bond Street	Eight Mile Creek	Layla
Brasserie	Eleven Madison Park	Le Colonial
Butterfield 81	Esca	Le Perigord
Cafe Centro	Estiatorio Milos	Local

Lutèce
Manhattan Ocean
  Club
Maya
Mercer Kitchen
Mesa Grill
Mi Cocina
Michael Jordan's
Michael's
Nadaman Hakubai
Nick & Toni's Cafe
Nicole's
Odeon
Orsay
Otabe
Ouest
Palio
Paola's

Park Avenue Cafe
Park View at the
  Boathouse
Payard Patisserie
Petrossian
Ping's
Ping's Seafood
Quilty's
Remi
River Cafe
Ruby Foo's
Salaam Bombay
Screening Room
Sea Grill
71 Clinton Fresh Food
Shaan of India
Shun Lee Palace
Smith & Wollensky

Solera
Surya
Tamarind
Tocqueville
The Tonic
Tribeca Grill
Triomphe
"21" Club
27 Standard
Union Square Café
Virot
Wallsé
Water Club
Zarela

☆ — Good

Abajour
Aleutia
Alva
American Park
Angelo & Maxie's
Arabelle
Asia de Cuba
Avra
Baldoria
Barrio
Blue Water Grill
Bobby Van's
Bouterin
Brasserie 8 $^1/_2$
Calle Ocho
Candela
Cendrillon
Chinghalle
Commune
Coup
Dawat
Della Femina
Delmonico's
Dim Sum Go Go
District
Dock's Oyster Bar

Downtown
14 Wall Street
Frank's
Goody's
Grand Sichuan
Gubbio
The Grocery
Il Buco
Il Giglio
Jack Rose
Jane
Korea Palace
L'Absinthe
La Grolla
La Nonna
Lentini
Le Zinc
Maloney & Porcelli
Maritime
Nicholson
NL
Novitá
Ocean Grill
Olives
One If By Land, Two
  If By Sea

Onieal's Grand Street
Papillon
Pastis
Peasant
Pop
Primavera
Provence
Red Bar Restaurant
The Red Cat
Redeye Grill
Riodizio
Scalini Fedeli
Sparks
Strip House
Tappo
The Tasting Room
Tavern on the Green
Trattoria dell'Arte
Trois Marches
Verbena
Viceversa
Village
Vine
Vox
West 63rd Street
  Steak House

Quick Guide to the Best Inexpensive Restaurants

Selected by Eric Asimov

Al Di La
Bali Nusah Indah
Bar Pitti
Bistro St. Mark's
Brawta Caribbean
    Café
Bright Food Shop
Café La Grolla
Carnegie Deli
Charles's Southern-
    Style Kitchen
Christos Hasapo-
    Taverna
Churrascaria Girassol
Coco Roco
Congee Village
Cooke's Corner
Cookies & Couscous
Cyclo
Da Ciro
Dakshin
Diner
East Buffet and
    Restaurant
El Cid
El Presidente
The Feeding Tree
Ferdinando's
    Focacceria
Flor's Kitchen
Funky Broome
Garden Cafe
Gennaro

Grand Sichuan
    International
Han Bat
Holy Basil
'ino
Jean Claude
Jewel Bako
Joe's Shanghai
    (Flushing branch)
Katsu-Hama
Katz's Deli
Komodo
Kori
La Esquina Criolla
La Flor
La Fonda Boricua
La Palapa
Lavagna
Le Jardin Bistro
Le Tableau
Le Zie
Little Basil
Locanda Vini & Olii
Lombardi's
Los Dos Rancheros
    Mexicanos
Luca
Lupa
Mama's Food Shop
Mavalli Palace
Mexicana Mama
Mirchi
Miss Williamsburg

Moustache
National Cafe
New Green Bo
Nha Trang
Our Place Shanghai
    Tea Garden
Pao
Pearl Oyster Bar
Pearson's Texas
    Barbecue
Pepolino
Po
Pongal
Prune
Queen of Sheba
Royal Siam
Sabor
Smith Street Kitchen
Snack
Soba Nippon
Soba-Ya
SoHo Steak
Taco Taco
The Sultan
Topaz Thai
Turkuaz
Ubol's Kitchen
Vatan
Velli
Wu Liang Ye
Xunta

For the latest restaurant reviews and directions by car or mass transit, check online at **New York Today**:

www.nytoday.com/restaurants

Restaurants of New York, A to Z

A $25 & Under NEW AMERICAN

947 Columbus Ave. (near 106th St.) (212) 531-1643
Credit cards: Cash only Meals: Br, L, D

A is more of a lounge than a restaurant, with several mis-matched tables and room for 15 or so. The menu offers only six dishes at a time. Chef Marc Solomon and his fiancée Blue Grant have turned A into an extension of their home, greeting every-one who comes through the door. A sweet 60's vibe pervades the premises, and when it's time to leave, hugs and kisses abound. They've wisely disencumbered themselves of distrac-tions. A place to wait? There's a bench outside. A wine list? Bring your own, if you don't mind sipping from a drinking glass. The two best dishes by far are broiled snails and a curried lamb pie. There are two desserts that are quite good: a dense chocolate and coffee cheesecake that actually tastes like fine espresso, and a subtle peach-and-mango cake.

Other recommended dishes: Rabbit pâté, roasted pear with goat cheese. **Price range:** Savory dishes, $8–$10; desserts, $6. **Wheelchair access:** Tightly packed tables, narrow entrance to restroom.

Abajour ☆ $$$ BISTRO/FRENCH

1134 First Ave. (at 62nd St.) (212) 644-9757
Credit cards: All major Meals: D, LN

A respectable neighborhood bistro with pleasing décor, an attractive menu and some well-priced wines: just what this neighborhood needs. Abajour's interior has a bright, summery look, and tall freestanding lamps allude to the restaurant's name, an adaptation of the French for lampshade (abat-jour). The menu fits the tone, with several smart little twists.

The humble-sounding country pâté, fresh-tasting and gener-ously portioned, shames a lot of the higher-priced meat spreads in the city. Fish and frites, the cheapest of the entrees, may be plain, but it makes a very good showing. Even better is a grilled prime sirloin steak smothered in roasted-garlic herb butter. Aba-jour does not make a big fuss about this steak, but it is an incredibly juicy, flavorful piece of meat.

Desserts do not make the pulse pound. Three little chocolate biscotti appear with the check. Seize them. They are as good as any of the desserts.

Other recommended dishes: Shaved fennel with cremini mushrooms; grilled tuna with parsnip purée; duck confit with bean purée; banana split; chocolate pot de crème; strawberry shortcake. **Wine list:** About 60 well-chosen American and French wines, seven by the glass, four by half bottle. **Price range:** Apps., $6.50–$14; entrees, $15–$29; desserts, $6.50. Prix fixe, $30. **Wheelchair access:** Restrooms on street level.

Acme Bar & Grill $ CAJUN/SOUTHERN

9 Great Jones St. (bet. Broadway & Lafayette St.) (212) 420-1934
Credit cards: D/MC/V   Meals: Br, L, D

More kitschy bar than grill, the food, nevertheless, is decent, filling and moderately priced. Music is loud (with live performances downstairs at Acme Underground) and the décor is clichéd, with all the familiar trappings: road signs, beer signs, Mason jars, etc. Marian Burros recommends the meatloaf.

Price range: Apps., $4.50–$8.50; entrees, $6.95–$14.95; desserts, $4–$4.50. **Wheelchair access:** Fully accessible. **Features:** Smoking permitted. **Services:** Catering, delivery, takeout, private parties.

Acquario $25 & Under   MEDITERRANEAN

5 Bleecker St. (near Bowery)   (212) 260-4666
Credit cards: Cash only   Meals: D   Closed Sun.

With its candles, brick walls and casual service, Acquario is a small, warm place straight out of the Village's bohemian past. The menu starts with salads and flows seamlessly through large appetizers — a couple of which can easily make a light meal — into main courses. Acquario's fresh sardines have a strong, briny aroma but a mild, wonderfully nutty flavor and are served with a small green salad. Fennel salad is also wonderful, though it's hard to find a more alluring dish than Portuguese fish stew.

Other recommended dishes: Boquerones (Spanish anchovies); risotto cakes; grilled chipilones (squid); grilled gambas (big shrimp); penne with bacalao (salted cod); crema Catalana (Spanish crème brûlée); warm chocolate cupcake. **Wine list:** Includes some unusual choices and terrific values. **Price range:** Apps., $5–$10; entrees, $12–$18. **Services:** Private parties.

Ada ☆☆ $$$$ INDIAN

208 E. 58th St. (at Second Ave.)   (212) 371-6060
Credit cards: All major   Meals: L, D

Ada aims to elevate the status of Indian cuisine in New York. The name, in Urdu, means something done with style or flair, and the owner has definite ideas about what style can do for Indian food. The décor, for one thing, steers clear of Indian fabrics, ornate brass plates and beaded curtains. The owner is intent on giving the food an upgrade as well. The results, for the most part, disarm criticism.

One of the best appetizers is a slow-grilled white-pea and potato cake accented with garam masala, fennel and cilantro, and surrounded by caramelized bananas coated with creme fraiche. Spices are used with great delicacy. Goan barbecue ribs, for example, have a down-home immediacy, but a dry rub of chilis and garam masala and the tang from an apple-vinegar marinade create a complex swirl of flavors. Tandoori usually means desiccated, artificially reddened meat. At Ada, the spices and marinades penetrate every fiber of the meats, which arrive in a state of melting tenderness. The syrupy, sour-sweet tamarind sauce makes the ideal foil for chicken suffused with the flavors of saffron, garam masala and chilies.

The dessert menu uses a few Indian ingredients strategically, with some success. Coconut panna cotta, covered with a slick of ice-wine gelee and tiny apple dice, has a perfect sweet-tart balance, and there's a surprise at the bottom of the dish, a firm layer of coconut-cardamom rice.

Other recommended dishes: Crab Malabar, escabeche of rock shrimp and tuna, seek kebabs, biryani, Kerala fish curry, ginger mint lamb chops, apple chutney and ladyfingers. **Wine list:** A spare list of 20 wines that have little to do with the food. **Price range:** Lunch: Apps., $10; entrees, $16; desserts, $9. Three-course prix fixe, $28. Dinner: three-course prix fixe, $55 or $65. **Wheelchair access:** Several steps down to the dining room. Restrooms down one flight or up one flight.

Adrienne $$$ FUSION
Peninsula Hotel, 700 Fifth Ave. (at 55th St.)   (212) 903-3918
Credit Cards: All major   Meals: L, D

Comfortable luxury in the newly refurbished Peninsula Hotel. Cozy seats, widely spaced tables and an eclectic menu with Asian notes featuring extravagant dishes like caviar-topped oysters, sautéed foie gras, halibut wrapped in banana leaves and crispy veal sweetbreads with parsley jus and salsify tapioca custard. Don't miss the seriously decadent white chocolate soufflé with caramel-bourbon sauce.

Price range: Apps., $10–$16; entrees, $21–$29; desserts, $8–$10. Prix–fixe business lunch, $38; pre–theater, $40; brunch, $45, $25 for children. Afternoon tea, $30. **Wheelchair access:** Fully accessible. **Services:** Private parties.

Aesop's Tables $$ NEW AMERICAN

1233 Bay St., Staten Island   (718) 720-2005
Credit cards: All major   Meals: L, D

From the bountiful garden at this warm little country restaurant, you can actually see stars. The menu features contemporary American items like asparagus, fennel and grapefruit salad, and seared chicken glazed with lingonberries and balsamic vinegar.

Other Recommended dishes: Lamb chops glazed with honey and balsamic vinegar; grilled steak rubbed with spices. **Price range:** Lunch: $4–$8. Dinner: apps., $4–$9; entrees, $14–$20; desserts, $5.**Features:** Smoking permitted, outdoor dining. **Wheelchair access:** Fully accessible. **Services:** Takeout, catering, private parties.

Afghan Kebab House $ AFGHANI

764 Ninth Ave. (bet. 51st & 52nd Sts.)   (212) 307-1612
155 W. 46th St. (bet. 6th & 7th Aves.)   (212) 768-3875
1345 Second Ave. (bet. 70th & 71st Sts.)   (212) 517-2776
74-16 37th Ave., Jackson Heights, Queens   (718) 565-0471
Credit cards: AE   Meals: L, D

Expect huge portions of mildly spiced kebabs and rice at these small, narrow places that are favorites with cab drivers. The food is filling and occasionally heavy, but you won't find many better buys near the theater district.

Alcohol: Bring your own. **Price range:** Apps., $3; entrees, $10–$15; desserts, $3. **Wheelchair access:** One step up at Ninth Ave. location. **Services:** Delivery, takeout, catering, private parties.

Alain Ducasse   ☆ ☆ ☆ $$$$ FRENCH

155 W. 58th St. (bet. Sixth & Seventh Aves.)   (212) 265-7300
Credit cards: All major   Meals: L (Thurs.-Fri.), D (Mon.-Fri.)

In its opening weeks, Alain Ducasse at the Essex House had the unmistakable look of a giant gilded turkey. But now, the outlines of a great restaurant can be seen. Mr. Ducasse, although not known as a chef plagued by self-doubt, has made changes, all for the better. Many of the annoying affectations have been dropped. No longer are diners asked to select the ergonomically perfect squab knife from a catalog's worth of choices. The adventurous but short wine list, which changes weekly, now arrives at the table backed up by a reserve list. The menu, now easier to read, offers two set-price formulas. The prices still make Ducasse far more expensive than any other restaurant in the city, which means that Mr. Ducasse must ravish his customers with every meal or invite their seething resentment. The service can seem overproduced and cluttered in the restaurant's confined space, but the waiters have worked out the dance steps, and what could be an overbearing formality is tempered by warmth.

Most important, the food is coming into sharp focus. Warm sea scallops, no bigger than a button, are sweetly melting, topped with a little dollop of osetra caviar. They come with a gauzy lemon cream sauce, just weighty enough to enrich the scallops but still transparent. A crust of lemon rock salt gives extra crunch and a precise spark of acidity to a lightly seared fillet of striped bass surrounded by plump clams. There's a kind of humility, too, in the dish described, in aw-shucks fashion, as "boiled country chicken with vegetables." It may be from the country, it's definitely boiled, but this is a rube dressed in Versace. Accessorized with white truffles, a simple chicken breast comes swathed in an insolently retrograde Albufera sauce, a chicken velouté that Mr. Ducasse has quietly upgraded with foie gras butter and a blend of Madeira, Cognac and port. This gold-plated 19th-century classic is executed here with absolute mastery. This is the kind of food that disarms criticism. You raise your eyes and give thanks.

There are still some quibbles. Mr. Ducasse seems convinced that to make an impression in Manhattan, he has to dazzle the natives, either by flashing shiny objects or distracting them with a shower of trinkets. The restaurant has more wheeled vehicles than Canal Street at rush hour. The Arizona beef looks gorgeous, but whatever the cattle are chewing out there in the great Southwest is not translating into flavorful meat. Desserts, although perfectly respectable, seem stolid and uninspired. And the cheese service still seems to draw out all of Mr. Ducasse's neuroses. The fairly orthodox cart carries a stingy selection of only six cheeses, two of them American and one English.

A "Bargain" Lunch

A bargain is a relative thing. In the rarefied world of Alain Ducasse, a $65 lunch counts as a supersaver discount. This modest three-course option (called the menu salad) is for those who want a taste of Ducasse before taking the ultimate plunge. It's a light lunch but an exceptionally fine one. The salad, served with the main course, arrives at the table unassembled. A waiter does the mixing and tossing, then applies a Caesar dressing. The well-orchestrated result is a salad that reminds you how refreshing a good salad can be, and that greens can have flavor as well as color. It nearly upstages the main course.

Main course choices may include shreds of peekytoe crab, sweet and juicy, pressed into a chilled round threaded with fresh mint and accompanied by a citrus marmalade. Another entree consists of sliced chicken breast enrobed in an ivory-colored sauce, a lightly interpreted Caesar dressing with Parmesan and anchovy flavors mediated by rich chicken stock.

Desserts, like a beautifully concentrated cherry granité and cherry marmalade with pistachio ice cream and goat-milk curd, make no pretense of restraint. You also get a glass of wine with the meal and mignardises after.

Wine list: An international list of about 150 wines changes weekly. It is supplemented by a 500-bottle list heavily slanted to Bordeaux and Burgundy. Both are pricey, with more than half the wines on the shorter list costing more than $100. **Price range:** Lunch and dinner, three-course prix fixe, $145; four-course, $160; five-course truffle menu, $250. **Wheelchair access:** Enter on Central Park South; restrooms on dining room level.

Al Bacio $ ITALIAN
1679 Third Ave. (at 94th St.)   (212) 828-0111
Credit cards: All major   Meals: Br, L, D

This low-key trattoria on the Upper East Side is a notch above the pasta mills that line the nearby streets, with pleasant, moderately priced pastas and pizzas. It's a nice place to bring children.

Alcohol: Beer and wine. **Price range:** Lunch: prix fixe, Mon.–Fri., $7.95. Dinner: apps., $5.50–$7.95; entrees, $8–$16.95; desserts, $4–$5. Brunch, $8.95. **Wheelchair access:** Dining room accessible with assistance; restrooms accessible. **Features:** Kid friendly. **Services:** Delivery, takeout, private parties.

Al Di La $25 & Under   ITALIAN
248 Fifth Ave., Park Slope, Brooklyn   (718) 783-4555
Credit cards: Cash only   Meals: D   Closed Tue.

The food at Al Di La is soulful and gutsy, with profound flavors. This neighborhood restaurant serves on bare wooden tables, but hints at a more sensual attitude with such luxurious touches as velvet drapes and chandeliers. The chef coaxes deep flavors out of simple dishes, and all the pastas are wonderful.

Recommended dishes: Braised rabbit with olives; steamed pork shoulder; sautéed liver; grilled hanger steak; baked sea bass; casunziei ravioli; bigoli in salsa; malfatti; tagliatelle with meat sauce; tripe Milanese; baccalá mantecato; apple crisp; poached pear. **Price range:** Apps., $5.50–$8; entrees, $8–$16. **Wheelchair access:** Small step in front; narrow entrance to restroom. **Services:** Takeout.

Aleutia ☆ $$$$

220 Park Ave. (at 18th St.)
Credit cards: All major

NEW AMERICAN
(212) 529-3111
Meals: L, D

When out-of-towners dream of an up-to-the-minute Manhattan restaurant, aswirl with youthful prime movers and pulsing with glamour, Aleutia is just the sort of place they want to be beamed into. The style starts at the door, where two futuristic L.C.D. panels seductively flash the menu in a slow, throbbing pulse of light. There's a lot more of it in the retro lounge, and still more in a dining room suspended over the main floor.

The food fits the script. It is fresh and contemporary, with lots of eye appeal and a sly way of interweaving Asian ingredients with down-home American favorites, like strip steak with creamed spinach and fried onion rings in a won-ton batter. The food is often very good. But just as often things go awry. Many dishes sound intriguing, and much thought has gone into the visual presentation. But after the buildup comes the letdown. There's nothing tricky, however, about exceptionally moist and flavorful free-range poussin with roasted mushrooms in herbed gravy and truffled whipped potatoes. And venison loin, smoked over a birch-wood fire, trembles at the threshold of greatness. Desserts tend to be overly sweet and heavy, with two pleasant surprises. The first is the startlingly fresh scoop of spearmint ice cream next to the nicely executed molten chocolate cake. The cardamom cappuccino float with cinnamon cajeta macadamia nut crunch, served in a parfait glass and topped with foamed milk, may be the best thing on the dessert menu.

Other recommended dishes: Slow-basted salmon, red and golden beet noodles with goat cheese. **Wine list:** A nicely chosen list of about 70 international wines, modestly priced, with 18 wines by the glass. **Price range:** Lunch: apps., $7–$9; entrees, $14–$18; desserts, $9; three-course prix fixe, $20. Dinner: apps., $10–$15; entrees, $25–$32; desserts, $9; five-course tasting menu, $65; seven-course tasting menu, $82. **Wheelchair access:** Restrooms are on street level.

The Algonquin $$

59 W. 44th St. (bet. Fifth & Sixth Aves.)
Credit cards: All major

AMERICAN
(212) 840-6800
Meals: B, Br, L, D, LN

The lobby and restaurant of the famous hotel have been redecorated to the tune of several million dollars. Even so, the ghost of Dorothy Parker will probably not take up residence. Now a lobby more than a restaurant, it offers modern dishes like grilled shrimp in a roasted garlic salsa, as well as hamburgers, lobster hash and Caesar salad. As long as you're not looking for a real meal, it's fine for a nibble before or after the theater.

Price range: Lunch: apps., $10–$13; entrees, $13–$24; desserts, $9. Dinner: apps., $11–$16; entrees, $18–$29; desserts, $9. **Wheelchair access:** Fully accessible. **Features:** Smoking permitted. **Services:** Catering, private parties.

Alison on Dominick ☆☆ $$$$ French
38 Dominick St. (bet. Varick & Hudson Sts.)   (212) 727-1188
Credit cards: All major   Meals: D

One of New York City's most surprisingly romantic restaurants is hidden away on an obscure SoHo side street. The light here is perfect: so soft and dim that everybody looks good. The music is perfect, too: loud enough to hear and low enough not to intrude. The design is so simple it seems unplanned, but it has an easy, offhand elegance. The food and wine list are primarily French and overwhelmingly wonderful.

Wine list: Nearly every wine on this small, well–chosen and reasonably priced list would be worth ordering. Pay special attention to the wines from Provence, which go well with the food. **Price range:** Apps., $11–$20; entrees, $27–$33; desserts, $9–$14. Prix fixe, 5:15–6 P.M., $20.02 and $30.02. **Wheelchair access:** Dining room on one level, but the restrooms are down a steep flight of stairs. **Services:** Catering, private parties.

Alley's End $25 & Under   Bistro/New American
311 W. 17th St. (bet. Eighth & Ninth Aves.)   (212) 627-8899
Credit cards: D/MC/V   Meals: D

Enter a portal and traverse a passageway, and you leave the workaday Chelsea world for Alley's End, a lovely network of dining rooms and gardens that feels as pastoral and isolated as an oasis. The brief American menu (with some international notes) manages to match the romantic draw of the interior.

Recommended dishes: Grilled quail and warm quinoa; grilled monkfish; wilted chicory salad. **Price range:** Apps., $6–$9; entrees, $14–$22; desserts, $6–$9. **Wheelchair access:** Five steps down from street level. **Features:** Good for business, romantic, smoking permitted. **Services:** Private parties.

All State Cafe $$ Cafe
250 W. 72nd St. (bet. Broadway & West End Ave.)
   (212) 874-1883
Credit cards: Cash only   Meals: Br, L, D, LN

This convivial little place is the epitome of the neighborhood hangout. The bar in front is almost always filled with people who seem to know everybody else there. Couples, both young and old, and families crowd the rear. In addition to drinks, beer and a sensible little wine list, All State serves fine burgers and other simple dishes.

Price range: Lunch: $7.50–$9. Dinner: apps., $6.50–$9.75; entrees, $11–$16; desserts, $3.50–$5. Brunch: $8.75–$11. **Wheelchair access:** Not accessible. **Features:** Smoking permitted. **Services:** Takeout.

Alouette $25 & Under   Bistro/French
2588 Broadway (near 97th St.)   (212) 222-6808
Credit cards: All major   Meals: Br, D

Early crowds seemed to overwhelm the kitchen, but Alouette now seems to have gotten both the food and the quality of service under control. Dishes are cleverly conceived, beautifully presented and moderately priced; each item promises excitement. Service has its ups and downs, and the second-floor dining room is warm and stuffy.

Recommended dishes: Morels and asparagus in veal stock; squid salad; warm potato tart; tuna; pike in saffron broth; roasted flounder; seafood pot-au-feu; hanger steak; vacherin (vanilla ice cream sandwiched between airy meringues). **Price range:** Apps., $5.50–$8; entrees, $15–$18.50. **Wheelchair access:** Two steps in front; restrooms are narrow. **Services:** Catering, private parties.

Alva ☆ $$$ New American
36 E. 22nd St. (bet. Park Ave. S. & Broadway)   (212) 228-4399
Credit cards: All major   Meals: L, D, LN   Closed Sun.

A friendly haven in a neighborhood overburdened with overheated restaurants, Alva is a casual American bistro serving interesting food and featuring an impressive wine list. The perfect meal can begin with an assortment of hors d'oeuvres, a little plate of tidbits that changes regularly but is always welcome. Then a plate of crisp-crusted grilled salmon, vegetables tossed with lemon balm and a small mountain of rich mashed potatoes. At lunch try the hamburger and the grilled chicken paillard with a warm bean salad. With the exception of the chocolate pudding, every dessert is wonderful.

Other recommended dishes: Crispy shrimp cocktail; gazpacho; shortcake; apple pie; cheese plate. **Wine list:** The long list has many interesting and hard-to-find wines at very fair prices. One criticism: some of the most tempting wines are far more expensive than the food. **Price range:** Lunch: entrees, $10–$16. Dinner: apps., $6–$11; entrees, $15–$26; desserts, $8. Prix-fixe dinner, 5:30–7 P.M.: $29.95, three courses (includes glass of wine or beer for patrons of Gramercy Theatre). **Wheelchair access:** Restrooms not accessible. **Features:** Smoking permitted. **Services:** Takeout.

Amaranth $$

21E. 62nd St. (at Madison Ave.)
Credit cards: All major

(212) 980-6700
Meals: L, D, LN

This is a casual, expensive bistro where beautifully dressed Upper East Siders kiss the air around each other's cheeks. Many dishes are bland; exceptions include a fine thin, crisp focaccia topped with arugula, goat cheese and tomatoes; a thick rich lentil soup, and tough but meaty short ribs. People go to Amaranth for the same reason that they go to dinner parties — for the company, not the food.

Price range: Lunch: apps., $7–$10.50; entrees, $15–$22; desserts, $7. Dinner: apps., $8–$16; entrees, $15–$24; desserts, $7. **Wheelchair access:** Fully accessible. **Features:** Smoking permitted. **Services:** Delivery, takeout, private parties.

Amarone $25 & Under

686 Ninth Ave. (near 47th St.)
Credit cards: All major

ITALIAN
(212) 245-6060
Meals: L, D

The rectangular dining room at this friendly restaurant, named after the powerful red wine from northeastern Italy, is bright and happy, suffused with the appetizing aromas of bread, herbs and olive oil. The centerpiece of the menu is a selection of fresh pastas with an ever-changing choice of sauces like strangolapreti ("priest stranglers"), fluffy twists of pasta served in a marinara sauce given a pleasantly bitter kick by broccoli rape.

Other recommended dishes: Pappardelle with shiitake mushrooms and truffle paste; agnolotti stuffed with veal, beef and Parmesan; farfalle with leeks, fontina and ham; watercress, pear and pecorino salad; broiled calamari; apple tart; hazelnut gelato. **Wine list:** Includes a dozen Amarones, mostly from excellent producers, but the list as a whole is too expensive. **Price range:** Apps., $4.50–$8.95; entrees, $7.95–$19.95. **Wheelchair access:** One step up at entrance. **Features:** Romantic, smoking permitted, outdoor dining. **Services:** Delivery, takeout, private parties.

American Park ☆ $$$

Battery Park (near State St.)
Credit cards: All major   Meals: Br, L, D

NEW AMERICAN
(212) 809-5508
Closed Sun.

Note: This neighborhood suffered substantial damage during the September 11, 2001 plane crashes that destroyed the World Trade Center. This restaurant may not be operational by the time you plan your visit.

This restaurant may offer Manhattan's most spectacular view: from the big-windowed room you look right out at the ferries chugging toward the Statue of Liberty. The mostly seafood menu is inventive and beautifully presented. The restaurant is so earnest and hard-working that you really want to admire it. So why is it that I have such a hard time appreciating it? It is mainly a matter of excess. The chef seldom uses a single ingredient when he can use two. A few dishes stand out: tuna tartar, perked up with ginger, shallots and toasted sesame seeds, is cool, clear and elegant. Black sea bass, simply roasted in the wood-burning oven and topped with cracked coriander, red onions and capers, is almost always excellent. At the end of the meal, the impulse to excess suddenly becomes an asset: The pastry chef has terrific fun turning chocolate mousse cake into the Statue of Liberty, scooping green tea ice cream onto coconut cake and serving a plum tart with white peaches and a perfectly restrained basil ice cream.

Other recommended dishes: Dry-aged sirloin; braised short ribs; pistachio and strawberry torte; warm citrus gratin. **Wine list:** Large, interesting, all-American and oddly chosen for the food. **Price range:** Apps., $9–$17; entrees, $18–$32; desserts, $8. Outdoor grill salads, sandwiches and snacks, $7–$11. **Wheelchair access:** Everything at ground level. **Features:** Good view, outdoor dining (patio). **Services:** Catering, private parties.

Amy Ruth's $25 & Under   SOUTHERN
113 W. 116th St. (bet. Lenox & Seventh Aves.)   (212) 280-8779
Credit cards: All major   Meals: B, L, D

Amy Ruth's succeeds in presenting Southern food that manages to be up-to-date without sacrificing time-honored traditions. Chicken is served with waffles, a common pairing, but you can also order whole-grain waffles, and they're all served with real maple syrup. The waffles, incidentally, are wonderful, crisp yet fluffy. The real stars of the menu include short ribs that are falling-off-the-bone tender in an earthy, oniony brown gravy, and deliciously spicy shrimp, perfect over fluffy white rice, and baked spareribs served in a sweet barbecue sauce. Each main course comes with two side dishes, and many of Amy Ruth's shine, like buttery string beans served almost al dente, and eggy potato salad. Sweet potato pie is a deep-dish version with a filling full of nutmeg and cinnamon and pineapple-coconut cake, an old church-picnic favorite, is big and terrific.

Other recommended dishes: Salmon croquettes; smothered pork chops; black-eyed peas; collard greens; peach cobbler. **Price range:** Breakfast, $3.95–$9.95; lunch and dinner, $7.95–$17.95. **Wheelchair access:** Everything on one level.

An American Place ☆☆ $$$$ NEW AMERICAN

565 Lexington Ave. (bet. 50th & 51st Sts.)   (212) 888-5650
Credit cards: All major   Meals: B, Br, L, D

Larry Forgione opened the original American Place in 1983.
With the single-mindedness of a Yankee farmer, he has plowed
his furrow, holding fast to a vision of American cuisine as an
infinitely renewable resource. Now located in a dressy-casual
hotel dining room, the food at An American Place has the right
blend of boldness and subtlety. The menu reflects Mr. Forgione's penchant for clearly expressed, big flavors, simple but
not simple-minded. The pot-roasted short ribs, two sizable
hunks of quiveringly tender meat, do not require a lot of fuss
and bother. This signature dish from the old American Place is
served with whipped potatoes that cut the richness of the meat
with a sharp horseradish edge and fresh herbs.

Desserts should be the mother lode for a tradition-minded
American chef, but they are a disappointment at An American
Place. The wisest course is to order the double chocolate pudding. Served with Schrafft's sugar cookies, it's a standout, one
of those regressive treats that are as satisfying as a trashy novel.

Ideas age quickly in New York, but Mr. Forgione's all-American approach to cooking hasn't. Eating at An American Place is
a little like rereading Thoreau or Emerson. No matter how well
you think you know them, they remain fresh, inspiring, and for
any thinking American, a source of genuine pride.

Other recommended dishes: Crab spring roll; cepes on toast;
Hudson Valley foie gras; salmon napoleon. **Price range:** Apps.,
$9–$15; entrees, $19–$35; desserts, $9. **Wheelchair access:**
Fully accessible. **Services:** Private parties.

Angelo & Maxie's ☆ $$ STEAKHOUSE

233 Park Ave. S. (at 19th St.)   (212) 220-9200
Credit cards: All major   Meals: L, D

Angelo and Maxie's celebrates a long-gone America where people smoked and drank and ate huge hunks of red meat. Order a
salad and a whole garden of greens appears in a big wooden
bowl. Meat comes big and bigger. Cocktails are served in
glasses that could double as hummingbird baths. The only
things that are not oversize are the prices, which are low
enough to encourage even more excess. The porterhouse steak
for two is the best of the beef, but Peter Luger certainly has no
cause for concern. The roasted chicken is moist, and the
salmon is a reliable piece of fish. Add some creamed spinach,
hash browns and onion rings, and any of them would make a
satisfying meal. If you can bear the thought of dessert, choose
the warm chocolate "soufflé," which is a very decent chocolate
cake. Service is cheerful and competent.

Other recommended dishes: Shrimp cocktail; Caesar salad; clams Casino; gravlax; grilled veal chop; hot fudge sundae. **Wine list:** The selection is excellent, the prices are reasonable, and if you want to splurge on a great Bordeaux, this is the place to do it. **Price range:** Apps., $5–$12.50; entrees, $9.50–$21; desserts, $4–$6. **Wheelchair access:** Fully accessible. **Features:** Kid friendly, smoking permitted (in the Cigar Room). **Services:** Private parties.

Anglers & Writers $$ NEW AMERICAN

420 Hudson St. (at St. Luke's Pl.) (212) 675-0810
Credit cards: Cash only Meals: L, D

Such a handsome, restful dining room! It's full of rustic wood and American antiques, with widely spaced tables and shelves of old tools and books adding a touch of serenity. The old-fashioned American food looks great too, but doesn't measure up to the furniture.

Alcohol: Beer and wine. **Price range:** Lunch: entrees, $4.95–$12.50. Dinner: apps., $4.50; entrees, $7–$13.50; desserts, $4.50. High tea: $12.50. **Wheelchair access:** Fully accessible. **Features:** Kid friendly, romantic.

Annie's $25 & Under NEW AMERICAN

1381 Third Ave. (near 77th St.) (212) 327-4853
Credit cards: All major Meals: B, Br, L, D

This versatile restaurant boasts a plain, unpretentious dining room, earnest, attentive service and a wide-ranging menu of surefire American winners with nods toward Mexico, Italy and Asia. The restaurant does a lot of things well enough to make it a pleasant neighborhood place, particularly for families. The food shows real spark, with the kitchen weighing in with spice when it could easily have served platitudes. Highlights include popcorn shrimp served with a peppery rémoulade, marinated skirt steak and ravioli stuffed with spinach. Breakfast is good, too.

Other recommended dishes: Green salad; chopped vegetable salad; mussels; goat cheese tart; sirloin steak; Cornish hen; lemon meringue tart; coconut cake. **Wine list:** Simple, fairly priced wine list. **Price range:** Lunch: apps., $4–$6.75; entrees, $5.95–$12.95. Dinner: apps., $4.95–$6.75; entrees, $7.75–$16.95. **Wheelchair access:** Fully accessible. **Features:** Kid friendly, smoking permitted. **Services:** Delivery, takeout, catering.

Annisa ☆ ☆ $$$ NEW AMERICAN

13 Barrow St. (bet. W. 4th St. & Seventh Ave.)   (212) 741-6699
Credit cards: All major   Meals: D   Closed Sun.

Annisa is a restaurant with a small room, a small staff and a
small menu. But with disarming ease, it manages to make a big
impression. Annisa, whose name means "women" in Arabic, is
a two-woman show. Anita Lo turns out the food; her partner,
Jennifer Scism, runs the front of the house. Both of them seem
to be very clear-eyed about the kind of restaurant they want, a
place with clean lines, a welcoming, inclusive atmosphere and a
quietly persuasive menu, filled with arresting ingredient and flavor combinations.

   Ms. Lo reaches far and wide for ideas and influences, without
strain. Throughout, her cooking is defined by good taste and
good judgment. She pairs a perfectly seared slice of foie gras
with her own version of Shanghai soup dumplings, stuffed with
a little foie gras mousse and thickened spicy soy broth. The
result is an appetizer that makes you fall in love with foie gras
all over again. Pan-roasted chicken in a high-low sauce of
sherry-accented truffles and pig's feet qualifies as a new-age
bistro breakthrough, original but perfectly sane. Fish is infallible
at Annisa, starting with a pellucid block of miso-marinated
sable, seared to a thick black crust on top and accompanied by
golden blocks of fried tofu in a briny bonito broth.

   For dessert, there's no resisting the attractive fluted carrot
cake, filled with bits of macadamia nut and served with a pouf
of crème fraîche. The apple tart, surrounded by a sticky pool of
caramel sauce, ranks very high, a beautifully executed classic
with a textbook crust and ideally tart apples.

Other recommended dishes: Lobster and avocado salad; zucchini blossom; soft-shell crabs; grilled squid salad; lamb tenderloin with lamb sausage; seared scallops. **Wine list:** An eclectic
list of about 75 wines chosen by Roger Dagorn of Chanterelle.
About half are under $40, and 30 are sold by the glass. **Price
range:** Apps., $8–$16; entrees, $23–$29; desserts, $8. **Wheel-
chair access:** Three steps up to dining room; restrooms not
accessible.

Antonio $$ ITALIAN

140 W. 13th St. (bet. Sixth & Seventh Ave.)   (212) 645-4606
Credit cards: All major   Meals: L, D

A sweet, reasonable little Italian restaurant in the Village with a
kitchen that really tries. "That's outrageously good!" says the
waiter to almost everything you order, and he is often right. The
menu is interesting, and the portions are generous. Grilled pizzas are good, and the pastas are hearty and appealing. A hefty
piece of grilled tuna is enhanced by a fine sweet-and-sour

sauce, and the short ribs are rich and wonderful. And no beet lover will want to miss the delicious orange-accented beets.

Price range: Dinner: apps., $6–$10; entrees, $12–$21; desserts, $6.50–$7.50. **Wheelchair access:** Fully accessible. **Features:** Outdoor dining. **Services:** Catering, takeout, private parties.

Aquagrill ☆☆ $$$ SEAFOOD

210 Spring St. (at Sixth Ave.)   (212) 274-0505
Credit cards: All major   Meals: Br, L, D   Closed Mon.

Aquagrill has the comfortable air of a neighborhood place, the sort of restaurant that ought to be serving burgers and beer. Instead there's an oyster bar in front and the menu is refreshingly original. Devoted almost entirely to fish, it offers unusual dishes like "snail-snaps" (bite-size popovers holding a single snail) and salmon in falafel crust. Soups are also satisfying. All the fish is well prepared and some with imagination, but the kitchen also has a way with plain fish as well. Yellow potato hash is, deservedly, a beloved signature dish. Desserts are homey and occasionally too sweet, but save room for the apple tart with cinnamon ice cream and caramel sauce. A recent visit suggests strongly, however, that Aquagrill is slipping. Service is indifferent, the cooking pallid, and the dining room cramped and noisy. The oyster list still impresses, but this but this very popular restaurant is riding on its reputation.

Other recommended dishes: Oysters; peppered tuna carpaccio; warm octopus salad; billi bi; sautéed mussels and snails; grilled swordfish; roasted cod with spinach and artichokes; Aquagrill sandwich of roasted crab cakes; grilled rare tuna sandwich; roasted grapefruit. **Wine list:** Excellent, out-of-the-ordinary wines at reasonable prices. **Price range:** Lunch: prix-fixe "shucker special," $14.50. Dinner: apps., $8.50–$14.50; entrees, $18.50–$26; desserts, $6–$10. **Wheelchair access:** One step into dining room; restrooms not accessible. **Services:** Takeout.

Aquavit ☆☆☆ $$$$ SWEDISH

13 W. 54th St.   (212) 307-7311
Credit cards: All major   Meals: L, D

Aquavit serves inventive Swedish-inspired cuisine in a former town house divided into a ground-floor cafe and a two-part downstairs dining room decorated with contemporary Swedish art. Marcus Samuelsson, Aquavit's restlessly inventive executive chef, is a fully mature artist with a distinctive style, the culinary version of counterpoint, in which precisely defined flavors talk back and forth to each other rather than blending into a single smooth harmonic effect. He keeps your palate on edge.

The menu sparkles with bright thoughts. Foie gras ganache is a light duck-liver pudding that releases a rich, liquid livery ooze when pierced with a fork. Salmon rubbed in Ethiopian spices has a remarkable depth of smoky flavor and a smooth texture. In between the cubes of fish are pure-white buttons of chilled goat cheese parfait topped with a little pyramid of osetra caviar. Aquavit's herring plate, served with an icy shot of aquavit and a Carlsberg beer, amounts to a dazzling showcase for the national fish. If the food is Swedish, it often looks Japanese. Mr. Samuelsson likes big plates, spare arrangements and bright colors. Mr. Samuelsson's pièce de résistance is his pellucid arctic char, pinkish orange and delicately smoked, served with creamy, sharply flavored nettle risotto and matsutake mushrooms. The dish looks complete. Then a waiter arrives with a Japanese tea kettle and pours a steaming mushroom consommé, or a spring-onion broth, over the fish. Meat cannot quite compete, but you will love the truffle-scented squash tart, a footlong strip tucked under slices of tender poached lamb.

For dessert, Aquavit's cheesecake looks like no other cheesecake on earth. It comes in three taco-like pastry shells arranged like a fan and surrounded by a pale green mint syrup and cracked black pepper.

Other recommended dishes: Porcini mushroom and sunchoke soup, oysters with mango-curry sorbet, lobster roll, poached veal with sweetbread croquettes. Wine list: A solid international list of about 250 wines, with 15 wines by the glass and a large selection of aquavits, many of them flavored at the restaurant. Price range: Lunch: apps., $9–$14; entrees, $24–$26; desserts, $8; five-course tasting menu, $48 ($73 with wines); three-course prix fixe, $35; four-course vegetarian menu, $35. Dinner: three- course pre-theater menu, served from 5:30 to 6:15 P.M., $39; three-course prix fixe, $67; seven-course tasting menu, $85 ($120 with wine); seven-course vegetarian menu, $58 ($93 with wine); 16-course "bite" menu, $110 ($170 with wines). Wheelchair access: Several steps down to the cafe, and another flight down to the dining room and restrooms.

Arabelle ☆ $$$$ FRENCH
Hôtel Plaza Athénée, 37 E. 64th St. (bet. Madison & Park Aves.)
(212) 606-4647
Credit cards: All major   Meals: B, L, D

Arabelle has a subtly luxurious feel, with pale pink wall panels, wispy gold curtains and a gold-domed ceiling. The moodily lighted lounge and bar just outside the restaurant's entrance should be on everyone's list of romantic meeting spots. The food is another matter. Mr. Saja, who worked at Le Régence before taking over the kitchen at Arabelle, proves that the restaurant world, too, has its fashion victims. In a clear case of overcompensation, he has avoided the fusty dishes and gold-plated war horses normally associated with fancy French restaurants in even fancier hotels. Instead, he has made a point of showing that he knows what foam is.

There's a little too much of everything here. As a result, ingredients often wage war on one another, or sit superfluously on a far corner of the plate, awaiting instructions. There are wonderful appetizers, however. Bits of citrus-cured salmon, clean-tasting and plushly textured, nestle in a shapely nest of microgreens and tiny, crunchy dice of jicama and malanga. Mr. Saja also makes a much better, more organized impression with his pan-roasted halibut with a golden crust, bathed in a well-judged truffled chicken jus, just the right level of richness to complement the fish.

Desserts have the virtue of being consistent with the rest of the menu. They use lots of herbs and even sneak in a little tomato. The cheesecake is closer to a sideways napoleon, with paper-thin rounds of roasted pineapple sandwiching dollops of cheese filling that brilliantly evokes Philadelphia cream cheese. I mean this as a compliment.

Price range: Lunch: apps., $11–$19; entrees, $21–$29; desserts, $13. Dinner: apps., $11–$19; entrees, $27–$39; desserts, $13. **Wheelchair access:** Entrance with ramp; small step into lounge. **Features:** Smoking permitted. **Services:** Private Parties

Arqua ☆☆ $$$ ITALIAN
281 Church St. (at White St.)   (212) 334-1888
Credit cards: All major   Meals: L, D

The setting of this restaurant named for Arqua Petrarca, a village in northern Italy, is alluring, but the noise can be deafening when all the chairs are occupied at night. Lunch is a more tranquil time, and the rustic fare is unfailingly good. Starters include grilled chicken and mushroom sausage on a warm lentil salad; fresh pickled sardines with sweet and sour onions; a soup of the day, and several homemade pastas. Some main dishes are pan-seared tuna loin with ginger sauce; baked duck breast with a sauce of black currant and cassis, and braised rabbit with white wine and herbs. Before the espresso, perhaps a ricotta cheesecake or a poached pear with caramel sauce and ice cream.

Price range: Apps., $8–$10; entrees, $16–$22; desserts, $8. Prix–fixe lunch, $20; prix–fixe dinner, $25. **Wheelchair access:** Not accessible. **Features:** Kid friendly, smoking permitted. **Services:** Private parties.

Artie's New York Delicatessen

$25 & Under   **Deli**

2290 Broadway (bet. 82nd & 83rd Sts.)   (212) 579-5959
Credit cards: All major   Meals: L, D

Artie's may not be ready to take its place among the deli elite, but it shows promise. And it already makes a fine egg cream. Artie's pastrami has potential, and the hot dogs are excellent, slender, garlicky and crisp around the edges, arriving already spread with mustard and sauerkraut. Potato pancakes are exceptionally crisp, with a solid center trailing crunchy slivers of potato. The dining room is bright and functional, and it's clear that Artie's has also been working on the deli atmosphere.

Other recommended dishes: Chicken soup; flanken in a pot.
Price range: Sandwiches, $4.95–$10.95; entrees, $7.95–$17.95.
Wheelchair access: Everything on one level.

Artisanal ☆☆ $$$ **Bistro**

2 Park Ave. (at 32nd St.)   (212) 725-8585
Credit cards: All major   Meals: L, D, LN

Artisanal is a big, very good-looking brasserie with more varieties of cheese than most human beings will encounter in a lifetime. Its cheese menu amounts almost to a dare: do you love cheese enough, and do you have the patience, to work your way through nearly 200 of them?

Artisanal is an easy restaurant to like. The interior, designed by Adam Tihany, is bold, cheery and inviting, with a zigzag-pattern tiled floor, lots of banquettes and a retail cheese counter with a tilted overhead mirror that lets everyone in the room admire the merchandise. The tradition-minded brasserie menu incorporates cheese without going overboard, although there are some close calls. Fondue, for example, is a food I can live without, but there it is, inevitably, in a special menu box all its own. Diners can order a small pot or a big one, filled with plain Swiss or combinations like Cheddar-bacon or Vacherin with porcini mushrooms. Anyone looking for a social icebreaker can order a basket of gougères, light pastry puffs mingled with just enough Gruyère to make them worth fighting over.

About half the menu at Artisanal is honest bistro cooking. The frites are just fine, the steaks respectable. The other half shows some genuinely inspired flashes. Rabbit in riesling sauce gets a sharp kick from rutabaga cleverly shredded in a tangy mustard sauce to resemble sauerkraut. And a half chicken pressed under a brick comes out crisp and moist, with a garlicky white-bean brandade.

After the entrees comes the moment of truth. You will have cheese. That's simply not an issue. Of the nearly 200 cheeses the restaurant handles, about 80 are ripe at one particular moment. Artisanal makes all of its 140 or so wines available by the glass, so no cheese need be eaten without the mathematically precise wine pairing.

Surprisingly, the cheesecake is disappointing. But the sly inclusion of Cheddar cheese in the tarte Tatin crust transforms this quintessentially French dessert into a close cousin of American apple pie with cheese on top.

Other recommended dishes: Bacon and onion tart, steak tartare, Dover sole with mushroom-asparagus fricassee. **Wine list:** A very good, modestly priced international list of about 140 wines, all available by the glass. **Price range:** Lunch: apps., $6–$16; entrees, $12–$33; desserts, $6–$10. Dinner: apps., $6–$20; entrees, $16–$36; desserts, $6–$10. **Wheelchair access:** Restrooms on street level.

Arturo's Pizzeria $ ITALIAN/PIZZA

106 W. Houston St. (near W. Broadway) (212) 677-3820
Credit cards: All major Meals: D, LN

A great old dive with lots of jazz and colorful characters behind the bar, serving genuine coal-oven pizza that is not quite at New York's top level, but is not too far behind.

Price range: Apps., $4.50–$9.75; entrees, $8–$26; desserts, $3. **Wheelchair access:** Restroom not accessible. **Features:** Outdoor dining. **Services:** Delivery, takeout, catering, private parties.

Asia de Cuba ☆ $$$ ASIAN/LATIN AMERICAN

237 Madison Ave. (near 37th St.) (212) 726-7755
Credit cards: All major Meals: L, D, LN

You won't eat very well at Asia de Cuba. But you will have so much fun being there that you may not notice. The manic energy of the place makes every night feel like a party. Try sitting at the long communal table (if you can get a reservation). The most successful invention is the oxtail spring roll, a wonderful combination of rich, fatty meat with crisp pastry and forceful flavors. A black bean, cucumber and tomato relish is the perfect foil. But who can think about all that when desserts are exploding all over the room? Guava Dynamite is the life of this party; it is just guava mousse wrapped in a chocolate tuile, but the sparkler on top is seductive.

Other recommended dishes: Thai beef salad with avocado, shredded coconut and orange segments; Latin Lover chocolate cake; coconut cake. **Wine list:** Pleasant, but this is very hard food to match with wine; rum seems more appropriate. **Price range:** Apps., $15–$24; entrees, $22–$34; desserts, $8–$10. Prix fixe, $65–$85 per person. **Wheelchair access:** Fully accessible. **Features:** Smoking permitted. **Services:** Private parties.

Atlas ☆☆☆ $$$$ FRENCH/BRITISH

40 Central Park S. (bet. Columbus Circle & Sixth Ave.)

(212) 759-7968

Credit cards: All major   Meals: D   Closed Sun.

Atlas has always been attractive, an oddly configured two-part restaurant with tucked-away booths and secluded corners to complement the window tables, with their sightlines over the sidewalk and Central Park, but there's no question that it is now one of the most exciting restaurants in the city. The starting point is French, with a reverence for good ingredients and classic technique. The animating principle, however, is working-class cheek — a determination to create friction by rubbing opposites together, or giving high-class treatment to low-status foods. Add an experimental urge, and you get a highly revved culinary engine.

One fixture at Atlas will catch your attention immediately. It's an ovoid dollop of green-apple and wasabi sorbet nestled in a baby abalone shell and sprinkled with a few crunchy grains of Maldon salt, England's fleur de sel. Out of nowhere, a waiter appears bearing a small glass beaker, from which he pours a drizzle of olive oil over the sorbet. The combination is magic — a jolt of fiery wasabi, a lively tingle of acidic fruit, then a palate-soothing smear of fresh, fruity oil.

The main courses at Atlas pull back from the edge just a bit. But cannon of lamb with braised artichokes in a coffee-cardamom fumet is not exactly conservative. Coffee and lamb, it turns out, were made for each other. Like star-crossed lovers, they simply took a long time to get together. Roasted beef fillet, fork-tender and exceptionally flavorful, takes a direct route, surrounded by a puree of roasted carrots and horseradish, baby onions poached in a cumin-accented broth and a wonderfully clear, intense jus.

Desserts have the right spirit of adventure. Chai tea ice-cream soda is a slightly preposterous, nervy confrontation between chocolate-orange sorbet and vanilla-clove soda that stubbornly refuses to be dreadful. And fig and almond butter cake, soaked in warm port syrup, is homey but elegant, with crème fraîche adding a welcome sour note.

Other recommended dishes: Parsley and licorice soup, eel with red wine glaze and watermelon, poached chicken on Basmati rice with tarragon and chestnuts, stuffed pig trotter. **Wine list:** A smart, well-chosen international list of about 200 wines, with three Champagnes by the glass and 10 wines served in two sizes of "fillip," either one-quarter or two-thirds of a bottle. **Price range:** Dinner, three-course prix fixe, $68. Pre-theater, 5:30–6:15, $48. **Wheelchair access:** Restrooms are on street level.

Aureole ☆☆ $$$$ New American

34 E. 61st St. (bet. Madison & Park Aves.)   (212) 319-1660
Credit cards: All major   Meals: L, D   Closed Sun.

Aureole is one of the city's most popular and revered restaurants. The reasons are perfectly understandable. Aureole serves appealing food in stylish surroundings. The service is polished, the atmosphere warm. Manhattan has no shortage of restaurants that could be described in the same way, but very few of them have achieved Aureole's invincible appeal.

Chef and owner Charlie Palmer likes big effects. His dishes tend to come on strong, make a big statement and then, as often as not, wear out their welcome. But when Mr. Palmer pulls it all together, his food has an unfussy, direct appeal that makes other chefs seem neurotic. The best entrees, like pan-seared quail with sautéed foie gras, corn bread and chanterelles, have a winning simplicity to them. The flavors are direct and concentrated, and there's an imaginative twist that adds intrigue to what otherwise might be a plodder. Two dishes jump off the high dive into sheer indulgence. Braised lobster with lobster ravioli luxuriates in a satiny tarragon-butter sauce that has a Gilded Age opulence to it. Stewed root vegetables add a brilliant common touch. The ballottine of duck, another platinum-card dish, pulls no punches. A whole deboned duck, juicy and tender, becomes the very expensive gift wrap for a stuffing of porcini mushrooms, roasted figs and foie gras.

Aureole continues to be what it has always been, a very civilized dining spot on the edge of a very tony Upper East Side. The restaurant has changed very little, in fact, but the world around it has changed a lot. If diners tend to inflate the Aureole experience, it's not hard to see why. The food comes in a very attractive setting, made more so by a subtle but effective makeover. Subtle hip-retro touches suggest a showplace modern living room, circa 1959.

Recently, Mr. Palmer updated the menu, lightening and brightening along the way. Appetizers now include tuna tartar with chili-spiced ponzu and pickled ginger, and roasted vegetable and goat cheese lasagna with olives and fennel salad. New main courses include roasted halibut with mussels basted in basil, served with fennel confit, and steamed nori-wrapped salmon, served with spicy prawn-filled dumplings and a lemongrass consommé.

Other recommended dishes: Eggplant caviar; goat cheese and tomato terrine; lemon custard with citrus mousse; crème brûlée. **Wine list:** A solid, reasonably priced 325-bottle list, mostly French and American, with 21 half bottles and 20 wines by the glass. **Price range:** Lunch: Apps., $8–$42; entrees, $20–$29; desserts, $8.50–$10; three-course "market lunch," $35. Dinner, three-course prix fixe, $69; tasting menu, $85. **Wheelchair access:** Four steps down at entrance, three steps down to the dining room. Restrooms are in the basement.

Avenue $25 & Under BISTRO/FRENCH

520 Columbus Ave. (at 85th St.) (212) 579-3194
Credit cards: All major Meals: B, Br, L, D, LN

This informal corner restaurant (with an unexpectedly French atmosphere and efficient service) serves breakfasts and light meals by day and full dinners at night. Avenue has toyed with the traditional menu, dividing appetizers into small, medium and large plates — which has nothing to do with size, but rather with the costliness of the ingredients. Smoked pork loin, sliced lamb and sliced steak are excellent. At brunch, try the hot chocolate, which is thick as pudding and rich as a chocolate truffle. From the terrific food to the daylong service and the good values, Avenue is a formula that works.

Other recommended dishes: Fried calamari; leek and Gruyere tartlet; risotto with morels, asparagus and peas; lobster bisque; walnut tart; chocolate cake; berry cobbler. **Price range:** Apps, $5.50–$14; entrees, $13.95–$16.95. **Wheelchair access:** Everything is on one level; restrooms are narrow. **Features:** Smoking permitted, outdoor dining. **Services:** Takeout.

Avra ☆ $$$ GREEK/SEAFOOD

141 E. 48th St. (bet. Third & Lexington Aves.) (212) 759-8550
Credit cards: All major Meals: L, D

Greek cuisine is a modest thing, a fairly limited catalog of simple pleasures, and Avra gives it honest, honorable representation. Fresh fish, barely touched, is the selling point here. In the open kitchen, a ball of fire blasts each side of a sea bass or red snapper imprisoned in a grilling basket; the fish gets a squirt of lemon, a drizzling of olive oil and a sprinkling of herbs, then heads to the table. It's an appealing formula, to which Avra brings its own brand of charm. The restaurant has a spacious, easy feeling to it, and just enough decorative pieces to suggest a country taverna without belaboring the point. The waiters make each table feel as though inside Avra's protective walls, all worldly cares have ended, all problems can be solved. It is a soothing place.

The seafood counter offers about a dozen fish listed on the menu and perhaps an extra two picked up at the market unexpectedly. All fish at the counter are priced by the pound. Generally speaking, the smaller fish weigh about a pound and make a good entree-size portion. Larger fish need to be shared by two or three people. For those who insist on meat, lamb loin chops, served with lemon potatoes and okra, are tender and flavorful. Avra's spanakopita is a flawless layering of good feta cheese, firm spinach and leeks, with crackling-fresh leaves of phyllo dough.

Other recommended dishes: Stuffed grape leaves; zucchini and eggplant chips; Greek bouillabaisse; grilled octopus; walnut cake; semolina custard. **Wine list:** About 130 wines, most moderately priced, with 23 Greek wines. **Price range:** Lunch: apps., $6.50–$12.50; entrees, $9.50–$26.50; desserts, $6.50–$7; three-course prix fixe, $20. Dinner: apps., $6.50–$14.50; entrees, $18.50–$26; desserts, $6.50–$7. **Wheelchair access:** There is a restroom on street level. **Features:** Smoking at bar.

AZ ☆☆☆ $$$ FUSION
21 W. 17th St. (bet. Fifth & Sixth Aves.)   (212) 691-8888
Credit cards: All major   Meals: Br, L, D

AZ is gorgeous, an improbable but enchanting blend of strict Asian geometry, Western Art Nouveau and turn-of-the century Viennese craft influences. The décor, in other words, matches the menu. The sultry bar and lounge on the ground floor has already begun to attract the young and the beautiful. But the lucky ones step into the silver steel elevator and head for the third-floor dining room. Tilted glass panels open up to the sky in clear weather, and a thin sheet of water flows down a stone slab near the entrance. It's a room to dream in, and a threat to steal the show.

When the food arrives, however, the stargazing stops and Patricia Yeo's highly inventive, extroverted and wildly successful brand of fusion cooking holds center stage. In dish after dish, she shows a rare combination of audacity and refinement, sustained with admirable consistency over the entire menu.

It takes nerve to come up with duck schnitzel. The dish sounds like a joke. The laughter stops after one bite, when the rich duck meat, wrapped in a paper-thin crunchy layer of breading, makes contact with brown butter, specks of hazelnut and a well-judged intervention of sweet and bitter flavors provided by sliced golden beets. Oxtail may not seem like the logical partner for tuna, but Ms. Yeo makes it work, brilliantly, marinating the meat in a liquid flavored with black beans, ginger, garlic and orange zest and then braising it in sake and veal stock. Ms. Yeo also works wonders with Asian teas. Chicken smoked in Lapsang souchong leaves absorbs the dusky perfume of the tea, which is nicely offset by a scallion pancake and a thick fig chutney.

There are times when execution does not quite keep pace with invention. In other words, some dishes are merely good. The dessert menu also feels a little quiet after the snap, crackle and pop of the appetizers and main courses.

Other recommended dishes: Crab and corn congee; pork chop with prunes; fig tarte Tatin; coconut financier. **Wine list:** A far-ranging, very original list of about 350 wines, with nearly 60 half bottles and 24 wines by the glass. **Price range:** Dinner:

three-course prix fixe, $52; six-course tasting menu, $75. **Features:** Smoking permitted, outdoor dining. **Services:** Catering, private parties.

Babbo ☆☆☆ $$$$ ITALIAN

110 Waverly Pl. (at Sixth Ave.) (212) 777-0303
Credit cards: All major Meals: D

Mario Batali and Joseph Bastianich are not playing it safe. They have taken one of the city's most beloved old restaurants, the Coach House, gutted its interior, and created a small, spare, intimate room with warm golden light. The menu isn't safe, either — loaded with dishes Americans are not supposed to like. Fresh anchovies and warm testa (head cheese) are among the appetizers, and pastas include bucatini with octopus, and ravioli filled with beef cheeks. Lamb's tongues and calf's brains are frequent specials. One of the best pastas is made with calf's brains wrapped in tender sheets and sprinkled with fragrant sage and thyme flowers. There is also a pasta tasting menu: five different pastas followed by two desserts. But a meal at Babbo is not complete without spicy, robust calamari. And all this comes at a relatively moderate price.

The entirely Italian wine list is filled with names unfamiliar to most Americans, and wine is not served by the glass but by quartinos (250 ml, or a third of a bottle). Try one. If you don't like it, the kitchen will take it back. If you leave room for dessert, ice creams are creamy and concentrated; sorbet tastes like frozen fruit. But the best ending is saffron panna cotta with poached peaches. *(Ruth Reichl)*

Other recommended dishes: Mint love letters; pappardelle Bolognese; squid; cherry crostata; corn ice cream. **Wine list:** Focused on Italy; unusual and fairly priced. **Price range:** Apps., $7–$11; entrees, $15–$35; desserts, $8; seven–course pasta tasting menu, $59; seven–course traditional tasting menu, $65. **Wheelchair access:** Fully accessible.

Bahia $25 & Under SALVADORAN

690 Grand St., Williamsburg, Brooklyn (718) 218-9592
Credit cards: All major Meals: B, L, D

Corn is the keystone of the Central American culinary universe, as is clear if you visit a Salvadoran restaurant like this bright and airy place. Although the extensive menu includes hamburgers, Caesar salad, Buffalo chicken wings and spaghetti puttanesca, the specialties are typical Salvadoran dishes like pupusas, corn pancakes that serve primarily as a vehicle for conveying the satisfying flavors of small amounts of meats and vegetables, which are stuffed into the center of the pancake. Bahia's pupusas are fine-grained, flattened on a griddle to a size slightly larger than would fit in a toaster, and come with a dish of marinated cabbage that looks like coleslaw. If you pile the coleslaw on the pupusa and eat them together, tangy, rich magic occurs, especially when you bite into the filling, which might include shreds of savory pork or earthy red beans pressed to the consistency of a paste, both the perfect texture to match the corn dough.

Corn shows up in many other dishes, like Salvadoran chicken tamales, in which cornmeal is steamed in green husks almost to a souffle-like consistency. Other dishes, even those without corn, can be fabulous, like a mess of fried yucca with chunks of fried pork, the crisp meat playing counterpoint to the starchy yuca, topped with marinated red onion and drizzled with tangy lime juice. Bahia does not serve alcoholic beverages, but don't pass up horchata, a sweet iced rice drink with cinnamon and cocoa that has a wonderful, almost malty flavor.

Other recommended dishes: Sopa de res, empanada de leche. **Price range:** Apps., $1.25–$10; entrees, $6.50–$15. **Wheelchair access:** Everything is on one level.

Baldoria ☆ $$$ ITALIAN
249 W. 49th St. (bet. Seventh & Eighth Aves.)   (212) 582-0460
Credit cards: All major   Meals: D   Closed Sun.

Baldoria (pronounced bal-DOR-ia, meaning "rollicking good time") is a big slice of neighborhood Italian, New York style, transferred, in a slicker format, to the theater district. They serve feel-good food in a feel-good atmosphere that inclines diners to overlook shortcomings. In restaurants like these, Frank Sinatra is more important than the chef.

Baldoria is a little more sophisticated than that, but not a lot. It is authentic, even naïve, and in an ironic, cynical age, that makes it tremendously appealing. It is possible to eat very well at Baldoria, or not. When it's good, Baldoria is quite good, although never quite as good as the overenergized waiters insistently tell you. The greens and the tomatoes are always fresh and flavorful, and they do a lot to regain lost ground in dishes like the tough, overbreaded veal Milanese. Pastas perform strongly, especially trenette with prosciutto, peas and onions in a light cream sauce and good, firm pappardelle with a dark, earthy mushroom sauce. Standard appetizers like vitello tonnato and clams sautéed in white wine are respectable, as are main courses like sweet sausages with pepper and onions. The osso buco struggles through, but veal in any other form comes out dry and overcooked. Get the costata di manzo, a thuggish-looking hunk of rib chop, weighing in at 54 ounces; it's an incredibly flavorful piece of beef, juicy, tender and perfectly cooked.

Other recommended dishes: Wild fennel and fava bean salad; seafood salad; asparagus risotto. **Wine list:** A work in progress, with about 100 wines, mostly Italian, with enough interesting selections to suggest a good list in the making. **Price range:** Apps., $7.50–$18; entrees, $18–$32; desserts, $7.50. **Wheelchair access:** Downstairs restroom on street level. **Features:** Good for business.

Bali Nusa Indah $25 & Under   INDONESIAN

651 Ninth Ave. (near 45th St.)   (212) 265-2200
Credit cards: All major   Meals: L, D

Indonesian restaurants are rare in New York, but this is a good one, offering fresh and lively Indonesian dishes in a tranquil and pretty setting. Most of the food is forcefully spiced, yet respectful of the flavors of each dish. Among the dishes worth trying are Javanese fisherman's soup; corn fritters gently flavored with shrimp; nasi goreng, the wonderful Indonesian version of fried rice, and sea bass broiled in a banana leaf. Most Asian restaurants are not known for their desserts, but there are exceptional ones here.

Other recommended dishes: Stuffed squid; spring rolls; fish mousse; pan–fried whole red snapper; beef with green chilies; chicken in chili sauce; pisang goreng (fried banana); lapis legit (mellow cinnamon cake with vanilla ice cream). **Alcohol:** Bring your own. **Price range:** Apps., $3–$4; entrees, $6–$13.50; daily specials, $13–$15; prix fixe, $11.95–$20. **Wheelchair access:** Everything is on one level; restrooms are narrow. **Features:** Kid friendly, good view, outdoor dining. **Services:** Delivery, takeout, catering, private parties.

Balkh Shish Kebab House $25 & Under
AFGHAN/MIDDLE EASTERN

23-10 31st St., Astoria, Queens   (718) 721-5020
Credit cards: Cash only   Meals: Br, L, D, LN

Balkh, named after a town north of Kabul, is a simple restaurant with a breezy garden in the rear. The waitresses are friendly and helpful, and the owners make it a point to stop by your table to make sure everything is all right. While kebabs are the restaurant's namesake, the highlight of the menu is the dumplings — either ashak, a lacy ravioli stuffed with scallions and served in a wonderful sauce of yogurt and grilled onions, or manto, stuffed with ground beef and served in the same sauce. Main course portions are enormous.

Other recommended dishes: Bolani (flat bread stuffed with potato purée); kabli kofta (brown rice blended with sweet cooked carrots, raisins and lamb); sabzey chalow (mild lamb and spinach curry); turshie (spicy pickled vegetables); tika (lamb) kebab; keema (beef) kebab; lassi (yogurt drink); rice pudding. **Alcohol:** Bring your own. **Price range:** Apps.,

$1.50–$6; entrees, $5–$8. **Features:** Kid friendly. **Services:** Delivery, takeout.

Balthazar ☆☆ $$ BRASSERIE/FRENCH
80 Spring St. (bet. Lafayette St. & Broadway)   (212) 965-1785
Credit cards: All major   Meals: B, L, D, LN

The bold-faced names have largely moved on, but this SoHo French brasserie continues to draw crowds for its affordable and delicious food. Try going for lunch, when tables are easier to come by and the food is just as good. The Balthazar salad is a fine mix of asparagus, haricots verts, fennel and ricotta salata in a truffle vinaigrette. Sautéed foie gras is excellent, as is an appetizer of grilled mackerel with a warm potato salad. The short ribs are awesome: rich and meaty, they are accompanied by fat-soaked carrots and buttery mashed potatoes. Lighter dishes are also attractive, like seared salmon served over soft polenta. (*Ruth Reichl, updated by Eric Asimov*)

Other recommended dishes: Rillettes; brandade; steak frites; steak au poivre; fettuccine with broccoli rape; cheeseburger; whole roast chicken; grilled brook trout. **Wine list:** Well chosen and fairly priced. **Price range:** Brunch: $13–$22. Lunch: apps., $6.75–$14; entrees, $11–$19. Dinner: apps., $7.50–$14; entrees, $16–$32; desserts, $6.50–$9. **Wheelchair access:** Fully accessible. **Features:** Kid friendly, smoking permitted.

Baluchi's $25 & Under   INDIAN
193 Spring St. (bet. Sullivan & Thompson Sts.)   (212) 226-2828
1565 Second Ave. (bet. 81st & 82nd Sts.)   (212) 288-4810
283 Columbus Ave. (bet. 73rd & 74th Sts.)   (212) 579-3900
361 Sixth Ave. (at Washington Pl.)   (212) 929-2441
240 W. 56th St. (bet. Broadway & Eighth Ave.)   (212) 397-0707
Credit cards: All major   Meals: L, D

At their best, this rapidly growing chain of mid-priced Indian restaurants can be very good. The name is adapted from Baluchistan, a region that stretches across the border between Iran and Pakistan. Appetizers include crisp potato cakes with creamy, spicy interiors and tandoori vegetable platter. Other recommended dishes are vegetable samosas, rogan josh (tender chunks of lamb in a yogurt sauce) and a searingly hot lamb vindaloo. The fires can be put out with mango ice cream or mandarin sorbet.

Price range: Lunch: 50 percent off dinner menu prices. Dinner: apps., $4.95–$7.95; entrees, $10.95–$15.95; desserts, $4.95. **Wheelchair access:** Restrooms not accessible. **Services:** Delivery, takeout, catering, private parties.

Bambou ☆ ☆ $$$ CARIBBEAN

243 E. 14th St. (bet. Second & Third Aves.)   (212) 505-1180
Credit cards: All major   Meals: D

The best Caribbean food in New York City is served in a room with such cozy elegance, it feels as if a warm breeze is blowing through it. The tables are filled with the beautiful and the famous. There is no better way to begin a meal here than with the eggplant soup, a thick dark liquid with the scent of curry and the deep, intoxicating taste of coconut. Bambou shrimp, each encrusted in coconut, are sweet and tasty, an appetizer that could almost be a dessert. Grilled marlin, a dense, meaty fish steak, comes on a buttery bed of mashed plantain that is the perfect foil for the subtle flavor of the fish. The tropical fruit plate glows with color and the coconut crème brûlée is fabulous.

Other recommended dishes: Steamed mussels with Bambou sauce; crab cake with avocado and molasses; grilled jerk chicken; spiced shell steak with callaloo; braised oxtail; rum cake. **Wine list:** Small but reasonable. The Pouilly–Fuisse goes well with the food. **Price range:** Apps., $8–$13; entrees, $18–$26; desserts, $8. **Wheelchair access:** Fully accessible. **Features:** Romantic, smoking permitted. **Services:** Catering, private parties.

Banania Café $25 & Under   BISTRO/FRENCH

241 Smith St. (near Butler St.), Brooklyn   (718) 237-9100
Credit cards: Cash only   Meals: L, D

Banania, named for a French children's drink, has an enticing menu of reasonably priced bistro dishes. There are Asian and Middle Eastern touches, so that though it feels French, it falls into that catchall international category that might be called contemporary. Calamari rings, for example, are dusted with cumin, roasted and served with carrot purée, a happy match of power and pungency. Among main courses, braised lamb shank is delicious — tender shreds of rosemary-flavored meat framed by chicory and a purée of white beans. Moist roasted cod is served with luscious potatoes mashed with black olives and roasted tomatoes. Desserts range from a classical tarte Tatin to crisp little wontons stuffed with puréed banana in a white-chocolate and ginger sauce.

Other recommended dishes: Pumpkin soup; sautéed foie gras; escargots; steak frites; poached chicken breast; Key lime tart; chocolate mousse. **Price range:** Apps., $5–$8; entrees, $12–$15. **Wheelchair access:** Everything on one level.

Bandol
$25 & Under FRENCH

181 E. 78th St. (bet. Third & Lexington Aves.) (212) 744-1800
Credit cards: AE   Meals: D   Closed Sun.

Bandol, named for a fine Provençal wine, offers dreamy
Mediterranean flavors that are especially transporting in a cold
spell. The food is very good, the atmosphere warm and neighborly. Even the overly familiar dishes like lamb shank, salmon
and scallops have clear, direct flavors that convey their appeal
rather than their popularity. Among the appetizers, the pissal-
adiére, a tart of onions, olives and anchovies served with a
green salad, is so good that you could eat two and call it a
meal. Fish soup is also traditional and excellent, served with
rouille, a thick, garlicky paste that spreads slowly through the
soup. While the main courses don't have the consistency of the
appetizers, they are still satisfying. Coq au vin is juicy and
lighter than usual, the chicken served over noodles with a red
wine sauce that pulls it all together. Grilled steak is juicy and
flavorful, served with crisp fries, while the tender lamb shank
offers primal enjoyment. The atmosphere is right and the food
delicious, but what about the wine? Here, Bandol falls short of
the ideal. The mostly French list is long but not very exciting,
and while it's not expensive, it is hard to find good values.

Other recommended dishes: Vegetable confit; grilled sea scallops; shrimp with anchovies and caponata; fricassee of snails
and mushrooms; terrine of foie gras; grilled salmon with tapenade; grilled shrimp; chocolate cake; apple tart; profiteroles.
Price range: Apps., $6–$10; entrees, $14–$18. **Wheelchair
access:** Entrance is narrow; restrooms are downstairs. **Features:**
Smoking section and at bar.

Barbetta $$$ ITALIAN

321 W. 46th St. (bet. Eighth & Ninth Aves.) (212) 246-9171
Credit cards: All major   Meals; L, D

Dappled sunlight filters through the branches of ancient trees
and a fountain creates cool music. Waiters move lazily across a
stone floor, pouring wine for impossibly elegant people. Can
this be midtown Manhattan? On an afternoon in late spring,
there is no nicer place for lunch than the garden at Barbetta; it
is the most beautiful in Midtown. The menu in this restaurant,
open since 1906, is so old it seems new. The best dishes are the
handmade pastas.

Price range: Lunch: avg. app., $8; entree, $21; dessert, $6.50.
Dinner: avg. app., $9; entree, $27; dessert, $9. **Wheelchair
access:** Restrooms not accessible. **Features:** Romantic, smoking
permitted. **Services:** Private parties.

Barking Dog Luncheonette $25 & Under

DINER

1678 Third Ave. (at 94th St.) (212) 831-1800
1453 York Ave. (bet. E. 77th & 78th Sts.) (212) 861-3600
Credit cards: Cash only Meals: B, Br, L, D, LN

With its dark wood paneling, comfortable booths, bookshelves and low-key lighting, the Barking Dog looks more like a library than a luncheonette. That, in part, explains its appeal to adults, along with its up-to-date American menu, which ranges from hamburgers, fried chicken and meatloaf to leg of lamb and roasted trout. If the children begin to fidget while waiting for the rich, bountiful desserts, distract them with the restaurant's dog tchotchkes, which can be a parent's best friend.

Alcohol: Beer and wine. **Price range:** Lunch: apps., $5; entrees, $9; desserts, $3.50. Dinner: apps., $5; entrees, $11; desserts, $4.50. **Wheelchair access:** Fully accessible. **Features:** Kid friendly, outdoor dining. **Services:** Delivery, takeout.

Barney Greengrass $$

DELI

541 Amsterdam Ave. (bet. 86th & 87th Sts.) (212) 724-4707
Credit cards: MC/V Meals: B, Br, L Closed Mon.

Why are all those people standing in line for such a dreary-looking establishment? For three reasons. In the first place, the restaurant sells truly great smoked and cured fish. Second, the kitchen makes awesome omelets and all manner of terrific deli dishes. Third, it's a true New York City institution, and for many people the weekend just wouldn't count without a visit to Barney Greengrass. (Note: Accepts cash only on weekends.)

Alcohol: Beer. **Price range:** Apps., $6–$14; entrees, $8–$35; desserts, $2.50–$5. **Wheelchair access:** Restrooms not accessible. **Features:** Kid friendly. **Services:** Delivery, takeout, catering.

Bar Pitti $25 & Under

ITALIAN

268 Sixth Ave. (near Houston St.) (212) 982-3300
Credit cards: Cash only Meals: L, D, LN

This casual cafe offers superbly simple Tuscan fare and draws an arty, fashion-conscious crowd. Bar Pitti's ease with people and with food is what makes it seem so Italian; its atmosphere of jangly controlled frenzy makes it a wonderful New York experience. Outdoor seating on Sixth Avenue is remarkably pleasant. The menu is small and familiar, and almost all the main courses are superb. Peak hours are not times for a quiet meal here, but even just before closing time, you will receive the same beautifully cooked food and offhand service.

Recommended dishes: Sautéed spinach; eggplant Parmesan; veal meatballs; mixed green salad; spinach–and–ricotta ravioli; taglierini with leeks and artichokes; baked striped bass; osso buco; veal over salad with white-wine sauce; lemon torte. **Alcohol:** Beer and limited wine list. **Price range:** Apps., $5–$8.50; entrees, $10.50–$19. **Wheelchair access:** Steps to restrooms. **Features:** Romantic, smoking permitted, outdoor dining.

Barrio ☆ $$ BISTRO

99 Stanton St. (at Ludlow St.)   (212) 533-9212
Credit cards: All major   Meals: Open 24 hours

Barrio lives up to the neighborhood in carrying on the melting-pot tradition. The name suggests Latino, but the menu speaks Esperanto. It abounds in small flourishes and flavor detours that add interest to fundamentally simple food that stresses fresh, organic ingredients. The strategy seems sensible. Barrio's round-the-clock, seven-day schedule makes it a cross between a diner and a bistro. That means the food needs to be sharp and hip, but not so clever that it scares away local residents hankering for a quick bite.

The lunch menu is mostly given over to soup, sandwiches and salads. But the soup could be a thick, silken blend of rutabaga and parsley root, sneakily spiced with cayenne and ginger, and the sandwiches outperform their bargain price of about $6, which includes crispy potatoes. The prix-fixe makes it possible to enjoy lunch with substantial main courses like braised veal cheeks on a sweet-sour bed of marinated beet greens.

Seared salmon with braised Swiss chard and sweet potatoes in a raisin-caper sauce skillfully knits sweet, sour and bitter flavors into a rich, complex dish. Plenty of dishes play it straight, however, like the very basic pearl-onion tart, or crispy shrimp served on Bibb lettuce with a fruity elderberry vinaigrette. Desserts could be better, though a cranberry tart with white chocolate ice cream gets things back on track.

Other recommended dishes: Smoked trout and pear sandwich (lunch), organic beef sirloin, pine-nut-crusted halibut with tomato fondue, apple crumble, napoleon. **Wine list:** An acceptable list of about 50 wines, with eight wines by the glass and four by the half bottle. **Price range:** Lunch: apps., $5.50–$7.50; entrees, $6–$9; desserts, $5–$5.50. Two-course prix fixe, $15; three courses, $18. Dinner: apps., $5.50–$11; entrees, $13–$27; desserts, $5.50–$7.50. **Wheelchair access:** Restrooms are accessible by portable ramp.

Bar Six $$ FRENCH/MEDITERRANEAN
502 Sixth Ave. (bet. 12th & 13th Sts.)   (212) 645-2439
Credit cards: All major   Meals: Br, L, D

The dining room is dark, smoky and loud, but the French-
Moroccan food at this narrow Village bistro is quite good. The
menu is limited and the kitchen, thankfully, does not try to do
too much.

Price range: Apps., $5.50–$9.50; entrees, $8–$19; desserts,
$5–$7. Prix fixe, 5:30–7:30 P.M., $18.50. **Wheelchair access:**
Restrooms not accessible. **Services:** Takeout.

Bar Veloce $25 & Under   ITALIAN/SANDWICHES
175 Second Ave. (near E. 11th St.)   (212) 260-3200
Credit cards: All major   Meals: D, LN

The sleek metallic style of this small Italian wine and sandwich
bar masks a warm and passionate establishment. The bar-
tenders wax enthusiastic over the list of fine Italian wines,
many available by the glass, which go well with the precisely
made sandwiches, like a Sicilian tuna tramezzino, a triple-
decker of soft crustless white bread with marinated tuna,
arugula, tomatoes and a minty pesto that brings the flavors
together.

Other recommended dishes: Smoked prosciutto with apple and
taleggio. **Price range:** Avg. sandwich, $7. **Wheelchair access:**
Restrooms not accessible.

Bayard's ☆☆ $$$ FRENCH
1 Hanover Sq. (bet. Pearl & Stone Sts.)   (212) 514-9454
Credit cards: All major   Meals: D   Closed Sun.

Bayard's may be the most distinctive, romantic dining room in
Manhattan, its Federal-style interior and maritime paintings
more Boston or Philadelphia than New York. It's a stage set
within the stage set of Hanover Square, eerily hushed at night
and nearly deserted. In an appropriately quiet way, Eberhard
Müller, formerly of Le Bernardin and Lutèce, has refashioned
the food to suit the surroundings. It may not be the most exciting food in town, but it makes perfect sense. It is cleaner, less
fussy and more direct.

It pays to remember that Mr. Müller is a farmer as well as a
chef. He grows his own produce, and it features prominently on
the menu, which glories in the fresh, earthy savor of pea
shoots, Savoy cabbage, celery root and beets. In the dead of
winter, his opportunities are limited, but spring and summer
unleash an avalanche of fruits and vegetables.

A restaurant like Bayard's, so distinguished-looking that you
feel you should be drafting the Federalist Papers there, demands

Dover sole, and it is excellent. A wrapping of slightly crunchy, steamed Savoy cabbage enfolds a hefty chunk of foie gras layered with a shaving of black truffle. The cabbage wrapper returns on the entree menu, this time encasing breast of chicken folded over a slice of foie gras, sitting in a shallow pool of chicken-vegetable broth. You would have to search far and wide for a better chicken dish.

Mr. Müller loves duck, and he expresses his love in very different ways. Tangy slices of smoked breast have the dark, rich complexity and the long finish of one of the Bordeaux on Bayard's knockout wine list, a lengthy document, peppered with bargains, that many restaurants would kill for.

The solid dessert list offers classics as well as highly inventive desserts like a chilled, silky saffron parfait with macerated dried dates, pears, apples and figs in a spicy syrup, and a Moroccan citrus soup with a refreshing Lillet granite.

Other recommended dishes: Roasted duck breast, Champagne sorbet with apple crisps. **Wine list:** An outstanding list, mostly French and American, with many older wines at bargain prices. **Price range:** Apps., $9–$16; entrees, $29–$38; desserts, $9–$10. **Wheelchair access:** A lift is at the side entrance on Stone Street. An elevator serves all levels.

Bayou $25 & Under CAJUN/SOUTHERN
308 Lenox Ave. (bet. 125th & 126th Sts.) (212) 426-3800
Credit cards: All major Meals: L, D

Bayou, a handsome Creole restaurant in Harlem, would do any New Orleans native proud. With its brick walls, retro brass lamps and woody touches, Bayou looks like countless other neighborhood bars and grills, but its big picture windows and second-floor setting offer an unusual New York panorama, unimpeded by tall buildings that might elsewhere blot out a view of a lightning storm or the sun setting over the Hudson. The menu is short, but includes standout appetizers like earthy chicken livers in a rich port wine sauce, and shrimp rémoulade, piquant with mustard and hot pepper and served with deviled eggs. The rich turtle soup is thick with bits of turtle meat and smoky andouille sausage, spiked with sherry and lemon. Fried oysters and spinach topped with melted Brie were exceptional. In many ways New Orleans is a city closer to the 19th century than to the 21st, and a dish like snapper Alexandria would have been quite at home on a menu 100 years ago. The sautéed fish, sprinkled with roasted pecans and drenched with lemon butter, was moist and altogether delicious. Bayou has two excellent desserts, a bread pudding with vanilla-whiskey sauce and a fudgy, wedge-shaped pecan brownie topped with peppermint ice cream and chocolate sauce. Both were passed around a table of five and nobody got seconds.

Other recommended dishes: Crawfish étouffée; shrimp Creole; deep-fried catfish. **Price range:** Apps., $4.50–$8.95; entrees, $12.95–$21.95. **Wheelchair access:** Restaurant up one flight of stairs. **Services:** Take out.

Beacon ☆☆ $$$ NEW AMERICAN

25 W. 56th St. (bet. Fifth & Sixth Aves.) (212) 332-0500
Credit cards: All major   Meals: L, D   Closed Sun.

This classy looking new midtown restaurant knows exactly what it's about. It offers civilized dining in a beautiful setting. Organized around an open kitchen and a huge wood-burning oven, it delivers uncomplicated big-flavored food emphasizing fresh, seasonal ingredients. The chef, Waldy Malouf, has a good thing going with this oven and he makes the most of it. Meat and fish pick up a smoky tang, roasted vegetables are served with entrees and even desserts feature roasted fruits.

Two of the best entrees are triple lamb chops, rubbed with cumin and puréed picholine olives, and a plain trout roasted over high heat with a bright vinaigrette of chervil, parsley, cilantro and shallots. For dessert soufflés are a point of pride but it's the carmelized apple pancake that grabs the brass ring.

Other recommended dishes: Grilled red onion salad; wood-roasted oysters; port shank; chocolate angel food cake. **Wine list:** Reasonably priced, touches all the bases without showing a strong personality. **Price range:** Lunch, apps., $14–$28; entrees, $12–$24; desserts, $7–$10. Dinner, apps., $8–$14; entrees, $19–$32; desserts, $7–$11. Pre-theater prix fixe, 5:30 P.M.– 6:30 P.M., $35. **Wheelchair access:** Main dining room and bar are on street level. Kitchen dining room is down several steps.

Becco $$ ITALIAN

355 W. 46th St. (bet. Eighth & Ninth Aves.) (212) 397-7597
Credit cards: All major   Meals: B, L, D

With a menu and a wine list that are decidedly unusual, Becco is one of the more intriguing restaurants in New York. Its dependable Italian food is served two ways. You choose a Caesar salad or antipasto plate and then either unlimited servings of the three pastas of the day, or any of a dozen enticing main courses, like roasted rabbit with prosciutto, osso buco or whole roasted fish of the day. The wine list is a fabulous value, with dozens of interesting, inexpensive, primarily Italian wines. If you have an ingrained need to spend more money, Becco also has a reserve list, ranging from $22 to $180.

Price range: Lunch: apps., $5–$10; entrees, $14–$20; desserts, $6.50–$7. Dinner: apps., $5–$10; entrees, $18–$30; desserts, $6.50–$7. Prix–fixe lunch, $16.95; prix–fixe dinner, $21.95.

Wheelchair access: Restrooms not accessible. **Features:** Smoking permitted. **Services:** Takeout, catering, private parties.

Bellini $$$ ITALIAN

208 E. 52nd St. (bet. Second & Third Aves.)   (212) 308-0830
Credit cards: All major   Meals: L, D   Closed Sun.

In an effort to set her restaurant apart from all the other chic Italian spots in town, Donatella Arpaia has recently decided to start featuring the food of Naples. Now, in addition to extremely pleasant service and lots of little freebies (bruschetta to start, zeppole to end), you can try unusual dishes like schiatelli, hand-made pasta topped with seafood sauce. The ambience is unusually relaxing, and lingering is welcomed.

Price range: Avg. app., $9; entree, $22; dessert, $8. **Wheelchair access:** Fully accessible. **Features:** Good for business. **Services:** Takeout, private parties.

Ben Benson's $$$$ STEAKHOUSE

123 W. 52nd St. (bet. Sixth & Seventh Aves.)   (212) 581-8888
Credit cards: All major   Meals: L, D, LN

It's not anyone's favorite steak place in the city, but it's a great also-ran. Ben Benson's caters to tyrannosaur-size appetites while treating its customers with the cuddly warmth of Barney. Carved eagles, bronze buffaloes and lions, deer antlers and other objets de testosterone are scattered about. When the room is crowded, the din echoes from one end to the other. (*Ruth Reichl*)

Wine list: Fair selection of mid-priced to expensive California red wines and chardonnays, weak on inexpensive wines. **Price range:** Apps., $6.25–$15.75; entrees, $16.95–$32.50; desserts, $5.50–$7.50. **Wheelchair access:** Restrooms not accessible. **Features:** Kid friendly, good for business, smoking permitted, outdoor dining. **Services:** Takeout, private parties.

Benny's Burritos $ MEXICAN/TEX-MEX

113 Greenwich Ave. (at Jane St.)   (212) 727-3560
93 Ave. A (at 6th St.)   (212) 254-2054
Credit cards: Cash only   Meals: Br, L, D, LN

If you like zeppelin-size California burritos, you can't do much better than Benny's. The drinks are big, the music loud and you can hold a complete dinner in two hands.

Price range: Apps., $1–$3.50; entrees, $5.50–$10; desserts, $3.50. **Wheelchair access:** Fully accessible. **Features:** Kid friendly, outdoor dining. **Services:** Delivery, catering, takeout, private parties.

Beppe ☆☆ $$$ ITALIAN

45 E. 22nd St. (bet. Park Ave. S. & Broadway)   (212) 982-8422
Credit cards: All major   Meals: L, D   Closed Sun.

Beppe, named for Chef Cesare Casella's grandfather, is packed
and worth a detour. The comfortable rustic Tuscan room has
exposed brick walls, wood beams, antique wooden floors and a
wood-burning fireplace that is damped down in the summer.
The walls are covered with photographs of Italians happily eating or making food. But is this really Tuscan food?

We'll settle for Mr. Casella's description — free-range Tuscan. But he is at his very best with the Tuscan dishes. Order
anything made with farro, the nutty whole grain, which is
served in soup and as farrotto, a risotto-style dish that changes
ingredients with the season. The warm seven-bean salad is stellar: perfectly cooked beans are mixed with thinly sliced red
onion and then bathed in a lusciously fragrant olive oil. Mussels
are plump and sweet, ablaze with garlic and pepper, and the
fried chicken would make a cook of the Deep South proud. The
spareribs are spicy, meaty and tender, and the bed of bitter
broccoli di rape provides a fine counterpoint to the richness of
the meat. The 11-herb pasta is perfectly cooked, and filled with
the flavor of those herbs.

The desserts at Beppe also play with Italian tradition to produce sweets appealing to the American palate. The cannoli are
really rolled lace cookies, cigarillo width, filled with flavored
mascarpone. The Tuscan riff on ice cream sandwiches is made
with toasted buccellati, the Tuscan version of panettone. An all-
American plum and cherry cobbler with the classic crumble
topping and vanilla-bean ice cream is a must. (*Marian Burros*)

Other recommended dishes: Antipasti, mussels, griddle pasta,
farrotto, fried chicken, spareribs, seven-bean salad, Tuscan fries,
peach crostata, cannoli, lemon soufflé cake. **Wine list:** Interesting variety of Tuscan wines, well priced. **Price range:** Lunch
and dinner, antipasti and soup, $7–$12; pasta, $16–$20; sec-
ondi, $23–$29; dessert, $7–$8. **Wheelchair access:** Wheelchair
accessible.

Bice ☆☆ $$$ ITALIAN

7 E. 54th St. (bet. Fifth & Madison Aves.)   (212) 688-1999
Credit cards: All major   Meals: L, D, LN

With a main dining room done in beige and wood with brass
sconces and indirect lighting, Bice is the handsomest Italian
restaurant in town. If you have lots of money, good ears and a
desire to see the fast and the fashionable, this offshoot of a
Milanese restaurant is for you. The food is predictable but good.
Fresh pastas, risotto, and the essentially uncomplicated main
courses — veal chop, chicken paillard and duck breast with

mango — are all recommended. The mostly Italian wine list is well chosen. Desserts include a napoleon with strawberry sorbet, ricotta cheesecake, hazelnut parfait, and caramelized banana tart with apricot compote. (*Ruth Reichl*)

Price range: Avg. app., $15; entree, $24; dessert, $9. **Wheelchair access:** Restrooms not accessible. **Features:** Good for business, smoking permitted, outdoor dining. **Services:** Takeout, private parties.

Big Wong Restaurant $ CHINESE
67 Mott St. (bet. Bayard & Canal Sts.) (212) 964-0540
Credit cards: Cash only Meals: B, Br, L, D

This bright, bare-bones Chinatown restaurant serves excellent barbecued meats and congee. At lunch, it is packed with jurors on lunch break from the courthouse nearby and local residents drinking tea from water glasses.

Alcohol: Bring your own. **Price range:** Apps., $3–$5; entrees, $5–$10. **Wheelchair access:** Not accessible. **Features:** Kid friendly. **Services:** Takeout.

Billy's Restaurant $$ AMERICAN
948 First Ave. (bet. 52nd & 53rd Sts.) (212) 753-1870
Credit cards: All major Meals: Br, L, D, LN

Billy's may have changed since it opened in March of 1870, but not so you'd notice. It's still the archetypal family restaurant, and it may be New York City's lowest-key celebrity-laden restaurant. A dish of cole slaw appears the moment you sit down, and the menu includes old favorites like Salisbury steak, lamb stew and shepherd's pie. Billy's also serves a well-aged rib steak, crisp roast chicken, calf's liver, pork chops and the like. The straight-ahead American fare is old-fashioned and fine, the atmosphere is casual and the waiters could not be nicer.

Price range: Apps., $6.95–$12.95; entrees, $13.95–$29.95; desserts, $4–$8. Brunch, $15.95. **Wheelchair access:** Fully accessible. **Features:** Kid friendly, smoking permitted. **Services:** Takeout, catering, private parties.

Biricchino $25 & Under ITALIAN
260 W. 29th St. (at Eighth Ave.) (212) 695-6690
Credit cards: All major Meals: L, D Closed Sun.

This unusual Italian restaurant is one of the better choices near Madison Square Garden. It offers a special feature: wonderful homemade sausages from its neighbor, Salumeria Biellese. The selection changes daily, but may include chicken and apricot;

duck with Grand Marnier; plump garlic sausages, or chicken and lemongrass.

Price range: Avg. app., $7; entree, $16; dessert, $5. **Wheelchair access:** Restrooms are downstairs. **Services:** Takeout, catering, private parties.

Bistro le Steak $25 & Under   Bistro/Steak

1309 Third Ave. (at 75th St.)   (212) 517-3800
Credit cards: All major   Meals: L, D

It's tempting to pass off Bistro le Steak as a too-obvious marketing scheme. The surprise is that Bistro le Steak hardly strikes a false note. It does look Parisian. The friendly staff conveys warmth and informality, and the food is both good and an excellent value. Steak is the specialty, but other simple bistro specialties are consistently satisfying. Wines are not as good a value, but desserts are terrific.

Other recommended dishes: Country paté; mussels; shrimp St. Tropez; house salad; Parisian cut sirloin; filet mignon; chocolate cake; lemon tart. **Alcohol:** Beer and wine. **Price range:** Apps., $4–$20; entrees, $15–$30; desserts, $10. **Wheelchair access:** Entrance is one step up; restrooms are downstairs. **Features:** Good for business, romantic.

Bistro St. Mark's $25 & Under   Bistro

76 St. Mark's Ave. (near Flatbush Ave.), Park Slope, Brooklyn
                                                 (718) 857-8600
Credit cards: All major   Meals: L, D

The subtle blue storefront of Bistro St. Mark's blends so inconspicuously with the surroundings that you might walk right by. A look at the menu provokes a double take, because this is no simple bistro fare. Bistro St. Mark's uses the guise of neighborhood conviviality to cloak serious and creative cooking.

The fine appetizers include glistening mackerel tartare topped with a luscious smidgen of caviar and dressed in capers and a bracing sauce gribiche, or the moist and delicious skate wing, dusted with ground walnuts and topped with a Roquefort sauce and tiny leaves of watercress. Even traditional dishes are far from standard fare, like the crisp Provençal tomato tart with anchovies and caramelized onions, and fresh, briny grilled sardines in a lemon vinaigrette. Halibut, served over a buttery potato purée, has a meaty depth, and richly flavorful braised beef cheeks, tinged with horseradish, arrive atop the same purée, surrounded by carrots and caramelized garlic cloves.

The loftlike dining room is spare and handsome, but with its soaring ceiling and hard surfaces, it tends to be loud.

Other recommended dishes: Scallop carpaccio, caramelized sea scallops, lemon cake. **Price range:** Apps., $5–$9; entrees, $14–$19. **Wheelchair access:** One level.

Bistrot Margot $25 & Under   BISTRO/FRENCH
26 Prince St. (near Mott St.)   (212) 274-1027
Credit cards: Cash and check only   Meals: Br, L, D

With its brick-red Parisian exterior, a French spelling of "bistro" and the inward-opening entrance that requires one to "poussez," Bistrot Margot is a Francophile's dream. By day, it is more like a cafe, serving light breakfasts, sandwiches and salads to patrons who feel free to while away the time with cafe au lait. At lunch and dinner, the bistro menu offers a small selection of simple, filling dishes, like marvelous Provençal lamb stew, lusty roast pork and beef stewed in red wine. While many things about Margot are delightful, there is a novice quality to the restaurant, expressed more as good-natured disorganization than anything else.

Other recommended dishes: Mesclun salad; charcuterie platter; tapenade; duck confit; shrimp with rice; raspberry tart; apple tart. **Alcohol:** Beer and wine. **Price range:** Apps., $5–$13; entrees, $9–$15.50; desserts, $6.50. **Wheelchair access:** One step up to dining room; restroom is large but not designed for wheelchairs. **Features:** Smoking permitted, outdoor dining. **Services:** Takeout, private parties.

Blue Hill ☆☆ $$ FRENCH
75 Washington Pl. (at Sixth Ave.)   (212) 539-1776.
Credit cards: All major   Meals: D   Closed Sun.

A few steps below sidewalk level in an old Greenwich Village town house, Blue Hill almost shrinks from notice. There's a small bar near the entrance, a few tables up front, some exposed brick and a few more tables and banquettes in the back. The décor barely exists, just enough to give off a vaguely pleasant impression. The menu is small, with tiny print. Prices are astoundingly low.

This quiet, adult setting admirably suits a style of cooking that is both inventive and highly assured. There are dull spots on the menu, dishes that please but do not excite. But the overall standard is high. High enough to make up for the excruciating banquette seating, where diners are pressed so close to one another that conversation becomes a survival exercise. Poached duck, an entree that deserves to be the restaurant's signature, shows the Blue Hill style to advantage. A skinned duck breast, poached in beurre blanc and duck stock, is paired with leg meat done as a confit, then crisped at the last minute and placed over pureéd artichokes. The bravura duck makes it difficult for competitors on the entree list, but the very simple hanger steak, surrounded by chewy spinach spaetzle and deliciously sweet little spring turnips, has nothing to be ashamed of, and salmon, cooked at a temperature so low that it barely breaks a sweat, could be seen as the piscine answer to the duck, an exercise in melt-in-your-mouth tenderness. The fish gets brilliant support from a fragrant pistou of spring vegetables.

Two of the four desserts are puddings. They are also clearly the best in this little pack. Chocolate bread pudding, a sizable cube of brioche, undergoes a miraculous transformation after marinating overnight in a loose chocolate ganache. Chocolate and bread interfuse to form a new compound, chocolate silk. It is a conversation-stopper.

Other recommended dishes: Ceviche of bass with grapefruit and mustard oil; skate with shrimp raviolo; braised cod with mushroom tart; rice pudding with passion-fruit foam. **Wine list:** A modestly priced, highly international list of 45 wines, with 11 wines and 5 sherries by the glass. **Price range:** Apps., $8–$14; entrees, $18–$23; desserts, $7–$8. **Wheelchair access:** Entrance is three steps down.

Blue Ribbon $$$ New American

97 Sullivan St. (bet. Prince & Spring Sts.)   (212) 274-0404
Credit cards: All major   Meals: D, LN   Closed Mon.

A favorite hangout for chefs, who like the late hours. Blue Ribbon offers a full menu until 4 A.M., and by then the sound level may have descended to a roar. The eclectic food is terrific.

Price range: Apps., $7.50–$18.50; entrees, $9.50–$29.50; desserts, $7–$9. **Wheelchair access:** Fully accessible. **Services:** Takeout.

Blue Ribbon Bakery $$ Bistro

33 Downing St. (at Bedford St.)   (212) 337-0404
Credit cards: All major   Meals: B, L, D, LN   Closed Mon.

Going downstairs at Blue Ribbon Bakery is a little like descending into the catacombs, a dark and mysterious space. In this clamorous place, people sit at small tables having serious discussions as they eat just about anything you can imagine. Blue Ribbon Bakery seems to want to be all things to all people. So you can have a hamburger, a sandwich, a bowl of hummus or a heap of beluga caviar. You can have less: just a plate of olives, a dish of french fries, a piece of cheese or a hot fudge sundae. And you can have more: sweetbreads in red wine sauce, breast of duck in raspberry sauce, New Orleans barbecue shrimp. The food I tried was delicious.

Price range: Apps., $3.50–$18.50; entrees, $7.50–$28; desserts, $6–$9. Prix-fixe menus, $35–$100. **Wheelchair access:** Fully accessible. **Services:** Takeout, catering, private parties.

Blue Ribbon Brooklyn $$ NEW AMERICAN
280 Fifth Ave. (at 1st St.) (718) 840-0404
Credit cards: All major Meals: D, LN

The Brooklyn outpost of the Blue Ribbon empire feels like many things at once. It's part saloon, part oyster bar, part bistro, part diner and part Jewish deli, if matzo ball soup is anything to go by. The extensive menu hops and skips from herring to clam stew to hummus to a fried catfish hero. The all-bases commitment reaches almost comical heights with the special platters, a United Nations of surf and turf interpretations. There's steamed lobster and New York strip steak served with French fries or fried catfish and fried chicken with mashed potatoes and gravy. Dragon and Phoenix is Oriental surf and turf, a pile of butter-flied shrimp, pigeon and bok choy. Europe is not forgotten. The paella royale, a $98 blowout, gathers a whole lobster, shrimp, salmon, striped bass, chicken, chicken sausage, mussels, clams, red peppers and peas in one teeming bowl.

The menu includes a special fruits de mer section with oysters, clams, crayfish, crabs and lobster sold by the piece or offered as plateaux de fruits de mer, priced at $62 or $95. The deluxe version, called the Blue Ribbon Royale, comes with two shots of Stoly. Seafood, however, is less than the half of it. Smoked, fried or grilled, seafood reappears throughout the menu, but it shares space with just about anything else: pirogies, steak tartare, cream of tomato soup, tofu ravioli and pork barbecue.

It's all-out to please the neighborhood's taste, and someone has decided that you just can't predict what those people in Brooklyn might want to eat, except when it comes to dessert. There are almost no wimpy desserts at Blue Ribbon. Fresh berries and sorbets are simply engulfed by a caloric tide of soda-fountain and diner favorites, like hot fudge sundae, banana split, root-beer float and banana walnut bread pudding in a banana caramel sauce.

Price range: Apps., $4.50–$14; entrees, $8–$30 (more for some specials); desserts, $6–$11. **Wheelchair access:** Steps to entrance. **Features:** Smoking permitted at bar. **Services:** Takeout.

Blue Ribbon Sushi ☆☆ $$$ JAPANESE/SUSHI
119 Sullivan St. (bet. Prince & Spring Sts.) (212) 343-0404
Credit cards: All major Meals: D, LN Closed Mon.

Blue Ribbon Sushi has good fish and an awesome list of sakes, but beyond that it has very little in common with a classic

Japanese sushi bar. If you have ever felt like a clumsy foreigner and worried about doing the wrong thing, this is the sushi bar for you. The menu is enormous, but the high point of the meal is always sushi and sashimi. The sushi chefs are at their best when inventing interesting specials like an appealing roll filled with fried oysters. And unfettered by tradition, they create unusual special platters filled with whatever happens to be best that day. Just name the price you are willing to pay and let them amaze you. (*Ruth Reichl*)

Other recommended dishes: Steamed soybeans; grated mountain yam with raw tuna; tiger's eye; squid "noodles"; ginger ice cream. **Wine list:** Minimal, but 11 sakes are nicely described and sold by the glass, cedar box or bottle. **Price range:** Apps., $4.25–$15.50; entrees, $11.75–$27.50; desserts, $4–$7. **Wheelchair access:** A few steps to dining room. **Services:** Takeout.

Blue Velvet 1929 $25 & Under   VIETNAMESE

227 First Ave. (near 14th St.)   (212) 260-9808
Credit cards: All major   Meals: L

Despite the suggestive name, this is in fact a low-key Vietnamese restaurant with a focus on the French. You can imagine Blue Velvet more as a colonial outpost, where patterned beige walls, a scattering of bamboo plants and a few palm fronds pass for exoticism, than as a Vietnamese hangout. The kitchen presents each dish simply but beautifully, graced with banana leaves, stalks of lemon grass and other modest adornments, with food carefully calibrated to intrigue but not intimidate. On the whole, it's pretty well done. Blue Velvet excels at delicate and fresh Vietnamese appetizers. Spring rolls are crisp and narrow, stuffed with minced chicken and herbs. They are delicious when wrapped in fresh lettuce leaves and dipped in nuoc cham, the invigorating sweet-and-sour Vietnamese condiment of fish sauce, lime juice and vinegar. Banh cuon are even better: chicken, shrimp, bean sprouts and shallots are wrapped in almost transparent crepes and steamed just enough.

Compared with the appetizers, main courses are a mixed bag. Sliced chicken breast is beautifully flavored with anise-like Thai basil, lemon grass and ginger and adorned with sweet potato crisps. Baby back ribs are exceptionally tender and flavorful, marinated in soy, honey and spices. Desserts include luscious roasted bananas that are as sweet as compote.

Other recommended dishes: Seafood soup; cool beef salad; gui cuon; grilled eggplant; roast duck with ginger; stuffed whole prawns; lemon tart. **Price range:** Apps., $5–$9.25; entrees, $9–$14.25. **Wheelchair access:** Everything on one level; restrooms are narrow.

Blue Water Grill ☆ $$ SEAFOOD

31 Union Sq. W. (at 16th St.)   (212) 675-9500
Credit cards: All major   Meals: Br, L, D, LN

Built as a bank in 1904, this is a big, breezy room with a side-walk cafe and a casual air. Along with pleasant service, large portions and reasonable prices can come large crowds and long waits. While it's not the most creative menu in the world, the food is well prepared and very good. Shrimp and oysters are good choices; so is the grilled fish. Desserts are not among Blue Water Grill's happy surprises, but the brownie sundae would make most people very happy. (*Ruth Reichl, updated by Eric Asimov*)

Other recommended dishes: Grilled marinated shrimp; steamers in pilsner beer broth; crab cake; seared yellowfin tuna; Moroccan spiced red snapper; grilled chicken. **Wine list:** The wine list has both pitfalls and happy surprises. Avoid the Sancerre; try the Bandol rose. Prices are fair. **Price range:** Lunch entrees, $10–$25; Dinner: apps., $6–$11; entrees, $18–$28; desserts, $5.50–$6.50. **Wheelchair access:** Restrooms not accessible. **Features:** Kid friendly, smoking permitted, outdoor dining (street-side patio). **Services:** Takeout, private parties.

Boat Basin Cafe $ AMERICAN

W. 79th St. & Riverside Park   (212) 496-5542
Credit cards: All major   Meals: L, D

One of New York's most eccentric and exciting little restaurants is in the formerly abandoned space at the west end of 79th Street. All the cooking is done on grills set up beneath the rotunda. The burgers are great, the menu keeps expanding and there isn't a nicer place for a drink at sunset. An added bonus: musicians who show up and play for tips.

Price range: Apps., $5–$9; entrees, $8–$17; desserts, $4–$5. **Features:** View of Hudson, smoking permitted, outdoor dining. **Services:** Private parties.

Bobby Van's ☆ $$$$ STEAKHOUSE

230 Park Ave. (at 46th St.)   (212) 867-5490
Credit cards: All major   Meals: L, D   Closed Sun.

Bobby Van's is a classic two-fisted steakhouse. With white tablecloths and lots of wood, this is a meat eater's paradise where most of the waiters are old pros who make you feel lucky to be in their hands. The Harry salad, a hearty mixture of green beans, chopped shrimp, bacon and tomatoes, is curiously tasty, and shrimp broiled with lemon and pepper are very appealing. Even the shrimp cocktail is good. The lobster is gorgeously cooked and so tasty that the big dishes of butter are completely unnecessary. The tenderloin is funky, rich and delicious. Desserts are so large they are almost obscene. There's a serious wine list and a bar in front filled with men drinking martinis and smoking cigarettes. They look as if they have been sitting there forever. (*Ruth Reichl*)

Other recommended dishes: Mixed green salad; porterhouse steak; veal chop; grilled fish; onion rings. **Wine list:** Many big red wines that go well with meat, at average prices. **Price range:** Apps., $7–$15; entrees, $23–$35; desserts, $5–$8.50. **Wheelchair access:** Fully accessible. **Features:** Good for business, smoking permitted. **Services:** Takeout, private parties.

Boca Chica $25 & Under   PAN-LATIN

13 First Ave. (at 1st St.)   (212) 473-0108
Credit cards: All major   Meals: L, D

Brazil, Bolivia, Argentina, Mexico, Cuba and the Dominican Republic are just some of the countries whose cuisines are juxtaposed on the enticing menu of this little pan-Latin restaurant. Top choices include camarones chipotle — shrimp in a tomato, chili and cilantro sauce; crisp, tangy chicharrones de pollo — the classic Dominican dish of chicken pieces marinated in lime, soy and spices; and pinones– sweet plantains stuffed with ground beef and pork. Service is sometimes slow when the boisterous dining room is filled.

Other recommended dishes: Shrimp, cheese, avocado and green chili quesadillas; heart of palm and yam salad; grilled pork chops with sweet and spicy sauce; vegetable burrito. **Price range:** Apps., $3.50–$6.50; entrees, $6.50–$15.95; desserts, $3.50. **Wheelchair access:** Restrooms not accessible. **Features:** Smoking permitted. **Services:** Takeout.

Bolo ☆☆ $$$ SPANISH

23 E. 22nd St. (bet. Park Ave. S. & Broadway)   (212) 228-2200
Credit cards: All major   Meals: L, D

Bobby Flay of Mesa Grill does a riff on Spanish cuisine in this colorful, casual and attractive restaurant. From the bold graphic collages on the wall to the Gaudí-style tiles around the oven, Bolo vibrates with the humorous edginess of Barcelona. The food has the same exuberance: little brown rings of fried squid come with a lemony parsley pesto and a lively anchovy vinaigrette, both excellent. The paellas are great, and desserts are lovely, especially the caramel sorbet.

Other recommended dishes: Bolo salad; pork loin; black-and-gold rice and beans; apple tortilla. **Wine list:** Spanish and American wines, well chosen and fairly priced. **Price range:** Lunch: apps., $7.50–$11; entrees, $13–$18. Dinner: apps.,

$8–$14; entrees, $22.50–$31; desserts, $8. **Wheelchair access:** Restrooms not accessible. **Features:** Smoking permitted. **Services:** Private parties.

Bond Street ☆☆ $$ JAPANESE
6 Bond St. (near Broadway)   (212) 777-2500
Credit Cards: All major   Meals: D   Closed Sun.

Cool and casually elegant, filled with thin, young, beautiful people and often horrendously noisy, this Nobu emulator is, nevertheless, a place of surprising sweetness where inventive Japanese dishes are as stylish as the customers. Ask for the chef's choice sashimi and sushi, called omakase, and the waiter will ask about your budget. A splurge will be rewarded with pristine slices of sashimi nestled against a crystalline block of ice decorated with fresh flowers. Sushi will follow. Soups are clear and clean flavored. Noodles are good, too — particularly green tea soba in a broth enhanced by crunchy bamboo shoots and slippery sheets of seaweed. Chilean sea bass, marinated in miso and grilled, is fine, and toro, the richest tuna, has the quality of a fine steak.

The more elaborate desserts are well crafted — chocolate fondue, sorbets and the cookies called Sweet Nothings. Or you can settle for a bite of candied ginger.

Other recommended dishes: Marinated sashimi salad with soba seed risotto; sashimi over frozen shiso vinaigrette; dobin mushi; broth with truffles and clams; kanpachi (amberjack) with chili daikon dressing; caviar sushi; steamed yuba dumpling. **Wine list:** Nicely chosen for the food. An appealing list of sakes as well. **Price range:** Sushi, $6–$28; apps., $4–$24; entrees, $18–$26; desserts, $7–$14. **Wheelchair access:** Dining room is up a flight of stairs. **Services:** Private parties.

Bongo $25 & Under   SEAFOOD
299 10th Ave. (near 28th St.)   (212) 947-3654
Credit cards: MC/V   Meals: D, LN

On any given day, Bongo serves half a dozen kinds of oysters, from Fanny Bays, which have a flavor shockingly like cucumbers, to Pemaquids, which are impressively salty, to Wellfleets, which have a pronounced mineral tang. With no more than a squirt of lemon, they are always impeccably fresh and gloriously sensual. The decadent allure of the oysters makes an amusing contrast to the suburban 20th-century modern style of the room, a quirky replica of 1950's living rooms. Aside from the oysters, the limited menu has a few other highlights, like wonderful, meaty lobster rolls served on crustless hot dog buns grilled in butter with sweet coleslaw, and an excellent smoked trout salad

Price range: Oysters, $1.50–$2.25 each (minimum order, half-dozen); salads, shrimp and lobster rolls, $6–$15.50; chilled lobster, $19.50. **Wheelchair access:** Step up at entrance; restrooms one step up from dining room.

Borgo Antico $$ ITALIAN
22 E. 13th St. (bet. Fifth Ave. & University Pl.)   (212) 807-1313
Credit cards: All major   Meals: Br, L, D, LN

Appealing northern Italian food in a laid-back atmosphere. Great if you're in the neighborhood.

Price range: Lunch: avg. app., $6; entree, $9.50; dessert, $6.50. Dinner: avg. app., $7; entree, $11.50; dessert, $6.50. **Features:** Smoking area. **Services:** Delivery, takeout, catering, private parties.

Bottino $$ ITALIAN
246 10th Ave. (bet. 24th & 25th Sts.)   (212) 206-6766
Credit cards: All major   Meals: D

Set in the midst of the budding West Chelsea gallery scene, this restaurant/wine bar has a delightful outdoor garden. Fifteen wines are offered by the glass to accompany items like bocconcini of fresh mozzarella, tuna carpaccio and bresaola with arugula. For more than a quick bite, Bottino offers grilled fish and pastas. There is an adjacent takeout section.

Other recommended dishes: Bocconcini; Norwegian salmon and penne with wild boar sausage. **Price range:** Lunch: apps., $6–$10; entrees, $10–$18; desserts, $7. Dinner: apps., $7–$14; entrees, $15–$27; desserts, $7. **Wheelchair access:** One step into dining room. **Features:** Smoking permitted, outdoor dining. **Services:** Delivery, takeout, catering, private parties.

Boughalem $25 & Under   BISTRO
14 Bedford St. (bet. Houston & Downing Sts.)   (212) 414-4764
Credit cards: AE   Meals: D

This is one of the most charming of the city's small, moderately priced bistros, with a stylish dining room that appeals to both uptown and downtown crowds, professional service and terrific food. Highlights include a circle of couscous that conceals a pungent array of grilled shrimp and roasted tomatoes embedded within; crisp little oval potato dumplings stuffed with minced shrimp, and terrific seared sea scallops.

Other recommended dishes: Grilled chicken; seared tuna steak; pan–roasted monkfish. **Price range:** Apps., $6–$9; entrees, $12–$19; desserts, $7–$8. **Features:** Romantic.

Bouley Bakery ☆☆☆☆ $$$$ FRENCH

120 W. Broadway (at Duane St.)   (212) 964-2525
Credit cards: All major   Meals: L, D

After an expansion and a slick renovation Bouley Bakery has
re-emerged as a resplendent, reinvented finer version of its former self. The restaurant crackles with a new energy, and
owner-chef David Bouley, as though responding to his new
jewel box of a theater, is turning out food that is nothing less
than inspired. It is stunningly good and consistently ascends to
the highest level.

As a chef, Mr. Bouley has it all—elegance, finesse and flair.
His flavors are extraordinarily clear and exquisitely balanced;
his use of seasoning is so deft as to be insidious. Even his most
complex creations have a classical simplicity to them. Mr.
Bouley cooks the way Racine wrote and Descartes thought. His
rack of lamb with glazed salsify and chanterelles is potent, with
an intoxicating overlay of sage. Even roast chicken takes flight
in his hands. It comes with an opulent Madeira sauce that
enfolds nicoise olives and organic tomatoes like a silken cloak.

Diners who demand the full monty when it come to desserts
will not be disappointed by "secret pleasures," a multilayer affair
of thin milk chocolate leaves separating layers of milk-chocolate
ganache and chantilly cream, all of it sitting on a toasted hazelnut dacquoise.

Bouley Bakery retains the feel of a neighborhood restaurant
where diners feel comfortable showing up in shirtsleeves. But
the staff shrewdly maintains a delicate balance between informality and a more disciplined level of service implicit in the food
and décor. The waiters seem passionate about the food and
deeply concerned that diners enjoy it to the full.

Wine list: An imaginative bistro list of about 90 wines, with a
dozen wines by the glass and a reserve list of 30 wines. **Price
range:** Lunch: apps., $7.50–$12; entrees, $24–$32; desserts,
$7–$9.50; six-course prix fixe lunch, $35. Dinner: apps.,
$9.50–$18; entrees, $27–$38; desserts, $7.50–$9; six-course tasting menu, $75. **Wheelchair access:** Everything at street level.
Services: Takeout, catering, private parties.

Bouterin ☆ $$$$ FRENCH

420 E. 59th St. (bet. First Ave. & Sutton Pl.)   (212) 758-0323
Credit cards: All major   Meals: D

Serving Provençal food in a Provençal atmosphere, this restaurant can be charming. The room has a casual cluttered feeling,
and it is all so sweet that it is easy to be indulgent. The best
dishes are the chef's old family recipes, like the hearty vegetable soupe au pistou, which tastes the way it might if had
been made on a wood-burning oven on a Provençal farm. The

tarte a la Provençale is a solid, savory wedge that seems like a snack that might be sold on the streets of Marseille. The rack of lamb wrapped in a herbal crust and sea bass in a bold bouillabaisse sauce each give a purely Provençal impression. The daube of beef, too, is delicious, the beef slowly stewed in red wine and garlic. (*Ruth Reichl*)

Other recommended dishes: Floating island; soufflés. **Wine list:** Little imagination has gone into the list, but the prices are fair. **Prices:** Apps., $8–$11; entrees, $20–$32; desserts, $5–$8. **Wheelchair access:** Entrance is four steps down. **Features:** Good for business. **Services:** Private parties.

Box Tree Inn $$$$ CONTINENTAL

250 E. 49th St. (bet. Second & Third Aves.) (212) 758-8320
Credit cards: All major Meals: L, D

The Art Deco dining room is beautiful, with its dark wood, stained glass and fancy fireplaces, and the Box Tree is considered one of New York's most romantic restaurants, but it is expensive and unbearably pretentious. It serves fancy, not very good Continental food for $86 a person, prix fixe. However, it is not impossible to find a few acceptable dishes to go with the dreamy décor. Appetizers are easiest. My favorite is the smooth terrine of duck liver. Main courses are the most difficult, but dessert holds no terrors. The vacherin, chocolate cake and raspberry brûlée are all perfectly pleasant. (*Ruth Reichl*)

Other recommended dishes: Snails with Pernod sauce; cold poached trout; chilled cucumber and yogurt soup; rack of lamb; broiled salmon. **Wine list:** Pretentious and overpriced. **Price range:** Prix–fixe lunch, $42; prix–fixe dinner, $86. **Wheelchair access:** Dining room is down a few steps. **Features:** Romantic. **Services:** Catering, private parties.

Brasserie ☆☆ $$$ BRASSERIE/FRENCH

100 E. 53rd St. (at Lexington Ave.) (212) 751-4840
Credit cards: All major Meals: B, Br, L, D, LN

The old Brasserie, which opened in 1959 and closed in 1995 after a kitchen fire, was so much a part of the city's fabric that the temptation must have been strong to reconstruct it, lovingly, piece by piece. But when patrons of the old Brasserie enter now, their jaws drop. The staircase down to the dining room, once a perilous descent for wobbly late-night revelers, has been transformed into a gentle slope of translucent steps. There's now a bar, with a bank of overhead monitors broadcasting images of customers who are captured on video as they spin through the restaurant's revolving door. The interior has been sheathed in a thin perforated pearwood veneer, arranged in overlapping panels that suggest airplane flaps. In futuristic booths along the side of the room, the tables are slabs of translucent lime-green acrylic. It's way too much design for one restaurant to contain, but the message could not be clearer. The Brasserie is ready for a new life.

For nostalgia, look to the menu. The onion soup is still there. It's only so-so, a pallid artifact. The goujonettes of sole are there, too — firm, expertly fried fingers of breaded fish with a thick, sharp mustard rémoulade for dipping. Chef Luc Dimnet delivers sensible, well-executed food with up-to-date touches but not too many neurotic kinks. Mr. Dimnet never met a root vegetable he didn't like. It's a two-way love affair. The carrots, potatoes and parsnips in his short rib pot-au-feu, another of the Brasserie classics indicated on the menu in boldface, have a startling freshness, as though they have just been pulled out of the dirt, and they redouble the dish's appeal. The nightly specials, on a fixed weekly rotation, begin Sunday with roast duck and wind up Saturday with venison stew. I recommend Wednesday, when the featured dish is stewed rabbit in a sharp mustard sauce, a full complement of root vegetables and a plateful of chewy spätzle.

For dessert try the chocolate beignets. Each powdered morsel, oozing with a perfectly measured mouthful of molten chocolate, reaffirms the genius of the doughnut concept.

Other recommended dishes: Roasted monkfish; seared salmon; crème brûlée; lemon profiteroles. **Price range:** Lunch: Apps., $7–$12; entrees, $14–$24; desserts, $7.50. **Dinner:** Apps., $7–$14; entrees, $14–$28; desserts, $7.50. **Wine list:** An intelligently selected bistro list of about 260 mostly French wines; 12 half bottles, 15 by the glass. **Wheelchair access:** Wheelchair lift to the right of the entrance. Handicapped restroom on dining room level.

Brasserie 8 ¹/₂ ☆ $$$ BRASSERIE/FRENCH

9 W. 57th St. (bet. Fifth & Sixth Aves.)   (212) 829-0812
Credit cards: All major   Meals: B, Br, L, D, LN

Visually, Brasserie 8 ¹/₂ is a knockout. The downward swoosh is a circular staircase in thick salmon carpeting. It winds down through an enormous hole in the floor to a low-slung illuminated onyx bar and an open-plan lounge, where deeply cushioned black leather chairs cluster. The anteroom feels like the departure lounge for the space shuttle. The dining room could be a galactic mess hall, with a white terrazzo tile floor and black leather booths. At the far end of the room, a stained-glass mural by Leger makes almost no impression. There's too much competition.

The traditional brasserie menu can be seen in a mostly standard raw bar selection, an iced seafood platter and a weekly rotation of specials like bouillabaisse on Fridays and confit of suckling pig on Thursdays. Wednesday deserves a check on the calendar. The plat du jour is a thick slab of Muscovy duck breast, coyly listed as a "steak," with a crisp, golden skin outside, pink, oozing meat inside and a sweet, sticky fig compote on the side. A perfectly fine steak au poivre, mussels marinière and a wonderfully gamy hanger steak round out the week. For dessert try the arresting milk–chocolate crème brûlée, iced with a rose marmalade and surrounded by candied rose petals.

There is a design flaw. The booths in the center of the room are so deep that most waitresses cannot reach the diners on the inside. It has placed a premium on male waiters with long arms, who are constantly called on to help. It makes "pardon my reach" the mantra for the evening.

Other recommended dishes: Potato and roasted garlic soup; haricots verts with macadamia butter; "reverse" chocolate soufflé; banana split. **Wine list:** An eclectic international list of about 150 wines, with a dozen half bottles and wines by the glass. **Price range:** Lunch: apps., $8–$15; entrees, $15–$29; desserts, $8. Dinner: apps., $8–$16; entrees, $18–$30; desserts, $8. **Wheelchair access:** Elevators to dining room; restrooms via corridor. **Services:** Private parties.

Brawta $25 & Under   Caribbean

347 Atlantic Ave., Boerum Hill, Brooklyn   (718) 855-5515
Credit cards: All major   Meals: Br, L, D

Brawta, Jamaican patois for "something extra," offers top-flight Jamaican food in a relaxed, colorful dining room. Rotis — peppery stews of chicken or mellow goat rolled up in huge, soft flatbreads — are superb, as is the spicy jerk chicken. Coco shrimp is an unusual and generous shrimp curry made with coconut milk. Don't miss the traditional Caribbean beverages, like sweet-and-spicy sorrel and the thick sea moss, a legendary boon to male virility. For dessert, try the bread pudding.

Price range: Apps., $4–$8.50; entrees, $9.50–$18; desserts, $3.50–$6. **Wheelchair access:** Fully accessible. **Services:** Delivery, takeout, catering, private parties.

Bricco $25 & Under   Italian

304 W. 56th St. (bet. Eighth & Ninth Aves.)   (212) 245-7160
Credit cards: All major   Meals: L, D   Closed Sun.

These inventive trattorias offer enough twists on the basic Italian formula to keep you intrigued, such as an appetizer of fresh anchovies the size of sardines, marinated but still firm and briny. Other excellent appetizers include tiny tender clams in a white wine and garlic broth and broiled rings of calamari, still smoky from the wood fire. Don't count on tranquility; when crowded, the dining rooms are loud.

Other recommended dishes: Octopus, fennel, and arugula salad; steamed clams; veal chop; filet mignon in creamy peppercorn–brandy sauce. **Price range:** Apps., $5.50–$6.95; entrees, $9.95–$19.95; desserts, $5.95. **Wheelchair access:** Fully accessible. **Features:** Smoking permitted. **Services:** Delivery, takeout, catering, private parties.

Bright Food Shop $25 & Under   ASIAN FUSION
216 Eighth Ave. (at 21st St.)   (212) 243-4433
Credit cards: Cash only   Meals: Br, D

This spare, minimalist former luncheonette serves an exciting blend of Asian and Southwestern ingredients. Scallop ceviche — chopped, marinated shellfish served on a crisp tostada — is a terrific appetizer. Green chili pozole is tart, vinegary and thick with chorizo and hominy, while the smoked trout and red peppers, wrapped in rice and seaweed, is a post-modern sushi roll. Bluefish salpicon, in which the fish is chopped and pickled with vinegar and chilies and served in corn tortillas, stands out among the main courses.

Other recommended dishes: Chips and salsa; tomato and shrimp soup; mushroom enchiladas; salmon with black sesame seeds; blackberry–and–nectarine crisp; chocolate pudding. **Alcohol:** Beer and wine. **Price range:** Apps., $4.75–$7.50; entrees, $12.75–$16.25; desserts, $5. **Wheelchair access:** Restrooms not accessible. **Services:** Takeout, private parties.

Brooklyn Diner USA $$ DINER
212 W. 57th St. (bet. B'way & Seventh Ave.)   (212) 977-1957
Credit cards: All major   Meals: B, Br, L, D, LN

From the street, this looks like just another restaurant-as-theme park. But when you walk inside and find the booths filled with guys drinking coffee and reading the paper, it almost feels like the real thing. Unlike the other nearby theme restaurants, this one is for grown-ups — grown-ups with big appetites. Breakfasts include the standard egg and pancake dishes, cereal, matzoh brie and corned beef hash. There are also oddities, like breakfast carbonara, which is ziti, eggs and pancetta. Lunch and dinner dishes reflect the entire Brooklyn melting pot.

Other recommended dishes: Hamburgers; hot dogs; salads; pot roast; baked zitti. **Price range:** Breakfast: $6.95–$17.95. Lunch: $10.95–$19.95. Dinner: apps., $5.95–$9.95; entrees, $10.95–$24.95; desserts, $5.95–$7.50. **Wheelchair access:** Fully accessible. **Features:** Kid friendly. **Services:** Delivery, takeout.

Brother Jimmy's BBQ $$ BARBECUE

1644 Third Ave. (at 92nd St.)   (212) 426-2020
428 Amsterdam Ave. (bet. 80th & 81st Sts.)   (212) 501-7515
1485 Second Ave. (bet 77th & 78th Sts.)   (212) 288-0999
Credit cards: All major   Meals: D, LN

These restaurants are loud, continuous frat parties, but the
Southern food and barbecue are pretty good, especially the
excellent spareribs, available with sauce or with a dry spice rub.
Is it worth braving the crowd? Takeout is a good option.

Other recommended dishes: Barbecued pork; collard greens;
yams with butter and nutmeg. **Price range:** Avg. app., $7;
entree, $15; dessert, $4. **Features:** Kid friendly, smoking permitted. **Services:** Delivery, takeout, catering, private parties.

Brunetta's Restaurant $ ITALIAN

190 First Ave. (bet. 11th & 12th Sts.)   (212) 228-4030
Credit cards: Cash only   Meals: D

A tiny, ultra-simple Italian restaurant with down-to-earth pastas
at extremely affordable prices, Brunetta's blossoms in the warm
weather, when a festive garden opens, doubling the size of the
restaurant.

Alcohol: Beer and wine. **Price range:** Apps., $4.95; entrees,
$9–$14.95; desserts, $4. **Wheelchair access:** Restrooms not
accessible. **Features:** Smoking permitted, outdoor dining. **Services:** Takeout, catering, private parties.

Bryant Park Grill $$ NEW AMERICAN

25 W. 40th St. (bet. Fifth & Sixth Aves.)   (212) 840-6500
Credit cards: All major   Meals: Br, L, D

Hugh Hardy designed one of New York City's airiest and most
attractive dining rooms just behind the library. The Grill is a
gorgeous pavilion with a bird mural stretching across one wall
and banquettes wrapped in a wonderful leaf-printed pattern.
Spacious and solid, with windows looking out on a vista of
grass, flowers, trees, shaded walkways and big buildings in the
background, the Bryant Park Grill looks more like Paris than
New York. The opening of the restaurant virtually revitalized
the park. So why is the light American food so disappointing?
(*Ruth Reichl*)

Price range: Lunch: apps., $5–$10; entrees, $15–$20; desserts,
$5–$7. Dinner: apps., $5–$11; entrees, $17–$24; desserts, $5–$7.
Prix–fixe dinner, 5–7 P.M. daily, $25. **Wheelchair access:** Fully
accessible. **Features:** Kid friendly, romantic, smoking permitted,
outdoor dining. **Services:** Catering, private parties.

Bulgin' Waffles $25 & Under   WAFFLES

49 1/2 First Ave. (near Third St.)   (212) 477-6555.
Credit cards: All major   Meals: B, L, D

This spare corner restaurant, which most resembles an American college-town coffeehouse, serves wonderful waffles. The namesake Bulgin' Waffle, the kind you might find in Belgium, is indeed big and thick, yet it's airy and fluffy. Even better are the smaller buckwheat wafflettes, exquisitely light and crisp, with more flavor than the big, white-flour waffles. You won't find those in Belgium, which is Belgium's loss. The biggest drawbacks at Bulgin' are that the waffles are served on paper plates with flimsy plastic cutlery and that you have to pay $.85 for pure maple syrup or any of the excellent fruit syrups.

Alcohol: Beer only. **Price range:** Entrees, $4–$5. **Wheelchair access:** Fully accessible. **Services:** Take out, private parties.

Bull & Bear Pub $$$ NEW AMERICAN

Waldorf = Astoria Hotel, 301 Park Ave. (at 49th St.)
    (212) 872-4900
Credit cards: All major   Meals: L, D, LN

One of the venerable restaurants of the Waldorf = Astoria Hotel, and one of the city's best examples of the steakhouse style of dining room. The wood-paneled dining room is a splendid space that evokes the past, and the capacious bar is a beauty, all by itself worth the price of admission. The food, however, is American, predictable and only fair.

Price range: Avg. app., $11; entree, $24; dessert, $6.50. **Wheelchair access:** Fully accessible. **Features:** Good for business. **Services:** Private parties.

Butterfield 81 ☆☆ $$$ NEW AMERICAN

170 E. 81st St. (bet. Third & Lexington Aves.)   (212) 288-2700
Credit cards: All major   Meals: D

Small, dark, cozy and casual; it looks like the perfect Upper East Side neighborhood hangout. Expect great food, good service and high prices. Chef Patricia Williams has introduced appetizers like red-hot shrimp with buttermilk slaw and entrees like striped bass with chorizo, leeks and cranberry beans.
(*Ruth Reichl, updated by William Grimes*)

Wine list: Exciting, well chosen and expensive, with only five wines below $30. **Price range:** Apps., $8–$12; entrees, $21–$30; desserts, $7–$9; three-course prix-fixe dinner, 5:30–6:15 P.M., $27. **Wheelchair access:** Dining room at street level; restrooms up a small flight of stairs. **Features:** Romantic, smoking permitted, outdoor dining. **Services:** Takeout, private parties.

Cabana Carioca $$ LATIN AMERICAN/BRAZILIAN
123 W. 45th St. (bet. Sixth & Seventh Aves.)   (212) 581-8088
Credit cards: All major   Meals: L, D

This Brazilian restaurant is a prime choice for inexpensive, filling and delicious food in the theater district. Dishes like roast
suckling pig, garlicky roast chicken and feijoada are not likely
to win awards for subtlety, but you will leave stuffed. The décor
is tacky, service can be spotty, but prices are reasonable and
lunch can be unbelievably cheap.

Price range: Apps., $1.95–$7.65; entrees, $9.95–$19.85;
desserts, $3. Lunch buffet, $6 and $9.95. **Wheelchair access:**
Not accessible. **Features:** Kid friendly, smoking permitted. **Services:** Takeout, private parties.

Cafe Asean $25 & Under   PAN-ASIAN
117 W. 10th St. (bet. Greenwich & Sixth Aves.)   (212) 633-0348
Credit cards: Cash only   Meals: L, D

The dining room looks like a stylized New England farmhouse,
but the menu is pan-Asian, with Vietnamese dishes being the
best bets. A friendly, welcoming atmosphere and pleasant garden make Cafe Asean quite the civilized place to eat.

Recommended dishes: Bun tom (rice vermicelli with grilled
shrimp), salads, goi cuon (shrimp and rice noodles). **Alcohol:**
Beer and wine. **Price range:** Lunch: apps., $4–$5; entrees,
$6–$7; desserts, $3–$5. Dinner: apps., $5–$6; entrees, $9–$13;
desserts, $3–$5. **Wheelchair access:** Restrooms not accessible.
Features: Romantic, smoking permitted, outdoor dining. **Services:** Takeout, catering, private parties.

Café Boulud   ☆☆☆ $$$$ FRENCH
20 E. 76th St. (near Madison Ave.)   (212) 772-2600
Credit cards: All major   Meals: L, D

Café Boulud is sleek and easy. In the crowded, sometimes noisy
dining room, cheerful waiters walk around wearing grins and
shirtsleeves. In the kitchen, Mr. Boulud and his chef are playing
with food. This is your opportunity to find out what happens
when a great chef at the top of his form stretches out and takes
chances.

The menu, which changes frequently, is divided into four
sections: La Tradition (classic country cooking), La Saison (seasonal dishes), Le Potager (vegetarian choices), and Le Voyage
(world cuisine). What that really means is, anything goes. It
gives the chefs the excuse to serve gutsy deep-fried fritters
stuffed with salt cod one night and a subtle cup of shrimp snuggled against pink grapefruit in an icy infusion of Earl Grey tea
on another.

Most days there are 30 or more dishes, and none are ordinary. A ceviche of scallops and oysters paved with caviar, listed as a seasonal dish, offers a stunning contrast to the hearty casserole of tripe, offered as a traditional dish. They are all completely delicious.

The most satisfying sections are La Saison and La Tradition. In the latter, you may find pig's feet laced with truffles, or salads scattered with skate or chicken livers. Equally inspired by the passing of the seasons, Mr. Boulud roasts fat sea scallops and serves them with crosnes, a crisp little white root vegetable. His scallion risotto is lavish with white truffles. Soup is another sure thing. The Potager and Voyage sections are less successful, but never dull. It is interesting to see how Mr. Boulud interprets the food of Spain or Mexico, like arroz verde with chorizo or ceviche of red snapper with lime and papaya, or how he works with cardamom, saffron, sumac and cumin. *(Ruth Reichl)*

Wine list: Exciting, with many selections at reasonable prices. The sommelier offer very intelligent advice. **Price range:** Lunch: apps., $10–$18; entrees, $19–$30; desserts, $6–$13; two-course prix fixe, $29; three-course prix fixe, $36. Dinner: apps., $9–$22; entrees, $22–$36; desserts, $9–$13. **Wheelchair access:** Fully accessible. **Features:** Outdoor dining (sidewalk). **Services:** Catering.

Cafe Centro ☆☆ $$$ FRENCH/MEDITERRANEAN

200 Park Ave. (at 45th St.)   (212) 818-1222
Credit cards: All major   Meals: L, D   Closed Sun.

This big, bold, bustling brasserie in the heart of Midtown serves good, affordable, French-Mediterranean food in a lively setting. The kitchen makes gutsy bistro food, expanded and spiced up for an American audience. The frisée aux lardons, a heap of curly endive rich with bacon, Cantal cheese and garlic toasts, is a veritable meal, but it's listed as an appetizer. The bouillabaisse is very tasty, too. There are other dishes at Cafe Centro that don't quite make it. But there are no disappointments among the desserts. *(Ruth Reichl)*

Other recommended dishes: Chilled seafood; Provençal fish soup; beef stew Provençal; T-bone steak; herb-roasted chicken; couscous; cassoulet; marquise au chocolat. **Wine list:** Well thought out and well priced with good wines by the glass, and a fine selection of beers. **Price range:** Apps., $8–$12; entrees, $18–$28; desserts, $5.50–$7.50. Prix–fixe dinner, $28; pretheater prix fixe, $24.50, Sat. only. **Wheelchair access:** Everything at street level. **Features:** Kid friendly, good for business, smoking permitted, outdoor dining. **Services:** Private parties.

Cafe Colonial $25 & Under   BRAZILIAN

73 E. Houston St. (at Elizabeth St.)   (212) 274-0044
Credit cards: All major   Meals: B, Br, L, D, LN

Perched on the edge of a trendy neighborhood, Cafe Colonial could easily be a cliché of bad food and worse attitude. The surprise is that the food is so good and the service so sweet. The restaurant has no culinary point to make. Top dishes include a terrific fried soft-shell crab sandwich; tilapia, sautéed until crisp around the edges yet still moist and flavorful within; and grilled squid, served in a cool salad with slices of excellent baguette.

Other recommended dishes: Mussels in spicy tomato sauce; watercress and radicchio salad; split pea soup; pan-roasted sea bass fillet; grilled salmon crusted with sesame seeds; Bahian shrimp in coconut sauce; crème brûlée; chocolate bread pudding. **Alcohol:** Beer and wine. **Price range:** Apps., $2.75–$8.50; entrees, $8–$16.25. **Features:** Romantic, smoking permitted, outdoor dining. **Services:** Delivery, takeout, private parties.

Cafe Con Leche $ LATIN AMERICAN

424 Amsterdam Ave. (bet. 80th & 81st Sts.)   (212) 595-7000
726 Amsterdam Ave. (bet. 95th & 96th Sts.)   (212) 678-7000
Credit cards: All major   Meals: B, L, D

These colorful, modern Hispanic restaurants specialize in robust Cuban and Dominican dishes. Portions are huge, prices are low, and while the newer uptown branch may be friendlier, the food is not yet up to the standard of the further downtown branch, where the roasted pork is a specialty.

Other recommended dishes: Meat or vegetable empanadas; conch with fried plantains; yucca patties; Dominican fried chicken; codfish stew; flan; rum cake. **Price range:** Lunch: apps., $2.75–$5.95; entrees, $4.95–$9.95; desserts, $2.50–$3.75. Dinner: apps., $2.75–$5.95; entrees, $6.95–$13.95; desserts, $2.50–$3.75. **Wheelchair access:** Restrooms not accessible. **Features:** Kid friendly, outdoor dining. **Services:** Delivery, takeout, catering.

Café de Bruxelles $$ BELGIAN

118 Greenwich Ave. (bet. Seventh & Eighth Aves.)
(212) 206-1830
Credit cards: All major   Meals: Br, L, D

The little zinc-topped bar at this cozy Belgian cafe is a warm and welcoming stop. The frites, served in silver cones with dishes of mayonnaise, go beautifully with the unusual Belgian beers, while mussel dishes and heartier Belgian stews are all very good. The small tables near the battered zinc bar are good for solo diners.

Price range: Lunch: apps., $4.50; entrees, $8–$12.75; desserts, $5.50. Dinner: apps., $4–$7.50; entrees, $13.75–$19.50; desserts, $6.50. **Wheelchair access:** Not accessible. **Features:** Romantic, smoking permitted. **Services:** Takeout.

Café des Artistes $$$ CONTINENTAL
1 W. 67th St. (bet. Central Park W. & Columbus Ave.)
(212) 877-3500
Credit cards: All major
Meals: Br, L, D

Its signature murals, leaded-glass windows and paneled wood walls contribute to the genteel impression at this grand cafe. The main room is more neighborly and louder than the intimate tables that ring the bar on the second level. The continental food, however, is surprisingly old-fashioned. Best for grazing before or after a concert.

Price range: Lunch: apps., $7–$18.50; entrees, $16–$24; desserts, $8–$25. Dinner: apps., $8–$30; entrees, $22–$40; desserts, $8–$25. **Features:** Good for business, romantic. **Services:** Private parties.

Café Frida $25 & Under MEXICAN
368 Columbus Ave. (bet. 77th & 78th Sts.)
(212) 712-2929
Credit cards: All major
Meals: D

No serapes in the dining room, no mariachi music in the background and no burritos on the menu. Café Frida is one of the new wave of Mexican restaurants in New York, presenting dishes like marinated lamb shank with avocado leaves and chiles en nogada, poblano chilies stuffed with meat and walnuts and draped in ethereal walnut cream. The food's not always consistent but when it hits, it can be superb.

Price range: Brunch: prix fixe, $9.95. Lunch/Dinner: apps, $8–$12; entrees, $13–$17. **Wheelchair access:** Not accessible.

Cafe Gitane $25 & Under CAFE
242 Mott St. (bet. Houston & Prince Sts.)
(212) 334-9552
Credit cards: Cash only
Meals: B, Br, L, D

Subversive thoughts (and plenty of cigarette smoke) are in the air at this hip Euro-spot, which fills with young people who come not only for the bohemian atmosphere but for a satisfying menu of salads, light meals and unlikely-but-delicious sandwiches like roast chicken with lettuce, chipotle mayonnaise, anchovies and Parmesan.

Alcohol: Beer and wine. **Price range:** Salads and sandwiches, $4–$10. **Wheelchair access:** Everything on one level. **Features:** Smoking permitted, outdoor dining. **Services:** Takeout.

Cafe Habana $25 & Under   LATIN AMERICAN

17 Prince St. (at Elizabeth St.)   (212) 625-2001
Credit cards: All major   Meals: B, L, D, LN

Much of the food here is hearty and enjoyable, certainly not
fussy or pretentious: great roast pork, terrific grilled steak and
good hamburgers. Its design is sleek and minimalist but true to
the look of the old luncheonette. Café Habana imitates its models with love and respect, not irony, preserving the diner's
cheap prices and function as a local hangout. Still, not all of the
dishes work as well as they should, particularly those with a
Mexican touch to them, and some of the basics need work, like
making rice properly and improving the cafe con leche.

Other recommended dishes: Shrimp in garlic sauce; mushrooms in garlic, lemon and olive oil; shrimp and crab croquettes; coconut flan; grilled corn. **Price range:** Apps.,
$2.75–$7.25; entrees, $4.95–$12.50. **Wheelchair access:** All on
one level; narrow way to restrooms. **Features:** Kid friendly. **Services:** Takeout, catering, private parties.

Cafe La Grolla $25 & Under   ITALIAN

411A Amsterdam Ave. (near 80th St.)   (212) 579-9200
Credit cards: All major   Meals: D

This cafe is tiny, holding no more than 30 people. The lighting
is a little too bright, the brick and yellow walls a little too plain,
but almost everything on the menu is delicious, and it is anything but generic Italian. Fried calamari arrives atop a hill of
caponata, a bright and brisk marinated eggplant salad. Salads
are excellent and individual pizzas are superb, with thin, crisp
crusts, exceedingly fresh mozzarella and fine toppings, like pungent anchovies with black olives. Agnolotti is rich and warming, the delicate ravioli squares filled with veal in a velvety
sage-scented reduction of beef broth, while sturdy strands of
whole-wheat bigoli were adorned with shreds of savory duck.
Fish are treated with the utmost respect, like flavorful trout
stuffed with clams and mussels and bathed gently in a lightly
creamy seafood broth. Meat dishes like calf's liver and roasted
pork tenderloin have a nice vinegary edge. Even desserts are
very good, especially a carefully constructed berry tart in a light
marzipan crust and a dark chocolate tart kissed with orange.
About all that is missing is a well-chosen Italian wine list.

Other recommended dishes: Panzanella, artichoke hearts with
almond pesto, pappardelle with veal ragu, monkfish. **Price
range:** Apps., $7–$10; entrees, $9–$20. **Wheelchair access:**
Everything is on one level.

Café Loup $$ BISTRO/FRENCH

105 W. 13th St. (bet. Sixth & Seventh Aves.)   (212) 255-4746
Credit cards: All major   Meals: Br, L, D

Every neighborhood should have a place like easy, comfortable Café Loup, where you can effortlessly feel like a regular. The menu of traditional bistro favorites doesn't challenge, but the restaurant does well by the standards, and that's really the point.

Price range: Lunch: apps., $6; entrees, $10.50; desserts, $6.50. Dinner: apps., $7; entrees, $13.50; desserts, $6.50. **Wheelchair access:** Restrooms not accessible. **Features:** Romantic, smoking permitted. **Services:** Takeout, private parties.

Cafe Luxembourg $$$ BISTRO

200 W. 70th St. (bet. West End & Amsterdam Aves.)
(212) 873-7411
Credit cards: All major   Meals: Br, L, D

The Art Deco room here has a timeless appeal, with cream-colored tile walls, a black-and-white terrazzo floor, sconces and cafe tables. Patrons cluster at the long zinc-topped bar in the early evening. The dining room is a tightly arranged maze of red banquettes and rattan-style chairs. At night the room is soft and seductive. The seasonal menu is orchestrated to offer everything from simple salads and steaks to more refined creations.

Price range: Lunch: apps., $6.75–$9; entrees, $10.50–$22; desserts, $5–$8. Dinner: apps., $7.50–$9.50; entrees, $17–$32; desserts, $5–$8. **Wheelchair access:** Restrooms are narrow. **Features:** Kid friendly, smoking permitted. **Services:** Private parties.

Cafe Riazor $25 & Under SPANISH

245 W. 16th St. (bet. Seventh & Eighth Aves.)   (212) 727-2132
Credit cards: AE   Meals: L, D

At this wonderful old-style subterranean Spanish restaurant in the middle of a residential block in Chelsea, stick with the classics — shrimp, chorizo, octopus, pork — and the sangria. The décor is strictly 1950's bohemian.

Price range: Lunch: apps., $4–$6.75; entrees, $6.25–$18.75; desserts, $2–$3.50. Dinner: apps., $5–$7.75; entrees, $9.50–$18.75; desserts, $2–$3.50. **Wheelchair access:** Not accessible.

Caffe Grazie $25 & Under   ITALIAN

26 E. 84th St. (bet. Fifth & Madison Aves.)   (212) 717-4407
Credit cards: All major   Meals: L, D

This Italian cafe is about as modestly priced as it gets near the
Metropolitan Museum. Featured are pasta dishes of orecchiette
blended with sausage, spinach and mozzarella in garlic and
olive oil and lobster ravioli in white wine sauce. There are also
entrees of pork medallions with prune sauce, and Mediterranean chicken with olives, capers and anchovies.

Other recommended dishes: Arugula with raisins, walnuts and
goat cheese; seared sea scallops; penne in fresh tomato sauce;
grilled mahi–mahi with pineapple salsa. **Price range:** Lunch:
apps., $6.50–$8.50; entrees, $10–$16; desserts, $6–$8. Dinner:
apps., $6.50–$9.50; entrees, $14.50–$21.50; desserts, $6–$8.
Wheelchair access: Three steps down to dining room. **Services:** Delivery, takeout, catering, private parties.

Calle Ocho ☆ $$ PAN-LATIN

446 Columbus Ave. (bet. 81st & 82nd Sts.)   (212) 873-5025
Credit cards: All major   Meals: Br, D

Since this restaurant arrived at the end of 1998, the Upper West
Side has been so dizzy with gratitude that the place is filled
every night. Lively and casual with a busy bar and lounge
scene, Calle Ocho has a cavernous main dining room seating
nearly 200 people. The cooking is as hectic as the nonstop high
volume Latin soundtrack. Start with the lobster ceviche, which
keeps the taste buds on full alert with a subtly insistent chili
flare. For the main course the Argentine hanger steak served
with grilled summer vegetables and tomato salsa is a meat
lover's delight. Thick, moist slabs of pork loin pick up a spicy
piquancy after being rubbed with adobo, a paste made from
ground chilies, and they find just the right surroundings in a big
dollop of chipotle mashed potatoes and roasted corn salsa.
Latin desserts are not for the meek. Sweet on top of sweet is
only half-sweet enough, so be prepared when you order banana
fritters with mamey ice cream and banana caramel sauce, or the
coffee-soaked sponge cake with caramel cream.

Wine list: Budget-priced bistro list, with emphasis on the wines
of Spain, Argentina and Chile, and some interesting sherries
and Spanish brandies. **Price range:** Dinner: apps., $8–$14;
entrees, $16–$24; dessert, $5–$8. Brunch, $19.99. **Wheelchair
access:** Main dining room is five steps up, but wheelchairs can
reach it through 100 W. 81st St.; bathroom is three steps down.
Features: Kid friendly, smoking permitted. **Services:** Takeout,
catering, private parties.

Calo & Co. $$ SPANISH/DINER

18 E. 41st St. (bet. Madison & Fifth Aves.)   (212) 683-1931
Credit cards: All major   Meals: B, L

This versatile newcomer to the Grand Central area offers
breakfast, lunch, tapas, drinks and carryout. The more ambitious restaurant dishes have a Spanish tinge, but you couldn't
really call Calo a Spanish restaurant. It's more like an upscale
diner.

Alcohol: Beer and wine. **Price range:** Apps., $4.95–$6.95;
entrees, $8.95–$14.95; desserts, $3.95–$5.95; prix fixe, $12.95.
Wheelchair access: Fully accessible. **Features:** Outdoor dining.
Services: Delivery, takeout, catering, private parties.

Cal's $$ CONTINENTAL/MEDITERRANEAN

55 W. 21st St. (bet. Fifth & Sixth Aves.)   (212) 929-0740
Credit cards: All major   Meals: L, D, LN

This is a neighborhood restaurant worth leaving your neighborhood for, combining the warmth of a local hangout with the
cool creativity of the Flatiron district's advertising firms and
photographers. The food is a lively blend of Continental and
Mediterranean cuisines, with a nice wine list and terrific hamburgers. Service is friendly, the interior is airy and inviting, and
the long, handsome bar can be a treat for solo diners.

Wine list: Modest list, mostly $25–$40. **Price range:** Lunch:
apps., $6–$8.75; entrees, $15–$20; desserts, $7. Dinner: apps.,
$6–$8.75; entrees, $16–$22; desserts, $7. **Wheelchair access:**
Everything on one level. **Features:** Romantic, outdoor dining.
Services: Takeout, private parties.

Cambodian Cuisine $25 & Under   CAMBODIAN

87 S. Elliott Pl., Fort Greene, Brooklyn   (718) 858-3262
Credit cards: MC/V   Meals: L, D

This may be the only Cambodian restaurant in New York City
and is worth checking out for that reason alone. Most dishes are
similar to Thai and Vietnamese foods — where lemongrass,
galangal, basil, lime juice and peanuts as well as various fish
sauces are characteristic — but some of the preparations are
unusual. In the signature dish, chicken ahmok, chicken breast
is marinated in coconut milk, lemongrass, galangal and kaffir
lime and steamed until it achieves a soft, pudding-like texture.
The voluminous menu also includes quite a few dishes that
seem more Chinese than Cambodian, and a list of interesting-
sounding desserts.

Other recommended dishes: Tchrok spey kdaob (sweet, pickled vegetables); hot-and-spicy ground beef appetizer; samlor

mchookrong (shrimp, tomato, and pineapple soup); nhioem salad (rice noodles and vegetables with lime-and-peanut sauce); Tonle Sap fish (fried fish in creamy lemongrass and basil sauce); kroeurng tao hoo (sautéed bean curd). **Price range:** Apps., $.95–$5.95; entrees, $3.50–$14.95; desserts, $3. **Wheelchair access:** Several steps down from sidewalk; restroom is narrow.

Campagna ☆☆ $$$ ITALIAN
24 E. 21st St. (bet. Broadway & Park Ave. S.)   (212) 460-0900
Credit cards: All major   Meals: L, D

The rustic charm of the setting befits the bold, alluring cooking the kitchen delivers at this popular restaurant that serves Italian food for the beautiful people. It's an unbeatable combination: big portions and a big scene. Pastas include spaghetti in white baby clam sauce; pappardelle tossed with spinach and cream, and goat cheese tortellini mixed with fava beans, asparagus, peas and prosciutto. For main courses, there are pan-roasted chicken breast in a balsamic reduction; grilled pork chop, aromatic of lemon and thyme, served with roasted fennel; veal scallopine topped with melted smoked mozzarella and marinated tomatoes, and salmon baked with olives, capers and sun-dried tomatoes.

On a recent visit, the restaurant chugged along as always, delivering robust, simple and satisfying Italian food, although the panzanella suffered from squishy bread cubes, and the signature "Finkel Fish," a grilled sole named after a prized customer, is as bland as a slice of wonder bread. (*Ruth Reichl, updated by William Grimes*)

Price range: Lunch: apps., $7.50–$11; entrees, $14–$25; desserts, $8–$10. Dinner: apps., $10–$16; entrees, $17–$35; desserts, $8–$10. **Wheelchair access:** Fully accessible. **Features:** Smoking permitted. **Services:** Takeout, catering, private parties.

Canal House ☆☆ $$$$ NEW AMERICAN
SoHo Grand Hotel, 310 W. Broadway (at Canal St.)
                                                 (212) 965-3588
Credit cards: All major   Meals: B, Br, L, D, LN

This austere, high-ceilinged dining room in the SoHo Grand Hotel, like the hotel itself, does not cater to the mainstream. This is American food for very knowing diners. Take the Manhattan clam chowder, one of the most abused dishes in the East Coast repertory. This one is very light and fresh. The menu tries to feed all appetites at all hours and does not make much of a distinction between appetizers and entrees. Don't dream of visiting Canal House without ordering the macaroni and cheese, which is nothing like the dish of your childhood. The straightforward American dishes are best: roasted chicken with mashed potatoes and sautéed greens, grilled lamb tenderloin with spoon bread, even a hamburger. (*Ruth Reichl*)

Other recommended dishes: Caesar salad; grilled shrimp with spicy lentils; marinated tomato salad; crab cakes; pan–roasted salmon. **Wine list:** Small, nicely chosen and fairly priced. **Price range:** Lunch: apps., $8–$13; entrees, $16–$24. Dinner: apps., $8–$15; entrees, $21–$29; desserts, $8. **Wheelchair access:** Elevator to second floor. **Features:** Kid friendly, smoking permitted. **Services:** Catering, private parties.

Candela ☆ $$ NEW AMERICAN

116 E. 16th St. (near Union Sq.) (212) 254-1600
Credit cards: All major Meals: Br, D

When the dishes click, the food is very exciting. But Candela is maddeningly inconsistent. The candle-lit dining room has a rustic, medieval air but it is vast, dark and clamorous (the perfect place for a Halloween date). What makes this especially disappointing is that the menu is so enticing. Every dish sounds delicious, and the menu is varied enough to offer something for almost anyone. The braised lamb shank is satisfying and flavorful; so is the monkfish. The angel food cake with balsamic-splashed strawberries is good, as is a wonderful apple tart, with its Calvados, rosemary and dried cranberries.

Other recommended dishes: Oysters; risotto cake; spicy chicken wontons; fried oysters over spinach; banana beignets. **Wine list:** Well chosen and fairly priced. **Price range:** Apps., $5–$9.50; entrees, $11.50–$22.50; desserts, $7; pre-theater prix fixe, 5:30–6:30 P.M., $19.99 (three courses). **Wheelchair access:** Fully accessible. **Features:** Good view, outdoor dining (sidewalk). **Services:** Private parties.

Candido Pizza $25 & Under PIZZA

1606 First Ave. (near 84th St.) (212) 396-9401
Credit cards: Cash only Meals: L, D, LN Closed Mon.

This is a classic New York City pizzeria with a coal oven. The crust is light, thin, unusually smooth, crisp and blackened on the bottom, and the toppings are all top quality. Though Candido is only a few years old, it offers the time-honored pizzeria trappings, like a high pressed-tin ceiling and, of course, Frank Sinatra and Tony Bennett in the background. Service is charming, draft beer is served at the right temperature with adequate carbonation, and there is a small selection of decent pasta dishes. But I can't imagine coming here for anything but pizza.

Alcohol: Beer and wine. **Price range:** Apps., $5–$9; entrees, $7–$14. **Wheelchair access:** Fully accessible. **Features:** Kid friendly, outdoor dining. **Services:** Delivery, takeout, catering, private parties.

Candle Cafe $25 & Under   VEGETARIAN
1307 Third Ave. (bet. 74th & 75th Sts.)   (212) 472-0970
Credit cards: MC/V   Meals: Br, L, D

This inviting little restaurant serves food fit not just for vegetarians but also for vegans, meaning no food of animal origins — no milk, no eggs, no cheese. Sometimes this works, but look out for familiar dishes that replace an essential ingredient with a nonanimal substitute. Cows would volunteer their services if they tasted cappuccino with soy milk.

Recommended dishes: French toast; grilled tempeh and mushroom burger. **Alcohol:** Beer and wine. **Price range:** Apps., $6.95–$8.95; entrees, $10.95–$14.95; desserts, $3.95–$5.95. **Wheelchair access:** Restrooms not accessible. **Services:** Delivery, takeout, catering, private parties.

Canteen $$$ NEW AMERICAN
142 Mercer St. (at Prince St.) (212) 431-7676
Credit cards: All major   Meals: Br, L, D

Canteen does make an impression. In an homage to the Lamborghini of the 1970's, half its circular booths and swivel chairs are upholstered in Day-Glo orange, the other half in deep chocolate. The chairs themselves, in a tall, body-hugging design, look as if they were engineered for Warp Speed 9. And the kitchen turns out extroverted food, updated diner and fanciful bistro dishes with an imaginative twist here and there. Chicken pot pie, a big one, comes with an herbed crust, and porcini mushrooms mingle with the chicken, carrot and potato chunks. Peekytoe crab tartar is modernized with a chipotle mayonnaise. One dish has no wrinkles. The "classic shrimp cocktail" is just that. It's served in a martini glass, of course, but the shrimp hanging over the rim are full of flavor, and the rough-textured cocktail sauce is vibrant, bursting with tomato sweetness and fired up with just the right horseradish burn.

Other recommended dishes: Chicken noodle soup; baked Alaska. **Wine List:** $24–$350. By the glass, $6–$12. **Price range:** Apps., $8–$14; entrees, $16–$26. **Wheelchair access:** Separate wheelchair entrance. **Features:** Smoking at bar. **Services:** Private parties.

Canton $$

45 Division St. (bet. Market & Catherine Sts.)   (212) 226-4441
Credit cards: Cash only   Meals: L, D   Closed Mon., Tue.

The perennial favorite of Westerners in Chinatown. The food is
good (and relatively expensive), but unless you're in the mood
for the tried and true, you will do better elsewhere.

Alcohol: Beer. **Price range:** Apps., $3.25–$6; entrees,
$15.95–$45 (lobster). **Wheelchair access:** Restrooms not accessible. **Features:** Kid friendly. **Services:** Takeout, private parties.

Capsouto Frères $$$ BISTRO/FRENCH

451 Washington St. (at Watts St.)   (212) 966-4900
Credit cards: All major   Meals: Br, L, D

Capsouto Frères was a TriBeCa pioneer, moving into a fine old
1891 landmark building long before the area became chic. But
the attractive, popular bistro serves surprisingly disappointing
French fare. Sometimes the desserts save the meal. The blood
orange soufflé, for instance, is just right. It is possible to have a
fine meal at the restaurant. All you have to do is order very
carefully. Or adjust your expectations. Best for brunch.

Other recommended dishes: Oysters on the half shell; arugula
salad with goat cheese; mushroom vol-au-vent; basil-cured
gravlax; cassoulet; steak frites; salade niçoise; grilled tuna with
bearnaise sauce; ice cream terrine. **Wine list:** Unimaginative
but fairly priced. **Price range:** Lunch: apps., $6–$12; entrees,
$14–$24; desserts, $6–$8; prix fixe, $19.99. Brunch: $8.50–$20.
Dinner: apps., $6.50–$15; entrees, $14–$27; desserts, $6.50–$9.
Wheelchair access: Two steps up to dining room; restrooms are
down a flight of stairs. **Features:** Romantic, smoking permitted,
outdoor dining. **Services:** Private parties.

Caravan of Dreams $25 & Under
KOSHER/VEGETARIAN

405 E. 6th St. (bet. First Ave. & Ave. A)   (212) 254-1613
Credit cards: All major   Meals: Br, L, D, LN

The food at this vegetarian restaurant, which looks more like a
college hangout than a health-food spot, is nothing to sneer at.
Caravan is more concerned about making food that tastes good
than about prescribing food that is good for you; as a result, a
dish like nachos, made with fresh organic blue corn chips, spicy
salsa and black beans, is wonderful, better than at most Mexican restaurants. At lunch, Caravan serves several egg dishes
and pancakes, like pear pancakes made of oat and wheat flours
and very good with maple syrup. One area in which Caravan
stints with dairy products is, sadly, dessert, but you can get a
very good cappuccino with real milk.

Other recommended dishes: Hummus; peanut sesame noodles; vegetable burger. Alcohol: Beer and wine. Price range: Apps., $5–$7; entrees, $9–$13; desserts, $4–$7. Wheelchair access: Dining room only. Features: Smoking permitted, outdoor dining. Services: Delivery, takeout, catering, private parties.

Carmichael's Diner $25 & Under   AMERICAN

11708 New York Blvd, Jamaica, Queens   (718) 723-6908
Credit cards: Cash only   Meals: B, L, D.

At this classic, old-style rectangular diner, booths are covered in orange vinyl, and each has its own jukebox. Ceiling fans keep things cool, the Formica tables and terrazzo floors are sparkling, and service is friendly and gracious. This is one of the few places in New York where you can get slices of authentic country ham, tough, leathery and salty but wonderful with grits and red-eye gravy. Salmon croquettes, a Southern breakfast staple, are flat, meaty and delicious. Home fries are savory and biscuits are buttery.

Price range: Breakfast: $5–$6. Lunch/Dinner: $6.50–$12.90. Wheelchair access: Fully accessible. Services: Takeout, private parties.

Carmine's $$ ITALIAN

200 W. 44th St. (at Seventh Ave.)   (212) 221-3800
2450 Broadway (bet. 90th & 91st Sts.)   (212) 362-2200
Credit cards: All major   Meals: L, D, LN

This duo of restaurants has been a hit from the day they opened and has inspired many imitators, serving garlic-laden family-style platters of old-fashioned Italian-American classics. With a big, noisy group, Carmine's is fine fun (and you can share), but don't expect subtlety. Do expect long waits.

Recommended dishes: Rigatoni with sausage and broccoli, porterhouse steak. Price range: Apps., $5.50–$19; entrees, $17–$47; desserts, $5–$12. All designed to share. Services: Takeout.

Carnegie Deli $$ DELI

854 Seventh Ave. (at 55th St.)   (212) 757-2245
Credit cards: Cash only   Meals: B, L, D, LN

Carnegie's sandwiches are legendarily enormous, big enough to feed you and a friend and still provide lunch for tomorrow. That doesn't stop people from trying to eat the whole thing, a sight that must gratify the deli's notoriously crabby waiters. The pastrami is wonderful, of course, but so are the cheese blintzes with sour cream, which are only slightly more modest. A raucous, quintessential New York City experience, from pickles to pastrami. Whatsamatter, you don't want no cheesecake?

Alcohol: Beer only. **Price range:** Apps., $6–$8; entrees, $10–$20; desserts, $5–$7. **Wheelchair access:** Restrooms not accessible. **Features:** Kid friendly. **Services:** Delivery, takeout, catering, private parties.

Carolina Country Kitchen $25 & Under

SOUTHERN

1993 Atlantic Ave., East New York, Brooklyn   (718) 346-4400
Credit cards: Cash only   Meals: B, Br, L, D

If it seems that the Southern food here is as good as it is down home, that's because much of it comes from down home. Patricia Lee, the owner, grew up in North Carolina, and much of her food is shipped from her father's farm there. Her barbecue is fine and her sweet potato pie unbeatable.

Other recommended dishes: Chopped chitterlings; hog maws; oxtail stew; fried or smothered pork chops. **Price range:** Entrees, $7.50–$9.20; desserts, $1.50–$3.50. **Wheelchair access:** Fully accessible. **Features:** Smoking permitted. **Services:** Takeout, catering, private parties.

Casa Adela $

CARIBBEAN

66 Ave. C (at 5th St.)   (212) 473-1882
Credit cards: Cash only   Meals: B, L, D

Adela specializes in Puerto Rican dishes that are both powerful enough to awaken the most jaded taste buds and filling enough to make you want to take a nap when you're done. Garlic is the key ingredient in dishes like pernil asado, moist chunks of roast pork occasionally adorned with crisp bits of skin, and mofongo, a potent blend of mashed plantains and crisp pork cracklings.

Price range: Entrees, $5.50–$8; desserts, $1.50. **Wheelchair access:** Fully accessible. **Features:** Kid friendly. **Services:** Delivery, takeout.

Casa Mexicana $25 & Under

MEXICAN

133 Ludlow St. (at Rivington St.)   (212) 473-4100
Credit cards: All major   Meals: L, D, LN

This may be the first Mexican restaurant in New York that owes as much to hip downtown Manhattan as to Mexico City. Walk through the front door and, in the dim candlelight of the boxy dining room, you can just make out the warm, rusty orange of the walls. In the rear is a bar, where patrons pause for sangria and wine before retiring later in the evening to the rosy red lounge area downstairs.

The most surprising thing about the menu is how little it resembles the usual array of Mexican street foods. The main courses include four steak dishes, duck breast, sea bass, halibut and scallops, along with a couple of chicken dishes and a single pork dish. The Azteca steak and the sirloin Tampiquena are fine pieces of beef, thick and crusty yet tender within. Pellizcadas, little disks of fried cornmeal with toppings like chorizo, chicken or crisp bits of pork, are always lively, as are tiny half-moon quesadillas, made with paper-thin, crisp tortillas.

The best dessert is a warm chocolate cake with a liquid center, topped with raspberry sauce and vanilla ice cream and surrounded by raspberries. It's not Mexican, but it is very good.

Other recommended dishes: Duck breast; caramelized sea scallops; pork tenderloin; tamalitos. **Price range:** Apps., $5–$11; entrees, $13–$21. **Wheelchair access:** Ramp at entrance.

Casimir $25 & Under   BISTRO/FRENCH
103 Ave. B (bet. 6th & 7th Sts.)   (212) 358-9683
Credit cards: AE   Meals: D, LN

The food at Casimir is uncomplicated, easy to enjoy, occasionally inspiring and several dollars cheaper than at comparable spots. All very appealing, unless you mind inattentive service, a long wait for food, a crowd shoehorned into cramped quarters and lots of cigarette smoke. Eating there feels more like a test of endurance than a pleasure. The menu includes a few surprises such as excellent pigs' feet, rich with marrow and dense with flavor, served off the bone in a crisp-topped cake over mashed potatoes. There is also a most un-French dish, a perfectly roasted fillet of Chilean sea bass, served over moist polenta with a tangy tomatillo sauce.

Other recommended dishes: Filet mignon, sautéed chicken livers, green salad with beets, celery and tomatoes. **Price range:** Apps., $5–$7; entrees, $13–$17; desserts, $5. **Services:** Private parties.

Caviar Russe $$$$ RUSSIAN
538 Madison Ave. (bet. 54th & 55th Sts.)   (212) 980-5908
Credit cards: All major   Meals: L, D

Caviar is naturally romantic, and Caviar Russe, with its blue and white walls and fanciful murals, seems to belong more in a fairy tale than in midtown Manhattan. In the old-fashioned rooms, brimming with tiny mother-of-pearl spoons and antique silver caviar dispensers, caviar is served in tiny tastes, nice if you want to deliberate about your indulgence, as well as in serious portions. While caviar unadorned is the main feature, the menu also has small, delicate dishes in which caviar is a supporting player, like chilled oysters topped with beluga, and a lobster claw set in cream-puff dough with caviar on top.

Price range: Apps., $7–$26; entrees, $16–$47; desserts, $9–$12. Tasting menus: five-course, $55; seven-course, $75. **Features:** Smoking permitted. **Services:** Private parties.

Caviarteria $$$$ EAST EUROPEAN

502 Park Ave. (at 59th St.)	(212) 759-7410
310 W. Broadway (at Canal St.)	(212) 925-5515
Grand Central Station (at 42nd St.)	(212) 682-5355
Credit cards: All major	Meals: B, L, D

Good caviar at very fair prices. Caviarteria intends to put a caviar bar in every community, but in the meantime we have a sort of caviar coffee shop on the Upper East Side, a far more substantial shop in SoHo and a new branch at Grand Central. If you yearn to learn about caviar, this is the perfect place to discover the differences between beluga, osetra and sevruga. Other options include a club du roi sandwich, made with an ounce of beluga and smoked salmon, and a beluga crepe made with an ounce of broken beluga eggs. The champagne selection tends toward the very expensive.

Alcohol: Beer and wine. **Price range:** Apps., $8–$25; entrees, $14–$125; desserts, $3–$8. **Wheelchair access:** Fully accessible. **Services:** Takeout, catering, private parties.

Cello ☆☆☆ $$$ FRENCH/SEAFOOD

53 E. 77th St. (at Madison Ave.)	(212) 517-1200
Credit cards: All major	Meals: L, D

Cello's minuscule, cocoonlike dining room provides a neutral backdrop for thrilling food. Executive chef Laurent Tourondel's entrees show remarkable refinement. With deceptive ease, he hits on flavor combinations that seem both distinctive and inevitable. Grilled Alaskan black cod, a monumental chunk of ideally moist fish, floats serenely in a lightweight but intense morel bouillon that diners can thicken with the garlic-parsley purée that's served on the side. In a special menu, Mr. Tourondel does variations on a single theme, a two-and-a-half-pound lobster. For the grand finale, Mr. Tourondel slow-roasts the tail, douses it in an emulsion made from the pan drippings and serves it with basil, fava beans, morels and gnocchi. Desserts are top-notch. The staff is attentive, but in a space as small as Cello's, attentive can feel a little hovery and tense.

Price range: Three-course prix fixe, $75; three-course lobster prix fixe, $97.

Cendrillon ☆ $$ ASIAN/FILIPINO

45 Mercer St. (bet. Broome & Grand Sts.)   (212) 343-9012
Credit cards: All major   Meals: Br, L, D   Closed Mon.

The most interesting Filipino restaurant in New York City, serving inventive food and terrific wines in a laid-back SoHo storefront. The best dishes on the menu are the cross-cultural
experiments, like shrimp curry with its strong notes of fish sauce
and coconut and its unusual blend of vegetables, or Cendrillon's
version of pinakbet, the Philippine vegetable melange, spiced
with habanero peppers and tossed with generous amounts of
shrimp and scallops. The black rice paella is a fine casserole
made with black rice mixed with crab, shrimp and Manila
clams. Salt-roasted duck is delicious, the legs crisp, the breast
richly flavored with plum, kumquat and ginger vinegar. Desserts
are sweet, ornate and fascinating.

Other recommended dishes: Spareribs; grilled octopus salad
with eggplant fritter; quail and rabbit adobo; ginger and lemongrass crème brûlée; tropical fruit terrine. **Wine list:** Both the
beers and wines are well chosen for this food and fairly priced.
Price range: Lunch and brunch: apps., $5.50–$7.50; entrees,
$7.50–$12. Dinner: apps., $6.50–$12.50; entrees, $15–$23;
desserts, $7.50–$9. **Wheelchair access:** Fully accessible. **Services:** Private parties, takeout.

Chanterelle ☆☆☆ $$$$ FRENCH

2 Harrison St. (at Hudson St.)   (212) 966-6960
Credit cards: All major   Meals: L, D   Closed Sun.

Some restaurants win admiration. Others inspire love.
Chanterelle does both. It's not hard to understand why New
Yorkers keep a warm spot in their hearts for Chanterelle. Few
restaurants are as welcoming or comfortable to enter. There's a
soft, casual edge to the atmosphere and the service. It is
unquestionably a fine restaurant, but the fresh face in TriBeCa
is well into middle age now. Admittedly, it's a Catherine
Deneuve sort of middle age, but Chanterelle is not quite the rav-
ishing young thing that turned TriBeCa into a glamour neighborhood.

David Waltuck, the chef and (with his wife, Karen) owner of
the restaurant, favors an opulent style. His strong suits are
depth and intensity of flavor, and he doesn't shy away from
thick, rich sauces in his quest to ravish the palate. The menu
changes every four weeks and includes splendid dishes like a
simple, pristine beef fillet, drenched in a red wine and shallot
sauce with more layers of flavor than a complex Burgundy. A
more indulgent beef fillet with oysters and oyster sauce is a
Gilded Age special worthy of Diamond Jim Brady. Mr. Waltuck
does pull off some dazzling effects, especially with a sushi-size
piece of salmon marinated overnight in mirin, soy and sake,

and then dry-cured for two days, and a delectable slice of salmon pickled in sweet ginger brine.

The restaurant's new pastry chef, Karen Zuckerman, has created some thrillers, including a trio of caramel desserts that becomes a quartet when she throws in a pear beignet to complement a maple crème caramel; a napoleon of peanut brittle and caramel mousse; and caramel-butterscotch ice cream. The peanut brittle is a life-changing experience.

The service at Chanterelle is gracious but perplexing, especially during the settling-in phase. I often found myself wondering where the waiter could be. The room itself looks as though it should be serene and hushed, but in fact the acoustics are poor, and when the place fills up, it takes some real lung power to carry on a conversation.

Chanterelle and its owners have shown admirable single-mindedness, consistency and immunity to fashion. In a city of neighborhoods, they created a neighborhood restaurant almost without equal — a warm, welcoming haven dedicated to cooking at a very high level. It's still there, and it's still pretty much the same. That is its appeal and its weakness.

Wine list: Impressive but pricey. About 400 mostly French wines; two dozen in half-bottles and a dozen by the glass. **Price range:** Lunch: apps., $7.50–$15; entrees, $19.50–$24; desserts, $9–$11; three-course prix fixe, $38. Dinner: three-course prix fixe, $79; six-course tasting menu, $94 or $154 with matching wines. **Wheelchair access:** Restrooms, with stalls for the disabled, on street level. **Features:** Good for business, romantic. **Services:** Private parties.

Charles' Southern-Style Kitchen

$25 & Under   SOUTHERN

2841 Frederick Douglass Blvd. (near 151st St.)   (212) 926-4313
Credit cards: All major   Meals: D, LN

Charles Gabriel, the chef and owner of this small restaurant (25 seats) and takeout spot in Harlem, is an artist at work. This is the sort of food you don't think about so much as feel, and the soulful feeling it provokes makes the term apt. The fried chicken may be the peak of Mr. Gabriel's artistry, but it is by no means all he does. Pork ribs are sweet and meaty, and falling-off-the-bone tender. Oxtails in an oniony brown gravy provoke sighs of contentment, while salmon cakes are light but forcefully flavored, a real treat if you can get them. Not everything is available all the time. Even the side dishes can't be predicted, which is too bad, because they, too, are wonderful.

Alcohol: None. **Price range:** Buffet: $6.99 from 1-4 P.M., $9.99 after 4 P.M. Lunch and dinner: Entrees, $6.50–$7.50, desserts, $2. **Wheelchair access:** Fully accessible. **Services:** Takeout, catering, private parties.

Chat 'n Chew $25 & Under   AMERICAN

10 E. 16th St. (bet. Fifth Ave. & Union Sq. W.)   (212) 243-1616
Credit cards: All major   Meals: Br, L, D

Middle American farm dishes and homespun décor set the tone
at this restaurant, which could lead you to believe it was off a
small-town courthouse square rather than off Union Square.
Portions are huge, desserts are luscious and the place is particularly appealing to children.

Price range: Apps., $4–$6; entrees, $7–$14; desserts, $4–$5.
Features: Kid friendly, outdoor dining. **Services:** Delivery, takeout.

Chelsea Bistro & Bar ☆☆ $$$ BISTRO/FRENCH

358 W. 23rd St. (bet. Eighth & Ninth Aves.)   (212) 727-2026
Credit cards: All major   Meals: D, LN

With a cozy fireplace, a great wine list and really good French
bistro food, this is a find in the neighborhood. While the wines
seem rather fancy for a bistro, the menu itself has fewer pretensions. Some of the dishes are superb. If the first thing you eat at
Chelsea Bistro is the fabulous mussel and clam soup, you will
be hooked forever. The fricassee of lobster and sea scallops is
almost as good. Some dishes are disappointing, but most of the
food is the satisfying fare you expect in a bistro. The hanger
steak is fine and rare, with a dense red-wine sauce. The restaurant serves predictable and good classic New York bistro
desserts. The bread pudding is slightly less conventional, if only
because it is enlivened with a shot of rum. (*Ruth Reichl*)

Other recommended dishes: Tartar of salmon; cassolette of
snails; goat cheese tart; braised lamb shank; haricots verts;
farm chocolate cake. **Wine list:** Large, well chosen and fairly
priced. **Price range:** Dinner: apps., $6.50–$8.50; entrees,
$17.95–$27; desserts, $7.50–$8.50; pre-theater prix fixe, $28.50.
Wheelchair access: Dining room is down two small steps. **Features:** Smoking permitted. **Services:** Private parties.

Chez Gnagna Koty's $25 & Under   AFRICAN

530 Ninth Ave. (near 39th St.)   (212) 279-1755
Credit Cards: MC/V   Meals: L, D, LN

This friendly, bright storefront has an extensive menu and is a
fine place to try West African cooking. Its specialty is stews —
enormous, hearty, well-flavored dishes served with a peppery
hot sauce. One of the best is yassa, grilled chicken in a piquant
lemon, mustard and onion sauce with rice. Bring your own
alcohol — or try bissap, a sweet red sorrel drink or spicy ginger beer.

Other recommended dishes: Thiebu djen (fish with green onions and herbs topped with cabbage manioc, tomato and carrots); maffe (creamy peanut sauce studded with lamb, chicken or fish); thiebu yap (chunks of tender lamb, mixed with rice). **Alcohol:** Bring your own. **Price range:** Apps., $3–$4; entrees, $7.50–$10; desserts, $3. **Wheelchair access:** Steps at entrance; narrow path to restroom. **Services:** Takeout.

Chez Jacqueline $$$ FRENCH

72 Macdougal St. (bet. Bleecker & Houston Sts.)   (212) 505-0727
Credit cards: All major   Meals: L, D

From its longtime perch in the middle of Greenwich Village, Chez Jacqueline offers solid, predictable French bistro food with a Provençal edge. It's a friendly neighborhood restaurant, but not particularly exciting.

Price range: Apps., $6.50–$9.50; entrees, $17.50–$23; desserts, $7. **Wheelchair access:** Fully accessible. **Features:** Outdoor dining. **Services:** Private parties.

Chez Josephine ☆☆ $$$ BISTRO/FRENCH

414 W. 42nd St. (bet. Ninth & 10th Aves.)   (212) 594-1925
Credit cards: All major   Meals: D, LN   Closed Sun.

This Theater Row pioneer has been entertaining us with its colorful parade of musicians, singers and dancers for more than a decade and is still going strong. Its reliably pleasing bistro fare and attentive service add to the charm. Highlights among starters include the crunchy endive salad topped with crumbled Roquefort and crushed walnuts, and the subtle goat-cheese ravioli in a delicate veal broth scented with fresh dill and finished with a sprinkle of toasted pine nuts. Favorites among entrees include lobster cassoulet replete with scallops, shrimp, lobster, seafood sausage and black beans; and sautéed calf's liver with honey mustard sauce and grilled onions. *(Ruth Reichl)*

Price range: Avg. app., $7; entree, $19; dessert, $7. **Wheelchair access:** Restrooms not accessible. **Features:** Romantic. **Services:** Private parties.

Chez Laurence $25 & Under   BISTRO/FRENCH

245 Madison Ave. (at 38th St.)   (212) 683-0284
Credit cards: All major   Meals: B, L, D   Closed Sun.

By day, Chez Laurence is a busy patisserie that serves some of the best brioche and croissants in the city. By night, the restaurant serves fine cuisine bourgeoise, including well-made bistro staples like cassoulet, a blend of deliciously tender beans, herbs, pork, chicken and three kinds of sausage; and swordfish served with mango chutney and swirls of whipped potato and sweet potato. Desserts are the weakest link, but the dinner experience is enjoyable enough to make you want to return.

Other recommended dishes: Charcuterie plate; saucisson with lentil salad; smoked salmon; medallions of pork; steak frites; fricassee of chicken; chocolate mousse with pear. **Price range:** Apps., $6–$10; entrees, $10–$18; desserts, $4.95; prix fixe, $21.95. **Wheelchair access:** Fully accessible. **Services:** Delivery, takeout, catering, private parties.

Chicama ☆☆ $$$

35 E. 18th St. (at Broadway)
Credit cards: All major

PAN-LATIN
(212) 505-2233
Meals: L, D, LN

Hung with Peruvian rugs and decorated with Peruvian religious statues, this restaurant has a eucalyptus-burning wood oven and a big ceviche bar, stacked with enormous lobsters and shellfish, not to mention the occasional Chilean barnacle. The noise level is up. And business is booming.

Some chefs merely cook. Others generate a special brand of excitement that somehow becomes part of the food. Douglas Rodriguez is one of these. Mr. Rodriguez cooks in two modes. The first is an exuberant, often flashy style that can be overwhelming, with plate-filling dishes that seem like the culinary equivalent of a carnival float. When it clicks, this style can be dazzling. Alio chicken, a house specialty, deserves its star billing on the lunch menu. It's a half chicken, smoky tasting after roasting over eucalyptus wood, served on a hash made from malanga root and suffused with a truffle mushroom mojo. Aj de gallina, or Peruvian hen stew, is another pull-out-the-stops production, with succulent pieces of guinea hen adrift in a viscous gravy flavored with walnuts, yellow chilies and olives. The ceviche bar shows Mr. Rodriguez in a calmer mood. The simple medium of raw fish allows him to play subtle variations, working with different chilies and fruit juices. There is a long list of serious beers, including some unusual South and Central American beers, like Cabro from Guatemala and Aguila from Colombia.

The dessert list is short and almost chaste. Vanilla flan infused with bay leaf may be, in a mild way, the most striking dessert on the menu, delicately herbal with a nicely paired accompaniment of carpaccio-thin pineapple slices decorated with a little goat cheese and accented with cracked pepper.

Other recommended dishes: Almost all ceviches; anticochu platter; smoked marlin salad; spinach and corn empanada; banana tres leches; churros (South American doughnuts). **Wine list:** About 120 modestly priced wines, half from Spain and South America. **Price range:** Lunch: apps., $10–$15; entrees, $15–$20; desserts, $7. Dinner: apps., $11–$17; entrees, $19–$39; desserts, $7. **Wheelchair access:** Restrooms on street level. **Features:** Smoking in front room. **Services:** Private parties.

Chimichurri Grill $$ LATIN AMERICAN/ARGENTINE
606 Ninth Ave. (bet. 43rd & 44th St.)   (212) 586-8655
Credit cards: All major   Meals: L, D   Closed Mon.

If you're looking for a casual place for a good dinner before or
after the theater, you can hardly do better than this minuscule
Argentine restaurant. Simultaneously sophisticated and home-
like, it combines all the elements that make the food of
Argentina so appealing: great grilled beef, a few Italian pasta
dishes and some pure home cooking, like the tortilla, a frittata
filled with potatoes, chorizo and onions. I could easily eat the
empanadas every day, crisp little turnovers filled with a mixture
of ground beef and olives.

Alcohol: Wine and beer. **Price range:** Lunch: apps., $5.25–$7;
entrees, $7.50–$17; desserts, $6–$7. Dinner: apps., $5.75–$9;
entrees, $14–$24; desserts, $6–$7. **Wheelchair access:** One step
up to restaurant; narrow restrooms. **Features:** Smoking permitted. **Services:** Takeout.

China Fun $ CHINESE
1653 Broadway (bet. 51st & 52nd Sts.)   (212) 333-2622
1221 Second Ave. (at 64th St.)   (212) 752-0810
246 Columbus Ave. (bet. 71st & 72nd Sts.)   (212) 580-1516
Credit cards: All major   Meals: Br, L, D, LN

The food in these quirky restaurants is sometimes good but
more often mediocre, always fast and always cheap. Décor is
appealingly industrial but tends to amplify the noise when
crowds are heavy. Try the dim sum, like the crisp pan-fried
radish cake, or the delicate shrimp dumplings. I also like the
noodle dishes and the roast pork.

Price range: Dumplings, $4.95; entrees, $9.50–$12.95. **Wheel-
chair access:** Fully accessible. **Features:** Kid friendly. **Services:**
Delivery, takeout, catering.

Chinghalle ☆ $$$ BRASSERIE/DINER
50 Gansevoort St. (bet. Greenwich & Washington Sts.)
                              (212) 242-3200
Credit cards: All major   Meals: D, LN

Chinghalle, an idiosyncratic rendering of the Italian word for
wild boar, makes a sly nod to the daytime business of the meatpacking district. The interior reflects the local dining culture
flawlessly, which is to say, most of the effort has gone into the
visuals; without the décor, it would be a diner, and not a great
diner, either. Once you're seated, things move at lightning
speed. It's not often that a party of four can go through a
pre-appetizer and three full courses in 70 minutes, but that's
simply cruising speed at Chinghalle.

Still, there are pleasures to be had. Homemade waffle potato chips have a pleasingly chewy heft to them, and the zucchini chips, fried in a thin tempura batter, are outstanding. There's an appealing sense of humor behind the boar sausage with baked beans, a crazy sort of signature dish that works, thanks to the foursquare, chunky sausage, flavorful beans and syrupy sauce. Penne in a robust boar sauce. Cornish hen, cooked coq au vin style, is the sort of unpretentious, full-flavored bistro dish that one could eat with pleasure five nights a week.

The pastry chef takes a populist approach, playing with American favorites like banana split, which is large enough for the table. Baked Alaska is also enormous; any sweeter and it would be a Hallmark Christmas special. The proper antidote is a gratifyingly sour Key lime pie (actually a tart). It's good, not great, a simple soul with unrealistically lofty aspirations. In that sense, it could be Chinghalle's signature dessert.

Other recommended dishes: Waldorf crab salad, salmon croquettes. **Wine list:** An acceptable but very short list (about 40 wines), modestly priced, with 11 by the glass. Price range: Dinner apps., $7–$13; entrees, $15–$19; desserts, $5–$12. **Wheelchair access:** Restrooms are on street level.

Chip Shop $25 & Under ENGLISH
383 Fifth Ave., Park Slope, Brooklyn   (718) 832-7701
Credit cards: Cash only   Meals: L, D

Bad English food is an old joke, and quite out of date. Yet the smirks persist, perhaps for good reason, at least when dealing with traditional English dishes. At this small, extremely English fish and chips restaurant, some items on the menu may sound funny — mushy peas (they are supposed to be mushy) and deep-fried Mars bars, for example — but much of the food is honest and forthright, filling and satisfying.

Not that the Chip Shop is your basic blue-collar fish and chippery. With the beat of acid jazz and trance music at high volume, the pitch is clearly toward a younger crowd. Still, the yellow dining room is cheerful and pleasant.

The mushy pea fritter is in fact a wonderful dish that encases the peas in a crisp, greaseless shell, much like an Indian pakora. It makes a fine appetizer. Fish here can be excellent, especially the moist cod, with its thin, crisp, nut-brown crust, which never seems to absorb enough malt vinegar. The Chip Shop offers some of England's greatest pub hits, like fine bangers and mash, plump pork-and-cereal sausages over mashed potatoes in a rich gravy of caramelized onions.

The Chip Shop does not yet have a liquor license, but you can take your own. And for dessert, the deep-fried Mars bar, with its crisp outer coating and gooey chocolate and caramel filling, is delicious.

Other recommended dishes: Stilton, apple and walnut salad; Scotch eggs; cod and chips; fish fingers; bangers and mash; steak and onion pie; chicken curry. **Price range:** Apps., $3–$6; entrees, $6–$11. **Wheelchair access:** Small step at entrance; aisle in dining room is narrow.

Cho Dang Gol ☆☆ $$$ KOREAN

55 W. 35th St. (bet. Fifth & Sixth Aves.)   (212) 695-822
Credit cards: All major   Meals: L, D

Cho Dang Gol serves uniquely rustic food that is very different from what is available at other Korean restaurants in the surrounding blocks. The specialty here is fresh soybean curd, made daily at the restaurant. The kitchen makes each dish with extreme care. Even the panchan, the little saladlike appetizers, are of remarkably high quality. For the uninitiated, searching out the best dishes is not easy. Cho-dang-gol jung-sik arrives in three bowls: one with rice dotted with beans, another with "bean-curd dregs" (which hardly conveys its utter deliciousness) and the third with a pungent soup-stew containing pork, seafood, onions and chilies. Also try chung-kook-jang, too, soybean-paste stew with an elemental flavor, and doo-boo doo-roo-chi-gi, a combination of pork, pan-fried kimchi, clear vermicelli and big triangles of bean curd.

Other recommended dishes: Doo-boo don-ki-rang-deng (tofu rounds with vegetables and beef); doo-boo kam-ja-jun (potato pancake with tofu and vegetables); cho-dang-goljae-yook bo-ssam (lettuce rolled around meat and seasonings). **Wine list:** Try beer, so ju (Korean sweet-potato vodka) or makkolli (the rough, milky rice liquor). **Price range:** Apps., $6.95–$18.95; entrees, $10.95–$29.95. **Wheelchair access:** Everything is on one level. **Services:** Takeout.

Choshi $ JAPANESE/SUSHI

77 Irving Pl. (at 19th St.)   (212) 420-1419
Credit cards: All major   Meals: L, D

A sushi bar in the guise of a college hangout, with graduate students sitting at worn wooden tables, writing in journals by candlelight. Service and atmosphere are pleasant, and the food is filling but not memorable.

Alcohol: Beer and wine. **Price range:** Apps., $5–$8; entrees, $12–$15; desserts, $1.50–$5. **Wheelchair access:** Not accessible. **Features:** Smoking permitted, outdoor dining. **Services:** Takeout.

Christer's ☆☆ $$$ SCANDINAVIAN

145 W. 55th St. (bet. Sixth & Seventh Aves.)   (212) 974-7224
Credit cards: All major   Meals: L, D

One of two upscale Scandinavian restaurants in Midtown, this
one is the more relaxed and humorous. It also shows how a fine
chef translates his love for American ingredients and ideas into
traditional dishes. Christer Larson, the chef and owner, specializes in seafood, salmon in particular. Everything he makes from
salmon is good, from seared smoked salmon with black beans,
corn, avocado and tomatillo salsa — more Southwestern than
Scandinavian — to gentle citrus-glazed salmon. His smorgas-
bord is wonderful, while his fricadelles, Swedish meatballs
made of veal, are hearty and comforting. Desserts like Pavlova,
an airy confection of ice cream, fruit and meringue, and a tart
of poached apples are perfect endings. (*Ruth Reichl*)

Price range: Lunch: apps., $7–$16; entrees, $19–$32; desserts,
$7–$8; prix-fixe, $25. Dinner: apps., $8–$17; entrees, $23–$36;
desserts, $7–$8; pre-theater prix-fixe, $36. **Wheelchair access:**
Not accessible. **Features:** Good for business, smoking permitted. **Services:** Private parties.

Christos Hasapo-Taverna $25 & Under
GREEK/STEAKHOUSE

41-08 23rd Ave., Astoria, Queens   (718) 726-5195
Credit cards: All major   Meals: L, D, LN   Closed Tue.

This cheerful, handsome Greek steakhouse recreates the traditional Greek pairing of a butcher shop and a restaurant. Meals
begin with fresh tzatziki, a combination of yogurt, garlic and
cucumber, and tarama, the wonderful fish roe purée. Appetizer
portions are big and easily shared, and there is a large selection
of grilled offal if you like to precede your meat with more meat.
Richly flavored steaks and chops dominate the menu, and some
nights more traditional fare, like piglet and baby lamb, is turned
on the rotisserie. Best desserts include baklava, a wonderful
apple cake, and a plate of prunes and figs marinated in sweet
wine.

Price range: Apps., $5–$15; entrees, $20–$25; desserts,
$3.50–$3.75. **Wheelchair access:** Two steps up to dining room;
front room and restrooms are on one level. **Features:** Parking
available, smoking permitted. **Services:** Takeout, catering, private parties.

Chumley's $

86 Bedford St. (bet. Bleecker St. & Seventh Ave. S.)

(212) 675-4449

Credit cards: Cash only

Meals: D

In the 1920's, this was a speakeasy, and it is still said that Mrs. Chumley stops in during the middle of the night to rearrange the furniture. Does this restaurant with no sign outside have character? You bet. Does it have good food? No. But it's fine for beer, burgers and nostalgia.

Price range: Apps., $5–$11; entrees, $7–$16. **Wheelchair access:** Fully accessible. **Features:** Smoking permitted. **Services:** Takeout, private parties.

Churrascaria Girassol $25 & Under BRAZILIAN

33-18 28th Ave., Astoria, Queens

(718) 545-8250

Credit cards: All major

Meals: L, D, LN

If you are excited by the idea of juicy, salt-edged steaks, rich sauces mellowed with palm oil and the prospect of unlimited meat courses, then Girassol can be a little bit of paradise. Not that anyone would ever imagine paradise looking like Girassol, a plain room with half a dozen tables and a small counter. During televised Brazilian soccer matches, diners leap out of their seats and scream with each goal and near miss.

That's part of the charm. No other churrascaria in New York is as truly Brazilian as Girassol, where everybody speaks Portuguese, and English can be a struggle. Nor are any on such a small-scale. The chef and owner, Lilian Fagundes, prepares almost everything from scratch. Her touch is evident in classic Brazilian dishes like an excellent feijoada, a richly flavorful black bean stew filling an iron kettle, thick with all manner of pork. Pile it on a plate with rice, and then add the adornments: shredded collard greens, the toasted manioc flour called farofa, and orange slices. Portions are large enough for two. Moqueca de peixe, a fish stew made rich and mellow with the combination of coconut milk and palm oil, is uncommonly good over rice, and if it's steak you want, the medalhão, a thick tenderloin that seems to have been marinated in soy and salt, is superb.

As good as these dishes are, most people seem to come for the rodízio. Compared with banquet-hall rodízios, which may serve as many as 20 cuts of meat, Girassol's selection of a half-dozen may seem paltry, but it is satisfying, beginning with dense pork sausages and crisp, juicy grilled chicken legs. Best of all is the grilled top sirloin, a tender, delicious salt-edged cut.

Girassol serves only beer and wine. There's a fruity Undurraga cabernet from Chile that goes well with almost everything. With so much food, appetizers are unnecessary, but don't miss out on the desserts. Dulce de leche with coconut, a grainy caramel pudding, is especially luscious.

Other recommended dishes: Feijoada, bean stew with pork or beef; fish stew; beef tenderloin; rodìzio; dulce de leche with coconut; passion fruit pudding. **Price range:** Apps., $1–$4; entrees, $9–$16. **Wheelchair access:** The entrances to the dining room and restroom are narrow.

Churrascaria Plataforma ☆☆ $$$

BRAZILIAN

316 W. 49th St. (bet. Eighth & Ninth Aves.)   (212) 245-0505
Credit cards: All major   Meals: L, D, LN

Two things are required to truly appreciate Churrascaria Plataforma: a large appetite to keep you eating and a large group to cheer you on. A caipirinha or two, the potent Brazilian drink, doesn't hurt either. This rodizio (all-you-can-eat Brazilian restaurant) is distinguished from the others by the high quality of the food and the charming attitude of the waiters. The salad bar is extraordinary, a long two-sided affair anchored at the corners by four hot casseroles. Go easy: This is only the appetizer, and it takes stamina to do justice to the main part of the meal. The waiters will entice you with ham, sausage, lamb, wonderfully crisp and juicy chicken legs, pork ribs, even the occasional side of salmon, which is delicious in its caper sauce. But it is beef that has pride of place: sirloin, baby beef, top round, skirt steak, brisket, short ribs, special top round. If the desserts are more interesting than wonderful, that is all to the good. The only reason to eat dessert after so much meat is to prove that you can. (*Ruth Reichl*)

Recommended dishes: Try everything. **Wine list:** Small and not particularly interesting; besides, everybody's drinking caipirinhas. **Price range:** All-you-can-eat rodizio meal, $38.95; children under 10, $19.50. **Wheelchair access:** Ramp to dining room, but restrooms are down a flight of stairs. **Features:** Kid friendly, smoking permitted. **Services:** Private parties.

Cibo $$$

ITALIAN

767 Second Ave. (bet. 41st & 42nd Sts.)   (212) 681-1616
Credit cards: All major   Meals: L, D

Friendly Italian food in the lobby of the former Daily News Building. Cibo means food in Italian, so it is not surprising that the menu is a familiar Mediterranean blend of salads, pastas, grilled and roasted poultry and seafood. While the room is modestly attractive and the prices are reasonable, little about the restaurant particularly stands out. The most popular entree is surely the giant lamb shank, which seems to be on half the tables.

Price range: Lunch: apps., $8–$11; entrees, $14–$29; desserts, $7–$8. Dinner: apps., $8–$14; entrees, $17–$32; desserts, $7–8. Prix–fixe brunch, $14.95; prix–fixe dinner, $27.95. **Wheelchair access:** Limited access. **Features:** Smoking permitted. **Services:** Takeout, private parties.

Cinque Terre ☆☆ $$ ITALIAN

22 E. 38th St. (bet. Madison & Park Aves.)   (212) 213-0910
Credit cards: All major   Meals: L, D

Cinque Terre is a small and friendly restaurant, with an unusual Ligurian menu and a staff that cares passionately about the wines of the region. The gallete di baccala e patate con cavolfiore e caviale — little salt cod cakes on a pond of puréed cauliflower, topped with grains of black caviar — is a beautiful dish, one that combines completely unexpected tastes and textures. Ligurian squid stew is cooked gently so that both the seafood and the vegetables maintain their integrity. Pansotti con salsa di noci, triangles of pasta stuffed with ricotta and a mixture of greens and herbs, is particularly irresistible. Each dessert here has been lovingly created, such as a chocolate hazelnut cake and a cheesecake sorbet. (*Ruth Reichl*)

Other recommended dishes: Salad of arugula, apples and blue cheese; minestrone; spaghetti with seafood; grilled marinated shrimp; roasted baby chicken; warm apple tart. **Wine list:** Small, but unusual, featuring wines from small Italian producers. **Price range:** Apps., $6–$11; pastas and entrees, $13–$26; desserts, $7–$8. **Wheelchair access:** Fully accessible. **Features:** Smoking permitted.

Circus Restaurant ☆☆ $$$ BRAZILIAN

808 Lexington Ave. (near 62nd St.)   (212) 223-2965
Credit cards: All major   Meals: L, D, LN

An upscale Brazilian restaurant that turns into a party every night. While churrascarias faithfully reproduce a form of restaurant popular in Brazil, Circus serves the food your mother might cook if you were raised in São Paulo or Bahia. It is a warm and cozy place, usually packed with Brazilians eager for a taste of home. Try picadinho, beef sautéed with wine and thyme, topped with a poached egg and accompanied by rice, beans and cooked bananas. Another particularly satisfying dish is an appetizer, bolo de milho e rabada, little polenta cakes baked with Manchego cheese and served with a robust oxtail sauce. Desserts are sweet and tropical. (*Ruth Reichl*)

Other recommended dishes: Black bean soup; seared tuna marinated in cane sugar and soy; salmon with shrimp sauce; feijoada; Maria mole; carmelized bananas with ice cream. **Wine list:** Mostly Iberian and Latin American with some United

States labels, often overpriced in low-end wines, some bargains among the older Spanish wines. **Price range:** Lunch: apps., $5–$10; entrees, $11–$19; prix fixe, $17.50. Dinner: apps., $6–$13; entrees, $16–$24. **Wheelchair access:** Two steps down to dining room, 10 down to restroom. **Features:** Smoking permitted, outdoor dining. **Services:** Delivery, takeout, catering, private parties.

Cité $$$ STEAKHOUSE

120 W. 51st St. (bet. Sixth & Seventh Aves.)   (212) 956-7100
Credit cards: All major   Meals: Br, L, D

If you visit this large, boisterous Art Deco restaurant and you see the wine flowing like water, it must be after 8 P.M., when one of New York's great wine deals goes into effect. From 8 to midnight, Cité — one of Alan Stillman's stable of restaurants, which also includes the Post House, Smith & Wollensky and the Park Avenue Cafe, among others — will pour as much as you want of four different wines, which usually include champagne, a decent white and a couple of decent reds. Along with the wine, Cité serves fine sirloin and other steakhouse staples. Sides like creamed spinach and french fries are top-notch.

Price range: Lunch: apps., $5.50–$12.50; entrees, $18.50–$26.50; desserts, $8.50. Dinner: apps., $5.50–$12.50; entrees, $18.50–$29.75; desserts, $8.75. Three-course pre-theater prix fixe, $42.50; three-course prix-fixe grill, $39.50; wine dinner, $59.50. **Wheelchair access:** Fully accessible. **Features:** Good for business, smoking permitted. **Services:** Takeout, private parties.

City Eatery ☆☆ $ ITALIAN

316 Bowery (at Bleecker St.)   (212) 253-8644
Credit cards: All major   Meals: Br, D, LN

City Eatery has the right stuff. The name, as plain as a brass doorknob, doesn't offer a clue as to what the kitchen might be serving. Neither does the spare, even severe, décor, which can seem cavernous and gloomy early in the evening. The food does the talking. "Polenta, truffled mushrooms" is a typically disarming dish, a simple but inspired matchup of creamy, feather-light polenta with truffled shiitake mushrooms. Butternut squash soup, which can be fat and bland, comes alive with a touch of curry spice, the bitterness of crispy shallots and the sour astringency of goat cheese.

Scott Conant, City Eatery's executive chef, loves meat. The cheaper the cut, the more love he lavishes on it. At the high end, he turns a grilled double rib steak into the juicy underpinnings for a messy-looking platter of sliced meat buried under an avalanche of truffles, mushrooms, shallots and Parmesan.

100

Roasted free-range kid, so tender it barely holds a shape, is piled high on a bed of potatoes, pristine peas and shallots, a country dish that the downtown city folk seem to have made the restaurant's signature, and for good reason.

The short dessert list holds up its end. The thin apple tart, its pastry crackling crisp, has the near-burnt quality that makes its scoop of caramel ice cream meaningful. Lemon cheesecake, halfway toward being a mousse, packs a powerful citric wallop.

Other recommended dishes: Rigatoni with braised rabbit, parsnips and mint; tuna poached in olive oil; braised short ribs, braised lamb shank with bitter greens; bittersweet chocolate cake. **Wine list:** A good, budget-priced list of about 60 mostly Italian and French wines. **Price range:** Dinner, apps., $6–$14; entrees, $11–$25; desserts, $7. Brunch, all dishes, $7–$12. **Wheelchair access:** Staff restroom on street level is available.

City Hall ☆☆ $$$ AMERICAN
131 Duane St. (near Church St.)   (212) 227-7777
Credit cards: All major   Meals: L, D, LN   Closed Sun.

The cavernous dining room has the spare quality of an old steakhouse, but the clean details, loud music and hip clientele give it an up-to-date air. The menu includes all the old classics, from iceberg lettuce to baked Alaska. Just as you are relaxing into this retro mode, however, you realize there is more to City Hall than old-fashioned fare. The plateau de fruits de mer, which feeds six to eight, is a $98 behemoth so impressive that people invariably gasp as it is carried across the room. You can't go wrong with oysters at City Hall, raw or cooked. Among the meat dishes try the huge double steak, still on the bone and served for two. For dessert, the apple bread pudding made with brioche is very, very good.

Time has begun to expose City Hall's weaknesses. It now seems like an unusually handsome restaurant serving very average food. The three-herring appetizer packs a punch, and the exuberantly presented all-American steaks, chops and seafoods have razzle-dazzle, but there's nothing much going on. You could do worse. You could do better. (*Ruth Reichl, updated by William Grimes*)

Other recommended dishes: Oyster pan roast; fried oysters; whole grilled fish; filet mignon; hamburger; hash browns; gratin of Yukon gold potatoes; curried onion rings. **Wine list:** Interesting and offbeat; try the New Zealand sauvignon blancs with the oysters, the Rhones with the steaks. **Price range:** Apps., $7–$16; entrees, $18–$32; side dishes, $7; desserts, $6–$8. **Wheelchair access:** Elevator to downstairs. **Features:** Smoking permitted. **Services:** Private parties.

Cocina Cuzco

$25 & Under   PERUVIAN

55 Ave. A (at 4th St.)   (212) 529-3469
Credit cards: Cash only   Meals: L, D, LN

Peruvian cuisine is a melting pot of Asian, European, African and ancient American influences. Cocina offers half a dozen ceviches, the marinated raw seafood dishes that show off the extraordinary variety of seafood along the Peruvian coast. The selection is not exotic but includes some excellent choices like ceviche de concha, clams marinated in lime and served on the half shell, covered with cilantro and tiny cubes of pickled onions and peppers. Each ceviche comes with slices of yam and yucca as well as cancha, the crunchy roasted corn kernels that go brilliantly with the soft seafood.

The chef has had long restaurant experience in Peru, and his main courses demonstrate many sides of Peruvian cuisine. Lomo saltado, stir-fried beef flavored with soy and onions and served over rice and French fries, shows the influence of the Chinese laborers who came to Peru a century ago. The influence of former African slaves can be seen in red snapper, crusted in thin slices of sweet potatoes, making it crisp on the outside and moist within. It is served with rice and beans, excellent fried yuca and salsa criolla, or marinated sweet onions. Desserts are delicious, like bread pudding flavored with dulce de leche, and mazamorra morada, a kind of sweet and fruity gelatin.

Other recommended dishes: Octopus with rosemary, papas a la huancaina, roasted pork, roasted chicken, skirt steak. **Price range:** Apps., $2.95–$9; entrees, $8.95–$13.95. **Wheelchair access:** Everything is on one level.

Coco Roco

$25 & Under   PERUVIAN

392 Fifth Ave., Park Slope, Brooklyn   (718) 965-3376
Credit cards: All major   Meals: L, D

This bright, pleasant restaurant offers some of the best Peruvian food in New York. The menu ranges from tender, delicious ceviches from Peru's coast to Andean dishes that have been enjoyed since the days of the Incan empire. Cancha, simply roasted, salted corn kernels, is served in a bowl before the meal and also shows up in several dishes, like tamalitos verdes, a tamale topped with roast pork and cilantro sauce. Roast chicken is excellent, and desserts like rice pudding and lucuma ice cream, made with a Peruvian fruit, are wonderful.

Other recommended dishes: Chicharrón; mixed seafood ceviche; clam ceviche; octopus in rosemary sauce; red snapper crusted in sweet potato; skirt steak; bread pudding. **Alcohol:** Beer and a modest list of inexpensive Argentine wines. **Price range:** Apps., $5.25–$7.95; entrees, $8.95–$16.95. **Features:** Kid friendly. **Services:** Delivery, takeout.

Coffee Shop $$ BRAZILIAN

29 Union Square W. (at 16th St.)   (212) 243-7969
Credit cards: All major   Meals: B, Br, L, D, LN

Big attitude, big crowd, very trendy. Great late at night when it's
filled with models or people who should be. Casual, inexpensive, open until 5:30 A.M. except Sundays.

Price range: Lunch: apps., $5–$8; entrees, $8–$15; desserts,
$5–$7. Dinner: apps., $6–$8; entrees, $8–$20; desserts, $5–$7.
Wheelchair access: Fully accessible. **Features:** Smoking permitted, outdoor dining. **Services:** Delivery, takeout, private parties,
catering.

Col Legno $25 & Under ITALIAN

231 E. 9th St. (bet. Second & Third Aves.)   (212) 777-4650
Credit cards: AE   Meals: D   Closed Mon.

This sedate Tuscan trattoria (whose name means "with wood,"
a musical term for playing a violin with the back of a bow)
offers simple, lusty yet delicate dishes invigorated by just a
touch of wood, achieved by a chef who plays the wood fire like
a musical instrument. Pastas are unusual and superb, while pizzas and grilled dishes, prepared in a big, wood-burning oven,
are all top-notch. Col Legno's desserts are simple but just right:
a huge glass of rich hazelnut gelato, or a tiramisu that actually
tastes of rum, espresso, chocolate and cream.

Alcohol: Beer and a brief list of inexpensive wines that go perfectly with the food. **Price range:** Apps., $3.95–$6.95; entrees,
$7.95–$16.95; desserts, $4.95. **Wheelchair access:** One step up
to dining room; restrooms are narrow. **Services:** Takeout, catering, private parties.

The Commons $$ NEW AMERICAN

1803 Second Ave. (bet. 93rd & 94th Sts.)   (212) 426-8350
Credit cards: All major   Meals: D, LN

This stylish wine bar and restaurant offers a rather complicated
contemporary menu. On first glance, you fear that the chef was
unfortunately given full freedom to indulge his creativity, but
the combinations turn out to make good sense. The sliced duck
filet with a soy ginger glaze, where the skin is crisp and the
meat sweet, is served with a soba noodle pancake on a bed of
Asian vegetables, while the terrific seared Maine scallops with
grilled mushrooms is served with asparagus risotto. The food
isn't cheap, but the wine list is reasonable, and the desserts are
excellent.

Price range: Apps., $6–7; entrees, $16–$18; desserts, $7–$8.
Wheelchair access: Fully accessible. **Features:** Good for busi-

ness, romantic, smoking permitted. **Services:** Catering, delivery, takeout, private parties.

Commune ☆ $$ ITALIAN/NEW AMERICAN

12 E. 22nd St. (bet. Broadway & Park Ave. S.)   (212) 777-2600
Credit cards: All major   Meals: L, D, LN

It is loud. It is young. It is crowded. The black-and-red décor is satanic in a strangely domestic way, with glowing red recesses at the tables that suggest a warm hearth. The food is just good enough to hold its own against the décor, but food is not really the main thing.

Matthew Kenney is a moderately talented chef with immoderate ambitions. The success of his restaurant, Matthew's, has spurred him to embark on an empire-building program. With each new venture, the food seems to dwindle in importance. Commune leans away a bit from the Mediterranean flavors and spices that dominated Mr. Kenney's earlier restaurants in favor of simpler, homier food. Lemon pops up in the surprising spoonful of preserved-lemon purée alongside a hefty slab of hot-smoked salmon, and in a wonderful tartar sauce that comes with two small crab cakes. Warm shrimp pick up a good, smoky bite from their bacon wrappers, nicely accentuated by a small dollop of thick tomato and chili jam. But many of the entrees suffer from the blahs. Steak au poivre, made with the absolute minimum of pepper, makes a decent-enough showing, but I found my attention wandering after the third bite. Saffron pasta with tender chunks of lobster poached in butter, rich and mildly exotic, has a whiff of distinction.

Other recommended dishes: Tuna tartar with lime-ginger dressing; parmesan polenta; truffled macaroni. **Wine list:** An imaginative, far-ranging list of nearly 170 wines, a third of them $40 or less. **Price range:** Lunch: apps., $7–$12; entrees, $13–$19; desserts, $8. Dinner: apps., $9–$14; entrees, $18–$26; desserts, $8. **Wheelchair access:** Restrooms on street level. **Features:** Good for business, romantic, smoking permitted. **Services:** Private parties.

Congee Village $25 & Under CHINESE

100 Orchard St. (bet. Delancey & Broome Sts.)   (212) 941-1818
Credit cards: All major   Meals: L, D, LN

The best congee in New York is in these friendly restaurants. Congee, also known as jook, is nothing more than Chinese hot cereal, a milky rice porridge. More than two dozen versions of congee are served here, some with additions as exotic as fish maws or frog, each served steaming in a pretty ceramic crock and flavored with cilantro, scallions and slivers of pungent ginger. The congee is especially good with a side of fried bread, which comes with a thick, sweet sauce but is better dunked in the congee.

At the uptown location, most of the rest of the menu is devoted to generic sweet and crispy Chinese-American dishes and a selection of surf-and-turf meals. The downtown restaurant offers excellent Cantonese and Hong Kong dishes, like tender, delicious and beautiful razor clams in a salty black bean sauce, and specials like sweet potato greens, shiny and deeply colored, flavored with reddish bits of dried pork and XO sauce.

Other recommended dishes: Congees (esp. pork with preserved egg, fish, roast duck with meatballs and chicken with black mushrooms). **Price range:** Congee, $2.50–$4.75; dim sum and soup, $1–$8.95; entrees, $5.50–$16.95. **Wheelchair access:** Entrance, dining room on one level; narrow ramp to restroom.

Cookies and Couscous $25 & Under MOROCCAN

230 Thompson St. (at W. 3rd St.)   (212) 477-6562
Credit cards: Cash only   Meals: L, D

This small (20 seats), bright restaurant has more going for it than the peculiar name might suggest. The short menu emphasizes flavorful seasonal ingredients. Soups and salads are all tasty but almost unnecessary because all the main courses are so big. All but one (the excellent Moroccan burger) are made with couscous and they too are excellent, whether served with vegetables alone or with meat as well. As for the cookies, they are all very good but not as interesting as the house-made sorbets and ice creams in subtle flavors like tart plum-anise, and soothing cinnamon-apple.

Price range: Apps., $5–$7; entrees, $10–$19; desserts, $3.
Wheelchair access: Fully accessible. **Services:** Takeout.

Cooke's Corner $25 & Under   AMERICAN

618 Amsterdam Ave. (at 90th St.)   (212) 712-2872
Credit cards: AE   Meals: D   Closed Mon.

This charmingly subdued little restaurant, with its small, well-designed menu and intelligent wine list, is free of what plagues so many restaurants in the neighborhood: loud music, a bar crowd and big-screen television sets. With its comfortable chairs, inlaid wood tables, subtle décor and low-key service, Cooke's is a restaurant that caters to grown-ups and makes no apologies for it. It even takes reservations.

The menu is quietly satisfying with attention to details. A salad of julienne fennel with blood orange sections and Bermuda onions, is an excellent combination of sweet and anise flavors, with fennel seeds tossed in for good measure. Gravlax is a salty-sweet surprise, served with a pile of cucumbers, dark bread and mustard-and-dill sauce.

Main courses include a juicy, flavorful roast chicken served over polenta with a mushroom stew, and a fine piece of maple-glazed salmon that was not overly sweet. Beef, braised for four hours until remarkably tender, has a lively Eastern European scent of caraway and coriander seeds and comes with buttery spaetzle. Halibut steak wears a grainy mustard coating that stands up to a robust tomato-shallot sauce. Desserts are weak, aside from a rich German chocolate cake with a dark chocolate sauce.

Other recommended dishes: Duck soup, mixed field greens, smoked trout, tofu "scallops." **Price range:** Apps., $5–$9; entrees, $12–$25 (some specials are $25, far more than regular menu items). **Wheelchair access:** Everything on one level.

Copeland's $$ SOUTHERN

547 W. 145th St. (bet. Amsterdam & B'way) (212) 234-2357
Credit cards: All major   Meals: B, L, D

The Southern buffet at this Harlem institution offers all the traditional specialties. Among the entrees are such specialties as Southern fried chicken, chitterlings and champagne, barbecued short ribs of beef and braised oxtails. It's not likely to surprise you, but it will fill you up.

Other recommended dishes: Clams casino; chitterlings vinaigrette. **Price range:** Lunch: avg. app., $3.50; entree, $10.50; dessert, $3. Dinner: avg. app., $4.50; entree, $25; dessert, $3.50. **Wheelchair access:** Fully accessible. **Services:** Delivery, takeout, catering, private parties.

Corner Bistro $ BAR SNACKS

331 W. 4th St. (at Jane St.)   (212) 242-9502
Credit cards: Cash only   Meals: L, D, LN

This old bar is renowned for its hamburgers, which are big and juicy but nowhere near the best in the city. It would be a great place to have in your neighborhood but is not worth a trip.

Price range: Apps./sides, $2–$3; sandwiches, $4–$5.50. **Wheelchair acceess:** Restrooms not accessible. **Features:** Smoking permitted. **Services:** Takeout.

Cosi Sandwich Bar $ SANDWICHES

165 E. 52nd St. (bet. Lexington & Third Aves.)   (212) 758-7800
(and a dozen other locations in Manhattan)
Credit cards: All major   Meals: B, L, D

These sleek, stylish assembly lines build sandwiches to your personal specifications. There are a few cookies, muffins and desserts, an espresso machine and a modest wine bar in the back. Cosi's Roman flatbread, which tastes of olive oil and salt, is the highlight; sandwich fillings are not as tasty. Nonetheless, these are fine places for quick bites.

Price range: $5.95–$7.95. **Wheelchair access:** Accessible at most locations. **Features:** Kid friendly. **Services:** Delivery, take-out, catering, private parties.

Coup ☆ $$

NEW AMERICAN

509 E. 6th St. (bet. Aves. A & B)
(212) 979-2815
Credit cards: All major
Meals: D

Like the rest of the East Village, Coup takes an ascetic stand on visual stimulation. The walls and the concrete floor are battle-ship gray. The chairs are painful. Severe, Japanese-style wooden slats make up the ceiling, and what little light is allowed comes from translucent white wall fixtures that look like glowing phar-maceutical capsules. Somehow, this sensory deprivation induces a feeling of tranquility. Beneath the cloak of mystery lies a deceptively normal neighborhood restaurant, one that is not only in, but of, the blocks around it. It fits stylistically. The food does not aim too high, but what it aims at, it hits. It's the kind of place that always seems like a good idea. The roast Cornish hen takes some beating. Brown as a berry and pleasingly plump, it's packed with chunks of coarse-grained sourdough bread and Michigan cherries. The stuffing is beyond praise. Coup also has a deeply limey Key lime pie and an honest, homey pineapple upside-down cake.

Other recommended dishes: Gravlax cured in lemon vodka; chili-rubbed shrimps; sautéed tuna and capellini; lamb shank with Japanese squash polenta; flan. **Wine list:** A budget-priced, not very exciting list of about 40 bottles. **Price range:** Dinner apps., $5–$9; entrees, $16–$21; desserts, $7. **Wheelchair access:** Everything on same level. **Features:** Smoking permitted, outdoor dining. **Services:** Private parties.

Craft ☆ ☆ ☆ $$$$

NEW AMERICAN

43 E. 19th St.
(212) 780-0880
Credit cards: All major
Meals: L, D

This is a handsome restaurant, with a clean, vaguely Mission-influenced look that supports the culinary theme. Craft invites diners to take a trip. The destination is a simpler, cleaner, more honest America; it's a vision of food heaven, a land of strong, pure flavors and back-to-basics cooking techniques.

But in pursuit of his vision, Tom Colicchio, the chef and an owner, has placed demands on his customers that make Craft one of the most baroque dining experiences in New York. At Craft, diners build their own meals. The menu has gone through many revisions, and it must be said that it's a lot easier to organize a dinner than it used to be, but the prevailing philosophy is still do-it-yourself, with side dishes and even sauces presented as options.

The saving grace at Craft, from the beginning, has been the high quality of the ingredients and their masterly handling by Mr. Colicchio and his chef de cuisine. Nothing at the restaurant sounds like much. Lunch could start with a half-dozen Belon oysters, followed by a thick slice of stuffed veal breast with roasted spring onions and roasted bluefoot mushrooms. Every bite is a revelation. The oysters sparkle. The veal, a humble cut of meat wrapped around some simple roast vegetables, has an honesty and a depth of flavor that will stop you cold.

Craft pulls off this quiet magic with deceptive ease. Roasted diver scallops, nearly the size of small muffins, stand, unadorned, coated in some simple pan juices. A sprinkling of preserved lemon lifts these chaste, marble-white beauties right off the plate. In a city famous for steak worship, the frighteningly large porterhouse, neatly sliced into rectangles, ranks as one of the finest large-scale hunks of beef you'll encounter.

The menu revisions have not yet reached dessert, which looms like the notoriously tricky 12th hole at Augusta National. To score par at Craft, diners must match a simple choice like crepes or brioche pain perdu with fruit, ice cream and any of eight sauces. Try a light, chiffonlike steamed lemon pudding or the custardy pain perdu, which can easily handle anything thrown at it. In a fit of exuberance, diners could easily construct a $30 dessert, on top of a $28 entree fitted out with $30 more in side dishes. If you like your food simple, in other words, be prepared to pay.

Other recommended dishes: Roast sweetbreads, potato gnocchi. **Wine list:** A rather short but carefully chosen international list of about 125 wines, with a dozen by the glass. **Price range:** Lunch: apps., $10–$14; entrees, $20–$26; side dishes, $6–$12; desserts, $4–$12; three-course prix fixe, $32. Dinner: apps., $10–$20; entrees, $22–$36; side dishes, $6–$12; desserts, $4–$12; five-course tasting menu, $68. **Wheelchair access:** Restrooms on dining room level.

Cuba Libre $25 & Under   PAN-LATIN

200 Eighth Ave. (at 20th St.)
Credit cards: All major

(212) 206-0038
Meals: Br, L, D.

At Cuba Libre the combination of loud voices, hard surfaces and raucous music is enough to make you want to scream, or shut up entirely. And while the food is not always consistent, some dishes are so good you simply want to eat and sigh.

An appetizer of oysters, coated in blue cornmeal and fried, would have been tasty left at that, but the oysters are perched on smoky collard greens and served with a mildly spicy salsa.

The resulting combination is superb. Two side dishes that serve equally well as appetizers are arepas, steaming corncakes as sweet as fresh-shucked cobs in August, and yuca fries, thin cylinders crisp on the outside and with a pleasing texture somewhere between that of a baked and a fried potato. They come doused with chimichurri, a blend of olive oil, parsley and garlic.

Among the main courses, the pork tenderloin is clearly best. The thin fillets are juicy and full of flavor, rubbed with ancho chili for a little jolt that stands up to the sweet side dish of mashed plantains and the hearty black bean sauce.

Other recommended dishes: Lobster empanada; chicken relleno; Dominican shellfish stew; tuna glazed with honey and red wine. **Price range:** Apps., $6.95–$8.95; entrees, $14.95–$18.95. **Wheelchair access:** Fully accessible.

Cucina Stagionale $ ITALIAN
289 Bleecker St. (bet. Sixth & Seventh Aves.)   (212) 924-2707
Credit cards: Cash only   Meals: L, D, LN

It's cramped, crowded and loud, so why are long lines of people almost always waiting to get in? The big plates of serviceable Italian food, offered at what seem to be impossibly low prices.

Alcohol: Bring your own. **Price range:** Apps., $4.95–$7.95; entrees, $7.95–$13.95; desserts, $4.95. **Wheelchair access:** Fully accessible. **Services:** Delivery, takeout, private parties.

Cupping Room Cafe $$ NEW AMERICAN
359 W. Broadway (bet. Broome & Grand Sts.)   (212) 925-2898
Credit cards: All major   Meals: B, Br, L, D

A SoHo pioneer that continues to serve good, straightforward American food, like burgers and chicken, and great coffee in a charmingly battered atmosphere.

Price range: Lunch: apps., $6.95–$9.95; entrees, 8.95–$13.95; desserts, $3.95–$7.95. Dinner: apps., $7.95–$11.95; entrees, $15.95–$22.95; desserts, $3.95–$7.95. **Wheelchair access:** Not accessible. **Features:** Smoking permitted. **Services:** Delivery, takeout, catering, private parties.

Cyclo $25 & Under VIETNAMESE
203 First Ave. (at 12th St.)   (212) 673-3957
Credit cards: All major   Meals: D, LN

This stylish little East Village restaurant serves some of the best Vietnamese food in New York City: It is inventive, impeccably fresh and meticulously prepared, while service is friendly and informative. Try cha gio, crisp and delicate spring rolls, and chao tom, grilled shrimp paste wrapped around sugar cane.

Don't hesitate to order fruit for dessert, like cubes of wonderfully fresh mango that are the perfect end to a stellar meal. The only problem is the constant crowds.

Other recommended dishes: Ca bam (seared monkfish); goi du du (green papaya salad); pho (oxtail broth with rice noodles); bun thit nuong (grilled pork over rice noodle pillows). **Price range:** Apps., $4.50–$8; entrees, $10–$15; desserts, $3.50–$7. **Wheelchair access:** Everything is on one level. **Features:** Kid friendly, romantic. **Services:** Delivery, takeout, catering, private parties.

Da Antonio $$$ ITALIAN

157 E. 55th St. (bet. Third & Lexington Aves.) (212) 588-1545
Credit cards: All major Meals: L, D

The pastas are superb at this gracious, quietly dignified restaurant. Agnolotti stuffed with sausages and broccoli rape is particularly good; the pockets of pasta are not only filled with the flavorful mixture but also topped with it. Service is lovely; the owner hands you a large Italian menu and leaves you to peruse it. When he returns to tell you about the specials, he actually describes each dish. You can almost dine on his enthusiasm.

Price Range: Lunch: apps., $5.95–$9.95; entrees, $12.95–$18.95; desserts, $7–$10. Dinner: apps., $7.95–$12.95; entrees, $15.95–$29.95; desserts, $7–$10. **Wheelchair access:** Four steps down to dining room, restrooms upstairs. **Services:** Takeout, catering, private parties.

Da Ciro $25 & Under ITALIAN

229 Lexington Ave. (near 33rd St.) (212) 532-1636
Credit cards: All major Meals: L, D

An excellent, often overlooked little Italian restaurant. Specialties, cooked in a wood-burning oven, include terrific pizzas like focaccia robiola, a wonderfully crisp double-crusted pizza encasing earthy, melted robiola cheese that has been drizzled with truffle oil. Also excellent is a casserole of wild mushrooms baked in a crock with arugula, goat cheese, olives, tomatoes and mozzarella. The pastas are simple but lively, and full-flavored desserts like bitter chocolate mousse cake and hazelnut semifreddo more than hold their own.

Price range: Apps., $5.95–$12.95; pastas, $12.50–$15.95; entrees, $15.50–$28. **Wheelchair access:** Everything on one level. **Features:** Good for business, smoking permitted. **Services:** Takeout, private parties.

Daily Chow

2 E. 2nd St. (at Bowery)   (212) 254-7887
Credit cards: All major   Meals: L, D, LN

Daily Chow brings together Thai and Korean dishes with Chinese, Japanese and Vietnamese preparations. It does enough things well and is so good-natured that a meal there can be thoroughly enjoyable. The centerpiece on the ground floor is a sort of salad bar used for the so-called Mongolian barbecue section of the menu, but this usually results in a prefabricated dish with little flavor. Preferable alternatives include Chinese scallion pancakes, crisp and savory, and Chinese shrimp with salt-and-pepper crust. A Japanese soy broth with soba noodles and tempura is simultaneously delicate and hearty.

Daily Chow falls short with wrapped and stuffed dishes, but Korean main courses are quite successful. Bulgogi, tender, flavorful shreds of beef, comes with spicy kimchi, while bibimbop, the famous rice, beef and egg dish, is served with vegetables in a hot stone crock so that the bottom layer turns crisp. One of the best dishes is a dessert, mango sticky rice, sweetened with coconut milk and served with mango slices. A ginger-flavored brownie with coconut ice cream is about as Asian as a Big Mac, but delicious nonetheless.

The food can certainly seem secondary. Daily Chow focuses on a drinking crowd, offering pitchers of cocktails with names like ginger kamikaze and Thai dye that seem to invite oblivion, though there is a small but well-chosen list of wines.

Other recommended dishes: Thai soups, Vietnamese pork chops, beef massaman curry. **Price range:** Apps., $3–$8.95; entrees, $7.95–$14.95. **Wheelchair access:** Ramp at entrance; restroom on ground floor.

Dakshin

1713 First Ave. (near 89th St.)   (212) 987-9839
741 Ninth Ave. (near 50th St.)   (212) 757-4545
Credit cards: All major   Meals: L, D

Perhaps no other cuisine pays as much attention to spices and seasonings as Indian, and yet so much Indian food in Manhattan is bland. So it is a great pleasure to find lively spicing in more than a few dishes at Dakshin. The kitchen's finesse with seasonings is immediately apparent in jhinga jal toori, small but flavorful shrimp in a sauce of tomatoes and onions made tangy by mustard greens and enhanced by the nutty, slightly bitter aroma of curry leaves. Dakshin's breads are excellent, especially mint paratha, rich with ghee and tasting powerfully and refreshingly of mint, and garlic nan, made smoky in the clay oven. Kebabs of minced lamb are especially flavorful, as are cubes of lemony boneless chicken breast. Seva batata poori, little round crisps topped with diced potatoes and crunchy slivers of lentil-flour angel hair, are made pleasantly tangy by a sauce of mint, tamarind and yogurt. Among the meat main courses, try the chicken Chettinad, with the chicken in a thick sauce made lively by black pepper and curry leaves. Dakshin's vegetable dishes excel, especially punj rattani dal. This creamy, mellow dish, made with five types of lentils and flavored with lots of garlic and ginger, is true home cooking.

Other recommended dishes: Mangalorean stir-fried chicken, tandoori assortment, lamb vindaloo, baby eggplant with ginger and coconut, bharta. **Price range:** Apps., $3–$6; entrees, $7–$17. **Wheelchair access:** Step at entrance.

Dalia's $25 & Under TAPAS

984 Amsterdam Ave. (near 109th St.) (212) 865-9541
Credit cards: All major Meals: D, LN

With its dark walls and soft lighting, Dalia's offers a warm haven on a part of Amsterdam Avenue that is as sedate as a chain saw. Portions are on the large side, closer to what the Spanish call *raciones*, or large appetizers, so three tapas can make a meal. A simple tapa like toast rubbed with garlic and olive oil and topped with ham and cheese is a fine starter, and the cold potato-and-onion omelet has a pleasant but unusual texture, courtesy of oatmeal that the chef had mixed in. Potatoes cut into cubes, fried until crisp and served with aioli are irresistible, while grilled chorizo is always a crowd-pleaser.

Other recommended dishes: Steamed clams; grilled sardines; omelets. **Price range:** Tapas, $4.25–$8.25. **Wheelchair access:** Everything on one level.

Dallas BBQ $ BARBECUE

132 W. 43rd St. (bet. Sixth & Seventh Aves.) (212) 221-9000
132 Second Ave. (at 9th St.) (212) 777-5574
21 University Pl. (at 8th St.) (212) 674-4450
27 W. 72nd St. (near Columbus Ave.) (212) 873-2004
316 Sixth Ave. (bet. Bleecker & 3rd Sts.) (212) 741-7390
1265 Third Ave. (bet. 72nd & 73rd Sts.) (212) 772-9393
Credit cards: All major Meals: L, D, LN

Lackluster ribs, burgers and chicken, but such big portions! Service is friendly and takeout is efficient.

Price range: Apps., $1.95–$7.95; entrees, $3.95–$12.95. **Wheelchair access:** Fully accessible. **Features:** Kid friendly. **Services:** Delivery, takeout, catering, private parties.

Da Mario $$

ITALIAN

883 First Ave. (bet. 49th & 50th Sts.)   (212) 750-1804
Credit cards: All major   Meals: L, D

It looks like dozens of other small Italian restaurants in New York City, but this one is distinguished by its Sicilian bent, its warmth and its careful cooking. Expect a fine-looking array of antipasti, a long list of fish specials and a we-can-make-any-thing-you-want sort of attitude. Good pastas, surprisingly good desserts and a wine list with a strong Italian emphasis.

Price range: Lunch: apps., $5.95–$8.95; entrees, $9.95–$18.95; desserts, $6; prix fixe, $16.95. Dinner: apps., $6.95–$10.95; entrees, $13.95–$23.95; desserts, $6; prix fixe, $26.95. **Wheelchair access:** Restrooms are small. **Services:** Takeout, private parties.

Danal $25 & Under

NEW AMERICAN

90 E. 10th St. (bet. Third & Fourth Aves.)   (212) 982-6930
Credit cards: MC/V   Meals: Br, L, D

The warm, cozy country atmosphere is one of the highlights at this enduring favorite. The reliably enticing homey American fare is the other. Menus change daily here, but typical offerings include a beet salad; grilled breast of duck with orange sauce; and roast monkfish finished with a soy-balsamic reduction. Danal also does a nice afternoon tea and a fine Sunday brunch. It's a great place for a date.

Other recommended dishes: Roast chicken; pork chops; smoked trout; beef tenderloin; banana bread pudding; chocolate macadamia tart. **Alcohol:** Beer and wine. **Price range:** Avg. lunch: $11. Dinner: avg. app., $6.50–$7; entrée, $18; dessert, $6. **Wheelchair access:** Not accessible. **Features:** Romantic, smoking permitted, outdoor dining. **Services:** Catering, private parties.

Da Nico $25 & Under

ITALIAN

164 Mulberry St. (bet. Grand & Broome Sts.)   (212) 343-1212
Credit cards: All major   Meals: L, D, LN

One of the few Italian restaurants in Little Italy that is actually worth trying. Rotisserie dishes, roasts and pizzas from the wood-burning oven are the best bets. Pizzas boast thin crusts and fresh, stylish toppings but could use another minute in the oven for additional crisping. The restaurant is an invitingly informal place in brick, wood and pewter with stools at a counter, tables in the food-filled front room facing the street and an airy, more secluded dining room in back.

Price range: Prix-fixe lunch, $6–$6.50; avg. dinner, $25. **Wheelchair access:** Fully accessible. **Features:** Outdoor dining. **Services:** Delivery, takeout, catering, private parties.

Daniel ☆☆☆☆ $$$$ FRENCH
Mayfair Hotel, 60 E. 65th St. (bet. Park & Madison Aves.)
(212) 288-0033
Credit cards: All major   Meals: L, D   Closed Sun.

Located in a luxurious hotel dining room, Daniel has moved forward, and upward, with grace and assurance. It is now the Daniel that New York wanted and expected all along, a top-flight French restaurant, sumptuous and rather grand, but still very much the personal expression of its chef and owner, Daniel Boulud. There's a definite tone at Daniel, a warmth usually associated with small neighborhood restaurants. Mr. Boulud has both feet planted in the rich gastronomic soil of the Lyonnais region, an area renowned for its robust cuisine. His menu is overwhelming, with a dozen appetizers and ten main courses supplemented by a daily list of specials and tasting menus. The dessert menu is two menus, with a second page devoted entirely to chocolate. The wine list is two bound volumes.

Mr. Boulud is ceaselessly inventive in a free and easy way. The influences come from all over the Mediterranean, and as far afield as Japan and India, pulled in and made French with total assurance. One of the more intriguing dishes on the menu is cod crusted in black truffles, served on a rustic bed of lentils and root vegetables in a mushroom broth. The cod, a fairly bland fish, becomes supercod, its meltingly tender meat suffused with the tang of smoke and earth. Cumin works its potent magic in roasted squab with a deceptively simple garnish of spiced pineapple, carrots and watercress. The unlikely addition of chickpea purée cooked as a giant French fry and spiced with just a hint of cumin transforms the dish. The flavors begin to bounce off each other, like popcorn kernels popping under heat.

There are lots of pleasant surprises like that at Daniel, culminating in a dessert menu remarkable for its elegance and restraint. The left side is devoted to fruit desserts, the right to chocolate, and it's understandable if eyes tend to drift rightward. One feels sorry for the lighter-than-air warm almond cake, almost a horizontal soufflé, served with muscat-raisin ice cream. How could it hope to upstage the glamour parade just across the way, led by thin leaves of chocolate filled with gianduja and amaretto or the glistening, nearly black chocolate bombe, a smooth sphere that opens up to reveal an inner core of cassis, vanilla crème brûlée and cashew nougat?

It is highly advisable to study the cheese trolley when it rolls around. The selection is well organized, the cheeses superb. Jean Luc Le Dû, the sommelier, has developed Daniel's list into a thrilling document, strong on classic French wines and top producers, but also filled with fascinating side trips, and subsections that feature specific producers, or vineyards, in depth.

Service, confident and expert, goes a long way to explain the neighborhood's love affair with Daniel. Diners feel well cared for. There's none of the hovering that passes for attentive service at lesser restaurants. The tone is pitch-perfect, and as a result, patrons feel at ease.

Other recommended dishes: Tuna Tartare; pork bellies and stuffed trotters with lentils and root vegetables. **Wine list:** An outstanding list, tilted toward French wines but highly international. Broad and deep, it has a good selection of half bottles and wines by the glass. **Price range:** Lunch: one course, $28; two courses, $36; three courses, $45. Dinner: three courses, $78; five-course tasting menu, $105; eight-course tasting menu $140. **Wheelchair access:** Entrance a few steps west of the main door.

Danube ☆☆☆ $$$$ VIENNESE/GERMAN
30 Hudson St. (at Duane St.)   (212) 791-3771
Credit cards: All major   Meals: L, D

David Bouley does not do things in a small way. Using fin-de-siécle Vienna as a culinary source, and a repository of romantic images, he has created Danube, the most enchanting restaurant New York has seen in decades. The Vienna of Schnitzler, Freud and Musil shimmers with a seductive light, captured brilliantly in Danube's décor. This is an opiate dream of lush fabrics, deeply saturated decadent colors and lustrous glazed surfaces. It's a swirl of opulent patterns and textures, dominated by the large, unabashedly excessive Klimts on the walls. If ever a restaurant was made for a four-hour meal, Danube is it.

In some cases, Mr. Bouley insists on authenticity. His Wiener schnitzel, with an impeccably light and greaseless crust, does not make the mistake of trying to be original. The kavalierspitz, a man-size slab of boiled beef shoulder served with puréed spinach, looks like a middle-class Sunday dinner.

But Mr. Bouley was not put on earth to boil beef. After anchoring the menu with a handful of classics, he has conjured up his own private Austria or, in some cases, taken leave of the country altogether. More typically, Mr. Bouley has lightened, modernized and personalized traditional dishes, or invented new ones using traditional ingredients, often with stunning results: the ravioli stuffed with Yukon Gold potatoes and braised veal is a triumph, coated in a powerfully reduced, syrupy veal stock and served with braised sunchokes. There are two thoroughly traditional desserts, both flawless: a Czech palacsintak, or crêpe, and a Salzburger nockerl, a mound-shaped soufflé dusted in confectioners' sugar and served with raspberries.

Other recommended dishes: Tyrolean wine soup with smoked trout crêpe; oxtail consommé with dumplings; beef cheeks in Zweigelt sauce. **Wine list:** A pioneering list of 240 wines, half of them Austrian. **Price range:** Lunch: apps., $8.50–$17; entrees, $28–$35; desserts, $9–$12; three-course prix-fixe, $35; five- or six-course chef's menu, $55. Dinner: apps., $9–$17; entrees, $29–$35; desserts, $9–$12. **Wheelchair access:** Restroom on first floor. **Features:** Good for business, romantic.

D'Artagnan ☆☆ $$$$ FRENCH

152 E. 46th St. (bet. Third & Lexington Aves.)   (212) 687-0300
Credit cards: All major   Meals: L, D   Closed Sun.

D'Artagnan has so much personality it could sell it by the pound. In a city chock-full of micromanaged restaurant images, it's a relief to see a restaurant that wears its heart on its sleeve, even at the risk of appearing foolish. The food is Gascon, from France's legendary region of foie gras, duck, Armagnac and prunes, and how could it be otherwise? The restaurant is an outgrowth of the D'Artagnan retail shop, which itself is a branch of the wholesale specialty meat business owned by Ariane Daguin, the daughter of the renowned Gascon chef André Daguin. (The name refers to Dumas's fourth musketeer, one of the Gascon soldiers who served Louis XIII and Louis XIV.)

In pursuit of the Gascon flavor, Ms. Daguin has turned D'Artagnan into a "Three Musketeers" theme park, with heavy oak tables, high-back chairs upholstered in red flocked velvet and musketeer tunics and crossed swords on the brick walls. The waiters do their best to pretend they are not outfitted in traditional Gascon garb. You have to love it.

This is not a restaurant for diners who pick at their food. The cuisine of the musketeers is meat in its richest forms, washed down with big sturdy reds like Cahors or Madiran. The food is authentic, robust, earthy and powerfully flavored, enlivened by Ms. Daguin's whimsical sense of humor. A sampler plate of foie gras begins in orthodox fashion, with terrine of duck foie gras, but it finds room for novelty items like a French Kiss (a prune boldly marinated in Armagnac and stuffed with foie gras mousse, possibly the finest adult candy ever invented). Foie gras appears in many guises. Perhaps the most seductive is the simple foie gras terrine, with a deep, dark, gamy tinge.

Cassoulet is a religion in Gascony, and the one served at D'Artagnan is a mighty heap of garlic sausage, duck-Armagnac sausage, duck leg confit, duck gizzard confit and the pancetta-like ventrèche embedded in a layer of garlicky coco beans dense enough to give the silverware a fight. Leg of lamb roasted on the rotisserie downstairs yields thick slices floating in an almost black sauce alive with the fire of Espelette peppers, the pimentos that heat the Basque stew known as piperade. Fish, however, doesn't have a chance.

The cheese course is small but pleasing, a rustic selection of Petit Basque, Roquefort and Coach Farm goat cheese. It comes with a thick jam swimming with the sour cherries known as griottes and meant to be eaten with the salty Petit Basque. For the most part, the desserts seem like a distraction before the important business of pouring the aged Armagnac. One Gascon speciality deserves attention: apple croustade, which relies for its effect on a thousand-layered pastry so froufrou that in French it's called a bridal veil.

Other recommended dishes: Quail with Armagnac-grape sauce, foie gras terrine with Sauternes jelly. **Wine list:** An admirably focused list of about 40 wines, most from southwestern France, nearly half available by the glass. **Price range:** Lunch: apps., $6.50–$19; entrees, $13–$26; desserts, $7–$9; two-course prix fixe, $20. Dinner: apps., $6–$19; entrees, $19–$26; desserts, $7–$9. Three-course pretheater menu, 5:30 to 7 p.m., $36. Six-course foie-gras tasting menu, $65. **Wheelchair access:** Main dining room upstairs.

Da Silvano $$$ ITALIAN
260 Sixth Ave. (bet. Houston & Bleecker Sts.)   (212) 982-2343
Credit cards: All major   Meals: L, D, LN

Menus in Tuscany don't change with the times, and this one hasn't either. For more than 20 years the restaurant has been turning out simple, authentic Italian dishes like marinated anchovies, trippa alla fiorentina and osso buco in a simple yet slightly raucous atmosphere. Good pastas, an interesting wine list and one of Manhattan's best opportunities for people-watching, especially from the outdoor cafe, have made this a perennial favorite.

Price range: Apps., $6.50–$12.50; entrees, $12.50–$28.50; desserts, $7.50 and up. **Wheelchair access:** Fully accessible. **Features:** Outdoor dining. **Services:** Takeout.

Dawat ☆ $$$ INDIAN
210 E. 58th St. (bet. Second & Third Aves.)   (212) 355-7555
Credit cards: All major   Meals: L, D

Once New York City's finest and most innovative Indian restaurants, it no longer seems so cutting edge. Most of the vegetable dishes — the small baked eggplant with tamarind sauce, the potatoes mixed with ginger and tomatoes, the homemade cheese in spinach sauce — are excellent. The set lunches are a bargain. Two dishes stand out: Cornish hen with green chilies, "a very hot specialty of Kerala's Baghdadi Jews," and sarson ka sag, a sour, spicy, buttery purée of mustard greens. Bhaja are also impressive: Whole leaves of spinach, battered so lightly that the green glows through the coating, are paired with light little potato-skin fritters. (*Ruth Reichl*)

Other recommended dishes: Aloo tikkiyas (potato cakes); sag gosht (lamb in spinach purée); tadka dal (simmered beans); zeera aloo (spicy potatoes); gajrela (grated carrots); kheer (rice pudding); mango ice cream. **Wine list:** The wine list irritatingly does not include the vintage years, and wines could be more creatively chosen to match the food. **Price range:** Apps., $5.75–$10.25; entrees, $15.95–$23.95; side dishes, $4.25–$12.95; desserts, $4.95. Prix-fixe lunch, $12.95 and $13.95. **Wheelchair access:** Everything on one level. **Features:** Smoking permitted. **Services:** Delivery, takeout, catering, private parties.

DB Bistro Moderne ☆☆ $$$$ Bistro
55 W. 44th St. (bet. Fifth & Sixth Aves.)   (212) 391-2400
Credit cards: All major   Meals: L, D   Closed Sun.

Daniel Boulud's newest venture is a lively, even raucous restaurant that tries to pass for a bistro but can't quite disguise its high-class leanings. The cooking, although simplified to suit the bistro concept and even countrified on occasion, plays to Mr. Boulud's strength, his refined rusticity. He simply shows that rock-solid technique, good ingredients and a sound idea translate into gustatory bliss. There's nothing fancy about Mr. Boulud's tarte Tatin heaped with roasted tomatoes, goat cheese, basil and black olives, but a perfect buttery crust and tomatoes brought to peak concentration of flavor make a little miracle out of this humble tart.

Gazpacho, tingling and vibrant, sticks to basics. It is clean, crisp and clear, with tender shrimp and small chunks of buttery avocado. Confit de canard, the Tuesday plat du jour, looks like meat in a bowl. It is potently flavored, with garlicky roast potatoes and mushrooms reeking of the earth. The bowl is a good idea. You can lean over it and simply inhale the fragrance, like a burnt offering. Years of catering to an Upper East Side clientele have given Mr. Boulud a supernatural hand with salads and spa fare. Cristina Aliberti, too, manages the trick of making very light desserts, like melon carpaccio with ginger sorbet as appealing as, say, her clafoutis tout chocolat, a small round chocolate cake, runny in the center, that looks like no clafoutis on earth. No one will object. Rich without being gooey, the clafoutis impersonator strikes me as the kind of chocolate dessert that can win over the most hardened chocolate skeptic.

Other recommended dishes: Tomato tarte Tatin; gazpacho with poached shrimp; marinated salmon with lovage oil; duck confit with mushrooms and garlic potatoes; boeuf en gelée with horseradish cream; chocolate clafoutis; mille-feuille of green figs and ricotta. **Wine list:** A shrewd international list of about 100 wines, with nine wines by the glass. **Price range:** Lunch, apps.,

$9–$16; entrees, $22–$26; desserts, $9–$11; prix-fixe, $22–$29. Dinner, apps, $12–$17; entrees, $28–$32; desserts, $9–$11. **Wheelchair access:** Entrance through hotel lobby leads to upper dining room. Restrooms are on upper dining room level.

Delhi Palace $25 & Under   INDIAN

37-33 74th St., Jackson Heights, Queens   (718) 507-0666
Credit cards: All major   Meals: L, D, LN

The menu promises the "haute cuisine of India," and the dining room has an almost stilted formality. The best dishes here are the rich, complex curries, each tailored for its particular dish. Shrimp vindaloo comes in a remarkable dark brown curry, tasting of vinegar and chocolate. Kadai gosht is another exceptional curry, with tender pieces of lamb in a tomato-and-onion sauce flavored with ginger and chilies. With the exception of reshmi kebab (tender pieces of chicken marinated in a lemon and garlic mixture), the Tandoori specialties are disappointing. Don't bother with the desserts; if you want a sweet, it's fun to shop in the nearby bakeries.

Alcohol: Beer and wine. **Price range:** Apps., $1.95–$5.25; entrees, $9.95–$12.95. **Wheelchair access:** Everything is on one level. **Services:** Takeout.

Della Femina ☆ $$$$ NEW AMERICAN

131 E. 54th St. (bet. Madison & Lexington Aves.)   (212) 752-0111
Credit cards: All major   Meals: L, D   Closed Sun.

Della Femina attracts a tony Upper East Side clientele with its cool, restrained, Yankeefied setting straight out of Martha Stewart. It looks like a television commercial for the good life, late 1990's style. The style of cooking is usually described as American with international accents: perfectly poached, unusually flavorful chunks of lobster stand out in a cool salad of young greens, herbs and mango, dressed with a basil-caviar vinaigrette. Roasted turbot, rich and firm, gets just the right support from spring-fresh green peas, morels and a tomato-tarragon essence. There can be inconsistencies but when the kitchen is on its game, Della Femina is very good indeed (although it is never a sure bet what the clueless waitstaff might bring, or when). Desserts, however, are consistently outstanding, especially the steamed lemon pudding.

Other recommended dishes: Roasted langoustines; grilled lamb; melon soup. **Wine List:** A fairly well-chosen French-American bistro list with six half-bottles and six wines by the glass. **Price Range:** Lunch: apps., $7–$12; entrees, $12–$24; desserts, $6–$8. Dinner: apps., $10–$25; entrees, $26–$42; desserts, $7–$9. **Wheelchair Access:** Four steps down to the dining room and restrooms.

119

Delmonico's ☆ $$$ ITALIAN/NEW AMERICAN
56 Beaver St. (at Williams St.)   (212) 509-1144
Credit cards: All major   Meals: B, L, D

An American icon has been restored to its former glory. Opulent, old-fashioned and dignified, the huge rooms are rich with stained wood and soft upholstery, and the tables are swathed in oceans of white linen. It can be noisy in the middle of the room. The best dishes are in the section headed "Pasta, Risotti." Linguine with clams is a classic that is very well done. Ricotta and spinach ravioli may lack delicacy, but they are generous little pockets topped with clarified butter and fresh sage, and they make a satisfying meal. There is one steak to recommend: the rib-eye may not have the pedigree of a porterhouse or Delmonico, but it is big, tasty and perfectly cooked. For dessert try the baked Alaska.

Wine list: Not brilliant, but there are a few good wines at fair prices. **Price range:** Apps., $8–$16 ($32 for the cold seafood platter); pastas, $16–$22; entrees, $21–$34; desserts, $6–$10. **Wheelchair access:** Steps to dining room. **Features:** Good for business. **Services:** Takeout, catering, private parties.

Destinée ☆☆ $$$$ FRENCH
134 E. 61st St. (bet. Lexington & Park Aves.)   (212) 888-1220
Credit cards: All major   Meals: L, D

Fancy French food, an intimate room and not entirely unreasonable prices: No wonder this small restaurant has been such a hit. It is a quiet little corner of France on 61st Street. But it is not modern France. This is food so decorative that each plate makes you gasp. The calamari are gorgeous, quickly seared and set on a green tangle of herbed pasta. Squid has never looked so lovely. Some main dishes feel fussy, but try the sea bass served in a crust of shellfish and capers richly scented with Indian spices. (*Ruth Reichl*)

Other recommended dishes: Salmon tartar; braised veal shanks; seared venison with spätzle; chocolate dome. **Wine list:** No bargains, but some excellent choices by the glass. **Price range:** Prix-fixe lunch, $20; a la carte apps., $8–$13; entrees, $19–$26; desserts, $8. Prix-fixe dinner, $55; six-course tasting menu, $69. **Wheelchair access:** Three steps down to the dining room. **Features:** Romantic. **Services:** Private parties.

Dim Sum Go Go ☆ $$ CHINESE
5 E. Broadway (at Chatham Sq.)   (212) 732-0797
Credit cards: All major   Meals: L, D

Dim Sum Go Go is a bright, happy extrovert clinging to the edge of Chinatown like a goofy sidekick. The restaurant's interior design is done on the cheap but with genuine flair. It has a clean, streamlined look, with perforated steel chairs, bright red screens and a clever wall pattern taken from medieval scrolls with dining scenes.

The chef has developed a quirky, very appealing menu that plays Western variations on Chinese themes, sometimes seriously, sometimes for the sheer fun of it, as in the Go Go hamburger, a steamed bun folded over a patty made from dim sum beef and served with taro French fries. The dim sum is presented on a separate miniature menu, with one page devoted to fish and meat dim sum, the other to vegetarian dim sum. On balance, they score better than average on the dim sum scale, but there's a sameness to the lineup that's hard to ignore if you order the attractively priced combination plates.

The better, more inventive food can be found on a larger menu of 60 dishes abounding in pleasant surprises. Bean curd skin is one of them, stuffed with bits of black mushroom and chopped spinach, then folded like a crêpe and fried. Swiss chard is used to wrap crunchy julienned vegetables, arranged around a tangle of frilly white fungus, supple yet crunchy, which the Chinese often use in medicinal soups. When a flick of the wrist will do the trick, the chef does no more. Just a few filaments of lemon zest, for example, provide the needed spark for a hefty spinach and bean curd soup.

Other recommended dishes: Smoked shredded duck with preserved ginger, fried halibut with vinegar-garlic sauce. **Wine list:** One white, one red, beers. **Price range:** Apps., $2.25–$9.95; entrees $8.95–$16.95; dessert, $2.75–$3. **Wheelchair access:** Restrooms down one flight or up one flight.

Diner
$25 & Under   NEW AMERICAN

85 Broadway, Williamsburg, Brooklyn   (718) 486-3077
Credit cards: Cash only   Meals: Br, L, D, LN

The owners of this tattered luncheonette underneath the Williamsburg Bridge had the good sense not to create a diner-theme restaurant. Instead, Diner brings the diner idea up to date, offering the sort of everyday food that appeals to the local art crowd. The basics — roast chicken, french fries, hamburgers, etc. — are fine, and other dishes can be superb, like skirt steak, perfectly cooked whole trout, black bean soup and eggs scrambled with grilled trout. The atmosphere is bustling and smoky.

Other recommended dishes: French salad; goat cheese salad; green salad; black-eyed pea soup; mussels; roasted fresh ham; rib-eye steak; flourless chocolate cake. **Price range:** Apps., $3.50–$8.50; entrees, $6.50–$15. **Wheelchair access:** Two steps at entrance; restroom not accessible. **Features:** Kid friendly, smoking permitted. **Services:** Takeout.

The Dining Room ☆☆ $$$ NEW AMERICAN

154 E. 79th St. (at Lexington Ave.)   (212) 327-2500
Credit cards: All major   Meals: D

The Dining Room is sincere and unassuming, an attractive setting for attractive, intelligently conceived food. On the ground floor, a handful of tables cluster near the front window to form a clubby dining area. The upstairs mood is a touch more formal, with fabric-lined booths that hark back to the golden age of train travel.

The menu, like the restaurant, is small, but it works some intriguing variations on familiar ingredients. An appetizer of seared foie gras with a thoroughly orthodox accompaniment of sautéed peach slices is a perfectly pleasant start to the meal, but bits of semisweet pickled watermelon rind really kick-start the dish. The chef seems to have all sorts of ideas like that in his repertory, like the sheets of spicy tasso ham which make a bright, racy counterpoint wrapped around dark quail meat and mushrooms. At the same time, there's nothing highfalutin about the dish, which rests on a neat pile of grits baked with Cheddar cheese. The chopped country salad, too, has modest pretensions, but it shames the competition in this increasingly popular category with an expertly juggled assortment of textures and flavors. The excitement subsides a little in the main courses, which are homey at heart, perfectly satisfying, but not quite as clever as the starters. Good ingredients carry most of the load, notably in the powerfully flavored lamb, served with a light, custardy corn pudding, and a he-man portion of prime rib, bolstered by a side dish of sweetly braised rib meat, potato gratin and wild mushrooms.

Two desserts fly right off the charts. A column of bread pudding, soaked in coconut milk, rests on a layer of tart crushed pineapple and then picks up the rich spice of ginger sorbet, poised atop a glassy sugar tuile. Chocolate caramel icebox cake is a simple compressed sphere concealing pleasurable depths — layer after layer of shortbread, chocolate-caramel mousse, molten caramel and meringue, swimming in a pool of caramel sauce and chocolate sauce.

Other recommended dishes: Pan-fried artichoke hearts, raw bar sampler, braised striped bass. **Wine list:** A respectable international list of about 80 wines, nearly half $40 or under, with 7 wines by the glass. **Price range:** Apps., $7–$14; entrees, $19–$28; desserts, $6–$9. **Wheelchair access:** Restrooms are on street level.

District ☆ $$$

NEW AMERICAN

130 W. 46th St. (bet. Sixth & Seventh Aves.) (212) 485-2999
Credit cards: All major Meals: B, L, D

There's a theatrical aspect to dining at District. It hits you full
force the moment you walk in the door and get a faceful of
David Rockwell's design. The walls look like flats, and ropes
behind the banquettes create the illusion that the scenery might
be raised at any moment. As a stage set, District is witty,
sophisticated and surprisingly cozy, especially if you land one
of the wraparound booths.

The kitchen can be perplexingly erratic, but when it hits the
marks, it's worth the ticket. The food is rich, florid, over the top
and, when it works, irresistible in a way that makes you feel
vaguely guilty. An enormous plate of beef carpaccio layered
over the largest portobello mushrooms in captivity arrives at the
table with an inexplicable basket of little Cuban sandwiches
filled with melted fontina cheese and truffles. The main
courses, too, sing at top volume. Slow-cooked salmon with
creamed lentils, bacon and chanterelles is a sprightly amuse-
bouche by comparison with the fearsome chicken cannelloni,
two buckwheat-pasta wrappers the size of Christmas crackers
that are filled with ricotta and chicken, then balanced atop a
crisped chicken leg done as a confit. The dish is rounded out
with a hefty serving of roasted squash and a sage and brown
butter sauce. The pastry chef likes lush, very sweet desserts,
but a tall, fluffy cheesecake with huckleberry compote scores a
direct hit.

Other recommended dishes: Potato-leek chowder with oysters;
roasted scallops with truffle-whipped butter; tuna mignon with
roasted peppers, onions and fennel. **Wine list:** An international,
rather dull list of about 60 wines, with six wines by the glass
and nine by the half bottle. **Price range:** Lunch: combined
appetizer and entree, $13–$19; desserts, $5. Dinner: apps.,
$8–$15; entrees, $21–$37.50; desserts, $7. Three-course pre-the-
ater menu, 5:30 to 6:30 p.m., $28. **Wheelchair access:**
Restrooms are on street level.

Diwan Grill $25 & Under

INDIAN

148 E. 48th St. (bet. Lexington & Third Aves.) (212) 593-5425
Credit cards: All major Meals: L, D

This sedate midtown Indian restaurant is easy to overlook, but
it is worth seeking out as almost everything is well prepared
and lively. Rogan josh, tender chunks of lamb in a complex
spicy sauce, sends waves of flavor passing through the mouth.
Seekh kebab, minced lamb rolled into cylinders and grilled, is
wonderfully spicy, and fish tikka, cooked in the clay oven, is

moist and gently but skillfully spiced. The dining room seems overly formal in a way typical of many Indian restaurants.

Other recommended dishes: Tandoori-roasted potatoes; stuffed peppers; samosas; roasted salmon; shrimp cooked with spinach; bhindi masala (okra strewed with tomatoes, onions, and coriander). **Price range:** Apps., $5–$10; entrees, $14–$20; desserts, $5. **Services:** Delivery, takeout, catering, private parties.

Diwan's Curry House $25 & Under   INDIAN
302 Columbus Ave. (at 74th St.)   (212) 721-3400
Credit cards: All major   Meals: L, D

Here are two things you almost never see in Indian restaurants: pork spareribs and a dining room decorated in a zebra-skin motif. Diwan's Curry House has them both. The zebra fabric lines the walls and upholsters the bar stools and divans in a lounge area, making the dining room look like an after-hours club with too many lights on. But those pork ribs are something else, bathed in yogurt and lemon juice, flavored with cumin, chilies and garlic, and grilled to crisp perfection.

Of course, almost nobody in India eats pork. They don't eat nan with garlic, rosemary and olive oil either, though it's quite good here. It all seems pretty bizarre. But the ribs and other dishes are welcome rewards. The menu's more conventional items can be excellent, like katori chat, little pastry cups containing a snack of potatoes, chickpeas and yogurt with a zingy tamarind-mint sauce, and bhel poori, a Bombay favorite, made with potatoes, onions, crisp puffed rice and a similar tamarind sauce. The curries are more of a mixed bag. Try the rogan josh, tender lamb in a yogurt sauce flavored with fennel and the tikka makhanwala, chunks of chicken in a spicy creamy tomato sauce. Be aware that the curries tend to be spicy.

Other recommended dishes: Garlic shrimp; tandoori shrimp; murg malai kebab; eggplant curry; rack of lamb. **Price range:** Apps., $5.95–$7.95; entrees, $10.95–$17.95. **Wheelchair access:** Restrooms are one flight down. **Features:** Smoking at bar. **Services:** Delivery, takeout.

Dock's Oyster Bar ☆ $$ SEAFOOD
633 Third Ave. (at 40th St.)   (212) 986-8080
2427 Broadway (at 89th St.)   (212) 724-5588
Credit cards: All major   Meals: Br, L, D, LN

These bustling fish houses with a sparkling shellfish bar from which to choose shrimp or lobster cocktails or oysters and clams on the half shell are crowded fish emporiums that give you your money's worth. Favorites among starters are the Docks clam chowder, Maryland crab cakes and steamers in beer broth. Engaging are entrees of grilled red snapper with coleslaw and rice, grilled salmon with coleslaw and steamed potatoes and Caesar salad with grilled tuna. Steamed lobsters come in one- to two-pound sizes, and there is a New England clambake on Sunday and Monday nights. (*Ruth Reichl*)

Price range: Apps., $6–$11; entrees, $15–$22; desserts, $5–$7. **Wheelchair access:** Fully accessible. **Features:** Kid friendly, smoking permitted.

Do Hwa $$ KOREAN
55 Carmine St. (at Bedford St.) (212) 414-2815.
Credit cards: All major   Meals: L, D   Closed Sun.

Do Hwa is the latest in a new breed of Korean restaurants that are trying to win converts by making their food more under-standable to curious Americans. In an imaginative step to demystify Korean food, the restaurant presents four tasting menus intended for parties of four. Three of the menus offer dishes from a specific region. The fourth is vegetarian. The Kaesong menu, with dishes from northwestern Korea, offers four appetizers and four entrees, all served at once. The appe-tizers include hot and spicy stir-fried squid and vegetables, and steamed sea kelp with asparagus. The entrees include kalbi jiim (stewed chunks of beef rib and potatoes) and kimchi chigae (pork and kimchi soup). All entrees come with panchan, the traditional palate-provoking condiments like kimchi, pickled radish or salted shrimp.

The set menus remove the burden of choice, but diners who want to forage can move on to a menu of traditional dishes. Most tables do not have grills for do-it-yourself barbecuing, but the kitchen makes kalbi (grilled beef short ribs) and deji bulgogi (grilled pork slices), eaten burrito style in a leaf of red lettuce flavored with garlic, shiso and chilies. It sounds like home cooking, and it is. The executive chef is the owner's mother.

Price Range: Apps $5–$10; entrees, $12–$22; desserts, $8. **Wheelchair access:** One step up from sidewalk. **Features:** Smoking at bar. **Services:** Takeout, catering, private parties.

Dok Suni $25 & Under KOREAN
119 First Ave. (bet. 7th St. & St. Marks Pl.) (212) 477-9506
Credit cards: Cash only   Meals: D, LN

The dining room has loud music, lots of cigarette smoke, would-be models and tame Korean food simultaneously made hip for the East Village and palatable for cautious Westerners. Potato pancakes are an unusual Korean starter, but they are delicious and go well with the soy-and-vinegar dipping sauce. Fried dumplings with a ground vegetable stuffing are tame com-pared with the spicy kimchee pancake. Main courses are also short on traditional Korean dishes. Bulgogi — grilled slices of marinated beef — is served with a mildly spicy sauce and large leaves of lettuce for rolling up the meat with rice. A seafood pancake, made with oysters, squid and shrimp, is mildly flavored, though the accompanying kimchee is spicy.

Price range: Apps., $4–$9; entrees, $8.50–$16. **Wheelchair access:** Restrooms not accessible. **Features:** Smoking permitted. **Services:** Takeout.

Donguri $$ JAPANESE/SUSHI
309 E. 83rd St. (at Second Ave.)   (212) 737-5656
Credit cards: All major   Meals: D   Closed Mon.

A tiny, rustic room that looks exactly like a small restaurant in Tokyo. Not a sushi bar and not a noodle parlor, Donguri serves small dishes like fried fresh shrimp in the shell and tofu topped with four varieties of miso. There are a few choice selections of sushi and a prix-fixe meal that changes daily.

Alcohol: Beer and wine. **Price range:** Apps., $4.50–$12.50; entrees, $12–$20; desserts, $3.50–$6. Tasting menus, $35 and $55. **Wheelchair access:** Restroom not accessible. **Services:** Takeout.

Downtown ☆ $$$ ITALIAN
376 W. Broadway (at Broome St.)   (212) 343-0999
Credit cards: All major   Meals: L, D, LN

Uptown has invaded downtown in this restaurant where most men wear suits and all the women are gorgeous. Clearly people go to Downtown to smoke, to look swell, to see and be seen. They get good Italian food at outrageous prices. Mussels and clams veneziana is a nice dish, and the thin slices of carpaccio a la cipriani are cut from a gorgeous piece of meat. And the baked tagliolini, made famous by the original Harry's Bar in Venice, is rich and creamy, elegant comfort food. The main courses are even better, including beautifully grilled chicken with nothing but a bit of zucchini and tomatoes on the side. The one sure thing is the prix-fixe meal, which includes a good salad, fine pasta, dessert and coffee. The service is always gracious and accommodating, and the scene is worth the voyage.

Other recommended dishes: Artichoke and avocado salad; fried calamari; pastas; semolina gnocchi; calf's liver with onions. **Wine list:** The vintages are not listed, the choices are unimaginative and many of the wines are sold out. Prices, however, are average. **Price range:** Apps., $9.50–$20.50; entrees, $21.50–$35.50; desserts, $10.50. **Wheelchair access:** Everything is at ground level. **Features:** Outdoor dining (sidewalk). **Services:** Delivery, catering, private parties.

Druids Bar & Restaurant $$ NEW AMERICAN

736 10th Ave. (bet. 50th & 51st Sts.)   (212) 307-6410
Credit cards: All major   Meals: Br, L, D

What makes this bar unusual is its surprisingly inventive menu
of contemporary American food. Sometimes it's very good, but
often it seems too inventive, as if the chef were striving to be
creative rather than rational. Still, it's worth trying, and the garden is an oasis on 10th Avenue.

Price range: Lunch: entrees, $8.50–$12.50. Dinner: apps.,
$7.50–$9.50; entrees, $15.95–$19.95; desserts, $6. **Wheelchair
access:** Fully accessible. **Features:** Smoking permitted, outdoor
dining. **Services:** Takeout, private parties.

Ear Inn $ BAR SNACKS

326 Spring St. (bet. Greenwich & Washington Sts.)
                                                (212) 226-9060
Credit cards: All major   Meals: L, D, LN

Since 1817 the landmark James Brown House, named after a
Revolutionary War-era tobacco trader, has housed some sort of
tavern. When New York was a great commercial port, it was a
sailors' dive. Since it became the Ear Inn, more than 20 years
ago, it has drawn an eclectic crowd of artists, writers, bikers
and construction workers for whom the air of an unpretentious
neighborhood watering hole has an unending appeal. The food
is basic and inexpensive. Try grilled shell steak, grilled salmon,
chicken pot pie and spaghetti with shrimp and scallops.

Price range: Apps., $4.50–$6; entrees, $4.50–$10; desserts,
$4.50. **Wheelchair access:** Fully accessible. **Features:** Smoking
permitted. **Services:** Takeout.

East Buffet & Restaurant $25 & Under CHINESE

42-07 Main St., Flushing, Queens   (718) 353-6333
Credit cards: All major   Meals: L, D

This huge, glossy Chinese eating hall seats 400 people in the
buffet hall and 350 in another room (separated by a reception
area) for sit-down service. Three islands run down the center of
the narrow buffet area. You will be astonished at the bounty
before you: more than 30 dim sum selections, a dozen soups,
40 dishes served cold and another 40 served hot. There are sta-
tions for poaching shrimp and clams, a satay station, a great big
platter of steamed crab legs, a raw bar and a sushi bar.

   Where to start? Try the superb cold appetizers. Dim sum can
be excellent, too: siu mai, firm little packets of shrimp and
pork, are delicate and flavorful, and the beef rice rolls are excellent. At one station, a carver slices moist and smoky slivers of
Peking duck and places them over a thick steamed pancake on

which you may then add hoisin sauce, cucumbers and scallions. Roast suckling pig is extremely tender. For dessert, try the gelatinous puddings in flavors like green tea, red bean, lotus seed and tapioca, or black sesame gelatin, rolled into cylinders and barely sweetened.

In the sit-down area try the extraordinary sticky rice, steamed in bamboo leaves and stuffed, tamale-like, with chopped pork. Unfamiliar cuts of meat abound here, like steamed pork full of small bones, worth the effort of gnawing at the flavorful meat.

Other recommended dishes: Tubular greens, cold noodles in hot oil, fried taro cakes, pork buns, shrimp balls, turnip cakes, steamed crab legs, congee, salt-and-pepper shrimp. **Price range:** Lunch, $9; dinner, $20–$24; brunch, $16. **Wheelchair access:** Elevator to dining room.

Edison Cafe $ DINER

Edison Hotel, 228 W. 47th St. (bet. Broadway & Eighth Ave.)
(212) 840-5000
Credit cards: Cash only   Meals: B, L, D

Known as the "Polish Tearoom," Edison Cafe is an institution and one of the last remnants of the old Times Square. Sitting in the faded glory of what was once a fancy restaurant, you eat great matzoh ball soup, potato pancakes and terrific sandwiches while waitresses straight out of Damon Runyon tell you their troubles.

Other recommended dishes: Blintzes; matzoh brei. **Alcohol:** Beer. **Price range:** Breakfast, $6. Lunch and dinner entrees, $8–$12. **Wheelchair access:** Fully accessible. **Features:** Kid friendly, good for business. **Services:** Takeout.

Eight Mile Creek ☆☆ $$$ AUSTRALIAN

240 Mulberry St. (at Prince St.)   (212) 431-4635
Credit cards: All major   Meals: D

When a restaurant announces that it will be serving Australian cuisine, you expect good comic material, not good food. The joke stops when the kangaroo salad arrives: large cubes of the loin languish in a marinade flavored with coriander seed, smoked paprika and poached garlic, and then are seared and served on lettuce-leaf wrappers dressed with a watercress vinaigrette and crispy rings of fried shallot. The meat is tender yet substantial, richly flavored but not gamy.

Eight Mile Creek is cheery, outgoing and warm, with a bar scene enlivened by a scattering of Australian expats. It is also very uncomfortable. The menu is short — eight appetizers, eight main courses, six desserts. But the chef, Ken Addington, makes every dish count. I'm not sure that oyster pie should be an appetizer, but I am sure that the pie at Eight Mile Creek is worth bending the rules for, a pastry-wrapped stew of precisely cooked oysters, still plump and juicy, suspended in a cream sauce chunky with salsify and leeks. Australia without lamb is an impossibility. Mr. Addington does not fool around too much with this sacred national trust, merely braising a whopping big shank and surrounding it with parsnips, chanterelles and roasted apple. The desserts often limit themselves to one thrilling twist, like the pavlova dotted with pink peppercorns for a touch of perfumed sweetness, or the rose water panna cotta dripping with pomegranate liquor.

Other recommended dishes: Mussels in coconut milk; marinated tuna; chicken dusted in lemon myrtle; sautéed diver scallops; chocolate and macadamia praline tart; beggar's purse of roast fig and chestnut. **Wine list:** An excellent, nearly all-Australian 42-bottle list, modestly priced, with some hard-to-find wines and some exciting Australian dessert wines by the glass. **Price range:** Apps., $8–$11; entrees, $17–$23; desserts, $8–$11. **Wheelchair access:** Restrooms on street level.

EJ's Luncheonette $ DINER
447 Amsterdam Ave. (bet. 81st & 82nd Sts.)   (212) 873-3444
1271 Third Ave. (at 73rd St.)   (212) 472-0600
432 Sixth Ave. (bet. 9th & 10th Sts.)   (212) 473-5555
Credit cards: Cash only   Meals: B, Br, L, D

These reproductions of classic 1950's luncheonettes are often packed. Despite the occasional contemporary dish, generous portions of old-fashioned recipes are what sell, along with huge desserts and malteds. It's hard to see what all the fuss is about.

Alcohol: Beer and wine. **Price range:** Lunch: apps., $2.50–$5; entrees, $6.95–$8.50; desserts, $2–$5. Dinner: apps., $2.50–$5; entrees, $9.95–$14.95; desserts, $2–$5. **Wheelchair access:** Fully accessible. **Features:** Kid friendly. **Services:** Delivery, takeout, private parties.

Elaine's $$$ ITALIAN
1703 Second Ave. (bet. 88th & 89th Sts.)   (212) 534-8103
Credit cards: All major   Meals: D, LN

Yes, movie folks hang out here. The literati do too. The question is, Why? It looks like an ordinary tavern and the food is mediocre.

Price range: Apps., $6.75–$13.75; entrees, $14.75–$38.75; desserts, $7. **Wheelchair access:** Restrooms not accessible. **Services:** Private parties.

El Cid
$25 & Under   **SPANISH**
322 W. 15th St. (bet. Eighth & Ninth Aves.)   (212) 929-9332
Credit cards: AE/D   Meals: LN   Closed Mon.

El Cid is delightful, with delicious food and a professional staff that handles any problem with élan. Tapas are a highlight, and you can make a meal of dishes like grilled shrimp that are still freshly briny; tender white asparagus served cool in a delicate vinaigrette; robustly flavorful peppers; tiny smelt fillets marinated in vinegar and spices; and chunks of savory marinated pork with french fries. The paella is exceptional. This is not a restaurant for quiet heart-to-heart talks. The simple décor features hard surfaces that amplify noise, producing a rollicking party atmosphere as the room gets crowded. And it does get crowded.

Price range: Apps., $4.25–$9.95; entrees, $14.95–$27.95; desserts, $4.95–$5.95. **Wheelchair access:** Two steps up to dining room; small restrooms. **Features:** Romantic. **Services:** Takeout, private parties.

Eleven Madison Park ☆☆ $$$ CONTINENTAL
11 Madison Ave. (at 24th St.)   (212) 889-0905
Credit cards: All major   Meals: L, D

The latest offering from Danny Meyer, who brought you Union Square Cafe and Gramercy Tavern, occupies the stately ground floor of a grand Art Deco building near the Flatiron building. Eleven Madison Park is a conscious homage to the area's past, and the menu is a thoughtful return to Continental cuisine. It could be seriously scary to an audience raised on new American cooking: appetizers include an astonishing amount of offal. It took courage to put a terrine of beef shank, veal feet and foie gras on the menu, but it is a beautiful dish. Sweetbreads are spectacular, too. Main courses are disappointingly uneven, but the skate grenobloise and the choucroute of salmon and trout are great. The desserts are irresistible, especially the plate of lemon desserts and butterscotch pot de crème. (*Ruth Reichl*)

Other recommended dishes: Couer à la crème; cookies; dark chocolate terrine. **Wine list:** A specialty in the second labels of the big chateaus of Bordeaux. Impressive list of Calvados. **Price range:** Lunch: apps., $8–$14; entrees, $17–$24. Dinner: apps., $8–$18; entrees, $19–$32; desserts, $8. **Wheelchair access:** Street level. **Services:** Private parties.

El Gauchito $25 & Under LATIN AMERICAN/ARGENTINE

94-60 Corona Ave., Corona, Queens (718) 271-8198
Credit cards: MC/V Meals: L, D Closed Wed.

This tiny storefront restaurant and butcher shop offers an authentic Argentine dining experience. Family groups crowd the few tables in the dining room, keeping up a lively banter in Spanish with the staff. The most popular dish seems to be the mixed grill, a huge plate of food that includes a plump pork sausage, a rich blood sausage and all manner of internal organs.

Alcohol: Beer and wine. **Price range:** Apps., $1.25–$6.50; entrees, $6.90–$12.90; desserts, $3–$3.50. **Wheelchair access:** Restrooms not accessible. **Services:** Takeout.

Elias Corner $25 & Under GREEK/SEAFOOD

24-02 31st St., Astoria, Queens (718) 932-1510
Credit cards: Cash only Meals: D, LN

Regulars at this bright, raucous Greek seafood specialist know to check the glass display case in front before selecting the freshest looking fish. Without a doubt, meals should start with a huge plate of delicious, pinky-size whitebait, dredged in flour and flash-fried whole. Other worthwhile starters include taramosalata, a lemony fish roe purée, and tzatziki, a blend of yogurt, mint and cucumber. The grilled fish are almost all delicious, basted with olive oil, lemon juice and herbs and cooked over charcoal until charred on the outside and juicy within. The small front room is less relaxed than the bright rear room, where big wraparound windows looking away from the overpass convey the feeling of a cruise ship. Elias is best in the off-hours, before the crowd arrives.

Alcohol: Beer and wine. **Price range:** Apps., $3.50–$8; entrees, $12–$17. **Wheelchair access:** Everything on one level, narrow entry to restroom. **Features:** Parking available. **Services:** Private parties.

El Paso Taqueria $25 & Under MEXICAN

1642 Lexington Ave. (at 104th St.) (212) 831-9831
Credit cards: Cash only Meals: B, L, D

One of the best restaurants in El Barrio is this extremely plain yet bustling little corner spot. It isn't much to look at; it doesn't even serve alcohol. But it excels at feeding people well, and that's nothing to take for granted. Tacos are a natural starting point. The fragrant soft corn tortillas are doubled up in authentic Mexican style to contain fillings like tangy marinated pork, spicy crumbled chorizo sausage and grilled beef, which stretch them to the bursting point. Essential to eating the tacos is the four-bowl relish tray that arrives with them, holding lime wedges, radish slivers and two exceptionally fresh, mildly spicy salsas, one made with tomatillos and cilantro, the other with tomatoes.

But the highlights at El Paso are the daily specials, all served with rice and refried beans. They might include puerco adobo, tender, vinegary pork served on the bone in a spicy tomato sauce subtly flavored with chilies and anise-scented avocado leaves, or cecina asada, a huge thin cut of beef that has been dried, salted and spiced, with sautéed chilies and cactus pads. On Saturdays and Sundays, El Paso serves pozole, the satisfying soup of pork and puffed corn.

Other recommended dishes: Pork ribs with mole poblano, flautas, meatballs in chipotle sauce, chilaquiles. **Price range:** Apps., $1.75–$7; entrees, $5–$10. **Wheelchair access:** Step at entrance; restroom is too narrow.

El Presidente $25 & Under CARIBBEAN/PAN-LATIN

3938 Broadway (bet. 164th & 165th Sts.)   (212) 927-7011
Credit cards: All major   Meals: B, L, D, LN

This small, bright restaurant near Columbia-Presbyterian Medical Center describes its food as Caribbean, which is technically true, though many people nowadays assume that Caribbean means Jamaican. El Presidente specializes in the foods of the Hispanic Caribbean — Cuba, Puerto Rico and the Dominican Republic — where flavors are powered by garlic, bell peppers and annatto rather than the heat of chilies. Pernil, or roast pork, is simple but wonderfully satisfying. El Presidente also serves an excellent charcoal-broiled skirt steak, with grilled onions and peppers, well-charred around the edges yet still juicy.

Other recommended dishes: Skirt steak. **Alcohol:** Beer and wine. **Price range:** Breakfast: $1.95–$5. Lunch/Dinner: apps, $1.50; entrees, $5.50–$14.75. **Services:** Delivery, takeout.

El Teddy's $$ MEXICAN/TEX-MEX

219 W. Broadway (bet. White & Franklin Sts.)   (212) 941-7071
Credit cards: All major   Meals: L, D, LN

The dining rooms of this spirited Mexican restaurant and bar look like an astral collision in a science-fiction movie, but all the silliness belies some spirited and intelligently composed food. Openers include sea scallop poached in lime juice, served with baby artichokes and lemon vinaigrette, and shucked oysters afloat in a shot glass of tequila and red sauce. There are several burritos, quesadillas, soups and salads. Entree possibilities include pan sautéed duck breast; grilled rare tuna on a shiitake cactus salad; and hredded beef with chorizo, avocado, tomato and homemade tortillas. Sweet final notes might be tequila-soaked baba filled with lemon Chantilly cream and a cold purée of guava with tropical fruit ceviche.

Price range: Lunch: apps., $5–$9; entrees, $9–$14. Dinner: apps., $5–$9; entrees, $14–$20. **Wheelchair access:** Fully accessible. **Features:** Smoking permitted, outdoor dining. **Services:** Takeout, catering, private parties.

Elvie's Turo-Turo $ FILIPINO
214 First Ave. (bet. 12th & 13th Sts.)   (212) 473-7785
Credit cards: Cash only   Meals: L, D

This friendly little restaurant offers a daily buffet of Filipino dishes. All you do is turo-turo, or point-point. This is not light food. Most dishes are beef or pork, with the occasional chicken and fish dish. The pork adobo, the national dish of the Philippines, is excellent. For dessert, point to sweet cassava cake.

Alcohol: Bring your own. **Price range:** Apps., $1.75–$3.75; entrees, $5.95–$7.50; desserts, $1.75–$3.50. **Wheelchair access:** Not accessible. **Features:** Outdoor dining. **Services:** Delivery, takeout, catering.

Emilio Ballato's $$ ITALIAN
55 E. Houston St. (bet. Mott & Mulberry Sts.)   (212) 274-8881
Credit cards: MC/V   Meals: L, D, LN

When John Ballato opened this restaurant on a quickly gentrifying stretch of Houston Street, it was on the outskirts of Little Italy. It's still that sort of a restaurant, offering decent, filling, old-fashioned Italian-American food in huge quantities.

Alcohol: Beer and wine. **Price range:** Apps., $6–$7; entrees, $10–$22; desserts, $4–$5.50. **Wheelchair access:** Fully accessible. **Services:** Private parties.

Emily's $25 & Under SOUTHERN
1325 Fifth Ave. (at 111th St.)   (212) 996-1212
Credit cards: All major   Meals: Br, L, D, LN

This pleasant but institutional restaurant offers a diverse Southern menu and draws an integrated crowd. If you go, go for the meaty, tender baby back pork ribs, subtly smoky and bathed in tangy barbecue sauce, or the big plate of chopped pork barbecue. The best sides include savory rice and peas (actually red beans) and peppery stuffing, and all dishes come with a basket of fine corn bread. Sweet potato pie is the traditional dessert, and Emily's version is nice and nutmeggy.

Other recommended dishes: Fried chicken; candied yams. **Price range:** Lunch: apps., $5.95–$9.95; entrees, $4.95–$10.65;

desktop, $4.25. Dinner: apps., $5.95–$9.95; entrees, $10.25–$24.95; desserts, $4.25. **Wheelchair access:** Everything on one level. **Features:** Smoking permitted, outdoor dining. **Services:** Delivery, takeout, catering, private parties.

Emo's
$25 & UNDER   KOREAN
1564 Second Ave. (near 81st St.)   (212) 628-8699
Credit cards: All major   Meals: L, D

A Korean restaurant outside the confines of Midtown is no longer unusual. What makes Emo's especially noteworthy is that, aside from American-style service and the addition of fresh salad greens to several dishes, it pulls few punches, offering robust, spicy, authentic fare that is full of flavor. The heat is especially welcome in a dish like yook huei, a kind of Korean beef tartare in which the raw meat is threaded with pine nuts and slivers of juicy Asian pear; hot sauce offers the right added note. It is less necessary with appetizers like pa jun, a crisp and delicious rice flour pancake with scallions, shrimp and squid, and with bin dae duk, a cakier pancake made with mung-bean flour and flavored with kimchi, the fiery pickled cabbage.

The highlights here are the superb main courses, like oh jing uh gui, wonderfully tender cylinders of barbecued squid scored to resemble pale pine cones and touched with hot sauce to add dimension to the squid's mellow flavor. A variation of this is jae yook gui, barbecued pork in a delectable smoky, spicy sauce. Along with the main courses comes the panchan, a group of a half- dozen little dishes that always include kimchi as well as other nibbles like tiny slightly sweet dried fish or a mild cubed potato salad.

There is an American-style bar that lines the entryway to the spare, narrow but airy dining room. Korean beer and barley liquor are available, of course, but so are martinis, micro brews and California wines.

Other recommended dishes: Marinated short ribs, miso stew with beef, codfish in soy-and-garlic sauce. **Price range:** Apps., $3–$7; entrees, $11–$18. **Wheelchair access:** One step in front, restroom is narrow.

Empire Diner
$$ DINER
210 10th Ave. (at 22nd St.)   (212) 243-2736
Credit cards: All major   Meals: B, Br, L, D, LN

One of the early entries in the modern revival of America's love affair with diners was this campy Art Deco gem that attracted a hip late-night crowd in the 1980's. Nowadays, the Empire is a tourist destination. The up-to-date diner basics with some Mediterranean touches are not bad at all — better than at most diners, in fact — which is reflected in the prices.

Price range: Apps., $6–$8; entrees, $10–$17; desserts, $4–$7.
Wheelchair access: Not accessible. **Features:** Kid friendly, outdoor dining. **Services:** Delivery, takeout, private parties.

Erminia $$$ ITALIAN
250 E. 83rd St. (bet. Second & Third Aves.)   (212) 879-4284
Credit cards: AE   Meals: D   Closed Sun.

Some people think of this little brick-walled restaurant with candles as romantic and charming; to me it's just crowded. But the Italian food is good and the service is usually charming.

Alcohol: Beer, wine, and Champagne. **Price range:** Apps., $7.95–$13.95; entrees, $16.95–$32.95; desserts, $7. **Wheelchair access:** Restrooms not accessible. **Features:** Romantic. **Services:** Private parties.

Esashi $25 & Under SUSHI
32 Ave. A (bet 2nd & 3rd Sts.)   (212) 505-8726
Credit cards: All major   Meals: D

Esashi is a modest, informal restaurant that stands out for its sushi and many other well-prepared Japanese dishes. The sushi selection is not particularly large or unusual, but everything is exceptionally fresh and beautifully presented. Gyu-tataki, paper-thin slices of beef seared on the edges and rare in the center, are tender and delicious, especially with a squeeze of lemon. Tiger eye, an unusually beautiful appetizer with a subtle flavor, is a strip of cooked skate wrapped around salmon with a layer of seaweed. Esashi has a wide selection of sakes, warm and cold.

Alcohol: Beer and wine. **Price range:** Apps, $3–$4; entrees, $11.25–$18. **Wheelchair access:** Fully accessible. **Services:** Takeout.

Esca ☆☆ $$$ ITALIAN/SEAFOOD
402 W. 43rd St. (at Ninth Ave.) (212) 564-7272
Credit cards: All major   Meals: L, D   Closed Sun.

At Esca — the name means "bait" — the most important word in the Italian language is *crudo*. It means raw, and that's the way the fish comes to the table in a dazzling array of appetizers that could be thought of as Italian sushi. Joe Bastianich and Mario Batali, the impresarios behind Esca, insist that their way with raw fish is a venerable Italian tradition. It matters not. The *crudo* appetizers at Esca are the freshest, most exciting thing to happen to Italian food in recent memory. In the hands of chef David Pasternack, the *crudo* formula shows remarkable flexibility. By changing olive oils, adding a bitter green, or throwing in a scattering of minced chilies, Mr. Pasternack works thrilling variations on a very simple theme. Pink snapper takes nothing more than a sprinkling of coarse sea salt. Fluke, another mild fish, is topped with a few spindly sea beans and tiny radish slivers.

The menu changes daily depending on what comes out of the sea. Look hard enough, and you can find a dish like guinea hen with fingerling potatoes and broccoli rape, or roast chicken with spring greens and cippoline onions, but it seems perverse to order anything but seafood. About half the menu consists of knockouts. Half is rather ordinary, although the surroundings at Esca can trick any diner into believing otherwise. The lemon-yellow walls and sea-green tiles give it a bright, cool look, and the solid wooden table in the center of the dining room, loaded down with vegetable side dishes, strikes a rustic note while communicating the food philosophy: fresh from the market, and prepared without fuss.

Other recommended dishes: Caprese salad; grilled octopus; bucatini with octopus sauce. **Wine list:** A connoisseur's and bargain-hunter's list of about 180 wines from all regions of Italy, with 10 wines sold in glass-and-a-half decanters called quartini. **Price range:** Lunch: apps., $7–$12; entrees, $16–$21; desserts, $8. Dinner: apps., $8–$14; entrees, $17–$26; desserts, $8. Six-course tasting menu, $65 ($85 with matching wines). **Wheelchair access:** Restrooms on street level. **Features:** Smoking at bar, after 11 P.M.

Esperanto $25 & Under   Pan-Latin
145 Ave. C (at 9th St.)   (212) 505-6559
Credit cards: AE   Meals: D, LN

This is a warm and welcoming place with Latin food that can be surprisingly subtle and delicate. Bolinho de peixe, deep-fried balls of codfish, are exceptionally light, crisp and flavorful, with a terrific dipping sauce galvanized by spicy mustard. Another good appetizer is salpicão, a Brazilian chicken salad with celery, apples and mayonnaise dressing. Aside from an inconsistent flounder, Esperanto's main courses are sturdy and hard to mess up. Steak is good and beefy, bathed in chimichurri, the Argen-tine condiment of garlic and parsley; and feijoada, the Brazilian stew of black beans and smoked meats, has a nice, gritty tex-ture and an almost yeasty flavor. Esperanto serves potent caipir-inhas or mojitos, a sort of Cuban mint julep, and features a brief wine list with some good, rustic reds. And don't miss the stellar coconut flan.

Price range: Apps., $4–$6; entrees, $9–$14. **Wheelchair access:** Steps are at entrance; restrooms are narrow.

Esperides $$

3701 30th Ave., Astoria, Queens
Credit cards: All major

This Greek restaurant in Astoria is on the upscale side, with a glossy, shiny, comfortable interior and careful service. The food is only fair, though, with seafood routinely overcooked. Best is the selection of cold appetizer spreads and the roast suckling pig, served on weekends only.

Price range: Lunch: apps., $3–$5.95; entrees, $6–$11.95; desserts, $3–$3.50. Dinner: apps., $3–$12.95; entrees, $8.50–$25.95; desserts, $3–$3.50. **Wheelchair access:** Fully accessible. **Features:** Smoking permitted. **Services:** Delivery, takeout, catering, private parties.

Estiatorio Milos ☆ ☆ $$$$

125 W. 55th St. (bet. Sixth & Seventh Aves.)
Credit cards: All major

If you love the Greek fish places in Astoria but wish the fish were better, try this. The room is clean, spare, blindingly white, and the entire focus is on the display of gorgeous fish by the open kitchen. Choose one and it is grilled simply and brought to the table. If you like big fish, bring a crowd. Most of the fish are cooked whole. And the lamb chops, a concession to meat eaters, are excellent. Appetizers are wonderful, too. The tiny squid are inky and fabulous eaten just as they are. The grilled sardines are oily and flavorful, and the octopus, charred and sliced, mixed with onions, capers and peppers, is truly delicious. The homemade yogurt — thick, slightly sour and served with a scattering of wild blueberries and drizzles of wild honey — is the ideal way to end these meals. (*Ruth Reichl*)

Other recommended dishes: Crab cakes; charcoal shrimp; tomato salad; swordfish skewers; sesame-crusted tuna.
Wine list: Intelligently chosen for the food and fairly priced.
Price range: Prix-fixe lunch, $32.95. Apps., $9.50–$20; fish for main courses is sold whole and by weight, from $25–$34 a pound; lamb chops, $32; desserts, $7.50–$25. **Wheelchair access:** A few steps up to the main dining room, but there are a few tables near the bar, at street level. **Features:** Outdoor dining (sidewalk). **Services:** Private parties.

Etats-Unis ☆ ☆ $$$

242 E. 81st St. (bet. Second & Third Aves.)
Credit cards: All major

This family-run restaurant with only 31 seats serves terrific, eclectic food. The menu is handwritten each day and comes wrapped up in one of the quirkiest, most personal wine lists in the city. While the room has a spare sort of elegance, the food is astonishingly exuberant, accepting no limits and recognizing no boundaries. The menu evolves quickly, changing bit by bit over the course of the week in response to the market and the chefs' moods. These fast changes are a luxury unheard of in larger kitchens. The food has the appealingly rustic character of the best home cooking. Desserts wear their plainness with pride: an apple pie that tastes as if it has just won a blue ribbon at a county fair and a fabulous chocolate soufflé. (*Ruth Reichl*)

Wine list: Small, personally selected, unusual and wide-ranging list. **Price range:** Apps., $9–$15; entrees, $24–$34; desserts, $7–$10. **Wheelchair access:** Everything on one level, but the restaurant is small and quite crowded. **Services:** Private parties.

Evergreen Shanghai $25 & Under   CHINESE

63 Mott St. (near Bayard St.)   (212) 571-3339
10 E. 38th St. (bet. Fifth & Madison Aves.)   (212) 448-1199
1378 Third Ave. (bet. 78th & 79th Sts.)   (212) 585-3388
Credit cards: Cash only at Mott St.   Meals: L, D, LN

When reading the long menu, eliminate the familiar dishes from other regions and concentrate instead on the Shanghai specialties. Look for cold appetizers like aromatic beef, a Chinese version of barbecued brisket, and smoked fish, sweet with light, smoky notes and hints of star anise. Great main courses include bean curd with crab sauce and yellowfish with seaweed. The staff is friendly, with enough English speakers to help with the selections.

Other recommended dishes: Raw crab with soy flavor; spicy cabbage; wine chicken; mock duck; stir-fried jellyfish; steamed crab and pork buns. **Price range:** Apps., $3.25–$6.25; entrees, $5.95–$24; desserts, $1.95–$2.95. **Wheelchair access:** Fully accessible. **Features:** Kid friendly. **Services:** Delivery, takeout, private parties.

Excellent Dumpling House $ CHINESE

111 Lafayette St. (bet. Canal & Walker Sts.)   (212) 219-0212
Credit cards: Cash only   Meals: L, D

Great dumplings and other Chinese dishes, served in a plain dining room. It's especially popular with the jury-duty crowd.

Alcohol: Beer. **Price range:** Apps., $1.75–$4.95; entrees, $7.50–$10.50. **Wheelchair access:** Fully accessible. **Features:** Kid friendly. **Services:** Delivery, takeout, private parties.

F&B

$25 & Under

269 W. 23rd St. (bet. Seventh & Eighth Aves.) (646) 486-4441.
Credit cards: Cash only
Meals: B, L, D

F&B, a sleek storefront decorated in soothing pastels with pleasant lighting, offers a self-consciously European visage. The name stands for frites and beignets, but hot dogs are the centerpiece, including the excellent Great Dane, a slender, red Danish sausage with bright snap to it. It is eaten just as it is in Denmark, on a roll with frizzled onions, marinated cucumbers, mustard, ketchup and remoulade. It sounds like a lot, but it's an easy mouthful, especially compared with the Top Dog, a plumper German-style sausage topped with tame sauerkraut and crumbled bacon. Frites are crisp and savory, and for an extra 50 cents, they are served with toppings including aioli, blue cheese and truffle oil.

Alcohol: Beer and Wine. **Price range:** Entrees, $1.75–$5.
Wheelchair access: One step down from street. **Services:** Delivery, takeout.

Fanelli

$

94 Prince St. (at Mercer St.) (212) 226-9412
Credit cards: All major
Meals: L, D, LN

Long before there was a SoHo, Fanelli's was dispensing beer and burgers to the local populace. The neighborhood has changed; Fanelli hasn't. The restaurant offers wonderful atmospheric pleasures as well as decent burgers and pasta. It's best during the off hours, when it's not crowded, loud and smoky.

Price range: Apps., $4.95–$7.25; entrees, $8.95–$15; desserts, $3.95. **Wheelchair access:** Fully accessible. **Features:** Smoking permitted. **Services:** Delivery, takeout.

Feeding Tree

$25 & Under

892 Gerard Ave. (near 161st St.), the Bronx (718) 293-5025
Credit cards: All major
Meals: B, L, D

This casual West Indian restaurant near Yankee Stadium looks like a bright takeout place, with a counter over a glass display case with assorted Jamaican groceries. But to the right of the counter is a closed door leading to a trim dining room, with sleek Formica tables and chairs, some green plants and a glossy bar. The touchstone of a Jamaican restaurant is its jerk, and Feeding Tree's jerk chicken is excellent, subtly spiced with thyme, allspice and chilies. As with all the main courses, the jerk comes with rice and peas (as kidney beans are called in Jamaica), an earthy and equally subtle counterpoint, as well as sweet plantains, not-too-sweet corn bread and a mixture of cabbage, carrots and green beans that is an antidote to the heat of the chilies.

The best dish on the menu is the magnificently mellow curried goat, tender chunks of meat in a mild green sauce. Beer goes well with this food, but so does sorrel, a sweet and spicy cold drink made from the flowers of a plant in the hibiscus family, steeped with ginger, cloves and other flavorings. The Feeding Tree doesn't offer much in the way of dessert, but try the coconut drops, little spicy patties flavored with coconut and ginger that are the Caribbean equivalent of pralines.

Other recommended dish: Beef stew, oxtail stew. **Price range:** Entrees, $6–$10. **Wheelchair access:** Entrance and restrooms are narrow. **Services:** Takeout.

Felidia ☆☆☆ $$$$ NORTHERN ITALIAN
243 E. 58th St. (bet. Second & Third Aves.)   (212) 758-1479
Credit cards: All major   Meals: L, D   Closed Sun.

Felidia is an old-fashioned restaurant, comfortable and rustic, and largely oblivious to food fashions. The menu, which changes with the seasons, concentrates on the foods of Italy's northeast: Friuli, the Veneto as well as Istria, now part of Croatia, and the home of owners Felice and Lidia Bastianich.

This is robust food served in generous portions, revolving around game, organ meats, and slow-cooked sauces. Homemade cotechino is highly spiced pork with mustard sauce; venison comes with wild rice, Swiss chard and a thin purée of apples. The plate of venison osso buco is piled high with quince, cranberries and spätzle so soft and light they seem to float off your plate into your mouth. And scrambled eggs on a bed of grilled porcini with white truffles shaved over the top is irresistible — even if it does cost $25. This is not to say you can't eat lightly. Felidia serves lots of seafood, including lobster and crabmeat salad, and an impressive octopus and potato salad. Roasted fish arrives at the table with its head and tail; filleted, slicked with olive oil and served with grilled tomatoes, it is simple and satisfying.

Although Felidia is hardly any American's idea of an Italian restaurant — no pizza, scaloppine or fried calamari — it does serve pastas like pappardelle in a primavera sauce. But it would be a shame to miss Felidia's unusual specialties. Krafi, for instance, festive ravioli filled with cheese, raisins, rum and grated lemon rind. Or fuzi, little twists with broccoli rape and sausage. Good desserts include apple strudel, and the wonderful sweet crepes called palacinke. (*Ruth Reichl*)

Most popular dishes: Buffalo mozzarella poached in red and yellow tomato-basil sauce; veal osso buco. **Chef's favorite:** Krafi. **Wine list:** One of the city's finest Italian lists; great wines at great prices and unusual regional specialties. The staff is

knowledgeable and helpful. **Price range:** Lunch: apps.,
$10–$14; entrees, $20–$32; desserts, $10. Dinner: apps.,
$12–$16; entrees, $27–$32; desserts, $10. **Wheelchair access:**
Restrooms not accessible. **Services:** Private parties.

Ferdinando's Focacceria $25 & Under ITALIAN

151 Union St., Carroll Gardens, Brooklyn   (718) 855-1545
Credit cards: Cash only   Meals: L, D   Closed Sun.

They filmed *Moonstruck* on this street, and you can see why.
This restaurant is a throwback to turn-of-the-century Brooklyn,
before Ebbets Field had even been built. Ferdinando's serves
old Sicilian dishes, like chickpea-flour fritters; vasteddi, a focaccia made with calf's spleen; and pasta topped with sardines
canned by the owner. It's worth a visit.

Alcohol: Beer and wine. **Price range:** Apps., $7; entrees,
$10–$13; desserts, $4. **Wheelchair access:** Fully accessible. **Ser-
vices:** Takeout, catering, private parties.

Fifty Seven Fifty Seven ☆ ☆ ☆ $$$$

NEW AMERICAN

Four Seasons Hotel, 57 E. 57th St.   (212) 758-5757
Credit cards: All major   Meals: B, L, D

Fifty Seven Fifty Seven is a restaurant that trumpets its hotel
affiliation. The diner steps into the imposing I.M. Pei lobby of
the Four Seasons Hotel and begins an architectural journey
through a procession of monumental spaces, up a flight of stairs
and into one of the city's stateliest dining rooms. Service is
solicitous and the menu offers something for absolutely every
taste. Vegetarians will find many choices: soups, large salads,
even a sampling tray of five vegetable dishes big enough to feed
two. Dieters will find starred offerings low in fat and salt. And
those with an appetite for meat and potatoes have many
options from rack of veal in a red wine sauce to grilled beef tenderloin with rosemary cream potato pie.

The food is decidedly American with a modern bent. The
menu changes frequently with a different prix-fixe offering
every day. Architectural though the entrees may be, the visually
restrained desserts are rich in flavor and texture. Consider a
smooth cylinder of cake wrapped in a sheet of chocolate. Inside
is a mound of rich chocolate mousse and a layer of halvah, the
sesame candy. Halvah adds a meringue-like crunch and a
shocking jolt of flavor.

With its solicitous service in a memorable public space, Fifty
Seven Fifty Seven is setting a new standard for an old tradition.
(*Ruth Reichl*)

Other recommended dishes: Creamless tomato soup; Cobb salad. **Most popular dish:** Crab cake. **Wine list:** Many hard-to-find wines, but prices are high. **Price range:** Breakfast, $32. Lunch: apps., $8–$15; entrees, $22–$31; desserts, $10; prix fixe, $45. Dinner: apps., $12–$22; entrees, $25–$32; desserts, $10; prix fixe, $55. **Wheelchair access:** Fully accessible.

F.illi Ponte ☆☆ $$$$ ITALIAN
39 Desbrosses St. (bet. Washington St. & West Side Hwy.)
                                 (212) 226-4621
Credit cards: All major   Meals: L, D

Despite the most elegant renovation in recent history, the former Ponte's steakhouse on the waterfront downtown has not lost its rakish charm. The room has been transformed into a great, rustic room with bare brick walls, beamed ceilings and a fabulous view of the Hudson. At night, the cozy cigar lounge is filled with live music. The menu has been transformed too: Expect admirable Italian fare and fine spicy lobster, though surprisingly pricy. The porchetta, spit-roasted baby pig, is superb. Fried calamari are sweet, crisp, irresistible. Shrimp cocktail is just about perfect. There is an excellent veal chop. Pastas are a letdown, but even so, eating in this beautiful old room as the light fades over the Hudson river is a pleasure. (*Ruth Reichl, Updated by Eric Asimov*)

Other recommended dishes: Antipasto; fried calamari; shrimp cocktail; risotto; linguine with clams; spaghetti with tomato sauce; spit-roasted chicken; cheesecake; ice cream. **Wine list:** Long, beautifully chosen list of mostly Italian and American wines. **Price range:** Apps., $8–$12; entrees, $17–$35; desserts, $8. **Wheelchair access:** Elevator available to second-floor dining room. **Features:** Romantic, smoking permitted, outdoor dining (sidewalk). **Services:** Takeout, catering, private parties.

Firebird ☆☆ $$$ RUSSIAN
365 W. 46th St. (bet. Eighth & Ninth Aves.)   (212) 586-0244
Credit cards: All major   Meals: L, D

When the Russian Tearoom closed, the crowd moved to this jewel box of a restaurant. And now that the Tea Room has reopened, is there any reason for them to go back? With a room as ornate and luxurious as a Fabergé egg, and a staff so polished, it really does seem that you have entered some more serene and lavish era. The caviar arrives with its own private waiter who turns the service into a performance, pouring hot butter onto the plate, spooning on the caviar and then delicately twirling the blini around the roe. The wild mushroom zhulien, roasted beet and walnut phkali and Georgian chicken satsivi, a small dish of shredded chicken dressed with crushed walnuts, are delicious appetizers. Among the first courses, the manti, hearty steamed lamb dumplings served in a dish of minted sour cream, and the herring in a blanket of potatoes, beets, onion and chopped eggs are worth ordering.

If you want to eat lightly, try the grilled sturgeon in a creamy mustard sauce. On a recent visit, Firebird continued to offer imaginatively updated Russian classics, like chicken tabaka with plum sauce, and grilled sturgeon with sorrel-potato puree. Desserts, once a weak point, have improved greatly. This is the place to try the traditional molded cheesecake, an Easter treat in Russia, called pashka. (*Ruth Reichl, updated by William Grimes*)

Other recommended dishes: Blini; smoked sturgeon; smoked salmon; pickles with sour cream and honey; vinagret; herring; grilled marinated lamb loin; Ukrainian borscht; steamed salmon with sorrel sauce; quail; Russian cookies. **Wine list:** Not nearly as impressive as the vodka list. **Price range:** Lunch: apps., $6.50–$16; entrees, $17.95–$21.50; prix fixe, $20.02. Dinner: apps., $8.25–$18; entrees, $26–$38; desserts, $9; prix fixe, $36.50 (Thu.–Sat.), $30 (rest of the week) **Wheelchair access:** First floor fully accessible. **Features:** Romantic, smoking permitted. **Services:** Takeout, catering, private parties.

First $25 & Under   NEW AMERICAN
87 First Ave. (bet. 5th & 6th Sts.)   (212) 674-3823
Credit cards: All major   Meals: D, LN

Ambitious, creative contemporary American fare at relatively modest prices, served late into the night. First also offers an intelligently chosen list of wines and beers and worthwhile weekly specials, like its Sunday night pig roast.

Recommended dishes: Grilled guinea hen paillard; crisp oysters with seaweed salad; pizzas; chicken wings; sandwiches. **Price range:** Avg. app., $9; entree, $17; dessert, $6. **Wheelchair access:** Not accessible. **Features:** Romantic, smoking permitted. **Services:** Private parties.

Fish Restaurant $25 & Under   SEAFOOD
2799 Broadway (at 108th St.)   (212) 864-5000
Credit cards: All major   Meals: Br, L, D

This is the only seafood restaurant in the neighborhood, and the fish is generally pretty good, though the menu swings between creative American preparations and Asian-inflected dishes as chefs come and go.

Price range: Lunch: apps., $2.95–$4.95; entrees, $7.95–$10.95; desserts, $4–$5. Dinner: apps., $2.95–$6.95; entrees, $10.95–$19.95; desserts, $4–$5. **Wheelchair access:** Fully accessible. **Features:** Outdoor dining. **Services:** Delivery, takeout, catering.

Fleur de Sel ☆☆ $$$$ FRENCH

5 E. 20th St. (bet. Broadway and Fifth Ave.) (212) 460-9100
Credit cards: All major Meals: L, D

Who doesn't pine for that little neighborhood restaurant, tucked
away on a side street, where the lighting is subdued, the chef is
French and the food is terrific? Well, here it is. Cyril Renaud, the
chef and owner, put in his time cooking at places like Bouley
and La Caravelle. He has hung the lemon-color walls with his
own paintings; the menus display his handiwork too, watercol-
ors with culinary themes.

The fixed-price menu is perfectly calibrated to the small
room, with five appetizers, seven main courses and five
desserts, and Mr. Renaud knows in a quiet sort of way how to
create excitement on the plate. It might be an unfamiliar ingredient, like kamut, the fat-kerneled ancient Egyptian grain
related to wheat, which makes a chewy, nutty accompaniment
to his lamb loin marinated in Dijon mustard and thyme. It
might be an unexpected flavor combination, like rose water and
apricots, the unlikely partnership in a puree, which seems to
coax extra richness and depth from seared foie gras. There's no
sense of strain to any of this. Two ovoid venison fillets from
New Zealand, finely grained, sit starkly on the plate, coated in a
nearly black licorice-and-beet sauce. Slices of venison sausage
transform the accompanying celery root and potato gratin into a
co-star while intensifying the venison flavor in the fillets. Two
plump pigeons from the Catskills, dark and livery inside, sit on
what looks like a beige lily pad, a giant galette filled with figs
and turnips.

The modest desserts round things out nicely. The concentrated flavor of the fruit sends the raspberry feuillete right into
orbit. It's a disarmingly simple-looking thing, two rectangular
pastry leaves, some fat fruit and a blob of white-chocolate
caramel ganache, but the pastry melts on the tongue, and the
ganache is almost criminally delicious.

Other recommended dishes: Ravioli stuffed with sweetbreads,
steamed sea bream with mushrooms, crèpe with Devonshire
cream. **Wine list:** About 50 wines, largely French and Californian, most under $50; four ciders from Normandy and Brittany.
Price range: Lunch, three courses, $28. Dinner, three courses,
$52. **Wheelchair access:** Restroom is on street level.

Florent $$ FRENCH

69 Gansevoort St. (bet. Washington & Greenwich Sts.)
(212) 989-5779
Credit cards: Cash only Meals: B, Br, L, D, LN

Breakfast at 7 A.M. at this pioneer of the meat-packing district,
when the transvestites are going out and the families are com-

ing in, remains one of the quintessential New York City experiences. Otherwise, the French-American food is decent and it won't break the bank. Open 24 hours Saturday and Sunday.

Price range: Lunch: apps., $3.75–$5.95; entrees, $5.95–$13.95; desserts, $3.50–$5; prix fixe, $7.25 or $10.95. Dinner: apps., $4.50–$9.95; entrees, $7.95–$17.95; desserts, $3.50–$5; prix fixe, $18.50. **Wheelchair access:** Fully accessible. **Features:** Kid friendly, romantic, smoking permitted, outdoor dining. **Services:** Delivery, takeout, catering, private parties.

Flor's Kitchen $25 & Under   VENEZUELAN

149 First Ave. (near 9th St.)   (212) 387-8949
Credit cards: All major   Meals: L, D, LN

Tiny, bright and colorful, this new Venezuelan restaurant offers many snacking foods like empanadas criollas—smooth, crisp pastries with fillings like savory shredded beef or puréed chicken. Among the arepas — corncakes with varied fillings — try the chicken and avocado salada. Two sauces — one made with avocado, lemon juice and oil; the second, a hot sauce — make dishes like chachapas (corn pancakes with ham and cheese) taste even better. Soups are superb, and desserts are rich and homespun.

Other recommended dishes: Pescado a la plancha (planked fish); arroz con pollo (chicken and rice); pabellon criollo (stewed shredded beef). **Price range:** Apps., $1.50–$3.25; entrees, $4–$9. **Wheelchair access:** Path to restroom extremely narrow. **Services:** Takeout.

44 $$$$ NEW AMERICAN

Royalton Hotel, 44 W. 44th St. (bet. Fifth & Sixth Aves.)
                                                  (212) 944-8844
Credit cards: All major   Meals: B, Br, L, D

Publishing people hold court at lunchtime, when nonentities are seated in the hall. Good American food at very high prices. Don't miss the waterfall in the men's bathroom.

Price range: Lunch: avg. app., $15; entree, $25; dessert, $9.50. Dinner: avg. app., $16; entree, $36; dessert, $9.50. **Wheelchair access:** Fully accessible. **Features:** Good for business, smoking permitted. **Services:** Catering, private parties.

The Four Seasons ☆☆☆ $$$$ NEW AMERICAN

99 E. 52nd St. (bet. Park & Lexington Aves.)   (212) 754-9494
Credit cards: All major   Meals L, D   Closed Sun.

About 40 years ago, the Four Seasons introduced the idea of changing seasonal menus to America. It is still a pioneer, and the two rooms designed by Philip Johnson have hardly aged: they are cool, elegant and completely unstuffy. The Grill Room is dark and masculine; the Pool Room — a vast and soothing square room with a marble pool — airy and romantic. The menu has an eclectic mix of ingredients, and in a time of know-nothing waiters and deafening dining rooms, the Four Seasons is a reminder that restaurants can still be comfortable and relaxing.

The Grill Room is still the power lunch place for those who count in fashion, finance and publishing. The distance between tables allows other diners to be seen but not heard. At lunch the menu is straightforward. Try the crab cakes, big meaty chunks of crab meat that seem held together by nothing more than the chef's will, or the bunless burger with creamed spinach and crisp onions. Other choices? A plain piece of grilled fish. Food is not the point here: people pay for the privilege of eating it in the world's most powerful company.

The Grill Room serves lunch at the bar where you can get fast service and a limited choice of cherrystone clams, the bar burger (which comes on a bun with tomatoes, lettuce and fried onion rings), tuna burgers, a Caesar salad with chicken and a simple plate of prosciutto.

The Pool Room is at its best with unfussy food like broiled Dover sole or rack of lamb and the perfect steak tartare. It is my favorite place. At night, the kitchen reserves its best dishes for the Pool Room. But wherever you are seated, it is hard to eat at the Four Seasons without luxuriating in an extraordinary sense of privilege. Eating here is an expensive experience. In the many years that the Four Seasons has been pampering its patrons, it has learned how to send each one out the door with a sense of having lived, if only for a few hours, the life of the very rich. (*Ruth Reichl*)

Wine list: Big, expensive and strong in Italian wines as well as the French and American bottles. It is surprising that such an old restaurant has such a young wine list. **Price range:** Lunch: apps., $12.50–$27.50; entrees, $32–$45; desserts, $14. Dinner: apps., $12.50–$27.50; entrees, $34–$55; desserts, $14. Prix fixe: pre-theater (Mon.–Fri.) or after-theater (Sat.), $55; dinner in Grill Room, $59. **Wheelchair access:** Elevator to dining room is available. **Services:** Private parties.

14 Wall Street ☆ $$$ FRENCH/NEW AMERICAN

14 Wall St., 31st Fl. (bet. Broadway & Broad St.)   (212) 233-2780
Credit cards: All major   Meals: B, L, D   Closed Sat., Sun.

Note: This neighborhood suffered substantial damage during the September 11, 2001 plane crashes that destroyed the World Trade Center. This restaurant may not be operational by the time you plan your visit.

This is a place for power meals with a view of the financial district. Once J.P. Morgan's residence, the dining rooms have a slightly old-fashioned air, looking more like a private dining area for a big corporation than an establishment that is open to the public. The service is very professional, and the food is pleasingly straightforward. Breakfast is a bargain, and at lunchtime the restaurant overflows with diners intent on serious food; they think nothing of sitting down to a lunch of foie gras, grilled lamb chops and crème brûlée. Salads are excellent, but the best main courses are the chef's signature dishes, like beautifully cooked liver with mashed potatoes, or brook trout stuffed with fennel, lightly smoked and served on a wooden plank. The most interesting dessert is a tasting of crème brûlée, three little pots of custard flavored with vanilla, pistachio and Armagnac.

Other recommended dishes: Foie gras; endive, pear and Roquefort salad; fish soup; sautéed calf's liver; rack of lamb; grilled salmon. **Wine list:** Best choices are French; no bargains. **Price range:** Apps., $8–$15; entrees, $19–$28; desserts, $8. **Wheelchair access:** Elevators to the dining rooms, which are on one level. **Features:** Good view, good for business, smoking permitted. **Services:** Catering, private parties.

Frank $25 & Under   ITALIAN

88 Second Ave. (near 5th St.)   (212) 420-0202
Credit cards: Cash only   Meals: Br, L, D, LN

This sweet, unpretentious restaurant, with its crowded, ragtag dining room, has been packed from the moment it opened. Start with an order of insalata Caprese, ripe tomatoes and mozzarella di bufala, and you may forget the tight surroundings. Among the entrees, polpettone, a savory meatloaf, with a classic, slow-cooked gravy, and orecchiette with fennel and pecorino Toscano are excellent. If you go early, you can expect special touches, like a free plate of tiny potato croquettes, or a dish of olive oil flavored with orange rind with your bread.

Other recommended dishes: Fennel salad; mussels; green bean, potato and egg salad; roasted trout; chicken with garlic and rosemary. **Alcohol:** Beer and wine. **Price range:** Apps., $3.95–$7.95; entrees, $6.95–$14.95. **Wheelchair access:** Narrow and small, particularly the restroom. **Features:** Romantic. **Services:** Takeout.

Franklin Station Cafe $ SOUTHEAST ASIAN

222 W. Broadway (at Franklin St.)   (212) 274-8525
Credit cards: All major   Meals: B, Br, L, D

It calls itself a French-Malaysian cafe, but the French part is
hard to discern. No matter: The curries and other Asian dishes
are enticing, as are the salads and sandwiches, served in a
pleasant if unremarkable setting.

Alcohol: None. **Price range:** Apps., $3–$6.50; entrees,
$6.50–$16.50; desserts, $3–$5. **Wheelchair access:** Not accessible. **Services:** Catering, delivery, takeout.

Frank's ☆ $$$ STEAKHOUSE

85 10th Ave. (at 15th St.)   (212) 243-1349
Credit cards: All major   Meals: L, D

A paradise for carnivores and smokers. The bare brick walls
and long bar announce this as a restaurant whose only desire is
to serve big portions to hungry people. Three or four shrimp in
a cocktail would probably provide enough protein for an average person: they are giant creatures of the sea, and absolutely
delicious. The T-bone steak is a great charred hunk with the
fine, funky flavor of meat that has been dry-aged for a long
time. The steak fries are long and thick, the sort of fries that
give potatoes a good name. The same family has been running
Frank's since 1912; they want you to feel at home, and you will.
(*Ruth Reichl*)

Other recommended dishes: Grilled chicken with mustard and
tarragon; veal chop; tripe stewed with onions and tomatoes;
greens with garlic and oil; cheesecake. **Wine list:** The list is
small and seems like an afterthought; if you want great wine
with your steak you'd be better off at Sparks or Smith & Wollensky. **Price range:** Lunch: apps., $6–$14; entrees, $8.50–$24;
desserts, $4–$9. Dinner: apps., $7–$15; entrees, $18–$30;
desserts, $4–$9. **Wheelchair access:** The restaurant is up five
steps. **Features:** Kid friendly, smoking permitted. **Services:**
Delivery, takeout, private parties.

Fred's $25 & Under   AMERICAN

476 Amsterdam Ave. (at 83rd St.)   (212) 579-3076
Credit cards: All major   Meals: B, Br, L, D, LN

This subterranean bar and restaurant offers homey American
fare and relaxed, friendly service, a combination that has made
it a neighborhood hit from the night it opened. It's a simple,
familiar formula, but Fred's, named for the owner's dog, does it
well. The standout appetizer is a butternut squash bisque, a
thick purée of squash flavored with apples, onions and cream.
The best main courses are meats, like an excellent, thick pork

chop cooked perfectly and served with roasted apples, potatoes roasted with rosemary and a mixture of broccoli and zucchini. Desserts are huge and eager to please, like an intensely fudgy brownie and a spicy apple-berry crisp.

Other recommended dishes: Mesclun with blue cheese, apple and roasted pecans; fried calamari; fillet of beef; beef stew; tuna steak; salmon fillet. **Price range:** Apps., $3–$8.95; entrees, $8.95–$16.95. **Wheelchair access:** Dining room is five steps down from street. **Features:** Kid friendly, smoking permitted, outdoor dining. **Services:** Takeout, private parties.

Fresco Tortilla Grill $25 & Under TEX-MEX

36 Lexington Ave. (bet. 23rd & 24th Sts.)	(212) 475-7380
253 Eighth Ave. (bet. 22nd & 23rd Sts.)	(212) 463-8877
769 Sixth Ave. (bet. 25th & 26th Sts.)	(212) 691-5588
215 W. 14th St. (bet. Seventh & Eighth Aves.)	(212) 352-0686
Credit cards: All major	Meals: L, D

Superb Tex-Mex fast food served in a tiny storefront. Fresco has been so successful that it's given rise to an indecipherable number of related branches and unrelated imitators, all with similar names. The original branch, on Lexington Avenue, is still the best.

Recommended dishes: Taco al carbon; tacos with ground chorizo; quesadillas; fajitas; sincronizadas. **Alcohol:** Bring your own. **Price range:** Entrees, $4.95–$13.95. **Wheelchair access:** Everything on one level. **Features:** Kid friendly, outdoor dining. **Services:** Delivery, takeout, catering, private parties.

Funky Broome $25 & Under CHINESE

176 Mott St. (bet. Broome & Kenmare Sts.)	(212) 941-8628
Credit cards: All major	Meals: L, D, LN

From its odd name to its brightly colored interior, Funky Broome suggests youth and energy rather than conformity. Though the menu is largely Cantonese and Hong Kong, Funky Broome has stirred it up a bit with some Thai touches and by making mini-woks centerpieces. The small woks are set over Sterno flames, which keep everything bubbling hot but can make it difficult to pass around the wok. Nonetheless, some of the dishes are unusual and good, like a delicious vegetarian casserole of nutty-tasting fried lotus roots in a gingery sauce with dried cherries, and plump and flavorful oysters stuffed with green onions and steamed in a red wine sauce. Seafood dishes are excellent, like decoratively scored squid served in a searing spicy sauce, and razor clams in a hot, garlicky black bean sauce. Salt and pepper seafood, a familiar Cantonese dish of fried shrimp, scallops and squid, is flawless. Funky Broome can breathe new life into hoary old dishes like crisp and tender beef with broccoli, while shredded chicken with Chinese vegetables is full of distinct and honest flavors.

Other recommended dishes: Sautéed bok choy greens; sautéed water spinach; shredded dried beef with shrimp paste and rice. **Price range:** Apps., $4.95–$15.95; entrees, $6.95–$15.95. **Wheelchair access:** Everything on one level. **Services:** Delivery, take out.

Gabriela's $25 & Under   MEXICAN
685 Amsterdam Ave. (at 93rd St.)   (212) 961-0574
311 Amsterdam Ave. (at 75th St.)
Credit cards: All major   Meals: B, L, D

This place is owned by the same people who own two Carmine's, three Ollie's Noodle Shops, two Dock's Oyster Bars and one Virgil's Real BBQ, but unlike those high-volume restaurants, named after fictional characters, there really is a Gabriela, and she makes terrific, authentic Mexican dishes. Taquitos al pastor, tiny corn tortillas topped with vinegary roast pork, pineapple salsa and cilantro, are a wonderful Mexican street dish. Gabriela's pozole, the traditional Mexican soup made with hominy, is a meal in itself, served in a huge bowl with chunks of tender pork or chicken. Entrees all come with tortillas so fragrant that the aroma of corn rises with the steam. And one last surprise: Gabriela's offers several superb desserts, including capirotada, a buttery bread pudding with lots of honey.

Other recommended dishes: Chips; guacamole; salad with nopales; tacos; tamales; carnitas; chochinta pibil; shrimp in chipotle sauce; jericalls; rice pudding. **Alcohol:** Beer, wine and tequila-based drinks. **Price range:** Apps., $2.95–$7.95; entrees, $5.95–$14.95. **Wheelchair access:** Entrance and dining room are on one level; restrooms are down one flight. **Features:** Kid friendly. **Services:** Delivery, takeout, catering, private parties.

Gabriel's ☆☆ $$$ ITALIAN
11 W. 60th St. (bet. Broadway & Columbus Ave.) (212) 956-4600
Credit cards: All major   Meals: L, D   Closed Sun.

This clubby and comfortable restaurant is a great choice before or after the symphony, with its great big portions and fabulous friendly service. Although the food is called Tuscan, it is not. It is far too American for that, too original. Look around the restaurant and the dish you see on almost every table is an earthy and seductive buckwheat polenta. The salads are inventive but they work. None of the pastas are ordinary, either. The real winner here is homemade gnocchi, little dumplings so light they float into your mouth and down your throat. Among the entrees, roast kid is a big, tasty hunk of meat. Desserts, with the exception of the wonderful sorbets and gelatos, are not very exciting. (*Ruth Reichl*)

Other recommended dishes: Grilled mushrooms, spicy mussel soup, pappardelle with rabbit and prunes, grilled baby chicken. **Wine list:** The mostly Italian list is quirky, personal and carefully chosen. **Price range:** Lunch: apps., $6.50–$10; entrees, $14–$19; desserts, $8–$12. Dinner: apps., $8.50–$12; entrees, $18–$32; desserts, $8–$12. **Wheelchair access:** Fully accessible. **Features:** Good for business. **Services:** Takeout, private parties.

Gage & Tollner $$ SEAFOOD/SOUTHERN

372 Fulton St., Brooklyn Heights, Brooklyn (718) 875-5181
Credit cards: All major Meals: L, D Closed Sun.

Gage & Tollner, the bastion of seafood and Southern cooking, lives on, its dignified face blinking a little awkwardly in the tackiness of Fulton Mall. Everything has been restored at Gage & Tollner, which opened in 1879 and moved to its current downtown Brooklyn location in 1892. It is a wonderfully old-fashioned room. The beautiful old gas-fired lights have been retrofitted, and they now flicker appealingly, making everyone look beautiful, and acoustic tiles have been removed, exposing the original vaulted ceiling. Unlike the room, the menu has barely changed in a century, with old favorites like soft clam bellies, lobster Newburg, she-crab soup and "blooming onions," which are cunningly fried whole. It's not likely to be the best lobster or the best steak you'll ever eat, but at Gage & Tollner it's the history and beauty, not the food, that's really the point.

Price range: Lunch: apps., $5.95–$11.95; entrees, $12–$21; desserts, $4.50–$6.95. Dinner: apps., $6.95–$11.95; entrees, $15–$27; desserts, $4.50–$6.95. **Wheelchair access:** Restrooms not accessible. **Features:** Parking available, smoking permitted. **Services:** Catering, private parties.

Galaxy $25 & Under NEW AMERICAN

15 Irving Pl. (at 15th St.) (212) 777-3631
Credit cards: MC/V Meals: B, Br, L, D, LN

The bar doubles as a hangout for Irving Plaza, the rock club next door, and the techno music doesn't always stay in the background. What makes it worthwhile is the unusual menu of Asian- and Latin-inspired dishes, like a salad of cold noodles in a light sesame-oil dressing over greens. The Galaxy also serves an excellent breakfast.

Price range: All dishes priced under $10. Prix-fixe brunch, $9.95. **Wheelchair access:** Not accessible. **Features:** Romantic, smoking permitted, outdoor dining. **Services:** Delivery, takeout, catering, private parties.

Gallagher's $$$ STEAKHOUSE

228 W. 52nd St. (bet. Broadway & Eighth Ave.)   (212) 245-5336
Credit cards: All major   Meals: L, D, LN

The slabs of prime beef hanging in the windows of Gallagher's
are a steak lover's delight, and if you know anything about
meat so much the better: you may go into the refrigerated room
with its hanging meat and pick your own steak. The best bet at
this shrine to long-gone prizefighters and sports stars is to stick
with the sirloin steak and other basics, like the fabulous steak
fries and terrific onion rings.

Price range: Lunch: apps., $7.50–$15.75; entrees,
$12.75–$42.75; desserts, $3.95–$5.75. Dinner: apps.,
$7.50–$15.75; entrees, $16.95–$42.75; desserts, $3.95–$5.75.
Wheelchair access: Side entrance available; restrooms not
accessible. **Features:** Kid friendly, good for business, smoking
permitted. **Services:** Private parties.

Garden Cafe $25 & Under NEW AMERICAN

620 Vanderbilt Ave., Prospect Heights, Brooklyn (718) 857-8863
Credit cards: All major   Meals: D   Closed Sun., Mon.

This family-run operation, near the Brooklyn Academy, serves
an ever-changing menu of artful American food that is always
satisfying. Standards like grilled veal chops and steaks are
superb, and the chef occasionally comes up with dishes like
jambalaya with Middle Eastern spicing. It's the kind of place
you wish was in your neighborhood.

Other recommended dishes: Green salad with lemon vinaigrette; lemon soufflé in raspberry sauce. **Alcohol:** Beer and
wine. **Price range:** Apps., $5.50–$6.75; entrees, $17.50–$20;
desserts, $6. Weeknight three-course dinner, $25. **Wheelchair
access:** Fully accessible.

Gennaro $25 & Under ITALIAN/MEDITERRANEAN

665 Amsterdam Ave. (near 93rd St.)   (212) 665-5348
Credit cards: Cash only   Meals: D

This newly expanded, simply decorated Italian restaurant is one
of the best things to happen to the Upper West Side in years,
serving wonderful dishes like an awesome osso bucco and terrific pastas. Appetizer specials are satisfying, like ribbolita, the
classic Tuscan vegetable and bean soup, served over thick slices
of bread. Cornish hen roasted with lemon is also excellent. Gennaro serves its own pear tart, flaky and delicious, and a rich
flourless chocolate cake.

Other recommended dishes: Butternut squash soup; grilled
scallops with white beans; grilled vegetables; beef carpaccio;
orecchiette with broccoli and provolone; tortelloni with spinach

and ricotta; braised lamb shank; grilled quail. **Alcohol:** Beer
and wine. **Price range:** Apps., $5.75–$8.50; entrees,
$8.50–$14.95; desserts, $5.25–$6. **Wheelchair access:** Entrance
and dining room on one level; restroom is narrow. **Services:**
Delivery, takeout.

Ghenet $25 & Under   AFRICAN/ETHIOPIAN
284 Mulberry St. (near Houston St.)   (212) 343-4888
Credit cards: All major   Meals: L, D

This friendly, enticing restaurant offers an introduction to
Ethiopian food, not quite as spicy or as gamy as you might find
elsewhere, but good just the same. Highlights include kategna,
simply a length of injera — the smooth, brownish bread made
from fermented tef toasted until crisp and painted with berbere,
a fiery sauce, and kibe, a clarified butter that resembles the
Indian ghee. The main courses are tasty but mildly spiced: Siga
wat, cubes of tender, delicious beef, comes in a sauce milder
than usual, since "wat" ordinarily means hot; doro wat is also
tamer than expected, a chicken stew served, as is traditional,
with a hard-boiled egg.

Other recommended dishes: Misir; engouday tibs; azifa; yebeg
alecha; yegomen wat; yemsir wat. **Alcohol:** Beer and wine.
Price range: Apps., $3.95–$4.95; entrees, $8.75–$13.95. **Wheelchair access:** Restrooms not accessible.

Gino $$ ITALIAN
780 Lexington Ave. (bet. 60th & 61st Sts.)   (212) 223-9658
Credit cards: Cash only   Meals: L, D

You saw it in *Mighty Aphrodite*, zebra wallpaper and all. Unless
you're a regular customer, the charms of this old-time Italian
restaurant might elude you.

Price range: Dinner: apps, $5.95–$12.95; entrees,
$13.50–$26.95; desserts, $3.95. **Wheelchair access:** Restrooms
not accessible. **Services:** Takeout.

Globe $$ NEW AMERICAN
373 Park Ave. S. (bet. 26th & 27th Sts.)   (212) 545-8800
Credit cards: All major   Meals: Br, L, D

A truly peculiar restaurant where the quality of the wide-ranging menu varies wildly from day to day. Simple dishes like roast
chicken and sautéed fish are generally the best bets, but also
steamed shrimp and tuna tartar. The odder and more complex
dishes can be problems. Décor is either pretentious or playful,
depending on your mood.

Price range: Lunch: apps., $6–$8; entrees, $10–$14.95; desserts, $6–$8. Dinner: apps., $5–$10; entrees, $14.95–$22; desserts, $6.50–$8.50. **Wheelchair access:** Fully accessible. **Features:** Smoking permitted. **Services:** Takeout, catering, private parties.

Golden Unicorn $$ CHINESE

18 E. Broadway (at Catherine St.)   (212) 941-0911
Credit cards: All major   Meals: B, Br, L, D

Consistently reliable Chinatown restaurant with excellent dim sum.

Price range: Apps. from $2.50; entrees from $14. **Wheelchair access:** Restrooms not accessible. **Features:** Kid friendly. **Services:** Takeout, catering, private parties.

Good $25 & Under   NEW AMERICAN/PAN-LATIN

89 Greenwich Ave. (at Bank St.)   (212) 691-8080
Credit cards: All major   Meals: L, D   Closed Mon.

Steven Picker, the chef and owner of Campo, a restaurant in Greenwich Village, found common threads among the foods of South, Central and North America and wove them into one menu. Apparently not enough people liked this approach because Mr. Picker closed Campo and replaced it with Good.

But here's a secret: several of Campo's old dishes remain, and some interesting new dishes have been added, so it's still possible to eat unusually, eclectically and very well. Crisp peanut chicken is one of those welcome old dishes. Grilled calamari, a newcomer, takes its cue from Asia. The flavorful squid, served atop cucumber ribbons, arrives in a lime-and-mint dressing. The burger is big and meaty and sure to satisfy; even better is the grilled flank steak with Mr. Picker's parsley-garlic sauce. Also try the sautéed rock shrimp, flavored with garlic and served over gloriously mushy grits with corn relish. There is a good piece of tuna, glazed in molasses and served with delicious collard greens. And definitely take the chilaquiles, a Mexican solution to the problem of what to do with leftover tortillas: grill them and toss them with other leftovers (in Good's case, chicken, onions, cilantro and chili sauce).

The service is warm and professional. The signature dessert, house-made doughnuts, are rather dry and tasteless, but the demitasse of Oaxacan chocolate served with them is delicious.

Other recommended dishes: Arepa with scallops; Camembert crisp with pear chutney; flank steak; pork sandwich; tuna glazed in molasses. **Price range:** Apps., $5–$8; entrees, $10–$17. **Wheelchair access:** Everything on one level. **Features:** Romantic.

Good Enough to Eat $$ NEW AMERICAN
483 Amsterdam Ave. (bet. 83rd & 84th Sts.) (212) 496-0163
Credit cards: All major Meals: B, Br, L, D

This folksy, homespun restaurant was one of the first to redis-
cover the appeal of American comfort food. Still, it's hard to
fathom why Upper West Siders stand in line for an hour or
more for weekend brunch. The french toast and eggs Benedict
are no better here than at dozens of other places, the nightly
meals of meatloaf and roast chicken are no great shakes, and
the service is adequate. Go figure.

Price range: Lunch entrees, $6–$11. Dinner: apps., $4–$6.50;
entrees, $9–$18.50; desserts, $1–$5. **Wheelchair access:** Fully
accessible. **Features:** Kid friendly. **Services:** Delivery, takeout,
catering, private parties.

Good World Bar and Grill $25 & Under
SCANDINAVIAN
3 Orchard St. (at Division St.) (212) 925-9975.
Credit cards: All major Meals: D, LN

If for no other reason, Good World Bar and Grill beckons
because it's a bar in an old barbershop near Chinatown that
serves Scandinavian food. As a restaurant, it's unpolished. Yet,
it offers a spirit of adventure, a departure from the routine, that
makes Good World's world a good world indeed. It's not
entirely Scandinavian, but the lack of rigor reflects the laid-back
spirit of the place, with its spacey service but appealing downtown ambiance. Skagen is shrimp with crème fraîche and dill,
served on toast. It's pretty good, a nice prelude for the exceptionally tender and tasty sautéed squid, or the fabulous fish
soup, a bisque that tastes like the essence of the sea, made with
sour cream and onions and full of shrimp and mussels. Basic
dishes like Swedish meatballs and potato pancakes can be
unpredictable. Good World is on far firmer ground with seafood
dishes, like an offering of three kinds of herring.

Other recommended dishes: Grilled sardines; crab cakes;
three-berry pie. **Price range:** Apps , $3–$6; medium and large
plates, $8–$16. **Wheelchair access:** Everything is on one level.

Goody's ☆ $ CHINESE
1 E. Broadway (at Chatham Sq.) Chinatown (212) 577-2922
Credit cards: All major Meals: L, D

Great Shanghai food from the people who went on to open the
Joe's Shanghai chain. Don't miss the soup dumplings, xiao long
bao. Goody's pride is the crab meat version, tinted pink by the
seafood that glows through the sheer, silky skin. But there are
other unusual dishes, like fabulous turnip pastries, yellowfish

fingers in seaweed batter, and braised pork shoulder, a kind of candied meat. This dish is so rich that it must be eaten in small bites. Goody's kitchen also works magic with bean curd, mixed with crab meat so it becomes rich and delicious.

Other recommended dishes: Steamed pork buns; dried bean curd with jalapeños. **Alcohol:** Beer. **Price range:** $15–$20. **Wheelchair access:** Restrooms are narrow. **Services:** Delivery, takeout, private parties.

Gotham Bar and Grill ☆☆☆ $$$$

NEW AMERICAN

12 E. 12th St. (bet. Fifth Ave. & University Pl.)   (212) 620-4020
Credit cards: All major   Meals: L, D

Gotham Bar and Grill is a cheerful, welcoming restaurant in an open, high-ceilinged room with a lively bar along one side. Through some trick of design, each table offers intimacy: seated, you have the sense of watching without being watched. Starched men in suits mingle with rumpled guys in blue jeans. Gotham's service is a big part of its ambiance. Waiters take their cues from the customer — anticipating their every wish and making diners feel remarkably well cared for.

And then there's the food. The chef, Alfred Portale, famous for his vertical dishes, is working with an architecture of flavor, composing his dishes so that each element contributes something vital. His food seems modern but is almost classic in its balance. His signature dish is seafood salad, a spiral of scallops, squid, octopus, lobster and avocado that swirls onto the plate like a mini-tornado. Dressed only in lemon and olive oil, it depends on the flavors of the seafood itself; textures are underlined by smooth avocado, crisp leaves of lettuce and crunchy bits of flying-fish roe. Tuna tartar is lively with lime, scallions and ginger. Mr. Portale clearly has fun with the pastas, which change daily.

Main courses are more straightforward. Fish is always paired with something — like leeks and morels, artichokes, braised escarole or tomato confit — to bring out its most important qualities. Desserts, like the wonderful chocolate cake, are intense and very American.

On a recent visit, the restaurant showed no signs of slowing down or slacking off. In fact, it would be hard to think of another three-star restaurant of comparable age that continues to perform, dish after dish, with such admirable consistency. The food is taller than ever, but it may be better than ever. The range of flavors and treatments is impressive, from rustic delights like seared mackerel with a salad of cracked wheat, onions and peas, to indulgent exercises like a slice of foie gras surrounded by black plums and drizzled with 25-year-old balsamic vinegar. It's a tight fit in the back room, but the waiters manage to pirhouette their way through the maze impressively. (*Ruth Reichl, updated by William Grimes*)

Other recommended dishes: Octopus salad; seared mackerel; sautéed skate wings; herbed ricotta ravioli; grilled salmon; seared tuna; roast chicken; grilled steak; rack of lamb. **Wine list:** The waiters are very helpful in navigating the unusual and well-chosen list. It would be nice if there were more lower-priced bottles. **Price range:** Lunch: apps., $11.50–$16.50; entrees, $16–$20; desserts, $8–$9; three-course prix fixe, $19.99. Dinner: apps., $14–$21; entrees, $28–$38; desserts, $8–$9. **Wheelchair access:** A ramp for the steps to the dining room, but restrooms are downstairs. **Services:** Private parties.

Grace $$ NEW AMERICAN
114 Franklin St. (bet W. Broadway & Church St.) (212) 343-4200
Credit cards: All major Meals: Br, L, D, LN

It's hard to know whether Grace is a restaurant with a bar or a bar with a restaurant. Visually the bar comes first, and it's impossible to miss. Weighty, glossy and a mile long, it dominates the front room. The extensive bar list includes an apple martini made with vodka and Berentzen Apfelkorn, a tangerine margarita and a superior winter warmer made with hot spiced cider, Maker's Mark bourbon, fresh lemon juice and a stick of cinnamon.

The dining room, though, is more than an afterthought, with a grazing menu that's strong on bright, assertive flavors with smartly targeted Southwestern and Asian ingredients. The dishes can be as minimal as a sandwich of melted raclette and Westphalian ham, or mussels steamed in Belgian beer and served with a side of fries, and there's a fundamental simplicity to even the more complicated choices. The round cakes of shredded barbecued duck with a sweet pepper relish have a pleasingly down-home quality to them.

Other recommended dishes: Chipotle-marinated skirt steak; mascarpone polenta cakes; seared tuna in pepper crust. **Wine list:** American and French wines from $20–$50; by the glass, $6–$10. **Price range:** Small plates, $8–$13. Dinner: apps, $8–$11.50; entrees, $9–$14, desserts, $5–$8. **Wheelchair access:** Steps up to dining room. **Features:** Smoking at bar. **Services:** Take out, private parties.

Gradisca $25 & Under ITALIAN
126 W. 13th St. (bet. Sixth & Seventh Aves.) (212) 691-4886
Credit cards: Cash only Meals: D

Gradisca epitomizes the local trattoria, downtown style. The dining room is rustic: tables covered in butcher paper, walls of brick and rough-hewn wood, which are covered in officially sanctioned graffiti, and candles throwing so little light you can barely make out the menu. Its waiters conform to a more modern stereotype: young, hip and lanky in tight black T-shirts. Piadinas are excellent starters. These round, unleavened flatbreads from the Romagna region of northern Italy are cooked on a griddle and then stuffed with things like prosciutto and fresh mozzarella, or spinach and pecorino. Gradisca even serves spaghetti carbonara as it was intended, simply with eggs and bacon. The list of main courses is small, but includes two superb selections: sliced leg of lamb that is tender and full of flavor in its red wine sauce, and a big pork chop that holds its own under a cloud of crisp leeks.

Desserts standouts include salame di cioccolato, a deliciously dense, bittersweet chocolate torte made to resemble salami slices, and a jiggly, satisfying amaretto semifreddo.

Other recommended dishes: Carrot soup, eggplant with tomato and anchovies, pappardelle with lamb ragu, spaghetti with cuttlefish and black ink sauce, lasagna. **Price range:** Apps., $5–$8; entrees, $12–$20. **Wheelchair access:** Two steps at entrance.

Gramercy Tavern ☆☆☆ $$$$ NEW AMERICAN
42 E. 20th St. (bet. Broadway & Park Ave. S.)   (212) 477-0777
Credit cards: All major   Meals: L, D

When Gramercy Tavern opened in 1994 the owners, Danny Meyer and Tom Colicchio, said they intended to redefine grand dining in New York. The large and lively Tavern has fulfilled this promise. Chef Tom Colicchio cooks with extraordinary confidence, creating dishes characterized by bold flavors and unusual harmonies. His best dishes take flavor to extremes. Marinated hamachi is brushed with lemon and olive oil; roast beets and herbs are scattered across the top. The clean, fresh taste of the fish comes soaring through with the clarity of a flute. Salmon is baked in salt until the flesh has the texture of velvet. A silky, just-cooked breast of chicken with truffles stuffed under the skin in a lively broth perfumed with rosemary is chicken soup raised to an entirely new level.

To experience Mr. Colicchio's cooking at its best, consider the chef's extraordinary market menu. At $90, it is expensive, but perfect for special occasions. Sample the parade of extraordinary desserts including sorbets, with startlingly different textures, and a barely sweet chocolate cake with bay leaf cream.

Service is solicitous but unceremonial. For a less expensive alternative, the handsome bar in front offers a casual but excellent menu. (*Ruth Reichl*)

Other recommended dishes: Sweetbreads with bacon; tuna tartar with sea urchin and cucumber vinaigrette; wild mushroom and salsify ragout; seared tuna; roast cod with savoy cabbage;

spiced loin of lamb; roast squab with fava beans; warm chocolate tart; panna cotta; tarte Tatin; lemon soufflé tart. **Most popular dish:** Grilled fillet with puréed potatoes and balsamic
relish. **Chef's favorite:** Rabbit with sherry vinegar, olives and
garlic sausage. **Wine list:** Interesting, accessible and well
priced. **Price range:** Lunch: three-course prix fixe, $36. Dinner:
three-course prix fixe, $65; seasonal tasting menus, $78–$90.
Wheelchair access: A ramp in front and everything is on one
level. **Services:** Private parties.

Grand Sichuan ☆ $ CHINESE

125 Canal St. (near Bowery) (212) 334-3323
Credit cards: Cash only Meals: L, D

Grand Sichuan may serve the best Sichuan food in Chinatown,
but it is an extremely modest storefront establishment near the
entrance to the Manhattan Bridge. The beef tendon is breathtaking, sprinkled with ginger and flooded with a startlingly hot,
clear oily sauce. Bean curd with chili sauce, made with hot
bean sauce, small bits of chopped pork and finely ground
Sichuan peppers, was utterly seductive. Sautéed loofah, a tender vegetable similar to cucumber, is gently cooked in chicken
stock and provides a perfect contrast. The restaurant also serves
a triumphant braised whole fish in a fragrant hot bean sauce
that seems to blend all the flavors of Sichuan. (*Ruth Reichl*)

Other recommended dishes: Tea-smoked duck; chicken with
wonder sauce; dan dan noodles with chili sauce; prawns with
garlic sauce; double-cooked fresh bacon with chili sauce;
Sichuan double-cooked pork. **Alcohol:** Beer. **Price range:**
Apps., $1.50–$5.25; entrees, $6.95–$15.95. **Wheelchair access:**
One step up to dining room; restrooms downstairs. **Features:**
Kid friendly. **Services:** Delivery, takeout, private parties.

Grand Sichuan International $25 & Under

CHINESE

229 Ninth Ave. (at 24th St.) (212) 620-5200
745 Ninth Ave. (bet. 50th & 51st Sts.) (212) 582-2288
Credit cards: All major Meals: L, D

These restaurants are notable not only for their terrific Sichuan
and Hunan food, but also for a remarkable approach to their
clientele. The owner hands out a 27-page pamphlet that
explains five Chinese regional cuisines and describes dozens of
dishes the restaurant serves. The eating is as interesting as the
reading, with wonderful dishes like sour stringbeans with
minced pork and tea-smoked duck. While Sichuan food is
indeed spicy, that is only part of the story, as you see when you
taste a fabulous cold dish like sliced conch with wild pepper
sauce, coated with ground Sichuan peppercorns, which are not
hot but bright, effervescent and almost refreshing.

Other recommended dishes: Sichuan wontons with red oil; cold Sichuan noodles; broad beans in scallion sauce; prawns with garlic sauce; red-cooked pork with chestnuts; bean curd with spicy sauce. **Alcohol:** Beer. **Price range:** Apps., $1–$3.95; entrees, $5.95–$16.95. **Wheelchair access:** Aisle to restrooms is very narrow. **Features:** Kid friendly, good for business. **Services:** Takeout.

Grange Hall $25 & Under   AMERICAN

50 Commerce St. (at Barrow St.)   (212) 924-5246
Credit cards: AE   Meals: Br, L, D

Grange Hall celebrates Depression-era American food of the Midwest with flair, from fat little loaves of white bread to succotash, pork chops and lake fish. The food is usually pretty good, the décor is inspiring and the all-American wine and beer list is appealing.

Price range: Lunch: entrees, $7–$8; desserts, $5. Dinner: apps., $4–$8; entrees, $10.50–$21; desserts, $5.75. **Wheelchair access:** Fully accessible. **Features:** Romantic, smoking permitted. **Services:** Takeout, private parties.

Grano Trattoria $25 & Under   ITALIAN

21 Greenwich Ave. (at 10th St.)   (212) 645-2121
Credit cards: MC/V   Meals: Br, L, D, LN

The dining room, with its marble tables, Italian tile floor and open kitchen, seems the essence of an urban neighborhood trattoria, and the food, when it is on the mark, is delicious. But dishes are remarkably inconsistent. The surest bets here are the appetizers, like a superb special of red bean soup, or grilled soppressata, a large cured sausage, served with polenta. Salads are offered in can't-go-wrong combinations, like arugula, pear and Parmesan. Ravioli in a light tomato sauce with spinach and eggplant is excellent. Service is friendly, and occasionally Grano offers unusual game dishes.

Other recommended dishes: Eggplant cakes; roasted beet salad with fennel, arugula and Parmesan; shrimp, green beans and roasted peppers; orecchiette with veal sausage, broccoli rape and tomato; chocolate mousse. **Alcohol:** Beer and wine list with some excellent values. **Price range:** Lunch: apps., $5–$7; entrees, $8.50–$15; desserts, $6. Dinner: apps., $6–$8; entrees, $7–$16; desserts, $6. **Wheelchair access:** Everything is on one level. **Features:** Smoking permitted, outdoor dining. **Services:** Delivery, takeout, catering, private parties.

Gray's Papaya $

2090 Broadway (at 72nd St.)
402 Sixth Ave. (at 8th St.)
Credit cards: Cash only

FAST FOOD
(212) 799-0243
(212) 260-3532
Meals: Open 24 hours

Nowhere but New York City do you find the combination of hot dogs and tropical drinks, and Gray's is one of the best practitioners. It's hard to find a cheaper meal than a couple of these juicy, garlic-tinged hot dogs, washed down with papaya juice.

Alcohol: None. **Price range:** French fries, $1.50; two hot dogs and a drink, $1.95. **Wheelchair access:** Everything on one level.

Green Field $25 & Under

108-01 Northern Blvd., Corona, Queens
Credit cards: All major

LATIN AMERICAN
(718) 672-5202
Meals: L, D, LN

With a dining room the size of a soccer field, this Brazilian barbecue restaurant does a huge business with its all-you-can-eat menu. The best selections are the sausages and the tenderloin steak charred on the outside and flavored with olive oil and rosemary. At the end, a simple piece of fruit from the salad bar is just right for dessert. The food is good, and the routine of signaling for more from the spit-wielding waiters is fun. The key is not to fill up at the huge salad bar.

Other recommended dishes: Pork loin; rib-eye steak; turkey wrapped in bacon; beef ribs; chicken hearts; venison. **Price range:** $19.95 all-you-can-eat. **Wheelchair access:** Everything is on one level. **Features:** Parking available. **Services:** Catering, private parties.

Grill Room ☆☆ $$$

2 World Financial Center
Credit cards: All major

NEW AMERICAN/SEAFOOD
(212) 945-9400
Meals: L, D

Note: This neighborhood suffered substantial damage during the September 11, 2001 plane crashes that destroyed the World Trade Center. This restaurant may not be operational by the time you plan your visit.

When Larry Forgione of An American Place opened his latest homage to star-spangled food in the World Financial Center, he had the wisdom to look forward instead of back. Wall Street has changed, and the Grill Room means to feed modern traders with up-to-date appetites. The menu is as unfussy as the décor, straightforward American fare with no exotic ingredients. Meals begin with warm biscuits so rich and crumbly they're impossible to stop eating. Many of the first courses are spectacular.

Crab cakes wrapped into a spring roll are light and perfectly right. Little fried popcorn shrimp are irresistible, too. The dense chowder is the essence of corn, beautifully swirled with vegetable purées. The American theme continues with the main courses, which are heavy on protein. Of all the meats, the pot-roasted short ribs are best. The desserts are rich and wonderful. Strawberry shortcake is a dream. All of this comes at a high price. But then, the great restaurants of Wall Street were never cheap. And none of them had a view of the Hudson like this.

Other recommended dishes: Napoleon of smoked salmon; shrimp cocktail; fried Ipswich clams; oysters; scallops wrapped in pastrami-cured bacon; cedar-planked salmon with parsley sauce; yellowfin tuna; dry-aged steak; Vidalia onion rings; double-chocolate pudding; peach-raspberry cobbler; bourbon chocolate-chip ice cream. **Wine list:** All American with many good wines, too few of them inexpensive. **Price range:** Apps., $8–$12; entrees, $15–$29; desserts, $5–$7. **Wheelchair access:** Elevators from 225 Liberty St. **Features:** Smoking permitted. **Services:** Takeout, catering, private parties.

The Grocery ☆ $$ NEW AMERICAN
288 Smith St. (bet. Union & Sackett Sts.)   (718) 596-3335
Credit cards: MC/V   Meals: D   Closed Sun.

The Grocery likes to project the image of the little restaurant that could, a struggling Brooklyn storefront operation where things can and will go wrong, but in a way that makes you laugh. Don't be fooled by the act. Despite serious service problems, it is a focused, high-quality restaurant that, in fits and starts, rises to heights that make it much more than a nice neighborhood spot.

Many restaurants sell themselves as market-driven, but the Grocery follows through on the pledge. Fresh produce, good fish and flavorful meat are the foundation of the Grocery's cuisine, an internationalized style of bistro cooking with an Italian insistence on pristine ingredients. A seared tuna appetizer gets the lightest possible dusting of cumin, a note that's amplified in a cumin-yogurt sauce. A bright-red pile of shaved beets, tart and sweet, sends this little dish right into orbit. The duck breast is winningly simple, served on a bed of fluffy bulgur soaked in a well-reduced, very fruity red-wine sauce punctuated by black currants and bits of carrot. The menu finishes strong with excellent, homey desserts with an exotic touch here and there. Two steamed puddings vie for supremacy. Chocolate pudding, moistened with rum and sherry, seems unbeatable. It cannot quite compete, however, with the steamed ginger pudding, a spicy dream of a dessert, surrounded with poached nectarines and a puff of vanilla whipped cream.

The Grocery has the charm and the drawbacks that make many of Brooklyn's restaurants a pleasure-pain trade-off. It's in a small, simple storefront, and seating is cramped. In warm weather, the backyard garden, with its spreading fig tree, offers relief from the crowded, very noisy conditions in the dining room. In either location, prepare to wait. And wait.

Other recommended dishes: Steamed clams in garlic-herb broth; baked halibut with fava beans and bacon; grilled trout; plum upside-down cake. **Wine list:** A modestly priced, eclectic 35-bottle list, with nine wines by the glass. **Price range:** Dinner: apps., $6–$8; entrees, $16–$19; desserts, $6–$7. **Wheelchair access:** One step down to garden. Restrooms not accessible.

Grove $25 & Under BISTRO/FRENCH

314 Bleecker St. (at Grove St.)   (212) 675-9463
Credit cards: All major   Meals: Br, L, D, LN

This gracious restaurant with a lovely garden in back serves French-inflected American food. It doesn't carve out new territory, yet it is terrifically appealing. The dining room and service are warm and welcoming, and the food is moderately priced. An appetizer like roasted red pepper and grilled tomato with slivers of basil is simple but wonderful, and main courses are just as good, like the thick grilled pork chop with tender greens and sautéed apples, or incredibly good chicken breast pounded thin, breaded and topped with an arugula and tomato compote. Desserts are a weak link.

Other recommended dishes: Fried calamari; carrot soup; penne with tomato, mushrooms and eggplant; hanger steak; grilled salmon; raspberry crisp. **Alcohol:** Beer and a short, inexpensive wine list. **Price range:** Apps., $5–$10; entrees, $14–$20; desserts, $6. **Wheelchair access:** One step to front door; garden is accessible, downstairs and restrooms are not.

Guastavino's ☆☆ $$$$ ENGLISH/FRENCH

409 E. 59th St. (bet. First & York Aves.)   (212) 980-2455
Credit cards: All major   Meals: L, D

Sir Terence Conran has made good on the theatrical possibilities in the tiled vaults under the Queensboro Bridge. Named after the father and son team that created the tiled ceilings in the bridge's vaults (as well as the ceilings in the Grand Central Oyster Bar and several other sites), the restaurant encourages the eye to linger on the powerful pillars that lead upward to cathedral-like ceilings. The raw, almost brutal granite blocks that make up the caissons of the bridge have been left exposed. But the overall design is sleek and international. Guastavino's almost begs diners to look everywhere but at their plates, and to talk about everything except the food. It's not so much a restaurant as an opportunity to live, for two or three hours, a certain mood, and a certain sense of style, that suits every time zone and speaks every language.

Guastavino's two kitchens operate independently, and while the food may not light up the night, at its best it is well conceived and well executed.

Guastavino Restaurant

This first-floor restaurant is a 300-seat brasserie, clamorous and casual, with a glorious brasserie-style shellfish display in front of the kitchen. The downstairs menu sticks to straightforward brasserie fare, with a few international additions, like matzo ball soup, a lively but overly vinegared salad of scungilli and hot peppers, and an exceedingly tame Cuban stew of tripe, short ribs and oxtail. Prawns, oysters and lobsters from the raw bar fairly crackle with freshness, but two of the more hefty appetizers are notable: a plate-size portobello mushroom buried under a landslide of melted taleggio cheese, and cabbage stuffed with pancetta and tomato. One entree deserves elevation to the upstairs menu, a moist and tender baby chicken sprinkled with walnuts, doused in walnut and sage butter, and surrounded by a sticky reduction sauce. Sweetbread schnitzel turns out to be a pleasant surprise, gently crunchy outside, rich and creamy inside. A good old-fashioned Pavlova leads the list of desserts, followed closely by a concentrated lemon tart.

Club Guastavino

Up a curved marble staircase, the more formal and intimate Club Guastavino, which seats 100, hangs over the first floor like a giant balcony, retaining a swaddled sense of isolation and privilege, enhanced by more luxurious materials and boothlike velvet-upholstered sofas. The smaller tables that overlook the first floor feel like ringside seating, with an unobstructed view of the percolating bar scene. Farther away from the glass railing, a quieter, more loungey atmosphere takes over. There's a lot of presentation at Club Guastavino. Waiters run over, laden with platters of roasted baby lamb or, one evening, bearing an entire roasted pig. Both the lamb and the pig deserve the fanfare. The pig, in particular, feels almost sinful to eat.

Quenelles are the merest puffs of pike mousse floating in an almost obscenely voluptuous crayfish sauce. A roast quail appetizer also scores a direct hit. The little birds, done to a turn, are stuffed with a fluffy black pudding enriched with pine nuts and dates. Like the quenelles, pan-roasted veal kidneys with a Cognac and mustard sauce may be a dish as old as the hills, but they march right on the stage and take it over.

The desserts show a light, fresh touch. Tangerine parfait tastes like a Creamsicle that's come into a lot of money, and a very simple, elegant-looking terrine of mango and coconut sorbet manages to be opulent and refreshing at the same time.

Other recommended dishes: Corn chowder; côte du boeuf; chocolate vacherin. **Wine list:** Guastavino Restaurant offers an international bistro list of 80 modest wines, plus 12 half bottles, 10 wines by the glass and about 30 splurge wines from the Club Guastavino list. Club Guastavino's list of about 400 wines, many of them very inexpensive, is a judicious international mix, with 20 half bottles. **Price range:** Guastavino Restaurant: Apps., $8–$18; entrees, $14–$30; desserts, $7–$9. Club Guastavino: Lunch, three courses, $35. Dinner, three courses, $65. **Wheelchair access:** Elevators to both restaurants, and accessible restrooms on both floors.

Gubbio ☆ $$$ ITALIAN

233 W. Broadway (bet. White & Franklin Sts.) (212) 334-8077
Credit cards: All major   Meals: L, D   Closed Sun.

A meal at Gubbio — named after one of Umbria's most attractive hill towns — unfolds in pleasant surroundings. The dining rooms are spacious, and there's a soothing quality to the heavy rustic wooden table where the antipasto plates sit. You will dine simply but well on dishes like grilled focaccia topped with a warm onion confit and marinated sardines, or zuppa di farro, a thick, peasant soup chunky with beans and scented with rosemary oil. Umbrians mean business with pasta. Pisarei e fasó, a traditional bread and cheese gnocchi, are feather light, served with beans and a smoky tomato sauce. Tortelli, stuffed with stewed veal then coated in a thick veal stock and topped with firm slices of asparagus, could be the finest thing on the entire menu, one of those dishes you finish and then actually think about ordering seconds. Fish puts in a feeble performance, but the meat courses make a much stronger impression. Firm, smoky-tasting Castelluccio lentils perfectly complement full-flavored lamb chops in a red wine and herb sauce; and pork, the meat supreme in Umbria, gets the full treatment in a medallion smothered in stewed cabbage and smoked ricotta.

The pastry chef offers up the obligatory gelati, sorbetti, panna cotta and tiramisu, but he cuts loose a little with his delizia di cioccolato, a modest cylinder of deep chocolate cake with an even deeper chocolate glaze, drizzled with orange syrup and surrounded by candied kumquats.

Other recommended dishes: Sautéed shellfish; sliced skirt steak with potato and artichoke torte; cheesecake. **Wine list:** Emphasis on Tuscany and Piedmont; many under $40. **Price range:** Lunch: apps., $6.50–$10.75; entrees, $12.50–$18.50; desserts, $6. Dinner: apps., $7.50–$12.75; entrees, $16.60–$24.50; desserts, $6.50–$7.50. **Wheelchair access:** Wheelchair entrance on White St. **Features:** Smoking permitted. **Services:** Takeout, private parties.

Gus's Figs $25 & Under   MEDITERRANEAN

250 W. 27th St. (bet. Seventh & Eighth Aves.)   (212) 352-8822
Credit cards: All major   Meals: L, D, LN

Figs captures the dreamy, generous, sun-soaked aura that
makes the Mediterranean so endlessly appealing. The chef
excels at blending flavors and textures in main courses like
moist, flavorful chicken, braised in a clay pot and served over
creamy polenta. Top dishes include tender pieces of lamb
served over a soft bread pudding made savory with goat cheese
and pine nuts and sweetened with figs; and pan-roasted cod
with grilled leeks, orange sections and pomegranate vinaigrette.

Other recommended dishes: Bruschetta; phyllo tasting plate;
grilled polenta cake; beet and goat cheese salad; cassoulet;
kakavia; grilled tuna; whole grilled snapper; almond cake;
poached pear. **Price range:** Apps., $5–$9; entrees, $13–$19.50.
Wheelchair access: Restrooms and dining room are on one
level; a ramp is planned for entrance. **Features:** Good for business, romantic, smoking permitted. **Services:** Delivery, takeout,
catering, private parties.

The Half King $25 & Under   PUB/IRISH

505 W. 23rd St. (bet. Tenth & Eleventh Aves.)   (212) 462-4300
Credit cards: All major   Meals: B, L, D

Owned by Sebastian Junger, author of *The Perfect Storm*, and
named for an 18th-century American Indian leader, the Half
King is unlike any conventional notion of a writers' bar. The
music is so loud that conversation is hard and brooding impossible. The patrons are so young they probably wouldn't know a
typewriter from a martini. One more thing sets the Half King
apart from all other writers' bars: food that you can actually
enjoy.

The starting point is Irish pub grub, skillfully elevated from
its proletarian moorings while retaining its heartiness and simplicity. The starters include a light cake constructed of potatoes
and goat cheese, wrapped in excellent smoked salmon and
accompanied by a good green salad, and an artfully composed
salad of artichokes, sweet beets and creamy goat cheese. Main
courses include a superbly flavorful pork roast, and a surprisingly delicate fillet of sole. Lamb steak is full of forthright flavor,
and the shepherd's pie, made with chopped beef, is ample and
hearty. There is an inexpensive, serviceable wine list and a
selection of beers on tap. Desserts are good and rustic, like a
rough-hewn berry, peach and apple crumble, and a rugged
lemon tart that is thankfully more tart than sweet.

By day, the bar is almost empty, and it's easier to notice the
handsome simplicity of the woody décor, with its occasional
nautical artifacts. A small garden in the rear is pleasant at
lunch, or at breakfast, when you can sample the delicious

house-made scones, served warm with clotted cream and jam, or the huge Irish breakfast.

Other recommended dishes: Seafood chowder, smoked salmon salad, seaweed salad, hamburger. **Price range:** Apps., $4–$10; entrees, $9–$16. **Wheelchair access:** Everything is on one level.

Hallo Berlin $25 & Under   GERMAN

402 W. 51st St. (at Ninth Ave.)   (212) 541-6248
626 10th Ave. (at 44th St.)   (212) 977-1944
Credit cards: Only at 10th Ave. location   Meals: L, D

For inexpensive German specialties, it's hard to do better than Hallo Berlin. The half dozen kinds of mildly spiced sausages are excellent; and rouladen, beef fillets sliced thin and rolled around bacon and cucumber, are almost like sausages themselves. Fat white meatballs, a mixture of pork and beef, are boiled and then bathed in a creamy caper sauce and come with mashed potatoes, peas and carrots. All this food goes perfectly with the selection of German beers, though the setting — a few rickety tables — is barely more comfortable than a bench on the sidewalk.

Other recommended dishes: Potato pancakes; rollmops; wurst; rouladen; smoked pork chops. **Alcohol:** Beer and wine. **Price range:** Apps., $1–$3; entrees, $8.95–$14.95; desserts, $3–$4. **Wheelchair access:** 10th Ave. location fully accessible; 51st St. dining room is two steps from street. **Features:** Kid friendly, smoking permitted, outdoor dining. **Services:** Delivery, takeout, private parties.

Han Bat $25 & Under   KOREAN

53 W. 35th St. (bet. Fifth Ave. & Broadway)   (212) 629-5588
Credit cards: All major   Meals: L, D   Open 24 hours

Korean restaurants are no longer uncommon in this part of Midtown. But this spare, clean, round-the-clock restaurant is unusual because it specializes in the country dishes of southern Korea. Typical Korean dishes, like scallion and seafood pancakes, fiery stir-fried baby octopus and bibimbab, are all excellent. Meals here are served family style and include several little appetizers; almost all dishes are served with rice, a welcome balm to the spicier fare, and crocks of the rich beef soup, which is full of noodles and scallions but needs a shot of salt.

Other recommended dishes: Binde duk; jaeyuk bokum; bul go ki; nakji bokum; gobdol bibambab. **Alcohol:** Beer and wine. **Price range:** Apps., $5.95–$9.95; entrees, $6.95–$15.95. **Wheelchair access:** Everything is on one level. **Features:** Smoking permitted. **Services:** Delivery, takeout.

Hangawi ☆☆ $$$ KOREAN/VEGETARIAN

12 E. 32nd St. (bet. Fifth & Madison Aves.)   (212) 213-0077
Credit cards: All major   Meals: L, D

Eating in this calm, elegant space with its smooth wooden
bowls and heavy ceramic cups is utterly peaceful. Diners
remove their shoes on entering and sit at low tables with their
feet dangling comfortably into the sunken space beneath them.
They are surrounded by unearthly Korean music, wonderful
objects and people who move with deliberate grace. Even people accustomed to eating on the far side of food may find these
greens, porridges and mountain roots exotic. Much of the menu
can be sampled by ordering the emperor's meal, which includes
a tray of nine kinds of mountain greens surrounded by 10 side
dishes: water kimchi, cold spinach, sweet lotus root with
sesame, chili cabbage and the like. (*Ruth Reichl*)

Price range: Apps., $5.95–$10.95; entrees, $14.95–$24.95;
desserts, $3.50–$5.95; prix-fixe dinners, $29.95 and $34.95. **Features:** Romantic. **Wheelchair access:** Dining room and
restrooms are a few steps up; see details above for seating. **Services:** Private parties.

Harry Cipriani $$$$ ITALIAN

Sherry Netherland Hotel, 781 Fifth Ave. (bet. 59th & 60th Sts.)
   (212) 753-5566
Credit cards: All major   Meals: B, Br, L, D

If any institution is emblematic of Americans' love affair with
all things Italian, it is Harry Cipriani, that rakish and cosmopoli-
tan restaurant in the Sherry Netherland modeled after the
famous Harry's Bar in Venice. Low ceilings, lots of smoke and
absurdly high prices. Still, if they know you well enough to hold
the attitude, you could convince yourself that this is Venice. The
small menu changes daily.

Price range: Apps., $12–$27; entrees, $24–$38; desserts,
$10–$12. **Alcohol:** Beer and wine. **Wheelchair access:** Fully
accessible. **Services:** Takeout, catering, private parties.

Harry's at Hanover Square $$$ CONTINENTAL

1 Hanover Sq. (bet. Stone & Pearl Sts.)   (212) 425-3412
Credit cards: All major   Meals: L, D   Closed Sat., Sun.

This restaurant and saloon, long a landmark for Wall Street
workers, is fittingly housed in the landmark India House, which
was built in 1851. Harry's menu, with dishes like steak Diane,
fillet of sole amandine and shrimp fra diavolo, might variously
be described as classic, traditional or old-fashioned. There's
nothing frumpy about Harry's wine cellar, though, which is one
of the best in New York City and is known for having the lowest

prices for expensive wines. The restaurant's owners recently announced their intention of making this a steakhouse.

Other recommended dishes: Baked clams oreganato; smoked trout; marinated herring; gazpacho; fresh Dover sole; calf's liver with bacon; veal piccata or scaloppine; crème caramel; peach Melba. **Price range:** Lunch: apps., $4.25–$12.95; entrees, $10.50–$34.95; desserts, $3.50–$6.50. Dinner: apps., $6.75–$13.50; entrees, $11.75–$34.95; desserts, $3.75–$6.50. **Wheelchair access:** Not accessible. **Services:** Catering, delivery, takeout, private parties.

Harvest $25 & Under   AMERICAN
218 Court St., Cobble Hill, Brooklyn   (718) 624-9267
Credit cards: All major   Meals: Br, L, D, LN   Closed Mon.

A lively, appealing neighborhood restaurant that is plagued by inconsistency. Harvest feels like the best restaurant in a small college town, and the menu of American regional food like roasted beet salad, gumbo and meatloaf whets the appetite, but the execution is too often half-baked. Try the rib-eye steak, which is more like a thick slice of lean roast beef. The best desserts are the individual fruit pies from the Moondog Bakery, and brunch is the best meal of all.

Other recommended dishes: Spinach salad; shrimp salad; pancakes; meatloaf. **Alcohol:** Beer and wine. **Price range:** Apps., $3–$6; entrees, $9–$14; desserts, $4–$5. **Wheelchair access:** Step at entrance (ramp is available); restrooms are up one flight. **Features:** Outdoor dining. **Services:** Delivery, takeout, private parties.

Havana NY $25 & Under   CUBAN/LATIN AMERICAN
27 W. 38th St. (bet. Fifth & Sixth Aves.)   (212) 944-0990
Credit cards: All major   Meals: L, D   Closed Sat. & Sun.

This bustling Cuban restaurant is a lunchtime hot spot, serving tasty, inexpensive food in pleasant surroundings. Walk past the bar, past the elderly cigar smokers eating their lunches and watching the television, and you will see that Havana NY opens into a trim brick-walled dining room. The food is typically robust, flavored with lusty doses of garlic and lime, yet it can be delicate, too, as in an octopus salad, which is marinated in citrus until tender like a ceviche and served with lettuce, rice, beans and plantains. Another dish, Chilean sea bass, is moist and subtly flavored, not the sort of dish that would succeed in an assembly-line kitchen. These are a far cry from the restaurant's stock in trade, though, dishes like the excellent grilled skirt steak, served with a pungent chimichurri sauce, essentially garlic and parsley, that is delicious spread over the steak. Vaca frita is thin strips of sautéed beef in a tangy sauce of lime and bitter orange juice, with plenty of onions cooked until soft, translucent and almost sweet. Pork dishes don't quite match the beef dishes, but roast pork, falling-apart tender, is especially good when livened up with mojo, a garlic-and-citrus sauce. All the main courses are enormous, served with rice, beans and sweet plantains — so appetizers are usually unnecessary. Service is swift and likable. In fact, there's little not to like about Havana NY.

Other recommended dishes: Masitas de cerdo; fried yucca fingers; beef empanadas. **Price range:** Apps., $2.50–$6.95; entrees, $8.95–$12.95. **Wheelchair access:** Step at entrance; steps to dining room and restrooms. **Features:** Smoking. **Services:** Delivery, takeout.

Haveli $ INDIAN
100 Second Ave. (bet. 5th & 6th Sts.)   (212) 982-0533
Credit cards: All major   Meals: L, D, LN

This Indian restaurant, around the block from the endless stretch of them on East 6th Street, is more expensive than its counterparts, but it's better, though not as good as its outsize reputation would have it. The menu spans the realm of Indian vegetarian and grilled specialties.

Price range: Lunch entrees, $3.25–$9.25. Dinner: entrees, $7.25–$23.50; desserts, $2.75–$5.50. **Wheelchair access:** Fully accessible. **Services:** Catering, delivery, takeout, private parties.

Heartbeat ☆☆ $$ NEW AMERICAN
149 E. 49th St. (at Lexington Ave.)   (212) 407-2900
Credit cards: All major   Meals: B, Br, L, D

New York's hippest spa food brings models to mingle with moguls in a slick setting. You could describe Heartbeat that way, but it would be doing the restaurant a disservice; this is a very comfortable, crowded and surprisingly quiet room with good service and good food. This approach works best when the food is simply left alone, like mackerel ceviche with a lemon-chervil sauce, or whole roasted quail with a mushroom-and-fig hash. Try the simple grills, the good meats and the Japanese-accented dishes. Be prepared for the tea sommelier to show up at the end of the meal. (*Ruth Reichl*)

Other recommended dishes: Sliced raw tuna with radish salad; chilled oysters with caviar; fillet of natural beef tenderloin; roasted baby chicken with pear; chocolate dome; bowls of berries; pineapple with passion fruit mousse. **Wine list:** Interesting and fairly priced. **Price range:** Lunch: apps., $8–$14; entrees, $16–$26. Dinner: apps., $9–$14; entrees, $18–$30; desserts, $8–$10. **Wheelchair access:** Dining room is up a few steps, but there is an elevator.

170

Hell's Kitchen
$25 & Under   MEXICAN

679 Ninth Ave. (near 47th St.)   (212) 977-1588
Credit cards: All major   Meals: D, LN

For almost three years, Sue Torres was the chef at Rocking Horse Cafe Mexicano in Chelsea, a showcase for the possibilities of Mexican food beyond the tyranny of nachos, burritos and refried beans. If you're interested in what Ms. Torres can do when she's inspired, head directly for the interpretations of Mexican dishes. Her appetizer of tuna tostadas is brilliant. In another appetizer, shreds of rich duck confit are encased in a flaky corn pastry, creating little empanadas that go beautifully with a sweet mole sauce made with figs.

Ms. Torres devotes part of her menu to quesadillas, house-made flour tortillas layered with cheese and other fillings. In size, they are like small main courses; in spirit, they succeed because they retain their clear Mexican identity even with creative enhancements. The great potential shown in her appetizers and quesadillas unfortunately fades with the main courses. The best is a pork loin flavored with chili and set over steamed corn and pineapple. After the main courses, desserts rebound to another high. Sorbets are wonderfully intense and served over fruit with a surprising touch of chili. Other good choices include a fabulous coconut flan.

In atmosphere, Hell's Kitchen is international, with music that is more Cuban than Mexican. There is a small wine list, with some good choices. Incidentally, the loud music and hopping bar suggest that conversations will be difficult, but the acoustics are surprisingly good.

Other recommended dishes: Chayote and portobello roll; fried calamari; sirloin steak; banana empanada; artichoke and mushroom quesadilla; cold peach soup; chocolate terrine. **Price range:** Apps., $6–$8; entrees, $13–$18. **Wheelchair access:** One step up at entrance.

Henry's Evergreen
$25 & Under   CHINESE

1288 First Ave. (near 70th St.)   (212) 744-3266
Credit cards: All major   Meals: L, D

This bright and appealing restaurant follows the decorating scheme of many other Chinese restaurants, but a glance beyond the tanks of fish and the gleaming bar reveals something else: polished wood wine racks stuffed with bottles. The biggest part of the surprising wine list is devoted to California reds, and includes some midlevel zinfandels and pinot noirs as well as some whites that go brilliantly with the food. Many of the dishes are fresh and appealing. The real excitement, though, is discovering how good the wine and food combinations can be.

For example, Tria zinfandel goes beautifully with pan-seared turnip cakes, crisp on the outside with a custardy consistency within, or tender steamed cilantro-and-shrimp dumplings. A superb, steely Alsatian riesling, Trimbach Cuvée Frédéric Émile has enough depth to go with sautéed meat dumplings, which are savory but not spicy as billed, or with the rich shredded duck salad accented with cilantro. It is perfect with sautéed shrimp cakes flavored with chives, with mussels steamed in a ginger-flavored broth and, of course, with lean roasted pork loin tasting mildly of anise. Dim sum and appetizers tend to be the best part of Henry's menu; main courses are much less consistent. Shredded chicken in oyster sauce with vegetables is a plain but satisfying dish, as is lean chicken breast cooked in a clay pot. Both were excellent matches with a Sanford pinot noir, a good value at $49.

Other recommended dishes: Cold sesame noodles, steamed Asian flatfish, white scallops in XO sauce. **Price range:** Apps., $3.20–$10.50; entrees, $7.95–$27.50. **Wheelchair access:** One step at entrance, ramp available; restrooms downstairs or patrons may use ground-floor restroom of McDonald's next door.

Herban Kitchen $25 & Under HEALTH FOOD
290 Hudson St. (near Spring St.) (212) 627-2257
Credit cards: All major Meals: L, D, LN

Herban is representative of a new generation of hedonistic health-food restaurants where good organic ingredients are made even better in the kitchen. Most people would be happy to make a meal of appetizers here, starting with the basket of country bread that comes with a tasty mushroom-lentil spread. A main course called un-fried free-range chicken is a complete surprise: it is baked and has the crusty, savory quality of fried chicken, while remaining moist and tender. Aside from a salmon burger on a whole-wheat bun, fish dishes are less successful. Check out the list of organic wines and beers.

Other recommended dishes: Fish cakes; red pepper soup; hummus; green salad; barbecued chicken. **Alcohol:** Beer and wine. **Price range:** Apps., $5–$8; entrees, $11–$18; desserts, $6.50. **Wheelchair access:** Small step in front; everything else on one level. **Features:** Outdoor dining. **Services:** Delivery, takeout, catering, private parties.

Hog Pit $25 & Under SOUTHERN
22 Ninth Ave. (at 13th St.) (212) 604-0092
Credit cards: All major Meals: D, LN Closed Mon.

Nothing remarkable about this small bar in the meatpacking district, except that the kitchen unexpectedly turns out fine Southern food. The baby back ribs are terrific: meaty, tender enough to fall off the bone and bathed in a peppery sauce sweetened by molasses and brown sugar. Hush puppies are the real thing: cornmeal blended with garlic, celery and onion, and deep-fried until crisp, and the tart fried green tomatoes come with a crisp, greaseless cornmeal crust. The staff is friendly, the jukebox is loud, the room is smoky and the beer is cold.

Other recommended dishes: Fried chicken; meatloaf; coconut pie; banana pudding. **Price range:** Apps., $4–$5.95; entrees, $6.25–$12.95. **Wheelchair access:** Everything is on one level; restrooms are narrow.

Holy Basil $25 & Under THAI

149 Second Ave. (bet. 9th & 10th Sts.)   (212) 460-5557
Credit cards: All major   Meals: D, LN

This is one of the best Thai restaurants in the city, turning out highly spiced, beautifully balanced dishes like green papaya salad, elegant curries and delicious noodles. The dining room looks more like a beautiful church than a restaurant, jazz usually plays in the background and the wine list offers terrific choices.

Other recommended dishes: Yum pla muok (cool but spicy squid salad); chicken laab; green papaya. **Price range:** Dinner: apps., $4–$7.50; entrees, $8–$16; desserts, $4–$8. **Wheelchair access:** Not accessible. **Features:** Romantic, smoking permitted. **Services:** Delivery, takeout, catering.

Honmura An ☆☆☆ $$$ JAPANESE/NOODLES

170 Mercer St. (bet. Houston & Prince Sts.)   (212) 334-5253
Credit cards: All major   Meals L, D   Closed Mon.

The buckwheat noodles known as soba have been eaten in Japan for 400 years. But making soba is not easy. The Japanese say it takes a year to learn to mix the dough, another year to learn to roll it, a third to learn the correct cut. The soba chefs at Honmura An have clearly put in their time — the soba here is wonderful and worth their high price. Knowing this can put you in the proper spirit. The spare, soothing space will certainly put you in the mood. Warm towels and the perfect drink, cold sake in a cedar box with salt along the edge, will help you wipe away the outside world.

Many dishes are worth trying here, but nothing is remotely on a par with the noodles. To appreciate how fine they are, you must eat them cold. Seiro soba come on a square lacquered tray arrayed across a bamboo mat. On the side is a bowl of dashi, a mellow, rich, slightly smoky and incredibly delicious dipping sauce. Next to it are condiments to mix into the dashi according to your own taste. Pick some soba off the mat with your chopsticks, dip them into the dashi, and inhale them as noisily as possible (slurping is de rigueur). The noodles are earthy and elastic, and when you dip them into the briny bowl of dashi land and sea come, briefly, together. Soba also comes with various toppings: seaweed, mushrooms, even giant fried prawns. And you can get them hot, the noodles submerged in a bowl of soup with chicken, seafood or greens floating on top. In kamonan, the strands of soba luxuriate in an intensely fragrant duck stock, with slices of duck covering the top of the bowl. Honmura An also makes excellent udon — the fat wheat noodles. Served cold with a sesame dipping sauce, they snap when you bite into them. Served hot, in the dish called nabeyaki (a staple of cheap noodle shops), they virtually redefine the dish.

On a recent visit, Honmura An seemed secure in its position as one of the most fascinating and distinctive Japanese restaurants in the city, with tantalizing appetizers like slices of smoked duck breast with a rich border of fat; cold pressed whitefish, with the texture of a thick pasta; and giant shrimp flown in from the Tokyo fish market and turned into tempura. (*Ruth Reichl, updated by William Grimes*)

Other recommended dishes: Marinated wild greens with seaweed; Japanese green summer soybeans; seaweed salad; prawns rolled with soba, shiso and nori; giant prawn tempura. **Wine list:** Try the cold sake. **Price range:** Lunch: apps. $6–$18; entrees, $10–$18; desserts, $6. Dinner: apps., $8–$20; entrees, $13–$22; desserts, $6–$8. **Wheelchair access:** Dining room is up a full flight of stairs. **Services:** Private parties.

Hoomoos Asli $25 & Under   MIDDLE EASTERN

100 Kenmare St. (at Lafayette St.)   (212) 966-0022
Credit cards: Cash only   Meals: B, L, D, LN

There is nightly chaos at Hoomoos Asli, which diners are willing to endure, even enjoy, because of the owner's sparkling Israeli dishes and good cheer. "Please don't pronounce it humm-us," the menu says. The "hoomoos" it calls asli is a Turkish word meaning "the real thing," and it is wonderful, simply a smooth chickpea purée with a lemony tang and a deep flavor, served with fresh puffy pita bread.

The menu offers much more, including a selection of extremely fresh salads. Among the other dishes, try the mallawach, a Yemenite Jewish dish of flaky flatbread pan-fried until crisp on the bottom and topped with feta cheese, black olives, olive oil and zatar, a fragrant Middle Eastern spice.

Other recommended dishes: Baba ghanoouj; tabbouleh; carrot salad; Israeli salad. **Price range:** Apps., salads and hummus, $3.50–$6.50; entrees, $8–$17. **Wheelchair access:** Ramp at entrance; dining room and restroom on one level.

Hourglass Tavern $$ NEW AMERICAN

373 W. 46th St. (bet. Eighth & Ninth Aves.)   (212) 265-2060
Credit cards: All major   Meals: L, D

A tiny and unsung little place on Restaurant Row in the theater
district. The food isn't fabulous, but it's not expensive either,
and it is very pleasant when the theater crowd finally files out.
Dinner specials include soup or salad, and feature simple dishes
like grilled tuna, rib-eye steak, pork loin and crab cakes, all
served with mashed potatoes. Not in the mood for potatoes? Try
the seafood pasta.

Price range: Lunch: entrees, $8–$10; desserts, $4.50–$5.50.
Dinner: entrees, $12.75–$14.75; desserts, $4.50–$5.50. **Wheelchair access:** Not accessible. **Features:** Outdoor dining. **Services:** Private parties.

Hudson Cafeteria (Poor) $$$ FUSION

356 W. 58th St.   (212) 554-6500
Credit cards: All major   Meals: B, L, D, LN

Hudson Cafeteria has the mesmerizing power of a Superman
villain. A certain segment of New York's population simply cannot stay away. Perhaps there's something in the cosmopolitans
that the bar sends out by the thousands every night. Neither
long lines nor inadequate food can keep people away from the
place. Its stripped brick walls suggest a mini-storage vault.
Long rough-hewn wood tables, benches and episcopal chairs
create, quite convincingly, the feeling that you are eating in a
refectory. The center of the dining room is dominated by a large
open kitchen topped by a decorative frieze that shows sketchily
rendered human heads consumed by flames. The chefs end up
looking like demons stoking the fires of hell. The food makes
you think you've arrived there.

Very simple dishes in the menu's comfort-food section afford
some relief. Pot pie filled with chicken, morels and pungent bits
of smoked bacon and pearl onions really does fulfill its man-
date. Beef stew made with short ribs braised in red wine holds
its head high. It's everything beef stew can aspire to, which
isn't much, but under the circumstances, it seems like a lot.
Desserts aim straight for the big, fat American comfort zone but
somehow drift off course. The best of the bunch is a tall apple
pie with a shockingly direct, flaky crust.

Other recommended dishes: Turkey-mushroom meatloaf,
banana cream pie. **Wine list:** A lowest-common-denominator
list of 40 very modestly priced wines. **Price range:** Apps.,
$7.50–$14.50; entrees, $7.50–$30; desserts, $4.50–$7. **Wheelchair access:** Restrooms are on dining level.

Hudson River Club ☆☆ $$$$ NEW AMERICAN

250 Vesey St., 4 World Financial Center
Credit cards: All major

(212) 786-1500
Meals: Br, L, D

Note: This neighborhood suffered substantial damage during the September 11, 2001 plane crashes that destroyed the World Trade Center. This restaurant may not be operational by the time you plan your visit.

This very sedate, very expensive restaurant has upscale American food, a dazzling view of the river, a largely male clientele and a great bar. Despite its spectacular setting, Hudson River Club is not a romantic restaurant. Everything about the place, from its no-nonsense name to its large tables, comfortable seats and solicitous service, makes it a perfect place for a business meeting. It is also one of the few waterfront restaurants in which seafood is not the main draw. The kitchen makes some of the most delicious hearty stews you'll find in a New York restaurant. Try the braised rabbit pot pie or one of the dishes from the game menu. If you've never tasted grouse, this is the place to indulge. To end the meal with a laugh, try the cheesecake. Out comes a large porcelain teacup with a spoon and a tea bag on the side. The cup is white chocolate filled with cheesecake, the spoon is a cookie and the tea bag is made of phyllo. (*Ruth Reichl*)

Other recommended dishes: Lemon meringue pie; sorbets; Hudson Valley cheeses. **Wine list:** There are excellent wines, including hard-to-find regional American labels, but few bargains, and wine by the glass is very expensive. The beer list is impressive. **Price range:** Lunch: apps., $11–$16, entrees, $24–$30; desserts, $8–$12. Dinner: apps., $13–$20; entrees, $29–$36; desserts, $9–$12. **Wheelchair access:** The restaurant can be reached by elevator and all the restrooms are accessible. **Features:** Good view, good for business, smoking permitted. **Services:** Catering, private parties.

Icon ☆☆ $$ NEW AMERICAN

W Court Hotel, 130 E. 39th St. (bet. Lexington & Park Aves.)
(212) 592-8888

Credit cards: All major

Meals: B, Br, L, D

Icon is swanky, slinky, murky. Located in the W Court Hotel, it has a mildly lurid décor and a lighting philosophy perfectly designed for illegal trysts and furtive meetings. It comes with a boutique hotel attached, ensuring a steady flow of youngish, stylish diners. Once your eyes adjust to the gloom, they behold a pleasing sight. Icon has a rich, indulgent feel, with its red-velvet chairs and banquettes, its steely gray ceiling and its fat pillars. Visually, it is soothing to the nerves. Aurally, it's touch and go. As the evening progresses, a thumping rock soundtrack forces diners to shout across the table, and the whoops of gaiety from Wet Bar across the lobby become intrusive.

The food at Icon is better than the setting might suggest. Paul Sale, the executive chef, lets his ingredients do a lot of the work, and he changes the menu frequently to take advantage of seasonal produce. There's no trickery at all in his warm Fishers Island oysters, for example. They're served on the half shell, swathed in a luxurious saffron cream, with crisp strands of leek for textural contrast, and they are sublime. Braised oxtail, presented in a fat, round slice, was tender and deeply flavored. Seared foie gras in a hard-cider reduction was another winner. Desserts are not flashy; quiet good taste is more the style. Litchi mousse, a satiny yellow-orange disk on a dense pastry foundation, glows on the plate, garnished simply with a tropical fruit compote and a single crisp of phyllo dough.

Other recommended dishes: Arctic char with savoy cabbage and smoked salmon bacon; stuffed chicken with herb risotto; apple tart. **Price range:** Lunch: apps., $7–$10; entrees, $16–$21; desserts, $7. Dinner: apps., $7–$12; entrees, $19–$25; desserts, $8. **Wheelchair access:** Alternate entrance to restaurant down corridor to restrooms. **Features:** Good for business, smoking at bar.

I Coppi ☆☆ $$ ITALIAN

432 E. 9th St. (bet. First Ave. & Ave. A)   (212) 254-2263
Credit cards: All major   Meals: Br, D   Italian

This is an attractively rustic, family-run Italian trattoria with an open kitchen in the rear and a very knowledgeable staff. The room is warm and wonderful, the wine list is excellent and the food is good. Among the best appetizers are a Swiss chard and ricotta flan served with mixed greens. The best main courses are a revelation, robust but subtly different from other Italian menus around town. Try the lemony veal stew served with sautéed Swiss chard. Thin-crust pizzas are also very good, and desserts include an intensely rich chocolate almond cake served with thick whipped cream. (*Ruth Reichl*)

Other recommended dishes: Soft polenta with mushrooms and ground pork; grilled striped bass; homemade ravioli with herbs; stewed rabbit; panna cotta. **Wine list:** Excellent Tuscan list. **Price range:** Apps., $5–$12.50; pastas, $14–$18; pizzas, $10–$16; entrees, $15–$25; desserts, $6–$8. **Wheelchair access:** Staircase down to restrooms. **Features:** Outdoor dining (garden). **Services:** Private parties.

Il Bagatto $$ ITALIANᴵᵀᴬᴸᴵᴬᴺ

192 E. 2nd St. (bet. Aves. A & B)   (212) 228-0977
Credit cards: Cash only   Meals: D   Closed Mon.

Limousines and town cars aren't usually found idling outside
restaurants in the East Village, but fresh ingredients, simply prepared, have made this casual trattoria incredibly popular. Bottom line: the food is good, though over-hyped, but the low
prices make Il Bagatto an exceptional value if you don't mind
loud music, cigarette smoke and claustrophobic seating.

Price range: Apps., $4–$8; entrees, $8–$16; desserts, $5–$6.
Wheelchair access: With assistance. **Features:** Smoking permitted. **Services:** Takeout, catering, delivery.

Il Buco ☆ $$ MEDITERRANEAN

47 Bond St. (bet. Bowery & Lafayette St.)   (212) 533-1932
Credit cards: AE   Meals: L, D, LN

The room is dark, lighted by candles and filled with odd
antiques for sale; it could easily be a set for a 50's movie about
the Bohemian life. The food, which is more Mediterranean than
Italian, certainly fosters the illusion. Start with baby calamari,
sweet, tender and served with a fine fresh salsa. Go on to
seared tuna served with enormous white corona beans. Grilled
baby lamb chops are wonderful, too, sweet tiny little chops,
each no more than a couple of bites. Desserts are quite simple;
especially the dense, dry, orange pound cake. (*Ruth Reichl*)

Other recommended dishes: Marinated anchovies and pep-
pers; Serrano ham with melon; saffron risotto cakes with
sautéed wild mushrooms; gambas; orange cake; apple cake.
Wine list: The wine cellar was the inspiration for "The Cask of
Amontillado" by Poe. The list is short on chardonnay and
cabernet and long on good and unusual wines at fair prices.
Price range: Apps., $5–$22; entrees, $16–$28; desserts, $7.
Wheelchair access: Everything at street level. **Features:**
Romantic, smoking permitted. **Services:** Private parties.

Il Covo dell'Est $$ ITALIAN

210 Ave. A (near 13th St.)   (212) 253-0777
Credit cards: All major   Meals: L, D

The menu is Tuscan, and the atmosphere is uncompromisingly
Italian. Within 30 seconds of sitting down, a friendly arm is
draped around your shoulder and a booming voice is reciting
what seems like the longest list of specials ever assembled at
one restaurant. They can distract and detract from the very
attractive main menu, which stays regional without lapsing into
cliché. The restaurant (whose name the owner translates as
"the Hangout") serves Florentine gnudi — sticky balls of

spinach and ricotta — with a classic butter and sage sauce. The rest of the pasta list does what Italy does best, combining dough in a thousand formats with ingredients whose freshness jumps off the plate. Try the tagliatelli topped with a robust, concentrated meat sauce contributed by the chef's grandmother. Braised rabbit with olives and tomatoes stands out among the meat entrees, although it has a rival in a centuries-old dish called peposo alla fiorentina: boneless beef shank cooked very slowly with red wine, black pepper and sauted spinach.

Other recommended dishes: Shrimp croquettes; tagliolini with shrimp and asparagus; Livornese fish stew. **Wine list:** All Italian, several by the glass: $6–$15. **Price range:** Lunch: prix-fixe, $12.95. Dinner: apps $6.95–$8.95; entrees, $12.95–$19.95. **Wheelchair access:** Fully accessible. **Features:** Smoking at bar. **Services:** Delivery, takeout, catering, private parties.

Il Giglio ☆ $$$ ITALIAN
81 Warren St. (near Greenwich St.)   (212) 571-5555
Credit cards: All major   Meals: L, D   Closed Sun.

Small and nondescript, Il Giglio is notable for excess: there is too much food on the table and too many people in the room. With a wave of his hand, your waiter will cover the table with small offerings; he may also produce baskets of warm garlic bread. Every meal is a piece of theater, but the food can be disappointing. The best pastas are a deliciously simple spaghettini carbonara and some achingly rich mushroom and truffle ravioli adrift in an ocean of cream. The rack of lamb is a good dish, eight tiny, tasty chops arranged like the spokes of a wheel around a centerpiece of potatoes. Order fruit for dessert, and the waiter will carve oranges and strawberries to make them look like flowers. (*Ruth Reichl*)

Other recommended dishes: Prosciutto with melon; clams oreganato; salad of endive, arugula and radicchio; veal chop. **Wine list:** Small, unimaginative and expensive. **Price range:** Apps., $7–$14; entrees, $17–$40; desserts, $8–$12. **Wheelchair access:** Everything at street level.

Il Mulino $$$$ ITALIAN
86 W. 3rd St. (bet. Sullivan & Thompson Sts.)   (212) 673-3783
Credit cards: All major   Meals: L, D, LN   Closed Sun.

Big portions, long waits, a halcyon atmosphere. No wonder New Yorkers are so enthralled with this garlic haven. While the portions are large, so are the prices. Dinner might begin with a dish of shrimp fricassee with garlic; bresaola of beef served over mixed greens tossed in a well-seasoned vinaigrette, or aromatic baked clams oreganato. The pasta roster includes fettuccine Alfredo; spaghettini in a robust Bolognese sauce; trenette tossed in pesto sauce; and capellini all'arrabbiata, or in a spicy tomato sauce. The menu carries a dozen veal preparations, along with beef tenderloin in a shallot, white wine and sage sauce and broiled sirloin.

Price range: Apps., from $14.75; entrees, from $24; desserts, $12. **Wheelchair access:** One step up to dining room; difficult access to restrooms. **Services:** Takeout.

Ilo ☆☆☆ $$$$ NEW AMERICAN
Bryant Park Hotel, 40 W. 40th St. (bet. Fifth & Sixth Aves.)
(212) 642-2255
Credit cards: All major   Meals: L, D

At Ilo, a Finnish word meaning something like "bliss," Chef Rick Laakkonen creates complex dishes that seem simple. He knows how to coax pure flavors from his ingredients, and how to keep those flavors clear and distinct. Major ingredients bask in the spotlight. Grilled quail, as meaty and tender as any in recent memory, stand out heroically from their busy tableau, where a feather-light cheese flan is surrounded by spicy minced peppers, chilies, coriander and lime.

Ilo's rabbit shows that a dish can be rustic and rarefied at the same time. The rabbit is done country style, pan-roasted with olives and accented with oregano and preserved lemon. The slick addition here is cannelloni stuffed with sheep's milk ricotta that's flecked with bits of bitter dandelion. Every ingredient in the dish is as humble as a wooden shoe. The orchestration makes it perfectly at home on a white tablecloth. Tasting menu portions are mercifully calibrated to a normal appetite.

Chilled apricot soup is a regular on the dessert menu. It is a blazing slick of yellow, punctuated by a bright red stack of cherry sorbet disks topped with an orange tuile. A multipart citrus showcase, intended for two diners, that includes blood-orange granité, warm orange cake, lemon layer cake and vanilla-lime parfait. The components, taken individually, score high on the pleasure scale. Ilo's cheese cart is a serious, well-organized but not overwhelming affair with some unusual, even quirky cheeses. Sommelier Kim Anderson presents the wine list in an unusually informative and ingratiating way. It's worth waving her over, because the 250 or so wines on the list include many unusual grapes and lesser known regions.

Other recommended dishes: Artichoke soup with mushrooms, "tidal pool" seafood in broth, scallops with artichokes and chickpea pappardelle, beef tasting menu (tongue and oxtail terrine, tripe stew with chipolata, roast marrow bone, grilled ribeye). **Wine list:** An appealing, well-thought-out international list of about 250 wines, with attention paid to up-and-coming regions and varietals. **Price range:** Lunch: apps., $8–$16; entrees $19–$29; desserts $10–$22 (for two). Dinner: apps., $10–$18; entrees $26–$38; desserts $9–$22 (for two); beef tasting menu, $85 ($120 with wines); seven-course vegetarian tasting menu, $65; eight-course chef's tasting menu, $110 ($165 with wines). **Wheelchair access:** Six steps up from lounge to dining room; there is an elevator to the right of the staircase. Restrooms are down one flight, or by the lobby elevator.

Il Postino $$$$ ITALIAN

337 E. 49th St. (bet. First & Second Aves.)   (212) 688-0033
Credit cards: All major   Meals: L, D

One of those restaurants where the list of specials is four times as big as the menu. And four times as expensive. Although it's not worth the money, the northern Italian food is good.

Price range: Entrees, $19–29; daily specials, $35–$40. **Wheelchair access:** Restrooms not accessible. **Features:** Smoking permitted. **Services:** Delivery, private parties.

Il Posto Accanto $25 & Under ITALIAN/SANDWICHES

190 E. 2nd St. (near Ave. B)   (212) 228-3562
Credit cards: MC/V   Meals: D, LN   Closed Mon.

This dim, intriguing Italian sandwich and wine bar, next door to its parent, the popular though charmless trattoria Il Bagatto, has the effortless appeal of a crooked grin, a rumpled sweater and a dangling cigarette. The wine list is especially inviting, where varietals from all parts of Italy can be served in carafes containing the equivalent of a half- or quarter-bottle. Sandwiches are made to order, slowly and carefully. The best include the Boncompagni, combining the brisk bite of bresaola with the richness of goat cheese, the pungency of arugula and the warmth of truffle oil. The sandwich menu is supplemented with simple but delicious dishes like spinach sautéed in olive oil with pine nuts, an ideal combination of flavor and texture.

Other recommended dishes: Medaglione (prosciutto and mozzarella), frisee salad with duck and cracklings. **Price range:** Sandwiches, $6–$11. **Wheelchair access:** Restrooms not accessible.

Il Valentino ☆☆ $$ ITALIAN

Sutton Hotel, 330 E. 56th St. (near First Ave.)   (212) 355-0001
Credit cards: All major   Meals: L, D

In a city where purely pleasant restaurants have become increasingly rare, Il Valentino feels like an oasis. It is neither a small, cramped space nor one of those noisy new factories. The timbered ceiling and terra-cotta floor give the room a cool rustic feeling. But the restaurant's appeal is mostly due to its admirably limited ambitions. Il Valentino wants to feed you well, but it does not seem set on becoming a big-deal multi-star establishment. Il Valentino serves simple, tasty Tuscan fare. The artichoke salad is delicious, and the Caesar salad is impressive. But it is the pastas that really shine. Try the handmade garganelli, little quills tossed in a classic white veal, prosciutto and mortadellaragu. Main courses tend to be straightforward. Marinated grilled lamb chops in a mustard seed sauce and osso buco are excellent. But you don't go to Il Valentino for the best meal of your life. You go because the food is reliable, you don't have to wait for your table and you know you will be able to hear your friends when they talk. (*Ruth Reichl*)

Other recommended dishes: Vegetable antipasto; fried calamari and zucchini; spaghetti with seafood; risotto; ricotta cheesecake. **Wine list:** Small and mostly fairly priced. **Price range:** Lunch: apps., $5.50–$8; entrees, $10.50–$20; desserts, $5–$7. Dinner: apps., $6–$9.50; entrees, $16–$25; desserts, $6–$9. **Wheelchair access:** Through the Sutton Hotel lobby, which is at street level; dining room is on one level. **Features:** Smoking permitted. **Services:** Takeout, catering, private parties.

Inagiku ☆☆ $$$ JAPANESE/SUSHI

Waldorf = Astoria Hotel, 111 E. 49th St.
(bet. Lexington & Park Aves.) (212) 355-0440
Credit cards: All major Meals: L, D

Most nights you see two distinct groups of people eating at Inagiku: tourists and Japanese businessmen. While Inagiku could hardly be called a meat-and-potatoes restaurant, the menu is full of unfrightening dishes intended for the first group: excellent tempura, grilled chicken on skewers, fish broiled in teriyaki sauce and a whole range of interactive dishes that are fun to cook at the table. The Japanese businessmen choose completely different dishes. Waitresses bring a seemingly endless parade of small, beautifully arranged "classic little dishes." Eating in this fashion is light and appealing. It is also very expensive. The black cod marinated in sake lees and grilled is the richest, most irresistible morsel of fish I can imagine. Other appealing small tastes include grilled maitake mushroom, whole sea eel in tempura and excellent chawanmushi, steamed shrimp and ginkgo nuts buried in a silken egg custard. (*Ruth Reichl*)

Other recommended dishes: Sashimi extravaganza; tempura; salad of greens and creamy "tofucheese;" chicken teriyaki; grilled tuna steak; steak ishiyaki; shabu shabu; tuna with grated yam; mozuku; hiyashi bachi; whole anago tempura; green tea ice cream; Japanese sweets. **Wine list:** Good selection of wines and sakes by the glass; prices are high. **Price range:** Apps., $6–$20; entrees, $20–$29; desserts, $7. Tasting dinners at $58, $70 and $90. **Wheelchair access:** Dining room at street level; separate restroom available on same level. **Features:** Smoking permitted. **Services:** Takeout, catering, private parties.

'ino $25 & Under   ITALIAN/SANDWICHES

21 Bedford St. (bet. Sixth Ave. & Downing St.)   (212) 989-5769
Credit cards: Cash only   Meals: B, Br, L, D

Armed with only an Italian sandwich press and a small hot
plate, this inviting little Italian sandwich shop and wine bar
offers intensely satisfying variations on the sandwich theme.
The menu is divided into three parts: panini, sandwiches made
with crusty toasted ciabatta; tramezzini, made with untoasted
white bread, crusts removed and cut into triangles, and
bruschetta, in which ingredients are simply placed atop a slice
of toasted bread. One dish that doesn't fall into any category
but is nonetheless wonderful is truffled egg toast, a soft cooked
egg served on top of toasted ciabatta with sliced asparagus and
drizzled with truffle oil. It's like warm, delicious baby food.

Alcohol: Beer and wine. **Price range:** Apps., $2–$10; entrees,
$2–$10; desserts, $5. **Wheelchair access:** Fully accessible. **Features:** Romantic, smoking permitted. **Services:** Takeout, private
parties.

Inside $25 & Under   NEW AMERICAN

9 Jones St. (bet. 4th & Bleecker Sts.)   (212) 229-9999
Credit cards: All major   Meals: Br, D

Inside has the stripped-down appearance and the simplified
approach of a place ready for leaner economic times. The handsome wood bar in front and the professional greeting bespeak
the comfort of a more expensive restaurant, yet the almost bare
white walls make the dining room feel airy and streamlined.
Wicker chairs are comfortable but informal. The menu, which
changes weekly, is confined to a single sheet of yellow paper.

With dishes based on no more than three seasonal and simple ingredients, Inside can keep prices gentle. The best appetizer is a handful of shrimp with a light, crisp salt-and-pepper
crust, topped with a tangy grapefruit confit. Main courses are
similarly streamlined. Newport steak is thick and beefy. Tender
braised lamb with cinnamon and olives achieves an almost
Moroccan balance of savory and sweet.

The wine list is well selected, though more choices in the
$25 range would be appreciated. Desserts are similarly up and
down. Try the panna cotta, whether flavored with vanilla and
mango or strawberry, and a steamed chocolate pudding with
rhubarb.

Other recommended dishes: Portobello mushroom salad, beets
and endive salad, broccoli rape, creamed spinach, trout with
Jerusalem artichokes and dill, calf's liver, roast chicken, roast
cod. **Price range:** Apps., $6–$9; entrees, $13–$18. **Wheelchair
access:** All on one level; restroom entrances are narrow.

Ipanema $25 & Under LATIN AMERICAN

13 W. 46th St. (bet. Fifth & Sixth Aves.)   (212) 730-5848
Credit cards: All major   Meals: L, D

This relaxed, gracious Brazilian restaurant offers big portions of
solid fare like shrimp in garlic-and-wine sauce, and vatapa, a
silky purée of fish, shrimp and nuts. Caldo verde, an intense,
smoky soup with strips of kale and potato and slices of Portuguese sausage, is a delicious and warming appetizer. Feijoada,
the national dish of Brazil, is both an impressive presentation
and an unmanageable portion: an iron platter full of a rich
black bean stew and various types of smoked pork and sausage,
a bowl of rice, a dish of orange slices, a plate of crunchy cassava blended with egg and a portion of collard greens. Desserts
are as robust as the rest of the fare, not exactly a light close.
The décor has a certain midtown stiffness, but the owner and
host makes Ipanema a lighthearted pleasure.

Other recommended dishes: Linguica frita; hearts of palm
salad; broiled halibut; churrasco misto. **Price range:** Apps.,
$1.50–$8.75; salads, $5.95–$7.95; entrees, $14.50–$19.95;
desserts, $4. **Wheelchair access:** Everything is on one level.
Features: Smoking permitted. **Services:** Takeout, catering, private parties.

Irving on Irving $25 & Under AMERICAN

52 Irving Pl. (at 17th St.)   (212) 358-1300
Credit cards: All major   Meals: B, L, D

Flash is the last thing you'll find at this plainly-named little corner restaurant. By day, Irving offers counter service for breakfast and lunch, mostly pastries, soups, salads and sandwiches.
Tuscan bean soup is richly satisfying, hearty with bits of
sausage. Appealing salads like Asian cole slaw and nutty wild
rice with cranberries and almonds are reasonably priced. By
night, waiters and waitresses come out, and Irving on Irving
becomes a real restaurant, even though the metal serving counters still line the room. When crowded, the small room becomes
loud and clattery.

The chef has put together a menu of uncomplicated ingredients, prepared simply. Appetizers show off their humble origins,
like what the menu calls "poor man's crab cakes." These are
actually excellent codfish cakes: savory, meaty and crisp outside. While the main courses are not exactly made of humble
ingredients, they are resolutely plain, with the possible exception of the peppery grilled swordfish, which is finely textured
and full of flavor. Grilled flank steak is tender and slightly
sweet, courtesy of extended marination.

Irving has a decent though small list of wines by the glass
and beers. The best dessert is the cinnamon doughnuts, more

like small beignets, actually, made to order and served hot and airy in a brown lunch bag.

Other recommended dishes: Mini-burgers, sausages, roast chicken. **Price range:** Apps., $5.25–$12.50; entrees, $10.50–$16.75. **Wheelchair access:** Everything is on one level, but the restroom entry is narrow.

Isla $$$

CUBAN/PAN-LATIN

39 Downing St. (bet Bedford & Varick Sts.)   (212) 352-2822
Credit Cards: All major   Meals: D   Closed Sun.

The place looks like a cabana, with a sleek, blue-tiled facade and a long, louvered window facing the street. Inside, the décor blends beach, 50's kitsch and Miami modern in one highly inviting package. The place is cool. The chef is Mexican by heritage but he has created a Cuban fantasy, a freely improvised list of nuevo latino dishes like smoked chicken croquettes with chorizo and a saffron sofrito sauce, mussels in a sauce of smoked-tomatoes and sugar-cane brandy, strip steak with Madeira sauce and fried yuca, and pan-roasted bass with a salsa verde and an unusual accompaniment of scalloped potatoes layered with bacalao paste. The desserts are tropical and sweet. The killer is natilla con basitos: layers of butterscotch custard and gingerbread topped with meringue kisses.

Other recommended dishes: Café con leche flan; Tarte tatin with caramelized pineapple and coconut ice cream. **Wine list:** Focuses on Spain and South America. Several wines by the glass for $12. **Price range:** Apps. $14–$16; entrees, $18–$26. **Wheelchair access:** Fully accessible. **Features:** Romantic, smoking at bar.

Island Burgers & Shakes $25 & Under

AMERICAN

766 Ninth Ave. (bet. 51st & 52nd Sts.)   (212) 307-7934
Credit cards: Cash only   Meals: L, D

While no more than a little aisle, stylish Island, decorated in summer pastels, turns out a huge menu of burgers (44 variations) and chicken sandwiches along with terrific sides like house-made potato chips. The burgers aren't bad, but the grilled chicken sandwiches are exceptional.

Price range: Apps., $3.75–$4.25; entrees, $4.50–$8.50. **Wheelchair access:** Fully accessible. **Features:** Kid friendly. **Services:** Delivery, takeout.

185

Island Grill
$25 & Under   CARIBBEAN

2 Lafayette St. (at Centre St.)

Credit cards: All major

(212) 227-9566

Meals: L

This small Jamaican restaurant in TriBeCa offers an extensive menu of curries, rotis and jerk dishes. Try the delicious ackee and saltfish, a typical Jamaican blend of salt cod and ackee, a reddish orange fruit that is sautéed and resembles scrambled eggs. If you like spicy food, make sure to let them know. The dining room is colorful and pleasant, but the pounding music may make takeout more desirable.

Price range: Apps., $1–$3.50; entrees, $5.75–$7.75; desserts, $2.50. **Wheelchair access:** Fully accessible. **Services:** Catering, delivery, takeout.

Island Spice
$25 & Under   CARIBBEAN

402 W. 44th St. (bet. Ninth & 10th Aves.)

Credit cards: All major

(212) 765-1737

Meals: L, D

This little storefront, almost hidden behind metal gates that always seem to be closed, offers refined Caribbean cooking to a steady stream of show business types. Little beef patties, gently spiced bits of ground beef encased in half-moons of flaky dough, are a savory way to begin, and earthy red bean soup has a long, lingering, slightly smoky flavor. Island Spice's jerk barbecue (pork or chicken) is excellent. Island Spice serves beer and wine as well as Caribbean concoctions like sorrell, a tart, refreshing deep-red beverage made from hibiscus. Desserts are somewhat limited.

Price range: Lunch: apps., $2.75–$6.50; entrees, $6.50–$12.50; desserts, $3.50–$4.50. Dinner: apps., $2.75–$12.50; entrees, $8.95–$21.95; desserts, $3.50–$4.50. **Wheelchair access:** Not accessible.

Isola
$25 & Under   ITALIAN

485 Columbus Ave. (bet. 83rd & 84th Sts.)

Credit cards: All major

(212) 362-7400

Meals: Br, L, D

When Isola is crowded, its dining room, full of hard surfaces, can be unbearably loud, but the restaurant offers some of the best Italian food on the Upper West Side, with lively pastas like spaghetti in a purée of black olives and oregano, and fettuccine with crumbled sausages and porcini mushrooms. The wine list is nicely chosen.

Price range: Apps., $4.95–$7.95; entrees, $9.95–$18; desserts, $4.95. **Wheelchair access:** Fully accessible. **Features:** Smoking permitted, outdoor dining. **Services:** Delivery, takeout.

I Trulli ☆☆ $$$ ITALIAN

122 E. 27th St. (bet. Lexington Ave. & Park Ave. S.)

(212) 481-7372

Credit cards: All major   Meals: L, D   Closed Sun.

This is New York City's best and most attractive restaurant dedicated to the cooking of Apulia. It serves interesting, unusual food in an understated room, dominated by a glass-enclosed fireplace, that is both elegant and warm; there is also a beautiful garden for outdoor dining. The rustic food from Italy's heel does not have the subtle charm of northern Italian food or the tomato-and-garlic heartiness of Neapolitan cuisine. The menu relies on bitter greens (arugula, dandelions, broccoli rape) and many foods that Americans rarely eat. The pastas have a basic earthy quality. Orechiette are made by the owner.

A recent visit showed that I Trulli remains a good bet, with well-executed Italian dishes, good service and pleasant surroundings. The menu, rustic but shrewd, avoids the obvious, with appetizers like stuffed squid with zucchini, black olives and mint, pastas like Sardinian dumplings with ground sausage and saffron, and entrees like lamb chops in herb sauce with fava bean puree and dandelions. (*Ruth Reichl, updated by William Grimes*)

Other recommended dishes: Roasted rabbit; grilled mackerel with eggplant; cavatelli with broccoli rape and roasted almonds; layered chocolate chestnut cake. **Wine list:** Wonderful and well-priced list with unusual wines. **Price range:** Apps., $9–$14; entrees, $18–$32; desserts, $9. **Wheelchair access:** Restaurant is on one floor. **Features:** Good for business, romantic, outdoor dining (garden). **Services:** Private parties.

Jack Rose ☆ $$$ NEW AMERICAN/STEAKHOUSE

771 Eighth Ave. (at 47th St.)   (212) 247-7518.

Credit cards: All major   Meals: L, D

Jack Rose is an artful exercise in nostalgia. The smooth, dark wood floors and brown leather booths feel like the 1930's. The huge horizontal stone fireplace, the polished driftwood accents and the rec room paneling evoke postwar suburbia with a touch of lounge. It's a classic, four-square, no-punches-pulled all-American joint that specializes in seafood, steaks, chops and no funny stuff.

Scallops wrapped in good, strong bacon delivers a gutsy American flavor, and the spicy mayonnaise on the side of the plate doubles the pleasure. Pan-roasted halibut, a generous snow-white slab with a golden-brown crust, could not be simpler, but it gets the job done. Clams casino, one of the great Edsels of American cuisine, puts on a brave front, topped liberally with bits of shallot, bell pepper and bacon. And although Jack Rose reserves a lot of room on the menu for steaks, Peter

Luger has nothing to fear. The beef covers the plate, but it makes a pretty feeble impression on the palate.

The kitchen can still win you over with the oysters Rockefeller or a plump, moist chicken, roasted to a crisp mahogany, its skin still bristling with charred, smoking sprigs of rosemary and dripping with syrupy pan juices. Aside from the bread pudding and a more than respectable crème brûlée, the desserts never quite hit the spot. Jack Rose seems about halfway there. When you hit, you hit big. When you don't — nothing.

Wine list: A reasonable if uninspiring list of about 110 mostly American and French wines, with 17 half bottles and a dozen wines by the glass. **Price range:** Lunch, apps., $5.50–$11.95; entrees, $10.95–$28.50; desserts, $6. Dinner: apps., $5.50–$11.95; entrees, $15.95–$29.95; desserts $6. **Wheelchair access:** Restrooms are on street level.

Jackson Diner $ INDIAN

37-47 74th St. (bet. 37th & Roosevelt Aves.) (718) 672-1232
Credit cards: Cash only Meals: L, D

Good Indian food at microscopic prices has resulted in a considerable reputation for this plain restaurant in Jackson Heights. The food's not even close to being the best in the city, but the value is terrific, particularly with South Indian vegetarian dishes like rasa vada, lentil doughnuts served in a spicy broth, and masala dosai, huge, spicy crepes stuffed with potato and onions.

Alcohol: Bring your own. **Price range:** Apps., $2.50–$6.95; entrees, $7.50–$18.95; desserts, $2.95. Lunch buffet: weekdays, $5.99; weekends, $7.50. **Wheelchair access:** Restrooms not accessible. **Services:** Takeout, catering, private parties.

Jackson Hole $ HAMBURGERS

232 E. 64th St. (bet. Second & Third Aves.) (212) 371-7187
1611 Second Ave. (at 83rd St.) (212) 737-8788
1270 Madison Ave. (at 91st St.) (212) 427-2820
521 Third Ave. (at 35th St.) (212) 679-3264
517 Columbus Ave. (at 85th St.) (212) 362-5177
Credit cards: AE Meals: B, Br, L, D, LN

This chain serves huge hamburgers; it's a pity they're not very good. Jackson Hole's cooking technique results in steamed masses of juiceless gray meat, served with equally pallid fries.

Alcohol: Beer and wine. **Price range:** Hamburgers, $4.40–$9. **Features:** Kid friendly, smoking permitted, outdoor dining. **Services:** Delivery, takeout, private parties.

Jane ☆ $$

100 W. Houston St. (at Thompson St.)
Credit cards: All major

NEW AMERICAN/BISTRO
(212) 254-7000
Meals:

Jane is a restaurant with the soul of a cafe. There's an air of cool, loungy relaxation inside, the wood floors and the studiedly neutral décor massage the nerves, and the menu couldn't be more friendly if it were printed with Have a Nice Day at the bottom. Jane, whose name is meant to suggest simplicity and lack of pretension, sets itself modest goals. For the most part it delivers, at a fair price.

The appetizer portions are so large that some diners may have second thoughts about their entrees. The tuna and salmon tartare is delicious, a slickly conceived interweaving of pristine ahi tuna nuggets with salmon that has been cured gravlax style with dill and rice wine vinegar. Shrimp and tomato flatbread, plain as it might sound, makes a big impression. Entrees do not, on balance, live up to the appetizers. An exception is the dark, richly gamy hanger steak, swimming in a red wine sauce and onion marmalade. Jane knows what to do when dessert time rolls around. The bias is toward American flavors, but with a little twist here and there, like the lemon-thyme sauce that brightens a cylinder-shaped cheesecake dense enough to bend a spoon. Minted strawberries with Champagne cream sounds like food for the gods, and in this case, reality does not disappoint.

With 100 seats in the main dining room, Jane is far too large for what it is, and there are times when the place seems like a mess hall.

Other recommended dishes: Roasted chicken with potato torte and rosemary jus; banana bread pudding sundae. **Wine list:** A sturdy if unexciting international list of about 35 wines, most under $40, with a dozen wines by the glass. **Price range:** Lunch, apps., $5–$8; entrees, $8–$19; desserts, $7–$8. Dinner, apps., $8–$14; entrees, $17–$21; desserts, $7–$8. **Wheelchair access:** Restrooms downstairs.

Japonica $$$

100 University Pl. (at 12th St.)
Credit cards: AE

JAPANESE/SUSHI
(212) 243-7752
Meals: L, D

In the N.Y.U. neighborhood, this sparkling Japanese restaurant is as popular as spring break. And little wonder, for the food is pristine, beautifully presented and delectable. Japonica is larger than it appears at first glance, with a wraparound dining room done in natural wood, colorful Japanese lanterns overhead and a handsome sushi bar. Most items are appealing, including a deluxe sushi assortment, yakitori and beef dumplings.

Price range: Dinner: apps., $7–$18; entrees, $11–$30; desserts, $4.75–$6.25. **Wheelchair access:** Restrooms not accessible. **Services:** Delivery, takeout.

Jarnac $$$ BISTRO/FRENCH

328 W. 12th St. (at Greenwich St.)   (212) 924-3413
Credit Cards: All major   Meals: Br, L, D   Closed Mon.

Instantly recognizable as a bistro, Jarnac sits on a quiet corner at the fringe of the meatpacking district. When the windows are thrown open, it's a cozy spot that allows diners to watch the world walk by while they drink house wine by the carafe. The restaurant is named after a famous town in the Cognac district. The chef has developed a quirky menu that flits back and forth between old classics like veal Marengo and braised rabbit chasseur, and contemporary dishes like curried red lentil soup and roast confit of duck with rhubarb and ginger chutney.

Other recommended dishes: Menu changes every two weeks. **Wine list:** Eclectic, with wines from France, Australia, New Zealand and California. **Price range:** Apps.,$7–$9.75; entrees, $19.50–$23, desserts, $7.25–$8.25. **Wheelchair access:** Not accessible. **Services:** Private parties.

Jean Claude $25 & Under   BISTRO/FRENCH

137 Sullivan St. (bet. Prince & Houston Sts.)   (212) 475-9232
Credit cards: Cash only   Meals: D

The bustling dining room is authentically Parisian, with the scent of Gitanes and the sound of French in the air. For these low prices you don't expect to find appetizers like seared sea scallops with roasted beets or main courses like roasted monkfish with savoy cabbage, olives and onions.

Other recommended dishes: Sautéed duck breast with turnips, white beans, and citrus compote. **Alcohol:** Beer and wine. **Price range:** Apps., $6–$8; entrees, $12–$16; desserts, $6. **Wheelchair access:** Fully accessible. **Features:** Romantic, smoking permitted, outdoor dining. **Services:** Catering, takeout, private parties.

Jean Georges ☆☆☆☆ $$$$ NEW AMERICAN

Trump Hotel, 1 Central Park W. (at 60th St.)   (212) 299-3900
Credit cards: All major   Meals: B, L, D

On the surface, Jean Georges looks like just another expensive new restaurant. But take a deeper look: in his quiet way the chef and co-owner, Jean-Georges Vongerichten, has created an entirely new kind of four-star restaurant. He has examined all the details that make dining luxurious, and refined them for an American audience. The changes are so subtle that they are easy to miss, but nothing, from the neutral look of the dining room to the composition of the staff to the pacing of the meal, follows a classic model.

Most important, he has returned the focus to the food. Mr. Vongerichten introduced simplicity to four-star cooking years ago and here the food is essentially simple. And he is at the top of his form. If a walk in the woods were translated to flavor, it would be his porcini tart, a rich pastry spread with a deeply flavored walnut-and-onion paste and topped with sautéed mushrooms. Many dishes are bold. Sometimes the innovation is in the side dish. A gorgeous rack of lamb in a green garlic crust is served with a bouquet of vegetables that includes wild French asparagus, Cajun asparagus and mustard chives. The surprises do not end at dessert. The pastry chef is completely in tune with Mr. Vongerichten's sensibility.

The austerity of the design of the restaurant also puts the focus on food. The dining room is comfortable and expensive but so low-key it is easy to ignore. While some restaurants are more concerned with who is in the room than what is on the plate, the people at Jean Georges neither fawn nor intimidate. This is no celebrity restaurant; all over the dining room, waiters bend over the food, carving or pouring, intent only on their guests' pleasure. Ask for wine advice and the excellent sommelier uncondescendingly recommends reasonably priced bottles. (*Ruth Reichl, see p. 14 for Eric Asimov's up-to-date appraisal*).

Other recommended dishes: Marinated tuna and hamachi (yellowtail); lobster tartine; roasted pear spiked with vanilla beans. **Wine list:** Excellent, with many unusual wines, many affordable wines and a knowledgeable staff. **Price range:** Lunch: three courses, $35; four courses, $45. Dinner: three courses, $85; seven-course tasting menu, $115. Nougatine dining room: three-course prix-fixe lunch, $20; three-course prix-fixe dinner, $45. **Wheelchair access:** Separate entrance; dining room on one level. **Services:** Private parties.

Jekyll & Hyde Club $$ Theme
1409 Sixth Ave. (bet. 57th & 58th Sts.)   (212) 541-9505
Credit cards: All major   Meals: L, D, LN

Of all the theme restaurants around 57th Street, this one offers the closest to an amusement park atmosphere. From the moment you walk in and find the walls in the alcove closing around you, the suspense never lets up. While grown-ups grouse about the wait to get in (count on at least an hour), the wait to be fed (sometimes another hour) and the quality of the food, children are usually enchanted.

Price range: Apps., $4.95–$8.50; entrees, $8.95–$17.95; desserts, $3.95–$6.95. **Wheelchair access:** Fully accessible. **Features:** Kid friendly, smoking permitted. **Services:** Private parties.

Jewel Bako $25 & Under   Sushi

239 E. 5th St. (bet. Second & Third Aves.)   (212) 979-1012
Credit cards: All major   Meals: D   Closed Sun.

The first taste at Jewel Bako, a sparkling new Japanese restaurant in the East Village, will leave no doubt that here is great sushi. The absolute freshness of the fish, the unusual variety of selections and the beauty of the chef's creations combine to form a sublimely sensual experience. Add the welcoming charm of the husband-and-wife owners, Jack and Grace Lamb, and the warmth of the chef, Tatsuya Nagata, and you come close to the ideal for a neighborhood sushi bar.

With six seats at the sushi bar in the rear, the restaurant holds about 30 people. Jewel Bako, Japanese slang for jewel box, is aptly named. The clean lines of the small dining room, under an arched bamboo ceiling, echo the purity of the sushi. Mr. Nagata's approach is traditional. He avoids creating fancy rolls layered with avocado, instead focusing on the freshest and best ingredients. The sushi and sashimi selections, including bowls of richly satisfying miso soup, run $12 to $29, but order à la carte, allowing the chef to guide you. Don't say no if he suggests the top-of-the-line toro, as creamy and tender as melted butter. And don't pass up the starkly white fresh octopus, which practically melts in the mouth.

Each piece of sushi seems an almost perfect unit of rice and fish, often with a dot of complementary flavoring devised by Mr. Nagata, like an almost smoky vinegar jelly, a touch of hot chili or a breezy hint of shiso. Each unit is so well fashioned and thought out that you won't want to alter it by adding soy sauce or wasabi.

There is a refreshing dessert of stewed mission figs, served cool in a sweetened white wine and shiso broth.

Price range: Sushi and sashimi selections, $12–$29; à la carte, $3–$4.50 a piece; some specials higher. **Wheelchair access:** Everything is on one level.

Jezebel $$$ Southern

630 Ninth Ave. (at 45th St.)   (212) 582-1045
Credit cards: AE   Meals: L, D   Closed Sun., Mon.

The South seen through the lens of *Gone With the Wind*. Invented decadence, lots of drama, lots of fun. The food is also invented, but it's Southern and sinful. Palms and other foliage tower overhead, diaphanous shawls hang from ceiling pipes, candles flicker, and Southern bric-a-brac surrounds diners as they consume a combination of homey Southern cooking and undiluted soul food. Openers include crispy chicken livers in a peppery gravy; a chunky and thick fish chowder, and she-crab soup. Among the main dishes are shrimp creole, fried or broiled catfish, seafood gumbo, smothered pork chops, ham hocks and fried or smothered chicken. Collard greens, okra, yams and grits are popular accompaniments. The dessert list includes lemon, pecan and sweet potato pies and banana and bread puddings.

Price range: Lunch: apps., $6.75–$11.75; entrees, $11.75–$22.75; desserts, $6.75–$11.75. Dinner: apps., $8.75–$11.75; entrees, $18.75–$32.75; desserts, $6.75–$11.75. **Wheelchair access:** Fully accessible. **Features:** Kid friendly, romantic. **Services:** Takeout, private parties.

Jimmy Armstrong's Saloon
$25 & Under   Eclectic/Latin

875 10th Ave. (at 57th St.)   (212) 581-0606
Credit cards: All major   Meals: L, D, LN

A worn, dark, enjoyable corner bar with a twist: the owner is fascinated with Hispanic cultures, and he's gathered recipes from Cuba to Mexico to Spain and put together an unusual menu. Mr. Armstrong's passion is for sausages, like Morcilla, a Spanish blood sausage; or for a main course, finely ground garlic sausages called Adirondacks. Grilled Yucatan chicken allows the mingled flavors of meat and marinade to shine through. Even the more common dishes like pork chops and steak are well prepared and satisfying.

Other recommended dishes: Chorizo sausages; caldo gallego; escarole soup; Caribbean roast pork platter; ropa vieja; bread pudding. **Price range:** Apps., $2.95–$7.50; entrees, $7.50–$16.50. **Wheelchair access:** One step at entrance; restrooms are narrow. **Services:** Private parties.

Jing Fong $
Chinese

20 Elizabeth St. (bet. Bayard & Canal Sts.)   (212) 964-5256
Credit cards: All major   Meals: L, D

Chinatown's biggest restaurant serves awesome dim sum during the day. At night the cavernous dining room serves good Cantonese fare, but if you order ahead you can get a pretty terrific spread served in a private room. Ask for the banquet manager.

Price range: Lunch entrees, $1.90–$3.95. Dinner: apps., $3.95–$5.95; entrees, $8.85–$18.25; desserts, $1.90. **Wheelchair access:** Fully accessible. **Features:** Kid friendly. **Services:** Catering, takeout, private parties.

Joe Allen $$
New American

326 W. 46th St. (bet. Eighth & Ninth Aves.)   (212) 581-6464
Credit cards: All major   Meals: Br, L, D

Chili and celebrities in the heart of Broadway. The food's not great, but it's not expensive either. If you're looking for safe, unpretentious American food in the high-rent Restaurant Row, this is the place.

Price range: Apps., $4–$8; entrees, $9–$19.50; desserts, $5–$6. **Wheelchair access:** Fully accessible. **Features:** Smoking permitted. **Services:** Private parties.

Joe's Shanghai ☆☆ $ CHINESE

24 W. 56th St. (bet. Fifth & Sixth Aves.)	(212) 333-3868
9 Pell St. (bet. Bowery & Catherine St.)	(212) 233-8888
136-21 37th Ave., Flushing, Queens	(718) 539-3838
82-74 Broadway, Elmhurst, Queens	(718) 639-6888
Credit cards: All major	Meals: L, D

In addition to hip, handsome, friendly waiters (even, shocking for Chinatown, some women) and an exciting menu of Shanghai specialties, these spartan restaurants, serve awesome dumplings filled with soup. The xiao lung bao are modestly listed on the menu as "steamed buns," but they are Shanghai soup dumplings. The chef has perfected the art of wrapping hot liquid in pastry: the filling is rich, light and swimming in hot soup. Everybody orders steamed dumplings, but there are many other wonderful dishes, including smoked fish, strongly flavored with star anise, vegetarian duck, thin sheets of braised tofu folded like skin over mushrooms, and drunken crabs, raw marinated blue crabs with a musty, fruity flavor that is powerful and unforgettable. Also try the turnip cakes, the intensely chewy Shanghai noodles, the lion's head, fried bean curd with spinach and crispy yellow fish fingers with dry seaweed. (*Ruth Reichl*)

Other recommended dishes: Steamed crab buns; steamed pork buns; scallion pancake; wine-marinated chicken; razor clams with black-bean sauce and chilies; eel with yellow chives; fresh bacon with preserved vegetable; sweet red-bean shortcake. **Alcohol:** Beer; full bar in Midtown. **Price range:** A la carte $9.50 and up. **Wheelchair access:** Everything on one floor. **Features:** Kid friendly. **Services:** Takeout, catering.

John's Pizzeria $25 & Under   ITALIAN/PIZZA

408 E. 64th St. (bet. First & York Aves.)	(212) 935-2895
278 Bleecker St. (near Seventh Ave. S.)	(212) 243-1680
48 W. 65th St. (near Central Park W.)	(212) 721-7001
260 W. 44th St. (bet. Seventh & Eighth Aves.)	(212) 391-7560
Credit cards: All major (64th & 65th, AE only)	Meals: L, D

John's earns its reputation for great pizza every day. What sets John's apart is the expert economy of its pizza: no waste or excess, a thin and faintly smoky crust, just crisp enough to offer a delicate crunch, while the other ingredients are fine: creamy mozzarella, slightly spicy tomato sauce, crumbled fennel sausage from Faicco Pork Store in the Village. Of the four John's locations, the best are the original, a brusque, battered, sprawling place on Bleecker Street, and the Times Square outlet, a huge pizzeria in a beautiful old church.

Best dishes: Pizza. **Alcohol:** Beer and wine. **Price range:** $5.50–$10.95. **Wheelchair access:** Fully accessible. **Features:** Kid friendly, smoking permitted, outdoor dining. **Services:** Takeout, private parties.

Josie's $25 & Under NEW AMERICAN
300 Amsterdam Ave. (at 74th St.)   (212) 769-1212
565 Third Ave. (at 37th St.)   (212) 490-1558
Credit cards: All major   Meals: L, D, LN

Much of the food at Josie's is billed as organically raised. Many dishes are dairy-free, napkins are unbleached brown paper, and according to the menu, "water used for drinking, cooking and ice is Multi-Pure filtered." The surprise is that so much of the food is so good, with highlights like light potato dumplings served in a lively tomato coulis spiked with chipotle pepper, ravioli stuffed with sweet potato purée, superb grilled tuna with a wasabi glaze and wonderful gazpacho. Josie's offers about two dozen reasonably priced wines, some organic beers and freshly squeezed juices, including tart blueberry lemonade. Even the organic hot dogs are good.

Price range: Apps., $5–$7.50; entrees, $9.50–$16; desserts, $5.50. **Wheelchair access:** Restrooms not accessible. **Services:** Delivery, takeout, catering.

Jubilee $$$ FRENCH
347 E. 54th St. (bet. First & Second Aves.)   (212) 888-3569
Credit cards: All major   Meals: L, D

Small, crowded and exuberant, this is a great Sutton Place find. It offers simple and good bistro food, like steak frites and roast chicken. The restaurant makes something of a specialty of mussels, offering them in five guises with terrific french fries or a green salad, all for reasonable prices.

Other recommended dishes: Bouillabaisse; duck breast; lamb shank; roasted salmon; steak; marquise au chocolat. **Price range:** Lunch: apps., $6–$9; entrees, $13.50–$22; desserts, $5.50–$7.50. Dinner: apps., $6.50–$13.50; entrees, $13.50–$24; desserts, $5.50–$8.50. **Wheelchair access:** Not accessible. **Features:** Smoking permitted. **Services:** Takeout, private parties.

Judson Grill ☆ ☆ ☆ $$$ NEW AMERICAN

152 W. 52nd St. (bet Sixth & Seventh Aves.)   (212) 582-5252
Credit cards: All major   Meals: L,D   Closed Sun.

Judson Grill is big, bright and utterly urban, a mature restaurant with none of the irritating glitches of a new establishment. Its lighting is right, they've got the service down pat and the wine list has had time to develop its own quirky personality. In the skillful hands of the chef, Bill Telepan, the food is unassuming but extremely eloquent, so roaring with flavor that the minute you finish one bite you instantly want another.

Consider the vegetable soup — a clear golden broth filled with tenderly poached peas, beans and mushrooms. The liquid is alive with flavor, and the vegetables are faintly crisp and sweet. A spring vegetable salad is a riot of golden beets, fava beans, pea shoots, tiny asparagus, peas and cucumbers in a perfectly balanced lemon vinaigrette. Marinated yellowtail is enhanced by a spicy kohlrabi salad, radishes and mint. Grilled duck sausage, so lean that it hardly qualifies as sausage, comes with a terrific warm potato salad. Main courses are even better. The organically grown meats are especially impressive. Pork is wrapped in a black mustard crust and lamb is coated with herbs and served with wild greens and potatoes.

Desserts include the restaurant's Jack Daniel's ice cream soda and its chocolate sampler. Both are good, but the fruit concoctions are most appealing. (*Ruth Reichl*)

Other recommended dishes: Hearts of romaine salad; terrine of foie gras; Swiss chard and pancetta ravioli; tuna tartar; free-range chicken; sourdough onion rings. **Most popular dish:** Maine halibut. **Chef's favorite:** Foie gras terrine. **Wine list:** Interesting, intelligently chosen; affordable special values and big deal wines bought at auction. **Price range:** Lunch: apps., $9–$13; entrees, $21–$29; desserts, $7–$9.50. Dinner: apps., $9–$16; entrees, $22–$35; desserts, $7–$9.50. Five-course seasonal tasting menu, $65; with wines, $85. **Wheelchair access:** Fully accessible. **Services:** Private parties.

Jules $$ FRENCH

65 St. Marks Pl. (bet. First & Second Aves.)   (212) 477-5560
Credit cards: AE   Meals: L, D, LN

This French bistro looks French, sounds French and even smells French, or like French cigarettes. The menu is straightforward and unsurprising, and the food is workmanlike, but a good value.

Alcohol: Beer and wine. **Price range:** Lunch: apps., $6–$7.50; entrees, $7.50–$13; desserts, $4. Dinner: apps., $5.50–$7.25; entrees, $11.50–$18.75; desserts, $6–$7.50. Prix fixe, $16.50 (Sun.-Thur., 5:30-7 P.M.). **Wheelchair access:** Not accessible.

Features: Smoking permitted, outdoor dining. **Services:** Private parties.

Junno's $25 & Under   JAPANESE/KOREAN
64 Downing St. (bet. Bedford & Varick Sts.)   (212) 627-7995
Credit cards: All major   Meals: D   Closed Sun.

The food at this friendly Japanese-Korean fusion restaurant is not great, but it can be good, especially if you order wisely. Appetizers are especially good, like tataki of tuna with ponzu sauce, thin-cut rectangles of tuna that are seared around the edges and rare in the middle. The best main courses are the most robust, like a delectable Korean dish, grilled short ribs, sweetened by a soy marinade and served off the bone with a nice little salad.

Other recommended dishes: Ravioli of sweet shrimp; grilled squid; sliced braised pork; udon noodle soup with braised beef; roast ginger chicken; warm chocolate cake; pear sorbet. **Price range:** Apps., $4–$6; entrees, $8–$14. **Wheelchair access:** Everything is on one level. **Features:** Smoking permitted. **Services:** Private parties.

Kabul Cafe $ AFGHAN
265 W. 54th St. (bet. Eighth Ave. & Broadway)   (212) 757-2037
Credit cards: All major   Meals: L, D

This is one of several small, dim Afghan cafes that offer good value in the midtown area. Like the others, Kabul Cafe serves huge lamb and chicken kebabs with lots of rice, and good salads and other meatless entrees.

Alcohol: Beer and wine. **Price range:** Lunch: apps., $4–$5; entrees, $4.95–$11.95. Dinner: apps., $4–$5; entrees, $8.50–$13.95, desserts, $3–$4. **Wheelchair access:** Not accessible. **Features:** Kid friendly. **Services:** Delivery, takeout, catering, private parties.

Kaña $25 & Under   SPANISH
324 Spring St. (near Greenwich St.)   (212) 343-8180
Credit cards: All major   Meals: L, D, LN

Tapas are satisfying and traditional at this friendly, lively bar, where loud music and cigarette smoke are simply part of the milieu. Boquerones, anchovies pickled in a sweet-and-sour marinade, are delicious; another good choice is tuna escabeche, tender, tasty cubes of fresh tuna marinated in citrus with fennel and served cool. Hot tapas don't stray from the traditional, but they are lively and often prepared to order.

Other recommended dishes: Shrimp in green garlic sauce; sardines; chorizo; octopus in red wine. **Price range:** Entrees, $14–$16. **Alcohol:** Beer and wine. **Wheelchair access:** Everything is on one level. **Features:** Outdoor dining. **Services:** Takeout, catering, private parties.

Katsu-Hama $25 & Under JAPANESE

11 E. 47th St. (bet. Madison & Fifth Aves.) (212) 758-5909
Credit cards: All major Meals: L, D

Katsu-Hama doesn't offer much in the way of atmosphere or creature comforts, but it is an authentic Japanese experience. To enter it, you need to walk through a takeout sushi restaurant (Sushi-Tei) and pass through a curtain divider; there, you encounter an almost entirely Japanese crowd who've come for the restaurant's specialty: tonkatsu, or deep-fried pork cutlets. The cutlet comes bathed in a rich, robust curry sauce, for example, or it is served over rice with scallions and egg sauce, a cozy, oozy, Japanese comfort food. But the best is unadorned, dipped into a special condiment that resembles freshly made Worcestershire sauce blended with sesame seeds.

Alcohol: Beer and wine. **Price range:** $8.95–$13.95, including soup, shredded cabbage and rice. **Wheelchair access:** Everything is on one level; path to restrooms is narrow. **Features:** Kid friendly, good for business. **Services:** Delivery, takeout, catering, private parties.

Katz's Deli $ DELI

205 E. Houston St. (at Ludlow St.) (212) 254-2246
Credit cards: All major Meals: B, Br, L, D, LN

A wonderful Lower East Side artifact and originator of the World War II slogan, "Send a salami to your boy in the Army." It is one of the very few New York City delis that still carves pastrami and corned beef by hand, which makes for delicious sandwiches.

Alcohol: Beer and wine. **Price range:** Apps., $2–$5; entrees, $5–$10.95; desserts, $2.75–$3. **Wheelchair access:** Fully accessible. **Features:** Kid friendly. **Services:** Delivery, takeout, catering, private parties.

Kazan Turkish Cuisine $25 & Under TURKISH

95-36 Queens Blvd., Rego Park, Queens (718) 897-1509
Credit cards: All major Meals: L, D

Kazan is a spare, open dining room with a maroon rug and white walls adorned with a hookah and an old Turkish coffee urn. There is also a stone oven that produces exceptional pide, soft football-shape loaves of bread dotted with sesame seeds, which are just right with any of the superb cold appetizers. Eggplant is excellent, either charcoal grilled and puréed with garlic or left chunky and served with tomato and garlic. Don't ignore the tangy hummus, either, or fragrant, minty grape leaves stuffed with rice and pine nuts. Kazan's short selection of main courses also includes some real winners like shish yogurtlu, juicy chunks of tender grilled lamb served over a sauce of yogurt blended with tomatoes. Kasarli kofte is another standout, made with chopped lamb blended with mild kasseri cheese, which gives the meat an unusual airiness. Desserts like kadais, made with shredded wheat, walnuts, pistachios and honey syrup, are good, but extremely sweet.

Other recommended dishes: Yogurt with cucumber; yogurt with walnuts; white bean salad; minced vegetables; tarama.
Price range: Apps., $3.50–$4.50; entrees, $8.50–$13.95. **Wheelchair access:** Everything is on one level.

K.B. Garden $$ CHINESE
136-28 39th Ave., Flushing, Queens   (718) 961-9088
Credit cards: All major   Meals: L, D

Flushing's biggest and newest Hong Kong seafood palace is a cavernous room decorated with fish tanks. The size of a couple of football fields, it is filled at lunchtime with women wheeling dim sum carts through the vast space and calling out the names of their wares. You can go for dim sum (and expect to wait for a table on weekends) or call ahead and order a banquet for a group. There is just about anything you can imagine, from the usual har gow and shiu mai dumplings to braised duck feet, spicy tripe and green-lipped mussels topped with mayonnaise.

Price range: Apps., $2–$13.95; entrees, $7.95–$40. **Wheelchair access:** Fully accessible. **Services:** Takeout, catering, private parties.

Keens $$$$ STEAKHOUSE
72 W. 36th St. (bet. Fifth & Sixth Aves.)   (212) 947-3636
Credit cards: All major   Meals: L, D

Opened in 1885, Keens looks like something out of a tale by Dickens. The scene is wonderful: big tables filled mostly with men chowing down on big platters of meat as they inhale tankards of beer and any of the more than 60 single-malt Scotches. The restaurant served its millionth mutton chop decades ago, and that continues to be the best thing on the menu. The best of the appetizers is the shrimp cocktail, with oysters on the half shell a close second. All the standard side dishes are on hand: creamed spinach (with too much nutmeg), sautéed mushrooms, potatoes in any number of guises.

Price range: Lunch: apps., $6–$16; entrees, $13.50–$20; desserts, $6–$7. Dinner: apps., $6–$16; entrees, $18.50–$34.75; desserts, $6–$7. **Wheelchair access:** Not accessible. **Features:** Smoking permitted. **Services:** Takeout, private parties.

Kelley & Ping $$ NOODLES/THAI

127 Greene St. (bet. Houston & Prince Sts.)   (212) 228-1212
Credit cards: All major   Meals: L, D

This stylish combination Thai restaurant, tearoom and retail shop is best for a quick bowl of noodles or a cup of tea. The room is pleasant and the food is thankfully not too ambitious.

Alcohol: Beer and wine. **Price range:** Lunch: apps., $4–$6; entrees, $5–$8. Dinner: apps., $5–$7; entrees, $8–$14; desserts, $6. **Wheelchair access:** Fully accessible. **Features:** Kid friendly, smoking permitted. **Services:** Catering, delivery, takeout, private parties.

King Cole Bar $$$ HOTEL/LOUNGE

St. Regis Hotel, 2 E. 55th St. (bet. Fifth & Madison Aves.)
                                                          (212) 339-6721
Credit cards: All major   Meals: L, D, LN

Sure, you can order a top of the line Scotch or a vintage port at this swank hotel bar. But why not go for the Bloody Mary? After all, this is where the ubiquitous vodka-and-tomato juice concoction was invented, or so they claim. Only at the King Cole Bar it's still called by its original name, the Red Snapper. Maxfield Parrish's celebrated "Old King Cole" mural is in its traditional place behind the bar in this stylish paneled room. Hors d'oeuvres include Chinese spring rolls, crispy calamari, crudités, smoked salmon rosettes with beluga caviar and a $45 finger-food sampler. Among the entrees are grilled red snapper with pearl pasta; roasted poussin with garlic mashed potatoes; chicken or sirloin burgers, and steak and french fries. Desserts are apple pie à la mode, crème brûlée, fruit tart, and butterscotch pecan pie. For a simpler snack, there is a "classics" menu from which you may choose onion soup; chicken consommé with vegetable ravioli; Caesar salad; chicken club sandwich; croque monsieur, or a $45 caviar tasting. Madeiras, ports, Cognacs and Armagnacs are available, as are a wide selection of cigars.

Price range: Apps., $14–$23; entrees, $23–$32; desserts, $14. **Wheelchair access:** Fully accessible.

Kitchen Club $$ FRENCH/JAPANESE

30 Prince St. (at Mott St.)   (212) 274-0025
Credit cards: All major   Meals: L, D   Closed Mon.

The menu is ever-changing at this creative restaurant, where the Dutch chef and owner, Marja Samsom, offers her own blend of Asian and European dishes, like steamed shrimp served cold in a bento box and cod in sake sauce. The miniature Zen garden in front sets a tone of calm serenity.

Other recommended dishes: Mushroom dumplings; string bean salad with duck sausage; smoked eel; chicken with mushroom sauce; stuffed quails. **Alcohol:** Beer and wine. **Price range:** Apps., $9–$10.50; entrees, $15–$24; desserts, $6–$8. **Wheelchair access:** Fully accessible. **Features:** Romantic, smoking permitted. **Services:** Catering, private parties.

Kitchenette $ NEW AMERICAN

80 W. Broadway (at Warren St.)   (212) 267-6740
Credit cards: AE   Meals: B, Br, L, D

Breakfast is best at this small farmhouse-style restaurant in SoHo, not least because, unlike lunch, breakfasts are freshly prepared. Dishes like orange-poppy-seed waffles, blueberry pancakes and biscuits are homey and delicious. Lunch, unfortunately, is dominated by prepackaged sandwiches that have lost their zip by the time they are served.

Price range: Apps., $3–$6; entrees, $11–$16; desserts, $3–$4. **Wheelchair access:** Fully accessible. **Services:** Delivery, takeout, catering, private parties.

Knickerbocker Bar & Grill $$ AMERICAN

33 University Pl. (at 9th St.)   (212) 228-8490
Credit cards: All major   Meals: L, D, LN

Huge portions, huge menu, great service. An old reliable restaurant with good American food that never lets you down. No wonder it's a neighborhood favorite.

Price range: Lunch: apps., $5; entrees, $9.95–$15; desserts, $5–$6. Dinner: apps., $5.75–$11.75; entrees, $14–$18; desserts, $5–$6; prix fixe, $16.50. **Wheelchair access:** Not accessible. **Features:** Kid friendly, smoking permitted. **Services:** Catering, takeout, private parties.

Knödel $25 & Under

SCANDINAVIAN/FAST FOOD
Grand Central Terminal, Lower Level
Credit cards: All major

(212) 986-1230.
Meals: L, D

The restaurant is Scandinavian, but the plump and rich sausages are American, served on fresh potato rolls with assorted toppings like hot dogs, though derived from the European tradition of creative sausage making. The fine Knodel brat, for example, is mostly savory pork, with puréed fig for softer texture and, surprise, pine nuts, which fit in perfectly. Knodel also serves an excellent smoky, spicy andouille and a sweet and smoky chicken-and-apple sausage. Sides include sesame-scented Asian slaw, with red cabbage, carrots and raisins.

Alcohol: Beer and wine. **Price range:** Entrees, $5–$12. **Wheelchair access:** Fully accessible. **Services:** Delivery, Take out.

Kodama $$

JAPANESE/SUSHI
301 W. 45th St. (at Eighth Ave.)
Credit cards: All major

(212) 582-8065
Meals: L, D

Although the décor is drab and the menu almost frighteningly large, this remains a perennially popular restaurant with people who work at *The New York Times*. It is also a big hit with people rushing to the theater. The Broadway Box, a selection of many small dishes, is a bargain, sushi is safe if not superb, and there is always an available table when other nearby restaurants are overcrowded. The modest prices are another draw.

Price range: Apps., $4–$7.75; entrees, $8–$25; desserts, $2.25–$5.50. **Wheelchair access:** Not accessible. **Features:** Smoking permitted. **Services:** Delivery, takeout, private parties.

Komodo $25 & Under

ASIAN/MEXICAN
186 Ave. A (bet. 11th & 12th Sts.)
Credit cards: All major   Meals: D

(212) 529-2658
Closed Mon.

The annals of fusion cuisine are not exactly bulging with examples of Mexican-Asian restaurants. With a shared taste for ingredients like cilantro, chilies and rice, the regions have more grounds for compatibility than most. Yet only the Bright Food Shop in Chelsea, which is a decade old, and now Komodo in the East Village have seen fit to explore the possibilities. Komodo's small storefront dining room is clean, simple and cool; the fusion idea never outweighs the flavors on the plate, so the food never seems forced or needlessly flamboyant. A simple appetizer like beef satay is rubbed with ground ancho chilies and served with peanut sauce, a combination that differs so subtly from the original that it seems effortlessly natural. Even better are Asian guacamole rolls, in which the avocado is flavored with ginger and wasabi and combined with sweet potato and cumin. The list of main courses is small, but the grilled sirloin topped with oysters tempura and crisp fried leeks, an Asian version of an old carpetbagger steak, is excellent. For a more Mexican approach, snapper is wrapped in a corn husk and then grilled, leaving it soft, moist and infused with a mild corn flavor that stands up to cilantro, jalapeños and a jicama slaw. Good dessert choices include a rich chocolate pot de crème flavored with black litchi tea, and an apple empanada.

Other recommended dishes: Duck-mango spring rolls; tomatillo-corn-crab cakes; glazed salmon with wasabi cream; Vietnamese chicken. **Price range:** Apps., $3.95–$8.95; entrees, $9.75–$15.95. **Wheelchair access:** Everything on one level.

Korea Palace ☆ $$$ KOREAN

127 E. 54th St. (bet. Park & Lexington Aves.)   (212) 832-2350
Credit cards: All major   Meals: L, D

Great carved dragons guard the entrance to Korea Palace, giving the restaurant a fancy and slightly forbidding air; it is surprising to find that the interior has the casual, utilitarian look of a converted coffee shop. There is a huge selection of dishes, and the waiters speak English; it is a good choice for people trying Korean food for the first time. Another attraction: You can grill the sweet, salty and garlicky Korean barbecue at your table and watch the very efficient fans draw the smoke away from you and your clothing. In addition to spicy marinated squid with vegetables, kimchi and pork casseroles, the usual barbecue dishes and soups, the restaurant offers a fine selection of sushi. (*Ruth Reichl*)

Other recommended dishes: Mandoo gui (dumplings); chap chae (stir-fried clear noodles); haemul pajun (seafood pancake); Korean barbecue; stir-fried pork and kimchi; stir-fried octopus and noodles; kimchi casserole with bean curd; bibimbab (Korean rice with various toppings). **Wine list:** The wine list is well chosen and inexpensive, but soju, the Korean sweet-potato vodka, or beer are better matches for this powerful food. **Price range:** Apps., $8.50–$15.95; entrees, $10.95–$50.95 (for more than one person), desserts, $2.50–$13. **Wheelchair access:** Separate entrance for wheelchairs. **Features:** Smoking permitted. **Services:** Delivery, takeout, catering, private parties.

Kori $25 & Under   KOREAN

253 Church St. (near Leonard St.)   (212) 334-0908
Credit cards: All major   Meals: L, D, LN

It's easy to miss Kori, an attractive little Korean restaurant and bar on a drab block in TriBeCa. Consider yourself lucky if you find it, because Kori is unusual, a Korean restaurant that succeeds in merging East and West, old and new. Kori seems a wholly personal expression of its owner and chef, Kori Kim: up-to-date and appealing to Americans but tied to Korean traditions. She learned to cook in a big, traditional Korean family in Seoul, and she said her hope was to serve her customers exactly the same food she made for her family.

It is hard to imagine Ms. Kim serving food at home as polished as her dubu sobegi, a tofu croquette stuffed with savory ground Asian mushrooms and beautifully presented like a rectangular gift box, sliced diagonally into four pieces and held together with a seaweed ribbon. It's a subtle dish in a cuisine known for its power and rusticity. If it is power you want, Jo ge gui, littleneck clams marinated in soju, a clear Korean liquor, is both beautiful and spicy. Duk bokki, soft rice-flour cylinders with a pleasant bite to them, come in a red chili sauce that is pure fire. Main courses don't quite rise to the level of the appetizers, though they can be very good as well. Galbi jim is a wonderful stew of short ribs with sweet dates, chestnuts and turnips, while eel, marinated in sweet soy sauce and sautéed, is melt-in-your-mouth tender.

Kori is a bar as well, and noise and smoke occasionally waft through the narrow dining room. There are some excellent cocktails made with soju along with a small selection of wines.

Other recommended dishes: Bulgogi; marinated beef with Asian pear; mung-bean pancakes; octopus with noodles; bibimbop. **Price range:** Apps., $5–$12; entrees, $12.95–$21. **Wheelchair access:** Small steps at entrance. **Features:** Smoking in bar.

Kum Gang San $$$ KOREAN
138-28 Northern Blvd., Flushing, Queens (718) 461-0909
Credit cards: All major Meals: B, Br, L, D, LN Open 24 hours

A Korean restaurant with something for everyone: a waterfall outside, a piano player (in a tuxedo) inside and an enormous menu of Korean specialties. Good for Korean barbecue; open all night.

Price range: Lunch: apps., $4–$5; entrees, $5.95–$8.95; desserts, $2.95. Dinner: apps., $5; entrees, $10–$15; desserts, $2.95. **Wheelchair access:** Fully accessible. **Features:** Smoking permitted. **Services:** Takeout, catering, private parties.

Kuruma Zushi ☆☆☆ $$$$ SUSHI
7 E. 47th St., 2nd Fl. (bet. Madison & Fifth Aves.) (212) 317-2802
Credit cards: All major Meals: L, D Closed Sun.

Few restaurants are more welcoming to diners who do not speak Japanese, and few chefs are better at introducing people to sushi than Toshihiro Uezu, proprietor of Kuruma Zushi. One of New York City's most venerable sushi bars, it serves only sushi and sashimi and is, admittedly, expensive.

Serious sushi eaters always start with sashimi. Mr. Uezu sets boards in front of diners, heaps them with shiny, frilly green and purple bits of seaweed and begins slicing fish. Next to him an underling grates fresh wasabi. Very few places use fresh wasabi, but the flavor is much subtler and more delicate than the usual powdered sort. The man scoops up little green hillocks and sets one on each board. Beside them Mr. Uezu places pale pink rectangles of toro.

"Now sushi?" Mr. Uezu asks. He selects Japanese red snapper, crisp giant clam, small, sweet scallops. Raw shrimp, soft as strawberries, may be followed by marinated herring roe and gently smoked salmon that gleamed like coral, or sea urchin on pads of rice.

Increasing competition has made the restaurant seem a little less of a standout, and service at lunch can be glacial. But the list of seafood flown overnight from Japan is still impressive, and a recent visit showed the restaurant to be firmly entrenched among the best sushi parlors in Manhattan. (*Ruth Reichl, updated by William Grimes*)

Price range: Apps., $5–$15; entrees, $25–$100; desserts, $5.
Wheelchair access: Elevator to right in front of restaurant.

La Bouillabaisse $$ FRENCH/SEAFOOD
145 Atlantic Ave., Brooklyn Heights, Brooklyn   (718) 522-8275
Credit cards: Cash only   Meals: Br, L, D, LN

The fact that La Bouillabaisse draws crowds willing to wait an hour in line for a table is testimony both to the well-made dishes on its traditional French menu and to the paucity of choices in the area. In Manhattan, La Bouillabaisse fades into the crowd. Take your own bottle.

Alcohol: Wine. **Price range:** Apps., $3–$9.50; entrees, $6.95–$19; desserts, $4.50. **Wheelchair access:** Staff will provide assistance. **Services:** Catering, takeout, private parties.

L'Absinthe ☆ $$$$ BRASSERIE/FRENCH
227 E. 67th St. (bet. Second & Third Aves.)   (212) 794-4950
Credit cards: All major   Meals: Br, L, D

The etched glass, mirrors, polished brass and ancient clocks in this gorgeous restaurant give it the familiar warmth of a typical bistro and it serves some of the best old-fashioned food. The saucisson chaud, generous slices of poached sausage paired with potatoes and lentils, is perfect French bistro food, and the cold seafood platter is enough for six. The best of the main courses is the Moroccan-style salmon, the spicy, crusty fish served with couscous and preserved lemons. Desserts are always impeccable, like the lemon tart and the crème caramel, and there is not a crisper, more buttery or better warm apple tart in all of New York. Unfortunately, if you are not a regular all this is served with a dose of attitude. (*Ruth Reichl*)

Other recommended dishes: Pan-seared loin of lamb; hanger steak with red-wine sauce; warm chocolate cake. **Wine list:** The French and American list is short but beautifully chosen for this food, and it is fairly priced. **Price range:** Avg. dinner, $55. Prix fixe: brunch, $29.50; lunch, $29.50; tasting menu, $65. **Wheelchair access:** There is one small step up to the dining room; three steps down to restroom. **Services:** Private parties.

L'Acajou $$ Bistro/French
53 W. 19th St. (bet. Fifth & Sixth Aves.)   (212) 645-1706
Credit cards: All major   ,   Meals: L, D, LN

Regular customers make going to this well-worn Chelsea bistro feel like coming home. Reliable food, a terrific wine list and an ever-changing art show add to the slightly funky atmosphere.

Price range: Lunch: apps., $6.50–$8.50; entrees, $9–$17; desserts, $4–$6. Dinner: apps., $5–$18; entrees, $16–$26; desserts, $4–$6. **Wheelchair access:** Not accessible. **Features:** Smoking permitted. **Services:** Catering, private parties.

La Caravelle ☆☆☆ $$$$ French
33 W. 55th St. (near Fifth Ave.)   (212) 586-4252
Credit cards: All major   Meals: L, D   Closed Sun.

La Caravelle is a French restaurant of the old school, a great social stage where people go to look at one another. The pretty murals and flattering lighting make everyone look good, and the captains are skilled at making their customers feel as good as they look.

No restaurant in New York does a better job at guarding tradition while honoring the present. If you are searching for solid French cooking — airy quenelles in a creamy, rich lobster sauce, filet of Dover sole meunière or a truly satisfying vol-au-vent — you will find it here. And nobody does classic dishes like roasted chicken with Champagne sauce or canard à l'orange better. But that is just one part of the menu. New inventions are scattered among these old dishes. You can have foie gras as a terrine, or simply sautéed and served with an exciting confit of green tomatoes. Choose the restaurant's famous crab salad or the light crisp crab cakes laced with corn.

The food changes with the seasons. A memorable winter dish was circles of squid stuffed with dark rice and spinach and set in saffron sauce. Tart cranberry relish and sharp horseradish brought out the deep sweetness of roasted vegetables in a terrine of winter vegetables. The menu offers little red meat, but fish is particularly fine. The daurade royale stuffed with vegetables and steamed so that it tastes supremely of itself is fabulous. For dessert, the marquise au chocolat is intense enough to make a chocaholic swoon and soufflés are excellent. (*Ruth Reichl*)

Wine list: Mostly expensive; some lower-priced bottles. **Price range:** Prix-fixe lunch, $36. Prix-fixe dinner, $68; tasting menus, $90 and $110; pre-theater dinner, $48. **Wheelchair access:** Everything at street level.

La Cascade $25 & Under CHINESE
Sheraton La Guardia East Hotel, 135-20 39th Ave.,
Flushing, Queens (718) 460-6666
Credit cards: All major Meals: B, Br, L, D

Would you believe this is a Chinese restaurant? In fact, it serves highly unusual specialties like cross-bridge noodles from Yunnan, but you can get them only if you order a Yunnan noodle banquet at least a day in advance. It's not too expensive and it is great fun, but you need at least six people.

Price range: Banquet: $19.95, $25.95 or $35. **Wheelchair access:** Elevator to dining room; restrooms are on the same level. **Features:** Smoking permitted. **Services:** Catering, private parties.

La Cocina $ MEXICAN/TEX-MEX
762 Eighth Ave. (bet. 46th & 47th Sts.) (212) 730-1860
2608 Broadway (bet. 98th & 99th Sts.) (212) 865-7333
Credit cards: All major Meals: L, D

Somewhere between the margarita mills and the better, more authentic Mexican restaurants are places like La Cocina where you can find competently made tacos, enchiladas and flautas, but rarely will you find anything that makes you sit up and take notice.

Price range: Apps., $5.25–$6.25; entrees, $5.55–$7.25; desserts, $2.25. **Wheelchair access:** Restrooms not accessible. **Features:** Kid friendly. **Services:** Delivery, takeout.

La Côte Basque ☆☆☆ $$$$ FRENCH
60 W. 55th St. (bet. Fifth & Sixth Aves.) (212) 688-6525
Credit cards: All major Meals: L, D

For 36 years La Côte Basque was a bastion of civility on East 55th Street. When the restaurant lost its lease in 1994, there was much mourning. Even if a new home could be found, what would La Côte Basque be without its famous murals? In the end the murals turned out to be portable (they are painted on canvas), and the restaurant sashayed across Fifth Avenue and settled gracefully into intimate new quarters.

The food is still well prepared and well presented, but rarely so unmannerly as to call undue attention to itself. Similarly, the menu is smaller, more modern and easier to read than the one in the old restaurant. The daily seafood special is often a discreet heap of fresh crab meat and lobster daintily topped with grains of black caviar. The most exciting entree is cassoulet, a splendid pile of white beans cooked with pork loin, duck confit and fat chunks of garlic sausage until each bean bursts with fat and flavor. I liked the duck, too, with crisply lacquered skin. Dover sole, a frequent special, is the best of the fish. The fillet of black bass wrapped in "scales" of potato and served in a classic red wine sauce is a close second. These dishes are extremely well executed. And large. Each plate is piled with food, making the $68 prix-fixe dinner menu a good deal.
(*Ruth Reichl*)

Wine list: Mostly French and mostly expensive, with a few lower-priced selections. **Price range:** Prix-fixe lunch, $36; prix-fixe dinner, $68, with supplements. **Wheelchair access:** Dining room at street level. Restrooms downstairs but there is an elevator. **Services:** Private parties.

L'Actuel ☆ ☆ $$ BRASSERIE/FRENCH

145 E. 50th St. (bet. Lexingtion & Third Aves.)   (212) 583-0001
Credit cards: All major   Meals: B, Br, L, D   Closed Sun.

Behold the brasserie of the future. It feels French. It sounds French. But there's an unmistakable, enticing whiff of Spain, Italy, North Africa and the Caribbean in the air. L'Actuel is the most modern French restaurant in New York. The name of this sparkling brasserie can be translated as "right now," and the name means what it says. It's up-to-the-minute in a very French way, which is to say that it is pointedly international, while hanging on for dear life to the essential qualities that define a brasserie. It has an Alsatian choucroute, of course, and one worthy of the name: a cornucopia of smoked meats and sausages on a heaping pile of sauerkraut perfumed with juniper and cumin. It also has a tapas menu — but French tapas, like marinated grilled zucchini stuffed with goat cheese. There are plates of fruits de mer, because there must be, but you get a superior American cocktail sauce along with the mignonette, not to mention chewy, saline seaweed bread. The chef also makes a place on his menu for tartes flambées, the thin-crust pizzas of his native Alsace, but side by side with an orthodox cheese, onion and bacon tart smeared with a layer of crème fraîche, he offers a wild-card tart topped with wasabi and bluefin tuna

The place looks like several restaurants merged into one. The front of the dining room, with heavy, low-slung circular chairs, has the feel of a lounge. Toward the back, banquettes along one wall suggest a bistro, while across the room, dark, grilled wine cabinets seem as though they belong in a gentlemen's club. But like the menu, everything seems to make sense in an indefinable way. Fish dishes are impressive; so too the tajine of veal shank, served in a peaked Moroccan vessel, swimming in a rich braising liquid and served with a dense, unctuous macaroni gratin that is worth the price of the entree. Desserts are intriguing. The obligatory apple tart happens to be excellent, with a properly burnt crust.

Other recommended dishes: Roasted snapper stuffed with Provençal vegetables; warm chocolate cake; crème brûlée plate. **Wine list:** A geographically diverse 250-bottle list of mostly modest wines at modest prices, with 22 wines by the glass or carafe. **Price range:** Lunch: apps., $7–$13; entrees, $12–$24; desserts, $8–$9. Dinner: apps., $8–$14; entrees, $17–$24; desserts, $8–$9. Brunch, $25. **Wheelchair access:** Restrooms on street level.

Lady Mendl's Tea Parlour $$ ENGLISH

56 Irving Pl. (bet. 17th & 18th Sts.)   (212) 533-4466
Credit cards: All major   Meals: D   Closed Mon., Tue.

This haute Victorian parlor in the Inn at Irving Place offers a popular afternoon tea that is traditional but not slavishly so. Sandwiches might include excellent smoked salmon or thin-sliced cucumber brushed with mascarpone. Then, a scone with luxurious clotted cream and preserves, and finally desserts, like a luscious apricot tart or maybe some refreshing fruit. Teas are carefully chosen and include some unusual blends like Eros, a mixture of black tea, hibiscus and mallow flowers.

Price range: Five courses, $30 per person. **Wheelchair access:** Not accessible. **Features:** Romantic, smoking permitted. **Services:** Private parties.

La Esquina Criolla $25 & Under

ARGENTINE/URUGUAYAN

94-67 Corona Blvd., Corona, Queens   (718) 699-5579
Credit cards: All major   Meals: L, D

Like other Argentine and Uruguayan grills in the area, La Esquina Criolla is both meat market and restaurant. While some customers may take home one of the reasonably priced steaks, almost everybody in the throng on a Saturday night is filling up right there. Certainly, some grills are prettier than La Esquina

Criolla — "the Spanish corner," as one of the owners translates the name. But it's hard to imagine a sweeter restaurant, despite a language barrier. And you can't get a better steak value than La Criolla's shell steak, a thick cut with the mineral tang and charred crust that you ordinarily find only in a dry-aged steak.

Each table is set with a bowl of chimichurri, a condiment made primarily of garlic, parsley and olive oil, which goes well with the excellent entraña, a well-charred beefy skirt steak with robust flavors. Or lather it on the enormous mixed grill plate, which includes skirt steak, savory pork chorizo, blood sausage, which was mealy but flavorful, crisp tripe, short ribs and somewhat chewy sweetbreads. All meals are supplemented with vegetables like flawless yucca frita — puffy chunks of fried yucca — or fried plantains, both sweet and green. Cap it off with an excellent flan topped with creamy dulce de leche, which is like pure caramel.

Other recommended dishes: Roast chicken. **Price range:** Apps., $1.25–$3.50; entrees, $5.95–$18.95. **Wheelchair access:** Everything is on one level.

La Flor $25 & Under   Eclectic
53-02 Roosevelt Ave., Woodside, Queens   (718) 426-8023
Credit cards: Cash only   Meals: B, L, D

The gloomy corner of Roosevelt Avenue and 53rd Street in Queens is an unlikely spot to find a lively and unusual restaurant, but La Flor has become a culinary center for the neighborhood. In an ocean of franchise duplicates, formula menus and by-the-numbers décor, La Flor stands out both for its looks and its food. The chef has assembled a menu that puts specialties from Mexico side by side with French and Italian dishes. Sometimes he even creates a fusion dish, like his shrimp pastilla, Moroccan-derived but clearly his own, wrapping shrimp with rice and almonds in crisp phyllo dough and serving it in a mole poblano sauce.

The polyglot menu includes excellent individual pizzas, the crusts puffy and thick on the edges yet crisp and smoky underneath. The Mexican pizza, made with queso blanco, studded with chili rounds and juicy pieces of marinated pork, and scented with cilantro, is a standout. Almost everything with pork is good, like the tacos with carnitas, or a fat, satisfying sandwich of flavorful roasted leg of pork on a fine glossy bun, augmented by sweet pineapple slices, cheese and chipotle mayonnaise.

Breakfast includes bourbon-vanilla French toast, made with thick slices of multigrain bread, or fine huevos rancheros, a Southwestern scramble of eggs, onions, peppers and tomatoes. Best of all, though, are the baked goods, like fabulous cheese biscuits and those sticky buns. Desserts are a high point, too, from the sophisticated blueberry and walnut tart to the fudgy, spectacularly big chocolate cookie. La Flor does not have a liquor license, so you may bring your own.

Other recommended dishes: Sticky buns, shrimp pastilla, pizzas, tacos, Mexican sandwiches, spareribs, steak, house salad, corn salad, French toast, huevos rancheros, blueberry-walnut tart. **Price range:** Apps., $4–$6; entrees, $6–$13. **Wheelchair access:** One step at entrance; doorways are narrow.

La Fonda Boricua $ Latin American
169 E. 106th St. (bet. Third & Lexington Aves.)   (212) 410-7292
Credit cards: Cash only   Meals: B, L, D

Everything seems to move to a beat at La Fonda, a friendly place where the food is hearty and satisfying, particularly the beef stew, tender meat teamed with peppers and onions; arroz con pollo, smoky baked chicken with a mass of yellow rice; a chewy octopus salad made with onions, green peppers and olives; and pernil, peppery roast pork. All are served with a selection of three beans: white, pink or red.

Price range: Entrees, $4.50–$9; desserts, $3. **Wheelchair access:** Fully accessible. **Features:** Kid friendly. **Services:** Catering, takeout, private parties.

La Fusta $ Argentine/Latin American
8032 Baxter Ave., Flushing, Queens   (718) 429-8222
Credit cards: All major   Meals: L, D, LN

This old-style Argentine restaurant in Flushing offers exactly what you would expect: meat, meat and more meat. Grilled steaks are particularly good, and the mixed grill, including sausages, tripe and several kinds of steak, is huge and satisfying. The Italian dishes, the other usual component at Argentine restaurants, don't come off as well.

Price range: Apps., $2–$12.50; entrees, $2–$22.50; desserts, $2–$6. **Wheelchair access:** Fully accessible. **Features:** Kid friendly. **Services:** Catering, takeout, private parties.

La Goulue $$$ Bistro/French
746 Madison Ave. (bet. 64th & 65th Sts.)   (212) 988-8169
Credit cards: All major   Meals: L, D

Le Tout Paris descends on La Goulue when visiting New York City. Chic, attractive and expensive, this is one of those upscale bistros that tastes much better if you speak French.

Price range: Lunch: apps., $6–$12; entrees, $15–$22; desserts, $8. Dinner: apps., $8–$14; entrees, $19–$27; desserts, $8. **Wheelchair access:** Fully accessible. **Features:** Romantic, outdoor dining. **Services:** Takeout, private parties.

La Grenouille ☆☆☆ $$$$ FRENCH

3 E. 52nd St. (near Fifth Ave.)   (212) 752-1495
Credit cards: All major   Meals: L, D   Closed Sun., Mon.

La Grenouille is one of the few New York restaurants that still
serves many of the French classics, including quenelles de brochette, perfectly grilled Dover sole and the best soufflés in New
York. It is also the most frustrating restaurant in New York. This
is not because the food is bad or the service unpleasant. Just
the opposite; in fact, the restaurant displays such flashes of bril-
liance that each failure is a deep disappointment.

La Grenouille could so easily be a four-star establishment
with its golden light, magnificent floral displays and professional and caring staff. As we sink into our seats, our captain
bustles about making us comfortable and reciting the specials
with irresistible enthusiasm. He suggests the special chicken
liver mousse in crayfish-and-shrimp sauce. It is superb. Poached
chicken is memorable, a tasty bird served in a fine horseradish
sauce complemented by both celery and celery root. For dessert
there is a bitter chocolate tart with a barely sweetened, deep
chocolate sorbet.

Each meal I've had here has offered moments of joyful excellence, but unfortunately many dishes are entirely forgettable.
You can count on a good meal at La Grenouille. If you're lucky,
however, you may get a great one. (*Ruth Reichl*)

Other recommended dishes: Littlenecks Corsini; rack of lamb;
chicken in Champagne sauce; ice creams and sorbets. **Most
popular dish:** Dover sole grillée. **Chef's favorite:** Quenelles de
brochette. **Wine list:** Affordable bottles have been added to the
Old Bordeaux still available for the very rich. **Price range:** Prix-
fixe lunch, $45; dinner, $90; tasting menu, $110. **Wheelchair
access:** Everything at street level. **Services:** Private parties.

La Grolla ☆ $$ ITALIAN

413 Amsterdam Ave. (near 80th St.)   (212) 496-0890
Credit cards: All major   Meals: Br, L, D

La Grolla is a small, cramped but friendly restaurant offering
warm if not very good service. It showcases the rustic, simple
cuisine of Val d'Aosta, a tiny region of Italy wedged tightly
between the French and Swiss Alps. The food leans heavily
toward hearty fare intended to keep shepherds moving uphill in
freezing weather.

Start with fonduta, an Italian versian of fondue made with
Fontina cheese. The flavor is irresistible; nutty, with a distinct
tang. The seupa Valpellinzentsche, a peasant-simple soup thick
enough to bend a spoon, is a casserole of whole-wheat bread-
chunks, savoy cabbage and fontina cheese in an oxtail stock.
All the pastas are made on the premises but they are not all that
successful. The best was pappardelle with a wild-game ragout.

The restaurant does a fine roasted rabbit, and the chicken stew with rosemary and chestnuts is wonderfully sweet and savory. Desserts are straightforward and good. After dinner, try the grolla (for which the restaurant is named), a box with a mixture of coffee, grappa, Grand Marnier, sugar and orange zest that is set afire to burn off the alcohol.

Other recommended dishes: Venison carpaccio; artichokes with almond pesto; carbonada; ricotta cheesecake; panna cotta. **Wine list:** Modest, but modestly priced. Poor selection of wines by the glass, but interesting after-dinner wines and grappas. **Price range:** Lunch: apps., $5–$10; entrees, $11–$19; desserts, $6–$8. Brunch dishes, $5–$11. Dinner: apps., $6–$11; entrees, $12–$23; desserts, $6–$8. **Wheelchair access:** Everything at street level.

Lakruwana $25 & Under   SRI LANKAN
358 W. 44th St. (bet. Eighth & Ninth Aves.)   (212) 957-4480
Credit cards: All major   Meals: L, D

One of the city's very few Sri Lankan restaurants, Lakruwana offers a great opportunity to taste this spicy, unusual cuisine, close to Indian food but with its own spicy character. Try hoppers, delicate pancakes made of rice flour and coconut milk; masala wade, a deep-fried disk of lentils and onions eaten with a fiery sauce, and pittu, a rich, dry, light grain served with curries. Lentil soup is unlike any lentil soup I've ever had, puréed lentils blended with coconut milk to an unbelievably creamy consistency, garnished with parsley and crisp, buttery croutons. There's even a worthwhile dessert, watalappan, a light, creamy pudding that tastes of caramel and nutmeg.

Other recommended dishes: Cutlet; kotthu roti; shrimp biryani; lamb black curry. **Alcohol:** Bring your own. **Price range:** Apps., $3.75–$6.95; entrees, $11.95–$16.95; desserts, $3.90. **Wheelchair access:** Everything is on one level. **Services:** Delivery, takeout, catering, private parties.

La Locanda $25 & Under   ITALIAN
737 Ninth Ave. (near 50th St.)   (212) 258-2900
Credit cards: All major   Meals: L, D

La Locanda serves pastas and meat dishes that stand out for their simplicity and flavor, and offers an enticing and unusually arranged wine list. Start with the basket of bread and focaccia, freshly baked at La Locanda's bakery, Il Forno, which is just around the corner. Second, try one of the large and alluring salads, like insalata rifredda, essentially an Italian version of the frise salad, a bistro classic, made with goat cheese and cubes of pancetta. Pastas can be excellent, either as a shared appetizer or as a main course. The chef, Ivan Beacco, is refreshingly unfussy in his approach, allowing simple combinations of flavors to speak for themselves without muddying them with extra ingredients. Penne alla Genovese is perfectly al dente, with carrots, celery and onions cooked until meltingly sweet and flavored with a sprinkle of herbs.

Mr. Beacco's meat dishes also benefit from his restraint, which seems to make up for a tendency toward overcooking. His sliced leg of lamb, served like all the main courses with roasted potatoes and sautéed broccoli rape, is past the point of pink, but the sauce, simply lamb juices and herbs, imbues the meat with flavor. The same is true of veal shoulder, aromatic and delicious in its sauce of herbs, white wine and veal juices. The wine list is large for this sort of restaurant and worth noting, with good choices at low prices. For dessert, skip tiramisu and profiteroles, and opt instead for the rustic blueberry tart or the compact French-style strawberry tart.

Other recommended dishes: Rice salad; orechiette with broccoli rape; linguine with tiny clams and garlic; sautéed calf's liver; roasted pork with green olive and mustard sauce. **Price range:** Apps., $7.50–$11; pastas and entrees, $11–$21.50. **Wheelchair access:** Step at entrance; restrooms are small and entryway is narrow.

La Lupe $25 & Under MEXICAN/TEX-MEX
43-16 Greenpoint Ave., Sunnyside, Queens (718) 784-2528
Credit cards: Cash only Meals: L, D, LN

This neat, bright taquería has all the atmospheric hallmarks of authenticity, from the blaring jukebox to the big television set tuned to Spanish soap operas to the dour men silently sipping beer. Tacos are fine, the pozole — a soulful, mild soup thick with puffed hominy and chunks of pork — is terrific, and the long list of main courses includes some unusual dishes like pierna adobada, chunks of tender pork in an extremely spicy sauce, and pollo en salsa chipotle, chicken breasts that are flattened, grilled and served in moderately spicy sauce with the distinctive smoky flavor of chipotle chilies.

Other recommended dishes: Enchiladas de mole poblano; chilaquiles verdes. **Price range:** Almost everything is under $10. **Wheelchair access:** Restroom is downstairs. **Features:** Kid friendly. **Services:** Takeout.

La Maison de Sade $$$ THEME
206 W. 23rd St. (bet. Seventh & Eighth Aves.) (212) 645-2999
Credit cards: All major Meals: D, LN

If you dream of dining with the Marquis de Sade, pull up a chair. The waiters carry whips and would love to abuse you. The food is actually decent, but who's eating?

Price range: Apps., $4.95–$18.95; entrees, $12.95–$20.95; desserts, $6.95. Prix fixe: $19.99 (Sun.-Thur., 5-7 P.M.); $27–$37 (daily, parties of 6 or more). **Features:** Smoking permitted. **Services:** Catering, private parties.

La Metairie $$ FRENCH
189 W. 10th St. (at W. 4th St.) (212) 989-0343
Credit cards: All major Meals: Br, D, LN

A Village dream, that cozy, rustic little restaurant hidden among twisting streets. Good Provençal food and dim lighting make this a romantic retreat.

Alcohol: Beer and wine. **Price range:** Lunch: apps., $6–$16; entrees, $12–$22; desserts, $7.50. Dinner: apps., $7–$19; entrees, $18–$26; desserts, $8.50. **Wheelchair access:** Fully accessible. **Services:** Catering, private parties.

Landmark Tavern $$ BAR SNACKS
626 11th Ave. (at 46th St.) (212) 757-8595
Credit cards: All major Meals: L, D, LN

The English pub food is not the point at this great old-time watering hole. Entering the rickety town house restaurant feels like taking a step into the past, and it's great fun for gathering with friends for drinks and simple dishes like burgers and hearty soups. Steer clear of the more complicated stuff.

Price range: Apps., $4–$9; entrees, $14–$28; desserts, $10–$14. **Wheelchair access:** Fully accessible on first floor. **Features:** Smoking permitted. **Services:** Catering, private parties, takeout.

La Nonna ☆ $$ ITALIAN
133 W. 13th St. (bet. Sixth & Seventh Aves.) (212) 741-3663
Credit cards: All major Meals: L, D

La Nonna is a warm, inviting place that does a perfectly good job with its no-nonsense menu of thoroughly traditional Tuscan dishes. The emphasis is on meat and fish roasted or grilled in a wood-burning oven that you can see in the back of the dining room, framed by decorative Italian tiles. The dining room has a simple, inviting look, with well-spaced tables and antique engravings of Tuscan scenes on the walls. You can find better meals, but rarely in such agreeable surroundings.

The appetizers at La Nonna can be as simple as pink slices of prosciutto draped on thick slices of Tuscan bread coated with olive oil, or crostini piled high with chicken liver pâté. A hot, messy casserole of radicchio, anchovies and scamorza is a triple threat of assertive flavors and a great way to take the edge off the cold. The wood-burning oven, alas, turns out to be an underperformer. A marinated Cornish hen, flattened out and grilled to a nice, crisp char, makes the best advertisement for the oven. It is moist, tender and oozing with spicy juices.

Pasta turns out to be the most dependable category on the menu. The Gorgonzola gnocchi are as light as whipped cream. Another standout is strozzapreti, slightly sticky dumplings of Swiss chard and spinach firmed up with ricotta and Parmesan cheese, then doused with butter and sage. Anyone determined to get to the heart of the cuisine should proceed directly to the trippa alla Fiorentina. By some mysterious process, it becomes a deeply satisfying, earthy mix of sharp tomato flavor, fragrant rosemary, white wine and sweetly rich vegetables wrapped around chewy slivers of tripe.

Other recommended dishes: Pappardelle with duck ragú; Italian cheesecake. **Price range:** Lunch: apps., $5–$8.50; entrees, $10–$21.50; desserts, $7. Dinner: apps., $6–$9.50; entrees, $16.50–$24.50; desserts, $7. **Wheelchair access:** Three steps down to front door; restrooms on main floor. **Features:** Smoking at the bar.

La Paella $25 & Under SPANISH

214 E. 9th St. (bet Second & Third Aves.)
Credit cards: MC/V

(212) 598-4321
Meals: D, LN

Dark, crowded, smoky and loud, La Paella is like an American's fantasy of a Spanish tapas bar and includes the basic tapas repertory, like thick wedges of Manchego cheese with apple slices, delicate rounds of cold marinated squid and a puffy potato omelet. About 20 selections — sort of an introduction to tapas — are available each day, and almost all are very good, but it's best to order a chef's selection, a plate with enough to feed three people. The paellas are rich, full of flavor and enormous. For dessert, the crema catalana is so good that I'd consider naming the restaurant after this dish instead.

Alcohol: Beer and wine. **Price range:** Apps., $4–$9; entrees, $12–$17; desserts, $5. **Wheelchair access:** Restrooms not accessible. **Features:** Smoking permitted. **Services:** Delivery, takeout, catering, private parties.

La Palapa $25 & Under MEXICAN

77 St. Marks Pl.
Credit cards: All major

(212) 777-2537
Meals: L, D, LN

This bright and cheerful restaurant in the East Village, is the latest in a fleet of new Mexican restaurants that reveal the regional glories of Mexico rather than the familiar one-dimensional margarita-fueled Tex-Mex dishes. The fascinating menu shows off all sorts of complex flavor combinations based on traditional Mexican ingredients. A moist cod fillet is served in pipian verde, a sauce based on ground pumpkin seeds that is quite different from similar sauces. It's quiet and subtle, given its color by cilantro and extra taste by a mild chili that complements the cod perfectly. Though appetizers are the least interesting part of the menu, they are satisfying. Tacos are authentically Mexican and come with fillings like spicy chili-rubbed chicken, shrimp in a smoky adobo sauce or mild poblano chili with epazote and onions. Guacamole is chunky and well spiced.

The real excitement comes with the main courses, like thin slices of duck breast, fanned out in a wonderful sesame mole with a rich, almost malty chocolate flavor given added dimension by the underlying chili heat, served with savory rice and refried black beans. Chicken enchiladas are almost stewlike, in a soupy tomatillo sauce that is very spicy but tangy as well. For dessert, try rich Mexican chocolate ice cream and a spicy chili-laced peach sorbet. They also accompany other delicious desserts, like an empanada stuffed with cinnamon-flavored rice pudding.

Other recommended dishes: Jicama and pineapple salas, ceviche, catfish tamal, shrimp with garlic, pork chop, roast chicken. **Price range:** Apps., $4.50–$8.95; entrees, $11.95–$18.95. **Wheelchair access:** Everything is on one level.

La Perricholi $ PERUVIAN/COLOMBIAN
106-26 Corona Ave., Flushing, Queens   (718) 271-8687
Credit cards: All major   Meals: L, D

This friendly restaurant offers an expansive Peruvian menu with some Colombian dishes. Ceviches are fine, as is lomo saltado, stir-fried beef served over french fries. The menu includes some unusual items, like goat steak and tripe stew. The chicha morada, a soft drink made from purple corn, is fabulous. Lunches are quiet, but an imposing sound system may be loud at night.

Price range: Entrees, $3–$10. **Wheelchair access:** Not accessible. **Services:** Takeout.

La Pizza Fresca $25 & Under   ITALIAN/PIZZA
31 E. 20th St. (bet. Park Ave. S. & Broadway)   (212) 598-0141
Credit cards: AE   Meals: L, D, LN

Carefully made brick-oven pizzas with firm, crisp crusts and impeccably fresh toppings are the hallmark of this simple, handsome restaurant. Pastas, too, are worth trying, from the basic spaghetti al pomodoro to the more complex gnocchetti al pesto, tiny potato dumplings that are surprisingly light.

Other recommended dishes: Pizzas (margherita, salame piccante, quattro stagioni, acciughe); fagioli all'uccelletto. **Alcohol:** Beer and wine. **Price range:** $15–$25. **Wheelchair access:** Everything is on one level. **Features:** Outdoor dining. **Services:** Delivery, takeout.

L'Ardoise $25 & Under   FRENCH

1207 First Ave. (bet. 65th & 66th Sts.)   (212) 744-4752
Credit cards: All major   Meals: L, D

This unfashionable little restaurant is not much to look at, but
the well-prepared traditional French food and the quirky charm
of the proprietor more than make up for this. Bistro favorites
like warm frisée salad with lardons, steamed mussels, duck
confit and steak frites are all good bets.

Alcohol: Beer and wine. **Price range:** Entrees, $6.50–$7.95;
desserts, $5–$5.50. Prix fixe: $16.95 (5-6:30 P.M.); $16.95–$26.95
(after 6:30 P.M.). **Wheelchair access:** Fully accessible. **Features:**
Smoking permitted. **Services:** Catering, takeout, private parties.

La Taza de Oro $25 & Under   PUERTO RICAN

96 Eighth Ave. (bet. 14th & 15th Sts.)   (212) 243-9946
Credit cards: Cash only   Meals: B, L, D

This little Puerto Rican restaurant has not changed at all in
decades. And why tamper with success? A cheerful waiter
greets diners with "Hello, capitan," though regulars are pro-
moted to general. The food is forceful and delicious, and the
portions are huge, from garlic-suffused roast pork to tender
octopus salad with marinated onions. The inexpensive café con
leche is better than almost any coffee bar's cappuccino, at a
third the price.

Alcohol: Bring your own. **Price range:** Apps., $2–$3; entrees,
$3.50–$10.50; desserts, $1.50. **Wheelchair access:** Not accessi-
ble. **Services:** Catering, takeout.

Lavagna $25 & Under   MEDITERRANEAN

545 E. 5th St. (at Ave. B)   (212) 979-1005
Credit cards: Cash only   Meals: D, LN   Closed Sun.

Lavagna's food is fresh and generous, with honest, straightforward flavors. The simple rectangular dining room is casual and
inviting, but can get loud when it's crowded. Pastas are best,
both simple dishes like rigatoni with crumbled fennel sausage,
peas, tomatoes and cream, and more complicated ones like
fresh pappardelle with rabbit stew. Cacciucco, the Tuscan fish
soup scented with saffron and anise, and served with mussels,
cockles and chunks of fish, is a great value.

Other recommended dishes: Grilled vegetables with goat
cheese and hazelnuts; grilled stuffed squid; sweetbreads with
polenta and mushrooms; roasted sardines; chicken grilled under
a brick; roasted sea bass; cheesecake; panna cotta. **Alcohol:**
Bring your own. **Price range:** Apps., $5–$7; entrees,
$11–$16.50. **Wheelchair access:** Everything is on one level.
Features: Romantic.

218

La Vineria $25 & Under   ITALIAN

19 W. 55th St. (at Fifth Ave.)   (212) 247-3400
Credit cards: All major   Meals: L, D

With its brick walls lined with wine bottles, its tile floor and its
timbered ceiling, La Vineria is a warm, modestly priced oasis in
a midtown neighborhood full of expensive restaurants and fast-
food joints. What's best at La Vineria is what's least expensive:
the salads and the fine, individual-size brick-oven pizzas. The
best thing at La Vineria is a pizza with the poetic name Miseria
e Nobilta, a 12-inch round of pizza topped with mozzarella and
Parmesan, and covered in huge arugula leaves and footlong
slices of prosciutto. It is pizza nirvana.

Other recommended dishes: Field greens; insalata caprese;
prosciutto and melon; quattro stagioni and boscaiola pizzas.
Alcohol: Beer and wine. **Price range:** Apps., $6.50–$12.50;
entrees, $11.50–$28.50; desserts, $6–$7. **Wheelchair access:**
Fully accessible. **Features:** Good for business. **Services:** Private
parties.

Layla ☆ ☆ $$$ MIDDLE EASTERN

211 W. Broadway (at Franklin St.)   (212) 431-0700
Credit cards: All major   Meals: L, D

Part of the Drew Nieporent-Robert De Niro empire, Layla is a
hip downtown setting for the Arabian nights, complete with
broken pottery shards on the wall and a belly dancer twirling
through the room after 9 P.M. Layla is tasty and lots of fun, featuring good Middle Eastern food from the wood-burning oven.
The smooth baba gannouj, briny taramosalata and tzatziki are
seductively delicious dips. The phyllo-wrapped sardines are fabulous. The lobster pastilla is one of those sweet, spicy Moroccan dishes that everybody loves. The lamb shank arrives in a
tagine, the conical north African casserole, atop grains of couscous. Both dishes are irresistible. Desserts are original and delicious, especially the eggy orange blossom crème brûlée. (*Ruth
Reichl, updated by Eric Asimov*)

Other recommended dishes: Hummus; tabbouleh; spiced carrots; falafel; lamb ravioli; spiced chicken; pomegranate
napoleon. **Wine list:** Entertaining to read and nicely chosen,
with good choices under $20. **Price range:** Lunch (Fri. only):
apps., $5–$12; entrees, $12–$18; desserts, $7–$10. Dinner: apps.,
$5–$14; entrees, $20–$29; desserts, $7–$10. **Wheelchair access:**
Four steps up to dining room. **Features:** Smoking permitted, outdoor dining (patio). **Services:** Takeout, private parties.

Le Bateau Ivre $25 & Under BISTRO/FRENCH

230 E. 51st St. (bet. Second & Third Aves.) (212) 583-0579
Credit cards: All major Meals: D, LN

This little wine bar and restaurant is so wholeheartedly French
that every one of the 250 wines on its list, including 150 available by the glass, is French. There are some good buys on the
list, but navigate carefully; there are just as many expensive
bottles. The menu is likewise straightforwardly French, with
some good choices like lobster bisque and grilled lamb. A generous portion of mussels marinières is perfectly cooked, and
roast chicken is juicy and inviting.

Other recommended dishes: Grilled salmon; hamburger; lamb
chops. **Price range:** Apps., $5–$9; entrees, $7.50–$18.50.
Wheelchair access: Everything is on the same level. **Services:**
Private parties.

Le Bernardin ☆☆☆☆ $$$$ FRENCH/SEAFOOD

155 W. 51st St. (bet. Sixth & Seventh Aves.) (212) 489-1515
Credit cards: All major Meals: L, D Closed Sun.

Most restaurants grow into their stars. Not Le Bernardin: at the
ripe old age of three months, it had all four stars bestowed
upon it. The restaurant has been in the spotlight ever since. In
1986, the brother-and-sister team of Gilbert and Maguy Le Coze
moved from Paris to New York, and Mr. Le Coze's cooking
changed American dining. His style, impeccably fresh fish
cooked with respect and simplicity, was so widely copied that
people forgot who had invented it. But as other restaurants followed the Le Cozes' lead, buying better fish and cooking it in
more interesting ways, Le Bernardin itself was maturing, presenting the most adventurous dishes in town. Most of the problems that plague other great establishments were solved here:
there were no rude reservations takers, no endless waits for
tables, no overcrowding in the dining room. The waiters knew
their jobs and kept their distance. Dinners were appropriately
paced. When you reserved a table at Le Bernardin, you could
count on being seated promptly, served beautifully and fed fab-
ulously.

When Mr. Le Coze died unexpectedly at 48 in 1994, after the
shock and the mourning, the wondering began: What would
happen to the restaurant? Those who predicted the decline of
Le Bernardin did not reckon with Miss Le Coze. She hired Eric
Ripert, a talented young chef, and together they gave the restaurant an infusion of energy. Today, the comfortable dining room
is prettier and less ponderous. Flowers are everywhere, giving
the teak-lined room a lighter feeling. Meanwhile, Mr. Ripert
seems to be having wonderful fun in the kitchen.

The key to Le Bernardin's food has always been to coax forward the flavor of each fish. If you think all raw fish tastes the same, take a bite of the black bass ceviche topped with a confetti of coriander, mint, jalapeños and diced tomatoes; then follow it with tuna carpaccio, a tender circle dotted with lime peel. The one is clean and fresh-tasting, the other so soft it is like velvet in the mouth. Versions of each have been on the menu since the restaurant opened, but there are also new discoveries here.

Impressive starters include the deeply flavored fish soup and the extraordinarily delicious fricassee of shellfish with sweet and delicate mussels, clams and oysters. Main courses are even more admirable. Each fish has been stripped to its basic elements and dressed up to emphasize them. A fat chunk of cod, cooked until the outside is crisp and brown and the inside white and creamy, is served on green beans, tomatoes and tiny potatoes. Presented in a pungent vinaigrette alive with the strong flavor of vinegar and the brightness of olives, this superbly simple dish is fresh and vibrant. Delicate halibut is simply poached in a saffron bouillon.

Le Bernardin once showed New York how to eat fish; now it is showing the city how a four-star restaurant should behave. (*Ruth Reichl*)

Other recommended dishes: Salmon gravlax; mackerel; lobster stew in a hearty red wine sauce with fresh fettuccine. **Wine list:** The list, which once featured mostly expensive wines, has been expanded to include a few less expensive bottles. **Price range:** Lunch prix fixe, $45; dinner prix fixe, $77; tasting menu, $95 and $125. **Wheelchair access:** Fully accessible. **Services:** Private parties.

Le Bilboquet $$$ FRENCH
25 E. 63rd St. (bet. Park & Madison Aves.)   (212) 751-3036
Credit cards: All major   Meals: L, D

You probably can't get in. Don't worry; if you did they wouldn't treat you very nicely unless you were wearing great clothes and sporting a European accent.

Price range: Apps., $6–$17; entrees, $15–$22; desserts, $7. **Wheelchair access:** Restrooms not accessible. **Features:** Smoking permitted. **Services:** Private parties (only for people they know).

Le Cirque 2000 ☆ ☆ ☆ $$$$ FRENCH/ITALIAN
New York Palace Hotel, 455 Madison Ave. (bet. 50th & 51st Sts.)

(212) 303-7788

Credit cards: All major   Meals: L, D

Behold Le Cirque 2000, a giddy swirl of wealth and privilege, of gilt without guilt, a glittering social pageant that cries out for a Balzac or a Wharton. As pure spectacle, there is nothing in New York like it.

Le Cirque is more and less than a restaurant. First and foremost, it is a social institution and an emblem of status that recalls the Gilded Age powerhouses like Delmonico's and Sherry's. Diners go to Le Cirque to see and be seen. They check in, have their self-esteem validated by Sirio Maccioni and settle in for a sumptuous evening surrounded by their own kind, preferably, but not necessarily, in the smaller of the two dining rooms, with its higher ratio of moguls to mortals.

More than any restaurant since Le Pavillon, Le Cirque is a one-man show. It is Mr. Maccioni, and Mr. Maccioni is it. An evening at Le Cirque without a table-side visit from him is social death. Diners put themselves in his practiced hands, not the kitchen's. But food was never the most important thing about Le Cirque, and at the moment, it may not even be the second or third thing. Pierre Schaedelin, who had been the executive sous-chef, is now executive chef. He has modified the menu a bit, dropping many of the Asian accents and moving toward a simpler, more robust style.

As a social dynamo, the restaurant thrums along, even if the roster of regulars often makes it seem like Le Cirque 1982 rather than Le Cirque 2000. But the kitchen merely equals the performance of the better two-star restaurants in town.

The cuisine, as always, is hard to make sense of. Is the place French, Italian or Mediterranean? I'm tempted to call it New Age Continental. One thing is certain, no one leaves hungry. The meal starts with a daunting amuse-bouche that can consist of as many as four mini-dishes of near-appetizer size. Rather than priming the appetite, they come close to killing it.

The menu moves back and forth between two poles: an almost rustic simplicity and sometimes heavy, lavishly presented fancy food. I am happy to report that one of Le Cirque's signature dishes, black sea bass wrapped in sheets of crisp, paper-thin potato and lavished with Barolo sauce, lives up to my blissful memory of it. Tuna tartare with mustard-sesame vinaigrette seemed merely dutiful at first bite, but then little threads of marinated red cabbage, woven throughout, began speaking up. With one deft little touch, the predictable became sensational.

Simpler dishes delivered. Beef short ribs, one of the rotating daily specials, was a mighty cube of savory meat, glued to the plate in a rich reduction sauce and tricked out with little dollops of marrow in the bone, eaten with a tiny silver spoon. Roast tenderloin, from a special menu of dishes done on the grill or rotisserie, made good on its simple promise.

The more ambitious entrees missed the mark, however. A whopping big veal chop, dried out on the outside, was simply overwhelmed by a mélange of sautéed mushrooms, asparagus spears wrapped in bacon and a fat tourte stuffed with potato, leek and foie gras. It was a lot to take in.

Le Cirque's gaudy, even silly undertone swells to a mighty wave at dessert time. All over the dining room, ridiculous sugar sculptures and chocolate trees make their way to tables where diners grin like kids at a birthday party. Adam Tihany's circus-theme décor, much ridiculed when the new Le Cirque opened in the spring of 1997, suddenly makes perfect sense, right down to the happy clown buttons on the velvet-clad chairs. The famous chocolate stove, one of several Le Cirque classics, carries on. But it has been joined by newer desserts, like "Lady's Hat," a big Easter parade saucer of pastry sheet arranged over roasted fruit and sorbets. One of the best of these new additions is a milk chocolate and tea tart, unctuous and rich, with a big scoop of caramel ice cream. It's a dessert for a 5-year-old. And by the end of the meal at Le Cirque, that seems just about right.

Other recommended dishes: Lobster salad. **Wine list:** An outstanding list, mostly French, of 710 wines, about 100 of them priced under $50. There are 50 half bottles and 18 wines by the glass. **Price range:** Lunch: apps., $12–$35; entrees, $28–$39; desserts, $10–$12, three-course prix-fixe, $44. Dinner: apps., $16–$35; entrees, $28–$39; desserts, $10–$12. **Wheelchair access:** Enter on 50th Street and take the elevator to the restaurant. Restroom in private dining room on lobby level can be reached via elevator.

L'ecole $$ FRENCH

French Culinary Institute, 462 Broadway (at Grand St.)
(212) 219-3300
Credit cards: All major   Meals: L, D   Closed Sun.

Eating at the practice restaurant of the French Culinary Institute is a far surer bet than, say, getting your hair cut at the local barber college. The students are well drilled in the classics and well supervised by teachers such as Jacques Pepin and Andre Soltner. Even mistakes have a certain charm, and it's hard to beat the price.

Price range: Prix fixe: lunch, $17.95; dinner, $25.95. **Wheelchair access:** Can use service entrance. **Services:** Private parties.

Le Colonial ☆☆ $$ VIETNAMESE

149 E. 57th St. (bet. Lexington & Third Aves.)   (212) 752-0808
Credit cards: All major   Meals: L, D

Nostalgic for the old days when the French filled Saigon and the wind whispered in the palm trees? Then this is for you. In fickle Manhattan, Le Colonial is no longer a rallying point for the chic and the beautiful, so you're left with Vietnamese food for the not terribly adventurous. Vietnamese cuisine, as interpreted here, is sedate Asian fare that is more delicate than Chinese food, less spicy than Thai and notable mostly for its abundance of vegetables and its absence of grease. Spring rolls at Le Colonial are so delicate you tend to forget that they are fried. The spicy beef salad is still a standout. Grilled spareribs were fragrant, chewy and just lightly herbal. The steamed fish has a pleasantly savory taste, and vegetable dishes like grilled eggplant in a spicy basil lime sauce, or steamed okra in ginger-lime sauce make a more vivid impression than any of the meat dishes. (*Ruth Reichl, updated by William Grimes*)

Other recommended dishes: Salad rolls; Vietnamese ravioli; shrimp in curried coconut sauce; grilled eggplant; fried rice. **Wine list:** Small but well priced and mostly French. **Price range:** Apps., $7–$12; entrees, $14–$23; desserts, $6–$8. Pretheater prix fixe, $24. **Wheelchair access:** Second floor bar/lounge not accessible. **Features:** Romantic, smoking permitted. **Services:** Private parties.

Le Gamin $$ CAFE/FRENCH

183 Ninth Ave. (at 21st St.)   (212) 243-8864
50 Macdougal St. (bet. Houston & Prince Sts.)   (212) 254-4678
536 E. 5th St. (bet. Aves. A & B)   (212) 254-8409
27 Bedford St. (bet. Downing & Houston Sts.)   (212) 743-2846
5 Front St. (at Old Fulton St.), Brooklyn   (718) 246-0170
Credit cards: Cash only   Meals: Br, L, D, LN

These little restaurants are like slivers of France, where the Parisian atmosphere is as thick as Gitane smoke. They offer a typical cafe menu of salads, sandwiches and omelets, but the best dishes are the crepes. With a frothy bowl of café au lait, a ham and melted cheese crepe, followed by a lemon crepe, makes a wonderful light meal.

Price range: Crepes, $3.50–$9; salads, $6.50–$11; desserts, $4–$5.50. **Wheelchair access:** Fully accessible. **Features:** Smoking permitted. **Services:** Takeout.

Le Gigot $25 & Under   FRENCH

18 Cornelia St. (bet. 4th & Bleecker Sts.)   (212) 627-3737
Credit cards: AE   Meals: Br, L, D   Closed Mon.

This little restaurant, with its little zinc bar and mirrored wall
crisscrossed with polished wood, pulses with the welcoming
spirit of a Parisian hangout. The Provence-inflected food adds to
the illusion, with excellent bistro fare like leg of lamb in a red
wine reduction; lamb stew; endive salad with apples, walnuts
and Roquefort, and rounds of baguette smeared with goat
cheese and smoky tapenade. There are disappointments, like
the steak frites: the soft, flavorless steak doesn't live up to the
surroundings. Nor does the bland, beige veal stew. The wine
list, too, needs rethinking. The best desserts are the sweet,
moist, caramelized tarte Tatin, the excellent bananas flambé,
and the great little cheese course.

Alcohol: Beer and wine. **Price range:** Apps., $7–$9; entrees,
$12–$17; desserts, $7. **Wheelchair access:** One step up to din-
ing room. **Features:** Romantic.

Le Jardin Bistro $25 & Under   FRENCH

25 Cleveland Pl. (near Spring St.)   (212) 343-9599
Credit cards: All major   Meals: Br, L, D

Just when you begin to doubt that the dish ever had any
appeal, you taste Le Jardin's steak frites, the meat chewy and
delicious, the fries crisp, salty and really hard to stop eating.
The rest of the roster of traditional bistro dishes — mussels,
cassoulet, sweetbreads — is outstanding, and the charming garden in the rear looks as if it's been there forever. The appetizers
are generally large, and excellent. Desserts also reflect the simple, generous spirit of the restaurant. If Le Jardin has any flaw,
it may be the fish dishes.

Other recommended dishes: Hanger steak; tuna tartar; foie
gras mousse; eggplant gâteau; salad with sweetbreads; venison
flank steak; chocolate marquise; crème brûlée; tarte Tatin; sorbets. **Alcohol:** Beer and wine. **Price range:** Apps., $4.75–$7.50;
entrees, $12.50–$21; desserts, $5–$6.50. **Wheelchair access:**
One step up to dining room; restrooms are narrow. **Features:**
Romantic, smoking permitted, outdoor dining. **Services:** Private
parties.

Le Madeleine $$ FRENCH

403 W. 43rd St. (bet. Ninth & 10th Aves.)   (212) 246-2993
Credit cards: All major   Meals: L, D

Proust would not have been inspired here. The menu hasn't
changed in years at this little restaurant, which crowds up on

matinee days and before the nightly curtains. The food is competently prepared but unexciting, and the menu of familiar French dishes won't surprise.

Price range: Apps., $5–$9; entrees, $8–$23; desserts, $6–$8. **Wheelchair access:** Fully accessible. **Features:** Outdoor dining. **Services:** Private parties.

Le Madri $$$$ ITALIAN
168 W. 18th St. (bet. Sixth & Seventh Aves.) (212) 727-8022
Credit cards: All major Meals: Br, L, D

Le Madri's splendid, airy Tuscan-style setting is effectively evoked by its vaulted ceiling supported by columns, strategically aimed overhead lights and well-spaced tables, and exposed tiled wood-burning oven in the dining room. The original idea was great: import some Italian mamas to do some serious Tuscan home-cooking. The moms may all have gone home, but this continues to be the model for dozens of northern Italian restaurants with similar menus. Very attractive, quite expensive.

Price range: Lunch: apps., $8–$12; entrees, $15–$20; desserts, $8.50. Dinner: apps., $10.50–$13; entrees, $25–$35; desserts, $8.50. **Wheelchair access:** Not accessible. **Features:** Good for business, smoking permitted, outdoor dining. **Services:** Delivery, takeout, private parties.

Le Max $$ FRENCH
147 W. 43rd St. (bet. Sixth Ave. & Broadway) (212) 764-3705
Credit cards: All major Meals: L, D

One of those old-fashioned theater-district restaurants: a large room and an even larger menu. The food is not fabulous, but it's a good choice if you are trying to please a bunch of people with different tastes.

Price range: Lunch: apps., $4.95–$7.95; entrees, $12.95–$20.95; desserts, $4.95–$5.95. Dinner: apps., $5.95–$9.95; entrees, $13.95–$22.95; desserts, $4.95–$5.95. **Wheelchair access:** Fully accessible. **Features:** Smoking permitted, outdoor dining. **Services:** Private parties.

Lentini ☆ $$$$ ITALIAN
1562 Second Ave. (at 81st St.) (212) 628-3131
Credit cards: All major Meals: D

Chef Giuseppe Lentini has no revolutionary ideas. He seems to operate according to the touching precept that if you are Italian and cook the food you love, the customers will come. Location and atmosphere make this a neighborhood restaurant. Some of the dishes do, too, like spaghetti with clam sauce, fried calamari and chicken cacciatore. But look more closely at the menu, scan the ambitious wine list and its equally ambitious prices, and it becomes clear that Mr. Lentini wants to be more than a nice little local standby.

Mr. Lentini's tomato sauces deserve close study. They can be light or so concentrated that you can almost slice them like terrine. The tomato sauce that arrives with a heaping plate of fried calamari is chunky, dense and powerfully concentrated, a sauce in name, but a condiment in fact. Pastas are also a very good bet. The comma-shaped gramegna, made at the restaurant, has a medium weight to suit a light tomato sauce with little cubes of swordfish and eggplant. The swordfish, miraculously, comes out perfectly moist. For dessert, try cassata, a dense, even sludgy mass of sweetened ricotta and spongecake that's topped with loose marzipan, then iced and festively decorated with candied fruit. The service wanders erratically, and advice on the extensive wine list is doled out stingily.

Other recommended dishes: Zucchini blossoms stuffed with smoked mozzarella; seafood-stuffed artichoke with fava bean purée; gramegna pasta with swordfish; spaghetti with sea urchin and saffron; veal loin with mushrooms; risotto with radicchio and Gorgonzola; Sicilian cassata. **Wine list:** An unexpectedly ambitious and often pricey list of more than 200 wines, nearly half of them Italian, with 26 half bottles and a large selection of grappas. **Price range:** Dinner, apps., $8–$13; entrees, $18–$30; desserts, $8–$10. **Wheelchair access:** Two steps to entrance.

Lento's $ ITALIAN

7003 Third Ave., Bay Ridge, Brooklyn   (718) 745-9197
833 Union St., Park Slope, Brooklyn   (718) 399-8782
Credit cards: Cash only   Meals: L, D, LN

It's hard to lump these sibling restaurants together. The original branch in Bay Ridge is a relic from the days of restaurants and pizzas past. It's just a simple brick corner tavern with a good-time neighborhood feel to it, but at one time Lento's had an air of formality that made restaurant-going a dignified business, traces of which still linger. The pizza, too, is a throwback, with a wafer-thin, extra crisp crust that makes up with texture what it lacks in elasticity or smoky flavor. The mozzarella is mellow, the tomato sauce is slightly spicy and the sausage is chunky and flavorful. The newer Park Slope branch, a handsome spot in a former firehouse, makes decent pizza but is no match for the older place.

Price range: Avg. app., $6.50; entree, $8.50; dessert, $2.50. **Wheelchair access:** Fully accessible. **Features:** Smoking permitted, outdoor dining. **Services:** Delivery, takeout.

Le Périgord ☆☆ $$$$ FRENCH

405 E. 52nd St. (east of First Ave.)   (212) 755-6244
Credit cards: All major   Meals: L, D

For more than 35 years Le Périgord has been a dignified pres-
ence on the dining scene. It's a French restaurant the way
French restaurants used to be. The waiters, well on in years,
wear white jackets. The even more senior captains wear tuxe-
dos. On the dessert trolley you know with dead certainty that
you will find floating island, chocolate mousse and tarte Tatin.

Le Périgord recently had a face-lift. The notoriously low
ceilings were raised half a foot, the banquettes were reuphol-
stered in tomato-red fabric, and the walls took on a gentle yel-
lowy peach blush. More important, the restaurant hired a new
chef, Jacques Qualin, who brought a new spark to the kitchen,
most notably in a stunning turbot with a crust of bread crumbs
and Comté cheese, so thin it scarcely seems to exist, except for
an unmistakable crunch with each bite, and a glorious overlay
of pungent, hazelnut flavor sharpened with the faintest possible touch of mustard. A light Champagne sauce enfolds the
fish like a sheet of silk. The turbot is impossible to equal. Mr.
Qualin's showy side turns up in his terrine of arctic char, the
fish ingeniously wrapped in a fish-stock-and-herb gelee so that
each slice, flavored with coconut emulsion and ginger oil,
comes out in a pattern of four pink squares defined by a thick
green border.

Mr. Qualin must be given high marks for shaking things up
at one of New York's most torpid restaurants. If only he could
remake the staff. Some nights, the restaurant can seem like a
cross between Fawlty Towers and Katz's Delicatessen. Waiters
try to remove your plate, even as you grip it tightly, fighting for
a last bite. The dessert trolley gets stuck in narrow passages,
causing the floating islands to bob furiously. The staff swarms,
then disappears. Is there a dormitory upstairs?

The diners do not seem to mind. Inside Le Périgord, they
can swaddle themselves in a quietly civilized atmosphere, a
million miles removed from the tumult of the city outside.

Other recommended dishes: Peekytoe crab soup, watercress
soup with caviar, sauteed foie gras with figs and cardamon
chutney, foie gras terrine, veal chop. **Wine list:** A fusty, mostly
French list dominated by a handful of negociants and in need of
an overhaul. **Price range:** Lunch: apps., $8–$15; entrees,
$22–$30; desserts, $9; three-course prix-fixe, $32. Dinner: three-
course prix-fixe, $57. **Wheelchair access:** Three steps down to
the dining room; restrooms are in basement.

Le Petit Hulot $$ BISTRO/FRENCH

973 Lexington Ave. (bet. 70th & 71th Sts.) (212) 794-9800
Credit cards: All major Meals: L, D

The French bistro menu is predictable but reliable, and the
small room does its best to look as if it's in Paris. Best in the
summer when you can eat in the charming outside garden.

Price range: Lunch: apps., $6–$8; entrees, $10–$15; desserts,
$7. Dinner: apps., $6–$12; entrees, $16–$23; desserts, $7.
Wheelchair access: Not accessible. **Features:** Smoking permitted, outdoor dining. **Services:** Takeout, private parties.

Le Quercy $$ BISTRO

52 W. 55th St. (bet. Fifth & Sixth Aves.) (212) 265-8141
Credit cards: All major Meals: L, D

It's been here forever, but it is still the sort of place where you
might find French chefs on their nights off. Good cassoulet,
good value.

Price range: Lunch prix fixe, $21. Dinner: apps., $6–$10;
entrees, $12–$18; desserts, $6; pre-theater, $24.75; prix fixe,
$29. **Wheelchair access:** Fully accessible.

Le Refuge $$$ FRENCH

166 E. 82nd St. (bet. Third & Lexington Aves.) (212) 861-4505
Credit cards: AE Meals: L, D

Small, crowded, hectic and noisy, this perennially popular East
Side bistro is surprisingly expensive. But then, the neighborhood doesn't seem to mind the prices.

Price range: Lunch: avg. app., $9.50; entree, $17; dessert,
$7.50. Dinner: avg. app., $10.50; entree, $15–$24. **Wheelchair
access:** Fully accessible. **Features:** Romantic, smoking permitted, outdoor dining. **Services:** Takeout, private parties.

Les Halles $$ BRASSERIE/FRENCH

411 Park Ave. S. (bet. 28th & 29th Sts.) (212) 679-4111
Credit cards: All major Meals: Br, L, D, LN

If you're in the mood for good steak frites, you can hardly do
better than this butcher shop and restaurant named for the old
Paris market district. Small, lively and affordable, it offers a satisfying experience.

Price range: Apps., $5.75–$9.50; entrees, $14.50–$29; desserts,
$5.50–$8.50. Prix fixe for two, $49.50. **Wheelchair access:**
Fully accessible. **Features:** Smoking permitted, outdoor dining.
Services: Catering, takeout, private parties.

Leshko's $25 & Under

DINER/NEW AMERICAN

111 Ave. A (at 7th St.)
Credit cards: AE

(212) 473-9208
Meals: B, L, D, LN

For decades, Leshko's has held down a corner near Tompkins Square Park in what was once called the Pierogi Belt, in deference to the neighborhood's Slavic population. In 1999, new owners changed both the décor and the food. The menu offers a well-prepared selection of New York-American favorites with a few East European touches like pierogi, red cabbage and spätzle thrown in for old time's sake. Better choices include hearty bacon-smoky split pea soup, served with an oil-rubbed toasted crouton in the center; or a bowl of tender steamed mussels with fennel and leeks. Leshko's menu of main courses may be predictable, but that doesn't make a dish like juicy slow-roasted chicken, redolent of sage and lemon, less enjoyable, especially with its side of mushroom-and-onion spätzle. A thick pork chop was perfectly grilled, the meat moist and tasty, flavored with rosemary and accompanied by chunky apple sauce and fat, crisp onion rings. Chicken pot pie is first-rate, and while meatloaf with mushroom gravy is nothing to sneer at, the meatloaf sandwich, served on brown bread with sweet-and-tart housemade ketchup, is unbeatable. Desserts are resolutely uninspiring.

Other recommended dishes: Green salad; endive and watercress salad; shrimp cakes. **Price range:** Apps., $4.95–$7.95; entrees, $10.95–$15.95. **Wheelchair access:** Ramp at entrance; narrow restroom entrance. **Services:** Takeout.

Le Singe Vert $$

FRENCH

160 Seventh Ave. (bet. 19th & 20th Sts.)
Credit cards: AE

(212) 366-4100
Meals: Br, L, D, LN

Like its East Village sibling Jules, Le Singe Vert offers decent French bistro fare in an area that is not overrun with it, making it highly popular. The food is neither exciting nor memorable nor cheap, making Le Singe a neighborhood restaurant, but no more.

Price range: Lunch: apps., $7; entrees, $14–$15; desserts, $5. Dinner: apps., $6–$9.50; entrees, $14.50–$22; desserts, $6.50. **Wheelchair access:** Restrooms not accessible. **Features:** Outdoor dining. **Services:** Private parties.

Lespinasse ☆☆☆☆ $$$$ FRENCH

St. Regis Hotel, 2 E. 55th St. (near Fifth Ave.)   (212) 339-6719
Credit cards: All major   Meals: D   Closed Sun., Mon.

Open the door and be dazzled by the golden light of chandeliers
and intoxicated by the aroma of white truffles. Flowers from
lavish bouquets bend to caress your shoulders as you pass.
Numerous servers hover nearby, eager to anticipate every wish.
In this rarefied atmosphere, the butter never gets warm and no
glass is ever empty. As you might expect, the menu descriptions
are elaborate, the prices stratospheric. When was the last time
anybody charged $35 for soup in New York? The only strategy
is to abandon yourself to the experience and pretend, if only for
a few hours, that money has no meaning. And so you give in to
the luxury of the $35 soup, a virginal concoction of leeks, pota-
toes and white truffles crowned by sweet little langoustines.
Butternut squash soup seems even more decadent, a luscious
orange mush studded with bits of duck breast and chunks of
foie gras.

The shower of foie gras and truffles does not abate with the
arrival of the main courses. Truffles are stuffed under the skin
of the astonishingly delicious hen, served for two. Truffles show
up again in the little pot of rice accompanying the bird. More
truffles appear with the excellent roasted pheasant, again in the
inventive venison plate, and again on the extremely pleasing
spit-roasted duck, which is served with caramelized figs and
port sauce.

The cheese cart is impressive. And so are the desserts. The
combination of the food, the quiet setting and the solicitous service creates an experience so opulent and old-fashioned that it
can be a serious shock to walk outside and find no coach waiting to take you home.

Other recommended dishes: Leek and potato soup with white
truffle; braised rack of veal; quince tart; bittersweet chocolate
tart; pineapple napoleon; chocolate soufflé with pistachio ice
cream; selection of ice creams. **Wine list:** Excellent and expensive; the gracious sommelier is eager to discuss his list and help
you unearth an affordable bottle. **Price range:** Apps., $22–$35;
entrees, $34–$46; eight-course tasting menu, $125; vegetarian
tasting menu, $95. **Wheelchair access:** Dining room is up a
flight of stairs, but there is an elevator.

Le Tableau $25 & Under   MEDITERRANEAN

511 E. 5th St. (bet. Aves. A & B)   (212) 260-1333
Credit cards: Cash only   Meals: Br, D   Closed Mon.

This simple storefront restaurant turns out superb Mediterranean fare. Unconventional dishes stimulate the mouth with
new flavors and textures, like a spicy calamari tagine that incorporates anchovies, hummus and olive purée. Main courses are

familiar, yet they are presented in inventive ways, like tender, juicy roast chicken served on a bed of garlicky escarole and white beans, with a thin layer of mashed potatoes poking through. Desserts can be excellent, like a mellow pumpkin bread pudding, a honey-nut tart and an apple tajine. The dining room is dimly lighted with candles and can become noisy, especially when a jazz trio begins playing in the late evening.

Other recommended dishes: Foie gras terrine with brioche; roasted shrimp; steamed mussels; mesclun salad; pasta with wild mushroom ragout; roasted monkfish; sliced leg of lamb; peppered duck breast; confit. **Alcohol:** Bring your own. **Price range:** Apps., $4.75–$8.50; entrees, $9.50–$14.75. **Wheelchair access:** Everything is on one level. **Features:** Outdoor dining. **Services:** Private parties.

Le Taxi $$$ FRENCH

37 E. 60th St. (bet. Madison & Park Aves.)   (212) 832-5500
Credit cards: All major   Meals: L, D

The food's not great but the atmosphere is. Young, lively and noisy, it's a decent place for French bistro food on a pricey stretch of Manhattan.

Price range: Lunch: apps., $7–$10; entrees, $14–$20; desserts, $8–$12. Dinner: apps., $10–$15; entrees, $20–$30. **Wheelchair access:** Fully accessible. **Features:** Smoking permitted, outdoor dining. **Services:** Delivery, takeout, catering, private parties.

Levana $$$ KOSHER/NEW AMERICAN

141 W. 69th St. (bet. Columbus Ave. & Broadway)
                                                (212) 877-8457
Credit cards: All major   Meals: L, D   Closed Sat., Sun.

New York City's most pretentious glatt kosher restaurant serves fancy, expensive fare to Orthodox yuppies. If you're looking for kosher creativity, this is the place.

Price range: Apps., $5–$14.50; entrees, $17–$39.95; desserts, $7.50–$12.50. Prix fixe: lunch, $19.99; dinner, $27.95. Tasting menu, $55. **Wheelchair access:** Three steps down to dining room, staff will assist. **Features:** Smoking permitted. **Services:** Takeout, catering, private parties.

Le Veau d'Or $$$ BISTRO

129 E. 60th St. (bet. Lexington & Park Aves.)   (212) 838-8133
Credit cards: All major   Meals: L, D   Closed Sun.

If you like things that don't change, you'll like this. Opened in 1937, it has been serenely serving the same menu in the same room for years. Even the staff seems the same, and sometimes that can be a relief.

Price range: Lunch, $17–$25; dinner, $24–$34 (no à la carte). Prix fixe, $19.99. **Wheelchair access:** Two steps up. **Features:** Smoking permitted. **Services:** Private parties.

L'Express $ BISTRO
249 Park Ave. S. (bet. 19th & 20th Sts.)   (212) 254-5858
Credit cards: All major   Meals: B, Br, L, D, LN

It's open 24 hours a day, and though you can find better little French restaurants at 8 P.M., you won't find many better at 3 in the morning. L'Express offers a solid bistro menu with unexpectedly earthy surprises like pigs' feet and tripe. The staff is likable and the food has been improving since the restaurant opened.

Price range: Lunch: apps., $4.75–$6.95; entrees, $7–$14; desserts, $4–$6. Dinner: apps., $5–$7.25; entrees, $9.95–$17.95; desserts, $4–$6. **Wheelchair access:** Fully accessible. **Features:** Smoking permitted. **Services:** Takeout.

Le Zie $25 & Under   ITALIAN
172 Seventh Ave. (at 20th St.)   (212) 206-8686
Credit cards: Cash only   Meals: L, D

This modest little trattoria offers some terrific Venetian dishes, like an inspired salad that features pliant octopus and soft potatoes acting in precise textural counterpoint. The chef has a sure hand with pastas like rigatoni with rosemary, served al dente in a perfectly proportioned sauce. Risotto with squid is also superbly cooked. Striped bass fillet with fennel and white beans is moist and wonderfully flavorful. Desserts are a weak point.

Other recommended dishes: Cichetti; bresaola with arugula and Parmesan; frico; baby eggplant with lima beans and endive; braised rabbit. **Alcohol:** Bring your own. **Price range:** Apps., $5.95–$8.95; entrees, $8.50–$16.95. **Wheelchair access:** Everything is on one level. **Services:** Takeout.

Le Zinc ☆ $$ BISTRO
139 Duane St. (bet. Church St. & W. Broadway)   (212) 513-0001
Credit cards: All major   Meals: Br, L, D, LN

New Yorkers are thought of as a finicky, demanding bunch. All the more surprising, then, that certain restaurants, agreeable but hardly special, manage to catch fire. Le Zinc is one of them. In 2000, David and Karen Waltuck, the owners of Chanterelle, took it over, did some minimal redecorating, and put the kitchen in the hands of Chanterelle's sous-chef. His low-key bistro menu, with an Asian accent here and a down-home touch there, qualifies as upmarket Manhattan comfort food, solid, reliable and reasonably priced.

A big pile of battered and deep-fried onions, labeled as fritters, come with a spicy Thai-style curry dip that makes them the perfect partner for a well-hopped, bitter beer. Chewy grape leaves, hot off the grill, encase a spicy lamb sausage that's remarkably light and clean-tasting. Le Zinc offers a menu-within-a-menu of charcuterie, and there's no doubt about it, the terrines here are superior, from the elegant galantine of rabbit, delicately seasoned with fines herbes, to the rough-hewn venison terrine, studded with dried cherries. Main courses make the usual bistro stops, with competently executed dishes like skirt steak in a red wine reduction, skate with brown butter and capers, and rib steak and French fries. Monkfish also is well treated here, allowed to show off its admittedly modest qualities, draped tastefully in a subdued red wine sauce. Le Zinc serves a nice, thick pork chop in a classic charcutière sauce, a vinegary sauce sharpened with mustard and slivers of cornichon. Maple crème caramel is luscious, with a seductive smoky-burnt taste.

Note well: Le Zinc takes no reservations. Diners who show up before 7:30 can expect to be seated right away. After that, prepare to wait. If a table turns up in less than 20 minutes, it's a square deal.

Other recommended dishes: Duck wings; moo shu pork; chicken grandmère; galette with apples, pears and cranberries; passion fruit tart. **Wine list:** A good French-dominated international list of about 85 wines, many of them modest country wines, with nearly 40 wines by the glass. **Price range:** Lunch: apps., $3.50–$10.50; entrees, $8–$15; desserts, $5–$6.50. Dinner: apps., $4.75–$15; entrees, $12–$19; desserts, $4.50–$6.50. **Wheelchair access:** Separate ramp entrance; restrooms on dining room level.

Le Zoo $25 & Under   BISTRO/FRENCH
314 W. 11th St. (at Greenwich St.)   (212) 620-0393
Credit cards: All major   Meals: D, LN

This popular little restaurant can get crowded, loud and zoolike, but the food is good and often creative. Where you might reasonably expect to find steak frites, roast chicken and pâté de campagne, there are instead such combinations as monkfish with honey and lime sauce, or wonderfully flavorful sliced scallops served in puff pastry with a leek-and-chive coulis. The dessert selection is small and classically French, offering satisfying choices. The restaurant does not take reservations, but once you are seated, the atmosphere becomes relaxed, casual and unrushed, though not quiet.

Other recommended dishes: Sweetbreads with wild mushrooms and fava beans; smoked salmon and asparagus; grilled trout on greens; loin of lamb; halibut; chocolate marquise; raspberry bavarois. **Alcohol:** Beer and wine. **Price range:** Apps., $5.50–$9; entrees, $12.50–$16; desserts, $5.50–$6.50. **Wheelchair access:** Fully accessible. **Features:** Romantic. **Services:** Private parties.

Lhasa
$25 & Under   TIBETAN

96 Second Ave. (near 5th St.)   (212) 674-5870
Credit cards: All major   Meals: L, D

This new Tibetan restaurant is a mellow, quiet place with an attractive patio and a staff that is friendly, calm, alert and responsive. With its Chinese and Indian influences, you'd expect that Tibetan food would be spicy, but in fact it's mild — that blandness is authentic, a reversal of the usual formula of toning down food for Americans. Some of the better dishes include shrimp patties, firm disks filled with chopped shrimp that are delicious with their minty dipping sauce; wonderfully savory fried momo, or dumplings, stuffed with chicken, and tsel gyathuk ngopa, or egg noodles, sautéed until almost crisp and topped with spinach, carrots and bok choy. The food at Lhasa is quiet and uplifting, and quiet is sometimes a good thing.

Other recommended dishes: La phing; tsel bhalae; phing tsel; Lhasa khatsa; then thuk; bhaktsa makhu; deysee; mango lassi. **Alcohol:** Beer and wine. **Price range:** Apps., $3–$6.50; entrees, $6.75–$12.50. **Wheelchair access:** Everything is on one level. **Services:** Takeout.

The Library
$$$ NEW AMERICAN

Regency Hotel, 540 Park Ave. (at 61st)   (212) 339-4050
Credit cards: All major   Meals: B, Br, L, D, LN

The restaurant at the Regency Hotel is the home of the power breakfast. This is something else again, a cozy library that looks as if it had been taken, unchanged, from an English estate. Filled with overstuffed sofas, portraits and books, it looks like a room imagined by Evelyn Waugh. A fine refuge for small snacks and light meals. It serves a truly fabulous lobster pot pie with chanterelle mushrooms and puff pastry. Sweets include a terrific chocolate pudding.

Price range: Entrees, $15–$25; desserts, $9. Late-night menu, $15–$22. **Wheelchair access:** Fully accessible. **Services:** Private parties.

Lin's Dumpling House $ CHINESE

25 Pell St. (at St. James Pl.)   (212) 577-2777
Credit cards: Cash only   Meals: L, D

Joe's Shanghai has been such a success in Chinatown that it's
not surprising that other restaurants want to get in on a good
thing, hence Lin's Dumpling House. This bi-level place offers
passable renditions of soup dumplings but on the whole is sec-
ond-rate.

Price range: Apps., $4.75–$6.25; entrees, $9.95–$14.95. **Wheelchair access:** Fully accessible. **Services:** Delivery, takeout, private parties.

Lipstick Cafe $ AMERICAN

Lipstick Building, 885 Third Ave. (bet. 53rd & 54th Sts.)
     (212) 486-8664
Credit cards: All major   Meals: B, L   Closed Sat. & Sun.

The cavernous lobby space is an unappealing place to sit, but if
you're getting food to go it is delicious. In the morning there is
coffee, fresh juice and good pastries (great jelly doughnuts),
and later the offerings include salads and interesting sandwiches.

Alcohol: Beer and wine. **Price range:** Breakfast, $3–$5. Lunch:
apps., $5–$6; entrees, $6–$15; desserts, $5. **Wheelchair access:**
Restrooms one flight down. **Features:** Kid friendly, outdoor dining. **Services:** Takeout, private parties.

Little Basil $25 & Under   THAI

39 Greenwich Ave. (at Charles St.)   (212) 645-8965
Credit cards: All major   Meals: D

Little Basil is no mere knockoff of Holy Basil, its older Thai sibling. Instead, it takes a different route, serving dishes that retain
the exquisite balance of Holy Basil's cooking while adding
Western touches and a beautiful presentation. Dishes like lamb
shank draped in herbs and delicate steamed dumplings strewn
with dried shrimp are not exactly Thai home cooking, yet the
food remains true to the essence of Thai cuisine, with salty,
sour, hot and sweet flavors unfurling in careful relation to one
another. Like Holy Basil, Little Basil tries hard to come up with
interesting, inexpensive wines to go with the food.

Other recommended dishes: Steamed mussels; yum nuer;
green papaya salad; mee krob; pet kaprow; whole striped bass;
talay thai; seared shrimp in sweet curry; coconut flan. **Alcohol:**
Beer and wine. **Price range:** Apps., $4–$9; entrees, $9–$16.
Wheelchair access: Everything is on one level. **Services:** Delivery, takeout.

Little Havana $25 & Under   CUBAN/CARIBBEAN

30 Cornelia St. (bet. Bleecker & W. 4th Sts.)   (212) 255-2212
Credit cards: All major   Meals: D   Closed Mon.

This restaurant combines classic Cuban dishes with an appreciation for organic, healthful ingredients. The result is lighter
Cuban food that sacrifices none of the flavor. Ceviche is a ster-
ling appetizer, especially when the flavor of the shrimp is acti-
vated by a splash of the hot sauce served in tiny pitchers, and
lentil soup is wonderfully subtle. The menu is small, befitting
the size of the restaurant, but the main courses include a couple
of terrific choices. Sautéed shrimp is superbly shrimpy, and filet
mignon is tender and buttery. Roast pork, a Cuban staple,
seems dry at first, but it comes to life with tomatillo sauce. The
one real disappointment was tamales with an odd flavor and
not much pork in the stuffing. Service is solicitous and caring.

Other recommended dishes: Market salad; kale and butternut
squash; sautéed boneless chicken breast; cheesecake. **Alcohol:**
Beer and wine. **Price range:** Apps., $5.50–$8.50; entrees,
$10–$15. **Wheelchair access:** A couple of steps in front;
restroom is very narrow. **Services:** Catering, private parties.

The Little Place $25 & Under   MEXICAN

73 W. Broadway (at Warren St.)   (212) 528-3175.
Credit cards: Cash only.   Meals: B, L, D   Closed Sat. & Sun.

This is no more than a small counter with another half-dozen
stools opposite, serving homespun Mexican dishes and soups,
sandwiches and breakfasts. The tamales are especially good:
moist chicken encased in a tube of corn dough steamed in a
corn husk and painted with either a complex mole sauce or a
tangy green salsa made with tomatillos. The Little Place also
serves excellent chili made with ground beef and black beans,
and terrific soups like savory potato-spinach.

Other recommended dishes: Beef or chicken fajitas. **Wheelchair access:** Not accessible. **Specials:** Take out, delivery.

Locanda Vini & Olii $25 & Under   ITALIAN

129 Gates Ave., Clinton Hill, Brooklyn   (718) 622-9202
Credit cards: Cash only   Meals: D   Closed Mon.

This mom-and-pop trattoria was a pharmacy for 130 years. The
woodwork has been lovingly restored, and many old features
have been left intact, like small wooden apothecary drawers,
rolling wood ladders and old counters used for a small bar and
to display desserts. Even so, if it were one more trattoria with
the same old food, it would provoke yawns. But Locanda's
menu is full of surprising dishes. Instead of a dish of olive oil to

accompany the fragrant Tuscan bread, they set out arugula blended with pine nuts and oil like a pesto, nicely bitter and just right with the bread. Appetizers may be as unexpected as tongue marinated in white wine and herbs, boiled, thinly sliced and sautéed until mellow and served with a parsley sauce.

Superb choices abound among the pastas, especially the maltagliati, fat strands of carrot-colored pasta in a light ricotta sauce with soft fava beans, diced prosciutto and sage. Beyond pasta, Locanda offers a small, changing selection of main courses like tender braised pork ribs, or excellent braised lamb, baked in a small round bread. The small list of wines includes some excellent choices from little-known producers. The best dessert may have been the simplest: small circular biscotti, flavored with anise and barely sweet.

Other recommended dishes: Shrimp with chickpeas, seafood charcuterie, bresaola with pears, venison cacciatorino, lasagna with chickpea and sausage sauce, guitar-string pasta with sardine, dill and raisin sauce, penne with walnut sauce, pappardelle with duck ragú, pici with porcinis, ricotta cheesecake with rose water. **Price range:** Apps., $5–$8; entrees, $6–$16. **Wheelchair access:** Two steps at entrance; restroom is narrow.

Lola $$$ NEW AMERICAN

30 W. 22nd St. (bet. Fifth & Sixth Aves.) (212) 675-6700
Credit cards: All major Meals: Br, L, D, LN

This is a festive place that presents American cooking with a touch of soul and a touch of Asia. Lola also offers three seatings for its popular gospel brunch on Sundays. Dinner openers include cayenne ribbon onion rings, potato soup with seared scallops and seared tuna with sesame seaweed. Among the main dishes are grilled pork chop, paella, fried chicken with black beans and plantains, and rack of lamb. The brunch menu includes caramelized banana hallah french toast, smoked trout with goat cheese and scrambled eggs, and poached eggs with yuca hash. Apple charlotte mousse cake and maple walnut streusel cake are some of the desserts.

Price range: Lunch: two-course prix fixe, $20; desserts, $6.50. Dinner: apps., $8.50–$13; entrees, $22.50–$35; desserts, $8.50. Prix-fixe gospel brunch, $29.75. **Features:** Smoking permitted, outdoor dining. **Services:** Delivery, takeout, catering, private parties.

Lombardi's $25 & Under PIZZA

32 Spring St. (bet. Mulberry & Mott Sts.) (212) 941-7994
Credit cards: Cash only Meals: L, D, LN

The dining room reeks of history at this reincarnation of the original Lombardi's, which is often credited with introducing pizza to New York City. The old-fashioned coal-oven pizza is terrific, with a light, thin, crisp and gloriously smoky crust topped with fine mozzarella and tomatoes. The garlicky clam pizza is exceptional.

Alcohol: Beer and wine. **Price range:** Apps., $6; pizzas, $10.50–$20. **Wheelchair access:** Fully accessible. **Features:** Kid friendly, smoking permitted, outdoor dining. **Services:** Delivery, catering, private parties.

Los Dos Rancheros $25 & Under   MEXICAN
507 Ninth Ave. (at 38th St.)   (212) 868-7780
Credit cards: Cash only   Meals: B, L, D

The dining room may be bare-bones (unpretentious is an understatement), but the restaurant serves authentic, delicious Mexican fare, like pollo con pipián, chicken with a fiery green sauce made of ground pumpkin seeds, and excellent soft tacos with fillings ranging from chicken to braised pork to tongue and goat.

Price range: Apps., $1–$2; entrees, $2–$7.50; desserts, $2. **Alcohol:** Beer and wine. **Services:** Delivery, takeout, private parties.

Lot 61 $$ NEW AMERICAN
550 W. 21st St. (bet. 10th & 11th Aves.)   (212) 243-6555
Credit cards: All major   Meals: D, LN

Some places just can't decide whether they want to be galleries, bars or restaurants. Lot 61, a cavernous room filled with low-slung sofas and cocktail tables, is among them. The huge former garage in the newly hip western edge of Chelsea is filled with good art that was commissioned for the site. It serves good food, too, of the upscale snack variety. With everything from figs and foie gras to french fries, this is bar food with attitude.

Price range: Apps., $6–$15; entrees, $12–$20; desserts, $5–$7. Tasting menu, $35. **Wheelchair access:** Fully accessible. **Services:** Catering, private parties.

Lotfi's Moroccan $25 & Under   NORTH AFRICAN
358 W. 46th St. (bet. Eighth & Ninth Aves.)   (212) 582-5850
Credit cards: All major   Meals: D   Closed Sun.

The couscous is top-notch, and that's just the beginning at this low-key Moroccan restaurant, one of the best deals on Restaurant Row. Lemon chicken and lamb tagine are both distinctively North African dishes, seasoned with a mixture of spices and sweets, while kebabs are expertly grilled. Lofti's is pleasant and solid, with tapestries in dark green and maroon, handsome Art Deco mirrors and brass lamps.

Other recommended dishes: Carrot and raisin salad; hummus; harira; almond breewats. **Price range:** Avg. app., $3.95; entree, $13.95; dessert, $2.95. **Wheelchair access:** Several steps down from street; restrooms are accessible. **Services:** Takeout, catering, private parties.

Luca $25 & Under ITALIAN

1712 First Ave. (near 89th St.) (212) 987-9260
Credit cards: All major Meals: D

This superb neighborhood Italian restaurant is spare but good-looking, with beige walls and rustic floor tiles. The menu offers dishes skillfully cooked to order that emphasize lusty flavors. The antipasto for two is very generous and very good. Pastas, like bigoli with a buttery shrimp-and-radicchio sauce, are terrific, as are main courses like grilled calamari and crisp grilled Cornish hen.

Other recommended dishes: Warm pear and Gorgonzola tart; bigoli al ragu d'agnello; ravioli with pumpkin; risotto with shrimp and asparagus; grilled calamari; Cornish hen; potato-crusted salmon; granita. **Alcohol:** Beer and wine. **Price range:** Apps., $5.95–$9.50; entrees, $8.50–$19.95. **Wheelchair access:** Everything is on one level. **Features:** Good for business, romantic. **Services:** Catering, private parties.

Luca Lounge $25 & Under ITALIAN/PIZZA

220 Ave. B (near 13th St.) (212) 674-9400
Credit cards: Cash only Meals: D, LN Closed Mon.

If further evidence is needed of the encroaching gentrification of Alphabet City, look not farther than Luca Lounge. As busy as the bar area is here, you can still find tranquillity in the big, pretty garden on two levels in the rear and in the narrow, paneled dining room. You can also find a selection of excellent antipasti and salads (especially radicchio with tuna, olives and tomatoes, and spinach with pecorino cheese and sweet green apples), served individually or in family portions, and little pizzas with wafer-thin, very crisp crusts and a small selection of traditional toppings. I especially liked the margherita, cheese and tomato with basil, and the quattro stagioni, in which the pizzette is divided in quadrants and topped with cheese, artichoke hearts, olives and mushrooms.

Wheelchair access: One step up at entrance. **Features:** Smoking permitted. **Services:** Takeout.

Lucien $25 & Under

BISTRO/FRENCH

14 First Ave. (bet. 1st & 2nd Sts.)
(212) 260-6481
Credit cards: AE
Meals: L, D, LN

This crowded, smoky, somewhat disheveled little French place
serves old-fashioned homey meals. The menu is familiar, but
the prices are modest and, best of all, the cooking is for the
most part very well executed. Three plump sardines, drizzled in
lemon, vinegar and thyme, make an excellent appetizer; one of
the best main courses is lapin moutarde, tasty, tender pieces of
rabbit in a creamy mustard sauce over egg noodles. Desserts are
superb, especially a fabulous tarte Tatin.

Other recommended dishes: Fish soup; bavette (flank steak);
passion fruit tart. **Alcohol:** Beer and wine. **Price range:** Avg.
lunch, $8–$9; dinner, $14.75; dessert, $5.50. **Wheelchair
access:** Fully accessible. **Features:** Smoking permitted. **Services:** Takeout, private parties.

L'Ulivo Focacceria $

ITALIAN/PIZZA

184 Spring St. (bet. Thompson & Sullivan Sts.)
(212) 431-1212
Credit cards: Cash only
Meals: L, D, LN

From the people who own Savore just up the street, an upscale
focacceria serving thin-crust pizza, pasta and the like in an
attractively Italian setting. Pizzas come in a dozen varieties;
there are also various kinds of carpaccio, vitello tonnato, salads,
a few desserts and various wines. And the espresso is excellent.
The small room (52 seats) is very attractive and prices are reasonable, making this a fine place to stop for a snack when you
are in SoHo.

Alcohol: Beer and wine. **Price range:** Apps., $8–$12; entrees,
$12–$16; desserts, $5; pizza, $11–$12. **Wheelchair access:**
Fully accessible. **Services:** Catering, takeout, private parties.

Lundy Brothers $$

SEAFOOD

1901 Emmons Ave., Sheepshead Bay, Brooklyn   (718) 743-0022
Credit cards: All major
Meals: Br, L, D, LN

Once a beloved Brooklyn institution with famous waiters, it has
been resurrected as a shadow of its former self. Still, the 800-
seat restaurant serves good, affordable seafood overlooking
Sheepshead Bay.

Price range: Apps., $8–$12; entrees, $9–$20; desserts, $3–$6;
$13.95 "Sunset Dinner" available Mon.-Fri., 5-7 P.M. **Wheelchair access:** Fully accessible. **Features:** Parking available,
smoking permitted, outdoor dining. **Services:** Takeout, catering,
private parties.

Lupa $25 & Under ITALIAN

170 Thompson St. (at Houston St.) (212) 982-5089.
Credit cards: All major Meals: L, D Closed Mon.

Word has gotten out about the intensely delicious Roman trattoria food, the breadth of the wine list and the warmth of the staff
at Lupa, so it can be as crowded and clamorous as a Roman
rush hour. Appetizers range from the classic to the bizarre. Prosciutto di Parma arrives in thin, nutty slices, while beet carpaccio is not only amusing, but also delicious. Pastas are simple
and tasty, like spicy spaghetti with oil, garlic and hot pepper, or
luscious sweetbread agnolotti with sage and butter. Saltimbocca, thin slices of veal layered with prosciutto, is good and
juicy, while crisply fried baccala with fennel and mint is
unusual and delicious. Lupa's 130-bottle wine list seems to
explore every little-known nook of Italy, but the resident wine
expert takes great delight in directing you to the perfect choice,
which is often cheaper than the one you might have settled for.
The best dessert choice is something from the cheese tray.

Other recommended dishes: Roasted littleneck clams; oxtail
stew; bavette with caciocavallo cheese and pepper; squid-ink
tagliarini with spicy calamari; sardines; ricotta with Sardinian
honey. **Price range:** Apps., $5–$9; entrees, $9–$15. **Wheelchair
access:** One step in front; restrooms are narrow.

Lusardi's $$ ITALIAN

1494 Second Ave. (bet. 77th & 78th Sts.) (212) 249-2020
Credit cards: All major Meals: L, D, LN

A casual East Side restaurant that caters to an affluent crowd.
Filled with regulars who love the reliably good northern Italian
food and the suave staff.

Price range: Apps., $9.50; entrees, $18; desserts, $6.50. **Wheel-
chair access:** Restrooms not accessible. **Services:** Delivery,
takeout.

Lutèce ☆☆ $$$ FRENCH

249 E. 50th St. (212) 752-2225
Credit cards: All major Meals: L, D

One of the oldest, most celebrated French restaurants in New
York, Lutèce was always a byword for refined cuisine and high
style. But like many long-running shows, it has shown signs of
fatigue in recent years. Early in 2001 it closed for renovations,
hired a new manager, and imported a chef, David Féau, from
the Michelin two-star Guy Savoy in Paris. The new Lutèce tries
to project a fresher, more contemporary image while retaining
an old-fashioned sense of luxury and formality. The chaste,
very elegant dining room retains the garden motif, but brick pil-

lars covered in white plaster have been placed at intervals around the dining room. The ceiling has been hung with white linen, and stark white stucco coats the walls, their color picked up by a stunning arrangement of white tulips, amaryllis and amaranth in the center of the room.

Mr. Féau brings a youthful touch to a classic French style, with respectful innovations that never violate good taste. Certain dishes convince you that Lutèce has found the right chef to bring it back to the first rank, especially a gently cooked John Dory with a subtle peppermint jus and pommes soufflées, and sautéed black bass with a rich vanilla jus and wilted spinach. In each case the sauce flattered the fish, with the transformative effect of studio lighting in an old Hollywood glamour photo.

Mr. Féau integrates Asian spices and ingredients with a fine hand. A light touch of curry makes his squab with mascarpone and meaty fava beans an exercise in sheer opulence. A cumin and rosemary crust imparts an exotic, savory perfume to baked loin of lamb, served with a sweet, silken parsnip gratin offset by a sharp, to-the-point lemon sauce.

Among the desserts, a superior pistachio soufflé with sour cherries and a tart cherry sorbet stands head and shoulders above its confrères, a presentable group that includes an apple soufflé served in a hollowed-out roasted apple.

The service at Lutèce remains an anachronism. In the restaurant's very limited confines, many captains move about, trying to stay out of the way of white-jacketed members of the lower orders. The captains radiate charm and good humor, but there seems to be limited communication between the two classes and the whole system suggests severe overmanning.

Other recommended dishes: Lobster soup. **Wine list:** An impressive if uneven list of more than 400 wines, mostly French, with about 35 half-bottles and 15 wines by the glass. **Price range:** Lunch: three-course prix fixe, $38. Dinner: three-course prix fixe, $72. **Wheelchair access:** Two steps down to narrow entrance. Restrooms are one flight up.

Luxia $$ CONTINENTAL

315 W. 48th St. (bet. Eighth & Ninth Aves.)   (212) 957-0800
Credit cards: All major   Meals: L, D, LN

A pleasant garden, an inviting tiled bar and solicitous service make Luxia an attractive choice in the theater district. The menu qualifies as continental — European without any distinct ethnicity — and the food is decent though not memorable.

Price range: Apps., $6–$13; entrees, $12.95–$24. **Wheelchair access:** Fully accessible. **Features:** Smoking permitted, outdoor dining. **Services:** Catering, private parties.

Luzia's $25 & Under   PORTUGUESE

429 Amsterdam Ave. (bet. 80th & 81st Sts.)   (212) 595-2000
Credit cards: All major   Meals: Br, L, D   Closed Mon.

One of New York's Portuguese restaurants began life as a take-out place. Then the neighborhood fell in love with the small restaurant and started staying for dinner. Larger than it used to be but still cozy, Luzia's serves wonderful Portuguese comfort food, like caldo verde, shrimp pie and cataplana, the soupy stew of pork and clams. It also produces remarkably delicious non-Portuguese dishes, like beef brisket that is tender and peppery. Luzia's has great flan, and a nice list of Portuguese wines.

Other recommended dishes: White bean salad; clams and mussels; shrimp pie; grilled sausage; bacalhau; braised chicken legs; Portuguese steak; chocolate hazelnut cake; fruitcake. **Alcohol:** Beer and wine. **Price range:** $20–$25. **Wheelchair access:** Everything is on one level. **Features:** Smoking permitted, outdoor dining. **Services:** Delivery, takeout, catering.

Mad.28 $$ ITALIAN

72 Madison Ave. (bet. 27th & 28th Sts.)   (212) 689-2828
Credit cards: All major   Meals: Br, L, D, LN   Closed Sun.

To eat in this large, brick-walled room is to have a multimedia experience. CD's blast through the air, movies are projected onto the walls and cooks toss pizzas in the open kitchen. Is it noisy? Yes. Is it good? Yes, if you like strawberry and Gorgonzola salads, less so if all you're looking for is a simple plate of pasta or a pizza.

Price range: Apps., $8–$14; pizza, $11–$16; entrees, $11–$25; desserts, $8. **Wheelchair access:** Fully accessible. **Features:** Smoking permitted, outdoor dining. **Services:** Delivery, takeout, catering, private parties.

Maeda Sushi $$$ SUSHI

16 E. 41st St. (bet. Fifth & Madison Aves.)   (212) 685-4293
Credit cards: All major   Meals: L, D

Yasuo Maeda's new restaurant is absolutely traditional. Although the kitchen makes a few concessions to non-Japanese customers by offering some nonsushi dishes, this is not the place to try tempura. It is, however, a fine sushi bar, the sort of restaurant that would reward the effort of making yourself known to Maeda-san. You, too, can probably snag those great slices of kanpachi. But only after you have become known.

Price range: Apps., $6–$14; entrees, $14.50–$45; desserts, $3.50–$5. Tasting menu, $80. **Wheelchair access:** Not accessible. **Features:** Smoking permitted. **Services:** Takeout, private parties.

Malatesta Trattoria $ ITALIAN

649 Washington St. (at Christopher St.) (212) 741-1207
Credit cards: Cash only Meals: L, D

If this little restaurant, which opened in the summer of 1998, reminds you of Piadina on West 10th Street, it's for a good reason: they share the same owners and offer similar menus, specializing in piadinas, the unleavened griddled bread that comes with stuffings like cheese and arugula. Malatesta, though, has yet to bring its food up to the level of Piadina, and its windowed corner site lacks the romance of Piadina's subterranean dining room.

Alcohol: Beer and wine. **Price range:** Apps., $5–$6; entrees, $9–$18; desserts, $5–$6. **Wheelchair access:** Not accessible. **Features:** Romantic. **Services:** Takeout, private parties.

Malaysian Rasa Sayang $$ PAN-ASIAN

75-19 Broadway, Jackson Heights, Queens (718) 424-9054.
Credit cards: Cash only Meals: L, D Closed Tue.

A blend of Malay, Chinese and Indian, with dashes of Thai and even Portuguese, Malaysian is one of the great polyglot food cultures and therefore fits right into the complicated ethnic puzzle of Queens. The restaurant presents a modest face. The color and drama are found in the kitchen, where the cooking is fresh, vibrant and fiery. On one visit, the waiter tried to protect a group of diners from the menu. "Too strong flavored for you," he said about the sambal shrimp, a spicy stir-fry of minced chilies, scallions, galangal and shrimp in a potent shrimp-paste stock. Strong flavored was exactly right. He forgot to add sublime. "Too spicy for you," the owner added about Asam curried fish head, one of the house specialties. It comes to the table bubbling in a clay pot with chunks of moist fish and cubes of deep-fried bean curd swirling in a vivid three-alarm tomato broth fragrant with anise. Asam laksa, another standout, is Malaysia's meal in a bowl, a spicy sweet-sour fish soup with fat round noodles and crunchy strips of cucumber. Milder dishes are just as impressive.

Other recommended dishes: Baby oyster omelet; deep-fried bean curd; Rojah salad. **Price range:** Entrees, $4.50–$20. **Wheelchair access:** Fully accessible. **Services:** Delivery.

Maloney & Porcelli ☆ $$$ SEAFOOD/STEAKHOUSE

37 E. 50th St. (bet. Park & Madison Aves.) (212) 750-2233
Credit cards: All major Meals: L, D

This is a comfortable, wood-toned, masculine room decorated with eagles and filled with lawyers and investment bankers. This is theme eating for grown-ups, a place where the food is more fun to discuss than consume. Crackling pork shank is an original and delicious dish, a great ball of meat, deep fried until the skin turns into cracklings, then slowly roasted. A hefty grilled rib eye comes with the bone sticking over the edge of the plate, and sirloin steaks are crusty and flavorful. End the meal with drunken doughnuts: warm twists of sugar-dusted dough and three pots of liquor-laced jam. (*Ruth Reichl*)

Other recommended dishes: Crab cakes; shellfish; Caesar salad; salmon pastrami; swordfish; London broil; steamed lobster; cheesecake; profiteroles with caramel ice cream and hot fudge. **Wine list:** Good and fairly priced, with an innovative list of 40 wines under $40. **Price range:** Apps., $7.75–$14.75; entrees, $18.50–$32; desserts, $8. **Wheelchair access:** Fully accessible. **Features:** Good for business, smoking permitted, outdoor dining. **Services:** Catering, private parties.

Mama's Food Shop $25 & Under AMERICAN
200 E. 3rd St. (bet. Aves. A & B) (212) 777-4425
Credit cards: Cash only   Meals: L, D   Closed Sun.

A simple takeout shop and restaurant where you point at what you want and they dish it up, but the food is outstanding: grilled salmon, fried chicken and meatloaf. Vegetable side dishes are especially good, like brussels sprouts, carrots, beets and mashed potatoes.

Price range: Entrees, $7–$8.50; desserts, $3. **Wheelchair access:** Fully accessible. **Features:** Smoking permitted. **Services:** Delivery, takeout, catering, private parties.

Mandoo Bar $25 & Under KOREAN
2 W. 32nd St. (bet. Fifth & Sixth Aves.) (212) 279-3075
Credit cards: All major   Meals: L, D

This bright little Korean place leaves no doubt about its signature dish. Mandoo (pronounced MAHN-do) is the Korean word for dumplings, and as you enter past a glass-enclosed kitchen, you can see the chefs rolling and cutting dough, stuffing and folding it into little flower-shape or half-moon dumplings until trays are full and they are ready to be cooked. Start with a platter of baby mandoo, bite-size half-moons stuffed with beef, pork and leeks and notable for a wrapper so sheer that it is almost transparent. Or try a small portion of crisp, savory pan-fried mandoo, filled with pork and minced cabbage. Boiled dumplings are fine, though the wrappings are a little doughy, and the flower-shape steamed meat-and-cabbage dumplings are very good. All the dumplings come with a dipping sauce, which you can make to your specifications.

Dumplings account for half the dishes on the menu, but some of the best selections are not dumplings at all. Slender rectangles of fried tofu make an excellent appetizer (hot pepper sauce gives them a jolt). Bibimbop, a casserole of rice, vegetables and ground beef served in a stone crock, is fresh, light and delicate.

The spare, handsome dining room is filled with blond wood tables, which have cushioned benches rather than chairs. Service is swift and courteous, and food arrives quickly. Mandoo Bar is the kind of place where you can drop in for a meal and be done in under an hour.

Other recommended dishes: Casserole with rice cakes, cellophane noodles, fish cakes and hot sauce; pa jun. **Price range:** Apps., $4–$9; entrees, $6–$24. **Wheelchair access:** Steps at entrance and to restrooms.

Manhattan Chili Co. $ MEXICAN/TEX-MEX
1500 Broadway (at 43rd St.)   (212) 730-8666
1697 Broadway (at 53rd St.)   (212) 246-6555
Credit cards: All major   Meals: Br, L, D, LN

At these busy little low-priced restaurants, you can get chili any which way, with spicing calibrated from mild to scalding. Tacos and fajitas are also well made.

Price range: Apps., $3.50–$7.95; entrees, $8.50–$15.95; desserts, $4.95–$5.50. **Features:** Kid friendly, smoking permitted. **Services:** Delivery, takeout, private parties.

Manhattan Grille $$$ SEAFOOD/STEAKHOUSE
1161 First Ave. (bet. 63rd & 64th Sts.)   (212) 888-6556
Credit cards: All major   Meals: Br, L, D

An unusually sedate steakhouse, with comfortable chairs, accommodating service and a menu that offers just about anything you want to eat.

Price range: Lunch: entrees, $9–$24; desserts, $3.50. Dinner: apps., $6.75–$15.75; entrees, $18–$32; desserts, $7.50. **Wheelchair access:** Restroom not accessible. **Features:** Smoking permitted. **Services:** Takeout, private parties.

Manhattan Ocean Club ☆☆ $$$ SEAFOOD
57 W. 58th St. (bet. Fifth & Sixth Aves.)   (212) 371-7777
Credit cards: All major   Meals: L, D

Tony, comfortable and trim as a luxury yacht, this is the steakhouse of fish restaurants. It has a masculine air, and you sense that the people who come here would rather eat steak, but their doctors won't let them. Eating here is an indulgence; the prices are high, especially if you begin with a shellfish bouquet for which you are charged for each clam, shrimp and oyster. Cold shrimp are big and tender, the lump crabmeat sweet and delicate. Soups like the creamy clam chowder are less expensive but no less delicious (the fish soup is so intense it is almost a meal in itself). The simple preparations are the most appealing here but one of my favorite dishes is the oysters buried in tiny morels covered with cream and baked in the shell. The dish is an edible definition of luxury. Desserts are almost all big and sweet. For sheer exuberance nothing beats the small mountain of caramel, pecans, whipped cream and ice cream. (*Ruth Reichl*)

Other recommended dishes: Red snapper with rosemary crust; steamed lobster; warm chocolate tart. **Wine list:** White wines from California and France dominate the list, which is good and fairly priced. **Price range:** Lunch: apps., $7.75–$13.50; entrees, $19.50–$26.50; desserts, $8.75; summer prix-fixe lunch, $20. Dinner: apps., $8.75–$31; entrees, $22.50–$29.75; desserts, $9.75. **Wheelchair access:** Not accessible. **Services:** Private parties.

Maratti $$$ ITALIAN/SEAFOOD

135 E. 62nd St. (bet. Park & Lexington Aves.)   (212) 826-6686
Credit cards: All major   Meals: L, D

Walk right past the attractive downstairs bar and up the stairs, and you'll find a room with not only a view, but a fireplace as well. One dish not to be missed: the extraordinary seafood risotto, made with a stock so rich and flavorful you find yourself moaning with pleasure. Also try the spaghetti with lobster and bass, and any whole grilled fish.

Price range: Lunch: apps., $7–$12; entrees, $14–$24; desserts, $8. Dinner: apps., $9–$12; entrees, $16.50–$34. **Wheelchair access:** Elevator available. **Services:** Takeout, catering, private parties.

March ☆☆☆ $$$$ NEW AMERICAN

405 E. 58th St. (near First Ave.)   (212) 754-6272
Credit cards: All major   Meals: D

A romantic gem, March offers its patrons refined American cuisine in a cozy, antique-filled town house. Its celebrated chef-owner, Wayne Nish, has created an opportunity for culinary diversion by replacing the usual three-course restaurant menu — appetizer, entree and dessert — with one that allows you to choose several smaller courses. Your food will arrive in the order in which it is listed on the menu. Select carefully: if you order only the salads and sashimi-like dishes you will surely leave hungry.

At March, no dish is more than a few bites, but those are so pretty and powerful that you are almost always satisfied. Mr.

Nish has a Japanese bent, and many dishes are his variations on sushi and sashimi. They are so beautiful they look more like jewelry than food. Hamachi sashimi is a single slice of yellow-tail brushed with a bit of olive oil and white soy sauce and sprinkled with chives and sesame seeds. Carpaccio of lobster is topped with caviar, sea urchin and shiso. Seared blue fin is an extraordinary piece of tuna encrusted with sesame seeds and topped with sea urchin roe. Cleanly fried tempura is wrapped in zucchini slices.

Most people consider the last five menu offerings as main courses. These, which might include veal medallions or venison or grilled and braised duck, are just a little bigger than the other dishes. March's co-owner, Joseph Scalice, who is passionate about wines, will help you select different glasses of wine for each course from an extensive list.

Extensive renovations have given March a new two-level dining area where the garden used to be, with one room downstairs and the other, smaller room on the mezzanine, both illuminated by a slanting skylight and decorated with 17th century Venetian botanical prints. The seats have increased to 85 from 50, and two options have been added to the fixed-price format. In addition to the four-course and seven-course menus, diners will now find five courses or six courses, with wines to match for a supplement. For all the changes, March retains its intimate feel, and on a recent visit Mr. Nish was still turning out inspired food like lobster carpaccio with three roes (osetra, mentaiko and uni) and Long Island duck with celery root and port wine sauce. The dessert menu includes sophisticated takes on homey desserts, like butterscotch pot de crème with crème fraîche and ginger snaps, and upside down sour cream cake with blueberries and buttermilk ice cream. *(Ruth Reichl, updated by William Grimes)*

Most popular dish: Beggars' purses (diminutive dumplings filled with caviar, truffles or foie gras). **Chef's favorite:** Beggars' purses. **Wine list:** Excellent, with a wide variety of styles and prices. **Price range:** Four courses, $72 (with specially selected wines, $116); Five courses, $90 (with specially selected wines, $145); Six courses, $108 (with specially selected wines, $174); seven courses, $126 (with specially selected wines, $203). **Wheelchair access:** Dining room up two small steps; restrooms down a steep flight of stairs. **Services:** Private parties.

Marichu $$ BASQUE/SPANISH

342 E. 46th St. (bet. First & Second Aves.)   (212) 370-1866
Credit cards: All major   Meals: L, D

Unusual Basque dishes in an unusual location, near the United Nations, draw a crowd of diplomats and others interested in selections like clams in a garlic-and-wine sauce and tender baby squid served in a nutty sauce of leeks, onions, tomatoes and ink. With the exception of several unappealing salmon dishes, it is best to stick with seafood: try the crowd-pleasing shrimp in sizzling garlic sauce, the fillet of red snapper in a garlic vinaigrette with scalloped potatoes, or red peppers stuffed with a creamy purée of codfish in an intense sauce made with dried red peppers.

Other recommended dishes: Fish soup; sautéed medallions of monkfish; natillas; tarta de Arrese; chocolate mousse. **Price range:** Tapas, $2–$7; apps., $6.50–$9; entrees, $14–$24; desserts, $5–$7; prix-fixe, $32. **Wheelchair access:** Dining room is one step up; restrooms are narrow. **Features:** Good for business, romantic, smoking permitted, outdoor dining. **Services:** Private parties.

Marika (Satisfactory) $ FRENCH/AMERICAN
208 W. 70th St. (bet. Amsterdam & West End Aves.)
(212) 875-8600
Credit cards: All major Meals: Br, D, LN

If looks were everything, Marika would shoot right to the head of the list of Manhattan's top restaurants. Rogers Marvel, the architectural firm, has organized it into a series of discrete low-slung rooms, tied together by a 90-foot illuminated glass bar, bluestone columns and a jazzy scheme of horizontal lines and bright primary colors that allude to Mondrian's "Broadway Boogie Woogie." It's not hard to feel you're in the spiffiest spot on the West Side, and there's a warmheartedness to go with the hard-edged style.

After a rocky start, in which the original chef was fired and replaced by Neil Annis of Lespinasse, Marika looks as though it may survive its critical panning. Mr. Annis' direct and unfussy menu suits the neighborhood, but is stylish enough for the surroundings. There's a touch of wit here and there, most strikingly in the roasted chicken, accompanied by giant French fries stacked like Lincoln Logs. The menu has a distinctly seasonal feel, with spring vegetables scattered throughout. A scattering of peas, fiddlehead ferns, baby carrots and asparagus tips enlivens a plate-filling raviolo with grilled rabbit and langoustines, and soft-shell crabs, cooked tempura-style, are surrounded by corn relish and a thin pool of basil coulis.

Other recommended dishes: Risotto with lobster; cod with pancetta, spinach and potato purée; rack of pork with onion crust. **Wine list:** About 200 wines, mostly American, with a page dedicated to 30 wines under $33, and 15 wines by the glass. **Price range:** Apps., $9–$15; entrees, $22–$34; desserts, $9. The cafe offers a smaller, less expensive menu. **Wheelchair** access: Restrooms are on street level.

Maritime ☆ $$$

SEAFOOD

1251 Sixth Ave. (at 49th St.)
Credit cards: All major

(212) 354-1717
Meals: L, D

As a piece of design, Maritime is one slippery fish: gleaming white wall tiles suggest an urban fish market, but the dark, solid wood wainscoting and cabinets feel more like a men's club. The menu is not easy to get a handle on, either. The oysters are straightforward enough; so are the two-fisted lobster and corn chowder and a crowd-pleasing shrimp cocktail. A fair number of the dishes at Maritime, however, are overthought and overwrought, like a bizarre and too-sweet appetizer of serrano ham with fig pancakes, mint and sheep's milk yogurt. But some results can be terrific. Lobster in a Portuguese tomato sauce is plump and flavorful, and the spicy chorizo "tater tots" that dot the plate make a witty point. Seared sea scallops are just rich enough to carry pumpkin ravioli and a porcini truffle sauce, thanks to an offsetting, neutralizing layer of wilted Swiss chard. Two desserts break out of the pack: the Southwestern banana split and a florid apple crisp. The service, while not exactly expert, has an all-out eager-to-please quality that helps paper over shortcomings.

Other recommended dishes: Curry fried oysters; squid fritto misto; crab cigars; banana split with chocolate tamale. **Wine list:** A pleasingly diverse, slightly quirky 132-bottle list, organized by taste characteristics, with 14 half bottles and nine wines by the glass. **Price range:** Lunch: apps., $6.50–$13.50; entrees, $16–$25; desserts, $7. Dinner: apps., $7.50–$13.50; entrees, $18–$25; desserts, $7. **Wheelchair access:** Enter through plaza (main entrance has two steps). Restrooms on street level.

Maroons $25 & Under

SOUTHERN/JAMAICAN

244 W. 16 St. (bet. Seventh & Eighth Aves.)
Credit cards: All major

(212) 206-8640
Meals: L, D, LN

This new restaurant is divided into a small, handsome dining room and a separate homey lounge. The menu, too, is a split proposition, neatly divided between Southern and Jamaican dishes. Appetizers are largely excellent, like meaty, spicy jerk chicken wings, and cod fritters that are tasty, light and puffy. From the South come fine little crab cakes and a generous pile of baby back ribs. Seafood entrees are especially enticing, like Jamaican fried fish and baked catfish, moist and positively beefy. Service is friendly but occasionally spacey.

Other recommended dishes: Yuca puffs; broiled snapper; oxtail ravioli; jerk chicken; carrot cake. **Wine list:** Unfortunately most bottles are $30–$35. **Price range:** Apps., $4–$8; entrees, $12–$19. **Wheelchair access:** One step down at entrance, restrooms and dining room are on one level.

Marumi $25 & Under   JAPANESE/SUSHI

546 La Guardia Pl. (bet. 3rd & Bleecker Sts.)   (212) 979-7055
Credit cards: All major   Meals: L, D

This versatile, reliable Japanese restaurant near N.Y.U. offers a
cross-section of casual Japanese dining. The service is swift,
efficient and charming and will even go the extra mile in pre-
venting bad choices. It's rare that you get such an interesting
assortment of sushi at an inexpensive restaurant, like mirugai,
or geoduck clam. Other worthwhile dishes are broiled eel, noodle soups and the economic bento box meals. The hefty tempura is about the only dish I would skip.

Alcohol: Beer. **Price range:** Apps., $4–$5; entrees, $9–$15;
desserts, $3–$3.50. **Wheelchair access:** Restrooms not accessible. **Features:** Good for business. **Services:** Takeout.

Master Grill $25 & Under   BRAZILIAN

34-09 College Point Blvd., Flushing, Queens   (718) 762-0300
Credit cards: All major   Meals: L, D

Possibly the most elaborate Brazilian rodizio in the city, Master
Grill feels like an enormous banquet hall, with seating for 1,000
people and a samba band playing full tilt. It's all great fun if
you're in the mood. The buffet itself is the size of a small
restaurant, where you can fortify yourself with all manner of
marinated vegetables, fruit, seafood, pasta, rolls, roasted potatoes and fried plantains. While the buffet dishes are nothing
special, they are easy to fill up on before the meat starts arriving. The parade of all-you-can-eat grilled meats, from chicken
hearts to six kinds of beef, goes on as long as you can hold out.

Recommended dishes: 15 varieties of grilled meat. **Price
range:** All you can eat for $18.95; desserts, $6. **Wheelchair
access:** Everything is on one level. **Features:** Parking available,
smoking permitted. **Services:** Private parties.

Mavalli Palace $25 & Under   INDIAN/VEGETARIAN

46 E. 29th St. (bet. Park & Madison Aves.)   (212) 679-5535
Credit cards: All major   Meals: L, D   Closed Mon.

This low-key Indian restaurant turns out terrific vegetarian fare
that is exciting and full of flavor. Those who think vegetarian
food can't possibly be satisfying may change their minds after
tasting superb dishes like rasa vada, savory lentil doughnuts in
a spicy broth, and baingan bharta, a fiery blend of eggplant and
peas. Mavalli means mother goddess, and the restaurant's sym-
bol is a goddess figure, hand out, waiting to serve. The staff,
though merely mortal, takes orders efficiently and brings food
out swiftly.

Other recommended dishes: Dahi vada; samosas; aluchat; mooli paratha; raita; masala dosai; uttappam; Kashmeeri pullav; lassi. **Price range:** $4.25–$16.75. **Wheelchair access:** Restrooms are one flight down. **Features:** Good for business. **Services:** Takeout, private parties.

Max $25 & Under ITALIAN

51 Ave. B (near 4th St.)	(212) 539-0111
1274 Amsterdam Ave. (at 123rd St.)	(212) 531-2221
Credit cards: Cash only	Meals: L, D, LN

A tiny Italian restaurant wholly without pretensions, the Avenue B location has been packed since it opened (the uptown location was added in 2001). The draw is exactly what has always attracted people to neighborhood restaurants: well-prepared food, served with warmth. Best of all, Max is cheap.

Max's buffalo-milk mozzarella is an excellent place to start. The cheese is fresh, nutty and slightly salty, and a perfect partner for prosciutto. It is also fine in the insalata Caprese, the familiar offering of mozzarella, tomato and basil. Fennel shows up in both a refreshing salad sweetened with balsamic vinegar, and on a plate of tasty grilled vegetables, with roasted peppers and zucchini. For the most part, Max's pastas are very enjoyable. Fettuccine al sugo Toscano has a wonderfully mellow meat sauce with layers of flavor that unfold in the mouth, while rigatoni Napoletano is served southern Italian style, with meatballs and sausages left intact in the sauce. The most expensive dish on the menu, osso buco, was nonetheless a good value; the veal shank was tender enough and came with a zesty lemony topping, but the meat was a tad underseasoned. Still, it came perched atop a mound of fine risotto, creamy but with a perfect bit of resistance in the grains, subtly flavored with saffron. Max has a brief list of wines under $25 and, oddly given the food prices, a broader selection for $25 to $40. Desserts include a good tiramisu and an excellent caramel panna cotta.

Other recommended dishes: Black linguine with shrimp; rigatoni alla Siciliana; rack of lamb; meatloaf Neopolitan style; crème brûlée. **Price range:** Apps., $4.95–$8.95; entrees, $8.95–$14.95. **Wheelchair access:** Ramp to restroom. **Features:** Smoking permitted.

Max & Moritz $25 & Under FRENCH-AMERICAN

426A Seventh Ave., Park Slope, Brooklyn	(718) 499-5557
Credit cards: All major	Meals: Br, D

Max & Moritz is rightfully popular for its moderate prices and cooking. While French-American dishes like goat cheese soufflé and steak au poivre are generally fine, look for Austrian accents like beef goulash. Wild mushroom ravioli, flavored with a few restrained drops of truffle oil, is earthy and solid, while French onion soup is prepared in the classic manner, with roof-of-the-mouth-searing cheese and sweet, caramelized onions. Except for a wimpy chocolate pôt de crème desserts do not disappoint. Best are a parfait of sour cherries and maple cream and a slender apple tart flavored with marzipan and topped with a scoop of cinnamon ice cream.

Other recommended dishes: Smoked salmon and celery root timbale; roast duck; pork chop; steak; pan-roasted cod; lamb shank. **Alcohol:** Beer and wine. **Price range:** Apps., $5–$7; entrees, $12–$17; desserts, $5–$6. **Wheelchair access:** Restrooms not accessible. **Features:** Outdoor dining. **Services:** Takeout, catering, private parties.

Maya ☆☆　　$$$　　　　　　MEXICAN/TEX-MEX
1191 First Ave. (bet. 64th & 65th Sts.)　　　(212) 585-1818
Credit cards: All major　　　　　　　　　　　Meals: D

Some of New York's most interesting Mexican food is served in this bright, festive but often noisy room. Although you can stick to margaritas and guacamole, you'll miss the best part if you don't try some of the more unusual dishes. Rock shrimp ceviche is breathtaking, the seafood salad simply delicious and I loved the roasted corn soup with huitlacoche dumpling, the chunky guacamole and the tacos al pastor, two little tortillas served with marinated pork and fresh salsa. The most impressive main courses are chicken mole (the dark sauce is truly complex) and pipian de puerco, grilled pork marinated in tamarind and served on a bed of puréed roasted corn. Desserts are not impressive, however; the flan is flat, the sorbets too sweet. (*Ruth Reichl*)

Other recommended dishes: Seafood chile relleno; chilaquiles; pan-roasted striped bass with cactus salad; red snapper tacos; grilled shrimp and lobster. **Wine list:** Negligible. Try the house margaritas or a shot of tequila with a shot of sangrita (a tart mixture of juices). **Price range:** Apps., $7.50–$9.50; entrees, $16.50–$24.50; desserts $6–$7.50. **Wheelchair access:** Everything is at street level. **Services:** Takeout, catering, private parties.

Mayrose　$　　　　　　　　　　　　　　DINER
920 Broadway (at 21st St.)　　　　　　　(212) 533-3663
Credit cards: All major　　　　Meals: B, Br, L, D, LN

Diner food in a trendy setting. With its high ceiling and loftlike feel, Mayrose looks good and attracts an arty crowd, but the food rarely rises above the ordinary. Stick with basic sandwiches, burgers and the like. Portions are big and prices are moderate.

Alcohol: Beer and wine. **Price range:** Apps., $3.50–$5.95; entrees, $6–$13.95; desserts, $2–$4.95. **Wheelchair access:** Fully accessible. **Features:** Kid friendly. **Services:** Delivery, take-out, catering.

McHale's $$ BAR SNACKS/HAMBURGERS
750 Eighth Ave. (at 46th St.)   (212) 246-8948
Credit cards: Cash only   Meals: L, D, LN

This neighborhood bar has a single specialty: great hamburgers that are big and juicy. There's really no point in ordering anything else, except maybe a beer or two. A nice place in which to be a regular.

Price range: Apps., $5–$9; entrees, $10–$18; desserts, $3.50. **Wheelchair access:** Not accessible. **Features:** Smoking permitted. **Services:** Takeout.

McSorley's Old Ale House $ BAR SNACKS
15 E. 7th St. (bet. Second & Third Aves.)   (212) 473-9148
Credit cards: Cash only   Meals: L, D, LN

Anybody who has ever read a book by Joseph Mitchell owes himself or herself a visit to this venue. (Yes, they do let women in now.) This old saloon has history on its side, but that's the extent of the attraction. The sawdust-strewn floor smells like the day after at a fraternity house, and the limited menu of burgers and sandwiches does little but pad the stomach for more beer.

Price range: Apps., $3; entrees, $4–$4.25. **Wheelchair access:** Fully accessible. **Features:** Smoking permitted.

Mee Noodle Shop $25 & Under   CHINESE
219 First Ave. (at 13th St.)   (212) 995-0333
547 Second Ave. (bet. 30th & 31st Sts.)   (212) 779-1596
922 Second Ave. (at 49th St.)   (212) 888-0027
795 Ninth Ave. (at 53rd St.)   (212) 765-2929
Credit cards: AE   Meals: L, D

A little chain of Chinese restaurants that is a cut above takeout, with huge portions of cheap, tasty noodles. Ingredients are fresh, and dishes like lo mein with roast pork and mee fun with chicken are carefully prepared. Mee offers seven kinds of noodles. The portions are huge — complete meals in themselves — and delicious.

Other recommended dishes: Dan dan noodles; scrambled eggs with shrimp; dry sautéed green beans; scallion pancakes; cold sesame noodles. **Alcohol:** Beer. **Price range:** $3.75–$12. **Wheelchair access:** Everything is on one level. **Features:** Kid friendly. **Services:** Delivery, takeout, catering, private parties.

Mekong

$25 & Under

VIETNAMESE

44 Prince St. (near Mulberry St.)
Credit cards: All major

(212) 343-8169
Meals: L, D

The atmosphere at Mekong is thoroughly Americanized, with a relaxed SoHo ambiance, but the food is authentically Vietnamese, achieving a balance of flavors and textures highlighted by fresh herbs and pungent fish sauce. Grilled pork with lemongrass over rice noodles and stewed fish in a fiery caramel sauce are two of the better dishes. Sautéed squid with curry sauce is peppery, a contrast to a cooler dish like chicken sautéed with green peppers, which seems almost Chinese except for the lemongrass. This preparation also works in a vegetarian guise, with seitan, or wheat gluten, replacing the chicken. Mekong also offers a well-chosen, moderately priced wine list.

Other recommended dishes: Shredded chicken salad; steamed rice crepes; grilled shrimp with sugar cane; shrimp rolls; hot-and-sour fish soup; beef with black pepper, butter and onions; stewed fish with caramel sauce; squid with curry sauce; chicken with green peppers; seitan with green peppers. **Price range:** Entrees, $10–$22. **Wheelchair access:** Everything is on one level. **Features:** Romantic, outdoor dining. **Services:** Delivery, takeout, catering, private parties.

Meli Melo

$$

NEW AMERICAN

110 Madison Ave. (bet. 29th & 30th Sts.)
Credit cards: All major   Meals: L, D

(212) 686-5551
Closed Sun.

The intriguing global menu is moderately priced, but never quite takes off, implying more ambition than the food delivers. Everything is correct but never incites the imagination or the taste buds. Still, it's nice to have in the neighborhood.

Price range: Lunch: apps., $5–$7; entrees, $10.50–$14.95; desserts, $5–$6. Dinner: apps., $6–$8; entrees, $13.95–$19.95; desserts, $5–$6; four-course prix fixe, $28.50. **Wheelchair access:** Fully accessible. **Features:** Smoking permitted, outdoor dining. **Services:** Private parties.

Meltemi

$25 & Under

GREEK/SEAFOOD

905 First Ave. (at 51st St.)
Credit cards: All major

(212) 355-4040
Meals: L, D

This friendly Greek restaurant offers big portions of simply prepared seafood, like grilled octopus with oil and lemon, and typical Greek offerings like grilled whole porgy and red mullet. Appetizers are generous, and two portions can easily feed four people. Grilled seafood is the centerpiece here, and I've rarely had grilled shrimp as good as Meltemi's, served butterflied, full of flavor and so delicate you can even eat the shell. The enthusiastic staff adds to Meltemi's enjoyable atmosphere.

Other recommended dishes: Assortment of cold spreads; loukanika laconias; Greek salad; beets in vinaigrette; swordfish steak; tuna steak; desserts. **Price range:** Lunch: apps., $4.95–$9.95; entrees, $10.95–$14.95; desserts, $3.95. Dinner: apps., $5.95–$9.95; entrees, $14.95–$28.95. **Wheelchair access:** Restrooms not accessible. **Services:** Takeout.

Menchanko-Tei $25 & Under   JAPANESE/NOODLES

43 W. 55th St. (bet. Fifth & Sixth Aves.)   (212) 247-1585
131 E. 45th St. (bet. Lexington & Third Aves.)   (212) 986-6805
Credit cards: All major   Meals: B, L, D, LN

Great big bowls of noodles are the thing at Menchanko-Tei, which means House of Mixed Noodles in Japanese. The house special, fat egg noodles in a fragrant chicken broth, is full of shrimp, little rice cakes and ground fish. Japanese business executives seem to have found homes away from home at the three Manhattan branches of this noodle shop. The food is authentic and inexpensive. Especially good if you can get someone to translate the specials, written only in Japanese.

Alcohol: Beer and wine. **Price range:** Apps., $3–$8; entrees, $7–$13; desserts, $3. **Wheelchair access:** Fully accessible. **Features:** Good for business. **Services:** Takeout, catering.

Mercer Kitchen ☆☆ $$$$ FRENCH

Mercer Hotel, 99 Prince St. (at Mercer St.)   (212) 966-5454
Credit cards: All major   Meals: B, L, D, LN

Jean-Georges Vongerichten strikes again in this chic SoHo restaurant filled with models and movie stars. The place is a designer's dream: brick walls, heavy wooden tables, gorgeous table-top appointments. The space is so mysteriously beautiful it makes each vegetable shimmer like a jewel in the dark. The food is equally innovative: mushrooms set into a marinade of white raisins and coriander; slowly baked rabbit with farfalle, olives and radicchio; or serious snacks like black sea bass with lime juice, coriander and mint. But the kitchen occasionally spins out of control, which can make it seem like a laboratory for food ideas not yet fully realized. Desserts, however, are simple and appealing, especially the fruit terrines, which are like summer puddings.

Wine list: Interesting, affordable and very well chosen for the food. **Price range:** Lunch: apps., $8–$14; entrees, $9–$15. Dinner: apps., $9–$15; entrees, $19–$35; desserts, $8. **Wheelchair access:** Restaurant is in a basement, but has an elevator.

Merge

$25 & Under

NEW AMERICAN

142 W. 10th St.

(212) 691-7757

Credit cards: AE

Meals: D

The music at Merge is too loud, and the dining area close to the bar is too smoky, but the service is friendly and efficient, and best of all, the food is not only delicious but also a great value. Appetizers are especially good. The notion of sushi fruit salad may not inspire immediate hosannas, but the combination of coconut and mango with Asian coleslaw and thin slices of tuna and salmon is an extraordinary blend of flavors and textures. More conventionally, a grilled paillard of guinea hen is given an earthy boost by a plum and foie gras sauce, while fettuccine with a rabbit ragout is a hearty winter warmer, though salty. Hanger steak is juicy and beefy, and the fine pan-roasted cod is worth ordering just for the accompaniments of braised cabbage, bacon and garlic potato chips. The wine list includes a few good choices under $30, but most cost more. Desserts also include some winners, like a sweet potato panna cotta with a caramel sauce. For a truly retro experience, you can make your own s'mores at the table.

Other recommended dishes: Fried oysters, roasted pork chops. **Price range:** Apps., $6–$8; entrees, $15–$20. **Wheelchair access:** Entrance and dining on one level; restrooms are down a flight.

Meridiana

$25 & Under

ITALIAN

2756 Broadway (near 106th St.)

(212) 222-4453

Credit cards: All major

Meals: D

This unusual Italian restaurant, styled like the ruins of Pompeii, has been buffeted by ownership changes, but still manages to produce exceptionally tasty fare like grilled sausages with peppers and roasted potatoes and well-made spaghetti carbonara. Meridiana's strength is its pastas, most of which are available in half orders as appetizers. Among the best were the sultry, spicy penne all'arrabbiata, made with sun-dried tomatoes, and tagliolini al nero, thin black noodles in a chunky, peppery tomato sauce with grilled shrimp. The waiters and waitresses are plucky and gracious, taking extra steps to let diners know they are on their side.

Other recommended dishes: Chicken salad; panzanella; tricolor salad; ravioli; ziti with sausage; veal with mushrooms; chocolate mousse cake; tiramisu. **Price range:** $4.50–$18. **Wheelchair access:** Fully accessible. **Features:** Outdoor dining. **Services:** Delivery, takeout, catering, private parties.

Mesa Grill ☆☆ $$$$ Southwestern

102 Fifth Ave. (bet. 15th & 16th Sts.)   (212) 807-7400
Credit cards: All major   Meals: Br, L, D

An instant hit on opening its doors in 1991, Mesa Grill is still a downtown favorite, crowded and clamorous at lunch, and even more crowded and clamorous at night. Despite the cookbooks, the television shows, and a second restaurant, Bolo, chef-owner Bobby Flay has somehow managed to keep Mesa Grill alive and kicking.

Southwestern food is not a cuisine. It's a grab bag of spices, flavors, colors and romantic associations that range from lurid sunsets to big green jalapeños to the paintings of Georgia O'Keeffe. Mr. Flay goes after big flavors and he knows how to get them. The thick, reduced bourbon and ancho chili glaze on his pork tenderloins, for example, is a swirl of sweetness, smoke and spice, nicely underlined by a tamale filled with creamy sweet potato and pecan butter. He also uses chilies and spices for flavor, not for heat. Sixteen-spice chicken sounds like a tongue-scorcher. It turns out to be a subtly handled, tingling orchestration of flavors, with an off-sweet sauce of caramelized mangos and garlic.

Mr. Flay has kept only one dish from bygone years, a corn tamale stuffed with corn and firm, flavorful shrimp, in a roasted garlic sauce. It is the house classic — simple, straightforward and irresistible. Elsewhere on the menu, new arrivals have kept the formula fresh, like a whole fish, fried so crisp it would shatter if dropped, with a winningly simple sauce of roasted tomatillos, ancho chilies and chipotle peppers, served with a side dish of smoky, spicy black rice. Gooseberry salsa adds real zip to a barbecued swordfish steak, and an orange sauce jazzed up with ancho chilies gives something like sex appeal to a roasted tuna steak.

Service at lunch can be very slow and disorganized; at dinner it can be so fast that it's hard not to feel rushed. Tables are close together, the volume level wavers between loud and deafening and a thundering soundtrack can be heard late in the evening. Mesa Grill is not the restaurant for a heart-to-heart talk, but it's ideal for a screaming fight. A good way to get one going is to cruise the margarita list. It is an inspirational document, and a rebuke to the appalling inventions that have made the drink synonymous with everyone's worst cocktail memory.

Other recommended dishes: Barbecued duck in blue corn pancake; orange and blackberry meringue cake; wild-berry bread and butter pudding. **Wine list:** About 50 American wines, most under $40. **Price range:** Lunch: apps., $6.50–$11; entrees, $10.50–$19; desserts, $7.50–$8.50. Dinner: apps., $8–$13; entrees, $24–$39; desserts, $7.50–$8.50. **Wheelchair access:** Restrooms on street level. **Services:** Catering, private parties.

Meskerem $25 & Under   AFRICAN/ETHIOPIAN

468 W. 47th St. (bet. Ninth & 10th Aves.)   (212) 664-0520
Credit cards: All major   Meals: L, D, LN

A meal at Meskerem, a plain, almost generic restaurant, demon-
strates how good Ethiopian food can be. The stews, which are
eaten with pieces of a spongy sourdough bread called injera,
are intensely spicy but three-dimensionally so, with flavors that
build and change in the mouth.

Alcohol: Beer and wine. **Price range:** Avg. app., $4; entree,
$8–$11; dessert, $2.95. **Wheelchair access:** Fully accessible.
Services: Delivery, takeout, catering, private parties.

Metisse $25 & Under   BISTRO/FRENCH

239 W. 105th St. (bet. Amsterdam Ave. & Broadway)
    (212) 666-8825
Credit cards: All major   Meals: D

A true neighborhood restaurant with an owner who prowls his
small dining room relentlessly to make sure all is well. Main
courses seem less consistent than the appetizers, but roast
chicken is superior, flavored with rosemary and served in a
vinaigrette with crisp sliced potatoes and braised carrots. Roast
leg of lamb and pork medallions are also good. Desserts count
for something, too, especially the warm chocolate cake with the
runny inside, and the brioche topped with caramelized apples
and caramel sauce.

Other recommended dishes: Oxtail on open-face ravioli;
potato ravioli; tuna tartar; goat cheese terrine; sautéed sweetbreads; lamb chops. **Price range:** Apps., $5–$8; entrees,
$12.50–$19.50. **Wheelchair access:** Four steps down from the
street; restrooms are narrow. **Features:** Romantic. **Services:**
Takeout, private parties.

Metrazur $$$ MEDITERRANEAN/NEW AMERICAN

404 East Balcony, Grand Central Terminal   (212) 687-4600
Credit cards: All major   Meals: L, D

In a city with no shortage of stunning views, there are few
prospects more impressive than Grand Central Terminal's
main concourse. Seen from the marble-railed balconies, the
frantic choreography of New Yorkers moving at top speed
seems like the very pulse of the city. Metrazur (on the east
balcony), with its spare, cool décor and low-slung lines,
makes the visual swirl and the busy hum of Grand Central
part of the meal. There's never any doubt that you are eating
in a train station. There's also no doubt that you are eating
mediocre food.

Once they get over the first flush of excitement at sitting down to eat beneath the great domed zodiac, diners will find themselves staring at food so undistinguished it nearly disappears on the plate. At its best, it's easy-listening food. Thyme-roasted halibut, on a pillow of chive whipped potatoes, is simple and pleasing. Roast chicken with rosemary and glazed potatoes is perfectly satisfactory. But the Metrazur bouillabaisse is almost daringly bland. Fire-roasted lobster scores higher, with wonderfully rich lobster meat but, again, an overly decorous carrot reduction. Tuna loin crusted with coriander and parsley is more like it.

The desserts have the inevitable feel of a Top 10 list. All are acceptable. The lone standout was a down-home peach-pistachio crisp, dense and gooey, with a scoop of pistachio ice cream.

Other recommended dishes: Shrimp and lobster spring roll; scallops with leeks; grilled sirloin with chanterelles. **Wine list:** A well-chosen international selection of about 70 wines, with five half-bottles and 11 wines by the glass. **Price range:** Apps., $7–$13; entrees, $22–$27; desserts, $8. Three-course pre-theater dinner, $29. Brunch, $19.50. **Wheelchair access:** Elevators in Northeast Passage, next to Track 23.

Metro Fish $$$ SEAFOOD

8 E. 36th St. (bet Madison & Fifth Aves.) (212) 683-6444
Credit cards: All major Meals: L, D

No matter what the calendar says, inside Metro Fish the date is 1955. Or it could be 1935. Metro Fish is the kind of restaurant that invites diners to ask about "the fisherman's catch" and boasts that its clams and oysters are "shucked to order." There's nothing self-consciously retro about any of this. The consciousness is pre-retro. Metro Fish offers, with a straight face, dishes like clams Casino, coconut fried shrimp and a broiled seafood platter. All entrees include baked potato, french fries or mashed potato. Children are in seventh heaven here: at last a fine-dining menu they can understand.

The décor runs to maritime kitsch, with a gaping shark here, a clipper ship there and a moody portrait of Jonathan Livingston Seagull thrown in for who knows what reason. The menu includes a few Greek and Italian touches, like fried calamari, grilled octopus and a Greek appetizer sampler of taramosalata, stuffed grape leaves and feta, but most of the dishes come straight from the grand American tradition of plain shore dining. There is no surf and turf, but Metro Fish offers a grilled Black Angus steak, an aged prime rib-eye steak and sliced steak with mushrooms. It is characteristic that fully 20 years after Paul Prudhomme burst onto the scene, Metro Fish still lets diners order their fish broiled, poached, blackened or Cajun-grilled.

Wine list: An international list with most bottles $22–$25, or by the glass for $5. **Price range:** Lunch: apps, $6.95–$12.95; entrees, $13.95–$18.95. Dinner: apps, $7–$14; entrees, $20–$34. **Wheelchair access:** Fully accessible. **Features:** Smoking at bar. **Services:** Private parties.

Metsovo $25 & Under   GREEK

65 W. 70th St. (near Columbus Ave.)   (212) 873-2300
Credit cards: All major   Meals: D

Metsovo's dim, romantic dining room is a far cry from the usual bright blue and white artifact-bedecked Greek restaurant. Instead of seafood, this restaurant, named after a town in north-western Greece, specializes in hearty stews, roasts and savory pies from the hills that form a spine through the region. The house specialties form the heart of the menu and are the best choices. Try Epirus mountain pies, which are offered with different fillings each day. They are all delicious. Tender chunks of baby lamb and a mellow stew of robust goat blended with thick yogurt and rice were also very good. Once you get through the house specialties, though, you're back in familiar territory. With the appetizers this is not a problem, but the grilled dishes are overcharred and dry. You may never receive the same selection of desserts twice, so hope for the luscious fig compote, or the wonderfully thick and fresh yogurt.

Other recommended dishes: Taramosalata; tzatziki; skordalia; eggplant salad; chopped salad. **Price range:** Apps, $4.95–$8.95; entrees, $13–$25. **Wheelchair access:** Steps up to entrance; stairs to restrooms. **Features:** Romantic. **Services:** Private parties.

Mexicana Mama $25 & Under   MEXICAN

525 Hudson St. (at W. 10th St.)   (212) 924-4119
Credit cards: Cash only   Meals: L, D

While this colorful restaurant's small menu doesn't register high on a scale of authenticity, the food succeeds in a more important measure: it tastes good. Rather than using the traditional mutton or goat, for example, a dish like barbacoa is made with beef, braised and then cooked slowly in a corn husk until it is fall-away tender, like pot roast. Authentic? No. Tasty? Definitely. Other worthy dishes include pollo con mole, a boneless chicken breast that is surprisingly juicy, with a terrific reddish-brown mole that is made with sesame seeds, chocolate and just enough chili heat to balance the sweetness of the chocolate.

Other recommended dishes: Tacos de puerco; flautas triologia; vanilla flan. **Price range:** Apps., $8; entrees, $8–$17; desserts, $5–$7. **Wheelchair access:** Restrooms not accessible. **Services:** Takeout.

Mezze $$ MEDITERRANEAN

10 E. 44th St. (bet. Fifth & Madison Aves.)   (212) 697-6644
Credit cards: All major   Meals: B, L   Closed Sat., Sun.

Mezze, one of Matthew Kenney's restaurants, is an attractive, informal, Middle Eastern fantasy with takeout service downstairs and a sit-down cafe upstairs. It is packed at lunchtime, with people lining up to choose from more than a dozen salads and flatbread sandwiches, like roasted vegetables with preserved lemon, Moroccan spiced carrots and spicy chicken salad. There are also flatbread pizzas, a new breakfast menu and main courses like spiced shrimp with tomato jam and a lamb shank with couscous. Mezze is open by day; dinner is delivery only.

Price range: Apps., $5–$8; entrees, $9–$17; desserts, $3.50–$5.50. **Wheelchair access:** Not accessible. **Services:** Delivery, takeout, catering, private parties.

Mi Cocina ☆☆ $$ MEXICAN

57 Jane St. (at Hudson St.)   (212) 627-8273
Credit cards: All major   Meals: L, D

You can get imitation Mexican food and Tex-Mex food and even upscale Mexican food all over the city. But if you're looking for the real thing, you can't do better than this small Greenwich Village storefront. Floor-to-ceiling windows open up the slender rectangular space of the restaurant, with its sparkling kitchen framed in colorful tiles. A superior starter is the empanaditas de picadillo: little turnovers filled with shredded beef, raisins and olives. Sopitos con queso de cabra are cornmeal crusts topped with goat cheese, salsa, onions and cilantro. Main courses include chicken enchiladas and fajitas, made with grilled skirt steak or breast of chicken, onions, peppers, guacamole, black beans and salsa. White almond flan, chocolate mousse cake and crepes filled with brandied raisins and walnuts are the desserts. *(Ruth Reichl)*

Price range: Apps., $7–$18; entrees, $16–$25; desserts, $8–$12. **Wheelchair access:** Fully accessible. **Features:** Kid friendly, outdoor dining (garden). **Services:** Takeout, catering.

Michael Jordan's ☆☆ $$$$ STEAKHOUSE

23 Vanderbilt Ave. (in Grand Central Terminal)   (212) 655-2300
Credit cards: All major   Meals: L, D

Despite a celebrity owner and a big-deal designer (David Rockwell), the real star of this place is Grand Central Terminal. You sit in comfort on the balcony gazing at the starry ceiling while harried commuters dash madly through the marble halls below. The menu is what you would expect, but the food, for the most part, is equal to the space. Shrimp cocktail is excellent and the meat robust, prime, aged and old-fashioned. All the standard cuts are available, but the flavorful rib-eye steak is best. The hamburger, made from chopped prime sirloin, is absurd; it's so enormous it looks more like an inflated basketball. Desserts are not inspiring. (*Ruth Reichl*)

Other recommended dishes: Iceberg lettuce salad; broiled marrow bones; porterhouse for two; New York strip steak; steamed or broiled lobster; chopped sirloin; crisp fried onions; hash brown potatoes; creamed spinach; hot fudge sundae. **Wine list:** Excellent wines at fair prices; terrible wines by the glass. **Price range:** Apps., $8–$16; entrees, $18–$34; side dishes, $6.95; desserts, $5–$8.50. **Wheelchair access:** Elevator to restaurant. **Services:** Catering, private parties.

Michael's ☆☆ $$$ NEW AMERICAN
24 W. 55th St. (bet. Fifth & Sixth Aves.)   (212) 767-0555
Credit cards: All major   Meals: B, L, D   Closed Sun.

Home of the power lunch. All of publishing goes to Michael's because the room is attractive and filled with good art. The menu offers one of the city's finest selections of fancy salads (some large enough to feed a small nation). The best food on the menu is unabashedly American, including grilled chicken, grilled lobster, good steaks and chops, and California cuisine. There are several daily fish selections. For dessert, the classic collection of tarts and cakes is very enticing. (*Ruth Reichl*)

Other recommended dishes: Gravlax; sweetbreads with capers, lemon and parsley; pork tenderloin with molasses; squab. **Wine list:** Wide-ranging with a fine selection of French and American wines at fair prices. **Price range:** Apps., $12–$18; entrees, $22–$34; desserts, $9. **Wheelchair access:** Three steps down into dining room. **Services:** Private parties.

Mickey Mantle's $$ AMERICAN
42 Central Park S. (bet. Fifth & Sixth Aves.)   (212) 688-7777
Credit cards: All major   Meals: L, D

Televisions everywhere showing great games past and present. As sports bars go, Mantle's is more restaurant than bar, with fine burgers, chicken and desserts. A standing ovation if you're a Mantle fan, otherwise have someone wake you when it's over. A perfect place for children after a day in Central Park.

Price range: Apps., $5.50–$8.95; entrees, $11.95–$25; desserts, $4.50–$6.95. **Wheelchair access:** Fully accessible. **Features:** Kid friendly, outdoor dining. **Services:** Takeout, catering, private parties.

Midway (Fair) $$$

145 Charles St. (at Washington St.)
Credit cards: All major

BRASSERIE
(212) 352-1118
Meals: L, D, LN

The menu here is all-American. It looks good on paper, and it won't break the bank. But a big problem is the chef's timidity with herbs and spices and some bizarre primeval fear of salt. Parts of various dishes are delicious. And in a few, everything works — like the garlic and artichoke soup, more like a delicate emulsion one night, a chowder another, gently flavored with garlic and strewn with a bit of crunch from the artichokes. It's a felicitous combination, as is the crisply grilled portobello mushroom with bits of Parmigiano-Reggiano, pleasingly bitter baby arugula and an intense balsamic reduction. The beef sashimi is fresh and appropriately paper thin, with a nice soy-sesame dressing.

But despite the tomato and apricot-mustard coulis, the tuna tartare was bland. Entrees do not fare as well as the appetizers, but on a good night the chicken can be nicely seasoned, tender and moist, the potato purée creamy and rich. The wines are expensive, though, especially for a restaurant where you can have a huge burger and fries for $11. Service can also be slow. But on weekends the energy in the room makes the blandness of the food seem less important. (*Marian Burros*)

Other recommended dishes: Garlic artichoke soup, "all natural chicken," roasted parsnip and celery root, potato purée. **Wine list:** Mostly American, and mostly overpriced. **Price range:** Lunch, $20; dinner, $40. **Wheelchair access:** Everything on one level.

Mignon $25 & Under

394 Court St., Cobble Hill, Brooklyn
Credit cards: Cash only   Meals: L, D

FRENCH
(718) 222-8383
Closed Mon.

Even when it's very busy, service in Mignon's lace-curtained dining room is friendly, courteous and efficient, food arrives at an acceptable pace, and best of all, it's delicious. The chef and owner, Pablo Trobo, shows a sensitive hand with seafood. Chilled seafood bisque, with the intense, rich flavors of shrimp and lobster reduced to their essences, is a great appetizer. Cod coated with ground almonds is terrifically moist and flavorful, while both sautéed monkfish and grilled red snapper are also perfectly cooked. Desserts include a wonderful fruit tart.

Other recommended dishes: Stuffed sardine; smoked duck breast with figs and blueberries; merguez en brochette; duck confit; steak au poivre; linzer torte; poached pear tart. **Price range:** Apps., $4–$9; entrees, $13–$18.50. **Wheelchair access:** Everything is on one level.

Milan's

$25 & Under   EAST EUROPEAN

719 Fifth Ave., Park Slope, Brooklyn   (718) 788-7384

Credit cards: Cash only   Meals: L, D   Closed Mon.

This bright, friendly place is one of the few restaurants in New York to offer genuine Slovakian cooking as well as traditional Eastern European cooking. That means hearty, solid fare heavy on meats, cream, cabbage and potatoes. Bygos, a blend of chopped kielbasa and smoked meats, cabbage and cream sauce, is an unusual turn on the formula, while goulash — chunks of tender beef in a meat, tomato and herb sauce — is terrific, served with slices of steamed white bread.

Other recommended dishes: Potato pancakes; halusky. **Alcohol:** Beer and wine. **Price range:** Apps., $3.50–$4; entrees, $5.50–$9; desserts, $2–$3.50. **Wheelchair access:** Fully accessible. **Features:** Smoking permitted. **Services:** Takeout.

Mill Korean

$25 & Under   KOREAN

2895 Broadway (bet. 112th & 113th Sts.)   (212) 666-7653

Credit cards: All major   Meals: L, D

This place is a reincarnation of the Mill, a greasy spoon luncheonette for generations of Columbia students. It still has lime rickeys and egg creams, but the emphasis is now Korean, with terrific offerings like sweet-and-spicy beef short ribs and huge portions of bibimbap, the egg and rice mixture served with meat or vegetables. A scallion pancake, big as a small pizza, is savory and delicate, as is a similar pancake, with shrimp and squid. Tiny pork dumplings are terrific either fried or steamed, and a couple of these dishes can make up an entire meal, especially when supplemented by kim chee and other free hors d'oeuvres.

Alcohol: Beer and wine. **Price range:** Apps., $6–$7; entrees, $7–$11. **Wheelchair access:** Fully accessible. **Features:** Kid friendly. **Services:** Delivery, takeout, catering.

Mi Mexico

$ MEXICAN

3151 Broadway (near 125th St.)   (212) 665-7338

Credit cards: All major   Meals: L, D, LN

The pozole at this little taquería (served Thursdays through Sundays only) is rich and filling, full of pork, onion, cilantro and delicious, springy puffs of white corn. Pipian de pollo, a chicken coated in a tangy sauce made with crushed pumpkin seeds, is bright with a nice, peppery edge to it, while a tamale with red pepper and chicken is lean and intense. Tacos, though, are too heavy on the iceberg lettuce, except for the spicy beef, coated with a red pepper paste, which was spicy enough to shine through.

Price range: Apps., $5–$9; entrees, $7–$8; desserts, $1–$2.50.
Wheelchair access: Not accessible. **Services:** Delivery, takeout.

Miracle Bar & Grill $$ SOUTHWESTERN
112 First Ave. (bet. 6th & 7th Sts.) (212) 254-2353
415 Bleecker St. (bet. Bank & W. 11th Sts.) (212) 924-1900
Credit cards: All major Meals: Br, L, D, LN

The original Miracle Grill has an East Village charm and a
lovely garden that give context to the Southwestern food; the
new West Village spot is simply a busy, charmless place that
puts too much emphasis on the menu of unexciting dishes. It's
best for drinks.

Price range: Apps., $4.95–$8.95; entrees, $5.95–$18.95;
desserts, $4–$6. **Wheelchair access:** Restrooms downstairs.
Features: Smoking permitted. **Services:** Takeout, catering, private parties.

Mirchi $25 & Under INDIAN
29 Seventh Ave. (near Morton St.) (212) 414-0931
Credit cards: All major Meals: L, D

Mirchi's clean and simple design, casual service and loud
Indian-by-way-of-London techno music suggest other youth-ori-
ented restaurants with bar crowds rather than other Indian
restaurants. Yet the food is strictly Indian, with not even a hint
of fusion. The focus is street foods and other small plates, a
deceiving concept since many portions are quite large. Mirchi's
other point of departure is forceful spicing, with occasionally
very high heat (the word mirchi means hot, as in chilies).
Chicken tak-a-tak, shredded chicken essentially stir-fried on the
tawa (pronounced tav-AH), an Indian equivalent of a wok, is
exceptional, with a peppery bite augmented by garlic, ginger
and chili. Among the main courses jaipuri lal maas is a fabulous and subtle lamb dish, made, the menu says, with 30 red
chilies. Yet the chunks of lamb are not fiery but hauntingly
spicy, as if the chilies had left a ghostly imprint of their power,
capturing the full flavor of the pepper. Mirchi's wine list is a
great idea, though it offers too many chardonnays and merlots,
which are overwhelmed by spicy food.

Other recommended dishes: Grilled shrimp in tamarind sauce,
hyderabadi baingan, ragda pattice, chicken chat, dhoklas,
kicheri. **Price range:** Apps., $4–$9; entrees, $9–$19. **Wheelchair access:** Everything is on one level.

Miss Maude's Spoonbread Too

$25 & Under SOUTHERN

547 Lenox Ave. (near 137th St.) (212) 690-3100
Credit cards: All major Meals: Br, L, D

Miss Maude's practically invites you in for a meal. Its walls are
adorned with kitchen tools and black-and-white family photos,
while each of its shiny red or yellow tables holds a fat, fresh
rose. The generous portions of Southern dishes are not only
robust and hearty, but also sometimes subtle, which should be
no surprise, since Miss Maude's is owned by Norma Jean Dar-
den, the caterer and cookbook author, who also owns Miss
Mamie's Spoonbread Too.

Meals begin with a basket of mildly spicy corn bread, grainy
and not too sweet, and are served Southern style, with large
portions of two sides. The smothered pork chops are thin but
flavorful enough to stand up to the peppery brown gravy. Close
behind are the excellent fried shrimp with traces of cornmeal in
the delectable crust. Fried chicken is as it should be, with a
crisp, oniony crust that remains united with the meat. Short
ribs are tender and very meaty, as are pork ribs baked with a
barbecue sauce that is sweet and citrusy, but also packs some
spicy heat. Side dishes are good, but except for banana pudding, produced in all its soft vanilla-wafer glory, the desserts are
a disappointment.

Other recommended dishes: Macaroni and cheese, meatloaf,
collard greens, candied yams, potato salad. **Price range:** Dinners, $9.95–$12.95. **Wheelchair access:** Everything is on one
level.

Miss Saigon

$25 & Under VIETNAMESE

1425 Third Ave. (bet. 80th & 81st Sts.) (212) 988-8828
473 Columbus Ave. (bet. 82nd & 83rd Sts.) (212) 595-8919
Credit cards: All major Meals: L, D

These two restaurants offer a fresh and tasty introduction to
Vietnamese food, with dishes like lemongrass-scented pork
with garlic and sesame seeds, piquant green papaya salad and
hearty pho bo, the traditional North Vietnamese oxtail soup.
These are pleasant dining rooms but not the places to explore
Vietnamese cooking at its pungent best.

Alcohol: Beer and wine. **Price range:** Lunch: avg. app., $4.95;
entree, $6.95; dessert, $5. Dinner: avg. app., $5.95; entree,
$12.95; dessert, $5. **Wheelchair access:** Not accessible. **Features:** Kid friendly, outdoor dining. **Services:** Delivery, takeout,
private parties.

Miss Williamsburg $25 & Under DINER/ITALIAN

206 Kent Ave., Williamsburg, Brooklyn,   (718) 963-0802
Credit cards: Cash only   Meals: D   Closed Mon.

Once the greasiest of spoons, this diner has been scrubbed until gleaming inside and now serves dishes of pasta rather than burgers and fries. Miss Williamsburg offers a small selection of uncomplicated, inexpensive dishes that qualify both as good Italian food and great diner food. Mussels, sautéed with greens and onions, are served in a tasty white wine and lemon sauce, perfect for sopping up with a slice of crusty bread. Among the pastas, try spaghetti alla chittara, thick shoelaces of house-made spaghetti with a perfectly proportioned sauce of chopped fresh tomatoes, arugula and roasted garlic, or the spinach-and-ricotta ravioli. Two main courses stand out: a thin and moist pork loin, and straccetti alla rugantino, thin, ragged strips of sautéed beef blanched almost beige in a white-wine sauce, all texture and lively flavor. The one absolute winner among desserts is a honey-flavored mousse with pine nuts.

Other recommended dishes: Vegetable salad; octopus salad; lasagna; skewers of shrimp and squid; roast chicken; grilled pork chop. **Price range:** Apps., $4–$6; entrees, $8–$14. **Wheelchair access:** Small flight of steps at entrance; restrooms are narrow.

Miyagi $25 & Under JAPANESE/SUSHI

220 W. 13th St. (near Greenwich Ave.)   (212) 620-3830
Credit cards: All major   Meals: L, D   Closed Sun.

Miyagi is a pretty little Japanese restaurant which seats just 45 people in the small dining room and sushi bar. It has the casual, welcoming air of an ideal neighborhood restaurant, with waitresses who are decorous despite jeans and T-shirts. The napkins and tablecloths are paper, the chopsticks are small and somewhat splintery, but Miyagi reserves elegance for what counts, like etched glass sake carafes that look like spherical pine cones and, of course, the freshest ingredients.

The menu has many familiar choices and just enough off-beat selections to keep things interesting. Consider what Yoshikatsu Makigi, the chef and owner, calls fried Alaska: ground salmon, asparagus and mint wrapped in seaweed like a sushi roll and expertly deep fried, then served in bite-size pieces with a miso dressing. It's a perfect melange of flavors and soft and crunchy textures.

Another excellent choice is greens tossed with delicate soy milk skins in a mustard-and-miso dressing. Miyagi's sushi and sashimi are just what you hope for in a midpriced restaurant: fresh and clean, with the cool distant flavor of the ocean. Beyond the sushi horizon is another world of Japanese cooking.

Negimaki, broiled beef rolled with scallions and cut into bite-size pieces, is a savory meal, while tonkatsu, a pork cutlet covered in fine bread crumbs, deep-fried and served with a fruity dipping sauce, is crisp and hearty. But the best dish is a simple broiled mackerel, which is full of flavor and virtually melts in your mouth.

Miyagi offers one unusual dessert along with the standard red bean and green tea ice creams. Gelatinous rice dumplings, which have more than a little bounce to them, are surrounded by a deliciously sweet paste of adzuki beans, which makes the whole dish worthwhile.

Other recommended dishes: Steamed monkfish liver; hijiki; spinach with sesame sauce. **Price range:** Apps., $2.50–$8.25; entrees, $10–$15; sushi and sashimi combinations, $14 –$22. **Wheelchair access:** Steps at entrance; tiny restroom.

Molyvos ☆☆☆　　$$$　　　　　GREEK
871 Seventh Ave. (near 55th St.)　　　　　(212) 582-7500
Credit cards: All major　　　　　　　　　　Meals: L, D

Casual, hospitable and lively as a Greek taverna, Molyvos offers food by people who passionately want you to love it. The friendly, caring service begins with mezedes, little tastes that captivate with the intensity of their flavors. Tiny mint-laced triangles of spinach are wrapped in layers of pastry so thin they crunch as you bite into them, then instantly melt away. Tzatziki, the dip made of cucumbers, garlic and sheep's milk yogurt, has a truly Greek tang. Melitzanosalata, the roasted eggplant dip with garlic and lemon, has a fine smokiness, and taramosalata, fish roe whipped with olive oil, is salty and satisfying. Skordalia, the garlic and potato purée, arrives with a handful of large, tender white beans crowned with chopped onions. Tyro keftedes, small pungent balls of fried cheese, are perfect between sips of ouzo. (There are 10 to choose from.)

The mezedes make a marvelous meal all by themselves. But that would mean missing the rest of the large menu with fine dishes from all the Greek islands. There are unusual dolmades — leaves of lettuce stuffed with salt cod and rice and served in an egg-lemon sauce. Marinated lamb shank, braised in wine with orzo and tomatoes, is soft, savory and delicious. Rabbit is stewed with onions in the sweet red wine of Patra. Even Greek standards like moussaka and pastitsio are impressive.

Portions are huge, and much of this food is straightforward, relying primarily on good ingredients. Fresh fish are simply grilled whole over wood. The grill gives shrimp, with the heads still on, a fine char without robbing them of their juiciness.

Desserts are as good (and as big) as everything else. The light, honey-drizzled fritters would easily feed an entire table.

Custard comes wrapped in that fabulous phyllo, and mastic ice cream, which has a faint flavor of pine, is served with fresh and marinated figs. (*Ruth Reichl*)

Other recommended dishes: Steamed mussels; steamed salmon wrapped in grape leaves; stuffed cabbage. **Most popular dish:** List of mezedes. **Chef's favorite:** Ocean black-fish plaki. **Wine list:** Many fine choices. Greek wines are excellent, and the sommelier is eager to help. **Price range:** Lunch: apps., $6.75–$12.50; entrees, $12.50–$20.50; desserts, $7. Dinner: apps., $6.75–$12.50; entrees, $18.50–$27.50; desserts, $7. **Wheelchair access:** Three steps up to dining room. **Services:** Takeout.

Mombar $25 & Under   MIDDLE EASTERN
25-22 Steinway St. (bet. 25th & 28th Aves.), Astoria, Queens
(718) 728-9858
Credit cards: Cash only   Meals: D, LN   Closed Mon.

There's no sign for Mombar (pronounced MOOM-bar), just a couple of huge eyes built into the storefront, one made of stucco, the other of tile shards. A door forms a sort of nose between the eyes, and what you see on entering is not so much a restaurant as a work of art. From the elaborate mosaic floor to the windows of stained glass, the old office postal chutes on the wall that have been transformed into tinted lights, and the unique and beautiful tabletops, every surface is covered with the creations of Moustafa El Sayed, the owner, chef and resident artist. Mombar has no menus; someone simply recites the choices. They almost always include the restaurant's namesake, mombar, a house-made Egyptian sausage of lamb, beef and rice with dill and garlic, served warm with chickpeas. (A vegetarian version is also served.) With food, too, Mr. Sayed is an artist: he serves personal interpretations of dishes and seems as if he's cooking at home. He blends the ingredients of his delicious couscous, concealing the semolina grains under tender lamb, zucchini, olives, raisins and dried cherries, rather than serving the components separately, North African style. Chicken tagine is a moist and smoky North African stew with olives and vegetables, while rabbit cooked in a clay pot is a hearty southern Egyptian blend, with zucchini, dried apricots, raisins, pine nuts and caramelized cauliflower. Mombar usually has several house-made desserts, like baklava dripping with honey or couscous cake, the grains compressed with prunes and dried apricots, luscious with strawberries and sour cream.

Other recommended dishes: Assorted appetizers; grilled striped bass; roasted duck with molasses. **Price range:** Apps., $5–$7.50; entrees, $18. **Wheelchair access:** Ramp at entrance.

Mona Lisa Gourmet Pizza $ PIZZA

190 Bleecker St. (at Macdougal St.)   (212) 979-1152
Credit cards: All major   Meals: L, D, LN

This traditional-looking pizzeria offers a selection of 24 pies,
ranging from the appealingly simple tomato and basil pie with
sliced plum tomatoes drizzled with olive oil and topped with
basil, to a Tex-Mex chicken pie. The less-complex pies are best,
with an extraordinarily light crust that manages to be airy yet
crisp and tasty. I can vouch for the triple mushroom, made with
fresh portobellos, shiitakes and creminis; the Mona Lisa, just
like the tomato and basil but with mozzarella and Parmesan,
and the vegetable supreme, which is topped with moisture-pro-
ducing eggplant, zucchini and peppers, and still achieves a
crisp crust. But even with all the choices, my favorite is the Da
Vinci, just tomato sauce, cheese and dough. Sometimes perfection is hard to improve upon.

Alcohol: Beer and wine. **Price range:** Slices, $1.75–$2.50; pies,
$11–$17.50. **Wheelchair access:** Fully accessible. **Features:** Kid
friendly. **Services:** Delivery, takeout, catering, private parties.

Monsoon $25 & Under   VIETNAMESE

435 Amsterdam Ave. (at 81st St.)   (212) 580-8686
Credit cards: All major   Meals: L, D, LN

The signs were pointing downhill for this Vietnamese restaurant,
which opened to crowds eager for its fresh, carefully prepared
and subtly spiced dishes but it devolved to being a takeout specialist. It's unfortunate evidence that Vietnamese food has
become an institution. A recent renovation, however, has spruced
up the place.

Recommended dishes: Summer rolls; chao tom; steamed lady
fingers; grilled pork chop; stir-fried chicken; stir-fried or
steamed rice noodles; pho; canh chua; green papaya salad;
banana pudding. **Alcohol:** Beer and wine. **Price range:** $8–$20.
Wheelchair access: Everything on one level; entrance and
restrooms are narrow. **Features:** Kid friendly. **Services:** Delivery,
takeout, catering, private parties.

Montrachet ☆☆☆ $$$$ FRENCH

239 W. Broadway (near White St.)   (212) 219-2777
Credit cards: All major   Meals: L (Fri. only), D   Closed Sun.

After 14 years, TriBeCa's first serious restaurant has achieved a
pleasant patina of age without losing its casual charm and
thoughtful service. In l998, when Rémi Lauvand took over the
kitchen, Montrachet became more Gallic than ever with muscu-

lar French cooking that seems just right for the small bistro-like dining rooms.

Start with the cool terrine of foie gras set off by a quince confit and crisp little haricots verts. As it hits the warm brioche toast, it begins to melt until it is utterly voluptuous. Afterward, try the memorable roast chicken served with a rich potato purée and a robust garlic sauce. Then, of course, some cheese, if only to finish the last of the wine chosen from a fine list of Burgundies and Bordeaux. And finally, because everything has tasted so good, perhaps a tarte Tatin made with seasonal fruits.

Main dishes tend to be straightforward, relying on excellence of execution rather than originality. Red snapper arrives looking like a minimalist painting: spare and plain, the dish frames the succulent fish. Turbot, steamed with leeks and paired with marrow, or accompanied by baby spinach in ravigote sauce, is elegant in its simplicity.

When a restaurant is named for a wine region it is difficult to pass up a cheese course. Montrachet offers a small selection of fine, ripe cheeses: each makes a fine prelude to dessert. Try the napoleon. It looks like the classic airy pastry, but mascarpone filling gives this confection an entirely new character. (*Ruth Reichl*)

Other recommended dishes: Blini with smoked trout and caviar; sautéed foie gras with pickled pumpkin and root vegetables; sweetbreads; loin of lamb with eggplant and onion compote. **Most popular dish:** Roast peaches in ginger cream. **Chef's favorite:** Warm braised rabbit salad with dandelions. **Wine list:** Excellent, with a specialty in Burgundies. **Price range:** Lunch: apps., $9–$16; entrees, $17–$23; desserts, $8; prix fixe, $20 and $28. Dinner: apps., $11–$26; entrees, $23–$34; desserts, $9. Prix fixe, $36, $44, $78 and $90. **Wheelchair access:** Three steps up to the dining rooms.

Morrell Wine Bar & Cafe $$$ New American

1 Rockefeller Plaza (on W. 49th St.) (212) 262-7700.
Credit cards: All major Meals: Br, L, D

The cafe may be small, but the wine list is large, about 2,000 bottles supplied by Morrell Wine Shop next door, with about 50 wines available by the glass. And the closet-sized kitchen somehow manages to send out satisfying, well-conceived dishes, with an eye on the wine list. An appetizer of smoked duck breast, served with pears and wild greens, is glazed with cracked black pepper and syrah. Roast loin of beef with truffled mashed potatoes swims in a cabernet jus. And the dessert list includes wine-inflected dishes like a tawny port flan and a vanilla-bean pound cake topped with dried fruits macerated in muscat, the opulent, apricot-scented white wine from the south of France.

Wine list: 2,000 bottles, ranging in price from $16–$6000. 110 wines by the glass, $5–$49. **Price range:** Apps, $8–$16; entrees, $17–$28. Mon. night wine dinner, $50. **Wheelchair access:** Fully accessible. **Features:** Smoking room, smoking at bar. **Services:** Private parties.

Moscow $$$ RUSSIAN

137 E. 55th St. (bet. Third & Lexington Aves.)   (212) 813-1313
Credit cards: All major   Meals: L, D, LN

You'll know it by the dancing bears outside. Inside you'll find a dreamy little jewel box of a restaurant that looks like the inside of a Fabergé egg, and an even better-looking bar. The food, unfortunately, doesn't match the setting. But there's a cabaret downstairs with very lively music.

Price range: Apps., $6–$18; entrees, $18–$24; desserts, $8. **Wheelchair access:** Fully accessible. **Services:** Catering, private parties.

Mottsu $25 & Under   JAPANESE/SUSHI

285 Mott St. (bet. Houston & Prince Sts.)   (212) 343-8017
Credit cards: All major   Meals: L, D, LN

This hip, neighborly, low-key place serves fresh, artful, moderately priced sushi. Top choices include the tuna, the eel hand roll made with cucumber, and an almost cedary smoked salmon.

Alcohol: Beer and wine. **Price range:** Lunch: apps., $6–$9; entrees, $8.50–$11. Dinner: apps., $6–$9; entrees, $13.50–$21. Prix fixe, $15 (5-7 P.M.); tasting menu, $38. **Wheelchair access:** Fully accessible. **Features:** Good for business, romantic. **Services:** Delivery, takeout, catering, private parties.

Moustache $25 & Under   MIDDLE EASTERN

90 Bedford St. (bet. Grove & Barrow Sts.)   (212) 229-2220
265 E. 10th St. (bet. First Ave. & Ave. A)   (212) 228-2022
Credit cards: Cash only   Meals: L, D, LN

These small, excellent Middle Eastern restaurants specialize in "pitzas," exceptional pizza–like dishes made with pita dough, including lahmajun, the Turkish specialty with a savory layer of ground lamb on crisp crust, and zaatar, a crisp individual pizza topped with a smoky, aromatic combination of olive oil, thyme, sesame seeds and sumac. Falafel is run-of-the-mill, but a sandwich of sliced lamb in pita bread with onion and tomato is brought to life by a minty lemon mayonnaise.

Other recommended dishes: Pita bread; hummus; baba gannouj; spinach and chickpea salad; foul; zatter bread; lamb sandwich; loomi; basboussa. **Price range:** $3–$12. **Wheelchair access:** Everything is on one level. **Features:** Outdoor dining. **Services:** Delivery, takeout, catering, private parties.

Mughlai
$25 & Under   INDIAN
320 Columbus Ave. (at 71st St.)   (212) 724-6363
Credit cards: All major   Meals: L, D

Mughlai offers tantalizing glimpses of the pleasures of Indian food. Its menu offers the litany of familiar dishes, but it also invites diners to try uncommon regional dishes. Almost always at Mughlai, the less familiar dishes are better. Dal papri, potatoes and chickpeas blended in a tangy tamarind-and-yogurt sauce and served cool, is a superb appetizer, a sort of Indian potato salad that invigorates the palate. Pepper chicken, a dish from the southwestern state of Kerala, is another adventure: the pieces of stewed chicken, coated in ground black pepper, seem to dance invitingly across the mouth. Also excellent are baghare baigan, small eggplants in an aromatic sauce of ground peanuts, sesame, tamarind and coconut. But old standbys such as chicken vindaloo or Tandoori dishes are as disappointing as the other dishes are invigorating.

Other recommended dishes: Aloo papri chat; shammi kebabs; achar gosht; lamb pasanda. **Price range:** Apps., $4.50–$8.95; entrees, $6.95–$18.95. **Wheelchair access:** One step up at entrance; restrooms are narrow. **Services:** Delivery, takeout, catering, private parties.

Nadaman Hakubai ☆☆
$$$$ JAPANESE
Kitano Hotel, 66 Park Ave. (at 38th St.)   (212) 885-7111
Credit cards: All major   Meals: B, L, D

New York City's most expensive restaurant serves kaiseki cuisine in private, brightly lighted tatami rooms. Nadaman Hakubai offers serenity and the extraordinary sense of experiencing another culture. A visit to one of this restaurant's tatami rooms is like a quick trip to Japan. Kaiseki cuisine, associated with the tea ceremony, is food for the soul as well as the body, meant to feed the eye with its beauty and the spirit with its meaning. The courses — served by kimono-clad hostesses — follow a strict order and each is intended to introduce the coming season. The way to enjoy this is to abandon yourself to the experience, appreciating the peace, the subtlety of the flavors and the sense that you are being pampered as never before. Unless you are an extremely adventurous eater, you will probably not like every dish you are served. But in spite of the occasional disappointment, each evening at the restaurant has been an immensely rewarding experience. Worth $150? Think of it this way: A trip to Japan would cost considerably more. (*Ruth Reichl*)

Wine list: There is a wine list, but the waitresses tend to be baffled by it. It is best to stick to sake and beer. **Price range:** Kaiseki dinners in private tatami rooms, $100 minimum per person, for a minimum of four people. Traditional Japanese breakfast in the dining room is $25 or $28; mini kaiseki lunch, $60; kaiseki dinners in the main restaurant begin at $80 (and are not particularly recommended). **Wheelchair access:** The restaurant is below street level, but there is an elevator. **Features:** Good for business. **Services:** Private parties.

Nam Phuong $25 & Under   VIETNAMESE

19 Sixth Ave. (at Walker St.)   (212) 431-7715
Credit cards: MC/V   Meals: L, D

With its dim lights, wall-length mirrors and neon signs, this pleasant Vietnamese restaurant fits well into its TriBeCa neighborhood. Nam Phuong serves delicious soups like pho tai, a traditional northern Vietnamese recipe with a rich, almost velvety cilantro-scented beef stock filled with paper-thin slices of tender steak and rice noodles. The southern version of pho, hu tieu, is equally good, the rice noodle soup full of sliced pork and shrimp. A nice counterpart to the soups is the cool, refreshing shredded chicken salad flavored with mint, lemongrass and lime and spiced with chilies. Iced Vietnamese coffee, made with condensed milk, is like a coffee milkshake, while lemonade is sweet and refreshing, made with green Vietnamese lemons.

Other recommended dishes: Spring rolls; barbecued beef rolls; steamed rice crepes with sausage; chao tom; sautéed seitan; grilled pork on rice noodles; tropical fruit shake. **Price range:** Apps., $3.95–$8.50; entrees, $7.50–$23.95. **Wheelchair access:** Everything is on one level. **Features:** Romantic. **Services:** Delivery, takeout, catering, private parties.

Naples 45 $$ ITALIAN/PIZZA

200 Park Ave. (at 45th St. & Vanderbilt Ave.)   (212) 972-7001
Credit cards: All major   Meals: B, L, D

The room is cavernous and clamorous, and you might as well be eating in Grand Central for all the peace you'll get. Still, the menu of Neapolitan specialties is enticing, and the pizza, sold by the meter, is superb.

Price range: Apps., $3.95–$6.95; entrees, $11.50–$18.50; desserts, $3.50–$5.50. **Wheelchair access:** Fully accessible. **Features:** Kid friendly, smoking permitted, outdoor dining. **Services:** Delivery, takeout, catering.

National Cafe $25 & Under CUBAN/LATIN AMERICAN
210 First Ave. (near 13th St.)   (212) 473-9354
Credit cards: All major   Meals: L, D

If you order a roast pork sandwich at this tiny Cuban restaurant, you can watch its construction. The server picks up a leg of pork and carefully carves pieces of the tender meat, piling them high on a hero roll. Then she places a chicharrón (a crisp piece of fried pork skin) on top. The result is delicious and filling, like almost everything else on the menu.

Alcohol: Beer and wine. **Price range:** Apps., $2.25–$3; entrees, $6.50–$9; desserts, $2.25–$2.50. **Wheelchair access:** Not accessible. **Services:** Delivery, takeout.

Negril Caribbean $25 & Under CARIBBEAN
362 W. 23rd St. (bet. Eighth & Ninth Aves.)   (212) 807-6411
Credit cards: All major   Meals: L, D, LN

This lively, colorful establishment with its sea blue ceiling, pale yellow walls and trompe-l'oeil windows opening onto a sunny Jamaican beach pulsates with Caribbean vibrations under the beat of background reggae music. The food is reliably pleasing and prepared with gusto. Complete meals are served here, and most main courses come with soup, steamed vegetables and a side dish. Among better options are the seafood roti, or spicy seafood stew combining shrimp, lobster and fish with chickpeas, peppers and tomatoes; flavorful oxtail stew in lima bean sauce; slow-cooked goat in a mild curry sauce; and steamed whole red snapper, which has first been marinated with lime, peppers, onions, peas and tomatoes.

Price range: Lunch: entrees, $7.50–$8.50. Dinner: apps., $2.95–$13.95; entrees, $8.95–$16.50. **Wheelchair access:** Entrance and some tables are on one level; restrooms are several steps up. **Services:** Delivery, takeout, catering, private parties.

New Green Bo $ CHINESE
66 Bayard St. (bet. Mott & Elizabeth Sts.)   (212) 625-2359
Credit cards: Cash only   Meals: L, D, LN

This bright, plain restaurant in Chinatown looks like many other bright, plain restaurants in the neighborhood, except that it offers delicious Shanghai specialties like soup dumplings, smoked fish and eel with chives.

Price range: Apps., $1.95–$6.95; entrees, $2.75–$24; desserts, $2.95. **Features:** Good for business. **Services:** Delivery, takeout, private parties.

New World Grill $25 & Under   NEW AMERICAN

329 W. 49th St. (bet. Eighth & Ninth Aves.)   (212) 957-4745
Credit cards: All major   Meals: Br, L, D

For its enticing mix of flavors that roam the globe from the
American Southwest to Asia and Italy, New World Grill
remains a steady lure. The restaurant is a bright, gazebolike
structure with 35 seats wrapped around a handsome bar. Its
hidden courtyard, away from the noises of the streets, is especially inviting. For starters, there are grilled portobellos and
Romaine lettuce dressed in balsamic vinaigrette, and grilled
marinated shrimp and calamari served over a mound of
mesclun. Main courses include a vegetarian plate of grilled
and roasted vegetables with wilted spinach and a pairing of
black rice; seared tuna drizzled with a ginger-sesame dressing
and accompanied by a salad of wild Asian greens, and grilled
chicken breast served with poblano mashed potatoes.

Price range: Lunch: apps., $4–$6.50; entrees, $8–$16. Dinner:
apps., $4.50–$6.50; entrees, $12.50–$19; desserts, $5–$6.
Wheelchair access: Everything on one level. **Features:** Good
for business, outdoor dining. **Services:** Delivery, takeout, catering, private parties.

Next Door Nobu   ☆☆☆ $$$$ JAPANESE

105 Hudson St. (near Franklin St.)   (212) 334-4445
Credit cards: All major   Meals: D, LN

Slightly more casual than Nobu, Next Door Nobu takes no
reservations and does not serve lunch. To dine here, come
early: later arrivals may wait up to 90 minutes for a table. But
the food is as accomplished (and as expensive) as Nobu's. And
while the menu features many of the same dishes, it strives for
its own identity, with an emphasis on raw shellfish, whole fish
served for an entire table, noodles, and texture.

Black cod with miso makes a fine dish. The flesh is so
sweet, so rich, so extraordinarily flaky that it tastes more like a
dessert than an entree. Whole fish are an exercise in texture.
Fried scorpion fish becomes so crunchy that you find yourself
munching on the crispy little bones. The same fish grilled, however, has a soft texture and gentle flavor.

Noodles range from the portly white udon, which slip sinu-
ously into your mouth, to the more austere soba with their
subtle chewiness. The few meat dishes on the menu are
memorable. The sliced Kobe beef tataki comes with little side
dishes — grated daikon, scallions and sliced garlic — that add
both flavor and texture.

And this textural roller coaster continues with dessert. A not-
too-sweet chocolate soufflé, paired with green tea ice cream, is
hot, cold, sweet and astringent. But mochi ice cream balls are

the most appealing way to end a meal. Mochi, the pounded rice candy of Japan, is stretchy and sticky when warm, but hardens into a cold tackiness when frozen. This one dessert says it all: Texture is an important part of Japanese cooking, and Next Door Nobu does it very well. (*Ruth Reichl*)

Other recommended dishes: Raw oysters; clams and sea urchins; toro tartar with caviar; whole grilled or fried fish; seafood udon; sushi and sashimi. **Wine list:** Interesting, well-chosen, but the special sake, served cold in chilled bamboo glasses, seems perfect for this food. **Price range:** Soup and salad, $3.50–$13; noodle dishes, $10–$15; hot dishes, $8–$32; sushi and sashimi, $3–$8 a piece; desserts, $8–$13. **Wheelchair access:** Three steep steps up to dining room. **Services:** Catering, private parties.

Nha Trang $25 & Under   CHINESE/VIETNAMESE

87 Baxter St. (bet. White & Walker Sts.)   (212) 233-5948
148 Centre St. (near Walker St.)   (212) 941-9292.
Credit cards: All major   Meals: L, D

Nothing fancy about Nha Trang. It's just a plain storefront with a bright dining room, but you may have to jostle with hordes of jurors for the excellent Vietnamese food. Nha Trang on Baxter Street was one of the pioneering Vietnamese restaurants in Chinatown, and it's still one of the best. Rather than turn away customers, the owners opened a second, equally plain restaurant a block west on Centre Street. With an emphasis on fresh herbs and vegetables, Vietnamese is one of the most satisfying cuisines in warm weather. Nha Trang's cool beef salad is a perfect summer lunch, the pleasantly charred meat resting on crisp lettuce, sprouts and marinated carrots, with fragrant mint and basil and some chili heat, all dressed with nuoc cham, the sweet and pungent Vietnamese condiment.

Familiar dishes are flawless here, like chao tom, grilled shrimp paste wrapped around a short stalk of sugar cane. You remove the shrimp, place it on a large lettuce leaf with mint and marinated vegetables and dip it in nuoc cham. Grilled dishes are also superb, like little cylinders of sweet and savory barbecued beef over rice vermicelli. Vietnamese iced coffee, made with sweetened condensed milk and tasting like a coffee milkshake, can be a fine dessert.

Other recommended dishes: Beef with rice-noodle soup; summer rolls; barbecued pork chop; grilled chicken; soft-shell crabs; chicken curry; water spinach. **Price range:** Apps., $3.75–$9; entrees, $4–$16. **Wheelchair access:** Everything is on one level.

Nicholson ☆ $$$ FRENCH

323 E. 58th St. (bet. First & Second Aves.)   (212) 355-6769
Credit cards: All major   Meals: D   Closed Sun.

Nearly everything about Nicholson seems designed to neutralize all known standards of restaurant criticism. To begin with, Nicholson occupies a peculiar spot, perched at the edge of the entrance to the upper roadway of the Queensboro Bridge. It looks like a guardhouse, and it's not much larger. It has a very distinctive dining room, whose décor was once described as Spanish-Portuguese belle époque, and under the new owner and chef, Patrick Woodside, things have become only more complex. The cane-work settees with their silk throw pillows remain. So do the brightly colored Spanish wall tiles with a satyr motif, the pastel panels filled with cupids, and the stenciled ceiling border depicting lily pads and lizards. An erratic Modernist streak now runs through the design. The atmosphere at Nicholson is almost indescribable. Stillness reigns, interrupted only by the gentle creak of the parquet floor, signaling the approach of a waiter, who, in truth, seems less like an employee than a faithful family retainer, just as the restaurant feels a bit like a room in the far west wing of Crotchet Castle.

Like the décor, the food at Nicholson swings wildly between extremes. It can be romantic and elegant, or almost insanely misjudged. Truffle cream, truffles, caviar and mushrooms loom large in Mr. Woodside's cooking vocabulary. One evening, some combination of the four showed up on every dish except the chocolate soufflé. So it was no surprise, in this eight-course excursion, to see truffle cream surrounding the croustillant of shrimp and langoustine. What was surprising was the espresso-chicory sabayon, looking unfortunately like beach foam, that came with a lovely shell-pink pavé of salmon. Mr. Woodside regained firmer ground with a pan-roasted pork tenderloin in a red-wine reduction flavored with oxtail. It was one of two entree choices. The alternative was a lobster treated Souvaroff-style, a 19th-century overload preparation here involving morels, chanterelles, spring onions and, surprise! — truffle cream.

After the grand tour, it's a short, sweet trip at dessert time. Nicholson limits itself to a few classic souffles, led by a superb but breathtakingly alcoholic apple-Calvados souffle, and old-fashioned pleasers like a poached peach with Champagne sabayon.

Other recommended dishes: Endive and Asian pear salad; braised squab with truffle cream; grape tomato salad; lamb carpaccio glazed with mint and basil; navarin of John Dory with fennel broth. **Wine list:** A not very interesting list of 60 bottles, most of them French and American, but with some real bargains at the low end. **Price range:** Four courses, $64; six courses, $78; eight courses, $98 ($135 with matching wines). **Wheelchair access:** Entrance is five steps down; restrooms on dining room level. **Features:** Smoking permitted. **Services:** Catering, private parties.

Nick & Toni's ☆☆ $$$ MEDITERRANEAN
100 W. 67th St. (bet. Broadway & Columbus)   (212) 496-4000
Credit cards: All major   Meals: L, D

A great neighborhood restaurant, Nick & Toni's is a lot like the neighborhood it serves: casual, crowded and noisy. But there is one thing that sets it apart from most of the neighborhood's restaurants: the food is really delicious. Nick & Toni's starts with good ingredients and leaves them alone. The menu changes constantly, but there are a few perennials, like the impeccable Caesar salad — crisp, lightly dressed, perfectly pungent. Often there is a fine pasta with just the right number of baby clams. You can drown in the delicious Ligurian fish stew. Desserts are simple and seasonal. (*Ruth Reichl*)

Other recommended dishes: Fritto misto di mare; wood-oven-roasted chicken and whole fish; grilled rib-eye steak; apple crisp. **Wine list:** Excellent choices, especially from the lesser-known regions of France; many by the glass. **Price range:** Apps., $6–$11; entrees, $11–$28; desserts, $8. **Wheelchair access:** One step up to dining room. **Services:** Takeout, catering, private parties.

Nicole's ☆☆ $$$ ENGLISH
10 E. 60th St. (bet. Madison & Fifth Aves.)   (212) 223-2288
Credit cards: All major   Meals: L, D

Nicole's (located in the Nicole Farhi store) hums and buzzes at lunchtime. It's filled with stylish, well-heeled diners, nearly all of them women. At night, the store closes, shadows descend, and Nicole's light and airy downstairs dining room takes on a somber tinge.

The notion of high-style dining in department stores and fancy boutiques is relatively novel here, but Nicole's does a lot to make it go down easy. The bright, appealing menu has a shrewd minimalist touch and just the right English notes. The chef is a precisionist about flavor, and picky when it comes to fresh ingredients. The smoked haddock chowder, more of a stew than a soup, thrives on the interplay between good-size, chewy nuggets of haddock with a smoky tang, and kernels of fresh corn that burst with sweetness. Nicole's does not go in for big, flashy effects. It's happy with clever little touches. The roasted duck breast is a good example: it derives just enough sweetness from a handful of baked figs, a small pile of roasted onions, and a little balsamic vinegar. A bed of red mustard greens provides a sharp counterpoint. The Moroccan cumin and lemon chicken is also irresistible. Nicole's wisely steers toward simple, homey sweets like lemon pudding, a fluffy mousse that develops density and texture as the spoon reaches deeper into the white ceramic pot. Nicole's also offers cheeses from Neal's Yard Dairy in London.

Other recommended dishes: Crab-lemon salad; grilled scallop skewer with lentils and pancetta; apple-walnut tart. **Wine list:** A modest but well-chosen 60-bottle list with 17 wines by the glass. **Price range:** Apps., $7.50–$16; entrees, $20–$32; desserts, $8. Bar menu, $7–$14. **Wheelchair access:** Two steps up to entrance.

92 $$ New American/Bistro

45 E. 92nd St (at Madison Ave.)   (212) 828-5300
Credit cards: All major   Meals: D

High up on the Upper East Side, whom you're eating with is often more important that what you're eating, and 92, Ken Aretsky's latest venture, reads the mood correctly. This is an American bistro-brasserie with a spare, unassuming interior and a menu to match. The hamburger with French fries is just that: a hamburger with French fries. In this fat-phobic territory, there's a turkey burger, too. The New England lobster roll does not do any strange twists and turns. It's a simple lobster roll with coleslaw and shoestring potatoes.

The appetizers go back and forth between light, Mediterranean dishes and all-American standards (crab cakes, mildly updated with jicama and carrot slaw). The entrees stick to beloved bistro dishes and cafe classics, like steak au poivre and meatloaf with mashed potatoes. There are two entree salads, a Caesar and a house salad called the 92, a mix of bibb lettuce, roast chicken, Montrachet cheese, bacon, hard-cooked eggs and beets in a balsamic vinegar dressing. The daily specials include fish and chips on Tuesday, fried clams on Friday and grilled lobster with roast corn salad and coleslaw on Saturday.

The desserts, prominently displayed near the entrance, may be the big draw here. A mile-high coconut layer cake broadcasts its seductive light throughout dinner. It is rivaled by an old-fashioned, homey strawberry shortcake, dense butterscotch pudding and two soda-fountain treats: a hot fudge sundae and a root beer float. There are no herbal desserts.

Price range: Apps., $8–$14; entrees, $14–$29. **Wheelchair access:** Everything on one level. **Features:** Smoking permitted at bar. **Services:** Takeout.

Nino's $$$

ITALIAN

1354 First Ave. (bet. 72nd & 73rd Sts.)   (212) 988-0002
Credit cards: All major   Meals: L, D

You've seen this restaurant, or one like it, many times before.
It's dark and comfortable, the tuxedo-clad waiters cook at the
table and the piano music is live. But the wine list neglects the
vintage years and the waiters insist on telling you so many
specials you can't begin to remember them all. Prices are
high. Best bet: lobster fra diavolo over linguine for two. Best
dessert: the free fresh fruit on ice.

Price range: Lunch: apps., $6–$10; entrees, $15–$25; desserts,
$8. Dinner: apps., $9–$15; entrees, $20–$30; desserts, $8.
Wheelchair access: Not accessible. **Services:** Delivery, takeout,
private parties.

Nippon $$$$

JAPANESE/SUSHI

155 E. 52nd St. (bet. Lexington & Third Aves.)   (212) 758-0226
Credit cards: All major   Meals: L, D

Large parties of Japanese people sit in the private tatami rooms,
obviously enjoying themselves. Perhaps they are eating better
than those of us in the main dining room; although the menu is
encyclopedic, nothing is notable, with the exception of the tempura, which is made at one end of the sushi bar.

Price range: Lunch: apps., $4.50–$10; entrees, $11–$28;
desserts, $3.50–$5. Dinner: apps., $4.50–$12; entrees, $19–$29;
desserts, $3.50–$6.50; tasting menus, $45, $60, $80 and $100.
Wheelchair access: Five steps to restrooms. **Services:** Takeout,
catering, private parties.

NL ☆ $$$

DUTCH/INDONESIAN

169 Sullivan St. (near Houston St.)   (212) 387-8801
Credit cards: All major   Meals: D

A Dutch restaurant seems like an inside joke. But NL, which is
short for Netherlands, has the last laugh. Roy Wiggers, formerly
the chef at Restaurant Stoop in Amsterdam, serves a clever mix
of beloved Dutch standbys, Indonesian dishes that have gained
honorary Dutch citizenship and invented dishes that use homey
Dutch ingredients like herring, potatoes, cheese and the yogurt
cream known as hangop. His devil-may-care style suits NL's
snappy décor, an appealing blend of Dutch modernism and
kitschy touches.

Dutch food is not fancy, and Mr. Wiggers does not fuss with
simple, traditional dishes like mosterdsoep, a tangy, light-bodied mustard soup accented with slivers of scallion. Herring
takes a modern spin, served as a dense tartare, its strong, oily
flavor cut with a citrus-soy vinaigrette and paired with a sweet

283

beet salad. Spice puts on its most vibrant performance in the Dutch-Indonesian hybrid known as rijsttafel, or rice table, small dishes and condiments served with rice. The NL version includes a too-dry chicken satay, beef rendang (spicy beef in a coconut sauce), and best of all, fried green beans in a chili-fired coconut sauce. Sauerkraut risotto sounds forbidding; it turns out to be one of the best things on the menu, once you get past the overcooked rice.

One thing the Dutch indisputably do well is cheese, but NL presents an abbreviated plate of Friesland cheese flavored with cumin and clove; Graven, a creamy blue cheese; and an arid Roomano. The cheese simply cannot compete with the poffertjes, soft, puffy mini-pancakes sprinkled with powdered anise and served with a scoop of vanilla butter. Just as good is the chocolate cake dusted with powdered sugar. On the side is a heaping spoonful of thick cream made with Advoocat, a Dutch liqueur similar to eggnog.

Other recommended dishes: Tuna rollmops, koninginnensoep, veal croquette, hazenpeper (hare stew). **Wine list:** A very short but decent list of about 20 wines, with five wines by the glass, six Dutch beers, and a good selection of Dutch spirits and liqueurs. **Price range:** Apps., $8–$14; entrees, $18–$25; desserts, $8–$13. **Wheelchair access:** Restroom on street level.

Nobu ☆☆☆　　$$$$　　JAPANESE
105 Hudson St. (at Franklin St.)　　　　(212) 219-0500
Credit cards: All major　　　　　　　　　Meals: L, D

Chic, casual and pulsing with energy, Nobu cannot be compared with any other restaurant. The spirit of invention of its chef-owner, Nobuyuki Matsuhisa — incorporating new ingredients into old dishes or retooling traditional recipes — lighted a spark in the kitchen, igniting each chef to new and increasingly daring feats. The result is something that seems like a Japanese dish but is not. Take the "sorbet." A little ball of white fluff, it looked like ice cream but turned out to be a grated turnip with a single enormous peeled grape inside. On top was a fan of marinated abalone. Each bite was clean, refreshing, delicious.

The best time to eat at Nobu is lunchtime. Order an Omakase meal and let the chefs choose your meal for you. No kitchen turns out a more spectacular plate of sushi. And sake lovers, once they have tasted Hokusetsu sake, will find it almost impossible to drink the stuff served in other restaurants. Desserts include a warm chocolate soufflé cake with siso syrup and green tea ice cream that comes in a bento box.

Popularity may be taking its toll. On a recent visit, the Benihana overtones, and a weakness for gaudy gimmicks, not to mention the tourist clientele, added up to a less than deluxe experience. Edwyn Ferrari, the new chef, can both dazzle and dismay with his omakase. The sushi maintains a high level of quality, however, and the black cod with miso is still one of the most luxurious taste experiences in New York. (*Ruth Reichl, updated by William Grimes*)

Other recommended dishes: The best way to appreciate this kitchen is to put yourself in the chefs' hands. **Wine list:** A lovely choice of wines that go well with the food. But the cold Hokusetsu sake shows this food off to best advantage. **Price range:** Lunch: avg. $40 per person; prix-fixe, $20.02. Dinner: avg. $60–$75 per person; tasting menus, $80 and up. **Wheelchair access:** The dining room is up a few steps, but there is a ramp at the back door. **Features:** Good for business. **Services:** Private parties.

Noho Star $25 & Under   AMERICAN
330 Lafayette St. (at Bleecker St.)   (212) 925-0070
Credit cards: All major   Meals: B, Br, L, D, LN

The big, airy room with the colorful columns and beautiful pressed-tin ceiling makes Noho Star a great place for a quiet breakfast, especially before heading to jury duty a few blocks away. The room is comfortable, and service is efficient. At other hours, the menu veers among burgers, chicken and dishes with Asian accents.

Price range: Lunch: apps., $5.25–$8; entrees, $8.50–$14.50; desserts, $1.50–$6. Dinner: apps., $5.75–$8.50; entrees, $13.50–$24; desserts, $1.50–$6. **Wheelchair access:** Fully accessible. **Features:** Outdoor dining. **Services:** Takeout.

Nostalgias $25 & Under   BOLIVIAN
85-09 Northern Blvd., Jackson Heights, Queens   (718) 533-9120
Credit cards: All major   Meals: L, D   Closed Mon.

This big, glossy restaurant is an excellent introduction to Bolivian food, which resembles Peruvian but with its own distinctive stamp. Papas a la huancaina looks almost identical to the Peruvian specialty of cold boiled potatoes served in a spicy cheese sauce, but the Bolivian dish is made with ground peanuts, yellow peppers, hard-cooked eggs and olives. Look for dishes like chicharrón de puerco, delicious pieces of subtly-spiced pork served on the bone with white corn and boiled purple potatoes. Another pork dish, lechòn, is powerfully suffused with garlic and served with both white and sweet potatoes. Saltenas, or empanadas, and soups are generally delicious.

Other recommended dishes: Khallo cochabambino; humintas; orejon; batidos; chairo paceño; pollo dorado; chola. **Alcohol:** Beer. **Price range:** Apps., $1.75–$4.50; entrees, $6–$10. **Wheelchair access:** Everything is on one level. **Features:** Kid friendly. **Services:** Takeout.

Novitá ☆　　$$　　ITALIAN

102 E. 22nd St. (bet. Park & Lexington Aves.)　　(212) 677-2222
Credit cards: All major　　Meals: L, D

The small room has been completely redecorated to give it the clean, elegant lines of a Milanese restaurant. Despite the elegance of the décor, the family-run restaurant has all the warmth of a mom-and-pop place. If you begin the meal with the ravioli of the day, you will not be disappointed. I also like the roast duck, which is served with pomegranate seeds and pine nuts in a rich Barolo sauce. And grilled slices of steak, bathed in a pungent balsamic vinegar sauce on a fine warm bean salad, are deeply satisfying. The nouvelle ricotta cheesecake, a sort of cookies-and-cream confection with tuiles and berries, makes me happy, too.

Other recommended dishes: Tuna carpaccio; risotto; grilled fish; panna cotta; warm chocolate tart. **Wine list:** The all-Italian list is small but well chosen and reasonably priced. **Price range:** Apps., $7.70–$10.50; pastas, $14–$16; entrees, $19–$22; desserts, $6.75; prix-fixe lunch, $20.02. **Wheelchair access:** Not accessible. **Features:** Outdoor dining (sidewalk). **Services:** Takeout, catering, private parties.

Ñ Tapas Bar　　$25 & Under　　SPANISH/TAPAS

33 Crosby St. (near Broome St.)　　(212) 219-8856
Credit cards: Cash or check only　　Meals: D, LN

At this small but stylish tapas bar, you can pick and choose among small dishes, like olives mashed with capers, garlic, olive oil and anchovies; octopus and steamed potato cubes, and of course the ubiquitous Spanish omelet with onions and potatoes. Ñ is also one of the best places in New York City to taste sherries, the fortified wines made in the Andalusia region of southern Spain. Try a delicate, flavorful manzanilla with boquerones, anchovies that taste like pickled herring. It's a classic combination.

Price range: Tapas, $2.50–$9.50. **Wheelchair access:** Not accessible. **Features:** Romantic, smoking permitted. **Services:** Catering.

Nyonya　　$　　ASIAN/MALAYSIAN

194 Grand St. (at Mulberry St.)　　(212) 334-3669
Credit cards: Cash only　　Meals: Br, L, D

A Malaysian restaurant done in the Chinatown style: bright, brusque and noisy. Food is inconsistent, spicy on one visit, bland on the next, but Nyonya is nonetheless popular. The wait for a table can be long, and chances are you will be rushed through the meal.

Alcohol: Beer. **Price range:** Apps., $1.95–$7.95; entrees, $3.95–$16.95; desserts, $1.50–$5. **Wheelchair access:** Fully accessible. **Services:** Takeout, catering.

Oceana ☆ ☆ ☆ $$$$ SEAFOOD
55 E. 54th St. (bet. Park & Madison Aves.)   (212) 759-5941
Credit cards: All major   Meals: L, D   Closed Sun.

Oceana's downstairs dining room is small and pretty, with an old-fashioned air. The intimate upstairs dining room is as handsome and luxurious as the dining room on a private yacht. Service is excellent, and you feel that you are about to set sail on a special voyage. You are.

Oceana's viewpoint is global — dishes are inspired by a wide variety of cuisines — while firmly rooted in an American idiom. What's more, the menu changes daily as chef Rick Moonen continues to experiment with new combinations.His careful spicing and the extremely intelligent use of ethnic accents brings out the essential nature of the fish. A recent visit confirmed the impression that Oceana remains one of New York's most inventive and underrated seafood restaurants, committed to seeking out the freshest possible supplies. The result is standout dishes like Norman turbot with a ragout of spring vegetables and mushrooms, Rossini-style roasted monkfish (served with foie gras, red onion confit, and perigueux sauce) and "kung pao" style squid and rock shrimp.

In summer, there is a huge variety of fruit desserts like rhubarb crumble or raspberry gratin with coconut and pineapple. One of the winter standards is sticky toffee pudding with vanilla ice cream. There are always six to eight sorbets and a similar number of ice creams on the menu. (*Ruth Reichl updated by William Grimes*)

Wine list: Well-chosen (especially the American wines) but expensive. **Price range:** Three-course prix-fixe lunch, $45; three-course prix-fixe dinner, $65; six-course tasting menu, $105; tasting menu with wines, $170. **Wheelchair access:** Not accessible. **Services:** Private parties.

Ocean Grill ☆ $$ SEAFOOD
384 Columbus Ave. (bet. 78th & 79th Sts.)   (212) 579-2300
Credit cards: All major   Meals: Br, L, D, LN

The room is big and attractively understated, with a raw bar in the front and a boisterous clientele. Crab cakes are crisp and plump and served with a fine roasted corn salsa. The grilled fish are all nicely handled, and the french fries are excellent. Cold poached salmon is very pleasant, and even the hamburger is good. The sundae, an intense combination of brownies, hot fudge and ice cream, would make any child happy, and the caramelized figs with ice cream were easily enough to please two grown-ups. (*Ruth Reichl*)

Other recommended dishes: Raw clams and oysters; fried calamari; grilled tuna; grilled swordfish; grilled salmon; chicken with mushroom sauce and mashed potatoes. **Wine list:** Decent and fairly priced. **Price range:** Lunch: apps., $5–$9; entrees, $8–$18; three-course prix fixe, $17.95. Dinner: apps., $5–$11; entrees $15–$22; desserts $5–$7; pre-theater prix fixe, $19.95. **Wheelchair access:** Not accessible. **Features:** Kid friendly, smoking permitted, outdoor dining (sidewalk). **Services:** Takeout.

Odeon ☆☆ $$ BISTRO/NEW AMERICAN

145 W. Broadway (at Thomas St.) (212) 233-0507
Credit cards: All major Meals: Br, L, D, LN

SoHo's first great American bistro is still cooking after all these years. The neighborhood has certainly changed, but time has stood still in the dining room. It is still unpretentious and comfortable, and it still feels as if it is filled with artists. Great for burgers, omelets, pasta and roast chicken in a slightly funky setting. Even greater for a martini. And it's still a destination until 3 A.M. (*Ruth Reichl*)

Price range: Lunch: avg. app., $7.50; entree, $13; dessert, $7. Dinner: avg. app., $8.25; entree, $18; dessert, $7. **Wheelchair access:** Fully accessible. **Features:** Kid friendly, outdoor dining (patio). **Services:** Takeout.

Old Devil Moon $25 & Under SOUTHERN

511 E. 12th St. (bet. Aves. A & B) (212) 475-4357
Credit cards: All major Meals: Br, D Closed Mon.

With mismatched chairs and tables, and walls covered with landscapes, animals and old postcards, Old Devil Moon looks like the product of a thousand flea markets. Southern cuisine is the specialty, with huge helpings of pork chops and chicken, sometimes with Asian touches. Breakfasts are terrific, especially when country ham is served. The desserts are generous, full flavored and very rich, like dense peanut butter pie, powerful devil's-food cake and fine seasonal fruit pies.

Other recommended dishes: Ham and eggs; biscuits and gravy; frittata; greens with white beans; johnny cakes; sweet potato scallion hash; gnocchi; spice-crusted chicken; pork chops; chocolate pecan pie. **Alcohol:** Beer and wine. **Price range:** Apps., $4.50–$8; entrees, $8–$22; desserts, $3.50. **Wheelchair access:** Everything is on one level, but the restrooms are narrow. **Features:** Kid friendly. **Services:** Takeout, private parties.

Old Homestead $$$$ STEAKHOUSE

56 Ninth Ave. (bet. 14th & 15th Sts.)   (212) 242-9040
Credit cards: All major   Meals: L, D

The Old Homestead has been sitting in the middle of Manhattan's meatpacking district since 1868. For sheer quantity, nothing can beat the Homestead. When you order a porterhouse for two, a prodigious steak arrives, as thick as a fat book and twice as heavy. Other significant cuts include chateaubriand for two, the heavy-cut sirloin and prime ribs served on the bone. If you want to spend more than $100 a pound for Japanese Kobe beef, the Old Homestead happily accommodates you (although the meat is pretty disappointing). Just call in advance.

Price range: Apps., $4.95–$10.95; entrees, $25–$32; desserts, $4–$10. **Wheelchair access:** Fully accessible. **Features:** Smoking permitted. **Services:** Delivery, takeout, catering, private parties.

Old San Juan $25 & Under PUERTO RICAN

765 Ninth Ave. (bet. 51st & 52nd Sts.)   (212) 262-6761
462 Second Ave. (at 26th St.)   (212) 779-9360
Credit: All major   Meals: L, D

One of New York's few Puerto Rican restaurants, Old San Juan serves unusual dishes like pasteles, similar to tamales except they are made with green bananas rather than corn; richly flavorful asopao, the soupy rice stew, and mild, tender stewed goat. It's not much for atmosphere, but service is friendly.

Price range: Entrees, $15; desserts, $3; lunch special, $7. **Wheelchair access:** Fully accessible. **Features:** Kid friendly, outdoor dining. **Services:** Delivery, takeout, catering, private parties.

Old Town Bar $ AMERICAN

45 E. 18th St. (bet. Broadway & Park Ave. S.)   (212) 529-6732
Credit cards: All major   Meals: B, L, D, LN

The worn wooden booths, towering pressed-tin ceiling and etched glass fixtures all wear years of accumulated smoke at this wonderful 1890's pub near Union Square. Old Town is mostly a bar, but it serves great hamburgers and terrific hot dogs.

Price range: Apps., $4.25–$8.50; entrees, $6–$10; desserts, $4. **Wheelchair access:** Lower level and restrooms fully accessible. **Services:** Private parties.

Olives ☆ $$

MEDITERRANEAN

W Union Square Hotel, 281 Park Ave. S. (at 17th St.)

(212) 353-8345

Credit cards: All major

Meals: B, Br, L, D

Chef Todd English seduced Boston with his first Olives, and his exuberant brand of cooking, which he calls "interpretive Mediterranean," made him a culinary star. Olives begat more Olives, in Washington, Aspen and Las Vegas. Mr. English has notched many other restaurants on his belt. And there are the television shows and the cookbooks.

He is fortunate in his Manhattan location. The W Union Square has been a magnet for young fun-seekers since the day it opened. They have slouched all over its lounge, packed the little bar at Olives and now populate Underbar, a floor down, in great numbers. The dining-room crowd is fairly sedate, and certainly older, but Olives is a hot ticket. Why?

The food is easy to like but hard to respect. Mr. English is the Thomas Wolfe of chefs: no sooner is a thought in his head than it's on the plate. But at least half the time the food at Olives really delivers. Do not look for light, because you won't find it, but it's hard to beat Mr. English for sheer palate-engulfing flavor. A case in point: an almost ridiculous assemblage of shredded artichokes on a crisp risotto cake bound with fontina cheese and drenched in black truffle vinaigrette. It is strange, and strangely irresistible.

Rack of venison, wrapped in sliced pears and roasted on rosemary branches, ranks as one of the best venison dishes in New York. A succulent osso bucco seems almost chaste, served with nothing more than broccoli rape and Gorgonzola agnolotti. Both venison and veal feature prominently in two of the better pastas, chestnut ravioli in a venison Bolognese sauce with creamy spinach, and mezzaluna, or pasta half-moons, stuffed with artichokes and blanketed under a ragu of braised veal breast and roasted tomatoes.

Desserts are the kind that make diners feel pleasantly guilty. The Napoleon, filled with layers of caramel and loaded up with hazelnuts, banana cream and a scoop of chocolate sorbet, seems halfway between a French pastry and an old-fashioned banana split. And two ice creams, playing a supporting role, almost deserve star billing: the port-butter ice cream that comes with his cinnamon gratin in a black-walnut crust, and the chestnut ice cream that sits alongside a warm bitter chocolate cake.

Other recommended dishes: Caramel Napoleon, bitter chocolate cake with chestnut ice cream. **Wine list:** A widely international list of 370 wines, reasonably priced, with many Champagnes and 25 wines by the glass. **Price range:** Lunch, apps., $8.50–$14.50; entrees, $12.50–$30; desserts, $8–$10.50.

Dinner, apps., $10.25 –$15; entrees, $17.50–$30; desserts, $8–$10.50. **Wheelchair access:** An elevator in the hotel lobby services the restrooms, on the second floor.

Ollie's Noodle Shop $ CHINESE/NOODLES

1991 Broadway (bet. 67th & 68th Sts.)	(212) 595-8181
2957 Broadway (at 116th St.)	(212) 932-3300
2315 Broadway (at 84th St.)	(212) 362-3111
200b W. 44th St. (bet. Seventh & Eighth Aves.)	(212) 921-5988
Credit cards: All major	Meals: L, D, LN

The next generation of Chinese neighborhood places has brought a new level of regional Chinese food to New York City's non-Chinese households. The food varies from almost-inedible to pretty wonderful, depending on the day and the location.

Price range: Apps., $1.30–$5; entrees, $6–$14.95; lunch special, $5.95. **Wheelchair access:** Fully accessible. **Features:** Kid friendly. **Services:** Delivery, takeout.

ONEc.p.s. (Satisfactory) $ BRASSERIE

Plaza Hotel, 1 Central Park S. (at Fifth Ave.)	(212) 583-1111
Credit cards: All major	Meals: Br, L, D

ONEc.p.s., whose little initials refer to Central Park South, does not manage to pull off the difficult trick of transforming the former Edwardian Room at the Plaza Hotel into a fresh-feeling brasserie. The signs of struggle are everywhere. To arrest the eye, the designer Adam Tihany has covered the ancient, massive chandeliers with cartoonish red lampshades. Installing a bar near the entrance lends some hum and buzz, but the place still wrestles with an identity crisis. Is ONEc.p.s. aiming to be a fine-dining experience to complement the room's handsome ceiling beams and stately curtained windows, or a breezy, slap-on-the-back sort of place?

Good food tends to silence awkward questions. Unfortunately, there's not a lot of it here. The menu reads well enough, but eating your way through it is a real trudge, a sobering encounter with murky sauces, mediocre ingredients and "fun" touches that fail to amuse. Simpler is better at ONEc.p.s. The shellfish "bouquet" for two or more diners, which can be ordered either steamed or chilled, is a respectable seafood platter with very good oysters and rather tasteless shrimp. Shrimp bisque makes a good showing, as does a rustic but pleasing salt cod and potato pancake. Main courses rise to just above the middling level about half the time, but a gutsy jumble of bacon, potato, onion and mushrooms makes the turbot grand-mere a satisfyingly countrified dish. Rack of lamb with shepherd's pie gets the job done. Ordering anything duck-related, however, is a one-way ticket to heartbreak. For dessert, try the tarte Tatin with a robust apple flavor or an excellent little pecan tart.

Other recommended dishes: Salt cod and potato pancake.
Wine list: An international, eclectic list of about 180 wines, with very slim pickings under $40. Eight wines are available in half bottles. **Price range:** Lunch: apps., $8–$19.50; entrees, $14.50–$27.50; desserts, $7.50–$10.50. Dinner: apps., $8.50–$27.50; entrees, $18–$28.50; desserts, $8.50–$12.50.
Wheelchair access: Ramp at main hotel entrance; accessible restrooms are available by elevator in the lobby.

One If By Land, Two If By Sea ☆

$$$$ Continental

17 Barrow St. (near Seventh Ave. S.)   (212) 255-8649
Credit cards: All major   Meals: D

Considered by many to be the most romantic restaurant in New York, it is almost always booked. The lights are low, the gas fire-places burn even in the summer and a pianist serenades you with music. Known mainly for the 1950's specialty Beef Welling-ton, the food has grown more ambitious of late. Wild field greens with Champagne vinaigrette and quenelles of Roquefort mousse is a perfectly fine salad. The seared tuna is fresh and rosy, and the lightly smoked and roasted rack of lamb is a fine piece of meat. Even poached peaches with pistachio ice cream are good.

Wine list: No bargains; generally better on American wines than European ones. **Price range:** Three courses, $64; seven courses, $75. **Wheelchair access:** Restrooms not accessible.
Features: Romantic. **Services:** Private parties.

Onieal's Grand Street ☆ $$$ New American

174 Grand St. (bet. Centre & Mulberry Sts.)   (212) 941-9119
Credit cards: All major   Meals: Br, L, D, LN

This is a beautiful, cozy restaurant with warm wood, a carved ceiling, fabric-covered banquettes, and lots of smoke; there are only 34 seats, making smoking legal. This small, clubby restau-rant is also dripping with history: ask about the tunnel in the basement. Many of the adventurous dishes are excellent, and seemingly simple dishes are often more interesting than they sound. (*Ruth Reichl*)

Wine list: Not nearly so inventive as the menu; prices are fair.
Price range: Apps., $6–$11; entrees, $17–$24; desserts, $8.
Wheelchair access: One step up to dining room. **Features:**
Romantic. **Services:** Takeout, catering, private parties.

Opaline $25 & Under FRENCH/AMERICAN
85 Ave. A (near 6th St.) (212) 475-5050
Credit cards: All major Meals: D, LN

Opaline is more raucous than intimate, an enjoyable place to
eat with a group. It's a subterranean space, one flight down
from the sidewalk, but the dining room, past a dim lounge area
and bar, feels airy. While Opaline calls itself French, and certain
French dishes do appear on the menu, the food is mainstream
American. Late at night, the lounge takes over, and tables are
pushed back for dancing.

Other recommended dishes: Potato-and-celery-root soup; fish
chowder; mussels; duck confit on frisée salad; mesclun salad;
polenta; sautéed monkfish; snapper; salmon with lentils; cassoulet; braised lamb shank; roast chicken; chocolate soufflé
cake; crème brûlée; lemon tart; cookies. **Price range:** Apps.,
$5–$12; entrees, $8–$26; desserts, $5–$7. **Wheelchair access:**
Elevator access to restaurant one floor below street level. **Services:** Private parties.

Orologio $ ITALIAN
162 Ave. A (bet. 10th & 11th Sts.) (212) 228-6900
Credit cards: Cash only Meals: D, LN

The most remarkable thing about this low-priced pasta restaurant in the East Village is the seating, long tables that run
around the perimeter of the blocky room. Good luck if you need
to get up in the middle of a meal. You, and everybody around
you, are in for an ordeal. The food is decent and a good value.

Price range: Apps., $5.50–$7.50; pastas, $7.50–$8.75; entrees,
$12.50–$14.50; desserts, $5. **Wheelchair access:** Restrooms not
accessible. **Features:** Outdoor dining. **Services:** Delivery, takeout, private parties.

Orsay ☆☆ $$$ BISTRO/BRASSERIE
1057 Lexington Ave. (at 75th St.) (212) 517-6400
Credit cards: All major Meals: Br, L, D

Orsay is a brasserie with a difference, although there's nothing
in the look of the place to suggest anything out of the ordinary.
In fact, the restaurant looks as if it was ordered from a kit, with
a lot of shiny brass, pristine leather banquettes and authentic
French waiter costumes. But the cuisine does not follow the
script. It has a fresh, wayward bent and an international style
that saves Orsay from being yet one more exercise in French
nostalgia. Even the old standbys, more often than not, veer off
in unexpected directions. Two healthy rougets, their skin grilled
to potato-chip crunchiness, get a lift from the feather-light
anchovy mayonnaise and four golden sticks of fried pureed

potato touched with a hint of cumin. A whiff of vanilla adds richness and complexity to thick pink slices of salmon with a black pepper crust, but that's only the beginning of the adventure, salmon-wise, at Orsay. A very strange dish labeled "le Britannique," with a shocking list of ingredients that includes Stilton, walnuts and Yorkshire pudding, is a triumph, its ingredients delicately interwoven to create a lovely interplay of unexpected flavors.

Another area of the menu worth lingering over showcases Orsay's hickory-chip smoker, which gives a dark, woodsy bite to salmon and to a dense, deeply flavored duck sausage. Oddly enough in this traditional setting, it's the traditional brasserie and bistro dishes that disappoint. Hanger steak is ordinary and rather tough. The T-bone is a better bet, and filet mignon, buttery-textured and enrobed in a thick pink-peppercorn sauce, hits it just right.

The pastry chef limits his flights of fancy to small embellishments. Piquant and acidic tamarillo sorbet helps cut the gooey sweetness of a fine fig tart. His restrained raspberry napoleon, with just a few pastry layers defining the form, is a perfectly executed classic, and warm apple tart is flawless.

Other recommended dishes: Crab salad with tomato sorbet.
Wine list: A thoughtfully chosen list of about 150 wines, mostly French and tilted toward Bordeaux and Burgundy, but with a decent showing of wines from Italy, Spain and Austria. A dozen half bottles. **Price range:** Lunch: apps., $7–$13; entrees, $14.50–$28; desserts, $8–$10. Dinner: apps., $8–$14; entrees, $15–$26; desserts, $9.50–$10. **Wheelchair access:** A restroom on the first floor.

Orso $$$ ITALIAN

322 W. 46th St. (bet. Eighth & Ninth Aves.)   (212) 489-7212
Credit cards: All major   Meals: L, D

Pretty and pricey. Italian food in the theater district that is most fun late at night, when theater people come around for dinner after they have removed their makeup. The menu changes constantly, but the food is reliable.

Price range: Apps., $6.50–$8.50; entrees, $17.50–$21.50; desserts, $5.50–$6.50. **Wheelchair access:** Not accessible.

Osso Buco $25 & Under ITALIAN

1662 Third Ave. (at 93rd St.)   (212) 426-5422
88 University Pl. (bet. 11th & 12th Sts.)   (212) 645-4525
Credit cards: All major   Meals: L, D

Osso Buco is a family-style Italian-American restaurant that manages to remove the meal from the mythology. Instead of the usual kitsch, Osso Buco's multilevel dining room is almost defiantly modest, with the sort of red, yellow and black color scheme that you might find in a chain franchise at a mall. The menu includes nothing surprising or unusual, but much of the food is tasty and satisfying, with far more high points than lows. And it's a good value: the family-style portions, described as double size, are closer to triple. Even so, Osso Buco is much more of a casual neighborhood place than a destination for big groups. It's hard to imagine better fried calamari: the light, crisp breading enhances the flavor of the squid rather than obliterating it. Trenette al pesto is a fringed ribbon pasta in a creamy, harmonious basil sauce; linguine in a garlicky white clam sauce is also good. Most of the tomato-based pastas are mundane and chicken dishes are likewise dull. But the veal dishes shine, particularly saltimbocca, a Friday night special that is the classic match of nutty prosciutto, sage and spinach with rich veal. Veal piccata, thin cutlets in a light sauce of lemon and white wine, and the restaurant's namesake, osso buco, a bright and hearty veal shank stew, are also good. Service at Osso Buco is efficient and professional, blissfully free of singing waiters and overly gregarious types.

Other recommended dishes: Tricolore salad; Caesar salad; baked clams; ravioli with meat sauce. **Price range:** Apps., $9.75–$15.75; entrees, $14.75–$48 (prices are for family-style portions). **Wheelchair access:** Steps in dining room and to restrooms. **Features:** Smoking at bar

Otabe ☆☆ $$$ JAPANESE

68 E. 56th St. (bet. Park & Madison Aves.)   (212) 223-7575
Credit cards: All major   Meals: L, D

Two separate dining rooms offer two different dining experiences. In the teppan room in the back it is a very upscale Benihana (with Kobe beef for those willing to pay the price). The elegant front dining room serves kaiseki-like cuisine. The kaiseki dinner is a lovely and accessible introduction to the most poetic food of Japan. Kaiseki is a ceremonial cuisine that is traditionally served in many small courses meant to reflect the season. Less ambitious eaters might want to sample fewer dishes; I particularly like uzaku, a dish of grilled eel on a bed of cucumber, and a fine, spicy miso soup. Soft-shell crab, fried and topped with a mixture of grated turnip and red peppers, is also appealing. Desserts are the big surprise at Otabe; more French than Japanese, they are original, beautiful and very delicious. The teppan room has a separate menu, and each course is cooked before your eyes by your personal chef. (*Ruth Reichl*)

Other recommended dishes: Mixed oshitashi (vegetables); chicken tataki; lobster tempura; eel teriyaki; teppan steak; teppan scallops; raspberry napoleon; apple trio; green tea crème brûlée; raspberry pancakes. **Wine list:** The small list seems like an afterthought. **Price range:** Lunch: apps., $4–$10; entrees, $14.50–$25; desserts, $3–$8. Dinner: apps., $4–$12; entrees, $14.50–$65; desserts, $5.50–$10. **Wheelchair access:** There is a ramp to the dining room. **Services:** Takeout, catering, private parties.

Ouest ☆☆ $$$

2315 Broadway (at 84th St.)
Credit cards: All major

NEW AMERICAN/BISTRO
(212) 580-8700
Meals: D

This place looks good and it feels good. Long before the food arrives, Ouest (pronounced WEST), with disarming confidence, has most diners eating out of the palm of its hand. It may have solved the longest-running problem in restaurantland. How do you create a lively atmosphere without obliterating the possibility of an intimate meal? Thickly padded booths with tall sides do the trick, semicircular in the front room, and nearly closed circles in the back room. (Pray for a booth, because the upstairs balcony seating is dark, cramped and loud.)

The cooking has a sane, rooted quality that makes it appropriate for what is, when all is said and done, a neighborhood restaurant. In the heart of Manhattan's smoked-fish-and-lox belt, Ouest rises to the challenge with long, velvet ribbons of intensely smoky sturgeon wrapped around a tangle of frisée, chunks of lardon and a simple poached egg. The chef pulls a very neat trick with his unctuous smoked duck breast, pounded out carpaccio style and surrounded by squiggles of thick mustard vinaigrette, the duck's richness undercut with bitter greens and a sunny poached-egg croquette.

Main courses drift toward the comfort zone, with purées and soft polenta to swaddle homey ingredients in a cushiony layer. Nuggets of pork tenderloin wrapped in bacon are appealingly pink and moist, nicely set off by a thick, garlicky white-bean purée and peppercorn sauce. Roast halibut with fava bean purée and mushroom broth has a solid, uncomplicated appeal, and the same can be said of the special section of the menu devoted to simple grilled meats. Those in an uncompromising meat mood should head straight for the short ribs, a full plate of braised beef with an outdoor-grill tang to it.

For dessert try the rhubarb crisp with strawberry juice, classic and all-American, with buttermilk sorbet adding a nicely sour note to offset the strawberry sweetness. For those who want to wallow unashamedly, there's the chocolate cake with banana ice cream and peanut brittle.

Other recommended dishes: Sweet-pea broth with Parmesan custard, mustard-crusted pork terrine, almond raspberry financier. **Wine list:** A budget-priced bistro list of about 100 wines, mostly French, Italian and Californian, with 10 wines by the glass. **Price range:** Dinner, apps., $7–$12; entrees, $16–$27; desserts, $6–$8. **Wheelchair access:** Restrooms on street level.

Our Place Shanghai Tea Garden
$25 & Under   CHINESE

141 E. 55th St. (at Third Ave.)   (212) 753-3900
Credit cards: All major   Meals: L, D

With its elevated service, thick linens and the ornate birds carved out of radish and turnip that adorn serving plates, Our Place has the feel of a fine yet informal banquet. The Shanghai dishes are rich and satisfying, beautifully rendered, yet accessible to Americans, who make up most of the clientele. The waiters are supremely attentive, dividing portions onto plates, putting umbrellas into drinks for young children and generally offering to do anything short of feeding you. Silver-dollar-size steamed soup dumplings are well-seasoned and nicely textured, either with pork and briny crab roe or just pork. Pieces of crunchy smoked fish, served cool, are not really smoky but sweet with an anise flavor in their jackets of caramelized sugar and five-spice powder. The kitchen excels at tofu dishes, like rich and delicious braised bean curd with crab meat and spinach, and knots of bean curd skin tossed with fresh soybeans and chopped mustard greens. Noodle dishes are also superb.

Other recommended dishes: Turnip pastries; cold vegetable duck; fresh bacon and bean curd skin; lion's head; fried yellowfish. **Price range:** Apps., $2.95–$8.95; entrees, $9.95–$24.95. **Wheelchair access:** Everything on one level; restrooms are narrow.

Oyster Bar and Restaurant $$$ SEAFOOD
Grand Central Station (at 42nd St.)   (212) 490-6650
Credit cards: All major   Meals: L, D   Closed Sun.

Everybody knows about the Oyster Bar, of course, but most people think only of the great vaulted outer dining room. In fact, the Oyster Bar has two other places to dine: the lunch counter, which looks like nothing so much as an old department store luncheonette, a fine place to sit by yourself and enjoy a rich oyster pan roast for lunch, and the saloon, a secluded, paneled room with a long bar and all the clatter and informality of a real saloon. This is where many local business executives have lunch, dining on seafood stews or any of the 16 varieties of oysters. One caution: smoking is permitted in the saloon, but that's O.K.; the important part of the name is Bar, not Restaurant.

Price range: Apps., $5–$10; entrees, $20–$27; desserts, $4–$6. **Wheelchair access:** Fully accessible. **Features:** Kid friendly, smoking permitted. **Services:** Takeout, private parties.

Oznot's Dish $25 & Under   MEDITERRANEAN

79 Berry St., Williamsburg, Brooklyn   (718) 599-6596
Credit cards: MC/V   Meals: Br, L, D, LN

In a neighborhood like Williamsburg, restaurants are routinely called quirky and offbeat. But Oznot's is truly unusual, a veritable flea market of mosaics, mismatched furniture and artwork set on a rickety, uneven wood floor. The blend of Mediterranean food is just as interesting.

Price range: Lunch: apps., $4–$6; entrees, $5–$9. Dinner: apps., $5–$9; entrees, $10–$22; desserts, $6. **Wheelchair access:** Not accessible. **Services:** Takeout, private parties.

Pachas $25 & Under   LATIN AMERICAN

93-21 37th Ave., Flushing, Queens   (718) 397-0729
Credit cards: All major   Meals: B, L, D, LN

The Colombian-Venezuelan menu at Pachas presents problems. For one thing, the cuisines of Venezuela and Colombia have many dishes in common, yet items on the Venezuelan menu seem to lack sparkle. Order from the much bigger Colombian menu and the difference will be clear. A simple arepa con queso, fragrant with corn, is served steaming with a block of dense, salty cheese on top. Even better is the sublime arepa buche, a blend of tender tripe, tomato and onion, boiled down to a soulful essence. On one visit, the waitress watched with a knowing look. "Colombian food can't be beat," she said.

In terms of amount of food per plate, she's probably right, especially if you order the bandeja Pachas, which includes a thin grilled steak, a footlong strip of fried pork skin with flavorful meat clinging to it, two fried eggs, a plump corncake, avocado slices, half a sweet plantain and, of course, rice and beans. It's known as the breakfast of mountaineers, and it's hearty enough. Even better is the muchacho relleno, pork loin stuffed with chopped peppers, tomatoes, onions and peas and covered with a peppery Creole sauce. Pachas has no liquor license but makes excellent batidos, or fruit shakes, in tropical flavors like lulo, a sweet and tart citrus.

Other recommended dishes: Arepas Colombian style with chicken and avocado, shredded beef, cheese or tripe stew; calentando; batidos. **Price range:** Apps., $1–$6.50; entrees, $6–$13. **Wheelchair access:** Everything on one level. **Services:** Takeout.

Pacifica $$

CHINESE

Holiday Inn, 138 Lafayette St. (near Howard St.) (212) 334-9003
Credit cards: All major

Meals: B, L, D

Surprisingly good Cantonese food in a Holiday Inn. One of Chinatown's more upscale experiences, this is a great place for dim sum or a banquet.

Price range: Breakfast, $6.95–$11.50. Lunch and dinner: apps., $2.50–$4.25; entrees, $8.75–$25; desserts, $2.50. **Wheelchair access:** Fully accessible. **Features:** Smoking permitted. **Services:** Catering.

Palacinka $25 & Under

CAFE/CREPES

28 Grand St. (at Sixth Ave.)

(212) 625-0362

Credit cards: Cash only

Meals: B, Br, L, D

This little restaurant, decorated with the sort of 1930's travel paraphernalia romanticized in J. Peterman catalogues, specializes in crepes. The cylindrical buckwheat-flour crepes are terrific and come with Gruyere and egg, or with roasted chicken, goat cheese and roasted peppers. Dessert crepes are also great, particularly the lime, which is made with white flour, dusted with sugar and drizzled with fresh lime juice.

Price range: Sandwiches and salads, $7–$9; savory crepes, $7–$8; sweet crepes, $3.50–$6. **Wheelchair access:** All on one level. **Features:** Kid friendly. **Services:** Takeout.

Palio ☆☆ $$$$

ITALIAN

151 W. 51st St. (bet. Sixth & Seventh Aves.)

(212) 245-4850

Credit cards: All major   Meals: L, D

Closed Sun.

The murals by Sandro Chia make the bar at Palio one of New York City's most magical spaces, and the formal upstairs dining room is elegant and charming. But the crowds have moved on, for good reason. Palio, once one of the city's premier Italian restaurants, has declined badly. Service borders on abusive. The food here was always a little unpredictable, and that's even truer now. A fabulous puréed Tuscan bean soup with sage and olive oil is everything you expect from great Tuscan cooking. Artichoke soup is heady and intense. Main courses can be disappointing, but some dishes are really impressive, such as the lobster ravioli and salmon wrapped in spinach in a creamy caviar sauce. On a recent visit, a soufflé—actually an earthy fricasee of vegetables and mushrooms wrapped in a tall pastry collar—was superb, but snapper with black olive sauce was gray and inedible. (*Ruth Reichl, updated by William Grimes*)

Other recommended dishes: All soups; lobster salad; beet salad; spaghetti with fresh tomato and basil; vitello tonnato;

wild boar; almond tortino. **Wine list:** Strong in Italian wines; a few surprisingly reasonable French bottles. **Price range:** Lunch: apps., $9–$16; entrees, $19–$38; desserts, $9–$14; lunch in the bar, $14.50–$20. Dinner: apps., $10–$16; pasta, $19–$25; entrees, $25–$36; desserts, $9–$14. Bar snacks after 8 P.M. are $12.50. **Wheelchair access:** Elevator to second-floor dining room. **Features:** Good for business, smoking permitted. **Services:** Private parties.

Palm $$$ STEAKHOUSE

837 Second Ave. (bet. 44th & 45th Sts.)   (212) 687-2953
840 Second Ave. (bet. 44th & 45th Sts.)   (212) 697-5198
250 W. 50th St. (bet. Broadway & Eighth Ave.)   (212) 333-7256
Credit cards: All major   Meals: L, D

Great steak, rude waiters and the world's best hash brown potatoes. The walls are covered with caricatures, the floor is covered with sawdust and if you want to experience the real New York rush, this is the place for you. If you can't get into the Palm, you may want to settle for second best, **Palm Too** (the 840 Second Ave. location). Then again, probably not. It is NEVER as good as the place across the street.

The newest addition (on 50th St.) doesn't have the original Palm's venerable gritty patina, built up over 73 years of charring steaks and meat-eating smokers. And the celebrity cartoons on the walls, many of them reproductions of the originals at the Palm on Second Avenue, do not have that baked-on aura. But it is pretty and spacious, with a big bar area with piano music, and several private rooms. A number of light lunch items like crab cakes and Cobb salad have been added.

Price range: Lunch: apps., $7–$14; entrees, $10.50–$35; desserts, $8. Dinner, apps., $10–$16; entrees, $16–$38; desserts, $8. **Wheelchair access:** Fully accessible. **Features:** Kid friendly, smoking permitted. **Services:** Delivery, takeout, catering, private parties.

Palm Court $$$$ NEW AMERICAN

Plaza Hotel, 768 Fifth Ave. (at 59th St.)   (212) 546-5350
Credit cards: All major   Meals: B, L, D, LN

Very pretty and unbelievably pricey. If you don't mind paying a small fortune for a chicken salad, this elegant old-fashioned place will make you feel you are eating in old New York.

Price range: Apps., $10.50–$19; entrees, $19–$29; desserts, $9.50. **Wheelchair access:** Fully accessible. **Services:** Catering, private parties.

Pampa $25 & Under   ARGENTINE

768 Amsterdam Ave. (bet. 97th & 98th Sts.)   (212) 865-2929
Credit cards: Cash or check only   Meals: D

The restaurant pickings are slim on Amsterdam Avenue in the
90's, where this rustic but pleasant and inexpensive Argentine
meatery stands out for its lean, flavorful steaks. Grilled steaks,
skirt steaks and filet mignon are all outstanding, as is the rotis-
serie-cooked Peruvian chicken. Vegetables? Worry about them
some other time.

Price range: Apps., $2–$8; entrees, $7.50–$14.50; desserts,
$4–$5.50. **Alcohol:** Beer and wine. **Wheelchair access:** Fully
accessible. **Features:** Outdoor dining. **Services:** Takeout.

Pam Real Thai Food $25 & Under   THAI

404 W. 49th St. (at 9th Ave.)   (212) 333-7500
Credit cards: Cash only   Meals: L, D

Most Thai restaurants in New York must appeal to a largely
American clientele, which leads many of them to compromise
by adding sweetness and toning down the long, slow buildup of
chili heat that is a Thai characteristic. At this sweet little restaurant, the compromises are not always obvious. The owner says
the restaurant tones down the heat for the supposedly tender
American palate, but your palate will revel in the kitchen's sure-
handed spicing.

Shredded green papaya salad, for instance, is not only both
tangy and sweet but fiery as well, strewn with chewy dried
shrimp and tiny red chilies, with a faint sense of pungent fish
sauce in the background. The chilies are not visible in the yum
nam sod, a salad of ground pork with lime dressing, onions and
roasted peanuts, but the heat builds into a healthy glow on the
lips and tongue, adding dimension and depth to the dish.

Pam's curries are superb, though the sliced red and green
bell peppers in those dishes would not be found in Thailand.
No matter. Try chu chee curry with pork, with its underlying
flavor of coconut milk laced with chili heat and a pungent but
refreshing dimension added by lime leaves. Also try pad kra
prow with beef, which has plenty of basil flavor, balanced by
garlic and chilies.

Pam is a resolutely plain place. The boxy dining room offers
some travel posters to take your mind off the industrial ceiling
tile.

Other recommended dishes: Crisp duck salad, panang curry,
duck with green beans. **Price range:** Apps., $3–$6; entrees,
$7–$14. **Wheelchair access:** Everything on one level.

Panaché $25 & Under

BISTRO/FRENCH

470 Sixth Ave. (near 12th St.)
Credit cards: All major

(212) 243-2222
Meals: L, D, LN

Named after a French summer cocktail that is two-thirds beer, one-third lemonade, Panaché is an unpretentious place, with a wood floor, leather banquettes and brass lighting fixtures. The chef has put together a menu that is generally down to earth and well anchored in bistro traditions. From the first bite of good, fresh French bread, you get the sense that simple things matter at Panaché. Appetizers do not have a dozen ingredients each, but they are nonetheless pretty and delicious, like fillets of herring, served with marinated potatoes. Fat slices of soft garlic sausage surround a mound of lentils bathed in a tangy vinaigrette. Main courses include a satisfying roast chicken with pearl onions, mushrooms and mashed potatoes; a cod duo, pairing a nicely roasted fillet with a sumptuous brandade, southern France's purée of potatoes, salt cod, olive oil and milk, augmented with a roasted garlic sauce; and salmon, cooked perfectly and enlivened by a heady horseradish sauce.

The crème brûlée is so good, you should expect all spoons at the table to zero in on it and finish it off in seconds.

Other recommended dishes: Frisée salad; chevre crusted with hazelnuts; potatoes lyonnaise; leg of lamb; veal with lemon, wine and capers; crepe with lemon syrup, mango cake. **Price range:** Apps., $5–$9; entrees, $12–$27.50. **Wheelchair access:** Ramp at entrance; restrooms are up a step.

Panino'teca 275 $25 & Under SANDWICHES/ITALIAN

275 Smith St. (near Sackett St.), Carroll Gardens, Brooklyn
(718) 237-2728
Credit cards: Cash only   Meals: L, D   Closed Mon.

The Italian sandwich and wine bar is an equivalent of the Spanish tapas bar, a relaxed place to drop in for a snack and a drink, with the option of moving on or making a night of it. Panino'teca is a small, boxy room, which seems plain until you look more closely and find unexpected details, like the series of reclining nudes laminated onto the bar.

The sandwich portion of the menu is divided into four sections: bruschetta; toasts, which, like the bruschetta, are served open-faced; tramezzini, triangular, crustless white-bread sandwiches, the kind a mother would never serve to her kids; and panini, pressed sandwiches made with small hero rolls. For sheer freshness, the bruschetta are highlights. The toppings include tomato and basil, which will remind you that the tomato is a fruit; creamy, fresh ricotta; a tart and pungent olive-anchovy paste; and puréed cauliflower deepened and enriched with a little white truffle oil. A tramezzini with prosciutto and fig jam is another winner, while a panini with bresaola, provolone and horseradish is earthy and sharp. Panino'teca's wine list is small but includes some good choices, like a fruity barbera from Abrate. For dessert, you can't go wrong with a panini slathered with Nutella, the chocolate and hazelnut spread, and a sweet caramel-apple shortcake is creamy and luscious.

Other recommended dishes: Figs stuffed with prosciutto; arugula salad with pancetta, potato, artichoke and tuna; tuna and roasted pepper tramezzini. **Price range:** Apps., $5–$9; bruschetta and sandwiches, $3–$7. **Wheelchair access:** One step at entrance; restrooms are narrow.

Pan Pan Restaurant $ SOUTHERN

500 Lenox Ave. (at Malcolm X. Blvd.)   (212) 926-4900
Credit cards: Cash only   Meals: B, L, D

This simple luncheonette in Harlem offers excellent waffles, served alone or in that classic combination of fried chicken and waffles, as well as other Southern breakfast specialties like salmon croquettes with grits and buttery biscuits.

Alcohol: Beer. **Price range:** Dishes from $1.85–$9.35. **Wheelchair access:** Restrooms not accessible. **Features:** Kid friendly. **Services:** Takeout, catering.

Pão $25 & Under   PORTUGUESE

322 Spring St. (at Greenwich St.)   (212) 334-5464
Credit cards: All major   Meals: L, D, LN

The small menu in this small (34 seats) restaurant offers traditional Portuguese cuisine with a contemporary touch. To begin, try roasted quail on cabbage braised with linguica — the mild Portuguese sausage — and black grapes; baked octopus in garlic-cilantro vinaigrette, and an excellent potato broth with shredded kale, chunks of potato and slices of sausage. Main dishes include pork and clams in a roasted-red-pepper sauce; grilled shrimp served with a clam-and-shrimp-studded lemony bread pudding, and sautéed salt cod with egg, onion and straw potatoes. Desserts are not to be missed, particularly the pudding with port-and-prune sauce and the rice pudding with citrus, nutmeg and cinnamon.

Price range: Lunch: apps., $4.25–$6.50; entrees, $8.95–$12.95; desserts, $3.75–$4.25. Dinner: apps., $5.95–$8.95; entrees, $13.95–$16.95; desserts, $5.25–$5.50. **Wheelchair access:** Everything on one level. **Features:** Good for business, romantic, smoking permitted, outdoor dining. **Services:** Takeout, catering, private parties.

Paola's ☆☆ $$$ ITALIAN

245 E. 84th St. (bet. Second & Third Aves.)   (212) 794-1890
Credit cards: All major   Meals: L, D

Everybody in New York seems to be looking for the perfect
neighborhood restaurant. This may be it. Paola's is one of New
York City's best and least-known Italian restaurants. Paola
makes some of the city's finest pasta, and the wine list is wonderful. No regular would even consider starting a meal here
without an order of carciofi alla giudea, as fine a version of
baby artichokes fried in the style of the Roman ghetto as you
will find in this country. But pastas are the soul of the menu.
Filled pastas such as cazunzei and pansotti are wonderful.
Entrees are a different matter, and the preparations can be
inconsistent. The safe choice here is the veal scaloppine.
Desserts, with the exception of a fine, light ricotta cake, seem
like an afterthought. (*Ruth Reichl*)

Other recommended dishes: Macco; mozzarella with tomatoes and basil; spinachi romana; mussels alla marinara; malfatti; potato gnocchi with radicchio and sausage; tortelloni
della casa; chicken and sausages in wine sauce. **Wine list:**
Many good and unusual Italian wines at reasonable prices.
Price range: Apps., $6–$14; pastas, $14–$18.95; entrees,
$16.95–$29; desserts, $8. **Wheelchair access:** One step up to
dining room. **Features:** Outdoor dining. **Services:** Catering,
private parties.

Papillon ☆ $$$ BISTRO

575 Hudson St. (near Bank St.)   (646) 638-2900
Credit cards: AE   Meals: Br, D, LN

Papillon looks like a neighborhood saloon, but it delivers twice
the quality at a third off the price of many Manhattan bistros.
Service ebbs and flows. And the rock-hard banquettes with
their awkwardly angled backs can impose cruel discipline. The
disparity between the surroundings and the food is so extreme
that some diners must wonder if dinner is being delivered from
another restaurant.

    The short menu bristles with happy combinations, mildly
offbeat ideas and clearly expressed flavors. Foie gras is set off
with potato croutons, Parma ham and mushrooms in a red-wine
jus sweetened with a little Madeira. The soups are superior,
with deeply concentrated stocks that show off one or two central ingredients. A very simple mussel bouillon relies on a whiff
of saffron for a magic lift. It has a counterpart among the
entrees, a small lobster, removed from the shell, floating in an
orange sea of intensely flavored bouillabaisse stock. The
French-sounding lamb confit is a round knob of lamb braised
for several hours, then wrapped in caul fat and given a final
touch-up in duck fat. A stately, plump filet mignon in a muscu-

lar bourguignon sauce comes with a partner, a whopping big potato shaped into a squat cylinder and jacketed in a thin layer of Swiss cheese.

The menu includes a vegetarian department, which may not move you. But hats off to the chef for breaking the spell of crème brûlée. It's disguised under the name "cassonade," the French term for brown sugar. It's a rich vanilla custard, not too dense, not too runny, served in a cup and topped with a crunchy layer of almond praline crushed to a powder.

Other recommended dishes: Steamed fish on root vegetables with smoked lardons, shredded crabmeat in pastry, chocolate tart, lemon tart. **Wine list:** A very short list, mostly French, of about 30 wines, half of them under $40. **Price range:** Apps., $7–$12; entrees, $16–$23; desserts, $7. **Wheelchair access:** Restrooms downstairs.

Paris Commune $ FRENCH
411 Bleecker St. (bet. W. 11th & Bank Sts.)   (212) 929-0509
Credit cards: All major   Meals: Br, D

The dim candlelight, the brick walls with dusty portraits, the floor as level as a wavy ocean all combine to epitomize the Greenwich Village grotto. Paris Commune is a friendly local hangout with a simple, appealing French-inspired menu.

Price range: Apps., $5–$8; entrees, $11–$20; desserts, $5. **Wheelchair access:** Restrooms not accessible. **Features:** Romantic.

Park Avalon $$ NEW AMERICAN
225 Park Ave. S. (bet. 18th & 19th Sts.)   (212) 533-2500
Credit cards: All major   Meals: Br, L, D

It's young, exuberant and very noisy. It is also reasonably priced and the American food is good. No wonder there are almost always lines. Especially good for the Sunday jazz brunch.

Price range: Lunch: apps., $5–$7; entrees, $9–$11; desserts, $5–$7. Dinner: apps., $6–$8; entrees, $14; desserts, $5–$7. **Wheelchair access:** Fully accessible. **Services:** Takeout, private parties.

Park Avenue Cafe ☆☆ $$$$ NEW AMERICAN
100 E. 63rd St. (near Park Ave.)   (212) 644-1900
Credit cards: All major   Meals: L, D

Park Avenue Cafe, which opened to great fanfare in January 1992, is still a good restaurant. But after a decade, the restaurant feels a little past its prime. This does not seem to bother the Upper East Siders who treat it as a beloved neighborhood fixture where they can relax in a fully realized J. Crew environment and eat sanely reinterpreted, high-spirited American food.

A Mediterranean accent now inflects the cooking. Two plump quail, surrounded by a bright red slick of chili-fired barbecue sauce and set on a johnnycake, has a Fourth of July picnic feel to it. But it competes with appetizers like artichoke ravioli with arugula, roasted tomatoes and figs wrapped in prosciutto and cavatelli with wild mushrooms and white truffle oil. Both pastas are among the best dishes on the menu, but the most sinfully indulgent experience is the formidable terrine of foie gras, served folksy style in a glass jar with fig jam smeared on the hinged lid. This is the whole hog, so to speak.

The signature "swordchop" still holds its place on the menu, a mighty slab of swordfish attached to the collarbone. It is juicy and big-flavored, served with tomato ditalini and lemon broth. It has been joined by a second gimmick dish, Duck, Duck, Duck!, which quick-witted diners will realize is duck prepared three ways, two of them suspect.

Richard Leach, the mad scientist whose desserts bristling with sugar antennas and Gehry-esque curved planes put him on the far edge of the architectural school, is still at work. The productions seem dated now, but they taste good, especially the cherry tart with almonds and vanilla mascarpone, and the beautifully realized chocolate cube, a thin wall of chocolate containing a solid espresso mousse. The restaurant's signature dessert, the admittedly ridiculous Park Avenue Park Bench, really does succeed as theater. With its chocolate slatted bench and leaning lamppost topped by a white chocolate globe, it exudes a strange, twilight melancholy. It's a subversive dessert, at odds with the prevailing mood of the restaurant, which looks like a Cracker Barrel made over by Martha Stewart. Fun American folk art enlivens the interior; green checkerboard upholstery and napkins send a wholesome message; and the hapless waiters wear silly ties with a hideous American flag pattern. It's an impressive display of nerdsmanship.

Other recommended dishes: Gazpacho, quail with barbecue sauce and johnnycake, cavatelli with wild mushrooms. **Wine list:** A reasonably priced if not terribly adventurous list of more than 200 wines with emphasis on California. **Price range:** Lunch, apps., $9–$16.50; entrees, $19.50–$28.50; desserts, $5–$8.50. Dinner, apps., $11.50–$16; entrees, $19.50–$42; desserts, $9–$12. Three-course prix-fixe, $65. **Wheelchair access:** One step up at entrance, six steps to restrooms.

Park Bistro ☆☆☆ $$$ BISTRO/FRENCH

414 Park Ave. S. (bet. 28th & 29th Sts.)   (212) 689-1360
Credit cards: All major   Meals: L, D

A classic French bistro, from the décor (photos of Paris in the 1950's) to the menu (magret, onglet and so forth). It offers seductive Gallic fare, good wines at reasonable prices and a cozy setting. After languishing in recent years, it looks as though the restaurant is on the upswing again with the arrival of Philippe Roussel, who has put some verve and style back in the kitchen. It's still one of the most atmospheric bistros in town, with one of the warmest welcomes.

Openers include house-cured salmon, gratin of fresh mussels, guinea-hen terrine, and a ragout of calamari, white beans and peppers. Among the entrees are grilled escalope of salmon, veal medallion, roasted and caramelized shoulder of pork with carrots and fennel, and a daube of beef with potato gnocchi. There is a daily selection of imported cheeses, and to top off the meal, thin warm apple tart with Armagnac and vanilla ice cream; fresh roasted fig tart, or the ubiquitous crème brûlée. There is a large and interesting selection of tea in addition to several coffees. (*Ruth Reichl, updated by William Grimes*)

Price range: Avg. app., $9; entree, $14–$20; dessert, $6.50.
Wheelchair access: Fully accessible. **Services:** Takeout, catering, private parties.

Park View at the Boathouse ☆☆ $$$
NEW AMERICAN

Loeb Boathouse, Central Park, E. 72nd St. entrance
   (212) 517-2233
Credit cards: All major   Meals: Br, L, D

Is this Manhattan's most romantic spot? Very possibly. Situated in the Loeb Boathouse next to Central Park's prettiest lake, it combines the country charm with views of skyscrapers peeking over the trees. The conversion from the Boathouse Cafe has added interesting, eclectic food and a good wine list. Even when you are eating one of the less fortunate entrees, the setting is so swell that you feel lucky to be there. The live jazz at the adjacent cafe, which is still called the Boathouse Cafe, is a real bonus. (*Ruth Reichl*)

Wine list: Interesting and filled with unusual choices and hard-to-find bottles. **Price range:** Brunch: apps., $8–$12; entrees, $14–$23. Lunch: apps., $10–$14; entrees, $18–$26. Dinner: apps., $8–$14; entrees, $18–$30; desserts, $7–$8. **Wheelchair access:** Indoor dining room at street level; ramp down to dock. **Features:** Kid friendly, good view, romantic, outdoor dining. **Services:** Takeout, catering, private parties.

Pascalou $25 & Under   BISTRO/FRENCH

1308 Madison Ave. (near 93rd St.)   (212) 534-7522
Credit cards: MC/V   Meals: Br, L, D

This likable neighborhood restaurant, which looks like a well-worn family restaurant in southwestern France, offers well-prepared French and Italian dishes, occasionally with Asian touches. There are a half-dozen pastas available, including seafood capellini and polenta with mozzarella, basil, pesto and grilled shrimp. Among the appetizers are warm Oriental shrimp salad with crab dumplings; blinis with smoked salmon and caviar, and mousse of foie gras. Entrees include roasted chicken with rosemary, calf's liver, shrimp curry with basmati rice, a fish of the day, and a wok-sautéed vegetable platter.

Other recommended dishes: Duck confit; bowtie pasta with mushrooms and truffle oil; lamb chops. **Alcohol:** Beer and wine. **Price range:** Apps., $7–$14; entrees, $13–$22; desserts, $6.50–$10. Prix-fixe dinner, 5-6:45 P.M., $18.45. **Wheelchair access:** Restrooms not accessible. **Features:** Kid friendly. **Services:** Delivery, takeout, private parties.

Pastis ☆ $$$ BRASSERIE/FRENCH

9 Ninth Ave. (at Little W. 12th)   (212) 929-4844
Credit cards: All major   Meals: L, D, LN

New Yorkers tolerate the most cramped and overcrowded living conditions in the United States, so they naturally gravitate to places of entertainment that are even more cramped and overcrowded. This instinct partly explains the overpowering allure of Pastis, a restaurant named after a drink that most Americans would not touch with a 10-foot pole. What do diners get for their suffering? A meal that's as good as it needs to be, but no better.

Pastis is the traditional restaurant that you whiz by in a thousand French towns — a little crumbly around the edges, burnished by time, with a faded advertisement for Suze or Byrrh painted on one wall. Riad Nasr and Lee Hanson, the chefs de cuisine at Balthazar, have devised a menu so traditional that virtually every dish could qualify for protection by the French Ministry of Culture. It's a deliberate invitation to simple pleasures. Grilled sardines, a typical appetizer, could use a little crunch around the edges, but the fish are hefty and flavorful. A frisée aux lardons is, as the French say, correct. There are a few American-style concessions, like hamburgers. But the point of the exercise lies in dishes like braised beef with glazed carrots, a rich, savory and unabashedly declassé hunk of meat; or trout amandine, the sort of thing that's so fusty it makes you think of blanquette de veau, carrots Vichy, crêpes suzette or floating island. All are on the menu. And all are good. If steak frites is the acid test of a dependable bistro, however, then

Pastis needs to work a little harder. Its béarnaise sauce — dense and creamy, with a sharp vinegar note — is fine, and the fries are too, but the steak is a little tough and stringy. The dessert menu is a minefield, but the crêpes suzette rise up in glory, and the floating island floats, a cloud with just enough substance to support its light custardy sauce.

Other recommended dishes: Grilled octopus salad; onion soup; rabbit pappardelle, tripes gratinées. **Wine list:** About 40 wines by the bottle, most from Bordeaux and Burgundy, with about 25 more modest bistro wines by the glass, half carafe, and carafe. **Price range:** Lunch: Apps., $5–$10, entrees, $12–$16, desserts, $6. Dinner: Apps., $6–$11, entrees, $14–$17; desserts, $7. **Wheelchair access:** Restrooms on street level. **Features:** Smoking at the bar .

Pastrami Queen $ Deli
1269 Lexington Ave. (at 85th St.)   (212) 828-0007
Credit cards: All major   Meals: B, L, D

Pastrami Queen doesn't feel quite comfortable yet in its new bilevel quarters. The pastrami is good — very good — though it no longer has the dry, garlicky power of the glory years of its legendary Queens predecessor, Pastrami King. It now tastes sweet, with hints of vinegar and garlic to round out the flavor. Even if it's no longer a top-echelon pastrami like those served at Carnegie Deli or Katz's Delicatessen, the two best in Manhattan, it's still great to have as an uptown outpost.

Price range: Apps., $2.50–$5.95; entrees, $9.95–$18.95; desserts, $1.95–$3.50. **Wheelchair access:** Restrooms not accessible. **Features:** Kid friendly, good for business. **Services:** Delivery, takeout, catering, private parties.

Patois $25 & Under   Bistro/French
255 Smith St., Carroll Gardens, Brooklyn   (718) 855-1535
Credit cards: All major   Meals: Br, D   Closed Mon.

This small storefront restaurant offers rich, gutsy bistro fare that can range from authentically French tripe stew — a mellow, wonderful dish, if not destined for popularity — to juicy pork chops and satisfying casseroles. Dishes don't always work, but it's nice that Patois is trying.

Other recommended dishes: Lamb and white bean casserole; warm leek, Roquefort and potato tart; grilled Provençal vegetables; steamed mussels; split-pea soup; chocolate cake; tarte Tatin. **Alcohol:** Beer and wine. **Price range:** Apps., $5–$8; entrees, $10–$17. **Wheelchair access:** One step at entrance; entrance to restroom is narrow. **Features:** Outdoor dining. **Services:** Catering, private parties.

Patria ☆☆☆ $$$

250 Park Ave. S. (at 20th St.)
Credit cards: All major

LATIN AMERICAN
(212) 777-6211
Meals L, D

With its colorful food and boisterous atmosphere, Patria feels like a party every night — one that celebrates Latin tastes and seduces customers with its flavors. The kitchen creates exuberant, outrageous nuevo Latino combinations with names like Honduran fire and ice, an extravagant tuna ceviche marinated with chilies, ginger and coconut milk. Each dish explodes in the mouth with a rich variety of tastes.

Peruvian ceviche, a mound of seafood in a citrus-scented marinade infused with squid ink, was surrounded by potatoes in the classic egg-and-cheese sauce of the Huancayo Indians. Empanada cabrales were an elegant contrast, a mixture of great Spanish cheese, warm pastry and greens in a dark walnut-pear vinaigrette.

At many restaurants, the main dishes are less interesting than the appetizers, but here the larger plates offer a greater opportunity for creativity. Guatemalan chicken is a gorgeous combination of grilled white meat and deep fried leg on a bed of green rice decorated with dots of mole sauce and an avocado salad. Rib-eye steak was so deeply smoked the taste seemed to fill the mouth. Boned red snapper came fried in a spicy batter and draped with cole slaw on a bed of coconut rice. It was absolutely delicious. Sweets are visually restrained but each has a surprising intensity of flavor. Try the flan, or the raspberry sorbet with its hint of cinnamon. For the sheer fun of it, have the smokeless Cuban cigar, a trompe l'oeil chocolate cigar with a book of sugar matches.

Lunchtime is quieter and the menu is slightly different. The lunchtime skirt steak is embellished with beet relish and black beans as well as chimichurri, the Argentine combination of parsley, vinegar, garlic and chilies. Some dishes need work, but even when not totally successful, the food is always interesting. (*Ruth Reichl*)

Other recommended dishes: Sugar cane tuna; clam pastel (a Puerto-Rican style tamale filled with clams, green tomato, avocado and rock shrimp); shrimp escabeche; Cuban sandwich. **Most popular dish:** The Original: plantain-coated mahi mahi with fufu (pieces of plantain with onion and bacon, served with pomelo horseradish and other garnishes). **Chef's favorite:** Churrasco: beef tenderloin, marinated and grilled with rice, beans and chimichurri sauce. **Wine list:** Emphasizes Argentina, Chile and Spain at fair prices and offers a large number of South African choices. The staff gladly describes them. **Price range:** Lunch: three-course prix fixe, $20. Dinner: Apps., $16–$22; entrees, $22–$34; tasting menus, $69–$79. **Wheelchair access:** Restrooms not accessible.

Patroon ☆ ☆ ☆ $$$$ NEW AMERICAN

160 E. 46th St. (bet. Lexington & Third Aves.)   (212) 883-7373
Credit cards: All major   Meals: L, D   Closed Sun.

When Ken Aretsky opened Patroon intending to create a contemporary "21," businessmen were charmed with the luxurious clubhouse atmosphere, the low lights, neutral colors and smooth textures, and the extremely professional service.

The menu features a few truly brilliant dishes. Duck à l'orange Patroon, served as an appetizer, is a stunning rendition of an old standard. There is a similarly innovative take on lamb breast, cooked into a rich terrine enlivened with accents of mango and tomato. It, too, makes an ideal appetizer. Lobster bisque is zinged with ginger, and terrine of foie gras is enlivened with green apples, plums and kale. Scallops can be magical, sometimes served topped with rounds of scallop terrine. Each terrine looks like a scallop but has a more delicate taste and a texture as seductive as custard. I loved that dish, and I simply wanted to stop eating and savor the flavor.

Patroon has a remarkably smart menu. It is American without being hokey, rich without being fussy. Sirloin with a side dish of crisp, light onion rings was a splendid piece of meat, beautifully charred over wood. Dover sole roasted over fennel, and with just a little lemon, is perfect. Chicken, carved at the table, was so fragrant that nobody who likes food could resist it. Prime rib was brought out raw and displayed in all its marbled beauty. Good desserts include hot fudge sundae, caramelized banana tart and pistachio profiteroles. (*Ruth Reichl*)

Other recommended dishes: Risotto of escargot; Caesar salad; clams and oysters; creamed spinach. **Most popular dish:** Scallops topped with a disk of scallop mousse. **Chef's favorite:** Rib eye of lamb with rosemary popovers filled with spiced fruit, nuts and grains. **Wine list:** Excellent, generally expensive, although the sommelier is helpful with affordable suggestions. **Price range:** Apps., $12–$25; entrees, $23–$38; sides, $9; desserts, $12. **Wheelchair access:** Restrooms not accessible. **Services:** Catering, private parties.

Patsy's Italian $$ ITALIAN

236 W. 56th St. (bet. Broadway & Eighth Ave.)   (212) 247-3491
Credit cards: All major   Meals: L, D

Rao's for the rest of us. If Damon Runyon were still around, this is where he'd eat. The menu features seriously old-fashioned New York Italian dishes like mozzarella in carozza served in enormous portions. Good hot appetizers like clams posillipo, chopped salads and lots of stuffed dishes with red sauce.

Price range: Lunch: apps., $9–$11; entrees, $14–$27; desserts, $6–$7. Dinner: apps., $10–$12; entrees, $16–$31; desserts, $6–$7. **Wheelchair access:** Restrooms not accessible. **Services:** Takeout, private parties.

Patsy's Pizzeria $25 & Under   PIZZA

509 Third Ave. (at 34th St.)	(212) 689-7500
67 University Pl. (bet. 10th & 11th Sts.)	(212) 533-3500
61 W. 74th St. (at Columbus Ave.)	(212) 579-3000
1312 Second Ave. (at 69th St.)	(212) 639-1000
2287 First Ave. (bet. 117th & 118th Sts.)	(212) 534-9783
Credit cards: Cash only	Meals: L, D

Patsy's Pizzerias are turning up all over town, as this chain continues to expand. As chains go, Patsy's is a good thing since the ambition is to make classic New York pizza. On the whole, they all do a pretty good job, with smooth, thin crusts and superb toppings.

Price range: Apps., $5.95–$9.95; entrees, $7.95–$14.95; desserts, $4.95–$5.95. **Wheelchair access:** Fully accessible. **Features:** Kid friendly. **Services:** Takeout.

Payard Pâtisserie ☆☆ $$$ BISTRO/FRENCH

1032 Lexington Ave. (at 73rd St.)	(212) 717-5252
Credit cards: All major Meals: L, D	Closed Sun.

This is the ultimate Upper East Side bistro, a whimsical belle epoque cafe and pastry shop, complete with mirrors, mahogany and hand-blown lamps. Just about everything here is extraordinary, from the inventive bistro menu to the amazing pastries sold in the bakery. A recent visit showed that chef Philippe Bertineau is still going strong, with inventive, impeccably executed dishes like a twice baked cheese soufflé with Parmesan cream sauce, sardines stuffed with quince chutney, and a simple sirloin steak with four-peppercorn sauce. The terrine of foie gras is the real thing, and irresistible. And then there is dessert: clear, true flavors, beautifully presented. (*Ruth Reichl, updated by William Grimes*)

Other recommended dishes: Bouillabaisse; duck confit; caramelized sweetbreads with orange and rosemary; croque-monsieur; pigs' feet salad; pan bagnat; french fries; pastries and ice creams. **Wine list:** Beautifully chosen and reasonably priced. **Price range:** Apps., $6–$15; sandwiches, $10–$12; entrees, $17–$25; desserts, $7–$15; tea, $14–$20. **Wheelchair access:** Main dining room and restrooms at street level. **Services:** Takeout, catering, private parties.

Pearl Oyster Bar $25 & Under SEAFOOD

18 Cornelia St. (bet. Bleecker & W. 4th St.)   (212) 691-8211
Credit cards: MC/V   Meals: L, D   Closed Sun.

It's just a marble counter with a few small tables, but Pearl has won over its neighborhood with its casual charm and Maine-inspired seafood. The restaurant is modeled on the Swan Oyster Depot in San Francisco, and when packed exudes a Barbary Coast rakishness. The menu changes seasonally, but grilled pompano was sweet and delicious, while scallop chowder was unusual and satisfying. Lobster rolls are big and delicious, and blueberry pie is sensational. Don't forget the oysters.

Other recommended dishes: Green salad; seared sea scallops. **Alcohol:** Beer and wine. **Price range:** Apps., $7–$8.50; entrees, $17–$25; desserts, $5. **Wheelchair access:** One step up at entrance; aisle to restroom is narrow. **Features:** Romantic. **Services:** Takeout, catering, private parties.

Pearson's Texas Barbecue $25 & Under
BARBECUE

71-04 35th Ave., Jackson Heights, Queens   (718) 779-7715
Credit cards: Cash only   Meals: L, D

The only pit barbecue restaurant in New York City has a new home, and the barbecue is better than ever. The smoke outside may be gone, but once you enter Legends, a pleasant-enough brick-and-panel bar, you know you're in the right place. In the rear, burnished slabs of pork ribs glisten behind a counter next to piles of plump sausages and chickens turned almost chestnut by smoke. Even so, the glory of Pearson's is its brisket, superb, tender and fully imbued with smoke from the rosy-brown, almost crisp exterior through to the pink center. It is so good that it needs none of the tomato-based barbecue sauce, which is offered in mild, medium and hot gradations. Pork ribs are excellent, meaty, smoky and well-flavored.

Other recommended dishes: North Carolina-style pork; chicken; sausages; ribs. **Price range:** Sandwiches, $5.95; barbecue by the pound, $4–$14. **Wheelchair access:** Everything on one level; restroom is narrow. **Features:** Kid friendly, smoking permitted, outdoor dining. **Services:** Take out, catering.

Peasant ☆ $$$ ITALIAN

194 Elizabeth St. (bet. Prince & Spring Sts.)   (212) 965-9511
Credit cards: All major   Meals: D   Closed Mon.

The concrete floor and the brushed-aluminum chairs send off warning signals. Is Peasant, despite the name, going to be an exercise in deprivation chic? But closer inspection suggests that all is not as it seems. At the far end of the room, a brick pizza oven radiates heat. On a counter in front of the open kitchen, apricots, tomatoes and grapes have been massed in abundant display. Even the forbidding chairs are form-fitting and inexplicably comfortable, and the black-clad waiters are Jimmy Olsens in disguise, full of gee-whiz enthusiasm.

Peasant has built a following by sticking to some very simple premises. Keep the food simple, rustic and Italian. Cook it over a wood fire. Serve big portions. Be nice. That's about it. When the formula works, Peasant sends out highly satisfying food, fresh and flavorful, with the rich tanginess that wood smoke imparts. The panzanella is just right, a generous plate of chewy bread cubes, red onion and cerignola olives, with a subtle application of balsamic vinegar for roundness and sweetness.

The wood fire adds a sublime crunch to the excellent crust of Peasant's little pizzas. (The most appealing of the three versions, topped with peperoncini and soppressata, is fiery enough to require a stern warning from the waiter.) Leg of lamb, slow-cooked on the rotisserie, is served on top of creamy polenta and garnished with an enormous head of bitter radicchio di Treviso grilled to a state of juicy limpness. The flavors here are potent and lingering. The pasta at Peasant is good, not great. Properly firm risotto, dotted with peas, shrimp bits and cherry tomatoes, pleases well enough. Gnocchi with morels is more like it: earthy, rich and — there's no other way to put it — peasantlike.

Among the desserts, the best choices are vanilla-soaked bread pudding, served with a caramel-swathed scoop of white chocolate gelato, and a heroically proportioned peach pie with a rough lattice crust.

Other recommended dishes: Buffalo mozzarella with roasted peppers; grilled sea bream; bread pudding. **Wine list:** Fifty Italian wines, half of them $40 or under, with an emphasis on lesser-known regions like Calabria, Emilia-Romagna and Puglia. **Price range:** Dinner, apps., $8–$12; entrees, $19–$24; desserts, $8. **Wheelchair access:** No steps into restaurant; restrooms on dining room level.

Penang $$ Malaysian

109 Spring St. (bet. Mercer & Greene Sts.)	(212) 274-8883
240 Columbus Ave. (at 71st St.)	(212) 769-3988
1596 Second Ave. (at 83rd St.)	(212) 585-3838
64 Third Ave. (at 11th St.)	(212) 228-7888
38-04 Prince St., Flushing, Queens	(718) 321-2078
Credit cards: All major	Meals: L, D, LN

What started as a small Malaysian storefront in Flushing has turned into an institution. The SoHo outpost is, as you might expect, the most exciting of the lot, if only for the people watching. But all of the branches offer surprisingly authentic

Malaysian flavors. The dish not to miss is the roti canai, a seductive, savory crepe served with coconut milk sauce.

Other recommended dishes: Roti tellur; fried calamari; won ton soup; chicken or beef satay; Penang noodles; mee goreng; beef rendang; kari ayam kering; sarang burung; clams with black bean sauce; grilled baby eggplant; kangkung; peanut pancake. **Price range:** Lunch: avg. app., $3.95; entree, $5.95; dessert, $6.95. Dinner: avg. app., $6.95; entree, $13.95; dessert, $6.95. **Wheelchair access:** Not accessible. **Features:** Kid friendly. **Services:** Delivery, takeout, private parties.

Pepolino $25 & Under   ITALIAN
281 W. Broadway (near Lispenard St.)   (212) 966-9983
Credit cards: AE   Meals: L, D, LN

There's a lot to like about Pepolino. The small, cheerful dining room seems to glow with warmth, the greeting is friendly, and the service is good-natured, though occasionally a little mixed up. The gnocchi at Pepolino are ethereal, as light as miniature clouds, making up with intense flavor what they lack in mass. Whether as malfatti, gnocchi made with spinach and served in a simple sauce of butter and sage, or in their more common potato incarnation, they are meltingly good. The chef also makes a glorious pappa al pomodoro, the Tuscan specialty of ripe tomatoes, shreds of stale bread and fragrant olive oil, cooked into a delicious mush. Pastas are marvelous, like spaghetti with braised leeks and Parmesan, and sturdy rigatoni with sausage and arugula. One dessert stands out clearly: a wonderfully dense chocolate cake, intensely flavored with coffee.

Other recommended dishes: Spinach soufflé; yellow pepper soup; salmon steamed with fennel and cannellini beans; snapper with leeks and beans. **Price range:** Apps., $5–$8.50; entrees, $11–$19. **Wheelchair access:** Long flight of steps to entrance.

Persepolis $25 & Under   PERSIAN
1423 Second Ave. (near 75th St.)   (212) 535-1100
Credit cards: All major   Meals: L, D

A friendly restaurant that specializes in simpler Persian dishes, like refreshing salads and gently spiced grilled meats. A dish of yogurt and cucumber, blended with a little mint, is the ideal cool complement to Persepolis's tiny rounds of fresh pita bread and rectangles of flat bread. Kebabs, served without heavy sauces, seem pleasantly light.

Other recommended dishes: Hummus; sherazi salad; tabbouleh; kebabs of salmon, filet mignon, chicken or chopped steak. **Price range:** Apps., $3.50–$4.95; entrees, $10–$26;

desserts, $3.95. **Wheelchair access:** Everything is on one level.
Features: Kid friendly, outdoor dining. **Services:** Delivery, take-out, private parties.

Pesce & Pasta $25 & Under   ITALIAN/SEAFOOD

1079 First Ave. (bet. 59th & 60th Sts.)   (212) 888-7884
262 Bleecker St. (bet. Sixth & Seventh Aves.)   (212) 645-2993
1562 Third Ave. (bet. 87th & 88th Sts.)   (212) 987-4696
Credit cards: All major   Meals: L, D, LN

This little chainlet succeeds because its places are like old-fashioned Italian restaurants done right. The atmosphere is simple, warm and gracious, and the best dishes tend to be the heartiest, where finesse and delicacy are not required. Soups are fine, and seafood specials are generally fresh.

Price range: Apps., $3.75–$7.50; entrees, $12.95–$15.50; desserts, $3. **Wheelchair access:** Everything on one level; restrooms are very narrow. **Services:** Takeout.

Peter Luger ☆☆☆ $$$$ STEAKHOUSE

178 Broadway, Williamsburg, Brooklyn   (718) 387-7400
Credit cards: Cash only   Meals: L, D

Peter Luger serves no lobsters, takes no major credit cards and lacks a great wine list. Service, though professional and often humorous, can sometimes be brusque. With its bare wooden tables, the place looks like a beer hall that has not changed since it opened in 1887. So why is it packed night and day, seven days a week? Simple: Peter Luger has the best steak in New York City. The family that runs the restaurant buys fresh shortloins and dry-ages them on the premises.

You know the steak is great from the fine, funky aroma that wafts across the table. When the waiter appears with the platter, he spoons a mixture of butter and meat juices across the sizzling porterhouse — served for two, three or four — in an exercise of pure theater. Finally he doles out slices of fillet and sirloin. As your mouth closes on the incredibly tender piece of beef, aroma and flavor explode on the palate.

An occasional diner will choose the thick and powerfully delicious lamb chops, or the fine salmon. And even side dishes have their moments. The thick slices of tomato served with strong onions and sweet sauce are tasty. Creamed spinach can be bright, rich and delicious; occasionally, it is dark and slippery in the mouth. German fried potatoes are usually crisp, fresh and irresistible, though sometimes they seem warmed-over. French fries have been terrific every time — hot and crisp with a powerful potato flavor.

But the steak's the thing here, an enormous porterhouse charred to perfection over intense heat. It is so good that if you're not careful you find yourself gnawing on the bone, picking the marrow out of the middle and covering yourself in greasy goodness.

The restaurant does well by desserts, serving a fine, rich cheesecake and a fluffy chocolate mousse cake. A little whipped cream? Why not? What's a little more cholesterol at this point? (*Ruth Reichl; see Eric Asmov's update on p. 13*)

Other recommended dishes: Apple strudel; fresh blueberry tart. **Wine list:** A limited wine list, but they do pour big, powerful cocktails. **Price range:** Lunch: Avg. price for two courses: $30. Dinner: avg. price for three courses, $60. **Wheelchair access:** Fully accessible. **Features:** Parking available. **Services:** Takeout, private parties.

Pete's Tavern $$ · American/Italian

129 E. 18th St. (at Irving Pl.) · (212) 473-7676
Credit cards: All major · Meals: B, Br, L, D, LN

O. Henry supposedly wrote "The Gift of the Magi" sitting at one of the tables covered with red-and-white-checked cloths, and not much has changed since his time. The food probably wasn't very good then, and it still isn't. But the tavern atmosphere is superb and the sidewalk seats are on one of Manhattan's more charming streets.

Price range: Lunch: avg. app., $7; entree, $11; dessert, $4.50. Dinner: avg. app., $9; entree, $14; dessert, $4.50. **Wheelchair access:** Restrooms not accessible. **Features:** Outdoor dining. **Services:** Delivery, catering.

Petrossian ☆☆ $$$$ · New American/Russian

182 W. 58th St. (at Seventh Ave.) · (212) 245-2214
Credit cards: All major · Meals: Br, L, D

Nobody in New York City serves better caviar, and nobody does it with more style. The dark room is covered with Art Deco splendor, the waiters wear blue blazers and an obsequious air, and the caviar arrives with warm toast, blini and beautiful little spoons. Vodka is served in icy little flutes that make it taste somehow better. Should you desire something else, the restaurant has introduced a fanciful menu with each entree accompanied by a reinvented blin, traditionally a buckwheat pancake. Brochette of lamb, for example, comes with an okra blin, seared bonito with a basil and sardine blin. This splash of creativity is, alas, not very successful. (*Ruth Reichl, updated by William Grimes*)

Price range: Prix-fixe brunch, $28. Prix-fixe lunch, $22 or $39. Dinner: apps., $7.50-14; entrees, $24–$34; desserts, $9; prix fixe, $38. **Wheelchair access:** Restrooms not accessible. **Features:** Good for business, romantic. **Services:** Takeout in cafe.

Philip Marie

$25 & Under   NEW AMERICAN

569 Hudson St. (at W. 11th St.)   (212) 242-6200

Credit cards: All major   Meals: D   Closed Mon.

This warm, welcoming husband-and-wife operation is the kind of place where you can smell the comforting aroma of a wood-burning fire, even though there's no fireplace. Service is efficient but casual, and the food — hearty American fare with some creative twists — inspires good feelings. Among the best dishes are a great lamb shank, braised in sour mash whisky and served with dirty rice, pine nuts and currants, and a delicious salad of smoked trout, pink grapefruit, radicchio and walnuts.

Other recommended dishes: Parsley salad with country ham, dried tomatoes and Wisconsin Asiago cheese; pumpkin fritters; roasted butternut squash soup; onion and toasted almond soup; steamed mussels; fish soup; whole striped bass stuffed with fennel; filet mignon; chocolate hazelnut torte. **Price range:** Apps., $4.95–$8.95; entrees, $13.50–$17.95. **Wheelchair access:** Ramp at entrance; restrooms down a flight of stairs. **Services:** Private parties.

Piadina

$25 & Under   ITALIAN

57 W. 10th St. (bet. Fifth & Sixth Aves.)   (212) 460-8017

Credit cards: Cash only   Meals: D, LN

This subterranean grotto is another classic Greenwich Village restaurant designed like a rustic Italian farmhouse. The menu offers simple Italian dishes and piadinas, the round, unleavened griddled bread that has been eaten for centuries in the Romagna region. A piadina is a wonderful appetizer for two, particularly with stuffings like prosciutto or cheese and arugula.

Other recommended dishes: Passatelli; mussels; polenta; green bean salad; fennel salad; chicken alla cacciatora; pork loin; red snapper; seared tuna; wild mushroom risotto. **Alcohol:** Beer and wine. **Price range:** Apps., $6; entrees, $11–$14; desserts, $6. **Wheelchair access:** Two steps down to dining room; restrooms are narrow. **Features:** Romantic, smoking permitted. **Services:** Takeout, catering, private parties.

Picholine ☆☆☆ $$$$ MEDITERRANEAN/FRENCH

35 W. 64th St. (bet. Broadway & Central Pk. W.)   (212) 724-8585

Credit cards: All major   Meals: L, D

Picholine, named after a Mediterranean olive, focuses on the food of southern France, Italy, Greece and Morocco. One of the best restaurants around Lincoln Center, it offers as much comfort to the pre- or after-theater dinner crowd as it does to more leisurely diners — although the moderately attractive room is not as impressive as either the service or the food prepared by the chef, Terrance Brennan.

Meals begin with good house-made breads, bowls of the tiny olives and olive oil. There is beautifully cooked whole fish for two, boned at the table. Salmon in horseradish crust is a signature dish and it is excellent. But there are also robust dishes from the north, like daube of beef short ribs with a horseradish potato purée, and a hearty cassoulet. Oyster fricassee, a blend of cream, gently poached Pemaquid oysters, salsify, leeks and potatoes, is fabulous. Topped with caviar, an option, it is even better.

The kitchen also has a way with game. A sauce laced with chocolate, more bitter than sweet, brings out the gamy quality of wild Scottish hare. Wild pheasant with roasted chestnuts, savoy cabbage, foie gras and puréed celery root was earthy and intense. Homey dishes — chestnut and fennel soup dotted with sausage, cassoulet rich with duck confit, and Moroccan spiced lamb, served on a bed of couscous with minted yogurt — are all wonderful. Finally, don't miss the wonderfully extravagant cheese cart, worth considering if only to hear the lovingly detailed descriptions of each cheese. (*Ruth Reichl*)

Other recommended dishes: Peekytoe crab meat salad; ceviche of black sea bass with sea urchin vinaigrette; grilled octopus; truffle-larded sea scallops. **Most popular dish:** White gazpacho soup with red gazpacho granite. **Chef's favorite:** Jamison loin of lamb with sweet garlic flan and artichokes Barigoule. **Wine list:** An expanded list with more French selections and nice choices among the smaller French wines as well as some good American pinot noirs. Knowledgeable, helpful staff. **Price range:** Lunch: apps., $8–$18; entrees, $19–$34; desserts, $8.50; prix fixe, $28–$32. Dinner: apps., $12.50–$25; entrees, $28–$38; desserts, $12.50; prix fixe, $54–$125. **Wheelchair access:** Two steps up to dining room. **Features:** Good for business. **Services:** Private parties.

Pico ☆☆☆ $$$$ PORTUGUESE

349 Greenwich St. (at Harrison St.)   (212) 343-0700
Credit cards: All major   Meals: L, D   Closed Sun.

Is Pico Portuguese? Yes and no. No and yes. Pico is named after an island in the Azores. It's a romantic reference, rather than a specific culinary source, and the chef has created his own private Portugal, a fantasy wrapped in a shimmering haze. Pico is cozy but not twee, dignified but not stodgy. It's alluring, with flattering lighting and an air of calm that makes you want to linger, rather than wave for the check.

Chef John Villa remains faithful to the simplicity of his source material while elevating it just enough to make it memorable and exciting. A purée of green olives, onion and walnuts, for example, brings a rich, burnished acerbity to grilled sea bream, with a nice, fresh lift provided by lemon confit and parsley. When the Ur-dish needs no repackaging, he stands back, letting flavors shine with a strong, unrefracted light. Steamed cockles, piled high in a bowl, match brine with brawn. They sit in a potent vinho verde broth strongly flavored with chunks of chouriço sausage. Salt cod, or bacalhau, is to Portugal what the potato is to Ireland. The chef whips up a brandade of cod, potato and olive oil gently sparked with piri-piri, shaping it into a cake and frying it until it's crisp outside, creamy inside. A fresh, slightly biting salad of blood oranges, roasted beets and radishes offsets the salt and oil. Suckling pig can be almost cloyingly rich, but Mr. Villa knows how to handle this Portuguese favorite, applying a honey-citrus glaze that leaves the skin crunchier than the surface of a good créme brûlée.

The star dessert at Pico is a heaped plate of cinnamon-dusted puffs of dough meant to be dipped in molten bittersweet chocolate or warm raspberry jam. They're called sonhos, or "beautiful little dreams," and it would be hard to think of a better way to end a meal at this little dream of a restaurant.

Other recommended dishes: Foie gras with spiced quince, seared tuna and mango, saddle of rabbit with smoked bacon, chocolate soufflé cake. **Wine list:** An international list weighted heavily toward Portuguese wines, presented by region, and ports. **Price range:** Lunch: two courses, $26; three courses, $32. Dinner: apps., $10–$15; entrees, $24–$34; desserts, $8 and $9. **Wheelchair access:** Restrooms are downstairs.

Pietro's $$$ ITALIAN/STEAKHOUSE
232 E. 43rd St. (bet. Second & Third Aves.)   (212) 682-9760
Credit cards: All major   Meals: L, D   Closed Sun.

One of New York's great old steakhouses has been serving terrific meat since 1932 along with standard Italian-American fare. Although it has never regained the character it had before it moved to its current home in 1984, the restaurant continues to be extremely reliable, with great Caesar salads and excellent service.

Price range: Apps., from $9; entrees, $19–$32; desserts, from $5.50. **Wheelchair access:** Restrooms not accessible.

Pig Heaven $25 & Under   CHINESE
1540 Second Ave. (near 80th St.)   (212) 744-4333
Credit cards: All major   Meals: L, D

Pig Heaven has a new, sleekly modern look, with a handsome bar, almond-shaped hanging lamps and a table of ceramic and carved decorative pigs. Its terrific Chinese-American food is spiced and presented in ways that please westerners, yet it is fresh and prepared with finesse. The best place to start is the pork selection, particularly roasted Cantonese dishes like suckling pig, strips of juicy meat under a layer of moist fat and wafer-thin, deliciously crisp skin. Most of the supposedly spicy Sichuan dishes here are good, but actually quite mild, and dumplings are excellent. There are other treasures, like moist pieces of hacked chicken in a creamy, slightly sweet sesame sauce and savory, crisp scallion pancakes. Desserts are a bizarre selection, including frozen praline mousse.

Other recommended dishes: White-cooked pork; pork soong; shredded pork with pickled Sichuan vegetables; beef with broccoli; Peking snowball. **Price range:** Appetizers, $2.75–$9.50; entrees, $7.95–$18.95. **Wheelchair access:** One step up at entrance. **Features:** Kid friendly.

Ping's ☆☆ $$ CHINESE

83-02 Queens Blvd., Elmhurst, Queens (718) 396-1238
Credit cards: AE Meals: B, Br, L, D, LN

Ping's looks like hundreds of other Chinese restaurants in New York City. The big square room is casual and brightly lighted, with a bank of aquariums near the back. Not until I approached the fish tanks did I appreciate how extraordinary the food was likely to be: in addition to the usual lobsters and sea bass, there were two types of live shrimp, three kinds of crab, both fresh- and salt-water eels and a number of fish rarely seen swimming around in restaurants. Fried giant prawns filled with roe and served with little sweet-potato dumplings were superb. Dungeness crab, topped with fried garlic, was irresistible, as was a home-style dish of greens with bits of pork and eggs. A perfect ending to the meal is steamed papayas wrapped in paper. For the best options, ask for the translation of the Chinese menu. (*Ruth Reichl*)

Other recommended dishes: Shrimp in shell; snails with special sauce; scallop in shell; shrimp rolls; superior shark's fin soup; congee; dou miao with eggs; stuffed bean curd; steamed or fried whole fish; fried Dungeness crab with garlic; lobster, any style; seafood noodles; steamed papaya; fresh fruit. **Alcohol:** Wine and beer. **Price range:** Apps., $2–$6.95; entrees, from $7.95 (all live seafood is market-priced). **Wheelchair access:** Everything at street level. **Services:** Delivery, takeout.

Ping's Seafood ☆☆ $$ CHINESE

22 Mott St. (bet. Worth & Mosco Sts.) (212) 602-9988
Credit cards: All major Meals: Br, L, D

Anyone who misses the gaudy sign outside gets the message a few steps inside the restaurant. Near the door, a high-rise of stacked fish tanks offers the menu headliners, a stellar cast that includes but is by no means limited to lobsters, eels, scallops, sea bass and shrimp. The seafood in the tanks ends up on your plate, pretty much shortcutting the freshness issue. The preparations are minimal — a ginger-garlic sauce for the lobster, for example, or black bean sauce for the eel — and the results are maximal. Shrimp in the shell, crackling crisp and salty, come to the table piping hot, exhaling a delicate, fragrant steam. You eat the shells, which crunch and then melt. Scallops, quickly steamed, come in three choices of sauce: garlic, black bean or XO, a Hong Kong innovation that's sweet and sour, hot and salty. Ping's XO is superlative, dense with tiny bits of dried shrimp and chilies.

Ping's has two siblings, on Queens Boulevard in Elmhurst (see above) and on East Broadway in Chinatown. The chef and owner, Chung Ping Hui, grew up in Hong Kong and has come back from Queens to concentrate on his newest restaurant, and the personal touch shows. There's a palpable élan in the air. The waiters seem not overjoyed (that would be too pushy and demonstrative), but quietly pleased at the food they're bringing out, setting dishes on the table to a chorus of oohs and aahs. Unusual for a Chinatown restaurant, they dare you to try things. For the adventurous eater, the quirky and often experimental food of Hong Kong always stands as a welcome challenge. One of the house signatures, a rather simple stir-fry of squid cut into long strands woven together with dried fish and crunchy matchsticks of jicama and celery, is a winner.

One of the more appealing rituals at Ping's is winter melon soup. You must call a day ahead, since the melon, which flourishes in the summer despite its name, has to steam for six hours. It comes as a bulging green bowl brimming with what initially seems to be nothing more than a mild-flavored chicken stock. The melon flesh, similar in color and texture to honeydew, is also subtly flavored and slightly sweet. As the ladle dips deeper into the gourd, interesting things begin to emerge — bits of fresh scallop and dried scallop, ham, dried white fungus, shrimp, frog and crab. This seems like the perfect emblem for Ping's, an exotic package with thrilling secrets inside.

Other recommended dishes: Fried bean curd with mashed shrimp; stir-fried pig's stomach and dried squid; abalone. **Wine list**: Minimal. **Price range**: Apps., $2–$5.95; entrees, $6.95–$30; live seafood priced according to market. **Wheelchair access**: Dining room up one flight of stairs; restroom down one flight. **Services**: Takeout.

Pintaile's Pizza $25 & Under   PIZZA

26 E. 91st St. (bet. Fifth & Madison Aves.)   (212) 722-1967
1443 York Ave. (bet. 76th & 77th Sts.)   (212) 717-4990
1577 York Ave. (bet. 83rd & 84th Sts.)   (212) 396-3479
Credit cards: MC/V   Meals: L, D

What could be a better vegetarian meal than pizza? Pintaile's, which has several branches scattered around Manhattan, specializes in pizzas with crisp, paper-thin crusts that are light in calories and heft yet full of flavor. The classic pie is the best, made with sliced plum tomatoes rather than sauce, with mozzarella, Parmesan and herbs. Vegans can order it without the cheese. Other nonmeat choices include wild mushrooms; goat cheese, eggplant, pine nuts and olives, and Greek pizza, made with feta cheese, olives and artichoke hearts.

Price range: $1.35–$14. **Features:** Kid friendly. **Services:** Delivery, takeout.

Pintxos $25 & Under   BASQUE/SPANISH

510 Greenwich St. (at Spring St.)   (212) 343-9923
Credit cards: AE   Meals: L, D   Closed Sun.

Pintxos is one of only two Basque restaurants in Manhattan, but it is also worth knowing about because it's such a sweet, charming place. The food is hearty yet subtle, with delicate flavorings that are surprising in food that seems so straightforward. Basque dishes earn the spotlight, like baby squid served over rice in a sauce of its own ink, or gambas a la plancha, a half dozen big prawns, grilled and served in their shells with heads intact. The all-Spanish wine list is very small but offers perfect choices for this fare.

Other recommended dishes: Squid in its own ink; grilled prawns; sautéed peppers; peppers stuffed with puréed cod; marinated anchovies; grilled lamb chops; sea bass in green sauce; octopus; chorizo. **Alcohol:** Beer and wine. **Price range:** Tapas, $1.25–$2.25; apps., $3–$7; entrees, $7.50–$16. **Wheelchair access:** Steps at entrance and at restroom. **Features:** Kid friendly, Smoking permitted. **Services:** Private parties.

Pio Pio $ PERUVIAN

84-13 Northern Blvd., Jackson Heights, Queens   (718) 426-1010
Credit cards: All major   Meals: L, D, LN

With brick walls, a pressed tin ceiling and big windows, this is an attractive restaurant and a good place for a date. The menu is brief and the specialty is the moist and beautifully spiced roast chicken. Tostones are excellent, as are the pisco cocktails. Ceviche is served only on weekends.

Alcohol: Beer and wine. **Price range:** Combination dinner, $20 for two people. Apps., $3–$14; desserts, $3. **Wheelchair access:** Fully accessible. **Features:** Smoking permitted. **Services:** Takeout, catering, private parties.

Pisces $25 & Under   SEAFOOD

95 Ave. A (at E. 6th St.)
Credit cards: All major

(212) 260-6660
Meals: Br, D, LN

When Pisces opened in 1993, it was one of the first serious restaurants on Avenue A, featuring a hybrid Southwestern-seafood cuisine that was light and delicious and a raw bar that was popular late at night. Those chefs have moved on, and with increased local competition, the crowds are no longer clamoring at Pisces' door, but the food continues to be excellent. The accents are now Asian rather than Southwestern, with dishes like crisp fried oysters with wasabi vinaigrette, grilled mako marinated in soy and lime, and baked bass with Asian vegetables.

Price range: Apps., $4.25–$7.50; entrees, $10–$18; desserts, $3.95-5.50. **Wheelchair access:** Dining room is one step up. **Features:** Smoking permitted, outdoor dining. **Services:** Takeout, private parties.

Pitchoune $25 & Under   BISTRO/FRENCH

226 Third Ave. (at 19th St.)
Credit cards: MC/V

(212) 614-8641
Meals: D

The formula for hip little French restaurants has been followed here: take a small dining room, decorate minimally and offer a short, creative menu of beautifully executed dishes. Though tightly packed, loud and hazy with cigarette smoke, Pitchoune offers fine Provençal dishes. Among the appetizers are a risotto of zucchini, mushrooms, spinach and herbs; roasted sweetbreads with onion marmalade, and steamed mussels in tomato broth. Main dishes include seared codfish with black-olive mashed potatoes; sautéed halibut with a napoleon of stewed onion wrapped in grilled zucchini and squash; steak frites, and three casseroles — sautéed monkfish, grilled quail, coq au vin — that may be ordered for two. Desserts include a rich molten chocolate cake; warm caramelized apple tart, and crème brûlée with vanilla beans. There is also a $19.99 pre-theater menu of appetizer, main course and dessert served until 6:30 P.M.

Price range: Apps., $6–$8; entrees, $16–$18; desserts, $6. **Wheelchair access:** Restrooms not accessible. **Features:** Smoking permitted, outdoor dining. **Services:** Takeout, private parties.

324

P.J. Clarke's $

BAR SNACKS/HAMBURGERS

915 Third Ave. (at 55th St.)
Credit cards: All major

(212) 759-1650
Meals: Br, L, D, LN

Decades ago, big shots used to gather here. Nowadays the place looks the worse for wear, but it still conveys a feeling of old-time New York City, where politicians met in bars and handed out jobs. A burger and a pint of Guinness is cheap when it comes with history.

Price range: Apps., $6–$7; entrees, $12–$25; desserts, $4.50.
Wheelchair access: Fully accessible. **Services:** Takeout, private parties.

The Place $

MEDITERRANEAN

310 W. 4th St. (bet. Bank & W. 12th Sts.)
Credit cards: All major

(212) 924-2711
Meals: L, D

The generic name does not convey the appeal of this cozy spot, where the food is interesting enough to attract a loyal neighborhood clientele but not enough to make it a destination. Wok-seared squid, sprinkled with crunchy peanuts and a sesame dressing, is excellent, while goat cheese and walnut ravioli has an earthy density that is a perfect counterpoint to the sweetness of the beet sauce.

Alcohol: Wine. **Price range:** Apps., $6–$9; entrees, $12–$12; desserts, $5–$8. **Wheelchair access:** Not accessible. **Services:** Catering, private parties.

Plan Eat Thailand $25 & Under THAI

141 N. 7th St., Williamsburg, Brooklyn
Credit cards: Cash only

(718) 599-0516
Meals: L, D, LN

This unusual, much-applauded Thai restaurant has its ups and downs, but more often than not serves spicy, meticulously prepared dishes like ground pork salad, sautéed bean curd and striped bass with crunchy greens. Plan Eat Thailand is often crowded and loud.

Price range: Apps., $2.75–$3.25; entrees, $4.75–$12.95. **Wheelchair access:** Narrow dining room and restroom. **Services:** Takeout.

Po $25 & Under ITALIAN

31 Cornelia St. (near Bleecker St.)
Credit cards: AE   Meals: L, D

(212) 645-2189
Closed Mon.

Eight years ago, before Mario Batali was a celebrity chef, he opened this small, vivacious trattoria. After years of semi-involvement, Mr. Batali has officially cut his ties to Po, and his departure is the best thing that could have happened. Without his full attention, it was able to rest on its association with celebrity. Now, it must stand on its own, and the food is as good as it was years ago. What's more, Po's prices have stayed remarkably reasonable.

The parade of lush flavors begins with the bruschetta offered at the start of each meal, a slice of toasted Italian bread piled high with tender Tuscan white beans, practically oozing with olive oil, sage and garlic. Appetizers are a strong point, with unusual combinations like delicate marinated anchovies draped over a delicious heap of faro, a barleylike grain that tastes of nuts and corn. A plump lump of goat's milk cheese makes a creamy centerpiece for caramelized leaves of endive, joined by sweet roasted red peppers and tart tapenade.

Salads, too, are exceptional, like roasted beets as rich as chocolate, served with artichoke leaves and melted taleggio cheese. Pasta standouts include rigatoni with cauliflower, cooked in white wine until soft, and seasoned with Parmesan, mint, sage and parsley. Spaghetti carbonara is just right, with no intrusion on the flavors of butter, cheese and pancetta.

Try the moist cod, crusted in flavor-enhancing porcini mushrooms, served over mild, mottled scarlet runner beans. A paillard of lamb, as long as a skirt steak, is almost beefy, daubed with aioli and served over sweet grape tomatoes.

Desserts include both a sublimely dense terrine of dark chocolate with a core of rich marzipan and a strangely artless chilled cappuccino with a scoop of coffee gelato tossed in.

Other recommended dishes: Marinated anchovies, steamed clams and mussels, cucumber salad, linguine with clams, grilled pork, quail. **Price range:** Apps., $7–$8; entrees, $12.50–$16. **Wheelchair access:** Small step at entrance; dining room and restroom on one level.

Polanka $25 & Under POLISH

22 Warren St. (near Church St.)   (212) 385-9987
Credit cards: All major   Meals: L, D   Closed Sun.

Polanka is a happy blend of disparate parts, bound together by some of the lightest, most delectable Polish cooking in New York. The path into Polanka looks well worn, a narrow strip of mosaic-tile flooring of a couple of clashing designs that passes several tables and a bar before opening into a wider tiled dining room. A strip of flashing floor lights borders the path to the bar, while the high ceiling and sloping walls are painted bright red and yellow. The effect is that of a woman with bright red hair and harlequin glasses; jaunty but peculiar. Polanka pulses at dinner, with different nights given over to D.J.s spinning salsa, blues, jazz, disco and trance. At lunch, the room is a bit more sedate. The floor lights still flash, but the D.J. gives way to a stereo playing great old Ray Charles hits as local business people dine on pirogies and kielbasa.

Polanka makes its own pirogies, the Polish stuffed dumplings that are often doughy but here are exceedingly light. They are served boiled or fried with a variety of fillings; try the ones with fluffy potatoes, fried for extra flavor and texture, and the meat pirogies, boiled because the ground pork is savory enough. Bigos, Polish sauerkraut stew, is made with amazingly soft, feathery sauerkraut, studded with chunks of pork, beef and smoky kielbasa, served with light, diamond-shaped potato dumplings. Service is extremely attentive, which makes up for occasional communication breakdowns.

Other recommended dishes: Boiled beef with horseradish sauce; cold borscht; Odessa salad; potato pancakes. **Price range:** Apps., $3.95–$9.95; entrees, $6.25–$10.95. **Wheelchair access:** Step at entrance, narrow vestibule and restrooms. **Features:** Smoking permitted. **Services:** Delivery, takeout.

Polistina's $25 & Under   PIZZA
2275 Broadway (near 82nd St.)   (212) 579-2828
Credit cards: All major   Meals: L, D

A pizzeria that's part of the Carmine's, Virgil's and Ollie's empire, Polistina's hallmark is a thin crust that achieves a remarkably consistent crispness and a pleasantly granular texture. Toppings are top-notch. The dining room is an antiseptic mix of booths and tables with an attentive crew. The wine list is well chosen, and the cannoli are terrific.

Alcohol: Beer and wine. **Price range:** Large pizzas, $16; toppings, $2–$3 each. **Wheelchair access:** Fully accessible. **Features:** Kid friendly. **Services:** Delivery, takeout, catering.

Pongal $25 & Under   INDIAN/KOSHER/VEGETARIAN
110 Lexington Ave. (near 27th St.)   (212) 696-9458
Credit cards: All major   Meals: L, D

With its brick wall, spare design and halogen lighting, Pongal looks like a generic neighborhood restaurant. Only the spicy aromas wafting in from the kitchen and the music playing in the background give it away. The delectable vegetarian cuisine of South India is the specialty at Pongal, where the food is kosher as well. The centerpiece dishes are the daunting dosai, huge crepes made of various fermented batters that are stuffed and rolled into cylinders that can stretch two-and-a-half feet. But they are light and delicious, filled with spiced mixtures of potatoes and onions. Pongal also serves a wonderful shrikhand, a dessert made of yogurt custard flavored with nutmeg, cardamom and saffron.

Other recommended dishes: Iddly rasam; iddly sambar; vada rasam; vada sambar; dahi vada; spinach pakoda; paper crepe masala; onion rava masala; mysore masala; utthappam; Pongal special; raita. **Alcohol:** Beer and wine. **Price range:** Apps., $3.95–$8.95; entrees, $7.95–$13.95; desserts, $3.95–$6.95. **Wheelchair access:** Entrance and dining room are on one level; restrooms are narrow. **Features:** Good for business, outdoor dining. **Services:** Delivery, takeout.

Pop ☆ $$$

PAN-ASIAN/BISTRO

127 Fourth Ave. (near 12th St.)
Credit cards: All major

(212) 767-1800
Meals: D

Pop is a bright, happy place with a noncommittal, nonemotive décor and a crowd-pleasing menu that hips and hops from one culinary source to another. The result is toe-tapping food. Who can order "shaved giant clam tartar" with a straight face? Pop feels just right, within fairly narrow limits, like an episode of "Friends." The plates are sprinkled with little surprises — fun, palate-pleasing footnotes like the ingenious slaw of fine-shaved brussels sprouts that comes with a thick, juicy veal chop in quince and pomegranate sauce. The dishes seem to hit the mark about half the time. A timbale of mushrooms and foie gras is nearly tasteless, but a perfectly straightforward wild mushroom soup is earthy and deeply flavored. That giant clam tartar, silly as it sounds, is the best appetizer on the menu, a meaty pile of raw clam chunks, supercharged with a sauce of ginger, chives and pepper oil and topped with crispy lotus-root chips. Whole broiled baby lobster is an all-stops-out production, coated with ginger, scallion and coriander, then doused in a kind of hot and sour soup made of lobster stock infused with seaweed and bonito flakes. Lift the lobster, and all sorts of wonderful ingredients make an appearance: bamboo shoots, shiitake mushrooms, Chinese mustard greens and pillowy tofu dice. For dessert, try the caramel bread pudding, which is simple and winning, and the strawberry cream cake, an all-out assault on the pleasure zones.

Other recommended dishes: Basil shrimp rolls; tuna tartar. **Wine list:** A short, eclectic list, reasonably priced except the Champagnes, with 19 wines by the glass. **Price range:** Apps., $9–$15 ($85 for one ounce of beluga caviar on toast); entrees, $24–$36; desserts, $8–$10. Five-course tasting menu, $75; six courses, $95. **Wheelchair access:** A restroom is available on the dining-room level.

Popover Cafe $ AMERICAN

551 Amsterdam Ave. (bet. 86th & 87th Sts.)   (212) 595-8555
Credit cards: MC/V   Meals: B, Br, L, D

This cutesy cafe, decorated with gingham and stuffed animals,
is hugely popular on the Upper West Side. The fluffy, impressive looking popovers are the specialty, naturally, but even
when lathered with strawberry butter, they are essentially
bland, tasteless hunks of dough. The menu otherwise offers
straightforward, unremarkable American diner food like meatloaf and chicken.

Alcohol: Beer and wine. **Price range:** Sandwiches,
$8.50–$10.25; entrees, $12.50–$19.95; desserts, $3–$5.50.
Wheelchair access: Fully accessible. **Features:** Kid friendly.

Porters New York $$$ NEW AMERICAN

216 Seventh Ave. (near 22nd St.)   (212) 229-2878.
Credit cards: All major   Meals: L, D

The glamour index seems to be inching up in Chelsea, which
has been strangely resistant to fine dining over the years. Neighborhood residents have preferred loose, casual spots and a
sprinkling of scene restaurants, but Porters New York maintains
the neighborhood feel while making a bid for stylishness in
food and décor. At Porters, the look might be called ocean liner
Deco, with floor-to-ceiling wood paneling, narrow curtains and
cylindrical light fixtures. The menu is essentially American,
with a restrained internationalism. The very good, very hefty
crab cakes come with a papaya and coriander salsa, warmed
with a touch of chili oil. The obligatory seafood tartar takes a
slightly unusual turn, wrapped in smoked salmon and surrounded with a coulis of roasted beets.

On one visit, porterhouse steak made a weak showing, but
fish came to the rescue, led by Chilean sea bass on basmati rice
with wilted spinach and mango coulis, It's all or nothing on the
dessert front — either dainty sorbets or big-calorie items like a
dark chocolate mousse cake with Jack Daniel's syrup or Bavarian cream cake served with custard sauce. In this case, its worth
giving in to one's weaknesses.

Other recommended dishes: Miso salmon with soba noodles;
duck foie gras. **Wine list:** Australian, New Zealand, Spain, Italian, France,150 different wines. $28–$400. By the glass, $7–$8.
Price range: Lunch: apps $7–$10; entrees, $14–$24. Dinner:
apps, $7–$13; entrees, $19–$30. **Wheelchair access:** Fully
accessible. **Features:** Smoking at bar. **Services:** Private parties.

Post House $$$$ STEAKHOUSE

8 E. 63rd St. (bet. Park & Madison Aves.)   (212) 935-2888
Credit cards: All major   Meals: L, D

Possibly New York City's most civilized steakhouse. This is the place for people who want their porterhouse with pomp and ceremony. They get it, along with good seafood, good service, high prices and a very good wine list.

Price range: Lunch: apps., $7–$13.50; entrees, $18.50–$34; desserts, $8. Dinner: apps., $7.75–$14.50; entrees, $22.50–$34; desserts, $8. **Features:** Kid friendly, good for business. **Services:** Takeout.

Pravda $$ RUSSIAN

281 Lafayette St. (bet. Prince & Houston Sts.)   (212) 226-4944
Credit cards: All major   Meals: D, LN   Closed Sun.

A subterranean room with interesting décor, comfortable chairs and good air circulation, Pravda is frequented by trendy, good-looking patrons who seem to wear a lot of black. Four main dishes are on the menu — chicken Kiev, beef stroganoff, skewered grilled lamb and a fish of the day — but the most interesting items are the Russian snacks, the several dozen vodkas, eight kinds of martinis (served in individual mini-shakers) and the mainstay: caviar. Spinach and cheese piroshki wrapped in rich, flaky pastry are terrific, as is the borscht: sweet, sour and filled with flavor. The blinis are superb: thin, tangy and worth the splurge on Scottish smoked salmon or sevruga, osetra or beluga caviar. Desserts include pear crepe, warm apple tart with spiced red wine sauce, and strawberry vodka sorbet.

Price range: Apps., $7.50; entrees, $12–$18; desserts, $6. **Wheelchair access:** Fully accessible. **Features:** Smoking permitted. **Services:** Private parties.

Primavera ☆ $$$$ ITALIAN

1578 First Ave. (at 82nd St.)   (212) 861-8608
Credit cards: All major   Meals: D, LN

The wood-paneled room has the patrician air of a private club, but the tables are very close together and the noise sometimes drowns out conversation. The restaurant serves Italian food for people who don't care how high the bill is. Regular customers know that the truffles will be grated with a lavish hand and the bill will be enormous. If you have to ask the price of the specials, you probably don't belong here. And the waiters will certainly let you know it. Still, all the pastas were never less than superb (fettucine was feather-light and fabulous) and some specials were excellent. The ricotta cheesecake was rich, light and buttery. (*Ruth Reichl*)

Other recommended dishes: Pasta specials; calf's liver with onions and white wine; veal piccata; baby lamb chops with balsamic vinegar. **Wine list:** Big names at big prices; the lesser wines are so sloppily listed that they often lack vintage years. **Price range:** Apps., $12.50–$24.50; pastas and risottos, $19.75–$24.50; entrees, $26.50–$39.50; desserts, $9.50–$12.50. **Wheelchair access:** Dining room is on one level, but the restrooms are down a flight of stairs. **Features:** Smoking permitted. **Services:** Private parties.

Prime Burger $ HAMBURGERS

5 E. 51st St. (bet. Fifth & Madison Aves.)   (212) 759-4729
Credit cards: Cash only   Meals: B, L, D

You feel as if you're entering a time warp when you enter Prime Burger. The décor is strictly 1950's and early 60's, and the seating system is quaint: Trays attached to the arms of chairs swing out to allow you to sit down. The burgers are terrific, and the seating makes eating them even more fun. Pies and cakes are first-rate.

Price range: Entrees, $3.25–$5.20; desserts, $2.25–$2.75. **Wheelchair access:** Not accessible. **Features:** Kid friendly. **Services:** Delivery, takeout, catering, private parties.

Provence ☆ $$$ FRENCH

38 Macdougal St. (near Prince St.)   (212) 475-7500
Credit cards: AE, V   Meals: L, D

A charmingly crowded French cafe straight out of the French countryside. But while the atmosphere is charming and romantic, the food feels tired. The wine list, however, is interesting. A few dishes still work well. Mussels gratinées, baked on the half shell and sprinkled with almonds and garlic, were very tasty. Bourride, a pale fish soup, is thickened with aioli; don't miss it. Pot au feu is also a fine example of hearty country cooking, and the bouillabaisse, served only on Fridays, was superb. (*Ruth Reichl, updated by Eric Asimov*)

Other recommended dishes: Pâté; roasted chicken; cod cheeks; pot au feu; steak frites; crème brûlée; marquise au chocolat. **Wine list:** Good, with an emphasis on out-of-the-ordinary French wines from small vineyards. **Price range:** Lunch: apps., $5–$8.50; entrees, $13–$22. Dinner: apps., $5–$9; entrees, $15.50–$26; desserts, $6–$8. Brunch prix-fixe, $19.50. **Wheelchair access:** Everything at street level. **Features:** Romantic, outdoor dining. **Services:** Takeout, catering, private parties.

Prune
$25 & Under

54 E. 1st St. (near First Ave.)
Credit cards: Major   Meals: D

(212) 677-6221.
Closed Mon.

The idiosyncratic name (the chef and owner's childhood nickname) is perfect for this unconventional little place. The menu isn't even divided into conventional categories, though price indicates whether a dish is small, midsize or a main course. You could describe the food as homey, or as faintly European. The food is excellent and unusual, fascinating and even funny, as with the slices of duck breast that taste of smoke, vinegar and black pepper, like pastrami, and are served with a small omelet flavored with rye. Voilá! Pastrami on rye. Appetizers are on the order of bar snacks, like a dish of fresh figs served with Serrano ham and pan-fried almonds. Roasted capon is as conventional a dish as Prune offers, yet it is marvelously juicy. The braised lamb shoulder is a perfect stew with tomatoes and vegetables in an assertive broth. Desserts are terrific, like cornmeal poundcake drenched in a sweet rosemary syrup.

Other recommended dishes: Grilled bacon chop; fried oysters; grilled shrimp with anchovy butter; roasted marrow bones; deviled dark-meat chicken; cod with cinnamon and thyme; pistachio pithivier. **Price range:** Apps., $4–$7; midsize dishes, $8–$10; entrees, $10–$17. Sun. prix fixe, $25. **Wheelchair access:** One step at entrance; restroom is narrow.

Puttanesca
$25 & Under

859 Ninth Ave. (at 56th St.)
Credit cards: AE

(212) 581-4177
Meals: L, D

At Puttanesca, a popular neighborhood trattoria that has expanded, the rule is, the simpler the better. Uncomplicated dishes, made with exceedingly fresh ingredients, include an excellent Caesar salad (I have not found the Caesar salad of my dreams, but Puttanesca's comes close), perfectly grilled vegetables and mussels steamed in white wine and garlic.

Other recommended dishes: Polenta with onions and zucchini; green salad; spaghetti with garlic and olive oil; spinach linguine with shrimp; mushroom fettuccine with seafood; sautéed rabbit; veal piccata; tiramisu; chocolate almond tart. **Price range:** Apps., $3.95–$7.95; entrees, $6.95–$16.95; desserts, $4.95. **Wheelchair access:** Fully accessible. **Features:** Romantic, outdoor dining. **Services:** Delivery, takeout, catering, private parties.

Quatorze Bis $$$

323 E. 79th St. (bet. First & Second Aves.)
Credit cards: All major

BISTRO/FRENCH
(212) 535-1414
Meals: Br, L, D

Although it has not been as funky and appealing since it moved uptown from 14th Street, this remains one of New York City's quintessential bistros, from the zinc bar and pure Parisian looks to the menu of steak frites and fruits de mer.

Price range: Lunch: apps., $8–$10; entrees, $9.95–$29; desserts, $6.50–$8; prix fixe, $16. Dinner: apps., $8–$10; entrees, $18.95–$29; desserts, $6–$8. **Wheelchair access:** Restrooms not accessible. **Features:** Kid friendly.

Queen $$

84 Court St., Brooklyn Heights, Brooklyn
Credit cards: All major

ITALIAN
(718) 596-5955
Meals: L, D

The dining room of this restaurant near the Brooklyn Court-house has a brightly dowdy, Middle American feel to it, but the food is strictly Italian, with huge portions of appetizers like sweet fava beans sautéed in butter and olive oil, with cremini mushrooms and tender baby artichokes, and first-rate pastas and grilled dishes. Main courses are also gargantuan.

Price range: Apps., $7–$11; entrees, $10–$22; desserts, $5.50–$7.75; prix fixe, 11:30 A.M.-5:30 P.M., $22.99. **Wheelchair access:** Fully accessible. **Features:** Good for business, parking available. **Services:** Delivery, takeout, catering, private parties.

Queen of Sheba $25 & Under

650 10th Ave. (at W. 46th St.)
Credit cards: All major

ETHIOPIAN
(212) 397-0610
Meals: L, D

With its brick-and-ocher walls and good-looking crowd, Queen of Sheba is one of the more inviting Ethiopian restaurants in New York. And the food is pretty good, too: beef and lamb stews flavored with a rousing dark-red hot sauce, and wonderful vegetarian dishes seasoned with complex spice blends, all eaten with pieces of injera, a spongy flat bread with the enticing flavor of sourdough.

Quilty's   ☆☆ $$$

177 Prince St. (near Sullivan St.)
Credit cards: All major

NEW AMERICAN
(212) 254-1260
Meals: L, D

Quilty's is small and tastefully decorated in pale cream tones, but it has been designed with such spare elegance that there is nothing to muffle the sound. The cooking is quirky and often exciting, and it deserves a more serene setting. One of my favorite appetizers was a salad of lettuces, fennel and sliced blood oranges tossed with big, warm squares of toasted hominy. There is occasionally one ingredient too many in the dishes, but I love the shiitake, sage and tangerine peel sprinkled on the delicate pappardelle served with braised rabbit. Among the desserts, I particularly like the frozen nougat, a dream of rich pistachios bound in an icy cream. (*Ruth Reichl*)

Other recommended dishes: Oysters in gewürztraminer cream; steamed shrimp with lime and coriander; mushroom fricassée; yellowfin tuna; steak frites; rack of lamb; bittersweet chocolate cake with chestnut ice cream; apple tart for two with black currant coulis; tangerine sorbet. **Wine list:** Small but choice, with offbeat selections. **Price range:** Lunch: apps., $5.50–$8; entrees, $7–$9. Dinner: apps., $8.50–$15.50; entrees, $23–$29; desserts, $8. **Wheelchair access:** Entrance is narrow and up one small step; restrooms are on the same level. **Features:** Outdoor dining. **Services:** Private parties.

Radio Perfecto $$ AMERICAN

190 Ave. B (bet. 11th & 12th Sts.)   (212) 477-3366
Credit cards: Cash only   Meals: Br, D, LN

Radio Perfecto is a boisterous spot that is hoping to capitalize on an up-and-coming area of the East Village. Its formula is moderately priced food and a convivial atmosphere. Rotisserie chicken and crisp fries are served, as well as other bistro dishes. The price is right, the value is good, but the food seems old hat.

Alcohol: Beer and wine. **Price range:** Apps., $4–$7; entrees, $8.95–$13.95; desserts, $5. **Wheelchair access:** Fully accessible. **Features:** Outdoor dining. **Services:** Delivery, takeout, catering, private parties.

Rafina $25 & Under   GREEK/SEAFOOD

1481 York Ave. (near 78th St.)   (212) 327-0950
Credit cards: All major   Meals: D

At this elemental Greek restaurant specializing in seafood, you know exactly what you'll get: simple ingredients, simply prepared. Charcoal-grilled octopus is crunchy outside, tender within, while grilled whole fish like porgy, red snapper and striped bass are enhanced by their simple marinade of olive oil, lemon juice, oregano and garlic, and they arrive moist and delicious. The pleasant, bright room is decorated in blue and white and bedecked in Greek seafood décor.

Other recommended dishes: Assortment of cold spreads; beets with skordalia; loukanika laconias; grilled octopus; swordfish steak; baby lamb chops; beef patties. **Price range:** Apps.,

$3.95–$8.95; entrees, $12.95–$24.95. **Wheelchair access:**
Everything is on one level; restrooms are narrow. **Features:** Kid
friendly, romantic. **Services:** Delivery, takeout, catering, private
parties.

Raga $25 & Under   FRENCH/INDIAN

433 E. 6th St. (bet. Ave. A & First Ave.)   (212) 388-0957
Credit cards: All major   Meals: D

A gulf separates this small, great-looking restaurant from the
block of Indian restaurants on the other side of First Avenue.
Raga is one of the first Indian fusion restaurants, combining
Indian spicing and ingredients with European ingredients and
presentation. The result is largely successful, with dishes like
terrific curried shrimp and filet mignon rubbed with garam
masala, but with occasional clinkers, too.

Other recommended dishes: Seared sea scallops; samosas;
prawns; crab cakes; grilled mahi-mahi; lamb stew; ginger crème
brûlée. **Alcohol:** Beer and wine. **Price range:** Apps., $5–$9;
entrees, $12–$17. **Wheelchair access:** Fully accessible. **Features:** Romantic. **Services:** Private parties.

Rain $25 & Under   PAN-ASIAN

100 W. 82nd St. (near Columbus Ave.)   (212) 501-0776
1059 Third Ave. (bet. 62nd & 63rd Sts.)   (212) 223-3669
Credit cards: All major   Meals: L, D

Rain is one of the most compelling of the recent crop of restaurants specializing in Southeast Asian cuisines. The dining rooms
seem perpetually busy, service is pleasant and helpful, and
much of the food is quite good. Cold vegetarian summer rolls
are wonderfully cooling, while green papaya salad is fiery yet
refreshing. Vietnamese charred beef salad, a spicy, beautifully
presented composition that balances cool herbal and citrus flavors with spicy heat, is top-notch, as is Thai chicken-and-
coconut soup. The best main courses are stir-fried beef in
peanut sauce and stir-fried Chinese eggplant with an excellent
yellow bean sauce.

Other recommended dishes: Grilled salmon; bananas steamed
in coconut milk; chocolate cake. **Price range:** Apps., $6.50–$10;
entrees, $12–$22.50; desserts, $5.50. **Wheelchair access:** Fully
accessible. **Features:** Kid friendly. **Services:** Takeout, catering,
private parties.

Rainbow Grill $$$$ ITALIAN

30 Rockefeller Plaza (49thSt. bet. Sixth & Seventh Aves.)

(212) 632-5100

Credit cards: All major   Meals: Br, L, D.

Dinner at the Rainbow Grill is not so much a meal as a real
estate transaction. You want to occupy 16 square feet in Midtown with an unsurpassed view? Prepare to pay. The old Promenade Bar atop 30 Rockefeller Center is gone, and so is the
elegance and romance. The Cipriani family, which now runs the
former Promenade Bar and the Rainbow Room, have whittled
down the bar operation and expanded the dining area,
installing double rows of tables to make the Rainbow Grill. It's
a little like an airplane. Diners with window seats get the view.
The rest get to watch their fellow diners. Under the new regime,
the Rainbow Room is used primarily for private parties. The
public can dine and dance on either Friday or Saturday night,
depending on the room's irregular schedule. The grill is open
for lunch and dinner seven days a week.

   The food at the Rainbow Grill is Italian, very simple and perfectly acceptable at half the price. The prices are brazen, especially in light of the cheap tables, cafeteria silverware and
drip-dry tablecloths. Like the waiters in their white dinner jackets, the menu strikes a traditional note, with straightforward
appetizers like prosciutto with melon, buffalo mozzarella with
tomatoes, and quickly grilled tuna squares surrounding a bed of
braised fennel. Main courses, too, stick to the middle of the
road, with dishes like veal Milanese, red snapper with tomatoes
and capers, and veal Marsala. The menu also includes a selection of dishes from Harry's Bar in Venice, like fish soup, risotto
alla primavera, calf's liver alla veneziana and carpaccio alla
Cipriani. Perhaps after the sticker shock, management decided
that the customers should not be further agitated by the food.
The view, by the way, is still spectacular.

Price range: Lunch: prix-fixe, $30 and $50, apps., $14–$125;
entrees, $34–$44, desserts, $11–$12; Dinner: prix-fixe: $60,
apps, $15–$125, entrees, $36–$48, desserts, $12–$13. **Wheelchair access:** Fully accessible. **Features:** Smoking at bar, good
view, good for business. **Services:** private parties.

Rao's $$$$ ITALIAN

455 E. 114th St. (at Pleasant Ave.)   (212) 722-6709

Credit cards: Cash only   Meals: D   Closed Sat., Sun.

You'd think that after more than a century of eating at Rao's,
people would get tired of the place, but no. This simple little
Italian restaurant, one of the few remnants of a once bustling
Italian neighborhood, continues to be one of the hardest tables
to get in New York. You can't get in unless you know somebody
or you are very persistent. If you do manage to get a seat, you'll

find old New York Italian food and characters straight out of Damon Runyon. The truth is, the atmosphere is better than the food. Most people will not have the opportunity to taste Rao's lemon chicken, veal chop or linguine with garlic and oil, but Rao's has made it easier for people to live vicariously. You can now purchase the Rao's cookbook and bottles of Rao's sauce, visit the Web site (www.raos.com) and even buy the Rao's CD of music to dine by.

Price range: Avg. meal, $65 per person. **Wheelchair access:** Three steps to dining room. **Features:** Smoking permitted.

Raoul's $$$

180 Prince St. (bet. Sullivan & Thompson Sts.)
Credit cards: All major

BISTRO/FRENCH
(212) 966-3518
Meals: D

This perpetually trendy spot has a genuine neighborhood feel and a hospitable staff serving decent French food. Although the booths are cramped and the prices are high, there is almost always someone famous in the room.

Price range: Apps., $5–$22; entrees, $16–$30; desserts, $6–$10. **Wheelchair access:** Restrooms not accessible. **Features:** Smoking permitted, outdoor dining. **Services:** Private parties.

Red Bar Restaurant ☆ $

339 E. 75th St.
Credit cards: All major

AMERICAN/BISTRO
(212) 472-7577
Meals: D

In a neighborhood aswarm with taco and sushi take-away joints, Red Bar offers warmth, style and good, unpretentious food. It has the casual, confident appeal that Ralph Lauren built a fortune on, an East Coast beach-influenced style that suits the Upper East Side like a navy blazer with gold buttons. Dark hardwood floors, red wainscoting and white skirting boards give a country-house feel. It has limited aims, and a menu that refuses to strain for effect.

Oysters, usually Malpeques, sparkle in their shells. Gravlax, cured at the restaurant, achieves a plush, velvety texture that makes the gravlax at other restaurants seem a little coarse. A buttery slab of foie gras terrine comes with artfully stacked dominoes of brioche toast and a point-counterpoint duo of condiments. Much of the menu is devoted to bistro standards, some presented very straightforwardly, others with a grace note or two. Sweet peppers are added to sauteed skate with lemon and capers, for example, but there's no fussing at all with the pan-roasted chicken with black olive mashed potatoes. Good ingredients make the simpler dishes shine in a modest way and lend support to more adventurous excursions like the rack of lamb covered in a pine nut crust and served with sauteed Swiss chard and buckwheat polenta.

The chef has a bit of a sweet tooth, and it detracts from some otherwise exemplary entrees. And while dessert should be the part of the menu dedicated to sin and indulgence, he makes polite desserts, although a dense frozen parfait made with three chocolates scores an unexpected bull's-eye.

Other recommended dishes: Steamed mussels in in a lemon grass and coconut broth; roast duckling with wild rice and cherries; herb-roasted cod with spinach in mushroom-port reduction. **Wine list:** A well-priced but rather predictable international list of about 90 wines, with 9 wines by the glass. **Price range:** Apps., $7–$14; entrees, $19–$29; desserts, $7–$8. **Wheelchair access:** Two steps up to the entrance; the restrooms are down one flight.

The Red Cat ☆ $$

BISTRO/AMERICAN

227 10th Ave. (near 23rd St.)
Credit cards: All major

(212) 242-1122
Meals: D, LN

A lot of restaurants make a big noise about being warm, welcoming and accessible. The Red Cat, with little ado, manages to be all three. It is stylish, but not snooty, cool but relaxed. The menu reflects the spirit of the place with a lineup of solid, well-executed American bistro dishes, with a little trick or twist on each plate. The sweet-pea risotto cake is served with poached oysters and charred corn and a touch of Champagne and cream. The obligatory steak dish comes with a ragout of roasted shallots, tomatoes and cracked olives. The short dessert list does not disappoint. The carmelized banana tart cannot be improved upon, but it is — by a scoop of praline ice cream. Unfortunately, when the kitchen slips, the food can seem dull and ordinary and the service can drift from casual to spaced out.

Other recommended dishes: Soft-shell crab; toasted orzo; mustard-crusted trout; chocolate truffle cake. **Wine list:** Plenty of $30 bottles, and 16 wines by the glass. **Price range:** Dinner: apps., $7–$14; entrees, $18–$28; desserts, $8. **Wheelchair access:** Not accessible.

Redeye Grill ☆ $$$

NEW AMERICAN

890 Seventh Ave. (at 56th St.)
Credit cards: All major

(212) 541-9000
Meals: Br, L, D, LN

The boisterous room seems as big as Grand Central Terminal and is lively at almost any hour. There's something for everyone on the vast menu, from smoked fish to raw clams, Chinese chicken, pasta, even a hamburger — late into the night. The small grilled lobster, served with a little potato cake and pristine haricots verts, was lovely. The steak of choice here would be the hanger steak, tender slices piled onto a biscuit. The plain

Jane cream-cheese bundt cake looks so modest you know it has to be the best of the desserts. Usually it is. (*Ruth Reichl*)

Other recommended dishes: Popped rock shrimp; red roof maki rolls; Cobb salad; cioppino; Asian-style sea bass; grilled fish; brick-pressed chicken; pastrami-style smoked salmon club sandwich. **Wine list:** Well chosen, interesting and well priced. **Price range:** Lunch: apps., $6.95–$11.95; entrees, $14–$30; desserts, $6.95–$9. Dinner: apps., $6.95–$19; entrees, $18–$35; desserts, $6.95–$7.95. **Wheelchair access:** The main entrance has steps but a side entrance has a ramp; restrooms are at dining room level. **Features:** Kid friendly. **Services:** Takeout, private parties.

Relish $25 & Under AMERICAN/DINER
225 Wythe Ave., Williamsburg, Brooklyn (718) 963-4546
Credit cards: All major Meals: L, D, LN

Diners for the most part are bygone expressions of Americana in the same way egg creams are relics of New York City's past. But in Williamsburg, Brooklyn, the classic diner has been resurrected three times with contemporary menus. (See entries for **Diner** and **Miss Williamsburg Diner.**)

The latest, Relish, is a diner of gleaming, embossed stainless steel. The chef, Joshua Cohen, is clearly at home in the modern vernacular, and his menu is rarely pretentious and often winning. It may be laughable for a diner to serve foie gras, but Mr. Cohen's version is quite good, a small tasty lump over a medley of sweet puréed quince and caramelized banana.

On a less exalted plane are excellent appetizers like beet carpaccio and thick stalks of grilled asparagus topped with roasted porcini mushrooms. One curious appetizer is both a nod to the neighborhood's older Polish population and the most daring item on the menu, if only because a cast-iron constitution may be necessary to withstand it: garlicky breaded kielbasa corn dogs, as cute as four little blimps surrounding a pile of greens. Among the main courses, roast chicken with pecan waffles is a great version of this Harlem classic. Hanger steak comes with a fine smoked tomato sauce that works well with the meat and a cauliflower purée that benefits from the gentlest touch of truffle oil.

The desserts could use a little work. Thin beignets concealing a well of chocolate sauce in the middle are the best bet. Relish offers a wine list that, with few bottles under $25, seems a little expensive. Oddly, and perhaps presaging a revival, Relish also serves a pretty good egg cream.

Other recommended dishes: Artichoke, fried clams, pork chop, fried catfish. **Price range:** Apps., $5.50–$11; entrees, $11–$17. **Wheelchair access:** Steps at entrance, steps to restrooms.

Remi ☆☆ $$$ ITALIAN

145 W. 53rd St. (bet. Sixth & Seventh Aves.)   (212) 581-4242
Credit cards: All major   Meals: L, D

Remi's stunning Gothic interior — a 25-foot-high ceiling, medieval arches and a room-length mural of Venice — and the kitchen's enticing and inventive Northern Italian fare make it easy to understand its continued popularity. The diverse menu includes starters of roast quail, wrapped in bacon; warm shrimp cakes garnished with mixed baby greens and grilled mushrooms, and grilled octopus paired with radicchio, dressed with a sun-dried tomato-and-celery vinaigrette. Enticing pastas and main courses include garganelli blended with Coho salmon in balsamic sauce; veal-and-spinach-filled cannelloni in rosemary sauce; baked red snapper in a seafood broth, and salmon in a horseradish crust, finished with red wine sauce. (*Ruth Reichl*)

Price range: Lunch: apps., $8–$13; entrees, $14–$22; desserts, $7.50. Dinner: apps., $8.50–$14; entrees, $16–$28; desserts, $7.50. **Wheelchair access:** Fully accessible. **Features:** Outdoor dining. **Services:** Delivery, takeout, catering, private parties.

René Pujol $$$ FRENCH

321 W. 51st St. (bet. Eighth & Ninth Aves.)   (212) 246-3023
Credit cards: All major   Meals: L, D   Closed Sun.

Walk in the door and you know instantly that you are in a restaurant run by pros. The classic French restaurant has been feeding the theater district for a very long time and it's still going strong. Unlike its neighbors, which serve bistro food, René Pujol proudly turns out high-end French fare in a civilized atmosphere.

Price range: Lunch: apps., $7–$12; entrees, $17–$27; desserts, $6; three-course prix fixe, $27. Dinner: apps., $7–$12; entrees, $20–$30; desserts, $6.50–$9; three-course prix fixe, $38. **Wheelchair access:** Not accessible. **Services:** Private parties.

Republic $25 & Under   ASIAN/NOODLES

37 Union Sq. W. (near 17th St.)   (212) 627-7172
Credit cards: All major   Meals: L, D, LN

This original, stylishly modern restaurant specializes in Asian noodles. Republic makes no claims to authenticity, but the food is fresh and well conceived, and the ethnic antecedents of most dishes are clear. Among the best noodle choices are slices of grilled beef marinated with galanga and mint and served on rice noodles, thin slices of pork marinated in garlic and soy and served on cold vermicelli, and strips of spicy chicken served in a rich Thai-style broth laced with coconut milk. Food is served quickly, and the backless benches, comfortable enough for a fast meal, don't encourage lingering.

Other recommended dishes: Chicken salad; grilled Japanese eggplant; sashimi salad; seaweed salad; seafood salad; barbecued pork; coconut chicken; vegetables with rice noodles. **Price range:** Apps., $4–$5; entrees, $6–$9; desserts, $3–$4. **Wheelchair access:** Dining area in front and a special bathroom are all on one level. **Features:** Kid friendly, outdoor dining. **Services:** Delivery, takeout, catering, private parties.

Restaurant Above $$$ FUSION/NEW AMERICAN

234 W. 42nd St. (bet. Seventh & Eighth Aves.)   (212) 642-2626
Credit cards: All major   Meals: B, Br, L, D

Larry Forgione is synonymous with American cuisine. But at Restaurant Above, in the Times Square Hilton, he has taken a lurching detour into the land of fusion. Mr. Forgione developed the Asian-influenced menu with his partner and the restaurant's two chefs, but Mr. Forgione leaves some tell-tale traces, as in an appetizer of fried Ipswich clams, a longtime signature but this time Easternized with a tartar sauce sharpened up with yuzu. Soft Asian tacos with barbecued duck and ginger plum sauce straddle at least a couple of continents, but in the world-traveler competition they lag well behind another appetizer, grilled sardine sushi on Himalayan red rice with ginger scallion pesto. Above swings freely, sometimes wildly, and the menu includes a fair share of overproduced duds. For every dish like the lettuce wrap with a lush, sweet-hot filling of spicy spring lamb, there's a garbled offering like tempura-style soft-shell crabs on soba noodles with poblano-cilantro sauce. Are you feeling lucky?

Appetizers are listed as "small plates," and the waiters, insisting that they are too small to stand alone as first courses, encourage multiple tastings. I found many of the small plates to be pretty large. But then the clientele at the Hilton may be used to Midwestern portions. Two desserts are worth saving room for. Ginger shortcake with sautéed peaches, cherries and vanilla cream makes the case that East and West can meet. And the chocolate and espresso ganache tart with macadamia nut brittle is a delirious trip into the heart of darkness. You won't be able to move for several minutes after eating it, so allow extra time.

Wine list: Extensive, primarily New World, featuring over 250 bottles, $35–$1700. By the glass, $7–$24. Chef infuses his own sake. **Price range:** Brunch: $9–$22. Lunch: apps, $5–$11; entrees, $18–26. Dinner: apps, $5–$12; entrees, $24–$29. Tasting platters, $17. **Wheelchair access:** Fully accessible. **Features:** Smoking section. **Services:** Private parties, bar menu.

Rhone $$$ BISTRO/FRENCH
63 Gansevoort St. (bet. Greenwich & Washington Sts.)

(212) 367-8440

Credit cards: All major   Meals: D   Closed Sun.

In the French pecking order, the wines of Bordeaux and Burgundy are king and queen. The Rhone runs a distant third, but Rhone, the wine bar and restaurant in the meatpacking district, reverses the hierarchy. The region's big, spicy reds and succulent whites get top billing, from marquee names like Chateauneuf-du-Pape and Hermitage to lesser fry like Vacqueyras and Lirac. The wine list offers about 150 choices by the bottle and more than 30 by the glass, starting at $6 or $7 for a sturdy Cotes-du-Rhone or Vacqueyras and ascend to $20 for an Hermitage La Sizeranne from Chapoutier.

The food sticks to very simple bistro basics, for the most part, although the lobster truffle salad with smoked bacon and Yukon gold potatoes puts on the dog. Pork belly salad with artichokes and fava beans is more like it, and braised lamb shank with vegetables is a plateful of flavor. Other entrees include fish stew in a saffron rouille and grilled Black Angus steak with ratatouille and a potato pie. The desserts stick to classics like the lemon tart.

Wine list: All wines from the Rhone Valley. **Price range:** Apps, $8–$90; entrees, $24–$28. **Wheelchair access:** Fully accessible. **Features:** Smoking in bar area. **Services:** Private parties.

Rialto $$ NEW AMERICAN
265 Elizabeth St. (bet. Houston & Prince Sts.)   (212) 334-7900
Credit cards: All major   Meals: Br, L, D, LN

Rialto has a lot to like, from the casually appealing dining room to the pleasant garden, but the menu of American food is disappointingly bland, making it a place to visit for drinks and hanging out but not for a special meal.

Price range: Apps., $8–$12; entrees, $15–$18; desserts, $6. **Wheelchair access:** Restrooms not accessible. **Features:** Smoking permitted, outdoor dining. **Services:** Takeout, private parties.

Ribollita $25 & Under   ITALIAN
260 Park Ave. S. (near 21st St.)   (212) 982-0975
Credit cards: Cash only   Meals: L, D, LN

With its mishmash of stone archways and log beams, Ribollita looks the part of a country trattoria. The food, too, offers the sort of rustic, hearty flavors that are so easy to enjoy yet so hard to find, as if its kitchen were filled with loving Italian grandmothers. Tart, oozy stracchino cheese wrapped in a thin slice of ham, drizzled with truffle oil and served over toast, is a wonderfully satisfying dish, while polenta with Gorgonzola is like delicious baby food. The pastas are simple and direct.

Other recommended dishes: Ribollita; crespelle; orecchiette with broccoli rape and sausage; rabbit cacciatore; chicken and sausages; roasted pork loin; roasted trout. **Alcohol:** Beer and wine. **Price range:** Apps., $5–$7.50; entrees, $7.50–$17. **Wheelchair access:** One step in front (ramp provided). **Services:** Takeout, catering, private parties.

Rice $25 & Under   ECLECTIC

227 Mott St. (bet. Spring & Prince Sts.)   (212) 226-5775
Credit cards: Cash only   Meals: L, D, LN

This small 25-seat restaurant and takeout shop serves only rice dishes. The brick-and-metal dining room is as simple and no-frills as the food. Six kinds of rice are served, and you choose toppings to match the rice from a selection that might include sensational black beans in tomato sauce, cool Vietnamese chicken salad and Thai beef salad. Rice has a small selection of beers and an intriguing wine list that specializes in rieslings.

Other recommended dishes: Chicken curry; chicken satay; rice pudding; banana-leaf pastry. **Alcohol:** Beer and wine. **Price range:** Apps., $3.50–$5.50; entrees, $4.50–$11; desserts, $1.50–$3. **Wheelchair access:** Not accessible. **Services:** Delivery, takeout, catering.

Rice 'n' Beans $25 & Under   BRAZILIAN

744 Ninth Ave. (bet. 50th & 51st Sts.)   (212) 265-4444
Credit cards: AE/D   Meals: L, D

Brazilian home cooking is the hearty specialty of this friendly little restaurant, which serves steaming bowls of caldo verde, the wonderfully rich, smoky soup, and huge portions of such dishes as feijoada, a black bean stew heaped with pork, sausage, bacon and beef. Rice 'n' Beans is small and drafty, but the welcome is warm.

Alcohol: Beer and wine. **Price range:** Lunch: apps., $3; entrees, $5.40–$8.75; desserts, $3.75. Dinner: apps., $3; entrees, $8.50–$16.95; desserts, $3.75. **Wheelchair access:** Not accessible. **Services:** Delivery, takeout.

Rinconcito Mexicano $ MEXICAN/TEX-MEX

307 W. 39th St. (bet. Eighth & Ninth Aves.)   (212) 268-1704
Credit cards: All major   Meals: L, D   Closed Sat., Sun.

This tiny restaurant is little more than a smoky aisle in the garment center. English is barely spoken, but the food needs no translation: soft tacos with the freshest and most authentic ingredients, like sautéed pork, calf's tongue, goat, chorizo and pork skin. The aroma of corn rises from the steamed tacos, and the refried beans are still pleasantly grainy.

Alcohol: Beer. **Price range:** Avg. entree, $8; dessert, $3.50. **Wheelchair access:** Not accessible. **Services:** Takeout.

Rinconcito Peruano $25 & Under PERUVIAN

803 Ninth Ave. (at 53rd St.) (212) 333-5685
Credit cards: Cash only Meals: L, D

Don't be deceived by appearances at this humble Peruvian storefront. Dishes like papas a la huancaina, sliced potatoes that are all but invisible under a blanket of cheese sauce, may lack visual appeal, but the combination of the mellow potatoes, served cold, and the unexpectedly spicy sauce is delicious. Lomito al jugo con arroz is a wonderful combination of stir-fried beef served over rice with pickled onions and tomatoes, which add just the right amount of sweetness to offset the spicy brown sauce.

Price range: Apps., $2–$6; entrees, $7–$10; desserts, $1.50–$3.50. **Wheelchair access:** Not accessible. **Features:** Kid friendly. **Services:** Delivery, takeout.

Rio De Janeiro's Churrascaria $$

BRAZILIAN

127 W. 43rd St. (bet. Broadway & Sixth Ave.) (212) 575-0808
Credit cards: All major Meals: L, D, LN

Manhattan's newest Brazilian restaurant has opened in the theater district with the now familiar rodizio formula: a long salad bar and an endless parade of skewered meats enticing you to eat more than you really should. But with Churrascaria Plataforma also in the area, this spot has a lot to live up to.

Price range: Lunch: apps., $8–$10; all-you-can-eat rodizio, $18.99. Dinner: apps., $8–$10; all-you-can-eat rodizio, $27.99; desserts, $4–$7. **Wheelchair access:** Fully accessible. **Services:** Delivery, takeout, catering, private parties.

Riodizio ☆ $$$ BRAZILIAN

417 Lafayette St. (bet. 4th St. & Astor Pl.) (212) 529-1313
Credit cards: All major Meals: D Closed Sun.

Manhattan's first all-you-can-eat Brazilian restaurant: the waiters walk around with skewers filled with meat, poultry and fish, and you simply take what you want. If you have a group, this is a fun place to eat, but it's crowded and noisy. Dishes from the menu are good, too, like pamonhas do norte, a rich steamed pudding made of coconut and kernels of corn. Among the main dishes, I'd recommend the frango de peruana, roast chicken with sweet potatoes and a sort of mango slaw. Desserts are big, sweet and sort of silly. If you have a group this is a fun place to eat, but it's crowded and noisy. (*Ruth Reichl*)

Other recommended dishes: Camarao com coco (pot of shrimp in a sauce of coconut, lima beans, leeks, tomatoes and lime juice); pokeka (steamed salmon in a broth with collard greens, yuca, leeks, mushrooms and chilies). **Wine list:** The moderately priced list has wines from around the world, but they can't compete with the potent caipirinhas. **Price range:** Apps., $6.95–$8.95; entrees, $14.95–$15.95; unlimited food, $35. **Wheelchair access:** Everything on one level but the room is often crowded. **Features:** Kid friendly, outdoor dining. **Services:** Catering, private parties.

Rio Mar Restaurant $ SPANISH
7 Ninth Ave. (at W. 12th St.)   (212) 242-1623
Credit cards: AE   Meals: L, D, LN

A lively old Spanish restaurant with a menu of favorites like sautéed chorizo, shrimp in garlic sauce and seafood in a thick parsley sauce. There is often live Spanish music; if the musicians aren't there, the jukebox is sure to be playing.

Price range: Lunch, $6–$6.50. Dinner: apps., $6; entrees, $13–$14; desserts, $2–$3. **Wheelchair access:** Restrooms not accessible. **Features:** Smoking permitted. **Services:** Takeout, catering.

Risa $25 & Under   PIZZA/ITALIAN
47 E. Houston St. (near Mulberry St.)   (212) 625-1712
Credit cards: All major   Meals: L, D, LN

The best pizzas are quick works of simple art, delicate and carefully composed, with the best ingredients. Risa's pies taste as good as they look. The crust is thin and light, with a gentle, crisp snap. The cheese and tomato pie is impeccably fresh, and other toppings only enhance. Designer pies, like one made with speck (a smoked ham), arugula and mascarpone, are notable for their subtlety.

Beyond pizzas, Risa offers pastas that are fine if not especially unusual. Pappardelle with an excellent Sicilian-style ragu of shredded beef and sausage in a long-cooked tomato sauce is especially satisfying. Appetizers are a weak link, although calamari, lightly breaded and sautéed and served with a pile of greens, was full of flavor and texture. And the waffled flat bread, baked in the pizza oven and flavored with herbs, salt and pepper, is absolutely delicious. The dining room is low-key, with couples and the occasional family at the widely spaced tables with their comfortable leather banquettes.

Other recommended dishes: Arugula and fennel salad, gemelli di salsicca, Tagliolini al pesto, ravioli with bottarga. **Price range:** Apps., $5.50–$9; pizzas, $9–$12; entrees, $8.50–$19.50. **Wheelchair access:** Dining room is one flight up.

River Cafe ☆☆ $$$$

1 Water St., Brooklyn Heights
Credit cards: All major

NEW AMERICAN
(718) 522-5200
Meals: Br, L, D

Is this New York City's most romantic restaurant? With water-side seating, a spectacular view of downtown Manhattan, dim lighting, heaps of flowers and live piano music, it certainly must be. Such a view might have made the food irrelevant, but this has been a seminal restaurant in the annals of new American food. The food is excellent and innovative, and brunch is a special pleasure. So too is the dessert made of chocolate and shaped like the Brooklyn Bridge. (*Ruth Reichl*)

Other recommended dishes: Tuna and salmon tartars with wasabi and fish roe. **Wine list:** Fairly large, wide-ranging and well-selected. **Price range:** Lunch: apps., $10–$22; entrees, $13–$29; desserts, $10-13. Dinner (no a la carte): prix fixe, $70; tasting menu, $90. **Wheelchair access:** Restrooms not accessible. **Features:** Romantic, parking available, smoking permitted. **Services:** Private parties.

Rocking Horse $25 & Under

182 Eighth Ave. (near 19th St.)
Credit cards: All major

MEXICAN
(212) 463-9511
Meals: L, D

In the mid-1990's, when Rocking Horse in Chelsea was known as Rocking Horse Cafe Mexicano, it eliminated Tex-Mex cooking from its menu in favor of what its owners, Roe DiBona and Marvin Beck, called contemporary Mexican cuisine. This was instrumental in changing the way New York looked at Mexican food. Recently, after completing a renovation that expanded and brightened its dining room, the restaurant resurfaced with a new chef and a shortened name. The elimination of "Cafe Mexicano" is telling. While the food is still inspired by Mexico, the careful and complex seasonings, with chilies and other typical Mexican flavorings like avocado leaves, epazote and pumpkin seeds, are now muffled. Instead, the restaurant has adopted a more international style that is much less distinctive.

Price range: Apps., $5.95–$8.95; entrees, $12.95–$20.95; desserts, $5.95. **Wheelchair access:** Restrooms are downstairs. **Services:** Takeout, private parties.

Roettele A.G. $25 & Under

SWISS/GERMAN

126 E. 7th St. (near Ave. A)
Credit cards: All major

(212) 674-4140
Meals: Br, L, D

This unpretentious Swiss restaurant survives quietly in the East
Village as noisier, flashier restaurants come and go. Why?
Dishes like viandes des Grisons, simply thin slices of air-dried
beef, are well prepared, and desserts, like a moist, delicious
linzer torte, are particularly good. Roettele has a pleasant garden, and more kitsch than one might expect in the East Village,
including waitresses in lederhosen, an oompah soundtrack and
Christmas lights year-round.

Other recommended dishes: Smoked trout; pasta with tomatoes; sautéed scallops; poached salmon; chocolate mousse;
Swiss nut torte. **Alcohol:** Beer and wine. **Price range:** Lunch
entrees, $8–$12. Dinner: apps., $5–$8; entrees, $10–$17;
desserts, $5–$7; prix fixe, $12.95. **Wheelchair access:** A couple
of steps down from the street; corridors are narrow. **Features:**
Outdoor dining. **Services:** Takeout, catering, private parties.

Rosa Mexicano (Satisfactory) $

MEXICAN

61 Columbus Ave. (at 62nd St.)
Credit cards: All major

(212) 977-7700
Meals: Br, L, D

Overall, the cooking at Rosa Mexicano is pallid and dull. It's
Latin without passion or flair, but with enough bright spots
along the way to offer hope. The best comes first. When a guacamole cart comes rolling by, hail it. The cart superintendent
will construct a superlative avocado experience, mashing ingredients in the traditional lava-stone molcajete.

It would be tempting, but a mistake, to order ceviche next.
Seafood can wind up either too tough or mushy, and at Rosa
Mexicano it usually does. The one fish success story among the
appetizers is the tacos de pescado, small tortillas filled with
crisp pieces of pan-fried lenguado, or rex sole, topped with a
tangy lemon-jalapeno dressing. For whatever reason, the
kitchen seems most successful with deep, earthy flavors, as in a
small appetizer casserole of sautéed mushrooms, tomatoes and
onions, flavored with garlic, serrano chilies and the pungent
herb epazote. The entire savory mess lies on a moist bed of
cornmeal, a neutral layer with just the right counterbalancing
sweetness. Main courses from the grill are unexceptional, and
the nongrilled entrees make, at most, a mildly pleasing impression. Red snapper Veracruz style, baked in a tomato sauce flavored with capers, poblanos and green olives, has almost
enough personality to linger in the memory. Desserts are very
sweet and very forgettable, except for the delicia de chocolate, a
tall column of velvety mousse resting on a crunchy chocolate
and peanut butter disk.

347

David Rockwell's design for the restaurant has a splashy exuberance that's missing from the food. The colors tingle and vibrate, and he outdoes himself in the restaurant's most memorable feature, a glittering blue tile wall with a thin sheet of water running over its two-story surface.

Other recommended dishes: Tostada de huitlacoche; chicken breast stuffed with huitlacoche; budin azteca. **Wine list:** A nice list of about 50 wines, mostly American and Spanish, with one Mexican cabernet-merlot. There are more than 20 tequilas. **Price range:** Lunch: apps., $6–$11; entrees, $13–$20; desserts, $7. Dinner: apps., $7.50–$18; entrees, $17.50–$28; desserts, $7. **Wheelchair access:** Elevator to second-floor dining room and restrooms.

Rose Water $25 & Under   NEW AMERICAN
787 Union St., Park Slope, Brooklyn   (718) 783-3800
Credit cards: All major   Meals: L, D

Rose Water has provided a jolt of excitement to its residential neighborhood, though its innovative cooking, moderate prices and relaxed ambience would be exciting anywhere. Even the basket of house-made bread is unusual, with corn bread flavored with bittersweet fenugreek; a flat, unleavened bread stuffed with cheese like an Italian piadina; and pita dusted on the inside with paprika and powdered cherry pits. Lovers of esoterica will find much to ponder. Tatsoi, a delicate Asian green, appears in a fine frisee salad with fingerling potatoes and grapes. A brik is a crisp North African turnover filled with ground lamb, caraway and mint and surrounds with a pungent parsley sauce. Rose Water offers a pork chop with a fabulous flavor, crusted on the outside and served with sweet, lemony apple chutney and broccoli rape. A thin-sliced rump steak, flavored with cloves and served over roasted hot and sweet peppers, works very well. The brief wine list includes some intelligent, moderately priced choices, but desserts need work.

Other recommended dishes: Fattoush with chanterelles; striped bass with charmoula; salad with beets, feta and shallots; yogurt with rose hip preserves; cheese plate. **Price range:** Apps., $4.50–$7; entrees, $12.50–$16.50. **Wheelchair access:** Everything is on one level.

Royal Kebab and Curry House $ INDIAN
2701 Broadway (at 103rd St.)   (212) 665-4700
Credit cards: MC/V   Meals: L, D, LN

An unprepossessing corner spot that does a lot of takeout business, Royal is one of the better neighborhood Indian restaurants around. The menu includes the usual tandoori dishes and a few vegetarian specialties as well, but they are all well prepared.

Alcohol: Beer and wine. **Price range:** Apps., $2.25–$5.95; entrees, $5.95–$9.95; desserts, $1.95–$2.50. **Wheelchair access:** Not accessible. **Features:** Kid friendly. **Services:** Delivery, takeout, catering.

Royal Siam $25 & Under   THAI
240 Eighth Ave. (bet. 22nd & 23rd Sts.)   (212) 741-1732
Credit cards: All major   Meals: L, D

Royal Siam's generic décor of mirrored walls, Thai posters and glass-topped tables belie some of the most flavorful and attractively prepared Thai cooking around. Dishes to look for include tom yum koong, or shrimp and mushroom soup in a lemony seafood broth; tod mun pla, fish cakes paired with a bright peanut sauce; and nuur yunk namtok, or grilled steak served sliced on a bed of mixed greens with cucumber and tomato. You can't go wrong with dishes of sautéed squid in a sauce enriched with onion, chili pepper, basil and garlic; shrimp in a spicy sauce of curry and coconut milk, and barbecued chicken redolent of an aromatic blend of Thai herbs and spices.

Other recommended dishes: Steamed dumplings; tofu tod; yum pla muk; soft-shell crabs with basil and chili; koong pad bai kraprow; pad Thai; gluay buach chee. **Alcohol:** Beer and wine. **Price range:** Lunch: apps., $2.95–$4.95; entrees, $5.95–$8.95; desserts, $2.75. Dinner: apps., $3.95–$5.95; entrees, $8.95–$14.95; desserts, $3–$5. **Wheelchair access:** One step up to dining room; restrooms are narrow. **Services:** Delivery, takeout.

Ruben's Empanadas $25 & Under
    LATIN AMERICAN
64 Fulton St. (bet. Gold & Cliff Sts.)   (212) 962-5330
15 Bridge St. (at White & Hall Sts.)   (212) 509-3825
Credit cards: Cash or check only   Meals: L   Closed Sat., Sun.

From Cornish pasties to Jamaican meat patties, meat-filled pastries are found the world over. Empanadas are the South American version. Ruben's, a trim, clean storefront, is just right for grabbing a quick meal. A couple of empanadas, perfectly turned crusts that are crisp around the edges and plump with spicy chicken, savory Argentine sausage or other fillings, make a fine fast lunch.

Price range: Apps., $3–$8.50; entrees, $6.75–$10.50; desserts, $1.25–$3.50. **Wheelchair access:** Fully accessible. **Services:** Delivery, takeout, catering.

Ruby Foo's ☆☆ $$ PAN-ASIAN

2182 Broadway (at 77th St.)   (212) 724-6700
1626 Broadway (at 49th St.)
Credit cards: All major   Meals: Br, L, D, LN

The glitziest restaurant on the Upper West Side has everything
it takes to make the neighborhood happy: fabulous décor, interesting pan-Asian food and the sort of atmosphere that appeals
to families with children as well as singles on the prowl. Not to
mention affordable prices. The menu offers everything from
dim sum to sushi with side trips through Thailand, tailored to
American tastes. With the exception of dim sum, the weakest
link in the menu, the Chinese food is seductive. A memorable
Japanese dish is the miso-glazed black cod. But it is the Southeast Asian dishes that really sing. The green curry chicken has a
fiery coconut-based sauce that is irresistible. Desserts are purely
American and purely wonderful, especially the raspberry-pas-
sion fruit parfait. (*Ruth Reichl*)

Other recommended dishes: Baby back ribs with spicy black
bean sauce; crab cakes with Thai chili sauce; spicy hot and sour
lemongrass soup; green papaya salad; sushi and sashimi combination plate; chicken with cashews and chilies; seven-flavor
beef; crispy whole fish; Chinese eggplant with Thai basil;
chocolate cake. **Wine list:** Well chosen and reasonably priced.
Price range: Apps., $4.95–$8.95; entrees, $9.50–$19.50;
desserts, $5.25–$6.50. **Wheelchair access:** Fully accessible.
Features: Smoking permitted.

Rue des Crepes $25 & Under   CREPES

104 Eighth Ave. (near 15th St.)   (212) 242-9900.
Credit cards: All major   Meals: B, Br, L, D

In recent years, crepes have been associated more with kitschy
French-American restaurants of the 1950's than with French
street food, and Rue des Crepes does little to remedy that. The
little dining room resembles a cobblestone Left Bank street by
way of Disney World, complete with street signs and other con-
trived cues. But it matters little, because the crepes are very
good. Savory combinations, wrapped in soft buckwheat crepes,
include merguez sausage with white beans and garlic and
chewy flank steak with caramelized onions. Especially good are
sweet fillings, like Nutella and banana, and the simple lemon
and butter wrapped in white-flour crepes.

Alcohol: Beer and wine. **Price range:** Brunch: prix fixe, $11.95.
Other meals: entrees, $4–$9. **Wheelchair access:** Small step up
from street. **Services:** Delivery, takeout, catering.

Rumi-Huasi $25 & Under BOLIVIAN/LATIN AMERICAN

44-10 48th Ave. Woodside, Queens (718) 784-5111
Credit cards: Cash only   Meals: L, D, LN   Closed Tues.

If you're having a bad day, this restaurant has a prescription for you: sopa de pollo. The chicken soup speaks for itself, a rich, homey broth with a tender chicken thigh and white rice sprinkled with parsley and cilantro. The restaurant has a way with other soups, like sopa de cordero, a rich lamb broth spiked with cilantro. The rest of the menu is a carnivore's delight, particularly chicharrons, gnarled chunks of fried pork on the bone, basted with a garlic sauce and served with hominy. Weekends offer the widest selection, but unfortunately some of the dishes that sound most interesting are rarely available.

Other recommended dishes: Salteñas; fricase; breaded sirloin steak; pique a lo macho. **Price range:** Apps., $1.95–$9.95; entrees, $7.95–$9.95. **Wheelchair access:** Entrance is narrow; restrooms are downstairs.

Russian Tea Room $$$$ RUSSIAN

150 W. 57th St. (bet. Sixth & Seventh Aves.) (212) 974-2111
Credit cards: All major   Meals: L, D

The Russian Tea Room of old is no more, and the first flush of enthusiasm for the new-model Tea Room seems to have subsided. There may be enough tourists and misty-eyed locals of a certain age to keep the brand name alive, however. The downstairs looks much the same, although much brighter and shinier. But upstairs, the new owner has pulled out the stops: the room is meant to conjure up the glittering halls of the Peterhof Palace and the magic world of Afanasyev's fairy tales. It feels more like a pinball machine.

More than ever, the Russian Tea Room is not about the food. The modern touches often seem peculiar, and the traditional dishes lack soul. It somehow seems symbolic that the black bread, mainstay of the Russian people from time immemorial, is airy and flaccid. Still, some of the charms of Russian cuisine are on display here, notably in a thick, no-holds-barred borscht, packed with braised meats, fragrant with dill (and oddly enough, cilantro) and outfitted with horseradish dumplings. Siberian veal and beef dumplings, or pelmeni, are nicely done, and their light, flavorful chicken broth offers blessed relief from the heaviness of the rest of the menu. The caviar, a fail-safe choice, makes a luscious appetizer, swaddled in buckwheat blini and smothered in sour cream and butter. A new chef since the reopening and a reworked menu offer signs of hope, with menu additions like foie gras ballotine with a napoleon of pickled fruit, and blini stuffed with mushroom fricassee.

Other recommended dishes: Assortment of smoked and marinated fish; farmer's cheesecake. **Wine list:** A substantial, intelligent 250-bottle list with some interesting lesser-known wines to go with the big-ticket Bordeaux and Burgundies. **Price range:** Lunch, apps., $8.95–$14.50; entrees, $19.50–$28.50; desserts, $8.50. Dinner, apps., $8.95–$18.50; entrees, $19.75–$32.50; desserts, $10.50; five-course tasting menu $75 ($95 with caviar). **Wheelchair access:** Enter through door to right of revolving door. An elevator serves all floors.

Ruth's Chris Steak House $$$$ STEAKHOUSE

148 W. 51st St. (bet. Sixth & Seventh Aves.)   (212) 245-9600
Credit cards: All major   Meals: L, D, LN

The New York City branch of this national chain looks so bland you could be in Iowa. The steaks are big and decent, but why would you want to eat in a New Orleans steakhouse when you're in the middle of Manhattan?

Price range: Lunch entrees, $10.95–$33.95. Dinner: apps., $6–$12; entrees, $18.95–$33.95; desserts, $4.25–$7. **Wheelchair access:** Not accessible. **Features:** Kid friendly, good for business. **Services:** Takeout, private parties.

Sabor $25 & Under TAPAS/PAN-LATIN

462 Amsterdam Ave. (near 82nd St.)   (212) 579-2929
Credit cards: All major   Meals: L (weekends), D

The menu here has enough subdivisions to keep a law student busy for hours. Beyond tapas, other sections are devoted, in Spanish and English, to ceviches, empanadas, cheeses, charcuterie, skewers, salads, a raw bar, side dishes and tapas grandes, mercifully translated as "main courses."

Certain things stand out among the main courses, like a fine, beefy grilled skirt steak served with ajilimujili, a purée of fresh pepper, garlic and lime juice, over coarse, nutty mashed malanga. Other main courses are even more impressive, like a braised lamb shank, served off the bone over mildly sweet mashed boniato with a luscious red-wine sauce. Sabor's paella takes liberties but is delicious and beautifully presented. Also try the delightful tapas, like airy little smoked chicken croquettes with aioli and a crisp lobster quesadilla topped with guacamole. The small wine list includes some good inexpensive choices. The small dessert selection has one standout, a creamy dulce de leche cheesecake that tastes like pure caramel.

Other recommended dishes: Sirloin steak, grilled tuna, boquerones, grilled lamb sausages, tuna ceviche, Andalusian Caesar salad. **Price range:** Tapas, $4.50–$9.95; entrees, $10.95–$15.95. **Wheelchair access:** Big step at entrance; dining room and restrooms on one level.

Saigon Grill $25 & Under VIETNAMESE

2381 Broadway (at 87th St.) (212) 875-9072
1700 Second Ave. (at 88th St.) (212) 996-4600
Credit cards: All major Meals: L, D

While Saigon Grill's business is mostly takeout, it is also a pleasant place to stay and eat, with some of the best Vietnamese food on the Upper West Side. Noodle dishes and soups like pho bo, the North Vietnamese standard of oxtail broth with paper-thin slices of beef, are excellent, as is chao tom, the snack of grilled shrimp paste wrapped around sugar cane that is so often a throwaway at Vietnamese restaurants. A new branch recently opened on the Upper East Side — a bright, plain dining room also serving top-flight Vietnamese fare.

Alcohol: Beer. **Price range:** Apps., $3.95–$5.95; entrees, $6.50–$13.95; desserts, $2. **Wheelchair access:** Not accessible. **Features:** Kid friendly. **Services:** Delivery, takeout, catering.

Salaam Bombay ☆☆ $$ INDIAN

317 Greenwich St. (near Duane St.) (212) 226-9400
Credit cards: All major Meals: L, D

Salaam Bombay looks much like every other upscale Indian restaurant in New York City, large and pleasant. But it departs from tradition and showcases the richness of regional Indian cooking. At lunch there's a big, affordable buffet. At dinner an interesting assortment of vegetable dishes is where this kitchen really shines. Try ringna bataka nu shaak, a Gujarati eggplant and potato dish cooked with curry leaves and lots of spices, and kadhai jhinge, shrimp stir-fried with tomatoes, onions and lots of fresh and fragrant spices. For dessert, shrikhand, a dreamy, custardlike dessert, has a mysterious flavor that imparts a certain sense of wonder.

Other recommended dishes: Dahi batata poori (small, crisp shells filled with diced potatoes, yogurt and tamarind sauce); khaman dhokla (lentil and yogurt steamed cakes); kachori (lentil-filled dumplings); tandoori dishes; murg chettinad (chicken in yogurt sauce with black pepper); murg methi (chicken with fenugreek leaves); undhiyu (sweet potato, beans, eggplant, spicy lentil dumplings and fresh lentils); roomali roti (crepelike "handkerchief bread"). **Price range:** Lunch buffet, $11.95. Lunch and dinner: apps., $4.95–$10.95; entrees, $9.95–$19.95; desserts, $4.95–$7.95. **Wheelchair access:** The dining area is up a few small stairs. **Features:** Outdoor dining. **Services:** Delivery, takeout, catering, private parties.

Salam Cafe $25 & Under   MIDDLE EASTERN

104 W. 13th St. (bet. Sixth & Seventh Aves.)   (212) 741-0277
Credit cards: All major   Meals: D

Syrian dishes are the specialty, but the menu ranges as far as
Morocco and India. Top-notch appetizers include foule, the
Egyptian bean salad, fragrant with cumin and garlic. While you
could make a meal of the appetizers, you would miss excellent
main courses. Salam's short wine list surprisingly includes
some fine values in first-growth Bordeaux.

Other recommended dishes: Baba gannouj; hummus; yogurt
with mint and cucumber; Palestinian air-dried beef; meat pie;
Syrian sausages; Moroccan chicken; lamb kebabs; chicken ouzi;
baklava. **Price range:** Apps., $4–$8; entrees, $12- $20; desserts,
$3.75–$5.75. **Wheelchair access:** Two steps at entrance narrow
passage to restrooms. **Features:** Smoking permitted, outdoor
dining. **Services:** Delivery, takeout, catering, private parties.

Sal Anthony's Restaurant $$ ITALIAN

55 Irving Pl. (bet. 17th & 18th Sts.)   (212) 982-9030
Credit cards: All major   Meals: Br, L, D

An old-style Italian restaurant that has been on Irving Place
almost forever. The ambiance is friendly and the food is big,
robust and not too expensive.

Price range: Lunch prix fixe, $10.95. Dinner: avg. a la carte,
$26 per person; prix fixe, $18.95. **Wheelchair access:**
Restrooms not accessible. **Features:** Outdoor dining. **Services:**
Delivery, takeout, catering, private parties.

The Saloon $$ NEW AMERICAN

1920 Broadway (at 64th St.)   (212) 874-1500
Credit cards: All major   Meals: Br, L, D, LN

The cavernous, noisy Saloon is still going strong, serving
straightforward American food that is acceptable primarily for
the restaurant's convenience to Lincoln Center.

Price range: Apps., $6–$10; entrees, $10–$20; desserts, $5.50;
prix-fixe brunch, $12.50. **Wheelchair access:** Restrooms not
accessible. **Features:** Kid friendly, outdoor dining. **Services:**
Takeout, private parties.

Sal's and Carmine's Pizza $ PIZZA

2671 Broadway (bet. 101st & 102nd Sts.)   (212) 663-7651
Credit cards: Cash only   Meals: L, D

Unlike so many other neighborhood pizzerias, you know who is
making the pizza at Sal's and Carmine's. One of the two is

always there shaping the pies and spreading the sauce. They use the freshest mozzarella, and the difference is apparent when you taste the creaminess, so different from the rubbery sensation of so many pizzas. Sausage is also excellent. Sal's and Carmine's refuses to let a pie out of their sight until you take possession of it. Delivery is out of the question.

Price range: Pizzas, $10.50–$14 (plus $3 for additional toppings). **Wheelchair access:** Not accessible. **Features:** Kid friendly. **Services:** Takeout.

Samalita's Tortilla Factory $25 & Under
MEXICAN/TEX-MEX

1429 Third Ave. (at 81st St.)   (212) 737-5070
Credit cards: MC/V or check   Meals: Br, L, D

Done up in pastel yellows and blues, Samalita's has a self-conscious Southwestern look. The Mexican side of the menu is better, with the spicy Mexico City tacos as the top choice.

Other recommended dishes: Veracruz tacos; burritos; chips; guacamole. **Alcohol:** Beer and wine. **Price range:** Apps., $2.75–$5.75; entrees, $3.25–$12.95. **Wheelchair access:** Fully accessible. **Services:** Delivery, takeout, catering, private parties.

Sammy's Roumanian $$$ STEAKHOUSE/JEWISH
157 Chrystie St. (bet. Delancey & Houston Sts.)   (212) 673-0330
Credit cards: All major   Meals: D

The kitschy Borscht Belt party atmosphere, the enormous garlic-rubbed beef tenderloins and the bowls of schmaltz — rendered chicken fat — on every table make Sammy's a nostalgic paean to the days before cholesterol consciousness. The fluorescent lights and the rec room décor have a certain charm, but Sammy's real appeal is in the impossibly heavy food laden with schmaltz, and gribeness, the cracklings left over from making schmaltz, which are often mixed with caramelized onions. Beyond the tenderloin, Sammy's specializes in fried kreplach and stuffed cabbage. Vodka may be the only beverage powerful enough to wash this food down.

Price range: Apps., $5.95–$11.95; entrees, $12.95–$28.95; desserts, $3.95–$4.95. **Wheelchair access:** Dining room is three steps down. **Services:** Catering, private parties.

Sandobe Sushi $$ SUSHI
330 E. 11th St. (bet. First & Second Aves.)   (212) 780-0328
Credit cards: Cash only   Meals: D, LN

The East Village is thick with sushi restaurants and Sandobe is one of the more unusual ones. Sushi rolls are the specialty, with all sorts of creative combinations that sound like overkill but are quite good. Try the Justin roll — salmon, shrimp, eel and crabmeat — or the Erik roll — yellowtail, tuna, salmon and crabmeat. Ordinary sushi and sashimi are not as good. Be prepared to wait. Sandobe is usually crowded.

Alcohol: Beer and wine. **Price range:** Apps., $2.50–$4; sushi dinner, $20–$50. **Wheelchair access:** Not accessible. **Services:** Private parties.

San Domenico ☆ ☆ ☆ $$$$ ITALIAN
240 Central Park S. (near Broadway)   (212) 265-5959
Credit cards: All major   Meals: L, D

San Domenico is dignified and comfortable. Menu descriptions are long and complicated. The wine list has the weight of the Manhattan phone book, service is sedate and the food is fabulous. It is one of a handful of American restaurants trying to showcase the cooking of the aristocratic northern Italian kitchen, the cuisine known as alta cucina. Give this staid restaurant a chance and it will manage to capture your heart.

The restaurant's signature dish is uovo in ravioli con burro nocciola tartufato: a single large puff filled with ricotta and spinach perfumed with truffle butter. Snuggled inside is an egg that spurts golden yolk onto the plate as you begin to eat. Garganelli, hand-rolled penne, come tossed with caviar, chives and asparagus tips. But the kitchen does not need luxury ingredients to show its stuff. The simple spaghetti alla chitarra, in a tomato and basil sauce, is like no spaghetti you've ever tasted. Tripe is cooked twice: first poached, then braised with tomatoes and chickpeas. Finally it is tossed with parsley and cheese. The result bears no resemblance to anything faintly funky.

You could come to San Domenico and treat it like a trattoria, choosing simple dishes and enjoying the care with which they are cooked. Just as you could forgo reading one of the city's finest Italian wine lists and limit yourself to the first three pages, which offer suggestions for the various dishes. You could eat a hasty meal and leave satisfied, but you would be missing the best the restaurant has to offer. At the end of a long, slow meal, wind down with an espresso-colored cake made of chocolate, cornmeal and hazelnuts, or a plate of Gorgonzola with nuts and honey. (*Ruth Reichl*)

Wine list: Enormous list, best on Italian wines. **Price range:** Lunch prix fixe, $19.99. Dinner: apps., $9.50–$19.50; entrees, $26.50–$32.50; three-course prix fixe, $32.50; tasting menu, $60. **Wheelchair access:** Restrooms not accessible. **Services:** Catering, private parties.

Sandwiches $25 & Under   AMERICAN

60 Greenwich Ave. (near Seventh Ave. S.)   (212) 255-0930
Credit cards: Cash only   Meals: L

You get nonstop patter with your sandwiches at this spare little shop where the brothers Rodolpho and P. J. Ramirez are as entertaining as their sandwiches are good. As you wait in line by the counter, you have to endure a lot of bad jokes, but a bad sandwich is unlikely. These are not sandwiches of the new, designer variety; they are traditional and tasty. Meatloaf and chicken salad are both wonderful. And the fresh lemonade is great.

Alcohol: Beer and wine. **Price range:** Avg. sandwich, $6. **Wheelchair access:** Restrooms not accessible. **Services:** Delivery, takeout, catering.

San Pietro $$$ ITALIAN

18 E. 54th St. (bet. Fifth & Madison Aves.)   (212) 753-9015
Credit cards: All major   Meals: L, D   Closed Sun.

Expensive and uneven Italian food for well-heeled businessmen. San Pietro clearly can produce good food: the many regular customers seem to know how to navigate the menu and each time I've been at the restaurant the food on all the other tables has looked better than mine. The fish are usually excellent and there are some very fine pastas. Nobody bothers to pretend that new customers are favored patrons, and the service is often perfunctory.

Wine list: The Italian and American wines include many excellent bottles at fair prices. **Price range:** Lunch: apps., $10–$15; entrees, $18–$26; desserts, $9. Dinner: apps., $12–$18; entrees, $19–$32; desserts, $9. **Wheelchair access:** Fully accessible. **Features:** Good for business, outdoor dining. **Services:** Takeout, private parties.

Sapphire $$ INDIAN

1845 Broadway (at 63rd St.)   (212) 245-4444
Credit cards: All major   Meals: L, D

Sapphire may not be the last word in Indian cuisine, but it is good enough and good-looking enough to advance the cause. The extensive menu includes the usual hit parade of samosas, curries, tandoori treats and even mulligatawny soup. But it also includes some sleepers like chutney idli, a small cake of steamed lentil and rice flour topped with a coconut curry. Spicier and just as good is kadhi pakoda, another appetizer. Balls of cumin-spiced lentil flour are deep-fried and served with a mustard-flavor yogurt sauce. The lamb may be tough in dishes like achari lamb and lamb xacutti (pronounced ESH-uh-coo-tee). Chicken, on the other hand, is unfailingly moist, tender and flavorful, especially the chicken Nizami, a masala dish with cashews, coconut and sesame seeds. Two breads deserve special mention, the nan stuffed with garlic and kulcha, another soft flatbread baked in the tandoori oven, this one stuffed with crab meat.

Sapphire has a pleasingly understated opulence, with ornately carved Mogul-period wooden doors and windows, brought over from Rajasthan, and embroidered panels of Jodhpur silk hung from the ceiling like small banners.

Wine list: Wines from Morocco, Argentina, Australia, France and Italy, starting at $28. **Price range:** Lunch: buffet, $11.95. Dinner: apps, $4.95–10.95; entrees, $11.95–$20. **Wheelchair access:** Fully accessible. **Features:** Smoking in lounge. **Services:** Delivery, take out.

Sapori d'Ischia $25 & Under   ITALIAN

55-15 37th Ave., Woodside, Queens   (718) 446-1500
Credit cards: Cash only   Meals: D

By day, Sapori d'Ischia is a bright and thriving Italian specialty market. But a transformation occurs around 5 P.M. The trays of hot food are put away, along with the display of pizza by the slice. Candles are lighted, soft music begins to play and a waiter takes over, welcoming guests, handing out menus and offering wine. Almost every table has a "reserved" sign on it. If the transformation seems unlikely, so is the site, an industrial block where the restaurant is barely discernible among the garages and auto glass shops that line this part of 37th Avenue. The kitchen turns out fine individual pizzas, with thin, crisp, beautifully smooth crusts, but the small menu has other excellent choices, like budino di carciofi, or artichoke puree, an Ischian specialty that is soft as flan and set atop a luscious combination of grilled pancetta and peppers.

Another excellent appetizer is two grilled portobello mushrooms sandwiching oven-dried tomatoes, grilled eggplant, caramelized onions and mozzarella, a savory fusion of earthy and sweet. If the restaurant has an obvious weakness, it is seafood. Redemption comes with fettuccine al'Antonio, an extraordinarily rich dish of fresh pasta with cream and prosciutto prepared at the table in a bowl carved out of a wheel of parmesan. The waiter shaves some of the cheese, which melts into the creamy pasta, and adds a blessedly small bit of white truffle oil, which amplifies the richness without being obtrusive. Sapori offers only a few wines, including a pedestrian Chianti and an inky negroamaro.

Other recommended dishes: Polenta with mushrooms and robiola, rigatoni with eggplant and ricotta, steak. **Price range:** Apps., $7.50–$8; entrees, $7.50–$14. **Wheelchair access:** Everything is on one level.

Sarabeth's $$ AMERICAN
945 Madison Ave. (at 75th St.)   (212) 570-3670
1295 Madison Ave. (at 92nd St.)   (212) 410-7335
423 Amsterdam Ave. (at 80th St.)   (212) 496-6280
Credit cards: All major   Meals: B, Br, L, D

These nostalgic, floral sanctuaries from modern life have their
good days and their bad days. At brunch, for example, you are
almost as likely to receive an undercooked waffle or pancakes
that are still batter in the center as you are a fully cooked
meal. Too bad, because the grainy cornmeal waffles, served
with warm syrup and compote, are delicious, as are the
desserts. Pastries are excellent. Don't forget to buy some jam.

Price range: Avg. $17 per person. **Wheelchair access:** Fully acces-
sible. **Features:** Kid friendly. **Services:** Catering, private parties.

Sardi's $$$ AMERICAN
234 W. 44th St. (bet. Broadway & Eighth Ave.)   (212) 221-8440
Credit cards: All major   Meals: L, D, LN

It's next door to *The New York Times*, and even we rarely go
there. What used to be the quintessential theater district restaurant is now a sad example of faded glory; if you have great
memories of the place, don't spoil them.

Price range: Lunch: apps., $6–$11; entrees, $12–$28; desserts,
$4–$7. Dinner: apps., $5.50–$12; entrees, $18–$32; desserts,
$6–$9; prix fixe, $43.50. **Wheelchair access:** Fully accessible.
Services: Private parties.

Saul $25 & Under NEW AMERICAN
140 Smith St., Boerum Hill, Brooklyn   (718) 935-9844
Credit cards: MC/V   Meals: Br, D

The small menu in this sweet little brick storefront offers
strong, clear flavors, bolstered by background harmonies that
augment without overshadowing. Velvety butternut squash
soup is luscious and smooth, with crisp pumpkin seeds adrift
around a soft island of luxurious squash flan. Duck confit is
expertly made, framed by earthy black lentils, and big enough
for a main course, justifying a splurge on the sumptuous
sautéed foie gras. The main courses seem familiar—salmon,
chicken, pork loin—but they are beautifully handled and surprisingly good. Desserts are wonderful, like lush baked Alaska
with a chocolate cookie crust.

Other recommended dishes: Bacon and onion tart; roast
chicken; sautéed salmon; roast pork loin; seared scallops;
lemon custard cake; black plum tart. **Price range:** Apps.,
$5–$11; main courses, $15–$20. **Wheelchair access:** One step
at entrance

Savann $25 & Under   BISTRO/FRENCH

414 Amsterdam Ave. (near 80th St.)   (212) 580-0202
Credit cards: All major   Meals: Br, D

Casual and cozy in atmosphere, Savann attracts a loyal crowd
of neighborhood patrons for its pleasing and moderately priced
contemporary fare. When it opened a few years ago, it was like
a dream come true for Upper West Siders who had yearned for
a simple, reasonably priced restaurant that served not-so-simple
contemporary bistro food. Savann was just such a place, with
ambitious yet delicious dishes like roasted pumpkin soup with
olive oil, perfectly cooked wild mushroom risotto, and grilled
duck breast with polenta. But leadership changes have shaken
up the kitchen and the front of the house, and Savann is not all
it was when it opened.

Alcohol: Beer and wine. **Price range:** Brunch, $7–$14. Dinner:
apps., $5- $10; entrees, $14–$23; desserts, $7. **Wheelchair
access:** Fully accessible. **Features:** Romantic. **Services:** Takeout,
catering, private parties.

Savore $$ ITALIAN

200 Spring St. (at Sullivan St.)   (212) 431-1212
Credit cards: All major   Meals: L, D, LN

The room is wonderful, with the cool elegance of a real Tuscan
trattoria. The food is mostly authentic Tuscan fare, and mostly
very good. Antipasti include smoked goose carpaccio, a shrimp
dish of the day and a plate of Tuscan charcuterie with
bruschetta. The pastas are particularly recommended. Among
the main dishes are breast of duck in pomegranate sauce;
imported fish from the Mediterranean, and wild boar in the
style of the Maremma marshlands, which are famous for game.

Price range: Lunch: apps., $8–$12; entrees, $14–$18; desserts,
$6. Dinner: apps., $8–$14; entrees, $14–$22; desserts, $6.
Wheelchair access: Fully accessible. **Features:** Outdoor dining.
Services: Catering, private parties.

Sa Woy $$ THAI

1479 First Ave. (at 77th St.)   (212) 744-6374
Credit cards: All major   Meals: L, D

A dim, attractive room, with deep red walls and expensive Thai
food, much of which is classic "Royal" Thai cooking: ornate but
not spicy. Appetizers include Thai beggar's pouch, fat bundles
filled with shrimp, chicken and a number of very aromatic
herbs. Seafood salad, a mixture of shrimp, squid, mussels and
scallops in a marinade of fish sauce, mint and lime juice, has
good, clear flavors. Expect slow service and high prices.

Price range: Apps., $6.95–$7.95; entrees, $12.95–$24.95; desserts, $5.95–$7.95. **Wheelchair access:** Fully accessible. **Services:** Delivery, takeout, catering, private parties.

Sazerac House $

533 Hudson St. (at Charles St.)
Credit cards: All major

CAJUN/CREOLE
(212) 989-0313
Meals: Br, L, D

This dark, venerable restaurant was one of the first in New York to offer New Orleans food. Time has passed the Cajun fad by, and Sazerac with it. What you get now are big portions for moderate prices, but the food isn't all that interesting. It's best for neighborhood regulars.

Price range: Brunch, $4.95–$16.95. Lunch, $6.95–$12.95. Dinner: apps., $4.95–$8.95; entrees, $8.95–$17.95; desserts, $5.50. **Wheelchair access:** Restrooms not accessible. **Services:** Delivery, takeout, private parties.

Scalini Fedeli ☆ $$

165 Duane St. (at Hudson St.)
Credit cards: All major

ITALIAN
(212) 528-0400.
Meals: L, D

Scalini Fedeli means "steps of faith," and in this case, it's a leap. The original Scalini Fedeli is one of New Jersey's most highly regarded and popular dining spots. This new location has no edge. What it has, instead, is old-fashioned grace. The dining room, with its well-spaced tables and conservative country-Italian décor, is as soothing as a massage. The food is pleasing, for the most part, but it rarely takes flight, and when it does, the dish is likely to be disarmingly simple.

The pappardelle with a sauce of Scottish hare and venison is a small feast of gloriously rich, dark meats finished off with cream and truffles. The main courses are satisfying, decorous and rather unassuming. A good-size fillet of roasted Chilean sea bass, for example, finds an ideal matchup in a sauce of sun-dried tomatoes and Sicilian and Greek olives. Saddle of rabbit, swaddled in pancetta and served with a black olive sauce, makes a simple, pleasing entree, and the thick, brick-red venison chop is just the ticket for some of the more serious Barolos, brunellos and amarones on the wine list. For dessert, the panna cotta takes a back seat to the dense chocolate tart, and to the clever miniature cannoli, painted with chocolate and filled with espresso-flavored mascarpone cream.

Food isn't everything. That may sound dismissive, but it isn't. There are dozens of intangibles that go into a meal and contribute to a diner's sense of satisfaction. Scalini Fedeli rates very high on most of these.

Other recommended dishes: Red snapper with lemon and chive oil. **Wine list:** Some 225 French, Italian and American wines; 22 half bottles. **Price range:** Lunch: apps., $7–$10; entrees, $17–$23; desserts, $7. Dinner: three courses, $60. **Wheelchair access:** Two steps up to entrance. Restrooms are downstairs.

Screening Room ☆☆　　$$$　　NEW AMERICAN

54 Varick St. (below Canal St.)　　(212) 334-2100
Credit cards: All major　　Meals: Br, L, D

It's a bar. It's a restaurant. It's a movie theater. It is also dark, casual and slightly scruffy. The slightly funky bar serves appealing snacks like lobster rolls, onion rings and Philadelphia cheese steaks. The restaurant offers serious American food on the order of grilled duck and spectacular desserts. The best appetizer is the pan-fried artichokes, served on lemony greens topped with shavings of Parmesan cheese. The simplest dishes are the most impressive: roast chicken with potatoes and escarole; a fine piece of grilled tuna; cedar-planked salmon with chard, tomatoes and parsley purée. The pastry chef does not have a loser on the list. My favorite dessert is lemon icebox cake, a riff on lemon meringue pie. The toasted angel food cake is terrific too. (*Ruth Reichl*)

Other recommended dishes: Chopped salad; macaroni with spinach, leeks, tomatoes and Parmesan; hamburger; pan-roasted quail; roasted pear and sour cherry crisp; macadamia hot fudge sundae. **Wine list:** Appealingly wide range of prices and styles, though none below $20. **Price range:** Lounge menu, $5–$13. Brunch, $5–$17. Dinner: apps., $7–$10; entrees, $13–$22; desserts, $6–$8. **Wheelchair access:** Everything at street level. **Features:** Smoking permitted. **Services:** Takeout, private parties.

Sea Grill ☆☆　　$$$　　SEAFOOD

19 W. 49th St., Rockefeller Center.　　(212) 332-7610
Credit cards: All major　　Meals: L, D　　Closed Sun.

A refiguring of the Rockefeller Center concourse has made the Sea Grill smaller, and a redesign by Adam Tihany has given it a cooler, cleaner and snappier appearance. But the main draw remains unchanged. Look out the windows at night and you see the golden figure of Prometheus, splashed by colored jets of water. In winter, skaters circle the ice. In warm weather, the skating rink becomes an outdoor extension of the restaurant, with canvas umbrellas and potted shrubs.

Like the new design, the Sea Grill's menu aims at a new target: casual luxury. Much of the menu, with trimmed-back prices, has a brasserie feel to it, with heaping, almost alarmingly abundant shellfish platters, and a changing daily menu of day-boat fish that are simply grilled, sautéed or seared, Mediterranean style, a la plancha, on a thin steel grill, and served with wilted arugula and a lobster coral emulsion. There's a fresh new breeze blowing over the rest of the menu as well, with the accent on vibrant flavors and simple preparations. Fat, rosy mussels come in a subtly spiced Thai curry broth. A translucent sheet of striped sea bass carpaccio needs no more than a sprinkling of baby cilantro and a slick of olive oil and lime juice to come alive. Edward Brown, the longtime executive chef here, made a renowned crab cake at the old Sea Grill; it returns, a lumpy-looking thing, more ball than patty, displaying the rough-hewn virtues that distinguish a real crab cake from a thousand prettified pretenders.

For dessert, a "palette of sorbets" comes on a shiny silver platter shaped like a painter's palette, with a half dozen tiny ice-cream cones placed in the holes. Each cone holds a Kodachrome-colored scoop of sorbet the size of a marble and a bonus chunk of chocolate in the base. As a tourist pleaser, this one is hard to beat, but it gets serious competition from the mile-high chocolate parfait, served on a giant plate with a silhouette of the New York skyline executed in powdered cocoa.

Other recommended dishes: Salmon belly cured in sea salt; salmon with pea purée; honey vanilla panna cotta. **Wine list:** About 115 mostly French and American wines, organized by taste characteristics; 18 wines are available by the half-bottle, 14 by the glass. **Price range:** Lunch: apps., $8–$16; entrees, $19–$29; desserts, $9–$14. Dinner: apps., $8–$16, entrees, $21–$29; desserts, $9–$14. **Wheelchair access:** An elevator on 49th Street descends to the restaurant. Restrooms are on dining room level.

Second Avenue Kosher Deli $ DELI

156 Second Ave. (at 10th St.) (212) 677-0606
Credit cards: All major Meals: B, L, D, LN

This kosher deli is still rich in historic Lower East Side character, but the food hasn't lived up to its reputation since even before its guiding force, Abe Lebewohl, was killed in 1995.

Alcohol: Beer and wine. **Price range:** Avg. meal, $10–$12. **Wheelchair access:** Fully accessible. **Features:** Kid friendly. **Services:** Delivery, takeout, catering, private parties.

Seeda Thai 2 $25 & Under THAI/VIETNAMESE

309 W. 50th St. (bet. Eighth & Ninth Aves.) (212) 586-4040
Credit cards: All major Meals: L, D

For years, Seeda Thai served decent Thai food in the theater district. When Vietnamese food started to catch on, the restaurant was reincarnated in a new location as Seeda Thai 2, serving both

Vietnamese and Thai. Both sides of the menu are pretty good, from incendiary minced pork to chicken in peanut sauce with mint. While Seeda's building is, to put it kindly, unprepossessing, the restaurant offers good cheap meals near the theaters.

Price range: Lunch, $5.95–$6.95. Dinner: apps., $3–$5.95; entrees, $6.95–$14.95; desserts, $3–$4; prix fixe, $12.95. **Wheelchair access:** Not accessible. **Features:** Smoking permitted. **Services:** Delivery, takeout, catering, private parties.

Sel et Poivre $$

BISTRO/FRENCH

853 Lexington Ave. (bet. 64th & 65th Sts.)
Credit cards: All major

(212) 517-5780
Meals: L, D

Not the best bistro in town, but not the most expensive either. Good for a meal if you happen to be in the neighborhood. The $13.95 lunch provides a nice break when you're shopping.

Price range: Lunch: apps., $5.95–$10.95; entrees, $13.50–$19.95; desserts, $6–$8; prix fixe, $13.95 or $17.95. Dinner: apps., $5.95–$10.95; entrees, $15.95–$23.50; desserts, $6–$8; prix fixe, $19.95 (before 6 P.M.) or $26.95. **Wheelchair access:** Restrooms not accessible. **Features:** Smoking permitted, outdoor dining. **Services:** Delivery, takeout, catering, private parties.

71 Clinton Fresh Food ☆☆ $$

BISTRO/NEW AMERICAN

71 Clinton St. (near Rivington St.)
Credit cards: All major   Meals: D

(212) 614-6960
Closed Sun.

Cool, understated and hip, 71 Clinton makes every other restaurant in New York look as if it's trying too hard. Chef Wylie Dufresne starts with wonderful ingredients, and when manipulating them, he shows a purist's respect for clean flavors and harmonious combinations. He has a fresh, original take on every dish, but an innate sense of rigor tells him when enough is enough. And he excels at striking visual presentations.

The menu is tiny. Diners can choose from six appetizers, seven entrees and four desserts, with a special or two thrown in from time to time. The goat cheese tart, topped with crisp sliced potatoes and dotted with rich applewood-smoked bacon, is simply a superior tart, with a flawless crust and an earthy note provided by a drizzling of arugula oil. Mr. Dufresne's root- vegetable lasagna is a perfect cube made of layer after paper-thin layer of vegetables, surrounded by a tingling mushroom vinegar broth. At the savage end of the spectrum lie beer-braised short ribs, glazed with a slick reduction that makes the neat rectangle of meat look like a pastry. Venison chop, often a dried-out letdown, could not be juicier or more flavorful.

Desserts are simple, like an absolutely straightforward warm pineapple tart. A scoop of coconut ice cream, the size of a Ping-Pong ball, offsets the pineapple's acidity with smooth cream.

Other recommended dishes: Marinated salmon wrapped in avocado; shrimp-stuffed squid; black sea bass with edamame and rye-bread crust. **Wine list:** An original and distinctive list of about 30 wines, half of them available by the glass. **Price range:** Apps., $7–$10; entrees, $15–$22; desserts, $6. **Wheelchair access:** Restrooms on ground level.

Sevilla $25 & Under   SPANISH

62 Charles St. (at W. 4th St.)   (212) 243-9513
Credit cards: All major   Meals: L, D, LN

This old-style Spanish restaurant is a relic from the 1950's, or maybe even before. The yellowed menus indicate a kitchen that hasn't changed in decades, and who can argue with Sevilla's philosophy, which seems to be, the more garlic the better. Wash it all down with sangría.

Price range: Apps., $6.75–$9.50; entrees, $11.75–$32.75; desserts, $3.50. **Wheelchair access:** Fully accessible. **Features:** Outdoor dining. **Services:** Takeout.

Shaan of India ☆☆ $$ INDIAN

57 W. 48th St. (bet. Fifth & Sixth Aves.)   (212) 977-8400
Credit cards: All major   Meals: L, D

Most of the food at Shaan is delicious, but the big menu can be a minefield. Sometimes different dishes turn out to taste more or less the same, and it does not help that the waiters, who are quite formal, seem reluctant to step in with suggestions. But order right, and the food can be a complete delight. Dahi batata poori, tiny puffs of the great Indian bread stuffed with a searingly spicy mixture of minced potatoes, chickpeas and bean sprouts, are a great beginning, as is tawa chicken, moist, boneless pieces of white meat cooked with onions, peppers and lots of spices. Tandoori quail is an inspired use of the clay oven, and lobster, rolled into a smooth, spicy red sauce rich with chilies and ginger, is fabulous. Vegetable dishes like methi palak corn, baby corn in a sumptuous spinach sauce shot through with the strong taste of fenugreek, are a joy. (*Ruth Reichl*)

Price range: Lunch buffet, $13.95. Dinner: apps., $8.95–$10.95; entrees, $10.95-15.95; desserts, $4.95; pre-theater prix fixe, $21.95. **Wheelchair access:** Fully accessible. **Services:** Delivery, takeout, catering, private parties.

Shabu-Tatsu $25 & Under JAPANESE

1414 York Ave. (at 75th St.) (212) 472-3322
216 E. 10th St. (bet. First & Second Aves.) (212) 477-2972
Credit cards: All major Meals: Br, D

These two bright, festive and informal restaurants specialize in
sukiyaki and shabu shabu, dishes that are cooked on circular
metal grills set over burners in the center of each table.
Whichever you choose, the food is great fun to make and it's
delicious.

Other recommended dishes: Yook hwe; kimchi; boiled soybeans; yakiniku; ice cream. **Alcohol:** Beer and wine. **Price
range:** Brunch, $8–$9. Dinner: apps., $4–$6; avg. entree, $20;
desserts, $3.50. **Wheelchair access:** Fully accessible. **Features:**
Kid friendly. **Services:** Takeout, private parties.

Shaffer City Oyster Bar $$ SEAFOOD

5 W. 21st St. (bet. Fifth & Sixth Aves.) (212) 255-9827
Credit cards: All major Meals: L, D Closed Sun.

An old-time New York City oyster saloon, updated for the 20th
century. The atmosphere may be casual, but given the price of
seafood, this is not the all-you-can-eat affair of the past. The
menu offers everything from caviar to seafood risotto with tarragon and basil essence. Try the roasted halibut on a very spicy
turnip purée and, for dessert, the strawberry napoleon. But the
best things really are the oysters: raw, poached or deliciously
fried.

Price range: Lunch: apps., $6.50–$9.95; entrees, $9.95–$14.50.
Dinner: apps., $6.50–$11.95; entrees, $15.95–$26.95; desserts,
$6.50. **Wheelchair access:** Fully accessible. **Features:** Smoking
permitted, outdoor dining. **Services:** Takeout, private parties.

Shanghai Cuisine $ CHINESE

89 Bayard St. (at Mulberry St.) (212) 732-8988
Credit cards: All major Meals: L, D

This popular and crowded Chinatown restaurant offers the
usual enormous menu. The Shanghai dishes are clearly a cut
above the others, with terrific appetizers like smoked fish, soup
dumplings with pork or crab and mock duck. Look for crisp
baby yellow fish, fish head casserole and stewed pork among
the main courses.

Alcohol: Beer and wine. **Price range:** Apps., $1.50–$5.50; avg.
entree, $9.95–$10.95; desserts, $4.25. **Wheelchair access:** Fully
accessible. **Services:** Takeout, catering, private parties.

Shanghai Tide $25 & Under   CHINESE

135-20 40th Rd., Flushing, Queens   (718) 661-4234
77 W. Houston St. (at Wooster St.)   (212) 614-9550
Credit cards: MC/V   Meals: L, D

The bright, handsome Flushing branch, one of the best Chinese places in the area, serves many excellent Shanghai specialties. You know you're in for an unusual meal when you enter and see fish tanks full of lively eels. Service is unusually friendly and helpful. The newer SoHo branch doesn't achieve the same high level.

Recommended dishes: Crab-meat-and-pork juicy buns; wined crabs; jellyfish with celery; smoked fish; fried juicy buns; fried yellow fish with seaweed; deep-fried bamboo shoots; lion's head with cabbage; pork shoulder with greens; eel in brown sauce; Shanghai-style pan-fried noodles. **Price range:** Apps., $3.95–$5.95; entrees, $6.95–$13.95 (specials to $24.95). **Wheelchair access:** Restrooms not accessible. **Features:** Kid friendly, good for business. **Services:** Delivery, takeout, catering, private parties.

Shark Bar $$ SOUTHERN

307 Amsterdam Ave. (bet. 74th & 75th Sts.)   (212) 874-8500
Credit cards: All major   Meals: D, LN

Crowds still turn out to this bustling bar and meeting place, and since it is primarily a bar, you wouldn't expect the food to be important. But the Southern cooking is hearty and delicious and worth checking out.

Price range: Apps., $5.50–$7.95; entrees, $12.95–$18.95; desserts, $4.50. **Wheelchair access:** Not accessible. **Services:** Takeout, catering, private parties.

Sharz Cafe & Wine Bar $25 & Under   ITALIAN

177 E. 90th St. (bet. Third & Lexington Aves.)   (212) 369-1010
Credit cards: D/DC/MC/V   Meals: L, D

A legion of regulars appears nightly in this small cafe, attracted by the warm, homey feeling and the good food. The biggest part of the menu is devoted to pastas, like terrific spaghetti bolognese and a fine penne with chunks of fennel sausage in a tomato-and-cream sauce. The wine list is improving, with about 50 wines available by the glass.

Other recommended dishes: Blackberry-peach cobbler; chocolate custard; cheesecake. **Price range:** Apps., $5–$9; entrees, $10–$24; desserts, $5–$7. **Wheelchair access:** Fully accessible. **Services:** Delivery, takeout, catering, private parties.

Shinbashi $$$

JAPANESE

280 Park Ave. (at 48th St.) (212) 661-3915
Credit cards: All major   Meals: L, D   Closed Sun.

A venerable Japanese restaurant where the waitresses wear traditional Japanese dress and the traditional food is fine. The room is starting to show its age a bit, but that only adds to the charm.

Price range: Lunch: avg. app., $10; entree, $20. Dinner: avg. app., $15; entree, $25; dessert, $5. **Wheelchair access:** Fully accessible. **Services:** Takeout, catering, private parties.

Shopsin's General Store $ AMERICAN

63 Bedford St. (at Morton St.) (212) 924-5160
Credit cards: MC/V   Meals: B, L, D   Closed Sat., Sun.

You're not likely to find a stranger restaurant in New York. Housed in an old general store, it's been an old village hangout for years. Kenny Shopsin, the chef and owner and his wife, are as likely to yell at you as look at you, especially if they don't like your attitude. The food is as quirky as the owners, with many of Shopsin's own pancake and soup inventions. Sometimes they are good, sometimes not so good, but portions are always huge and the menu is encyclopedic.

Shun Lee Palace ☆☆ $$$ CHINESE

155 E. 55th St. (bet. Lexington & Third Aves.) (212) 371-8844
Credit cards: All major   Meals: L, D

No restaurant in New York City can produce better Chinese food. And no restaurant in New York City does it so rarely. Shun Lee is a New York institution, with a cool opulence that is almost a caricature of a Chinese-American palace. Regular customers are so pampered that first-timers look on enviously as they are shunted off to a table in the far less luxurious bar area. It is a restaurant in which you need to invest a little time for the staff to figure out what you like. The spareribs are long, meaty, almost fat-free and perfectly cooked. Hunan calamari, tossed with lots of peppers and crunchy bits of celery, is breathtaking. The chefs do impressive things with whole fish, and the restaurant's owner likes to appear at the table with live fish swimming around in basins and suggest various ways the kitchen might prepare them. (*Ruth Reichl*)

Other recommended dishes: Chicken soong; ants climb on tree; Sichuan cucumbers; crispy sole; deep-fried soft-shell crabs; Chinese cabbage; smoked duck; Shanghai shrimps in wine sauce; cellophane noodles with lobster and ginger; Sichuan rack of lamb; ice cream; sorbet; tapioca; sesame puffs. **Wine list:**

There are a few wines that go well with the food. **Price range:** Lunch prix fixe, $20.01. Dinner: apps., $3.50–$13.95; entrees, $8.75–$29.95; desserts, $4.95–$6.75. **Wheelchair access:** Fully accessible. **Features:** Good for business. **Services:** Delivery, takeout, catering, private parties.

Shun Lee West $$$ CHINESE
43 W. 65th St. (at Columbus)   (212) 595-8895
Credit cards: All major   Meals: Br, L, D, LN

A cavernous Chinese restaurant near Lincoln Center that is always packed. The kitchen can do great things, but they are rarely produced for a clientele that sticks mostly to the familiar. If you want the best food, call ahead and discuss the menu. Good Peking duck.

Price range: Lunch: avg. app., $9; entree, $15. Dinner: avg. app., $12; entree, $19; dessert, $6. **Wheelchair access:** Not accessible. **Features:** Kid friendly, good for business, smoking permitted. **Services:** Delivery, takeout, catering, private parties.

Silver Swan $25 & Under   GERMAN
41 E. 20th St. (bet. Broadway & Park Ave. S.)   (212) 254-3611
Credit cards: All major   Meals: L, D, LN

The excellent selection of more than 75 beers and ales is reason enough to enjoy Silver Swan's solid German fare in a friendly atmosphere. Rauchbier, or smoked beer, made with smoked malt, goes perfectly with kassler rippchen, smoked pork chops served with vinegary sauerkraut, while any of more than a dozen Bavarian wheat beers are just right with weisswurst, mild veal sausage, or bratwurst, juicy pork sausage. This is not the place to eat if you are longing for vegetables, which run the gamut from cabbage to potatoes, cooked until soft. Meat is another matter, however, starting with five varieties of schnitzel and ending with a satisfying sauerbraten.

Price range: Apps., $5–$8.95; entrees, $14–$27; desserts, $5. **Wheelchair access:** Everything on one level; hall to restrooms is narrow. **Features:** Outdoor dining, kid friendly. **Services:** Takeout, catering, private parties.

Smith & Wollensky ☆☆ $$$$ STEAKHOUSE
797 Third Ave. (at 49th St.)   (212) 753-1530
Credit cards: All major   Meals: L, D, LN

If you were trying to design a classic steakhouse, this is what it would look like — big, plain, comfortable and manly. It is also one of the few steakhouses that never lets you down: the service is swell, the steaks are consistently very, very good (if rarely great) and the portions are huge. The sirloins are aged for around two weeks to intensify the flavor and give the meat a dry edge. Beyond that, if you have noncarnivores to feed, the restaurant knows how to do it. The lobsters are perfect specimens, and the clams and oysters are excellent too. The chicken is cooked by people who actually seem to like chicken. Desserts, unfortunately, leave a great deal to be desired. Smith & Wollensky may not have the eccentric ugliness of Palm or the Damon Runyon airs of other New York steakhouses, but it has a no-nonsense down-to-earth plainness. This is a place for two-fisted eating. (*Ruth Reichl*)

Other recommended dishes: Shrimp cocktail; crab cocktail; clams; split-pea soup; rib-eye steak; lamb chops; swordfish; calf's liver; creamed spinach; onion rings; hashed brown potatoes; cheesecake. **Wine list:** Big, deep and filled with impressive and expensive wines; for less expensive bottles, ask for the Wollensky's Grill list. **Price range:** Lunch: apps., $6–$14.75; entrees, $14.50–$27.75. Dinner: apps. $6–$14.75; entrees, $18.50–$65; desserts, $6.50–$8.75. **Wheelchair access:** Not accessible. **Features:** Kid friendly, good for business. **Services:** Private parties.

Smith Street Kitchen $25 & Under
SEAFOOD/NEW AMERICAN

174 Smith St., Boerum Hill, Brooklyn   (718) 858-5359
Credit cards: All major   Meals: Br, L, D

With its worn velvet banquettes, handsome pressed tin walls and black-and-white photos, the small dining room here has an inviting lived-in look. Service is solicitous without being overfriendly, and perhaps best of all, the restaurant offers excellent value. Smith Street Kitchen specializes in seafood. The menu is small, but the appetizers include some exceptional selections, like a small tart filled with sweet lobster and smoky chorizo along with mushrooms, spinach and tomato confit. The seafood and pork combination makes for a gorgeous contrast, which is echoed in the seafood chowder, a creamy stew laden with clams, tiny scallops and bass, augmented by lardons, salty pearls of French bacon. The main courses are less consistent. Thick slices of grilled tuna left rosy in the middle and flavored with sesame oil are excellent, as is sautéed cod, aided by a moist basil-flavored risotto. Cassoulet, one of only two land-based dishes on the menu, seemed straight out of Languedoc.

The brief wine list includes some decent inexpensive choices, but most of the better bottles are in the $25 to $35 range. For dessert, the pear bread pudding can take its place among the bread pudding elite.

Other recommended dishes: Gravlax, steamed mussels, green salad, bouillabaisse, roasted branzino, apricot strudel. **Price range:** Apps., $5–$9; entrees, $15–$22. **Wheelchair access:** Small step in front; restrooms and dining room on one level.

Snack $25 & Under GREEK
105 Thompson St. (at Prince St.) (212) 925-1040
Credit cards: Cash only Meals: L, D

At 380 square feet, kitchen included, and with seating for 10, barely, Snack is one of Manhattan's smallest restaurants. But taste Snack's stifado, a wonderful stew of braised lamb, delicately spiced with cinnamon and oregano and touched with the sweet juices of a currant, apricot and almond pilaf, and you know right away that Snack is worth squeezing into.

Start with the impeccable cold appetizers: hummus is sharpened to a lively tang with copious lemon juice, while melitzanes salata, an eggplant spread, is chunky and deliciously smoky. Chicken boureki, a triangle of puff pastry layered with sesame seeds and stuffed with chicken, feta, mushrooms and herbs, is a close-your-eyes-and-sigh kind of dish. Snack does offer other gems among its small selection of main courses, including keftedes, or savory veal meatballs with pine nuts and almond slivers, are served with sweet prunes in a red wine sauce over tiny, paper-thin squares of pasta.

Desserts are simple and satisfying, whether yogurt with honey or a moist semolina "halvah" in a cinnamon-orange syrup. Snack does not have a wine-and-beer license but is expecting one soon.

Other recommended dishes: Skordalia, tzatziki, olive boureki, roast chicken. **Price range:** Apps., $3–$8; entrees, $8–$13. **Wheelchair access:** Steps at entrance; narrow way to restroom.

Soba Nippon $25 & Under JAPANESE
19 W. 52nd St. (bet. Fifth & Sixth Aves.) (212) 489-2525
Credit cards: All major Meals: L, D

Few things induce serenity like a bowl of cold Japanese soba noodles, and few places make better noodles than Soba Nippon. The long dining room is airy and comfortable if somewhat plain, though pretty bamboo sprays arch over the plain wood tables. Soba Nippon serves sushi, as well as teriyaki and donburi dishes, but soba is the specialty. The owner, Nobuyoshi Kuraoka, has his own buckwheat farm in Canada, and soba noodles — 80 percent buckwheat and 20 percent wheat — are made daily at the restaurant.

Try the cold soba noodles served plain, which sounds spartan but really is not. The pale brown noodles arrive on a flat basket with a dipping sauce of fish stock and soy. You can add scallions and wasabi, or simply dip the noodles and slurp them home, the better to appreciate their smooth texture and the hint of resistance as you chew. The cool, clean sensation is indeed calming. Eventually, a small, simmering pot of liquid is placed on the table. This is the broth in which the noodles were boiled, and it is said to be full of nutrients. Pour the broth into the dipping sauce — now add the scallions and wasabi — and drink. It's marvelous.

The cold soba is offered in half a dozen variations. One fine alternative to soba is cold inaniwa udon noodles, as thin as spaghetti, with a pure, clean flavor. Soba Nippon's hot soba soups are excellent as well, especially soba with agedashi tofu, a delicate broth with perfectly cooked noodles.

Other recommended dishes: Watercress in sesame sauce, sautéed burdock. **Price range:** Apps., $3.50–$13.80; entrees, $8–$17. **Wheelchair access:** Everything is on one level.

Soba-Ya $25 & Under JAPANESE/NOODLES
229 E. 9th St. (bet. Second & Third Aves.)   (212) 533-6966
Credit cards: All major   Meals: L, D

Noodles are the focus at this bright, handsome little Japanese restaurant, one of several nearby owned by the same group. The soba noodles — buckwheat, pale tan and smooth — are served hot in soups or cold, a better bet for appreciating their lightness and clear flavors. Appetizers are excellent, differing night to night but sometimes including cooked marinated spinach, rice with shreds of marinated sardines and fried squares of marvelously fresh tofu.

Alcohol: Beer and wine. **Price range:** Apps., $2.50–$8; noodles and rice bowls, $6.50–$14. **Wheelchair access:** Everything is on one level. **Features:** Good for business, romantic.

SoHo Kitchen & Bar $$ NEW AMERICAN
103 Greene St. (bet. Spring & Prince Sts.)   (212) 925-1866
Credit cards: All major   Meals: Br, L, D, LN

Food is an afterthought at this dim, cavernous wine bar with high ceilings and brick walls. It serves dozens of wines by the glass, by the half-size tasting glass and even by smaller tastes for comparing and contrasting a series of wines.

Price range: Apps., $5–$8; entrees, $10–$15; desserts, $5. Avg. Sunday brunch, $7.50. **Wheelchair access:** Fully accessible. **Services:** Takeout, private parties.

Soho Steak $25 & Under

BISTRO/FRENCH

90 Thompson St. (near Spring St.)
Credit cards: Cash only

(212) 226-0602
Meals: Br, D

This thoroughly French little restaurant, drawing a young, good-looking crowd, emphasizes meat but is no simple steakhouse. It is a cleverly conceived, bustling bistro that serves creative dishes for lower prices than you might imagine. Steak frites, of course, is top-notch. Few places offer this much value for this kind of money.

Other recommended dishes: Grilled foie gras; braised oxtail ravioli; lamb shank; filet mignon carpaccio; sautéed squab; grilled sirloin; seared filet mignon; roasted pheasant; venison; pear tart; cheese plate. **Alcohol:** Beer and wine. **Price range:** Brunch, $5–$12. Dinner: apps., $6.50–$9; entrees, $14–$16; desserts, $5–$7. **Wheelchair access:** Fully accessible. **Features:** Romantic, smoking permitted. **Services:** Takeout, private parties.

Solera ☆☆ $$$

SPANISH

216 E. 53rd St. (bet. Second & Third Aves.)
Credit cards: All major   Meals: L, D, LN

(212) 644-1166
Closed Sun.

As warm and rustic as an inn in Spain, Solera looks so cozy it is almost impossible not to be drawn into the long room, with its terra-cotta tiles and romantic lighting. It is also impossible to resist the display of tapas by the bar (white beans tossed with chorizo, the garlic shrimp in sherry vinegar). Walk past the bar, past the pungent display of cheeses, pull up a chair and prepare to be seduced by the food and wine of Spain. The appetizers are all fine, but the octopus with paprika and olive oil consistently amazes me — it is as tender as marrow. There are several versions of paella, all delicious but the seafood is the most impressive. Filet mignon is punched up with cabrales, the Spanish blue cheese (and one of the great cheeses of the world). Best of all are the crisp little lamb chops served with a ragout of beans and polenta laced with cheese. Desserts are unimpressive but the cheeses are wonderful. (*Ruth Reichl*)

Other recommended dishes: Casserole of clams with shiitake mushrooms; fried calamari with ali-oli; piquillo peppers with rabbit and pistachios; grilled vegetables with romesco sauce; brandada; duck breast in cider sauce; trout with spinach in cava sauce; crema catalana; Spanish cheeses. **Wine list:** The all-Spanish list is excellent and the staff knows it well. **Price range:** Prix-fixe lunch, $32. Dinner: apps., $9–$12; entrees, $25–$35; desserts, $8.50; tapas, $3–$9.50. **Wheelchair access:** Main dining room at street level. **Services:** Catering, private parties.

Sosa Borella $25 & Under   AMERICAN/ARGENTINE
460 Greenwich St. (near Desbrosses St.)   (212) 431-5093
Credit cards: All major   Meals: B, Br, L, D

This quiet spot is all you could seek in a neighborhood restaurant. From the enticing pastries in the morning to the extensive list of delicious sandwiches at midday to the Argentine menu that comes out at night, Sosa does well by its food. It's friendly, handsome and reasonably priced to boot.

Other recommended dishes: Sandwiches, including bresaola, smoked turkey with roasted peppers and brie, and prosciutto with mozzarella and roasted peppers; French toast; oatmeal fruit brûlée; strip steak; beef short ribs; empanada; apple tart. **Alcohol:** Beer and wine. **Price range:** Avg. breakfast, $8. Avg. lunch, $15. Dinner: avg. app., $8; entree, $18; dessert, $6. **Wheelchair access:** Fully accessible. **Features:** Kid friendly. **Services:** Delivery, takeout, catering, private parties.

Soul Cafe $$ SOUTHERN/CARIBBEAN
444 W. 42nd St. (bet. Ninth & 10th Aves.)   (212) 244-7685
Credit cards: All major   Meals: D, LN

A late-night scene, complete with big portions of soul food and live music. The plush, L-shaped supper club promises "Afro-centered cuisine with Southern flair and a touch of the Caribbean." By that it means largely Southern and Caribbean food that has been updated, often for diet-conscious customers. The menu includes appetizers like Maryland she-crab soup and grilled lamb ribs, and main courses like jerk duck, braised short ribs and red snapper crusted with sweet potatoes and plantains. Side dishes are traditionally Southern, like macaroni and cheese, candied yams and string beans.

Price range: Apps., $6–$12; entrees, $10–$23; desserts, $6. **Wheelchair access:** Fully accessible. **Services:** Takeout, catering, private parties.

Soul Fixins' $25 & Under   SOUTHERN
371 W. 34th St. (bet. Eighth & Ninth Aves.)   (212) 736-1345
Credit cards: All major   Meals: L, D   Closed Sun.

You can pull up one of the dozen or so seats at this small storefront, but Soul Fixins' Southern food travels well, and it's nice to be able to spread out in comfort with dishes like meaty spareribs bathed in gloriously smoky sauce and crisp fried chicken. Side dishes (two came with each main course) were uniformly good.

Other recommended dishes: Collards; green beans; candied yams. **Price range:** Avg. app., $5.95; entree, $9.95; dessert, $3. **Wheelchair access:** Fully accessible. **Services:** Delivery, take-out, catering.

Sparks ☆ $$$$ STEAKHOUSE

210 E. 46th St. (bet. Second & Third Aves.)   (212) 687-4855
Credit cards: All major   Meals: L, D   Closed Sun.

Even though the rooms are filled with antique furniture and the walls are lined with gilt-frame paintings, it still feels like a casual, two-fisted, down-to-earth place. Mostly men come for big steaks and bigger lobsters; there is almost always a wait, but the incredible wine list and pleasant service make it worth visiting. The steaks are prime and aged in a combination of wet and dry aging, but can be iffy. You can have a terrific steak here. You can have mediocre ones, too. Avoid froufrou food like medallions of beef in bordelaise sauce, or steak fromage (with Roquefort cheese). The kitchen seems to have utter contempt for someone wanting something so effete. Don't expect much from the hash browns, but the spinach is delicious. Hint: dine on Saturday night when you may not have to wait, and are unlikely to be seated next to a group of 13 drunken stockbrokers. The most reliable dish is lamb chops, which are always delicious, but if you want seafood, have lobster, although there have been times it was a disaster. (*Ruth Reichl*)

Other recommended dishes: Shrimp cocktail; crabmeat cocktail; chopped tomato and onion salad; asparagus vinaigrette; prime sirloin steak; cheesecake. **Wine list:** Large, impressive, extremely reasonable. **Price range:** Apps., $6.50–$15.50; entrees, $19.95–$89.95 (for a five-and-a-half-pound lobster). **Wheelchair access:** Everything at street level. **Features:** Good for business. **Services:** Private parties.

Spazzia $$ MEDITERRANEAN

366 Columbus Ave. (at 77th St.)   (212) 799-0150
Credit cards: All major   Meals: Br, L, D

Grilled pizzas figure among the appetizers here, along with Ligurian fish soup and the fried ravioli of Nice. The pasta section of the menu includes interesting dishes like tagliatelle with fresh tuna, botarga and preserved lemon. The atmosphere is casual, the wine list excellent, the prices moderate.

Other recommended dishes: Salt-baked trout; grilled lemon-marinated chicken; steak au poivre; grilled squid and black rice. **Price range:** Brunch, $9–$15. Lunch: apps., $3–$7; entrees, $10–$16; desserts, $6. Dinner: apps., $7–$12; entrees, $14–$23; desserts, $6. **Wheelchair access:** Fully accessible. **Features:** Kid friendly, outdoor dining. **Services:** Takeout, private parties.

Stage Deli $$ DELI

834 Seventh Ave. (bet. 53rd & 54th Sts.)   (212) 245-7850
Credit cards: All major   Meals: B, L, D, LN

A classic New York deli with giant sandwiches, giant crowds, giant prices. It hasn't been the same since Max Asnes left.

Price range: Avg. breakfast, $7–$8. Avg. lunch, $10–$12. Avg. dinner, $15–$20. **Wheelchair access:** Fully accessible. **Features:** Kid friendly, outdoor dining. **Services:** Delivery, takeout, catering, private parties.

St. Dymphna's $25 & Under   IRISH/AMERICAN

118 St. Marks Pl. (bet. First Ave. & Ave. A)   (212) 254-6636
Credit cards: All major   Meals: B, Br, L, D, LN

This Irish bar that serves food is a definite step up from those old shot-and-a-beer places with a buffet, but the watchword is still "the simpler the better." That means burgers, fish and chips, and the like. St. Dymphna, by the way, is the patron saint of the insane.

Price range: Irish breakfast, $9.95. Avg. lunch, $6–$7. Dinner: apps., $4–$5; entrees, $7.50–$14.95; desserts, $5. **Wheelchair access:** Fully accessible. **Features:** Outdoor dining. **Services:** Catering, private parties.

Stella $25 & Under   NEW AMERICAN

58 Macdougal St. (bet. Prince & Houston Sts.)   (212) 674-4968
Credit cards: AE   Meals: Br, D

For SoHo, Stella is a rare combination of elements — good food, good wine, good atmosphere, good value. Good taste, too, since Stella is blissfully free of Stanley Kowalski references. The best appetizers include a rich, buttery pea risotto and a wonderful salad of leeks, radishes, sweet cantaloupe and tender little radish sprouts all topped with warm, earthy goat cheese. Some of the main courses seem conceptually flawed, but the tender, meaty Cornish hen, served in a bowl with braised prunes, olives and capers, and a thick Newport steak covered in a salad of cherry tomatoes, arugula and capers are very pleasing.

There is an excellent list of New World wines. Only a few bottles, like a pleasant riesling from Argyle in the Willamette Valley, are under $25, but there are some good values in the $30 to $35 range, like a Cline Old Vines mourvedre from Sonoma for $30 and a Macari cabernet franc from Long Island for $32.

Stella's desserts are not flashy, but the humble strawberry shortcake made with biscuits and whipped cream is more than satisfying, as is the sedate chocolate bread pudding. Don't miss the house-made ice creams, especially in herbal flavors like rosemary. And if you have a little wine left, a plate of artisanal American cheeses is perfect for two.

Other recommended dishes: Chilled cantaloupe soup; grilled sardines; merguez; salad of goat cheese, cantaloupe, leeks and radishes; Cornish hen with prunes and olives; grilled Newport steak; strawberry shortcake; chocolate bread pudding; ice creams; cheese plate. **Price range:** Apps., $6–$8.50; main courses, $13.50–$18.50, with one at $25.50. **Wheelchair access:** One step at entrance, another step at restroom.

Stepmama $ SANDWICHES

199 E. 3rd St. (at Ave. B)
Credit cards: Cash only

(212) 228-2663
Meals: L, D

An offshoot of the excellent Mama's Food Shop across the street, Stepmama offers sandwiches, salads and soups, including an excellent meatloaf sandwich on seven-grain bread. French fries are hand cut, crisp and liberally salted. Seasonal chilled soups are especially refreshing.

Price range: Soups, $3.50; sandwiches, $4–$7. **Wheelchair access:** Fully accessible. **Services:** Delivery, takeout, catering.

Strip House ☆ $$$ STEAKHOUSE

13 E. 12th St. (bet. Fifth Ave. & University Pl.)
Credit cards: All major

(212) 328-0000
Meals: D

Strip House is not so much a steakhouse as a catalog of hip references to the idea of a steakhouse. As the name suggests, there's a burlesque theme hard at work here. The walls are lined with lust-red flocked wallpaper and the banquettes are upholstered in quilted red leather. Vintage photographs of old-time strippers cover the walls. It all makes for a cheery, comfortable atmosphere, with none of the backslapping locker-room style of the old-line steakhouses.

The chef plays with the steakhouse formula without actually getting rid of steaks. The result, although pleasing enough, is neither fish nor fowl. The meat here is respectable, but not much more than that. The rib chop is awfully fatty, but the swaggering porterhouse comes through in a big way, seared aggressively to achieve a deep crunch, all rubescent tender meat within. The filet mignon and New York strip steaks are perfectly acceptable. The rest of the menu, however, shows a more playful side. Lamb comes in a three-way dish listed on the menu as Ménage à Trois, consisting of a first-rate chop, a loin and a braised flank. The time-honored side dishes are reinterpreted a bit, and new ones have been added. The potato fix comes three ways, depending on your mood: as a purée of fingerling potatoes, as deep-fried spuds or as a dark-golden dome of potatoes, crusty after frying in goose fat.

Desserts bring mixed results, but the fruit savarin is excellent, accompanied by toasted brioche, an ethereal Marsala sabayon and crunchy slices of toasted almond. The caramelized apple tart with mascarpone ice cream and brown sugar hard sauce is as good as it sounds.

Other recommended dishes: Braised short-rib flan, vegetables en papillote, raspberry crepes suzette. **Wine list:** An attractively international list of more than 200 wines, with 26 half bottles and 13 wines by the glass. **Price range:** Apps., $9–$14; entrees, $22–$32; desserts, $8. **Wheelchair access:** Restrooms are on street level.

Sud
$25 & Under   FRENCH
210 W. 10th St. (bet. Bleecker & 4th Sts.)   (212) 255-3805
Credit cards: All major   Meals: Br, D   Closed Mon.

Nothing seems hip or cool about this little French-North African restaurant in Greenwich Village. The owners do not treat food as an art. They simply offer a small menu of standards that seems like a relic of the 1950's, yet everything is really good, like dense, deeply flavored salmon mousse, excellent portobello salad and filet mignon with buttery mashed potatoes.

Other recommended dishes: Pumpkin soup; endive and Roquefort salad; streak maître d'hôtel; salmon; couscous; linguine with scallops and mussels. **Alcohol:** Beer and wine. **Price range:** Avg. app., $6; entree, $16; dessert, $6.50. **Wheelchair access:** Not accessible. **Features:** Romantic, smoking permitted. **Services:** Delivery, takeout, catering, private parties.

The Sultan
$25 & Under   TURKISH
1435 Second Ave. (near 74th St.)   (212) 861-2828
Credit cards: All major   Meals: L, D

This friendly storefront restaurant offers mainstream Turkish dishes that are notable for their fresh, lively flavors. Meals begin with a basket of puffy house-made bread studded with tiny black sesame seeds, and a dish of tahini blended with pekmez, a thick grape syrup. Kebabs are universally good here, especially the lamb yogurt kebab, and whole trout is grilled perfectly, then filleted at the table. The dessert menu is predictable yet well prepared.

Price range: Apps., $4.95; entrees, $11.95–$16.95; desserts, $4.95. **Wheelchair access:** Fully accessible. **Services:** Delivery, takeout, catering, private parties.

Supreme Macaroni Co. $ ITALIAN

511 Ninth Ave. (bet. 38th & 39th Sts.)   (212) 564-8074
Credit cards: All major   Meals: L, D   Closed Sun.

Behind the grocery store is the gloriously old-fashioned Italian restaurant, from the days when pasta was macaroni, sauce was called gravy and wine was served in juice glasses. It all comes alive again here, where tomatoes, peppers and sausages rule. Isn't it nice that some things don't change?

Alcohol: Beer and wine. **Price range:** Avg. lunch, $11–$12. Avg. dinner, $18–$19. **Wheelchair access:** Fully accessible. **Features:** Kid friendly. **Services:** Takeout, catering, private parties.

Sur $25 & Under   ARGENTINE

232 Smith St., Carroll Gardens, Brooklyn   (718) 875-1716
Credit cards: All major   Meals: Br, D

This brick-walled, candlelit Argentine restaurant is warm and inviting without any of the usual gaucho clichés. The focus, naturally, is on beef, with top choices including the lean, almost grassy Argentine sirloin, served with a mound of crisp, salty french fries. Alternatives to beef include juicy and flavorful roast chicken and several pasta dishes. For dessert, try the crepes filled with dulce de leche, a sublime caramel-like confection of cream and sugar.

Price range: Apps., $3.50–$6.50; entrees, $12–$19. **Wheelchair access:** Everything on one level. **Services:** Private parties.

Surya ☆☆ $$ INDIAN

302 Bleecker St. (bet. Seventh Ave. S. & Grove St.)
   (212) 807-7770
Credit cards: All major   Meals: Br, D

The restaurant named for the sun (in Tamil) actually has a small garden in the back along with a sleek interior. Its menu features mostly south Indian dishes, often filtered through the technique of France. The main courses have a bold freshness. Rack of lamb is particularly impressive. But what is most splendid about Surya is the entirely meatless side of the menu. It is, in fact, difficult to come up with a more exciting place to eat vegetables in New York City. I would not eat a meal at Surya without ordering the okra, sautéed in a thick mixture of tomatoes, onion, garlic and kokum (a sour Indian fruit). I love the dosai, too, and the desserts are out of the ordinary.
(*Ruth Reichl*)

Other recommended dishes: Sautéed scallops; pepper shrimp; idli (lentil cakes); kaikari (crisp vegetable rolls); rack of lamb; biriyani; crisp salmon; chicken Chettinad; sautéed new potatoes with spices; sprouted lentils and spinach; stuffed breads and chutneys; shrikhand; halva. **Wine list:** Small and unimaginative. **Price range:** Apps., $7–$10; entrees, $11–$24; desserts, $6–$9. **Wheelchair access:** Everything on one level. **Features:** Smoking permitted. **Services:** Private parties.

Sushiden $$$ JAPANESE/SUSHI
123 W. 49th St. (bet. Sixth & Seventh Aves.)   (212) 398-2800
Credit cards: All major   Meals: L, D   Closed Sun.

Always reliable sushi from a sushi bar that is as welcoming to non-Japanese customers as it is to the Japanese. One of the few places that almost always has good toro.

Alcohol: Beer and wine. **Price range:** Avg. lunch, $20. Avg. dinner, $25–$30. **Wheelchair access:** Restrooms not accessible. **Services:** Takeout, catering, private parties.

Sushi Hatsu ☆☆☆ $$$$ JAPANESE/SUSHI
1143 First Ave. (near 62nd St.)   (212) 371-0238
Credit cards: AE/DC   Meals: D, LN   Closed Mon.

With a modest sushi bar in front, and a few tables in the rear, Sushi Hatsu serves breathtakingly good fish of an astonishing purity. It is so light you feel you could go on eating forever.

I sat at the sushi bar and put myself in the chef's hands, then asked for sashimi. This, I have learned during many years of sushi eating, brands you as a serious sushi eater. The chef nodded and set a board in front of me. The beautiful ritual began. The chef wielded the knife so deftly it barely seemed to skim the fish. He set some tiny octopuses before me. He followed that with toro, the rich belly of bluefin tuna. He cubed Spanish mackerel, piling it into a little pyramid interspersed with scallions. He sliced yellowtail — rich and almost smoky in its intensity. Scallops showered down across the counter, shimmering like pearls against the golden wood. The chef scooped out a large shrimp, steamed it lightly, shelled it and laid it across the board. It was all delicious.

Now the chef spoke. "Sushi?" he asked. Of course. A new board appeared. The waitress brought a folded wet cloth on a ceramic dish. Sushi is eaten with the fingers, and this solid finger bowl was a thoughtful touch. First came tai, a sweet, lean relative of sea bream. The chef picked up a large clam that was still moving and sliced it. The flavor was clear and piercing and clean. Next came scallops in icily delicious slices; then a variety of fish roe served in little seaweed bundles. Umi, sea urchin gonads, followed. These creamy golden bits with their surprisingly perfumed quality are, to me, almost eerily delicious. "More?" the chef wanted to know. "Just one more flavor," I replied. The chef spread a crisp piece of seaweed with umeboshi, the pungent salted plum paste, layered it with shiso leaves, sesame seeds, radish sprouts and crunchy slices of Japanese potato, rolled it up and handed it to me. This is a bracingly astringent end to all those rich fish flavors and the perfect finale for sushi.

The bill was huge. I had expected it to be. Good sushi is never cheap. But if you've got the money, they've got the fish. (*Ruth Reichl*)

Recommended dishes: Sushi at the sushi bar. **Wine list:** Beer and sake. **Price range:** $30 minimum at the sushi bar, but expect to spend $75 to $100 a person. Sushi at the tables begins at $12. **Wheelchair access:** One step to dining room; restrooms are small. **Services:** Takeout.

Sushi Masa $25 & Under JAPANESE/SUSHI
141 E. 47th St. (bet. Lexington & Third Aves.) (212) 715-0837
Credit cards: All major   Meals: L, D   Closed Sun.

The small bright dining room here is extremely inviting, the service warm and pleasant. But what makes this restaurant special is the combination of high quality ingredients and the reasonable prices. At lunch order the specialty of the house, Sushi Masa gozen, an assortment of dishes that is like a small banquet (salad, dobin soup, sashimi, broiled tuna and pickled vegetables). At dinner try chirashi sushi (which many Japanese customers were eating), raw fish on top of vinegared rice. The sushi and sashimi assortments are all fresh and attractively presented.

Other recommended dishes: Edamame; eel-don; oysters with ponzu sauce. **Wine list:** Has the usual selection of sakes, plum wines and light-bodied, inoffensive Japanese beers, but there is one more, a malty dark beer from Asahi. **Price range:** Lunch, $7.50–$25. Dinner, $12–$25. **Wheelchair access:** Steps at entrance; corridor to restrooms is narrow.

Sushi of Gari $$ JAPANESE/SUSHI
402 E. 78th St. (at First Ave.) (212) 517-5340
Credit cards: All major   Meals: D

This simple little Japanese restaurant on the East Side offers a nice selection of sushi along with a range of other Japanese specialties like tempura, noodles and fried dishes. Sushi, though, is the best bet, along with delicious appetizers like boiled spinach with sesame sauce and delicate little dumplings.

Alcohol: Beer and wine. **Price range:** Avg. $25–$30 per person. **Wheelchair access:** Fully accessible. **Features:** Good for business. **Services:** Takeout.

Sushi Rose $$

248 E. 52nd St. (bet. Second & Third Aves.)   (212) 813-1800
Credit cards: All major   Meals: L, D   Closed Sun.

JAPANESE/SUSHI

This tiny, attractive second-floor restaurant looks traditional and expensive, but it is neither. The chef works amazingly fast, slicing extremely large pieces of sashimi for which the restaurant charges rather moderate prices.

Alcohol: Beer and wine. **Price range:** Avg. lunch, $12. Avg. dinner, $20. **Wheelchair access:** Fully accessible. **Services:** Delivery, takeout, private parties.

Sushisay $$$

JAPANESE/SUSHI

38 E. 51st St. (bet. Park & Madison Aves.)   (212) 755-1780
Credit cards: All major   Meals: L, D   Closed Sun.

Classic enough to please a Japanese clientele; friendly enough to please an American one. Small and attractively spare, Sushisay saves its best fish for the sushi bar, its very best fish for the regular customers, the ones who get the special chopsticks.

Alcohol: Beer and wine. **Price range:** Avg. lunch, $30. Avg. dinner, $50. **Wheelchair access:** Not accessible. **Services:** Takeout, catering.

Sushi Yasuda ☆☆☆ $$$

JAPANESE/SUSHI

204 E. 43rd St. (bet. Second & Third Aves.)   (212) 972-1001
Credit cards: All major   Meals: L, D   Closed Sun.

Sushi Yasuda looks like it was headed for TriBeCa and took a wrong turn. In one of the city's dreariest restaurant neighborhoods, it glows like a strange mineral, with a cool, celery-green facade. Inside, the dining room is bathed in light. Floors, walls and ceiling are lined in blond wood. The severe banquettes are upholstered in green-gray fabric. The refusal to decorate is almost palpable. The mood is quiet, contemplative, austere. But Sushi Yasuda has a lot of downtown in its soul. The manager and the waitresses are young. The exemplary service has an open, friendly quality to it. At the same time, the menu is dead serious, a purist's paradise of multiple choices among fish species — nearly 30, a startling number for a small restaurant — and elegantly presented appetizers and side dishes. The restaurant is a showcase for Maomichi Yasuda, formerly the star sushi chef at Hatsuhana, one of Manhattan's deluxe sushi shrines.

Sushi Yasuda makes a point of carrying fish that most sushi restaurants either can't get their hands on or don't want to bother with. There are six mackerels and three yellowtails to choose from. The restaurant offers four kinds of eel, and the prized fatty tunas, chutoro (medium fatty) and otoro (super fatty), come in six ascending levels of fatness.

But sushi is only half the story. The daily menu includes a small, transparent sheet of special appetizers, and they are worth jumping for. The selection may include a textural medley of six seaweeds, arranged like small tumbleweeds on a white rectangular plate, or deep-fried eel backbones, as salty and crunchy as crisp bacon, but with a rich fish flavor. It is often said that the test of a real sushi restaurant is its omelet; Sushi Yasuda's is excellent — dozens of compressed, tissue-thin layers of egg with a crisp edge.

Dessert is not usually an exciting moment in a sushi restaurant. Mochi rice makes the difference here: Japan's answer to flubber, mochi is a highly glutinous rice that can be rolled out into a sticky, pasta-like wrapper ready for filling with something sweet, in this case home-made red-bean ice cream and green-tea ice cream. Simple, restrained and playful, the mochi twins are just the right characters to send diners away with a cheery wave.

Other recommended dishes: Steamed clams; nonfish maki rolls; egg custard. **Wine list:** No wines, but four Japanese beers, and a half-dozen sakes. **Price range:** Apps., $4.50–$9.50; sushi, $3–$6.50 a piece; desserts, $4–$6. **Wheelchair access:** Restrooms on street level.

Sushi Zen $$$ JAPANESE/SUSHI

57 W. 46th St. (bet. Fifth & Sixth Aves.) (212) 302-0707
Credit cards: All major   Meals: L, D   Closed Sun.

Exotic, inventive sushi that spans the range from exciting and wonderful to just plain weird.

Price range: Lunch, $20–$40. Dinner, $30–$50. **Wheelchair access:** Restrooms not accessible. **Features:** Outdoor dining.

Sweet 'n' Tart Cafe $25 & Under CHINESE

76 Mott St. (south of Canal St.) (212) 334-8088
20 Mott St. (bet. Chatham Sq. & Pell St.) (212) 964-0380
136-11 38th Ave., Flushing, Queens (718) 661-3380
Credit cards: Cash only   Meals: B, L, D, LN

The specialty here is tong shui, a range of sweet tonics intended to benefit specific parts of the body or to balance one's yin and yang. But Sweet 'n' Tart's more typical dishes are terrific as well, like Chinese sausage and taro with rice, served in a tall bamboo steamer, and congee with beef, pork and squid. Little English is spoken here, but waitresses describe dishes as well as they can.

Other recommended dishes: Noodles; dumplings; home-style rice dishes. **Price range:** $5–$14. **Wheelchair access:** Street level. **Services:** Takeout.

Sylvia's $ SOUTHERN

328 Lenox Ave. (bet. 126th & 127th Sts.)   (212) 996-0660
Credit cards: All major   Meals: Br, L, D

Tour buses pull up in front for a sanitized taste of Harlem. The food's not fabulous, but it offers everything you expect: fried chicken, collard greens and sweet potato pie. Best for the gospel brunch on Sunday.

Price range: Avg. breakfast, $3. Avg. lunch, $6.95. Dinner: apps., $4.95; entrees, $8.95–$13; desserts, $3. Gospel brunch, $15.95. **Wheelchair access:** Fully accessible. **Features:** Kid friendly. **Services:** Takeout, catering, private parties.

Syros $25 & Under GREEK/SEAFOOD

32-11 Broadway, Astoria, Queens   (718) 278-1877
Credit cards: All major   Meals: L, D, LN

Syros is named after the Greek island on which the owner grew up. It is attractive enough, in a conventional kind of way. It has the usual open kitchen and display cases of fish and meat. With a glass ceiling, the main dining room in the rear is warm and bright on sunny days and glows with candlelight at night. The Greek dips are particularly good: melitzanes salata, or puréed eggplant dip, is delightfully vinegary, while taramosalata, a fish roe purée, is bracing and pungent. The grilled fish is superb — perfectly cooked, moist and delicious.

On one visit, grilled porgy was unexpectedly large but still tender, full of fragile flavor, beautifully seasoned with no more than salt, oregano, lemon juice and olive oil. Grilled shrimp, big and butterflied, were likewise cooked just enough to release their delicate shrimpy flavor. Main courses come with sides like lemon roasted potatoes, a standard that is surprisingly good here, rice and dandelion greens, which are oily and not so good. Spanakopita, crisp layers of phyllo encasing spinach and feta cheese, is fresh and savory, while saganaki, fried kasseri cheese, is nutty and rich. Lemony fish soup is excellent, and even a T-bone steak is beefy and winning.

Other recommended dishes: Potato-garlic purée; tzatziki; grilled striped bass; grilled sardines; fried cheese. **Price range:** Apps., $3.95–$10.25; entrees, $9.25–$22. **Wheelchair access:** Restrooms are downstairs.

Tabla ☆☆☆ $$$$

11 Madison Ave. (near 25th St.)
Credit cards: All major   Meals: L, D

AMERICAN/INDIAN
(212) 889-0667
Closed Sun.

The newest of Danny Meyer's restaurants, Tabla vibrates with sound and sizzles with color. At the bar downstairs, cooks grill roti and naan in odd and interesting flavors. Upstairs, the dining room is darkly sensuous with walls stained in shades of jade and coral.

Then the food arrives — American food, viewed through a kaleidoscope of Indian spices. The powerful, original and unexpected flavors evoke intense emotions. Those who do not like Tabla tend to dislike it with a passion. For me, Tabla was love at first bite. I am thrilled by the taste of mustard fettuccine tossed with veal. I look up and find my guest staring at a bowl of wild mushroom soup. "It's horrible," he says. I take a bite; it is electric with the taste of tamarind and ginger. "It's fabulous," I cry. Another night, another friend. I am so taken with the black bass topped with flaked rice and served with pea greens that it is a while before I notice she has pushed her poussin away. I pick up a forkful. The flavors explode in my mouth. I have learned to ignore those who do not like Tabla. Desserts are also impressively offbeat: I can't resist the warm chocolate date cake or the vanilla-bean kulfi, an ice cream with character. (*Ruth Reichl*)

Recommended dishes: Spice and port-glazed sweetbreads; Tabla salad; black spice-roasted poussin; spice-braised oxtail; eggplant-stuffed braised red onion; cranberry walnut tart. **Wine list:** Beautifully chosen for the menu. **Price range:** Lunch: apps., $8–$18; entrees, $17–$23; desserts, $8. Three-course prix-fixe dinner, $52 (plus a few supplements). **Wheelchair access:** Restrooms at street level; main dining room up a long flight of stairs. **Features:** Outdoor dining. **Services:** Private parties.

Taco Taco $

1726 Second Ave. (bet. 89th & 90th Sts.)
Credit cards: Cash only

MEXICAN/TEX-MEX
(212) 289-8226
Meals: L, D

Every neighborhood should have a Mexican restaurant like this where the atmosphere is casual and pleasant but the food is serious. Tacos, naturally, are the mainstay, with fillings like pork with sautéed cabbage, tongue and crumbled chorizo. More ambitious dishes include tender pork marinated with smoky chipotle chilies and grilled. Even nachos are made with unusual care.

Alcohol: Beer and wine. **Price range:** Lunch: apps., $3–$5.95; entrees, $4.85–$8; desserts, $3. Dinner: apps., $3–$5.95; entrees, $8.95–$11.95; desserts, $3. **Wheelchair access:** Not accessible. **Services:** Delivery, takeout.

Tagine $25 & Under

537 Ninth Ave. (near 40th St.)
Credit cards: All major

MOROCCAN
(212) 564-7292
Meals: L, D, LN

Though Tagine is self-conscious enough to call itself a "dining gallery," it is, in the true bohemian spirit, a low-budget operation. The dim, alluring dining room seems a blizzard of colors and styles. In the front is a small stage, where jazz bands play nightly after 9:30; downstairs is a lounge area for other performances. The languorous service may lead you to believe that food is not the focus here, but you'll relax when appetizers arrive. Zaalouk, an eggplant purée rich with the dusky aroma of cumin and dressed with charmoula, a blend of garlic, lemon juice, coriander and olive oil, is wonderful on freshly baked bread. Plump grilled merguez sausages, surrounding a mound of pepper salad, are savory yet mild. All seem big enough to serve two.

The restaurant's signature tagines, fragrant stews served in traditional earthenware vessels with conical lids, are the least satisfying of the main courses, though the chicken tagine and lamb shank are quite good. Tagine offers a full bar and a brief wine list, including a grapey Moroccan red. Desserts can be excellent, like semolina cake soaked in orange blossom water.

Other recommended dishes: Roasted pepper salad, sautéed collard green, spinach andkale, couscous, pastilla, cookies. **Price range:** Apps., $4.50–$9.50; entrees, $13–$19.50. **Wheelchair access:** Everything is on one level.

Tai Hong Lau $$

70 Mott St. (bet. Bayard & Canal Sts.)
Credit cards: All major

CHINESE
(212) 219-1431
Meals: B, Br, L, D

A Chinatown favorite, especially among non-Chinese. The Cantonese food is very good and slightly more expensive than that of its neighbors.

Price range: Lunch: apps., $2–$4.80; entrees, $4.50–$11.75; desserts, $2–$4.80. Dinner: apps., $2.50–$12; entrees, $8.95–$16.95; desserts, $2–$4.80. **Features:** Kid friendly, outdoor dining. **Services:** Takeout, catering, private parties.

Taka $$

61 Grove St. (at Seventh Ave. S.)
Credit cards: All major   Meals: D

JAPANESE/SUSHI
(212) 242-3699
Closed Mon.

Three things distinguish this sushi bar from other Japanese restaurants in New York City. One is that the sushi chef is a woman, Taka Yoneyama, who is a joy to watch as she swoops and cuts. The second is her unusual presentation. Leave the choice to the chef and you will get tuna decorated with leaves of edible gold, or squid stuffed with spiced cod roe and shiso, cut into pinwheels and stacked like sculpture. The salmon roe scattered across the top glitters like jewels. Third is that Ms. Yoneyama is especially nice to children, even those who won't eat anything but rice. The plates are handmade and the restaurant is tiny. With its few tables and miniature sushi bar, Taka has the intimate scale found in Tokyo.

Alcohol: Beer and wine. **Price range:** Apps., $4–$8; entrees, $10–$27; desserts, $2.50–$6.50. **Wheelchair access:** Not accessible. **Features:** Kid friendly. **Services:** Takeout.

Tamarind ☆☆ $$$ INDIAN
41-43 E. 22nd St. (bet. Broadway & Park Ave. S.) (212) 674-7400
Credit cards: All major Meals: L, D

Tamarind, named for the sweet-and-sour fruit, looks and feels fresh. The menu treats Indian cuisine as a genuine culinary language, like French, able to assimilate nontraditional ingredients and techniques. It's a clear-cut victory for the cause of Indian food. The setting helps. Tamarind is stylishly decorated, with a cool ivory and white color scheme. The raised, wrap-around banquettes make diners seem aloof and regal.

Quality varies on the extensive dinner menu, but on balance, the winners outnumber the losers by about 3 to 1. Some innovations catch fire, like creamy she-crab soup with ginger juice and a sprinkling of saffron and chives. Other dishes are executed with great delicacy, like the Calcutta specialty known as raj kachori, a lightly spiced chickpea croquette with a paper-thin crisp skin. For whatever reason, anything involving shrimp succeeds wildly, like shrimp balchau, an exotic shrimp cocktail with a smoothly fiery chili-masala sauce containing tiny chunks of firm tomato. Vegetarian dishes also seem to bring out the best at Tamarind. Saag paneer, cubes of compressed white cheese cooked with spinach and ground spices, somehow manages to be spicily bland, with a soothing texture, making it an ideal partner for fire-breathers like lamb vindaloo. The tandoor does not perform flawlessly, though some dishes emerge moist and succulent from the oven, like noorani kebab, chunks of spiced chicken flavored with saffron. The lunch menu at Tamarind is ingenious, with five set menus, each representing a coherent Indian meal.

Other recommended dishes: Nargisi kofta (lotus-root dumplings), bhindi do piaza (okra with onions and dried mango), gulab jamun (doughnuts), pistachio ice cream. **Wine list:** About 50 mostly French and American wines, with eight wines by the glass, and three Indian beers. **Price range:** Lunch: set menus, $15–$17. Dinner: apps., $4–7; entrees, $15–$26; desserts, $4.50. **Wheelchair access:** Restrooms on street level.

Tanti Baci Caffe $25 & Under   ITALIAN

163 W. 10th St. (bet. Seventh Ave. S. & Waverly Pl.)

(212) 647-9651

Credit cards: MC/V   Meals: L, D

Tanti Baci (Italian for many kisses) is wonderfully cavelike in the cellar of a small building. The menu is appropriately basic, simply salads and a selection of pastas, you choose the sauce. There are many time-honored preparations in which the freshness of the ingredients shines through.

Recommended dishes: Fennel, carrot and arugula salad; potato and egg salad; white beans; insalate Caprese; pastas with pesto, oil and garlic, Bolognese sauce, or white clam sauce; penne with artichokes, mushrooms and prosciutto; tiramisu; chocolate mousse cake; sorbets. **Alcohol:** Beer and wine. **Price range:** Lunch: avg. app., $3.50; entree, $6.50; dessert, $3.75. Dinner: avg. app., $4.50; entree, $7.50; dessert, $4.75. **Wheelchair access:** One flight down from the street; the restroom is very narrow. **Features:** Romantic, outdoor dining, smoking room. **Services:** Delivery, takeout, catering, private parties.

Tapería Madrid $25 & Under   SPANISH/TAPAS

1471 Second Ave. (near 77th St.)   (212) 794-2923

Credit cards: All major   Meals: D, LN

From the low timbered ceiling to the wood plank floor and the long family-style tables with wide benches, Tapería Madrid has every appearance of a credible Spanish tapas bar. Add in the exuberant crowds, the dark, smoky room and the pitchers of sangria on almost every table, and you have the real thing, primarily a bar with a selection of tapas, small portions to go with a few glasses of wine or sherry. A glass of the dry and enticingly tangy fino sherry goes beautifully with olives, or with boquerónes, fresh anchovies marinated in olive oil and garlic. In fact, the sherries go with almost everything, like toast rounds rubbed with garlic and tomato and topped with thin slices of Spanish ham, or cubes of sweet beets with salty cured anchovies and roasted garlic. Desserts include a fine caramel flan, and there is a nice selection of Spanish cheeses.

Other recommended dishes: Marinated olives; scallops in white wine and lemon sauce; grilled sardines; Spanish sausage. **Wine list:** There is an excellent selection here. **Price range:** Tapas, $4.50–$10. **Wheelchair access:** Everything is on one level. **Features:** Smoking permitted by the bar.

Tappo ☆ $$$

403 E. 12th St. (at First Ave.)
Credit cards: All major

(212) 505-0001
Meals: D, LN

New York has plenty of neighborhoods, and no shortage of restaurants, but a really good neighborhood restaurant can be hard to find. Tappo, in the East Village, hits the mark. The food is simple and fresh; the setting feels like a farmhouse kitchen, dark and cool, with heavy ceiling beams and long wooden tables. Until the restaurant fills up, guests are seated at a civilized distance from one another.

The menu has a long, unchanging list of appetizers that mixes traditional Italian starters with less predictable Spanish and Middle Eastern dishes, but the best of them, regardless of origin, have the sparkle that can only come from fresh ingredients. Two baby octopuses, straight from the grill, come with a bright tabbouleh salad fragrant with parsley and mint. Some appetizers, like prosciutto di Carpegna with grilled green and white asparagus in a little oil, do the bare minimum, which is enough with asparagus of this quality. Entrees, which change nightly, are deliberately plain. Baby chicken sautéed in herbs and white wine is just the sort of unpretentious dish that a place like Tappo should serve, and the kitchen turns out a superior roasted branzino, firm-fleshed and moist, with a robust accompaniment of mixed mushrooms. The pastas can be excellent. Best of all is a big bowl of very firm rigatoncini lightly sauced with prosciutto, arugula and radicchio, but lobster-asparagus risotto pulls off a minor coup. It is sumptuous without being heavy, with a textbook creaminess that still allows flavors to shine through.

The dessert lineup changes, but a creamy ricotta cheesecake sprinkled with bits of chocolate usually appears, as well as a richly flavored flourless chocolate cake. The standout dessert, however, is a dense panna cotta drizzled with sweetly pungent 25-year-old balsamic vinegar.

Other recommended dishes: Cuttlefish with mango and lentils; seared tuna with corona beans; steak with arugula and Parmesan cheese. **Wine list:** An adventurous 130-bottle list, mostly Italian and French, with an emphasis on country wines, and 21 wines by the glass. **Price range:** Dinner, appetizers, $7–$14; entrees, $15–$26; desserts, $7. **Wheelchair access:** One step up at entrance; restrooms on dining room level.

Taprobane $

234 W. 56th St. (bet. Eighth Ave. & Broadway)
Credit cards: All major

SRI LANKAN
(212) 333-4203
Meals: Br, L, D

This is the second-best Sri Lankan restaurant in New York City, after Lakruwana. Unfortunately, these may be the only two Sri

Lankan restaurants in New York. Still, the food has improved since Taprobane opened, and it's worth tasting the spicy, unusual fare. It is similar to Indian food but with different spicing in the curries, and different dishes, like hoppers, delicate pancakes made of rice flour and coconut milk.

Price range: Lunch: apps., $4.50–$6; entrees, $5.50–$7.50. Dinner: apps., $5–$9; entrees, $9.90–$15.90. **Wheelchair access:** Not accessible. **Services:** Delivery, takeout, catering, private parties.

Taquería de Mexico $25 & Under
MEXICAN/TEX-MEX

93 Greenwich Ave. (bet. W. 12th & Bank Sts.)   (212) 255-5212
Credit cards: Cash only   Meals: B, Br, L, D, LN

This handsome taquería has the same owners as Mi Cocina, one of the city's top Mexican restaurants, and their meticulous care is evident in Mexican street food like tacos and taquitos al pastor. The restaurant has enlarged its menu and serves more complex dishes, like sautéed shrimp with cactus pads and roast chicken glazed with ancho adobo sauce. The stylish little dining room, with turquoise tables and colorful paintings and masks, looks at if it had been plucked out of Cuernavaca.

Other recommended dishes: Taquitos; tacos; tamales; guacamole; burritos; fajitas; tortas; Mexican beverages. **Alcohol:** Beer and wine. **Price range:** Lunch: apps., $2.95–$4.95; entrees, $6.95–$11.95; desserts, $2. Dinner: apps., $4.50–$7.95; entrees, $9.95–$16.95; desserts, $3.50; three-course prix fixe, $20. **Wheelchair access:** Everything is on one level. **Features:** Kid friendly. **Services:** Delivery, takeout, catering, private parties.

The Tasting Room ☆ $$$ NEW AMERICAN

72 E. 1st St. (at First Avenue)   (212) 358-7831
Credit cards: All major   Meals: D   Closed Sun.

The Tasting Room follows the new downtown paradigm in almost every respect. The room is spartan and cramped. The menu has been edited down to a handful of dishes, and the restaurant radiates a sense of mission, with earnest service. The formula seems to work. Diners pack the place night after night.

When the restaurant is not caught up in its own spell, it does the honorable work of serving good food at a moderate price in a pleasant atmosphere, with a clever format. The menu allows diners to combine several tasting portions into a meal or to order the usual appetizer and main course.

What sets the Tasting Room apart is its ferociously ambitious wine list, a nicely-priced, all-American roster that ventures well off the beaten track. In comparison, the menu is a mere footnote. Half of it makes an impression, half seems like easy-listening music, pleasant but bland. Rabbit, done as a braised saddle and a pan-fried leg, is nicely shown off with enormous, garlicky white lima beans, braised spinach and a medium-powered olive sauce, not too assertive to override the admirably moist rabbit meat. A simple pan-roasted sea bass gets the full treatment, set on a bed of roasted eggplant and surrounded by corn, garlic chives and an exceptionally clean, zesty sauce of saffron and orange. Fresh asparagus is steamed gently and teamed with shiitake mushrooms, slivers of apple and onion, and a chunk of eel escabeche. The combination is daring and successful.

For dessert, Renée's Mother's Cheesecake is a cheesecake to die for, lighter than air, with a barely-there crust and a restrained sweetness level. And when it's not runny, the dark chocolate tart cannot be resisted.

Other recommended dishes: Trout with bacon and spelt, duck legs with red and white hominy, citrus-cured cod with yuzu vinaigrette. **Wine list:** An all-American list of more than 350 wines, with unusual varietals like melon, pinot meunier and lemberger. There are a dozen wines by the glass. **Price range:** Apps,. $7–$15; entrees, $13–$29; desserts, $6. **Wheelchair access:** A small step up to the dining room. Restroom is on dining room level.

Tavern on the Green ☆ $$$$ NEW AMERICAN

Central Park W. (at 67th St.) (212) 873-3200
Credit cards: All major Meals: Br, L, D

This is America's largest-grossing restaurant, a wonderland of lights, flowers, chandeliers and balloons that can make a child out of the most cynical adult. Patrick Clark, who died in February 1998, was a terrific chef, and he's left a culinary legacy for his successors to follow. But even he was not able to overcome the tavern's unaccountably rude and lax service. Even so, the people keep coming, for the glittery setting and for dishes like mustard-and-herb-crusted rack of pork, served with braised red cabbage and potatoes mashed with horseradish. The trick is simply getting the food. (*Ruth Reichl*)

Other recommended dishes: Menu changes seasonally. **Wine list:** Large and wide-ranging with a few bargains among the high-end wines. **Price range:** Apps., $7.75–$65 (Beluga caviar); entrees, $18–$37. Prix-fixe lunch, Mon.-Fri., noon-3 P.M., $20.01–$25. Prix-fixe dinner, Mon-Fri, 5-6:30 P.M., $33–42. **Wheelchair access:** Fully accessible. **Features:** Kid friendly, good view, romantic, outdoor dining. **Services:** Private parties.

Tavern on Jane

$25 & Under AMERICAN

31 Eighth Ave. (at Jane St.) (212) 675-2526

Credit cards: All major Meals: L, D, LN

Tavern on Jane is a convivial, unpretentious neighborhood bar and grill. Like other old-fashioned taverns, it is a refuge. Regulars have their usual at the bar, and neighborhood residents grab a table and are ready to order. Tobacco has a special place here, with the bar area allocated to smokers. Directly in back of that is a sometimes smoky nonsmoking area, and then curling off to the side, with its own air-conditioning system, another nonsmoking room. But it's cut off from the more bustling areas and feels a little sterile.

The menu is a reliable step above pub grub. Menu standards include crisp and meaty chicken wings, a heaping platter of crunchy fried calamari and a big bowl of mussels in a tasty sauce of white wine and herbs. Of more interest are the daily specials, like excellent, meaty crab cakes with a mango salsa and a fine green salad, and meaty pork chops in an applejack sauce, big enough to cover the plate. Otherwise, the simplest dishes are preferable, like a beefy, chewy hanger steak, fish and chips with plenty of malt vinegar, and a good, honest hamburger. There is a perfunctory wine list with a few decent bottles under $25, but it's more of a beer place, with good draft selections. Skip dessert.

Other recommended dishes: Grilled shrimp with sesame noodles; gazpacho; lamb shank. **Price range:** Apps., $2.50–$8.95; entrees, $9.95–18.95. **Wheelchair access:** Restrooms are small and narrow, step in front. **Services:** Takeout, private parties.

Tea & Sympathy

$25 & Under ENGLISH

108 Greenwich Ave. (bet. 12th & 13th Sts.) (212) 807-8329

Credit cards: Cash only Meals: Br, L, D

In cold weather, the windows of this little English restaurant are frosted over, and a blast of cold air cuts through every time the door opens. It's the perfect atmosphere for the old-fashioned but delicious food, like shepherd's pie, Sussex chicken, bangers and mash, and the full English breakfasts. Afternoon tea, served with finger sandwiches and delicate scones, is wonderful, and service is always charming.

Price range: Lunch: apps. $4; entrees, $7–$15; desserts, $5.50. Dinner: apps., $5; entrees, $7–$15; desserts, $5.50. **Wheelchair access:** Not accessible. **Features:** Romantic. **Services:** Delivery, takeout, catering.

Tea Box Cafe $ JAPANESE

693 Fifth Ave. (bet. 54th & 55th Sts.)   (212) 350-0180
Credit cards: All major   Meals: L   Closed Sun.

Beautiful food in a serene setting, hardly what you expect to find in a department store. The exquisite East-West tea, served in the basement of the Takashimaya department store, is a nice way to while away an afternoon hour, and the Zen-like dining room attracts a crowd as stylish as the cafe's minimalist serving trays. Tea can include three open-face "sandwiches" like marinated cucumber on pressed rice; chicken and wasabi on Japanese bread, and a delicate spring roll, served with fried sweet potato and slivers of grapefruit. For dessert, slender butter cookies and two of the most luxurious chocolates imaginable.

Price range: Avg. entree, $15. **Wheelchair access:** Fully accessible. **Features:** Good for business.

Ten Kai $$ JAPANESE/SUSHI

20 W. 56th St., 3rd Fl. (bet. Fifth & Sixth Aves.)   (212) 956-0127
Credit cards: All major   Meals: L, D

Affordable sushi in an area best known for its pricier outposts. The quality is more good than great, but the fish is always reliable.

Alcohol: Beer and wine. **Price range:** Lunch: apps., $4–$7.50; entrees, $10–$25; desserts, $3.75–$5. Dinner: apps., $4–$10; entrees, $10–$26; desserts, $4–$5. **Wheelchair access:** Fully accessible. **Services:** Delivery, takeout, catering, private parties.

Tennessee Mountain $ BARBECUE

143 Spring St. (at Wooster St.)   (212) 431-3993
121 W. 45th St. (bet. Sixth Ave. & Broadway)   (212) 869-4545
Credit cards: All major   Meals: L, D

Both the original restaurant in SoHo and the new Times Square branch offer great quantities of ribs and other meats for reasonable prices. The problem is the food isn't that good; it's certainly not barbecue class. The SoHo branch is farmhouse-style, while the Times Square branch resembles a raucous sports bar.

Price range: Apps., $4.50–$8.95; entrees, $6.95–$18.50; desserts, $5.50. **Wheelchair access:** Restrooms not accessible. **Features:** Kid friendly. **Services:** Delivery, takeout, catering, private parties.

Teodora $$

ITALIAN

141 E. 57th St. (bet. Lexington & Third Aves.)   (212) 826-7101
Credit cards: All major   Meals: L, D

A diminutive restaurant with a menu that looks authentically Italian and prices that are extremely reasonable for the chic location. The food is pleasant and served with a generous hand, but is otherwise unremarkable. Skip the piadina (flatbread) and try one of the hearty homemade pasta dishes.

Alcohol: Beer and wine. **Price range:** Apps., $7.50–$9.50; entrees, $11–$28; desserts, $7. **Wheelchair access:** Restrooms not accessible. **Services:** Delivery, takeout, private parties.

Tequilita's $25 & Under

MEXICAN

5213 Fourth Ave., Sunset Park, Brooklyn   (718) 492-4303
Credit cards: Cash only   Meals: L, D

Sunset Park has a growing Mexican population, and Tequilita's, a cheerful little storefront, is one of the better taquerías that dot the neighborhood. Pozole is terrific, thick with hominy and pork, and the tacos are superb, with several unusual choices like chewy pig's ears and blood sausage. Chicken enchiladas are served with a spicy, subtle mole sauce.

Price range: Apps., $4; entrees, $6–$7.95. **Wheelchair access:** Not accessible. **Services:** Delivery, takeout, catering.

Thai Cafe $

THAI

923 Manhattan Ave., Greenpoint, Brooklyn   (718) 383-3562
Credit cards: Cash only   Meals: L, D

This simply appointed Thai restaurant earned a reputation first for its spicy, delicious food, then for giving rise to Plan Eat Thailand, the popular restaurant in Williamsburg. It remains a good choice for tasty, inexpensive Thai cooking.

Alcohol: Beer and wine. **Price range:** Apps., $2.95–$3.75; entrees, $5.95–$10.95; desserts, $3.50. **Services:** Takeout, private parties.

Thailand Cafe $

THAI

95 Second Ave. (bet. Fifth & Sixth Sts.)   (212) 477-1872
Credit cards: All major   Meals: D

Among the many Thai restaurants in New York, Thailand Cafe is notable for its friendly, informal service and atmosphere. The staff is charming and happy to schmooze. The food itself is serviceable, not particularly distinct but not bad either.

Alcohol: Beer and wine. **Price range:** Apps., $4.50–$6.95; entrees, $7.95–$16.95; desserts, $2.95. **Wheelchair access:** Fully accessible. **Services:** Delivery, takeout, catering, private parties.

Thali
$25 & Under   INDIAN/VEGETARIAN
28 Greenwich Ave. (near W. 10th St.)   (212) 367-7411
Credit cards: Cash only   Meals: L, D

Tiny Thali is strictly minimalist; you don't even get a menu. What you do get is fascinating vegetarian Indian fare served on the traditional thali, a circular metal tray that holds all the components of a meal. The ingredients change every night but can include an appetizer like khapoli potato wadas, flash-fried balls of potato and spices, or steamed cakes made with rice or chick-pea flour. Main courses may feature ingredients as unusual as karela, a bitter gourd; toori, or Chinese okra, and tinda, a small green squash.

Recommended dishes: There is only one selection each day, and the meal includes an appetizer, dal, two vegetable dishes, bread, rice and dessert. **Price range:** Avg. lunch, $6. Avg. dinner, $10. Avg. brunch, $8. **Wheelchair access:** Entrance is narrow but accessible; the restroom is very narrow. **Services:** Takeout, catering, private parties.

Three of Cups
$25 & Under   ITALIAN
83 First Ave. (at 5th St.)   (212) 388-0059
Credit cards: All major   Meals: Br, D, LN

Pizzas and roasted dishes from the wood-burning oven are the best bets at this warm restaurant with a medieval theme, signaled by the name, derived from tarot cards. The excellent thin-crust pizzas come with toppings ranging from the appealing, piquant puttanesca, to the quirky potato. Perhaps you can explain the allure of a potato pizza?

Price range: Apps., $3.50–$8; pastas, $7.50–$11; entrees, $9–$15; desserts, $5. **Wheelchair access:** Restrooms not accessible. **Features:** Outdoor dining. **Services:** Delivery, takeout, catering, private parties.

Tibetan Yak
$25 & Under   TIBETAN
72-20 Roosevelt Ave., Jackson Heights, Queens   (718) 779-1119
Credit cards: All major   Meals: L, D

Though it is almost directly under the Roosevelt Avenue elevated train tracks, near a busy intersection, Tibetan Yak feels like a respite from the urban crush. Its wooden tables are widely spaced, giving the room an airy, calm quality. The decoration is minimal, simply Tibetan symbols of luck painted on the walls, along with a painting of a yak so lifelike you can almost feel its hot breath and wet nose. As soon as you sit down, you're greeted with cups of buttered Tibetan tea, rich, slightly salty and wonderful. The service could not be sweeter, though the language barrier is strong.

Many dishes show a direct influence of China or India. Momo, or Tibetan dumplings, look exactly like Chinese pot-stickers. The Yak's momo are served steamed or fried, stuffed with meat or vegetables. While the fried beef momo are thick and clumsy, the steamed vegetable momo are ethereal, with a filling of slightly sweet cabbage and served with a delicate sesame-dressed salad. The best dishes are direct and true, with clear flavors enhanced with gentle and occasionally gutsy seasonings. Potatoes are roasted, then fried and served with spinach flavored with garlic and fresh herbs. Pork chili, thin slices of flavorful sautéed pork, comes with onions and peppers and offers the clear taste sensation of chilies without the heat. Order a dessert like Yak's dey-see, and you are taken back to a pre-industrial age. This dessert is essentially a bowl of rice, lightly sweetened, served with golden raisins and a dollop of yogurt over the top, and that's it.

Other recommended dishes: Noodles in barley and sugar, fried rice, noodles in broth with beef and spinach, bean thread noodles with vegetables, curry with chicken or lamb. **Price range:** Soups and salads, $2.50–$4; larger plates, $6–$9.95. **Wheelchair access:** Sharp angle at entrance, narrow hall to restrooms.

Tibet on Houston $25 & Under   TIBETAN

136 W. Houston St. (at Sullivan St.)   (212) 995-5884
Credit cards: Cash only   Meals: D   Closed Mon.

This is a simple, pleasant dining room with one wall covered in Tibetan prayer flags and another with paintings of the Buddha. Tibetan food is assertively seasoned with plenty of garlic, ginger and onions. It is not largely vegetarian and beef is a staple (chicken, pork and lamb are also available). The best appetizers are Tibetan sheet snails like shogok shabril, fried potatoes stuffed with minced beef, and jhasha khatsa which are deep-fried cubes of chicken in a curry marinade. Among the entrees the meat dishes are the most interesting. Particularly good is kongo shaptak — thin slices of grilled beef with chili and a smear of pungent blue cheese, and phagsh tsigma, spicy spareribs.

Other recommended dishes: Kathmandu spuds; lephing (bean cake); amdo thukpa (noodles and beef); bhaza maku. **Price range:** Apps., $2.75–$6.50; entrees, $8–$13. **Wheelchair access:** Three steps at entrance; restrooms are narrow. **Services:** Takeout.

Tierras Colombianas $25 & Under COLOMBIAN

82-18 Roosevelt Ave., Jackson Heights, Queens   (718) 426-8868
33-01 Broadway (at 33rd St.), Astoria, Queens   (718) 956-3012
Credit cards: Cash only   Meals: L, D

Excess is the way at this Colombian restaurant, one of the more
polished spots in Jackson Heights. The ultimate dish is the
mountain plate, which includes a tender steak that has been
pounded thin, immersed in lime juice and garlic and then
grilled; chicharrón, which is fried pork skin; a mountain of yellow rice with a sea of wonderfully plump pinto beans; fried
plantains; a thick wedge of avocado, and a small, circular arepa,
or corn cake, and sitting on top of all this food, a single fried egg.

Other recommended dishes: Grilled loin of pork; fried whole
red snapper; grilled top round steak; breaded fried chicken cutlets. **Price range:** Complete meals, $5–$17. **Wheelchair access:**
Entrance, aisles and restrooms are narrow. **Services:** Takeout.

Tiffin $25 & Under INDIAN/VEGETARIAN

18 Murray St. (bet. Church St. & Broadway)   (212) 791-3510
Credit cards: All major   Meals: L, D   Closed Sun.

At best, the vegetarian Indian food at Tiffin is fascinating and delicious. It's never less than interesting, and should be a must-try for
anybody curious about the range and breadth of Indian flavors.
Almost nothing is familiar about the food, which abounds in herbs
and spices not found in the usual Indian curry blends. Try the
exceptional samosas, the smoked tomato rasam, and the undhiya,
a Gujarati melange of potatoes and vegetables with adzuki beans
and plantains, strongly flavored with mustard and anise seeds.

Other recommended dishes: Mumbai dosas; chawal sevaiya;
jaipuri khazana; Mysore bese bele; apple and kiwi soup. **Alcohol:** Bring your own. **Price range:** Prix-fixe lunch, $9. Prix-fixe
dinner, $20. **Wheelchair access:** Restrooms not accessible. **Ser-
vices:** Delivery, takeout.

Time Cafe $ NEW AMERICAN

380 Lafayette St. (bet. Third & Fourth Aves.)   (212) 533-7000
2330 Broadway (at 85th St.)   (212) 579-5100
87 Seventh Ave. S. (at Barrow St.)   (212) 220-9100
Credit cards: All major   Meals: B, Br, L, D

With its big, airy dining room, and Fez, an adjacent bar and
performance space at the East Village location, Time Cafe has
always drawn a young, trendy crowd. The contemporary American food is such that, an hour later, you may not remember
what you ate. Still, it's popular enough to have given rise to offspring in the West Village and on the Upper West Side.

Price range: Lunch: sandwiches, $7–$10; entrees, $9–$14. Dinner: apps., $5–$8; entrees, $12–$20; desserts, $5–$6. **Wheelchair access:** Fully accessible. **Features:** Outdoor dining. **Services:** Takeout, catering, private parties.

Tin Room Cafe $ ITALIAN
1 Front St., Brooklyn Heights (718) 246-0310
Credit cards: All major Meals: L, D

This quaintly pretty little restaurant under the Brooklyn Bridge features live opera singers, a comfortable garden and an inexpensive menu. The food does not surprise or impress; go for the atmosphere.

Alcohol: Beer and wine. **Price range:** Lunch: apps., $3.50–$5.75; entrees, $5–$15.75; desserts, $4.50; two-course prix fixe, $7.95. Dinner: apps., $4.50–$6.75; entrees, $7.75–$24; desserts, $5.50; three-course prix fixe, $13.95. **Wheelchair access:** One small step at entrance. **Features:** Free parking for dinner. **Services:** Delivery, takeout, catering, private parties.

Tinto $25 & Under TAPAS
60 Henry St. (at Cranberry St.), Brooklyn Heights, Brooklyn
(718) 243-2010
Credit cards: All major Meals: D

Tinto looks the part of a Spanish tapas bar, with leather banquettes, dim chandeliers and candles. The inviting bar and dining room are full of wood, taken from an old upstate barn. The menu changes nightly and includes excellent cold tapas like red peppers, marinated and roasted until their sweet, robust flavor blossoms, and scallops ceviche, mellow and flavorful, lightly citrusy and served with a lawn of greens. Among the hot tapas, try bacon-wrapped dates, served pierced with a toothpick like 1950's canapes. An almond is buried in the middle for an extra bit of texture and flavor. By contrast, you're not likely to find lobster tacos in Barcelona — its loss. The chunks of lobster and potato cubes, served on small tortillas with a sweet mango-and-pepper sauce, are quite good. The few main courses do not match the tapas standard. The dessert selection is small, but the Crema Catalan and pecan tart are fine.

Tinto appreciates the natural affinity of dry fino sherry and tapas, and takes care to serve its sherries fresh and chilled. The restaurant also has a good list of Spanish wines, though only a few are under $30.

Other recommended dishes: Boquerones, beet salad, stuffed calamari. **Price range:** Tapas, $5–$9; entrees, $12–$17. **Wheelchair access:** Ramp at entrance, ramp to restrooms.

Tocqueville ☆☆ $$$ FRENCH

15 E. 15th St. (bet. Fifth Ave. & Union Sq. W.) (212) 647-1515
Credit cards: All major   Meals: L, D   Closed Sun.

In a small, trapezoidal room off Union Square, Tocqueville is a quiet haven of good taste, good food and good service. The menu is limited. The décor is done with a very light touch, suggesting luxury without overburdening the room. Although tiny, Tocqueville never feels cramped. The spacing between tables is generous, given the floor space, and the service, which could easily feel intrusive and hovering, achieves a laudable transparency.

The restaurant is the late-arriving offspring of Marco Polo, the catering place next door; owner Marco Moreira, with his supply lines already well established, had access to good raw materials, putting him ahead of the game before he started. His peas say spring, even when the world outside is stalled in winter. Scallops have a concentrated richness that helps them hold their own when paired with foie gras. The lamb has the herbal flavor that American lamb usually doesn't. Billy Bi soup, the oddly named classic from France's Atlantic coast, is beyond praise. Fat mussels float languidly in a concentrated saffron meuniere broth with a briny tang and just the right citric spark.

Mr. Moreira takes a robust approach to most entrees. His roasted rack of lamb is surrounded by braised artichokes, mushrooms and fava beans in a red-wine reduction. Sweet potato purée and a ragout of chestnuts, pearl onions and lardons make a deeply flavored complement to moist roasted venison loin.

Desserts also do honor to the menu. Warm chocolate cake, just gooey enough on the inside, comes with a scoop of green ice cream permeated with a pristine mint flavor. Upside-down banana tart is a little marvel, a small palisade of fat banana chunks encircling a disk of almond shortbread. Dripping with caramel, it's teamed up with a ball of brown-sugar ice cream.

Other recommended dishes: Sardines in brown-butter-and-olive vinaigrette; crottin de Chavignol; marinated lamb shoulder; seared scallops and foie gras; lemon gratin. **Wine list:** About 120 wines on an international list, about one-third of them priced at less than $40. There are 17 wines by the glass. **Price range:** Lunch: apps., $8–$14; entrees, $14–$24; desserts, $8. Three-course prix-fixe, $20. Dinner: apps., $8–$16; entrees, $22–$28; desserts $8. **Wheelchair access:** Restroom on street level.

Tomoe Sushi $25 & Under   JAPANESE/SUSHI

172 Thompson St. (near Houston St.) (212) 777-9346
Credit cards: All major   Meals: L, D   Closed Sun., Tue.

Long lines of people seem perpetually planted in front of this small, plain restaurant, waiting to order the terrific, inexpensive sushi. The large assortment can include clean, clear-flavored mackerel; yellowtail as soft as whipped butter; sweet shrimp, and glazed eel. The nonsushi menu includes excellent cold soba noodles and delicate shumai (shrimp dumplings).

Price range: Apps., $3.50–$6.25; entrees, $5.75–$30.75; desserts, $3. Dinner: apps., $4.25–$12; entrees, $12–$24.75; desserts, $3. **Wheelchair access:** Fully accessible. **Services:** Takeout.

The Tonic ☆☆ $$$ NEW AMERICAN

108 W. 18 St. (bet. Sixth & Seventh Aves.)   (212) 929-9755
Credit cards: All major   Meals: L, D   Closed Sun.

This is a tony new restaurant that perfectly exemplifies New York in the late 1990's. The Tonic has a raucous, old-fashioned tavern in front, and in back a tranquil restaurant filled with beautiful light that makes all the patrons look lovely. Excellent waiters serve robust American food like a wonderful pumpkin bisque, ravioli filled with sweetbreads and salsify, and scallop velouté. Among the main dishes, try cocotte of braised meats, a big casserole filled with beef cheeks, goose, lamb and veal shank with a marrow custard right in the middle. Or the spiced duck, and the extraordinary truffle-crusted salmon in red wine fumet tastes like absolutely nothing else on earth. (*Ruth Reichl*)

Recommended dishes: Warm eggplant terrine; roast chicken with porcini-potato purée; warm chocolate brioche pudding; trio of cheesecakes; orange terrine; semolina custard. **Wine list:** Interesting, fairly priced and served by knowledgeable personnel. **Price range:** Apps., $8–$19; entrees, $25–$28; desserts, $8.50. **Wheelchair access:** Dining room at street level. **Services:** Private parties.

Tony's Di Napoli $ ITALIAN

1606 Second Ave. (bet. 83rd & 84th Sts.)   (212) 861-8686
Credit cards: All major   Meals: D

Enormous family-style portions of garlic-laden southern Italian food are the attraction, as at Carmine's, but without Carmine's crowds. It's not great, but it's not expensive, either.

Price range: Dinner (family style, serves two-three): apps., $8–$12; entrees, $10–$26; desserts, $3–$12. **Wheelchair access:** Fully accessible. **Features:** Smoking permitted, outdoor dining. **Services:** Delivery, takeout, catering, private parties.

Top of the Tower $$$ NEW AMERICAN

Beekman Tower Hotel, 3 Mitchell Pl., 26th Fl.
(at 49th St. & First Ave.)   (212) 980-4796
Credit cards: All major   Meals: D, LN

Great view, fabulous Art Deco room, forgettable food. Go for a
drink, eat elsewhere (or go after dinner).

Price range: Three-course prix-fixe dinners, $35, $45 and $55.
Wheelchair access: Elevator to dining room. **Features:** Good
view. **Services:** Catering, private parties.

Topaz Thai $25 & Under THAI

127 W. 56th St. (bet. Sixth & Seventh Aves.)   (212) 957-8020
Credit cards: All major   Meals: L, D

This Thai restaurant offers fine Thai cooking in a convenient
midtown location. Soups, like the delicious tom kha gai, made
with chicken stock, coconut milk, chili peppers and lime, are
particularly good, as are spicy dishes like the soupy jungle curry
made with scallops and green beans. The restaurant has a peculiar nautical theme courtesy of a previous tenant — Art Deco
paneling, triangular sconces and wooden captain's chairs.

Other recommended dishes: Mee krob; curry puffs; yum woon-
sen; gai yang; spareribs. **Price range:** Apps., $3.75–$8.75; entrees,
$7.95–$17.95; desserts, $4.50. **Wheelchair access:** Entrance is too
narrow for a wheelchair. **Services:** Delivery, takeout.

Toraya $ JAPANESE

17 E. 71st St. (bet. Fifth & Madison Aves.)   (212) 861-1700
Credit cards: All major   Meals: L   Closed Sun.

Entering Toraya is like stepping into a hushed and peaceful
Japanese temple. This tea salon has a menu of unusual Japanese dishes, but the highlights are the beautiful, meticulously
fashioned pastries like zangetsu, a soft ginger-flavored pancake
folded over a filling of sweetened azuki bean paste, etched with
a pattern of chrysanthemum petals. They are delicate, delicious
and unforgettable.

Price range: Lunch items from $5; desserts, $2.30–$10. **Wheel-
chair access:** Not accessible. **Services:** Private parties.

Tossed $ AMERICAN/CAFE

295 Park Ave. S. (bet. 22nd & 23rd Sts.)   (212) 674-6700
Credit Cards: All major   Meals: L, D

This stylish, minimalist restaurant exalts the salad, offering
more than a dozen enticing combinations, plus a design-it-your-
self menu. Tossed draws a fashionable, good-looking crowd,

including visitors from the various modeling agencies in the neighborhood, though it's doubtful that an excellent salad like rock shrimp with citrus chipotle dressing would qualify in any model's diet. Beyond salads are enticing soups and sandwiches.

Price range: Entrees, $6.95–$15.95; desserts, $4.95–$5.95.
Wheelchair access: Restrooms not accessible. **Services:** Delivery, takeout, catering, private parties.

Totonno Pizzeria $25 & Under   PIZZA

1524 Neptune Ave., Coney Island, Brooklyn   (718) 372-8606
1544 Second Ave. (bet. 80th & 81st Sts.)   (212) 327-2800
Credit cards: Cash only at Coney Island   Meals: L, D
Closed Mon., Tue. (Coney Island)

The original Totonno's, one of the early giants of New York City coal-oven pizza, is legendary both for its irregular hours and its devotion to artisanal pies served in humble surroundings. With its site in a small Italian bastion near Coney Island, Totonno's almost feels as if it's in another city, but the pressed tin walls are covered with testimonials from the glory days. The mozzarella is fresh and creamy, and the crust is soft and pillowy, bready rather than crisp. Measured against the vast sea of pizzas, Totonno is still near the top, but measured against its past, Totonno doesn't keep up. Unlike the humble Coney Island pizzeria, the Upper East Side branch is duded up for the neighborhood.

Alcohol: Beer and wine. **Price range:** Pizzas, $14–$15.70.
Wheelchair access: Not accessible. **Features:** Kid friendly.
Services: Takeout, private parties.

Tout Va Bien $$ BISTRO/FRENCH

311 W. 51st St. (bet. Eighth & Ninth Aves.)   (212) 974-9051
Credit cards: All major   Meals: L, D

A classic New York City bistro in the theater district that has been around for 50 years serving just what you would expect in a rustic atmosphere. Even the soundtrack is predictable.

Price range: Apps., $5–$8; entrees, $12–$18; desserts, $5.
Wheelchair access: Not accessible. **Features:** Smoking at the bar. **Services:** Takeout, private parties.

Town ☆☆☆ $$$ NEW AMERICAN

Chambers Hotel, 15 W. 56th St. (bet. Fifth & Sixth Ave.)
   (212) 582-4445
Credit cards: All major   Meals: L, D

There's nothing flashy about Town, but it has an unmistakable sense of style that starts with the dining room, one floor down from the lobby in the new Chambers Hotel. David Rockwell, who designed the hotel as well as the restaurant, has brought in lightness and air by lining the room in translucent sheets of blond wood and square panels wrapped in taupe suede. Strands of crystal beads suspended from the ceiling catch the light like giant Champagne bubbles frozen in mid-ascent.

It's a civilized, very adult setting that suits Geoffrey Zakarian's elegant, clean cooking, which seems almost effortlessly assured. With no visible signs of strain, he manages to enliven his dishes with just the half twist that makes them distinctive, as in a simple roasted skate served with three sorbet-shaped quenelles: pea-peppermint, apple-miso, and eggplant with hazelnut oil and quatre-épices. The foie gras terrine is a work of art — tempting layers of solid meat suspended in mousse and topped by a thick, fearless layer of yellow fat.

The execution at Town rarely falters. Quail is more often than not a tough, chewy disappointment, but at Town the little birds maintain a buttery succulence that makes them just a little firmer than the tiny foie gras fritters that come with them. Thick slabs of spice-crusted duck, deeply flavored, need no knife, and Mr. Zakarian proceeds to do wonderful things to them. He adds a hearty buckwheat pilaf and caramelized endive stuffed with thin slices of apple. Slow cooking causes the endive and apples to exchange flavors and textures until they are impossible to tell apart.

Some dishes are simplicity itself. Fresh pea soup with brittle shards of fried prosciutto and a few intact peas bobbing here and there gives an upgrade to traditional split pea and ham soup. A risotto of escargots doused with black truffle broth seems unfair. How can it fail? It's like having the chef write you a large check.

The dessert list is strong, and one is a showstopper with a strong New Orleans accent. It starts with a basket of sugar-powdered beignets filled with molten chocolate. Then comes a perfect frozen dome with a matte-brown cocoa surface. It's a chilled version of café brûlot, a flaming liqueur-laced coffee. The ingredients are solidified into a thick layer of coffee ice cream flavored with rum, orange and lemon zest, and Grand Marnier.

Other recommended dishes: Scallops with scallop sausage, red grapefruit gratin. **Wine list:** A solid list, mostly American, of about 200 bottles, with 18 half bottles and 10 wines by the glass. **Price range:** Lunch: apps., $9–$18; entrees, $18–$21; desserts, $9–$10. Dinner: apps., $10–$16; entrees, $21–$29; desserts, $9–$10. **Wheelchair access:** Elevator in hotel lobby descends to restaurant.

(handwritten annotations at top: "excellent!", "artichoke hearts,", "thin pizza", "veal chops", "fries")

Trattoria dell'Arte ☆ $$$ ITALIAN

900 Seventh Ave. (bet. 56th & 57th Sts.) (212) 245-9800
Credit cards: All major   Meals: Br, L, D, LN

There are reasons this trattoria near Carnegie Hall has been a hit since 1989: The antipasto is superb, the rest of the northern Italian food is reliably good, the service is professional and the place is always lively. And always packed. If you run out of things to say, you can always discuss Milton Glazer's outrageous design. Pastas, which can be had in half portions as starters, are among the best options: they include spinach-and-cheese ravioli, lobster linguine, a risotto of the day and a house special of tordelli bolognese. Dessert specialties include chocolate cake with chocolate sauce and a lighter version of Christmas panettone, the traditional yeast cake with candied fruit. (*Ruth Reichl*)

Price range: Apps., $8–$11; entrees, $17–$36. **Wheelchair access:** Front room only is accessible. **Features:** Outdoor dining. **Services:** Takeout, private parties.

Trattoria I Pagliacci $25 & Under ITALIAN

240 Park Ave. S. (near 20th St.) (212) 505-3072
Credit cards: Cash only   Meals: Br, L, D, LN

On entering this small Italian restaurant, the yeasty aroma of freshly baked focaccia combines with the scent of rosemary and garlic, of olive oil and sausage. It's like an olfactory still life of an Italian grocery store. The best pastas are simple and delicious. This is a happy place that attracts a late crowd. It sometimes can be hard to hear over the recorded jazz and buzz from other tables.

Other recommended dishes: Grilled portobello mushroom; grilled squid; pappardelle with mushrooms and chicken; tagliatelle with meat sauce; roasted lamb; grilled pork chop; hazelnut gelato in espresso; tiramisu. **Alcohol:** Beer and wine. **Price range:** Lunch: apps., $3–$6; pastas, $6–$8; entrees, $9.50–$11.50; desserts, $4.50. Dinner: apps., $4.50–$7; pastas, $7–$9; entrees, $11.50–$14; desserts, $4.50. **Wheelchair access:** One step up to dining room; restroom is narrow. **Services:** Takeout.

Trattoria L'incontro $25 & Under ITALIAN

21-76 31st St. (near Ditmars Blvd.), Astoria, Queens
(718) 721-3532
Credit cards: All major   Meals: L, D   Closed Mon.

At a time when many chefs solicit appreciation for their fashionable creativity, L'Incontro is a throwback, offering familiar

Italian dishes prepared by a chef who tries to avoid inserting himself between the ingredients and the clientele. The restaurant looks like an impersonal, assembly-line place. Yet L'Incontro has all the warmth of a corner mom-and-pop — or more accurately, mom-and-son. The owner and chef, Rocco Sacramone, is aided by his mother, Tina Sacramone, who oversees the pasta-making operation.

Pastas are excellent, particularly the fresh ones made by Mrs. Sacramone and, like the appetizers, enhanced by their simplicity. Cavatelli, a short, ribbed pasta, is well matched with crumbled sausage, cabbage and just a touch of truffle oil, while thin taglierini comes with nubs of asparagus and peas, all wrapped in a swatch of prosciutto. Even spaghetti and meatballs shine, thanks to a lively tomato sauce. Nothing could be simpler or better than an appetizer of cacciatorino with mozzarella and roasted peppers. Thin slices of the earthy cacciatorino, a dried sausage, went beautifully with the pillowy, nutty-tasting mozzarella, and the tart sweetness of the peppers was a refreshing counterpoint. Tomato-and-rabbit ragù, served with gnocchi so light they are almost fluffy, and roasted rabbit are both very tasty. L'Incontro has a nice selection of wines under $25, as well as a few worthy splurges.

Other recommended dishes: Ggrilled escarole and beans; grilled octopus; pizza; breaded sole and shrimp; osso buco.
Price range: Apps., $4.50–$8.95; pizzas, $5.95–$8.95; entrees, $8.95–$24.95. **Wheelchair access:** Everything is on one level.

Trattoria Spaghetto $ ITALIAN
232 Bleecker St. (at Carmine St.)   (212) 255-6752
Credit cards: Cash only   Meals: L, D, LN

This restaurant had an outsize reputation in the old days, when it was known as the Bleecker Luncheonette, known particularly for its hearty green minestrone. Nowadays its just another cheap Italian restaurant, crowded to be sure, but perhaps because of how good the food was long ago.

Price range: Apps., $3.25–$6.50; pastas, $8.25–$9.25; entrees, $11.75–$14.75; desserts, $3. **Wheelchair access:** Fully accessible. **Services:** Takeout.

Tribeca Grill ☆☆ $$$ NEW AMERICAN
375 Greenwich St. (at Franklin St.)   (212) 941-3900
Credit cards: All major   Meals: Br, L, D

Robert De Niro's first venture into the restaurant business in what the neighbors sometimes call Bob Row is a cool, casual outpost of modern American cuisine with an almost constant flow of celebrity guests. And the food's good. The big, airy space with exposed bricks, colorful banquettes and comfortable tables centers on a massive handsome mahogany bar many may remember as the original bar of Maxwell's Plum. The beguiling fare remains a steady lure. (*Ruth Reichl*)

Price range: Apps., $8–$11; entrees, $12–$32. Brunch, $11–$18. Lunch prix-fixe, $20.01. **Wheelchair access:** Fully accessible. **Features:** Kid friendly, good for business, outdoor dining. **Services:** Catering, private parties.

Triomphe ☆ ☆ $ FRENCH/NEW AMERICAN
Iroquois Hotel, 49 W. 44th St. (bet. Fifth & Sixth Aves.)
                                           (212) 453-4233
Credit cards: All major   Meals: B, L, D

In a city with flash to spare, this restaurant has a rare commodity: charm. The setting is subdued and adult, with pristine white walls, dark walnut floors and a dome ceiling with precise, crenelated moldings. It is an awkwardly proportioned room, but clever decorating has smoothed out the worst of the problems. The food is appropriately simple and understated.

The small menu abounds in small pleasures supported by big flavors, like the chewy brioche croutons that shore up a rich, vermouth-scented stew of Malpeque oysters, packed with potatoes and leeks. Again and again, Triomphe quietly strikes the right note, as with a subtle herb broth that nicely underlines the natural sweetness of acorn-squash wontons covered in shavings of Parmesan cheese. When the main ingredient calls for more, the chef opens up the flavors. A hefty rib-eye steak comes with fat grilled cèpes and a muscular brandy demi-glace, and a thick slab of salmon gets the works: a caviar-dotted beurre blanc, a scattering of grilled shrimp and parsnip whipped potatoes.

The best bet on the short dessert list is the poached Bosc pear, primarily because of what comes with it, a deceptively labeled chestnut poundcake that turns out to be a tiny bun split in half, filled with chestnut jam and espresso anglaise and topped with whipped cream.

Other recommended dishes: Chicken livers, rabbit stew in red-wine sauce with crepes, halibut with jasmine rice and ginger-chili marinade. **Wine list:** A short, rather mundane list of 50 wines, mostly French and Californian, at budget prices, with 14 by the glass. **Price range:** Lunch, apps., $7–$10; entrees, $14–$28; desserts, $8. Dinner, apps., $7–$13; entrees, $23–$32; desserts, $8. **Wheelchair access:** Four steps up to hotel and restaurant. Restrooms are in hotel lobby, on same level as dining room.

Trionfo $$$ ITALIAN

224 W. 51st St. (bet. Eighth Ave. & Broadway)   (212) 262-6660
Credit cards: All major   Meals: L, D

Small and modestly decorated with good northern Italian food
and surprisingly high prices for the neighborhood. Regulars are
treated with great affection, but no one will feel slighted.

Price range: Avg. app., $10; pasta, $14; entree, $19; dessert,
$5.95. **Wheelchair access:** Restrooms not accessible. **Features:**
Outdoor dining. **Services:** Takeout, catering, private parties.

Triple Eight Palace $$ CHINESE

88 E. Broadway (bet. Division & Market Sts.)   (212) 941-8886
Credit cards: All major   Meals: L, D

Eight, in case you hadn't guessed, is a lucky number in China.
And you'll be lucky to eat the fine dim sum in this large, dim
restaurant just beneath the Manhattan Bridge.

Price range: Lunch, $7–$9. Dinner, $10–$15. **Wheelchair
access:** Not accessible. **Features:** Kid friendly. **Services:** Takeout, catering, private parties.

Trois Canards $$ BISTRO/FRENCH

184 Eighth Ave. (bet. 19th & 20th Sts.)   (212) 929-4320
Credit cards: All major   Meals: Br, L, D

Ducks are everywhere in this pleasant if slightly too cute
Chelsea bistro. The food is primarily bistro French with modern
touches. And yet, in the hip new art world that Chelsea has
become, this seems more like the old Chelsea than the new.

Price range: Lunch: apps., $5.95–$7.95; entrees, $9.95–$12.95;
desserts, $6–$7. Dinner: apps., $6.95–$8.95; entrees,
$14.95–$21.95; desserts, $6–$7. **Wheelchair access:** Restrooms
not accessible. **Features:** Outdoor dining. **Services:** Delivery,
takeout, catering, private parties.

Trois Marches   ☆ $$ FUSION/FRENCH

306 E. 81st St. (bet. First & Second Aves.)   (212) 639-1900
Credit cards: Cash only   Meals: Br, D

Eating at Trois Marches is like stepping into a French version of
"Big Night." Owned and operated by two brothers, Marc and
Pierre Tagournet, the restaurant (whose name refers to the three
steps you descend to the entrance) is just large enough to hold
the owners, a tiny bar and a few tables and banquettes, arrayed
against peach-colored brick walls. Marc, the chef, has the kind
of attention-grabbing ideas that make Trois Marches a little
more interesting than the competition. Some of the ideas work.
Some do not. One of the more inspired French and Asian

encounters is a fricassee of snails and shiitake mushrooms in a deeply flavored, syrupy veal reduction, with fried shallots scattered here and there for crunch. For shock value, it would be hard to beat the appetizer of grilled eggplant, served as a kind of barge filled with crab and complemented by daubs of peanut-butter sauce and fried basil. It has a loony sound to it, but daring in this case is rewarded. The desserts swing wildly between extremes. At one end lies an insipid, flabby tapioca flan. At the other, looking oddly like pieces of meat, are thick, toothsome chocolate crepes wrapped around semisweet chocolate mousse scattered with hazelnuts and walnuts.

Other recommended dishes: Cod fillet with ginger; beef with spices and beer curry reduction. **Wine List:** A work-in-progress, with the current list of about 20 wines being expanded to about 50 modest wines from France, California and Long Island. **Price Range:** Dinner, apps., $6–$10.50; entrees, $17.50–$24.50; desserts, $6. **Wheelchair access:** Three steps down to entrance.

Tropica $$$ SEAFOOD
200 Park Ave. (at 45th St. & Lexington Ave.)   (212) 867-6767
Credit cards: All major   Meals: L, D   Closed Sat., Sun.

Excellent seafood in a corporate setting, often with an Asian accent. It's hard to forget that you're in the very bottom of the MetLife building when you're eating here, surrounded by men in suits.

Price range: Apps., $8–$14.50; entrees, $19.50–$35; desserts, $8. **Wheelchair access:** Fully accessible. **Services:** Catering, private parties.

Tsampa $25 & Under   TIBETAN
212 E. 9th St. (bet. Second & Third Aves.)   (212) 614-3226
Credit cards: All major   Meals: L, D, LN

Tsampa is peaceful and contemplative, as one might imagine of a Tibetan restaurant, except when the juicer goes off with a horrible mechanical whine. But Tsampa stands out from other Tibetan restaurants because the food is unusually well spiced. Steamed momos — light, delicate crescent-shaped dumplings — come with a fiery dipping sauce that ignites the flavors. The earthy phing sha — chicken and collard greens blended with mung bean noodles — is a lively main course.

Other recommended dishes: Lentil soup; spicy udon noodles; grilled whole trout; grilled salmon; yam and pumpkin pie; rice with yogurt, raisins and pine nuts. **Alcohol:** Beer and wine. **Price range:** Apps., $4.95; entrees, $8.95–$12.95; desserts, $4. **Wheelchair access:** Everything is on one level. **Services:** Delivery, takeout, catering, private parties.

Tse Yang $$$ CHINESE
34 E. 51st St. (bet. Madison & Park Aves.)   (212) 688-5447
Credit cards: All major   Meals: L, D

Expensive and pretentious Chinese food for people who would
really rather eat with forks and not be bothered by bones. Both
the setting and the prices are regal.

Price range: Lunch: three-course prix fixe, $25.75. Dinner:
apps., $5.25–$18; entrees, $18.50–$52 (Peking duck); desserts,
$7–$10. **Wheelchair access:** Fully accessible. **Features:** Good
for business. **Services:** Private parties.

Tsunami $ JAPANESE/SUSHI
70 W. 3rd St. (bet. Thompson St. & La Guardia Pl.)
                                                    (212) 475-7770
Credit cards: All major   Meals: L, D

At this stylish sushi restaurant, a little boat cruises the length of
the oval bar, tugging a sushi barge. The problem is, the sushi is
routine, which makes this simply a mediocre sushi bar with a
gimmick.

Price range: Lunch: apps., $4–$7; entrees, $7–$12; desserts, $6.
Dinner: apps., $4–$7; entrees, $10–$22; desserts, $6. **Wheelchair access:** Not accessible. **Features:** Outdoor dining. **Services:** Delivery, takeout, private parties.

Tupelo Grill $$$ STEAKHOUSE
1 Penn Plaza (bet. Seventh & Eighth Aves. at 33rd St.)
                                                    (212) 760-2700
Credit cards: All major   Meals: L, D

A manly sort of place with a menu that reads like an ode to protein and waiters who look like they work out in a serious way.
The porterhouses for two, three or four come with plenty of
butter spooned over the top, the sirloin is good and the lamb
chops are small, soft and smooth as velvet. There are a couple
of sissy dishes, including the most bizarre chopped salad you
can imagine. Skip dessert.

Price range: Apps., $6–$18; entrees, $17–$33.50; desserts, $6.
Features: Smoking permitted. **Services:** Private parties.

Turkish Kitchen $$ TURKISH
386 Third Ave. (bet. 27th & 28th Sts.)   (212) 679-1810
Credit cards: All major   Meals: L, D

Wonderful Turkish food in a dimly romantic setting. The food
will remind you of the culinary links between Greece and

Turkey. Appetizers are the star of this large, trim, red-walled dining room. Phyllo dough is rolled parchment thin, tucked around sharp, house-made feta cheese and fried to make the crisp sigara boregi, while mint, cucumber and garlic are folded into thick yogurt to make cacik. Giant appetizer platters may also include sahanda sucuk, a garlicky beef sausage; yogurtlu ispanak, stewed dilled spinach with yogurt and garlic, and tarama salatasi, a zesty version of Greek red caviar spread. Reliable main courses include a succulent kasarli kofte, a spicy blend of ground lamb and beef; grilled lamb chops, and hunkar begendi, lamb stewed with tomatoes and served over a smoky eggplant purée.

Price range: Four-course prix-fixe lunch, $13.95. Dinner: apps., $5.50–$8.50; entrees, $13.50–$18.75; desserts, $5.50. **Wheelchair access:** Assistance available for three steps down; restrooms not accessible. **Services:** Delivery, takeout, catering, private parties.

Turkuaz $25 & Under   TURKISH/MIDDLE EASTERN

2637 Broadway (at 100th St.)   (212) 665-9541
Credit cards: All major   Meals: D

Rrestaurants at the southwest corner of Broadway and 100th Street have come and gone faster than Italian prime ministers over the last decade, but Turkuaz should outlast them all. Turkuaz differs not only because the food is good, but also because it has a clear identity. The dining room is draped in billowy fabric so that it resembles an Ottoman tent. Seat covers give standard restaurant chairs a lush appearance, and the staff is adorned in traditional Turkish costumes.

There is also an extensive menu featuring excellent cold appetizers, perfect when the going gets steamy and just right with a basket of puffy, fresh-baked Turkish bread. The lineup includes the usual Middle Eastern complement, like creamy hummus and smoky baba ghanouj, along with Turkish specialties like patlican salatasi, a tangy, garlic-enhanced eggplant purée, and acili ezme, a mash of tomatoes, green peppers, onions and walnuts blended with parsley, olive oil and lemon juice and given a pleasant jolt with red pepper flakes. Main courses tend to be simple and elementally satisfying, like beyti kebab, spicy chopped lamb charcoal-grilled with herbs and garlic, and tender, well-flavored lamb chops. For added complexity, adana yogurtlu, a blend of beef and lamb layered with yogurt and tomato sauce over crisp bread, is well put together, while hunkar begendi, chunks of lamb in an eggplant purée, is rich and creamy. Desserts include the usual baklava and kadayif, dripping with honey, as well as a neat variation on rice pudding, served with the top caramelized like crème brûlée.

Other recommended dishes: Cacik; haydari; shepherd's salad; lahmacun; pides; Turkish soft drinks. **Price range:** Apps.,

$3–$7.95; entrees, $8.50–$18.50. **Wheelchair access:**
Restrooms down a flight of stairs.

Tuscan Square $$$ ITALIAN
16 W. 51st St. (bet. Fifth & Sixth Aves.)   (212) 977-7777
Credit cards: All major   Meals: B, L, D

Pino Luongo has opened his first theme park restaurant in
Rockefeller Center. The theme here is Tuscany, complete with
plates, linens, clothing and, of course, food. The food can be
very good, from interesting antipasto plates to fine, spare plates
of pasta, but you never forget you're eating in a store.

Price range: Lunch: apps., $6–$10; pastas, $12–$17; entrees,
$18–$22; desserts, $7. Dinner: apps., $9–$12; pastas, $15–$18;
entrees, $20–$32; desserts, $9. **Wheelchair access:** Fully acces-
sible. **Features:** Kid friendly. **Services:** Delivery, takeout, catering, private parties.

Tuscan Steak (Satisfactory) $$$$ ITALIAN
622 Third Ave. (at 40th St.)   (212) 404-1700
Credit cards: All major   Meals: L, D, LN

As an equation, Tuscany multiplied by steak equals enormous
crowds. As a piece of stage design, Tuscan Steak makes a powerful impression. The piazza-like main room leads to a more
intimate dining area with wraparound booths. The mezzanine
bar and lounge, with invitingly intimate booths and tables, is a
most civilized setting to have an aperitif. A second bar and
lounge, on basement level, aims at a younger crowd.

The food is designed to render criticism null and void. The
first signature dish here is a basket of toasted bread slices
daubed with white truffle oil and crusted with garlic. The second is, of course, the steak, specifically, slices of T-bone
brushed with olive oil and rosemary, then thrown on the grill
and served with garlic purée. It's good. The rest of the menu
can be heavy-handed and overproduced, but some of it is quite
good, like the osso buco risotto with Barolo essence, big enough
and rich enough to make four break a sweat. At Tuscan Steak,
you get the feeling that the cooks have been issued shovels
rather than spoons. As often as not, pasta comes to the rescue.
Puffy gnocchi in a simple Gorgonzola cream sauce offer a welcome contrast to the more lavish productions on the menu.

The triple-cream cheesecake is fluffy and velvety at the same
time, a real killer. All the chocolate desserts are dense and
heavy, but the revisionist cannoli, wrapped in phyllo pastry and
sprinkled with citrus sugar, shines. There were too many of
them, of course. But at Tuscan Steak, more is more.

Other recommended dishes: Linguine with chopped clams,
roasted lobster. **Wine list:** A heavily Italian list of nearly 200

wines, mostly young, with 13 wines by the half bottle and 21 wines by the glass. **Price range:** Lunch: apps., $12–$16; entrees, $15–$39; desserts, $9–$13. Dinner: apps., $12–$19; entrees, $18–$65; desserts, $9–$13. **Wheelchair access:** Elevator behind coat check serves all three levels.

"21" Club ☆☆ $$$$ AMERICAN

21 W. 52nd St. (bet. Fifth & Sixth Aves.)   (212) 582-7200
Credit cards: All major   Meals: L, D   Closed Sun.

Of all the restaurants in New York City, none has a richer history. American royalty has been entertaining at "21" for most of this century. The restaurant continues to be operated like a club where unknowns are inexorably led to the farthest dining room where they can watch from a distance as the more favored clients are pampered and petted. Nothing much else has changed either. The menu has been modernized but with mixed results. The basics are still superb, however. Great steak, rack of lamb, Dover sole, and the "21" burger, and several traditional desserts such as rice pudding and crème brûlée are all worthwhile. (*Ruth Reichl*)

Other recommended dishes: Shrimp cocktail; clams and oysters; grilled foie gras with caramelized pears; venison carpaccio; squash and mushroom risotto; Caesar salad; steak tartare; seafood in red shellfish sauce; frozen apricot yogurt with kiwi sauce. **Wine list:** Huge with surprisingly fair prices. **Price range:** Lunch: apps., $14–$24; entrees, $25–$42; desserts, $10.50; three-course prix-fixe lunch, $29. Dinner: apps., $14–$25; entrees, $25–$42; desserts, $10.50; prix-fixe dinner, $33. **Wheelchair access:** The dining room is down a few steps but there is a ramp at the service entrance; the restrooms are on the same level. **Services:** Catering, private parties.

27 Standard ☆☆ $$ NEW AMERICAN

116 E. 27th St. (bet. Park & Lexington Aves.)   (212) 576-2232
Credit cards: All major   Meals: L, D   Closed Sun.

Part jazz club (in the basement), part casually elegant restaurant, 27 Standard is one of the forerunners of what promises to be Manhattan's hottest new restaurant district. The room is large and airy, the wine list is interesting and the American food is unusual and for the most part very tasty. Salads are superb and main courses imaginative. Don't miss the roasted oysters with braised leeks and chives. The large Black Angus sirloin steak is bathed in a fine red wine sauce and served on a lively watercress and onion relish. Crisply fried onions ride atop the steak and a plate of thickly cut, french-fried potatoes is set on the side. Dusted with garlic, they are irresistible. Desserts are the most ornate section of the menu.

Other recommended dishes: Ginger crab cakes; soup; salad; spiced yellowfin tuna with fennel and figs; grilled chicken breast; steamed salmon with radishes, ramps, mushrooms and chive purée; lemon semifreddo. **Wine list:** Small and well chosen, with some unusual wines at reasonable prices. **Price range:** Lunch: apps., $5.50–$8; entrees, $9–$16; three-course prix-fixe, $19.98. Dinner: apps., $6.50–$9.50; entrees, $16–$27; desserts, $7. **Wheelchair access:** Fully accessible. **Services:** Private parties.

26 Seats

$25 & Under   FRENCH

168 Ave. B (at 11th St.) (212) 677-4787
Credit cards: AE   Meals: D   Closed Mon.

The name 26 Seats says a lot about this sweet little French restaurant near Tompkins Square Park. The narrow dining room is what real estate people call intimate, yet it's relatively comfortable and the waitresses are friendly and kind to children (who take up less room, of course).

The menu's French country offerings, hitting familiar regional notes, are both satisfying and a good value. From Provence comes a pissaladière, a flat, wafer-thin crusted tart of caramelized onions, made pungent with anchovy fillets and olives. From Lyon, fat rounds of savory garlic sausage paired with look-alike rounds of boiled potato and hard-boiled eggs, all dressed in a balsamic vinaigrette.

Like the appetizers, the main courses are well-executed versions of familiar recipes, with the occasional pleasing twist. The nutty flavor of a perfectly grilled fillet of striped bass, for example, is matched well with a soft cake of sweet corn, while a coating of mustard and ginger gives life to a grilled chicken breast. The modest wine list includes several appropriately priced choices, like a sprightly muscadet, an Alsatian riesling from Pierre Sparr and a decent pinot noir from the South of France. For dessert, a wedge of apple tart is the best choice.

Other recommended dishes: Snails in garlic sauce, butternut squash soup, mesclun salad, endive salad, salmon, steak au poivre, magret de canard. **Price range:** Apps., $5.50–$8.50; entrees, $11–$16.50. **Wheelchair access:** Front step; narrow dining room and rest room.

Ubol's Kitchen

$25 & Under   THAI

24-42 Steinway St., Astoria, Queens (718) 545-2874
Credit cards: All major   Meals: L, D

This simply decorated but authentic (there's a Buddhist shrine in the rear) Thai restaurant does not stint on its spicing or seasoning. Dishes marked on the menu as hot and spicy can be counted on to be searing, while dishes traditionally rich in fish

sauce are suitably pungent. Top dishes include spicy salads and
curries. Bamboo salad is one of the more unusual Thai dishes,
made with strands of fermented bamboo shoots, chilies and
lime juice. (Ubol's is pronounced YEW-bahnz.)

Other recommended dishes: Spicy ground pork salad; spicy
squid salad; green papaya salad; chicken with coconut milk
soup; tamarind fish; green curry with fish balls; jungle curry
with chicken; Panang curry with chicken. **Alcohol:** Beer and
wine. **Price range:** Apps., $3.50–$9.95; entrees, $5.95–$14.95;
desserts, $2.50. **Wheelchair access:** Fully accessible. **Services:**
Delivery, takeout, catering.

Ulrika's $$ SWEDISH

115 E. 60th St. (bet Lexington & Park Aves.)   (212) 355-7069
Credit cards: All major   Meals: Br, L, D

No one ever woke up and said, "Let's eat Swedish tonight."
But then again there was no Ulrika's. This small, rustic restaurant showcases the homey food of Hyltebruk, a tiny town in
southern Sweden. The place is filled with Swedish furniture
(the barstools have seats that look like buttons), swanky
Swedish flatware and the work of local Swedish artists on the
wall. There is herring, of course. Mustard herring, pickled herring and matjes herring come on big appetizer plates with
chunks of firm, sharpish Vasterbotten cheese. The excellent
salmon gravlax, fishy tidbits in a sweet mustard sauce, go
down beautifully with the restaurant's own pilsner, a clean,
medium-bodied brew with a crisp, hoppy bite to it. Ulrika's
also creates its own flavored aquavits that include the unusual
Queen's Special, made with a raspberry-blueberry fruit purée
popular in Sweden.

Swedish cuisine is not refined, but it is earthy, flavorful and
satisfying. Fish soup, with two iceberglike hunks of cod and
salmon looming in the bowl, makes a good warm-up for beef á
la Rydberg, tender cubes of tenderloin in a mustard gravy
served with sautéed potatoes and an optional raw egg yolk,
which Swedes pour over the meat and potatoes, letting the heat
partially cook it. Lovbiff ("leaf beef") looks like a Swiss steak,
but it's actually beef tenderloin pounded to a thin sheet, spread
with a mixture of Vasterbotten cheese, bread crumbs and herbs,
then folded over several times to form a neat rectangle.

Two desserts deserve special mention. The pannkaks Tarta
could not be cuter: a stack of miniature pancakes oozing bright-
yellow cloudberry jam and festively decorated with blueberries
speared on a long toothpick. But there's one dessert that goes
straight to the heart, a little basket of assorted Swedish cookies.
For Americans it will feel like an early Christmas present.

Wine list: Varied, but mostly Americans. $24–$42. By the glass:
$6–$10. **Price range:** Brunch: $7–$21. Lunch: apps, $6–$12;

414

entrees, $14–$20; prix fixe, $22. Dinner: apps, $6–$15; entrees, $15–$23. **Wheelchair access:** Steps down from sidewalk. **Services:** Takeout, private parties.

Uncle George's $25 & Under GREEK
33-19 Broadway, Astoria, Queens   (718) 626-0593
Credit cards: Cash only   Meals: B, L, D   Open 24 Hours

A cross between a giant diner that's always open and a boisterous family restaurant, Uncle George's is an Astoria Greek classic. Portions are big, service is speedy and the menu offers every kind of Greek dish, from great grilled fish to the ubiquitous spanakopita (spinach pie) and pastitsio (macaroni, meat sauce and cream sauce). You won't leave hungry. With bright lights, plastic table covers and seats crowded into every spot, it's fair to say that Uncle George's doesn't attract people for the décor.

Other recommended dishes: Tzatziki; yogurt and fish-egg dip; mashed potato and garlic dip; sautéed octopus; stewed rabbit; baked eggplant; barbecued pork; lamb burgers. **Alcohol:** Beer and wine. **Price range:** Apps., $2–$5; entrees, $6–$12. **Wheelchair access:** Fully accessible. **Features:** Kid friendly, outdoor dining. **Services:** Takeout.

Uncle Nick's $25 & Under GREEK/SEAFOOD
747 Ninth Ave. (bet. 50th & 51st Sts.)   (212) 245-7992
Credit cards: All major   Meals: L, D, LN

Once a little hole in the wall, Uncle Nick's developed a loyal following and expanded into a handsome Greek seafood taverna in Clinton. The fresh, pristine fish and other Greek specialties have won it a devoted following. Appetizers are terrific. While the fish is always fresh, too often it is overcooked and arrives dry. Make clear to the staff how you want it cooked.

Other recommended dishes: Three-spread combination; dandelion salad; sautéed Greek sausage; saganakityri; swordfish kebab; salmon steak; souvlaki; chicken souvlaki; baklava. **Price range:** Apps., from $4.50; entrees, from $7.95; desserts, from $2.50. **Wheelchair access:** Fully accessible. **Services:** Delivery, takeout, catering, private parties.

Union Pacific ☆☆☆ $$$$ FRENCH/ASIAN
111 E. 22nd St. (near Park Ave. S.)   (212) 995-8500
Credit cards: All major   Meals: L, D   Closed Sun.

Union Pacific occupies one of the most beautiful, comfortable and soothing environments in Manhattan. Its curtain of falling water at the entrance has the cool, calm look of Japan. Service is professional and enthusiastic, and chef Rocco di Spirito has invented an exciting menu.

Begin with a flight of little dishes and you will encounter something like the inventive sashimi served at Nobu: slices of soft, sweet yellowtail wrapped around tuna tartar, muscular strips of fluke with yuzu (Japanese citrus), a few strawberries tossed with fava beans. These teases make you very hungry. Despite Asian touches in the main part of the menu, the focus here is largely French. The unusual wine list adds another dimension, emphasizing bright wines with enough acidity to make them friendly to this food. The sommelier is happy to be helpful.

Desserts are as interesting as entrees. There are a number of strawberry desserts, and crème brûlée is laced with passion fruit essence or lavender, topped with pineapple sorbet and served with a twist of sugar candy threaded with black sesame seeds. Afterwards, there are fruit pâtés, wonderful chocolates and soft macaroons. (*Ruth Reichl*)

Other recommended dishes: Foie gras cru with wild strawberries; sautéed foie gras with seasonal fruit garnish; tuna tartar; gulf shrimp with fresh coriander; halibut with chard; fricassee of vegetables; squab with long beans and wild tarragon; warm chocolate cake; cheese plate. **Wine list:** Unusual and interesting, with many Austrian wines. **Price range:** Lunch: apps., $12–$17; entrees, $17–$32; desserts, $8–$10; three-course prix fixe, $20.01. Dinner: three-course prix fixe, $65 with supplements; seven-course prix fixe, $115. **Wheelchair access:** Fully accessible. **Services:** Private parties.

Union Square Café ☆☆ $$$ New American

21 E. 16th St. (near Union Sq. W.) (212) 243-4020
Credit cards: All major Meals: L, D

There's a reason why Union Square Café, in the nearly 14 years since it opened, has become one of the city's most beloved dining spots, and a top destination for tourists. The restaurant treats its guests very well. It makes them feel welcome by catering to their every whim in an openhanded, Midwestern manner that disguises a disciplined, highly professional understanding of service that broke the mold in New York. Union Square's pioneering fusion of fine food and wine, casual atmosphere and stellar service has made it the most influential restaurant of its time in the city, and certainly one of the most popular. Anyone who doubts this should try to book a table.

It's not the food that's setting off the stampede, however. Union Square has not changed, but the world has changed around it. Michael Romano, the executive chef and part owner, does what he has always done, and done very well, which is to turn out jazzed-up bistro and trattoria fare with utter consistency. What looked like a flashy sports car a decade ago now seems more like a mid-size Buick cruising in the center lane at a precise 65.

The signature fried calamari, a dull cliché elsewhere in town, deserve their star billing at Union Square, where the kitchen effortlessly sends out golden brown, crunchy piles of the stuff, perfectly cooked outside and inside, and nicely complemented with an incisive, creamy anchovy mayonnaise. Although there are several foreign accents heard on the menu, Italian dominates, especially in the pasta dishes, which put many Italian restaurants to shame. Mr. Romano's pasta has an ineffable, nutty firmness, even in the thinnest forms, that stamps it as authentically Italian. The crabmeat and artichoke tortelli, served with a roasted tomato and oregano butter, is a standout.

In general, Union Square has mastered the art of pleasing without challenging. The spice-braised lamb, one of the restaurant's recurring daily specials, strikes a mildly exotic mediterranean-Indian note, with mint, a lemon-basmati pilaf and glazed carrots, but it is the food equivalent of an ethnic crossover hit, just sweet enough to be mainstream. The lemon-pepper duck, served with a peach-cherry chutney, continues in the same vein.

Desserts aim for an artful blend of homey and exotic, most memorably in the banana tart with a caramel shellac, a Union Square standby. The all-American entry on the dessert list is a terrific peach pot pie that's surrounded by little clusters of caramel popcorn.

The excitement in New York's dining scene may have moved elsewhere, but when it comes to the mysterious comfort factor that keeps diners ferociously loyal, and sends them on their way in a state of bliss, Union Square still sits on top of the heap.

Other recommended dishes: Squash blossom appetizer; salad of red and yellow tomatoes; fazzoletto, plum popover. **Wine list:** A serious, carefully chosen list of about 300 bottles, mostly French, Italian and Californian. Many wines under $40, and 15 wines by the glass. **Price range:** Lunch: apps., $8–$15; entrees, $12.50–$18. Dinner: apps., $8–$15; entrees, $21–$29; desserts, $8. **Wheelchair access:** Main dining room is four steps down. Balcony dining room and restrooms are not accessible. **Features:** Good for business.

Uskudar $25 & Under TURKISH

1405 Second Ave. (near 73rd St.) (212) 988-2641
Credit cards: All major Meals: L, D

This sliver of a Turkish restaurant is the very model of a successful neighborhood institution. On any given night, the inviting dining room, which seats no more than 24, is crowded with families, couples and the occasional lone diner. Named for a neighborhood in Istanbul, Uskudar has achieved its institutional status without the burgers, pastas and steaks that form the default menu of most local hangouts. The selection of appetizers includes excellent spreads: patlican, smoky eggplant mashed with garlic, sesame paste and herbs, is smooth and delicious, while ezme, a blend of tomatoes, onions, parsley and walnuts, is bright and lightly spicy.

Uskudar's kebabs are uncommonly juicy, particularly the shish kebab, with tender cubes of marinated lamb. But the best dishes are the stews. There's etli bamya, lamb with baby okra cooked just enough to show off the vegetable's mellow flavor. Hunkar begendi, another hearty lamb stew, is made with tomatoes and herbs and served over pureed eggplant, an enticing combination. Beverages include Turkish beer and some serviceable Turkish reds. Another possibility is sour cherry juice, which is sweeter than it sounds and resembles cranberry juice. Uskudar makes its own desserts, and though they are familiar, they are excellent, especially kadayif, shredded wheat crowned with ground walnuts and drenched in honey.

Other recommended dishes: Chicken with garlic, imam bayildi, grilled quail, apricots stuffed with almonds. **Price range:** Apps., $4.95–$6.95; entrees, $12.95–$15.95. **Wheelchair access:** Step at entrance; aisle and restrooms are very narrow.

Vatan $25 & Under   INDIAN/VEGETARIAN

409 Third Ave. (at 29th St.)   (212) 689-5666
Credit cards: All major   Meals: D, LN   Closed Mon.

This astounding Indian restaurant transports you to a bright, animated Indian village with thatched roofs and artificial banyan trees. Vatan specializes in the rich, spicy yet subtle vegetarian cuisine of Gujarat. For one price, a parade of little dishes is served, which might include khaman, a delicious fluffy steamed cake of lentil flour with black mustard seeds; delicate little samosas; patrel, taro leaves layered with spicy chickpea paste and steamed, and much more.

Other recommended dishes: There is only one selection, a fixed menu that includes a dozen or so small Gujarati vegetarian dishes, served in three courses. **Price range:** $19.95. **Wheelchair access:** Everything is on one level. **Features:** Kid friendly, romantic.

Va Tutto! $25 & Under   ITALIAN

23 Cleveland Pl. (near Kenmare St.)   (212) 941-0286
Credit cards: All major   Meals: L, D   Closed Mon.

Va Tutto!, Italian for "Anything Goes," is a warm and welcoming Tuscan-oriented restaurant with a lovely garden. For lunch try the panini povero, a sumptuous sandwich of scrambled eggs, mozzarella, tomato sauce and herbs that somehow holds together on crusty grilled bread. The best main courses are the pastas al forno, baked dishes like a thin wedge of lasagna with fennel sausage, roasted peppers and plum tomatoes, and sumptuous cannelloni stuffed with spinach, mushrooms and Parmesan. Also wonderful are ribbons of pasta with speck (an excellent ham from the Alto Adige), roasted tomatoes, peas and garlic, and rigatoni amatriciana, a traditional dish of tomatoes, onions, pancetta and red pepper. For dessert, try the house-made focaccia lathered with Nutella, that European chocolate-hazelnut spread, and a scoop of rich fig-flavored gelato. Soft chocolate bread pudding is galvanized by dried cherries and a scoop of hazelnut gelato. And Va Tutto! offers the rare panna cotta in which flavor triumphs over texture.

Other recommended dishes: Grilled calamari; wood-roasted chicken; grilled quail; insalata di funghi. **Price range:** Apps., $6.50–$9.50; entrees, $13–$23. **Wheelchair access:** Steps to the garden. **Features:** Smoking at bar or in garden.

Velli $25 & Under   ITALIAN
132 W. Houston St. (near Sullivan St.)   (212) 979-7614
Credit cards: Cash only   Meals: Br, L, LN

The newest of Jean-Claude Iacovelli's group of sophisticated, casually lively, moderately priced restaurants is a French bistro disguised as a trattoria. It is filled with people who have come to enjoy good food and good talk. Yes, the menu is Italian, but the vibe is decidedly French. The philosophy is clear: keep the menu and wine list short, the ingredients top quality and the prices reasonable. Appetizers are exceptional.

Recommended dishes: Filet mignon carpaccio; tuna carpaccio; grilled calamari; pappa al pomodoro; fettuccine with prosciutto, truffle oil and Parmesan; lobster in fennel broth; chocolate mousse. **Price range:** Apps., $4–$6; pastas, $7.50–$8; entrees, $12–$15; desserts, $5. **Wheelchair access:** Everything is on one level. **Features:** Romantic, smoking permitted. **Services:** Catering, private parties.

Verbena ☆ $$$ NEW AMERICAN
54 Irving Pl. (near 17th St.)   (212) 260-5454
Credit cards: All major   Meals: Br, D

Until recently, Verbena was a one-woman performance piece by Diane Forley, who, as chef and owner, served up an intriguing synthesis of American ingredients and Middle Eastern flavors. Then the restaurant closed for a face-lift and an expansion, and Ms. Forley married Michael Otsuka, another cultural synthesizer. They now share cooking duties, and ideas, in Verbena's kitchen.

The new Verbena looks attractive. The tight dining room retains its very adult sense of calm and style, and a cool, breezy and secluded courtyard garden has been created in the back, with white canvas overhead and flagstones underfoot. Now the bad news. Verbena's expansion has placed burdens on the kitchen that it does not manage very well. Waiters seem to be assigned one table too many. Dishes take about 20 minutes longer than they should to arrive at the table. And what arrives does not always thrill.

The partnership of Ms. Forley and Mr. Otsuka feels more like a comfortable compromise than an exciting new departure. The menu has a plainness to it now and a simplicity that can be boring. Roast chicken with green beans, herbed plum tomatoes and escarole, for example, is perfectly respectable, but not much more than that. The bolder dishes sometimes hit and sometimes miss, but the red snapper, firm and moist, easily stands up to a robust accompaniment of Yukon gold potatoes, pancetta, trumpet royale mushrooms and peas. The sirloin steak is a remarkably rich, tender cut, beautifully charred outside. The better side dishes include chive potato croquettes, a zucchini-onion galette, ginger-glazed carrots and herbed French fries served in a big, golden heap with fried parsley leaves.

Desserts are polite, but milk chocolate pot de crème, straightforward, honest and velvet textured, has a pure, clean chocolate flavor that separates it from the pack. At the start of the meal, your waiter will ask if you are interested in the Bing cherry upside-down cake. It is baked to order and needs extra time. Say yes. The cake is better than Mom ever made.

Other recommended dishes: Foie gras with cherry blossom marmalade, grilled lamb chops with zucchini galette. **Wine list:** An imaginative list of about 150 wines, half of them French, half American and Australian, with 35 half bottles and eight to 12 wines by the glass. **Price range:** Dinner, apps., $7.95–$12.50; entrees, $14.50–$28, desserts, $6.25–$12. Four-course tasting menu, $58; four-course vegetarian tasting menu, $52. **Wheelchair access:** Three steps down to entrance; two steps up to garden.

Veritas ☆☆☆ $$$$ New American

43 E. 20th St. (near Park Ave. S.)   (212) 353-3700
Credit cards: All major   Meals: D

Small, spare and elegant, Veritas could be called a wine cellar with a restaurant attached. Because at Veritas, the wine is more important than the food. The 1,300 entries on its wine list include such rarities as a Chateau Margaux 1900, a Mouton

Rothschild 1945 and Lafite-Rothschild 1953, and they are offered at extremely reasonable prices.

Veritas offers clean and unfussy food that works well with its wine. The chef, Scott Bryan, one of four owners, serves food that is quietly sly. A hamachi tartar topped with a substantial scoop of osetra, hints of mint, scallion and soy, is memorable. Sweetbreads are extraordinary, their texture underlined by chestnut purée, their sweet softness emphasized by lemon.

Main courses, to suit the powerful wines, are robust, powerful and simple — with surprisingly little red meat on the menu. Chicken, served with a rich, garlicky potato purée and a sprinkling of fava beans, is truly flavorful. Powered by an emulsion of foie gras and set on a bed of bacon-infused lentils, squab can stand up to any red wine.

The intensity does not abate with desserts. Try warm chocolate cake (called a soufflé here), or a startlingly delicious praline parfait with a polished reduction of clementines so good that it eases you right into sweet wine. (*Ruth Reichl*)

Other recommended dishes: Frothy lentil soup; wild mushroom ravioli; warm oysters; braised veal; crème fraîche panna cotta. **Wine list:** Enormous, memorable and well priced. **Price range:** Three course prix-fixe dinner, $68. **Wheelchair access:** Fully accessible.

Veselka $25 & Under EAST EUROPEAN

144 Second Ave. (at 9th St.) (212) 228-9682
Credit cards: All major   Meals: B, Br, L, D   Open 24 hours

At this renovated Eastern European luncheonette, bohemian angst meets Slavic charm over kasha and blintzes. Great breakfasts can include hearty buckwheat pancakes, thick potato pancakes or delightful cheese blintzes. Soups are also very good, especially the excellent Ukrainian borscht, rich with just a touch of sweetness.

Alcohol: Beer. **Price range:** Apps., $3–$5; entrees, $6–$9; desserts, $3–$5. **Wheelchair access:** Fully accessible. **Features:** Kid friendly, outdoor dining. **Services:** Takeout.

Vespa Cibobuono $ ITALIAN

1625 Second Ave. (bet. 84th & 85th Sts.) (212) 472-2050
Credit cards: All major   Meals: D

Simple pastas served in a pleasant nook of a dining room make Vespa a good choice for a decent meal if you're in the area, especially in warm weather when you can enjoy the garden.

Alcohol: Beer and wine. **Price range:** Apps., $7–$11.50; entrees, $10.50–$25; desserts, $6. **Wheelchair access:** Fully accessible. **Features:** Outdoor dining. **Services:** Delivery, takeout, private parties.

Viceversa ☆ $$ ITALIAN

325 W. 51st St. (bet. Eighth & Ninth Aves.)   (212) 399-9265
Credit cards: All major   Meals: L, D

With its crisp earth-colored awnings and gleaming facade, Viceversa (pronounced VEE-chey-VAIR-suh) stands out on one of Manhattan's grungier blocks like a Versace suit. Inside, the décor is so minimal that it seems to disappear in the course of an evening, a blur of light beige walls, dark hardwood floors and antique terra cotta vases. Managers and wait staff project an unmistakable Italian warmth, and the menu is honest and unpretentious, a solid lineup of mostly northern Italian dishes.

Stefano Terzi, the executive chef, has brought casoncelli alla bergamasca from his hometown of Bergamo, near Milan, and it deserves star billing in Viceversa's strong ensemble cast of pastas. It is a ravioli filled with chopped veal, crushed amaretti, raisins and Parmesan, then topped with butter, crisped sage leaves and fried pancetta — a salty, herbal sauce that offsets the sweetness of the stuffing. The calamari and artichoke tart looks a little like a failed experiment, but one bite tells you that looks aren't everything. This is a soul-satisfying dish, the kind you could eat with pleasure every day. For flavorful simplicity, it would be hard to top the tender slices of beef loin, coated in a rich, vibrant sauce of balsamic vinegar and shallots.

Viceversa pulls a few surprises at dessert time. A lovely banana semifreddo, topped with a roasted banana slice, gets an unexpected lift from balsamic vinegar reduced to a thick syrup and drizzled over the plate.

Other recommended dishes: Turban of eggplant; strozzapreti with duck ragù; halibut. **Wine list:** A limited, uninspiring, mostly Italian list, with nine wines by the glass. **Price range:** Lunch, apps., $6–$11.50; entrees, $12.50–$18.50; desserts, $5; three-course prix-fixe, $20. Dinner, apps., $8–$12.50; entrees, $16.50–$22.50; desserts, $6. **Wheelchair access:** Entrance is three steps down; restrooms are on the dining room level. **Features:** Smoking at bar, outdoor garden.

Via Quadronno $25 & Under   ITALIAN/SANDWICHES

25 E. 73rd St. (near Madison Ave.)   (212) 650-9880
Credit cards: All major   Meals: B, L, D, LN

Via Quadronno reflects both the requirements of the neighborhood and its own ties to Milan. The cafe stretches past a selection of gelati to a timbered rear room with a mural featuring a flying boar. It's not exactly comfortable seating; some tables come with backless stools, others with rickety folding chairs, perhaps in an effort to keep the shopping and tourist crowd moving in and out. Prices are also higher, especially for wine, which is served by the bottle. Sandwich prices are more reasonable, and the servings are generous, like the single-ingredient panini semplici, served on small, warm ciabatta. Mortadella may be little more than a rich bologna with pistachios, but it makes for a satisfying sandwich. The open-faced tartufata is not quite the blend of minced porcini mushrooms, olive oil and truffles as billed on the menu — maybe somebody waved a truffle near it — but it is nonetheless earthy and pleasing. The best part of the menu is the desserts, especially crisp, buttery and beautiful pear and plum tarts.

Other recommended dishes: Ham and fontina cheese, chocolate and hazelnut gelati. **Alcohol:** Beer and wine only. **Price range:** Entrees, $12.50–$22. **Wheelchair access:** One step at entrance, four steps to dining room. **Features:** Smoking permitted at coffee bar. **Services:** Takeout, private parties.

Vico $$$ ITALIAN
1302 Madison Ave. (bet. 92nd & 93rd Sts.)   (212) 876-2222
Credit cards: Cash or check only   Meals: Br, L, D

Small and chic, this Upper East Side trattoria wants to look like Milan with its pared down décor. The menu is good if predictable, and the prices are high.

Alcohol: Beer and wine. **Price range:** Lunch: apps., $6.50–$10.50; entrees, $9.50–$20.50; desserts, $7. Dinner: apps., $7.50–$12.50; entrees, $13.50–$32; desserts, $8. **Wheelchair access:** Fully accessible. **Features:** Outdoor dining. **Services:** Delivery, takeout.

Victor's Cafe 52 $$$ CUBAN
236 W. 52nd St. (bet. Broadway & Eighth Ave.)   (212) 586-7714
Credit cards: All major   Meals: L, D, LN

Asia de Cuba does a better job of capturing the halcyon glamour of Havana in the 1950's, but this old theater district standby treats the food of Cuba with more respect. If you want to taste ropa vieja (literally "old clothes," but it's a meat stew) in an upscale atmosphere, this is a good place to do it.

Price range: Lunch: apps., $7–$19; entrees, $9–$19; desserts, $5–$8. Dinner: apps., $7–$22; entrees, $12–$30; desserts, $5–$8. **Wheelchair access:** Not accessible. **Features:** Smoking permitted. **Services:** Delivery, takeout, catering, private parties.

Villa Berulia $$

ITALIAN

107 E. 34th St. (bet. Lexington & Park Aves.) (212) 689-1970
Credit cards: All major   Meals: L, D   Closed Sun.

A pleasant, unassuming neighborhood Italian restaurant in a
neighborhood with very few restaurants. The ceilings look like
cottage cheese, the wine list is not memorable and the menu is
filled with dishes you have seen before. But the welcome is
warm, and if you're looking for someplace to eat on East 34th
Street, this will do.

Price range: Lunch: apps., $5–$8; entrees, $14–$22; desserts,
$6. Dinner: apps., $6–$9.50; entrees, $14–$27; desserts, $6.
Wheelchair access: Fully accessible. **Services:** Takeout, private
parties.

Village ☆ $$

BISTRO/FRENCH

62 W. 9th St. (at Fifth Ave.)   (212) 505-3355
Credit cards: All major   Meals: D, LN

Village is simple and sleek. The plain red canvas awning out
front strikes the right note; inside it is cool and soothing, with
wood floors, maroon leather upholstery and hanging lights that
look like grooved melons. A long bar in solid mahogany dominates the front room, which is lined with cozy booths. The
main dining room, with tables and banquettes, gets a sense of
air and light from an enormous domed skylight.

The food is good, not great. Village wants to be a congenial
neighborhood place with good food at reasonable prices. It is all
of that. But every once in a while, pure inspiration flickers and
you get a glimpse of the superbistro that Village might have been,
or might yet become. It shows in the oyster pan roast, thick and
smoky with chipotle peppers and crème fraîche. For the most
part, the chef sticks to bistro and café classics, like herring with
cucumber and potato salad, or guacamole, which he executes in
straightforward fashion. Both steak au poivre and steak with
béarnaise sauce are correct, as the French say. Linguine with a
deeply flavored roasted tomato sauce can (and should) be
ordered in a deluxe version, with olives, shrimp and bacon. The
star dessert is an ice cream sundae stuffed with miniature brownies and cherries and buried under a thick chocolate sauce.

Other recommended dishes: Smoked crépinettes; grilled leeks
with mustard sauce; grilled shrimp; crème caramel; fruit tarts.
Wine list: A modest and modestly priced bistro list of 36
French and American wines, with seven wines by the glass or
carafe. **Price range:** Dinner: apps., $5–$11; entrees,
$16.50–$22.50; desserts, $5–$7.50; prix-fixe, $25. Café menu:
most dishes under $10, available Thurs.-Sat. until 1 A.M.
Wheelchair access: Three steps down to entrance. Restrooms
upstairs. **Features:** Smoking permitted.

Villa Mosconi $$ ITALIAN

69 Macdougal St. (bet. Bleecker & Houston Sts.) (212) 673-0390
Credit cards: All major   Meals: L, D   Closed Sunday

A good old red-sauce restaurant that has been in the Village for
years. If you're longing for a taste of old-time Italian-American
cuisine, you could do worse than this pleasant restaurant with
its pleasant garden.

Price range: Lunch: apps., $6–$12; entrees, $10–$20; desserts,
$3–$5. Dinner: apps., $7–$13; entrees, $10–$22; desserts,
$3–$6.25. **Wheelchair access:** Fully accessible. **Services:** Takeout, catering, private parties.

Vince & Eddie's $$ AMERICAN

70 W. 68th St. (bet. Columbus Ave. & Central Park W.)
(212) 721-0068
Credit cards: All major   Meals: Br, L, D

Never great, never terrible. Fairly standard American food in a
fairly standard rustic setting. The small garden is attractive,
and it's a fine place for a bite after a concert at Lincoln Center.

Price range: Apps., $6.95–$10.50; entrees, $15.50–$21.95;
desserts, $6.95. **Wheelchair access:** Fully accessible. **Features:**
Outdoor dining. **Services:** Takeout, catering, private parties.

Vine ☆ $$$ NEW AMERICAN

25 Broad St. (at Exchange Pl.)   (212) 344-8463
Credit cards: All major   Meals: L, D   Closed Sun.

Vine is pleasant, airy and woody, with views of the New York
Stock Exchange out the tall front windows. The brightly colored
photographs of candles, silverware and bottles on the walls,
doctored to look a little like photo-realist paintings, have a
mindlessly chipper quality. The food is quite decent, in a mid-
dle-of-the-road, easy-listening sort of way. In just about any
American city of half a million or fewer inhabitants, Vine would
automatically be the best place in town. Here, it merges into the
crowd. Such is the current state of cuisine in New York. The
food plows fairly familiar ground, usually described as new
American with international accents. But when it's good, it's
very good.

If you're searching for escargots that do not have the texture
and flavor of pencil erasers, Vine comes to the rescue with what
looks like a small potpie, beneath whose crust bubbles a thick,
garlicky lava pungent with Roquefort cheese and chock full of
tender, hefty snails and walnut bits. The chili-rubbed pork tenderloin, a high-rent down-home entree, also shows a bit of
flash, with a dense, creamy dollop of Cheddar grits and golden

fried okra in a light sheath of breading. At Vine, richer seems to be better, like the truffle-studded sweetbreads, with a potato and goat-cheese raviolo. One entree is a real eyeful: slices of sashimi-grade tuna, served rare, and surrounded by tall, sculptured obelisks of roasted parsnip and carrot, with paintlike spatterings of beet sauce, a carrot-ginger reduction and parsley water. It's a party on a plate — fun to look at, but ordinary to eat. On the dessert menu, the chocolate soufflé, adrift in a flood of chocolate soup, is serenely voluptuous. Top honors, however, go to the peanut butter mousse, balanced on a raft of caramelized bananas soaked in buttered rum. The dessert is almost too darling to eat.

Other recommended dishes: Confit and breast of duck; herbed potato pie; lemon soufflé tart. **Wine list:** A fairly predictable list of about 150 mostly French and American wines, with 16 wines by the glass. **Price range:** Lunch: apps., $9–$14; entrees, $19–$28; desserts, $10. Dinner: apps., $9–$16; entrees, $23–$29; desserts $10. **Wheelchair access:** Enter through Vine Market next door. **Features:** Good for business, smoking at bar. **Services:** Delivery, take out, catering, private parties.

Vinegar Factory $$ NEW AMERICAN

431 E. 91st St. (bet. York & First Aves.)　(212) 987-0885
Credit cards: All major　　Meals: D　　Closed Mon.-Fri.

Eli Zabar serves good food in his restaurants. The differences here are that the setting is minimal (although the deck is pleasant in good weather), it is open only on weekends, and, most important, this one is fairly affordable.

Alcohol: Beer and wine. **Price range:** Apps., $7–$10; entrees, $18-28; desserts, $6.50. **Wheelchair access:** Not accessible. **Features:** Kid friendly, outdoor dining. **Services:** Private parties.

Virage $25 & Under MEDITERRANEAN

118 Second Ave. (at 7th St.)　　(212) 253-0425
Credit cards: All major　　Meals: Br, L, D, LN

This corner restaurant, with its big glass windows and unusual mosaics, has quiet jazz playing in the background. It squeezes a wide selection of dishes into a Mediterranean mold, adding couscous as a side dish to otherwise culturally nondescript centerpieces like lamb chops, duck and chicken, or enlivening salads and vegetable platters with hummus or feta cheese. The food's pretty good, the people are friendly and the price is modest.

Other recommended dishes: Baked shrimp with asparagus and shiitake mushrooms; pistou; filet mignon of tuna; ravioli with Swiss chard; braised lamb shank; three-milk cake; chocolate mousse cake. **Alcohol:** Beer and wine. **Price range:** Apps., $3–$8; entrees, $7–$19; desserts, $5.50. Brunch, $8.95. **Wheelchair access:** Fully accessible. **Features:** Outdoor dining. **Services:** Delivery, takeout, private parties.

Virgil's Real BBQ $25 & Under   BARBECUE

152 W. 44th St. (bet. Broadway & Sixth Ave.)   (212) 921-9494
Credit cards: All major   Meals: L, D, LN

With its framed photographs of restaurants, cattle and pigs, aprons and other artifacts covering the walls, Virgil's is a wildly popular shrine to barbecue joints around the country. If the food isn't quite authentic, the formula comes close enough and it works. And the place smells great, as any barbecue place should. Highlights on the menu include hush puppies served with a maple syrup butter; smoked Texas links with mustard slaw; crab cakes; barbecued shrimp and Texas red chili with corn bread. For main fare, big barbecue platters carry enticing selections of Owensboro lamb, Maryland ham, Carolina pork shoulder, Texas beef brisket and more.

Price range: Apps., $4.95–$8.95; entrees, $10.95–$18.95; desserts, $4.95–$5.95. **Wheelchair access:** Fully accessible. **Features:** Kid friendly, good for business. **Services:** Delivery, takeout, catering.

Virot ☆☆ $$$ FRENCH

Dylan Hotel, 52 E. 41st St. (bet. Park & Madison Aves.)
                                                  (646) 658-0266
Credit cards: All major   Meals: L, D

Didier Virot, formerly the executive chef at JoJo and sous-chef at Jean Georges, is inventive with an antic streak. He takes risks. Some of them don't pay off. But diners will not leave Virot feeling that they've had an ordinary meal.

Mr. Virot starts with a main ingredient, indicated in big boldface type on the menu, and treats it like a star. He has an admirable sense of proportion, never letting his supporting cast of flavors and ingredients take over the stage. Ruby-colored slices of tuna, marinated with cucumber and coriander, take on the lightest possible layering of spice and green freshness. Big, fat shrimp, cooked to a light outer crisp on a skewer with some basil leaves and a light saffron- mustard dressing, work one of those minor miracles encountered more often in print than in restaurants. They remind you of what shrimp used to taste like. Mr. Virot has an eye as well as a palate. Roasted black sea bass in a meaty olive sauce picks up a lovely splash of color from burgundy carrots, braised in butter and Meyer lemon juice.

But when he slips, there's no mistaking it. Absolutely first-rate squab, dark and livery, never quite works out a livable relationship with the intriguing-sounding oatmeal porcini cake, which feels as if it should be good for you, a bad sign. A much happier experiment in the same line is the cake of basmati rice that accompanies a magnificent lobster sautéed with cardamom and bathed with a caramel ginger sauce.

For dessert, try the demure, flawless flat cake made from ricotta cheese and roasted pineapple, with a scoop of tart, concentrated pineapple sorbet, and with an awesomely dense almond crème brûlée sprinkled with jujube chutney — jewellike cubes of candied red date slowly cooked with cinnamon, anise and pepper, and drizzled with walnut oil.

Service is a little hushed and reverential at Virot, and the style can be traced directly to the chill, formal room, which can feel like the waiting room in a grand old train station. Upstairs a treasure awaits, the balcony lounge. It's dark and intimate and, for the moment at least, it feels like a secret hideaway.

Other recommended dishes: Gnocchi with Jerusalem artichoke in truffle cream, hazelnut souffle. **Wine list:** A mostly French and American list of nearly 350 wines, with many wines from Alsace and, in an extensive dessert-wine list, many Loire selections. There are 19 wines by the glass. **Price range:** Lunch and dinner, apps., $12–$14; entrees, $24–$30; desserts, $9. Lunch, two-course prix fixe, $29; dinner, three-course prix fixe, $49. Six- course tasting menus at lunch and dinner, $75 and $65 (vegetable). **Wheelchair access:** Wheelchair entrance to the right of main entrance. Lobby elevator serves second-floor restrooms.

Vivolo $$ ITALIAN
140 E. 74th St. (bet. Second & Third Aves.)   (212) 308-0112
Credit cards: All major   Meals: L, D

This venerable Italian restaurant in an East Side town house presents several dining options, including a comfortable dining room, a quicker, more casual cafe and a takeout service, where you can get simple, lively dishes like spaghetti with olive oil and garlic, and spezzatine di vitello, a flavorful veal stew with peas, carrots and sage over fat strands of bucatini.

Price range: Lunch: apps., $5–$7; entrees, $12–$14; desserts, $5–$7. Dinner: apps., $6–$8; entrees, $12–$21; desserts, $6–$8. **Wheelchair access:** Fully accessible. **Services:** Delivery, takeout, catering, private parties.

Vong $$$$ THAI/FRENCH
200 E. 54th St. (at Third Ave.)   (212) 486-9592
Credit cards: All major   Meals: L, D

Jean-Georges Vongerichten does Thai in this sensuous spot. If the food is not quite up to the standard of his other restaurants

(Jo Jo and Jean Georges), it is still extremely satisfying. The food combines Thai ingredients with mostly French techniques, and it is very good. So are the desserts, especially the white pepper ice cream.

After more than a decade in business, Vong has every right to slow down, but a recent visit suggested that it rolls right along at a good clip, with crisp service and fusion food that still feels fresh and exciting. The only place in town for roasted sweetbreads on licorice satay.

Price range: Prix-fixe lunch, $28. Dinner: apps., $12–$25; entrees, $20–$36; desserts, $8–$10; pre-theater prix fixe, $38; six-course tasting menu, $68 per person (whole table must order). **Wheelchair access:** Fully accessible. **Features:** Romantic, outdoor dining.

Vox ☆ $$ BISTRO/PAN-LATIN

165 Eighth Ave. (bet. 17th & 18th Sts.) (646) 486-3188
Credit cards: All major Meals: L, D

At Vox (short for "vox populi"), the voice of the people has apparently cried out for a modern-feeling bistro with Asian and nonclassical Latin accents. The parsnip soup, thick and sweet, picks up a bit of spice and earth from little chunks of hot merguez sausage and grilled porcini mushrooms. A refreshing tartar of salmon and Kumamoto oysters is also nicely handled, with pristine, briny flavors brought into relief by a light miso sauce. If Vox has a signature, it is probably "paella (646)." The numerals refer to Vox's area code, which is Manhattan's newest and therefore appropriate for this jazzed-up Spanish classic. It's a garlicky, assertive paella, resting on an unfortunately gummy bed of rice. The (646) should honor instead the sautéed black sea bass, served on fluffy basmati rice and almonds and smothered with raita, the Indian vegetable and spiced yogurt mixture. For dessert, Mexican chocolate soufflé cake has the off-sweet quality that moves chocolate into the adult-dessert category. And the banana-peanut financier seems more like an ethereal muffin, but among muffins, it is a god.

Vox seems to get a more diverse crowd than many other Chelsea restaurants. Gay diners feel welcome enough to be affectionate with each other, and elderly diners can be spotted here and there, at ease even though their shoes do not have four-inch soles.

Other recommended dishes: Sautéed skate with morcilla; parsnip soup; sturgeon with white bean purée; quince linzertorte. **Wine list:** An eclectic, even scrambled, 42-bottle list, with most wines under $40. **Price range:** Lunch, apps., $8–$12; entrees, $14–$17; desserts, $5–$7. Dinner, apps., $6–$12; entrees, $18–$23; desserts, $5–$7. **Wheelchair access:** Restrooms are downstairs. **Features:** Smoking in lounge only.

Walker's $

BAR SNACKS

16 N. Moore St. (at Varick St.)
Credit cards: All major

(212) 941-0142
Meals: Br, L, D, LN

This handsome old bar draws a legion of regulars and tempo-
rary regulars (jurors, that is) for a menu of burgers, salads and
other simple dishes. The atmosphere is thick with history and
cigarette smoke.

Price range: Apps., $2.75–$7.50; entrees, $8.50–$14.75;
desserts, $4.50–$5.50. **Wheelchair access:** Fully accessible.
Features: Kid friendly, outdoor dining. **Services:** Delivery, takeout, catering, private parties.

Wallsé ☆ ☆ $$$

AUSTRIAN

344 W. 11th St. (at Washington St.)
Credit cards: All major

(212) 352-2300
Meals: D, LN

It took a few twists and turns before Kurt Gutenbrunner found
his way back to Austria. He intended to move from Bouley,
where he served as sous chef for five years, to the post of executive chef at Danube, David Bouley's ambitious, bejeweled
shrine to the cooking of Austria-Hungary. When the project
stalled, however, Mr. Gutenbrunner became restless and left.
Now he has found a new setting in Wallsé, a corner restaurant
in the far West Village that he has turned into a modest showcase for the Austrian cooking he grew up with.

The name comes from Wallsee, Mr. Gutenbrunner's hometown, with a Frenchified spelling to make it easier to pronounce: it's VAHL-zay. The décor is chaste, with white walls,
black banquettes and black chairs that have just the hint of an
Art Nouveau wiggle in their design and a jolt of unexpected
color on their neon-yellow and red seats.

The menu and the wine list seem perfectly suited to what is,
in effect, a glorified neighborhood restaurant. Mr. Gutenbrunner
keeps his rather short list of dishes relatively simple, but within
his self-imposed limits, he achieves splendid results. A light
touch with horseradish cream makes a salad of smoked trout
and eel a highlight on the menu. Again and again, Mr. Gutenbrunner hits on a happy idea that elevates his down-home Austrian sources. The result is a highly personal style that qualifies
as high bistro. Viennese rostbraten, a workaday sort of dish
based on sirloin in a sweet and sour vinegar and wine sauce, is
paired with a hearty kohlrabi gratin, a multilayer affair with
sheets of slick, firm root vegetable alternating with thick cream,
cheese and onion. Wiener schnitzel at Wallsé is nothing more
than Wiener schnitzel, but it comes with butter-coated, waxy-
textured parsley potatoes. Tafelspitz, rather bland slices of
boiled beef in a thin broth, perk up with their sharp topping of
apple horseradish, and a giant round of potato rosti (hash

browns with a German accent) certainly doesn't hurt — but the ingenious touch here is a reinvented steakhouse staple, creamed spinach, which Mr. Gutenbrunner reinterprets as a velvety purée, thick enough to form peaks.

The best dessert is the quark dumplings. Banish every association that "cheese dumpling" suggests, and start afresh. In Mr. Gutenbrunner's hands, the combination of quark and flour translates into a feather-light sphere, not too sweet, that melts on the tongue like manna. It comes with fat apricot halves that are roasted and stuffed with red currants.

New York never knew it needed Austrian cooking. Now it may not be able to live without it.

Other recommended dishes: Salad of asparagus and chanterelles; sautéed rabbit strudel; halibut; chocolate hazelnut cake. **Wine list:** An imaginative, well-chosen list of 55 mostly Austrian and French wines, with nine wines by the glass. **Price range:** Apps., $8–$16; entrees, $19–$25; desserts, $8. **Wheelchair access:** One step up to dining room; rest rooms are downstairs.

Wall St. Kitchen and Bar $$ NEW AMERICAN
70 Broad St. (at Beaver St.)   (212) 797-7070
Credit cards: All major   Meals: L, D   Closed Sat., Sun.

The atmosphere is clamorous with traders who are still shouting, even off the floor, as they drink fascinating beers and eat delicious snacks like short-rib sandwiches.

Price range: Apps., $6–$9; entrees, $8–$19; desserts, $5. **Wheelchair access:** Fully accessible. **Features:** Smoking permitted. **Services:** Delivery, takeout, catering, private parties.

Water Club ☆☆ $$$$ NEW AMERICAN
500 E. 30th St. (at the East River)   (212) 683-3333
Credit cards: All major   Meals: Br, L, D

Compared with the views from River Café and Water's Edge in Queens, the East River view from the Water Club lacks drama. Nonetheless, it's a wonderful feeling to sit close to the water, even in the Water Club's somewhat stodgy yacht club atmosphere. The food, unfortunately, doesn't live up to expectations. Classics like Dover sole and prime sirloin simply do not shine through, while more complicated preparations like coriander-scented tuna with sautéed watercress and jasmine rice in a lobster-cilantro vinaigrette seem like trendy hodgepodges. Straightforward desserts like strawberry shortcake are worth waiting for.

Wine list: The mostly French and American selection is fairly priced. **Price range:** Lunch: apps., $8–$13; entrees, $16–$22;

desserts, $7; prix fixe, $20.01 or $28. Dinner: apps., $9–$15; entrees, $26–$35; desserts, $7; prix fixe, $38. **Wheelchair access:** There is a ramp to enter the restaurant and an accessible restroom on the main floor. **Features:** Good view, good for business, romantic, outdoor dining. **Services:** Catering, private parties.

West 63rd Street Steak House ☆ $$$$

STEAKHOUSE

44 W. 63rd St. (near Broadway)
Credit cards: All major   Meals: D

(212) 246-6363
Closed Sun.

This restaurant turns the New York steakhouse experience on its head. It is quiet and restful, and the service is solicitous. As plush and comfortable as a rich man's library, it has an attractive view of Lincoln Center and serves big potent drinks and excellent shrimp cocktail. Unfortunately the steaks aren't always very good. The porterhouse and T-bone are sometimes aged to perfection, sometimes not; you just can't count on them. The veal chop, however, is a fine piece of meat and the roasted baby chicken is flavorful. Among the many side dishes the french fries are excellent, and so is the nutmeg-free creamed spinach, but the home fries are unimpressive. Desserts are not recommended; just stick to the sorbet. (*Ruth Reichl*)

Other recommended dishes: Shrimp cocktail; littleneck clams; black bean soup; porterhouse for two; filet mignon; broiled lobster; onion loaf; creamed spinach, sorbet. **Wine list:** Unremarkable, but with a wide range of prices. **Price range:** Apps., $9–$17; entrees, $22–$34; sides, $8; desserts, $7–$9. **Wheelchair access:** Elevator to second floor dining room and restrooms. **Services:** Takeout, catering, private parties.

Wollensky's Grill $$$ NEW AMERICAN/STEAKHOUSE

201 E. 49th St. (at Third Ave.)
Credit cards: All major

(212) 753-0444
Meals: L, D, LN

An after-work crowd, usually of beefy men, packs this free-wheeling, casual, less-expensive annex to the well-known steakhouse Smith & Wollensky. It's cramped and noisy, but you can get good steaks, of course, excellent burgers and a nice variety of wines by the glass. A few sidewalk tables are available in warm weather if you don't mind the incessant traffic.

Price range: Apps., $10–$15; entrees, $10–$30; desserts, $3–$8. **Wheelchair access:** Fully accessible. **Features:** Kid friendly, good for business. **Services:** Takeout.

Woo Chon $$$

KOREAN

8 W. 36th St. (bet. Fifth & Sixth Aves.)   (212) 695-0676
41-19 Kissena Blvd., Flushing, Queens   (718) 463-0803
Credit cards: All major   Meals: B, Br, L, D, LN

Two locations, each in the heart of a Koreatown, offer an all-purpose Korean menu 24 hours a day. Good kalbi (marinated short ribs) to barbecue right at the table, a fine version of the Korean seafood pancake haemul pajun, and all the spicy kimchi you can eat.

Price range: Apps., $4.50–$9; entrees, $8.50–$21.95; desserts, $3–$6. **Wheelchair access:** Fully accessible. **Services:** Catering, private parties.

Wu Liang Ye $25 & Under

CHINESE

338 Lexington Ave. (bet. 39th & 40th Sts.)   (212) 370-9647
36 W. 48th St. (bet. Fifth & Sixth Aves.)   (212) 398-2308
Credit cards: All major   Meals: L, D, LN

Though each of these branches of a Chinese restaurant chain differs slightly in menu and atmosphere, they all specialize in lively, robust Sichuan dishes, notable for their meticulous preparation. Sliced conch is one of their more unusual dishes, firm, chewy and nutty, served with spicy red oil. Four kinds of dumplings are all delicate and flavorful.

Other recommended dishes: Cold noodles with sesame sauce; soup with fish fillets and pickled cabbage; crystal seafood and asparagus dumplings; crystal shrimp dumplings; steamed pork dumplings in hot oil; steamed seafood dumplings; tea-smoked duck with ginger; double-cooked fresh bacon with chili sauce; chef's bean curd with spicy sauce. **Price range:** $7.50–$20. **Wheelchair access:** Steps at entrance; dining room and restrooms are on one level. **Features:** Kid friendly. **Services:** Delivery, takeout, private parties.

Xunta $25 & Under

SPANISH/TAPAS

174 First Ave. (near 11th St.)   (212) 614-0620
Credit cards: All major   Meals: D, LN

Xunta (pronounced SHOON-tuh) has the authentic feeling of a Spanish tapas bar. It's informal, crowded, smoky and loud, with dozens of tapas. The selection of Spanish wines and sherries is just right.

Recommended dishes: Tortilla espanola; grilled sardines; octopus salad; pork with potatoes and peppers; little clams in a marinade of wine and garlic. **Price range:** Tapas, $2.75–$16.25. **Wheelchair access:** Two steps to restrooms. **Features:** Romantic. **Services:** Takeout.

Ya Bowl

$25 & Under   **JAPANESE**

125 W. 45th St. (bet. Sixth & Seventh Aves.)   (212) 764-3017
Credit cards: All major   Meals: L, D, LN   Closed Sun.

This sweet little Japanese restaurant on the fringe of Times Square looks like a New York living room. The raison d'être is the bowl meals: one-pot meals in which hot food is served over rice in a bowl. Salmon teriyaki is typical, a well-cooked salmon steak brushed with sweet teriyaki sauce, which drips into the rice below. Even better is the unusual sukiyaki, the beef-and-vegetable stew which is simmered in a sweet soy sauce and served with egg over rice. Skip the mundane selection of sushi.

Other recommended dishes: Chicken cutlet; chicken cutlet curry; soba noodles; edamame; boiled spinach; gyoza; chocolate-espresso cake. **Alcohol:** Beer and wine. **Price range:** Lunch, $6.50–$14.95. Dinner: apps., $4.50–$9.50; entrees, $10.50–$14.50. **Wheelchair access:** Fully accessible. **Features:** Kid friendly, good for business, outdoor dining. **Services:** Takeout, private parties.

Yakiniku JuJu

$25 & Under   **JAPANESE**

157 E. 28th St. (bet. Madison & Park Aves.)   (212) 684-7830
Credit cards: All major   Meals: D

This small and friendly restaurant specializes in cook-it-yourself shabu-shabu, sukiyaki and Japanese barbecue. To get in, you descend steps to a subterranean doorway. Then you pass through a low, narrow hallway, up a spiral staircase and, finally, into a small dining room of booths, each outfitted with a gas-powered grill (and a fire extinguisher). It is a tableau that cries out for an appetizer of "salted squid guts," which arrive in a pretty little dish atop a small pedestal, the squid cut into cylinders the size of small anchovies, immersed in a pasty liquid. Yes, it is chewy and salty. In fact, it is fermented, though only mildly pungent. Another unusual appetizer is takoyaki, croquettes the size of golf balls stuffed with pieces of octopus and flavored with dried seaweed, ginger and a fruity sauce. Barely crisp on the surface, they collapse into a delicious porridge in the mouth.

Main courses are big and come with soup and salad. The choices include yakiniku, in which you cook pieces of meat and vegetables directly on the grill; shabu-shabu, in which you swish the meat and vegetables through boiling broth; and sukiyaki, the traditional Japanese stew, in which you simmer meat and vegetables in a slightly sweet soy-based sauce.

It is worth mentioning that children may get a special charge out of cooking their own dinner, if they are old enough to negotiate chopsticks and a hot grill.

Other recommended dishes: Kimchi pancake. **Price range:**
Dinner for two, $30–$46; for four, up to $80. A la carte,
$10–$20. **Wheelchair access:** Two sets of stairs to the dining
room.

Zarela ☆ ☆　$$　MEXICAN/TEX-MEX

953 Second Ave. (bet. 50th & 51st Sts.)　(212) 644-6740
Credit cards: All major　Meals: L, D

Bright, bold and raucous as a party, the sort of place that looks
like a typical Mexican taquería. Happily, it is not. Zarela Mar-
tinez has written several excellent Mexican cookbooks, and she
does her native cuisine proud by serving some of the city's
most exciting and authentic Mexican food. Among the best
dishes are a fiery snapper hash, crisp flautas, tamales and fajitas. Good side dishes include creamy rice baked with sour
cream, cheddar cheese, corn and poblano chilies, and pozole
guisado, in which hominy kernels are sautéed with tomatoes,
onions, garlic and jalapeño peppers. (*Ruth Reichl*)

Price range: Lunch: avg. app., $8; entree, $12; dessert, $7. Din-
ner: avg. app., $8; entree, $18; dessert, $7. **Wheelchair access:**
Restrooms not accessible. **Services:** Delivery, takeout, catering,
private parties.

Zaytoons　$25 & Under　MIDDLE EASTERN

283 Smith St., Cobble Hill, Brooklyn　(718) 875-1880
Credit cards: All major　Meals: D, LN

Of the many moderately priced Middle Eastern restaurants
around, few offer the combination of genial, relaxed surroundings and simple but meticulously prepared food that Zaytoons
does. If you have had only the sort of hardened disks of pita
bread that come in plastic bags, tasting the baked-to-order pitas
at this little corner cafe may be a revelation. The soft, pillowy
bread is perfect for scooping up cool salads and dips like tangy
hummus; tart tabbouleh that tastes of parsley and lemon juice;
smooth, lightly smoky baba gannouj; and excellent cucumber-
and-yogurt salad with crumbled feta and plenty of refreshing
mint. The pitas also form the basis of savory Middle Eastern
pizzas and the terrific zatter bread, baked just to the brink of
crispness and served glistening with olive oil and fragrant with
thyme, salt and toasted sesame seeds. Kebabs are moist and
succulent, while basbousa, a light semolina cake with honey
and almonds, makes a pleasing dessert.

Other recommended dishes: Mujadarra, potato salad, grape
leaves, shawarma, mint iced tea. **Price range:** Apps., $3–$6;
entrees, $5–$9. **Wheelchair access:** One step at entrance.

Zen Palate $$

ASIAN/VEGETARIAN

663 Ninth Ave. (at 46th St.)
34 Union Sq. E. (at 16th St.)
2170 Broadway (bet. 76th & 77th Sts.)
Credit cards: All major

(212) 582-1669
(212) 614-9291
(212) 501-7768
Meals: L, D

Who would have expected a restaurant serving the austere food
of Buddhist monks to be so successful? There are now three
Zen Palates, each architecturally serene and beautiful, each
offering dishes like "Jewel of Happiness" (mini-mushroom
steaks with endive) and "Beauty Quest" (sautéed wheat
gluten). If you like meatless Asian cuisine, this is for you.

Price range: Apps., $6–$7; entrees, $9–$10; desserts, $3.50.
Wheelchair access: Fully accessible. **Services:** Delivery, takeout, catering, private parties.

Zito's East $25 & Under

PIZZA

211 First Ave. (bet. 12th & 13th Sts.)
Credit cards: All major

(212) 473-3400
Meals: Br, L, D

Bread-making, not pizza-making, is the tradition at this pizzeria. In the back of the long, narrow dining room are twin brick
coal-fired ovens, which produce superb pizzas with smooth,
flawless crusts. Sausage is excellent, and the mozzarella is
freshly made, outshining the rather ordinary tomato sauce.

Alcohol: Beer and wine. **Price range:** Apps., $3.95–$6.95; large
pizza, $11 and up; entrees, $4.75–$14.95; desserts, $2.50–$4.
Wheelchair access: Fully accessible. **Features:** Kid friendly.
Services: Delivery, takeout, catering, private parties.

Zocalo $$

MEXICAN/TEX-MEX

174 E. 82nd St. (bet. Third & Lexington Aves.)
Credit cards: All major

(212) 717-7772
Meals: D

An Upper East Side restaurant more notable for its interesting
margaritas than its typical Mexican fare. The narrow restaurant
is great for drinks and guacamole. The food is good, but if
you're looking for authentic Mexican food, go elsewhere.

Price range: Avg. app., $8.50; entree, $20. **Wheelchair access:**
Not accessible. **Features:** Smoking permitted, outdoor dining.
Services: Takeout, catering, private parties.

Zoë $$

NEW AMERICAN

90 Prince St. (bet. Broadway & Mercer St.)
Credit cards: All major

(212) 966-6722
Meals: Br, L, D

The big, bright tiled room with its open kitchen seems just right after a day in the SoHo galleries. The modern American food seems right too. And if you're in the mood for new American wines, you'll love the wine list.

Price range: Lunch: avg. app., $8; entree, $11; dessert, $6. Dinner: avg. app., $10; entree, $19; dessert, $7. **Wheelchair access:** Fully accessible. **Services:** Takeout, private parties.

Zum Schneider $25 & Under

GERMAN

107 Ave. C (at 7th St.)
Credit cards: Cash only

(212) 598-1098
Meals: L, D

Essentially an indoor beer garden, Zum Schneider is right in the heart of Alphabet City, and it's packing young people in nightly. It sets no new culinary standards; the simple menu hews closely to the Bavarian formula of wurst, pork and cabbage. But it has accomplished the unlikely feat of making a German place cool. With its cement floor, smoky bar, timbered walls and ceiling, and hip-hop playing in the background, it's easy to imagine Zum Schneider in an equally hip neighborhood in Munich. Tables (with benches) are occupied family style, and while food is delivered to the table, you generally must order at the bar.

The bar offers a dozen excellent seasonal draft beers, all German, and 10 more in bottles. Zum takes great care to serve each beer in the correct glassware. Kölsch, a crisp, delicate specialty of the Cologne region, is rarely seen in New York, so a small glass of the almost minty Reissdorf Kölsch makes an excellent aperitif as you decide what to eat. Try the pfannkuchen soup, literally pancake soup, a mild beef broth seasoned only with parsley and a bit of salt and containing slender strips of egg pancakes, the equivalent of light dumplings.

Everything else comes with a potato dish, either fried potatoes or chunky potato salad flavored with vinegar, parsley, onions and garlic, and a cabbage dish, either cinnamon-scented red cabbage or a huge mound of rather neutral sauerkraut. The best of the main courses is a plump, rosy smoked pork chop, which goes well with a Schneider Weissbier, a medium-dark, tart and fruity wheat beer. The menu inevitably leads to sausages, cooked to a juicy snap and just right with beers as different as the HB Mai-Bock, a distinctive seasonal dark brew, and the sprightly Jever pilsener. The three-sausage platter, with a mellow weisswurst, a spicy wiener and a mild bauernwurst served with both sweet and hot mustard, is your best bet.

Other recommended dishes: Schneider gröstl. **Price range:** $7–$12, with $3 and $6 appetizer portions. **Wheelchair access:** Main room and restroom are on one level.

Zuni $25 & Under SOUTHWESTERN

598 Ninth Ave. (at 43rd St.) (212) 765-7626
Credit cards: All major Meals: Br, L, D, LN

The original focus at this appealing little restaurant was Southwestern, and the atmosphere still reflects this, but the current menu is all over the map, with Southwestern dishes like chili-rubbed rib-eye steak, New Orleans specialties like jambalaya and geographically indecipherable offerings like sesame-crusted salmon with mango-and-black-bean salsa and basmati rice. If it's too confusing, settle for meatloaf and garlic mashed potatoes. It's usually all pretty good.

Price range: Apps., $6.95; entrees, $7.50–$14.95; desserts, $5.50. **Wheelchair access:** Dining room is one step up; restroom is one flight down. **Services:** Delivery, takeout, catering, private parties.

A Guide to Restaurants by Neighborhood

THE WEST SIDE

West 100's

		On / Near
Amy Ruth's	Southern	116 St/Lenox Av
Bayou	Cajun/Southern	Lenox Av/125 St
Charles' Southern-Style	*Southern*	*F. Douglass/151 St*
Copeland's	Southern	145 St/Amstdm
Dalia's	Tapas	Amstdm/109 St
El Presidente	*Caribbean*	*Bway/164 St*
Fish	Seafood	Bway/108 St
Meridiana	Italian	Bway/106 St
Metisse	Bistro/French	105 St/Bway
Mill Korean	Korean	Bway/112 St
Mi Mexico	Latin American	Bway/125 St
Miss Maude's Spoonbread	Southern	Lenox Av/137th St
Monsoon	Vietnamese	Bway/110 St
Ollie's Noodle Shop	Chinese/Noodles	Bway/116 St
Pan Pan	Southern	Lenox/Malcolm X
Royal Kebab	Indian	Bway/103 St
Sal's and Carmine's	Pizza	Bway/101 St
Sylvia's	Southern	Lenox Av/126 St
Turkuaz	*Turkish/Middle Eastern*	*Bway/100 St*

West 90's

		On / Near
Alouette	Bistro/French	Bway/97 St
Café Con Leche	Latin American	Amstdm/95 St
Carmine's	Italian	Bway/90 St
Cooke's Corner	*European/American*	*Amstdm/90 St*
Gabriela's	Mexican	Amstdm/93 St
Gennaro	*Italian*	*Amstdm/93 St*
La Cocina	Mexican/Tex-Mex	Bway/98 St
Lemongrass Grill	Thai	Bway/94 St
Pampa	Latin American	Amstdm/97 St

West 80's

		On / Near
Al Dente	Italian	Amstdm/80 St
Artie's New York Deli	Deli	Bway/82 St
Avenue	Bistro/French	Columbus/85 St
Barney Greengrass	Deli	Amstdm/86 St
Café Con Leche	Latin American	Amstdm/80 St
Café La Grolla	*Italian*	*Amstdm/80 St*
Calle Ocho ☆	Pan-Latin	Columbus/81 St
Dock's Oyster Bar ☆	Seafood	Bway/89 St
E J's Luncheonette	Diner	Amstdm/81 St
Fred's	New American	Amstdm/83 St
French Roast Cafe	Bistro/French	Bway/85 St
Good Enough to Eat	American	Amstdm/83 St
Haru	Japanese/Sushi	Amstdm/80 St
Isola	Italian	Columbus/83 Stt
Jackson Hole	Hamburgers	Columbus/85 St

Note: Restaurants in **boldface italics** are Eric Asimov's choices for the best inexpensive restaurants in New York

439

West 80's (continued)

		On/Near
La Grolla ☆	Italian	Amstdm/80 St
Lemongrass Grill	Thai	Amstdm/84 St
Little Jezebel	Southern	Columbus/85 St
Luzia's	Portuguese	Amstdm/80 St
Miss Saigon	Vietnamese	Columbus/82 St
Monsoon	Vietnamese	Amstdm/81 St
Ollie's Noodle Shop	Chinese/Noodles	Bway/84 St
Ouest	New American/Bistro	Bway/84 St
Polistina's	Pizza	Bway/82 St
Popover Cafe	American	Amstdm/86 St
Rain	Pan Asian	82 St/Columbus
Sabor	*Tapas/Pan-Latin*	*Amstdm/82 St*
Saigon Grill	Vietnamese	Bway/87 St
Sarabeth's	New American	Amstdm/80 St
Savann	French	Amstdm/80 St
Time Cafe	New American	Bway/85 St

West 70's

		On/Near
All State Cafe	American/Hamburgers	72 St/West End
Baluchi's	Indian	Columbus/73 St
Boat Basin Cafe	Cafe	79 St/Riverside
Café Frida	Mexican	Columbus/77 St
Cafe Luxembourg	Bistro	70 St/Amstdm
China Fun	Chinese	Columbus/71 St
Citrus	Southwestern	Amstdm/75 St
Dallas BBQ	Barbecue	72 St/Ctrl Pk W
Diwan's Curry House	Indian	Columbus/74 St
Estihana	Chinese/Kosher	79 St/Bway
Gray's Papaya	Fast Food	Bway/72 St
Josie's	New American	Amstdm/74 St
Marika	French/American	70 St/Amstdm
Metsovo	Greek	70 St/Columbus
Mughlai	Indian	Columbus/71 St
Niko's	Mediterranean	Bway/76 St
Ocean Grill ☆	Seafood	Columbus/78 St
Patsy's	Pizza	74 St/Columbus
Penang	Malaysian	Columbus/71 St
River	Vietnamese	Amstdm/76 St
Ruby Foo's ☆☆	Pan-Asian	Bway/77 St
Shark Bar	Southern	Amstdm/74 St
Spazzia	Mediterranean	Columbus/77 St
Zen Palate	Vegetarian	Bway/76 St

LINCOLN CENTER
West 60's

		On/Near
Café des Artistes	Continental	67 St/Cntrl Pk W
Gabriel's ☆☆	Italian	60 St/Bway
Jean Georges ☆☆☆☆	New American	Cntrl Pk W/60 St
John's	Italian/Pizza	65 St/Bway
Levana	Kosher/ American	69 St/Columbus
Nick and Toni's ☆☆	Mediterranean	67 St/Bway
Ollie's Noodle Shop	Chinese	Bway/67 St
Picholine ☆☆☆	Mediterranean/French	64 St/Bway
Rosa Mexicano	Mexican	Columbus/62 St
The Saloon	New American	Bway/64 St
Sapphire	Indian	Bway/63 St
Shun Lee West	Chinese	65 St/Columbus
Tavern on the Green ☆	New American	Cntrl Pk W/67 St
Vince & Eddie's	New American	68 St/Columbus
W. 63rd St. Steakhouse ☆	Steakhouse	63 St/Bway

THEATER DISTRICT — WEST 50's

West 55th–59th

		On/Near
Alain Ducasse ☆☆☆	French	58 St/6 Av
Atlas ☆☆☆	French/English	Cntrl Pk S/6 Av
Baluchi's	Indian	56 St/Bway
Brasserie 8 ¹/₂ ☆	Brasserie/French	57 St/
Bricco Ristorante	Italian	56 St/8 Av
Brooklyn Diner	Diner	57 St/Bway
Carnegie Deli	*Deli*	*7 Av/55 St*
Christer's ☆☆	Scandinavian	55 St/7 Av
Estiatorio Milos ☆☆	Greek/Seafood	55 St/6 Av
Hard Rock Cafe	Theme	57 St/7 Av
Jekyll & Hyde Club	Theme	6 Av/57 St
Jimmy Armstrong's	Pan Latin	10 Av/57 St
Joe's Shanghai ☆☆	Chinese	56 St/5 Av
Hudson Cafeteria	Fusion	58 St/9 Av
La Caravelle ☆☆☆	French	55 St/6 Av
La Côte Basque ☆☆☆	French	55 St/6 Av
La Vineria	Italian	55 St/5 Av
Le Quercy	French	55 St/6 Av
Manhattan Ocean Club ☆☆	Seafood	58 St/6 Av
Menchanko-Tei	Japanese	55 St/6 Av
Michael's ☆☆	New American	55 St/5 Av
Mickey Mantle's	American	Cntrl Pk S/6 Av
Molyvos ☆☆☆	Greek	7 Av/55 St
Patsy's	Italian	56 St/Bway
Petrossian ☆☆	Russian	58 St/7 Av
Puttanesca	Italian	9 Av/56 St
Redeye Grill ☆	New American	7 Av/56 St
Russian Tea Room	Russian	57 St/6 Av
San Domenico ☆☆☆	Italian	Cntrl Pk S/Bway
Taprobane	Sri Lankan	56 St/8 Av
Ten Kai	Japanese/Sushi	56 St/6 Av
Topaz Thai	*Thai*	*56 St/6 Av*
Town ☆☆☆	New American	56 St/6 Av
Trattoria dell'Arte ☆	Italian	7 Av/57 St

West 50th–54th

		On/Near
Afghan Kebab House	Afghani	9 Av/51 St
Africa No. 2	African	53 St/8 Av
Aquavit ☆☆☆	Scandinavian	54 St/6 Av
Ben Benson's	Steakhouse	52 St/6 Av
Brasserie Centrale	French	Bway/53 St
China Fun	Chinese	Bway/51 St
Ciao Europa	Italian	54 St/6 Av
Cité	Steakhouse	51 St/6 Av
Druids	New American	10 Av/50 St
Gallagher's	Steakhouse	52 St/Bway
Hallo Berlin	German	51 St/9 Av
Island Burgers	Hamburgers	9 Av/51 St
Judson Grill ☆☆☆	New American	52 St/6 Av
Julian's	Mediterranean	9 Av/53 St
Kabul Cafe	Afghani	54 St/8 Av
La Locanda	Italian	9 Av/50 St
Le Bernardin ☆☆☆☆	French/Seafood	51 St/6 Av
Limoncello	Italian	51 St/7 Av
Manhattan Chili Co.	Mexican/Tex-Mex	Bway/53 St
Mee Noodle Shop	Chinese	9 Av/53 St
Old San Juan	Puerto Rican	9 Av/51 St
Palio ☆☆	Italian	51 St/6 Av

Note: Restaurants in **boldface italics** are Eric Asimov's choices for the best inexpensive restaurants in New York

West 50th–54th *(continued)*

		On/Near
Remi ☆☆	Italian	53 St/6 Av
René Pujol	French	51 St/8 Av
Rice 'n' Beans	Brazilian	9 Av/50 St
Rinconcito Peruano	Peruvian	9 Av/53 St
Ruth's Chris	Steakhouse	51 St/6 Av
Seeda Thai 2	Thai/Vietnamese	50 St/8 Av
Soba Nippon	*Japanese/Sushi*	*52 St/6 Av*
Stage Deli	Deli	7 Av/53 St
Tout Va Bien	French	51 St/8 Av
Trionfo	Italian	51 St/8 Av
Tuscan Square	Italian	51 St/6 Av
"21" Club ☆☆	New American	52 St/6 Av
Uncle Nick's	Greek	9 Av/50 St
Viceversa	Italian	51 St/8 Av
Victor's Cafe 52	Latin American	52 St/Bway

THEATER DISTRICT — WEST 40's

West 45th–49th

		On/Near
Afghan Kebab House	Afghani	46 St/6 Av
Amarone	Italian	9 Av/47 St
Baldoria ☆	Italian	49 St/7 Av
Bali Nusa Indah	*Indonesian*	*9 Av/45 St*
Barbetta	Italian	46 St/8 Av
Becco	Italian	46 St/8 Av
Cabana Carioca	Latin American	45 St/6 Av
Churrascaria Plataforma ☆☆	Brazilian	49 St/8 Av
District ☆	New American	46 St/6 Av
Edison Cafe	Diner	47 St/Bway
Firebird ☆☆	Russian	46 St/8 Av
Hell's Kitchen	Mexican	9 Av/47 St
Hourglass Tavern	New American	46 St/8 Av
Ipanema	Latin American	46 St/6 Av
Jack Rose	New American/Steak	8 Av/47 St
Jezebel	Southern	9 Av/45 St
Joe Allen	New American	46 St/8 Av
Kodama	Japanese/Sushi	45 St/8 Av
La Cocina	Mexican/Tex-Mex	8 Av/46 St
Lotfi's Moroccan	North African	46 St/8 Av
Luxia	Italian	48 St/8 Av
Maritime ☆	Seafood	6 Av/49 St
MchHale's	Bar Snacks/Burgers	8 Av/46 St
Meskerem	African	47 St/9 Av
Morrell Wine Bar & Cafe	New American	Rockefeller Plz
New World Grill	Southwestern	49 St/8 Av
Orso	Italian	46 St/8 Av
Pam Real Thai Food	Thai	49 St/9 Av
Queen of Sheba	*Ethiopian*	*10 Av/46 St*
Rainbow Grill	Italian	Rockefeller Plz
Sea Grill ☆☆	Seafood	Rockefeller Plz
Shaan Of India	Indian	48 St/6 Av
Sushiden	Japanese/Sushi	49 St/6 Av
Sushi Zen	Japanese/Sushi	46 St/6 Av
Wu Liang Ye	*Chinese*	*48 St/6 Av*
Ya Bowl	Japanese	45 St/6 Av
Zanzibar	Mediterranean	9 Av/45 St
Zen Palate	Vegetarian	9 Av/46 St

West 40th–44th

		On / Near
Algonquin	American	44 St/6 Av
Bryant Park Grill	New American	40 St/5 Av
Carmine's	Italian	44 St/7 Av
Chez Josephine ✩✩	Bistro/French	42 St/9 Av
Chimichurri Grill	Latin American	9 Av/43 St
Dallas BBQ	Barbecue	43 St/6 Av
Esca ✩✩	Italian/Seafood	43 St/9 Av
44	New American	44 St/6 Av
Hallo Berlin	German	10 Av/44 St
Ilo ✩✩✩	New American	40 St/5 Av
Island Spice	Caribbean	44 St/9 Av
John's Pizzeria	Italian/Pizza	44 St/7 Av
Lakruwana	Sri Lankan	44 St/8 Av
Le Madeleine	French	43 St/9 Av
Le Max	French	43v/6 Av
Manhattan Chili Co.	Mexican/Tex-Mex	Bway/43 St
Ollie's Noodle Shop	Chinese/Noodles	44 St/7 Av
Restaurant Above	Fusion/New American	42 St/7 Av
Rio De Janeiro	Brazilian	43 St/Bway
Sardi's	New American	44 St/Bway
Soul Cafe	Southern	42 St/9 Av
Tagine	Moroccan	9 Av/40 St
Triomphe ✩✩	French/New American	44 St/6 Av
Virgil's Real BBQ	Barbecue	44 St/Bway
Zuni	Southwestern	9 Av/43 St

GARMENT CENTER / MADISON SQ. GARDEN

West 30's

		On / Near
Chez Gnagna Koty's	African	9 Av/39 St
Cho Dang Gol ✩✩	Korean	35 St/6 Av
Han Bat	*Korean*	*35 St/6 Av*
Havana NY	Latin American/Cuban	36 St/5 Av
Keens	Steakhouse	36 St/6 Av
Los Dos Rancheros	*Mexican*	*9 Av/38 St*
Mandoo Bar	Korean	32 St/5 Av
Rinconcito Mexicano	Peruvian	39 St/8 Av
Soul Fixins'	Southern	34 St/8 Av
Supreme Macaroni Co.	Italian	9 Av/38 St
Tupelo Grill	Steakhouse	33 St/7 Av
Woo Chon	Korean	36 St/6 Av

CHELSEA & ENVIRONS

West 20's

		On / Near
Biricchino	Italian	29 St/8 Av
Bongo	Seafood	10 Av/28 St
Bottino	Italian	10 Av/24 St
Bright Food Shop	*New American*	*8 Av/21 St*
Cal's	Continental	21 St/6 Av
Chelsea Bistro & Bar ✩✩	Bistro/French	23 St/8 Av
Cuba Libre	Pan-Latin	8 Av/20 St
Empire Diner	Diner	10 Av/22 St
Gus's Figs	Mediterranean	27 St/7 Av
F&B	Hot Dogs/Sausage	23 St/7 Av
Fresco Tortilla	Mexican/Tex-Mex	8 Av/22 St
Fresco Tortilla	Mexican/Tex-Mex	6 Av/25 St
Grand Sichuan	*Chinese*	*9 Av/24 St*
The Half King	Pub/American	23 St/10 Av
La Maison de Sade	Theme	23 St/7 Av

Note: Restaurants in ***boldface italics*** are Eric Asimov's choices for the best inexpensive restaurants in New York

West 20's (continued)

		On/Near
Le Gamin	French	9 Av/21 St
Le Zie	*Italian*	*7 Av/20 St*
Lola	New American	22 St/5 Av
Lot 61	New American	21 St/10 Av
Negril	Caribbean	23 St/8 Av
Porters New York	New American	7 Av/22 St
The Red Cat ☆	New American	10 Av/23 St
Royal Siam	*Thai*	*8 Av/22 St*
Shaffer City Oyster Bar	Seafood	21 St/6 Av

West 14th–19th

		On/Near
Alley's End	New American	17 St/8 Av
AZ ☆☆☆	Fusion	17 St/5 Av
Bar Six	Mediterranean	6 Av/12 St
Blue Water Grill ☆	Seafood	Union Sq W/16 St
Cafe Riazor	Spanish	16 St/7 Av
Coffee Shop	Diner	Union Sq W/16 St
El Cid	*Spanish*	*15 St/8 Av*
Frank's ☆	Steakhouse	10 Av/15 St
Fresco Tortilla Grill	Mexican/Tex-Mex	14 St/7 Av
L'Acajou	French	19 St/6 Av
La Taza De Oro	Latin American	8 Av/14 St
Le Madri	Italian	18 St/6 Av
Le Singe Vert	French	7 Av/19 St
Maroons	Southern/Jamaican	16 St/7 Av
Old Homestead	Steakhouse	9 Av/14 St
Republic	Pan-Asian	Union Sq W/17 St
Rocking Horse Cafe	Mexican/Tex-Mex	8 Av/19 St
Rue des Crepes	Crepes	8 Av/15 St
Tonic ☆☆	New American	18 St/6 Av
Trois Canards	French	8 Av/19 St
Vox ☆	Bistro/Pan-Latin	8 Av/17 St

THE EAST SIDE

East 100's

		On/Near
El Paso Taqueria	Mexican	Lex/104 St
Emily's	Southern	5 Av/111 St
Rao's	Italian	114 St/Pleasant
La Fonda Boricua	*Latin American*	*106 St/3 Av*
Patsy's	Pizza	1 Av/117 St

East 90's

		On/Near
Al Bacio	Italian	3 Av/94 St
Barking Dog	Diner	3 Av/94 St
Brother Jimmy's	Barbecue	3 Av/92 St
The Commons	New American	2 Av/93 St
Jackson Hole	Hamburgers	Madison/91 St
92	New American/Bistro	92 St/Madison
Osso Buco	Italian	3 Av/93 St
Pascalou	Bistro/French	Madison/93 St
Pintaile's	Pizza	91 St/5 Av
Sarabeth's	New American	Madison/92 St
Sharz	Mediterranean	90 St/3 Av
Vico	Italian	Madison/92 St
Vinegar Factory	New American	91 St/York
Yura & Co.	New American	3 Av/92 St

East 80's

		On/Near
Baluchi's	Indian	2 Av/81 St
Butterfield 81 ☆☆	New American	81 St/3 Av
Caffe Grazie	Italian	84 St/Madison

Candido Pizza	Pizza	1 Av/84 St
Carino	Italian	2 Av/88 St
Comfort Diner	American/Diner	86 St/Lex
Dakshin	*Indian*	*1 Av/89 St*
Donguri	Japanese/Sushi	83 St/2 Av
Elaine's	Italian	2 Av/88 St
Emo's	Korean	2 Av/81 St
Erminia	Italian	83 St/2 Av
Etats-Unis ☆☆	New American	81 St/2 Av
Jackson Hole	Hamburgers	2 Av/83 St
King's	English	82 St/2 Av
Le Refuge	French	82 St/3 Av
Luca	*Italian*	*1 Av/89 St*
Miss Saigon	Vietnamese	3 Av/80 St
Panorama Cafe	New American	2 Av/85 St
Paola's ☆☆	Italian	85 St/2 Av
Pastrami Queen	Deli	Lex/85 St
Penang	Malaysian	2 Av/83 St
Pesce & Pasta	Italian/Seafood	3 Av/87 St
Pig Heaven	Chinese	2 Av/80 St
Pintaile's Pizza	Pizza	York/83 St
Primavera ☆	Italian	1 Av/82 St
Saigon Grill	Vietnamese	2 Av/88 St
Samalita's	Mexican/Tex-Mex	3 Av/81 St
Sistina	Italian	2 Av/80 St
Taco Taco	*Mexican/Tex-Mex*	*2 Av/89 St*
Tony's Di Napoli	Italian	2 Av/83 St
Totonno Pizzeria	Pizza	2 Av/80 St
Trois Marches ☆	Fusion/French	81 St/1 Av
Vespa Cibobuono	Italian	2 Av/84 St
Viand	Diner	86 St/2 Av
Wu Liang Ye	*Chinese*	*86 St/3 Av*
Zocalo	Mexican/Tex-Mex	82 St/3 Av

East 70's

On/Near

Afghan Kebab	Afghani	2 Av/70 St
Annie's	New American	3 Av/77 St
Bandol	French	78 St/Lex
Bistro Le Steak	Bistro/Steak	3 Av/75 St
Brother Jimmy's	Barbecue	1 Av/76 St
Café Boulud ☆☆☆	French	76 St/Madison
Candle Cafe	Vegetarian	3 Av/74 St
Cello ☆☆☆	French/Seafood	77 St/Madison
Dallas BBQ	Barbecue	3 Av/72 St
The Dining Room	New American	79 St/Lex
E J's Luncheonette	Diner	3 Av/73 St
Haru	Japanese/Sushi	3 Av/76 St
Henry's Evergreen	Chinese	1 Av/70 St
La Tour	Bistro/French	3 Av/76 St
Le Petit Hulot	French	Lex/70 St
Lusardi's	Italian	2 Av/77 St
Nino's	Italian	1 Av/72 St
Orsay	Bistro/Brasserie	Lex/75 St
Park View ☆☆	New American	Central Pk/72 St
Payard Pâtisserie ☆☆	Bistro/French	Lex/73 St
Persepolis	Mediterranean	2 Av/75 St
Pintaile's Pizza	Pizza	York/76 St
Quatorze Bis	Bistro/French	79 St/1 Av
Rafina	Greek/Seafood	York/78 St
Red Bar Restaurant	American/Bistro	75 St/2 Av

Note: Restaurants in **boldface italics** are Eric Asimov's choices for the best inexpensive restaurants in New York

East 70's (continued)

		On/Near
Sa Woy	Thai	1 Av/77 St
Sant Ambroeus	Italian	Madison/77 St
Sarabeth's	New American	Madison/75 St
Shabu-Tatsu	Japanese	York/75 St
The Sultan	*Turkish*	*2 Av/74 St*
Sushi Of Gari	Japanese/Sushi	78 St/1 Av
Toraya	Japanese	71 St/5 Av
Usküdar	Turkish	2 Av/73 St
Viand	Diner	Madison/78 St
Via Quadronno	Italian/Sandwiches	73 St./Madison
Vivolo	Italian	74 St/2 Av
Willow	New American	Lex/73 St

East 60's

		On/Near
Abajour	Bistro/French	1 Av/62 St
Amaranth	Mediterranean	62 St/Madison
Aureole ☆☆☆	New American	61 St/Madison
Arabelle ☆	French	64 St/Park
California Pizza Kitchen	Pizza	60 St/2 Av
China Fun	Chinese	2 Av/65 St
Circus ☆☆	Brazilian	Lex/62 St
Daniel ☆☆☆☆	French	65 St/Park
Destinee ☆☆	French	61 St/Lex
Gino	Italian	Lex/60 St
Jackson Hole	Hamburgers	64 St/2 Av
John's Pizzeria	Italian/Pizza	64 St/1 Av
La Goulue	Bistro/French	Madison/64 St
L'Absinthe ☆	French	67 St/2 Av
L'Ardoise	French	1 Av/65 St
Le Bilboquet	French	63 St/Park
Le Taxi	French	60 St/Madison
Le Veau d'Or	French	60 St/Lex
The Library	New American	Park Av/61 St
Manhattan Grille	Seafood/Steakhouse	1 Av/63 St
Maratti	Italian/Seafood	62 St/Lex
Maya ☆☆	Mexican/Tex-Mex	1 Av/64 St
Nicole's ☆☆	English	60 St/Madison
Park Avenue Cafe	New American	63 St/Park
Patsy's	Pizza	2 Av/69 St
Post House	Steakhouse	63 St/Park
Rain	Pan-Asian	3 Av/62 St
Sel et Poivre	French	Lex/64 St
Sushi Hatsu ☆☆☆	Japanese/Sushi	1 Av/62 St
Ulrika's	Swedish	60 St/Lex
Viand	Diner	Madison/61 St

East 55th–59th

		On/Near
Ada ☆☆	Indian	58 St/2 Av
Adrienne	French	5 Av/55 St
Bouterin ☆	French	59 St/1 Av
Caviarteria	East European	Park Av/59 St
Da Antonio	Italian	55 St/3 Av
Dawat ☆	Indian	58 St/2 Av
Felidia ☆☆☆	Northern Italian	58 St/2 Av
Fifty Seven Fifty Seven ☆☆☆	American	57 St/Park
Guastavino's ☆☆	Brasserie/French	59 St/1 Av
Harry Cipriani	Italian	5 Av/59 St
Il Valentino ☆☆	Italian	56 St/1 Av
King Cole Bar	Hotel/Lounge	55 St/5 Av

Le Colonial ☆☆	Vietnamese	57 St/Lex
Lespinasse ☆☆☆☆	French	55 St/5 Av
March ☆☆☆	New American	58 St/1 Av
Moscow	Russian	55 St/3 Av
Nicholson ☆	French	58 St/2 Av
Otabe ☆☆	Japanese	56 St/Park
Our Place Shanghai	*Chinese*	*55 St/3 Av*
P.J. Clarke's	Hamburgers	3 Av/55 St
Palm Court	New American	5 Av/59 St
Pesce & Pasta	Italian/Seafood	1 Av/59 St
Shun Lee Palace ☆☆	Chinese	55 St/Lex
Teodora	Italian	57 St/Lex

East 50th–54th

		On/Near
An American Place ☆☆	New American	Lex/50 St
Artos	Greek	53 St/1 Av
Bellini	Italian	52 St/2 Av
Bice ☆☆	Italian	54 St/5 Av
Billy's	American	1 Av/52 St
Brasserie ☆☆	Brasserie/French	53 St/Lex
Caviar Russe	Russian	Madison/54 St
Cosi	Sandwiches	52 St/Lex
Della Femina ☆	New American	54 St/Park
Jubilee	French	54 St/1 Av
Korea Palace ☆	Korean	54 St/Park
L'Actuel ☆☆	French	50 St/Lex
La Grenouille ☆☆☆	French	52 St/5 Av
Le Bateau Ivre	Bistro/French	51 St/2 Av
Le Cirque 2000 ☆☆☆	New American	Madison/50 St
Le Perigord ☆☆	French	52 St/1 Av
Lipstick Cafe	New American	3 Av/53 St
Lutèce ☆☆	French	50 St/2 Av
Maloney & Porcelli ☆	Steak/Seafood	50 St/Park
Meltemi	Greek/Seafood	1 Av/51 St
Nippon	Japanese/Sushi	52 St/Lex
Oceana ☆☆☆	Seafood	54 St/Park
Prime Burger	Hamburgers	51 St/5 Av
San Pietro	Italian	54 St/5 Av
Solera ☆☆	Spanish	53 St/2 Av
Sushi Rose	Japanese/Sushi	52 St/2 Av
Sushisay	Japanese/Sushi	51 St/Park
Tea Box Café	Japanese	5 Av/54 St
The Four Seasons ☆☆☆	New American	52 St/Park
Tse Yang	Chinese	51 St/Madison
Vong	Thai/French	54 St/3 Av
Zarela ☆☆	Mexican/Tex-Mex	2 Av/50 St

East 45th–49th

		On/Near
Avra ☆	Seafood/Greek	48 St/Lex
Bobby Van's ☆	Steakhouse	Park Av/46 St
Box Tree Inn	Continental	49 St/2 Av
Bull & Bear	New American	Park Av/49 St
Cafe Centro ☆☆	Mediterranean	Park Av/45 St
Comfort Diner	Diner	45 St/2 Av
Da Mario	Italian	1 Av/49 St
D'Artagnan ☆☆	French	46 St/Lex
Diwan Grill	Indian	48 St/Lex
Heartbeat ☆☆	New American	49 St/Lex
Il Postino	Italian	49 St/1 Av

Note: Restaurants in **boldface italics** are Eric Asimov's choices for the best inexpensive restaurants in New York

East 45th–49th *(continued)*

		On/Near
Inagiku ☆☆	Japanese/Sushi	49 St/Lex
Katsu-Hama	*Japanese*	*47 St/Madison*
Kuruma Zushi ☆☆☆	Japanese	47 St/5 Av
Marichu	Spanish	46 St/1 Av
Mee Noodle Shop	Chinese	2 Av/49 St
Menchanko-Tei	Japanese/Noodles	45 St/Lex
Naples 45	Italian/Pizza	Park Av/45 St
Patroon ☆☆☆	New American	46 St/Lex
Shinbashi	Japanese	Park Av/48 St
Smith & Wollensky ☆☆	Steakhouse	3 Av/49 St
Sparks ☆	Steakhouse	46 St/3 Av
Sushi Masa	Japanese/Sushi	47 St/Lex
Top of the Tower	New American	49 St/1 Av
Tropica	Seafood	Park/45 St
Wollensky's Grill	New American	49 St/3 Av

East 40th–44th

		On/Near
Caviarteria	East European	Grand Central
Cibo	Italian	2 Av/41 St
Cucina & Co.	Mediterranean	Park/Vanderbilt
Dock's ☆	Seafood	3 Av/40 St
Knodel	Scandinavian/Sausages	Grand Central
Maeda	Japanese/Sushi	41 St/5 Av
Metrazur	Mediterranean	Grand Central
Mezze	Mediterranean	44 St/5 Av
Michael Jordan's ☆☆	Steakhouse	Grand Central
Oyster Bar	Seafood	Grand Central
Palm	Steakhouse	2 Av/44 St
Palm Too	Steakhouse	2 Av/44 St
Pietro's	Italian/Steakhouse	43 St/2 Av
Sushi Yasuda ☆☆☆	Japanese/Sushi	43 St/3 Av
Tuscan Steak	Italian	3 Av/40 St
Virot	French	41 St/Madison

East 30's

		On/Near
Artisanal ☆☆	Bistro	Park/32 St
Asia de Cuba ☆	Asian/Latin	Madison/37 St
Chez Laurence	Bistro/French	Madison/38 St
Cinque Terre ☆☆	Italian	38 St/Madison
Da Ciro	*Italian*	*Lex/33 St*
Evergreen Shanghai	Chinese	38 St/5 Av
Hangawi ☆☆	Korean/Vegetarian	32 St/5 Av
Icon ☆☆	New American	39 St/Lex
Jackson Hole	Hamburgers	3 Av/35 St
Le Totof Bistro	Bistro/French	33 St/Lex
Mee Noodle Shop	Chinese	2 Av/30 St
Metro Fish	Seafood	36 St/Madison
Nadaman Hakubai ☆☆	Japanese	Park/38 St
Patsy's	Pizza	3 Av/34 St
Villa Berulia	Italian	34 St/Lex
Water Club ☆☆	New American	30 St/East River
Wu Liang Ye	*Chinese*	*Lex/39 St*

East 20's

		On/Near
Alva ☆	New American	22 St/Park Av S
Beppe	Italian	22 St/Park Av S
Bolo ☆☆	Spanish	22 St/Park Av S
Commune ☆	Italian/New American	22 St/Bway
Eleven Madison Park ☆☆	New American	Madison/24 St
Fleur de Sel ☆☆	French	20 St/5 Av

Fresco Tortilla	Mexican/Tex-Mex	Lex/23 St
Globe	New American	Park Av S/26 St
Gramercy Tavern ✫✫✫	New American	20 St/Bway
I Trulli ✫✫	Italian	27 St/Lex
La Pizza Fresca	Italian/Pizza	20 St/Park Av S
Les Halles	French	Park Av S/28 St
Mad.28	Italian	Madison/27 St
Mavalli Palace	*Indian/Vegetarian*	*29 St/Park*
Mayrose	Diner	Bway/21 St
Meli Melo	New American	Madison/29 St
Novitá ✫	Italian	22 St/Park
Park Bistro ✫✫✫	Bistro/French	Park Av S/28 St
Patria ✫✫✫	Latin American	Park Av S/20 St
Pongal	*Indian/Veg.*	*Lex/27 St*
Ribollita	Italian	Park Av S/21 St
Silver Swan	German	20 St/Bway
Tabla ✫✫✫	Pan Asian	Madison/25 St
Tamarind	Indian	22 St/Bway
Tossed	Cafe	Park Av S/22 St
Trattoria I Pagliacci	Italian	Park Av S/20 St
Turkish Kitchen	Turkish	3 Av/27 St
27 Standard ✫✫	New American	27 St/Park
Union Pacific ✫✫✫	French/Asian	22 St/Park Av S
Vatan	*Indian*	*3 Av/29 St*
Veritas ✫✫✫	New American	20 St/Park Av S
Yakiniku JuJu	Japanese	28 St/Madison

East 14th–19th

On/Near

Aleutia	New American	Park Av/18 St
Angelo & Maxie's ✫	Steakhouse	Park Av S/19 St
Blue Velvet 1929	Vietnamese	1 Av/14 St
Candela ✫	New American	16 St/Union Sq
Chat 'n Chew	New American	16 St/5 Av
Chicama ✫✫	Pan-Latin	18 St/Bway
Choshi	Japanese/Sushi	Irving/19 St
City Crab & Seafood Co	Seafood	Park Av S/19 St
Craft ✫✫✫	New American	19 St/Bway
Galaxy	New American	Irving/15 St
Irving on Irving	New American	Irving/17 St
Lady Mendl's	English	Irving/17 St
L'Express	Bistro/French	Park Av S/19 St
Medusa	Mediterranean	Park Av S/19 St
Mesa Grill ✫✫	Southwestern	5 Av/15 St
Old Town Bar	American	18 St/Bway
Olives ✫	Mediterranean	Park Av S/17 St
Park Avalon	New American	Park Av S/18 St
Pete's Tavern	American/Italian	18 St/Irving
Pitchoune	Bistro	3 Av/19 St
Sal Anthony's	Italian	Irving/17 St
Steak Frites	Bistro	16 St/5 Av
Tocqueville ✫✫	French	15 St/Union Sq W
Union Square Cafe	New American	16 St/5 Av
Verbena ✫✫	New American	Irving/17 St
Zen Palate	Vegetarian	Union Sq E/16 St

EAST VILLAGE (BELOW 14TH ST.)

On/Near

Acme Bar & Grill	Cajun, Southern	Great Jones/Bway
Acquario	Mediterranean	Bleecker/Bowery
Bambou ✫✫	Caribbean	14 St/2 Av
Bar Veloce	Italian/Sandwiches	2 Av/11 St

Note: Restaurants in ***boldface italics*** are Eric Asimov's choices for the best inexpensive restaurants in New York

East Village *(continued)*   **On / Near**

Benny's Burritos	Mexican/Tex-Mex	Av A/6 St
Boca Chica	Pan-Latin	1 Av/1 St
Bond Street ☆☆	Japanese	Bond/Bway
Borgo Antico	Italian	13 St/5 Av
Brunetta's	Italian	1 Av/11 St
Bulgin' Waffles	Waffles	1 Av/3 St
Caravan of Dreams	Kosher/Vegetarian	6 St/1 Av
Casa Adela	Caribbean	Av C/5 St
Casimir	Bistro/French	Av B/6 St
City Eatery ☆☆	Italian	Bowery/Bleecker
Cocina Cuzco	Peruvian	Av A/4 St
Col Legno	Italian	9 St/2 Av
Coup ☆	New American	6 St/Av A
Cyclo	*Vietnamese*	1 Av/*12* St
Daily Chow	Pan-Asian	2 St/Bowery
Dallas BBQ	Barbecue	2 Av/9 St
Danal	New American	10 St/3 Av
Dok Suni	Korean	1 Av/7 St
East Village Thai	Thai	7 St/2 Av
Elvie's Turo-Turo	Filipino	1 Av/12 St
Emilio Ballato's	Italian	E. Houston/Mott
Esashi	Sushi	Av A/2 St
Esperanto	Pan-Latin	Av C/9 St
First	New American	1 Av/5 St
Flor's Kitchen	*Latin American*	*1 Av/9 St*
Frank	Italian	2 Av/5 St
Haveli	Indian	2 Av/5 St
Holy Basil	*Thai*	*2 Av/9 St*
I Coppi ☆☆	Italian	9 St/1 Av
Il Bagatto	Italian	2 St/Av A
Il Buco ☆	Mediterranean	Bond/Bowery
Il Covo dell'Est	Italian	Av A/13 St
Il Posto Accanto	Italian/Sandwiches	2 St/Av B
Jewel Bako	*Sushi*	*5 St/2 Av*
Jules	French	St. Marks/1 Av
Komodo	*Asian/Mexican*	*Av A/1 St*
La Paella	Spanish	9 St/2 Av
Lavagna	*Mediterranean*	*5 St/Av B*
Leshko's	Diner	Av A/7 St
Le Tableau	*Mediterranean*	*5 St/Av A*
Lhasa	Tibetan	2 Av/5 St
Luca Lounge	Italian	Av B/13 St
Lucien	Bistro/French	1 Av/1 St
Mama's Food Shop	*New American*	*3 St/Av A*
Max	Italian	Av B/4 St
McSorley's	Bar Snacks	7 St/2 Av
Mee Noodle Shop	Chinese	1 Av/13 St
Moustache	*Middle Eastern*	*10 St/1 Av*
National Cafe	*Spanish*	*1 Av/13 St*
Old Devil Moon	Southern	12 St/Av A
Opaline	French-American	Av A/6 St
Orologio	Italian	Av A/10 St
Penang	Malaysian	3 Av/11 St
Pisces	Seafood	Av A/6 St
Pop ☆	New American	4 Av/12 St
Prune	*American/Continental*	*1 St/1 Av*
Radio Perfecto	American	Av B/11 St
Raga	French/Indian	6 St/Av A
Riodizio ☆	Brazilian	Lafayette/4 St
Roettele A.G.	Swiss/German	7 St/Av A
Sandobe Sushi	Japanese/Sushi	11 St/1 Av

2d Ave. Kosher Deli	Deli/Kosher	2 Av/10 St
Shabu-Tatsu	Japanese	10 St/1 Av
Soba-Ya	*Japanese/Noodles*	*9 St/2 Av*
St. Dymphna's	Irish	St. Mark's/1 Av
Stepmama	Sandwiches	3 St/Av B
Tappo ☆	Mediterranean	12 St/1 Av
The Tasting Room ☆	New American	1 St/1 Av
Thailand Cafe	Thai	2 Av/5 St
Three of Cups	Italian	1 Av/5 St
Time Cafe	New American	Lafayette/3 St
Tsampa	Tibetan	9 St/2 Av
26 Seats	French	Av B/11 St
Veselka	East European	2 Av/9 St
Virage	Mediterranean	2 Av/7 St
Xunta	*Spanish/Tapas*	*1 Av/11 St*
Zito's East	Pizza	1 Av/12 St
Zum Schneider	German	Av C/7 St

LOWER EAST SIDE   On / Near

Casa Mexicana	Mexican	Ludlow/Rivington
Congee Village	*Chinese*	*Orchard/Delancey*
Good World Bar & Grill	Scandinavian	Orchard/Division
Katz's Deli	*Deli*	*Houston/Ludlow*
Sammy's Roumanian	Steakhouse	Chrystie/Delancey
71 Clinton Fresh Food	Bistro/New American	Clinton/Rivington

GREENWICH VILLAGE / WEST VILLAGE   On / Near

Anglers & Writers	New American	Hudson/St. Luke's
Annissa	New American	Barrow/7 Av
Antonio	Italian	13 St/6 Av
Babbo ☆☆☆	Italian	Waverly/MacDougal
Baluchi's	Indian	6 Av/Washington
Bar Pitti	*Italian*	*6 Av/Houston*
Benny's Burritos	Mexican/Tex-Mex	Greenwich Av/Jane
Blue Hill ☆☆	French	Washington/6 Av
Blue Ribbon Bakery	New American	Downing/Bedford
Boughalem	New American	Bedford/Halston
Cafe Asean	Southeast Asian	10 St/Greenwich
Cafe de Bruxelles	Belgian	Greenwich/7 Av
Café Loup	Bistro	13 St/6 Av
Chez Jacqueline	French	MacDougal/Bleecker
Chinghalle	Brasserie/Diner	Gansevoort/ Greenwich
Chumley's	Bar Snacks	Bedford/Bleecker
Cookies and Couscous	*Moroccan*	*Thompson/3 St*
Corner Bistro	Bar Snacks	4 St/Jane
Cowgirl Hall of Fame	Southern	Hudson/10 St
Cucina Stagionale	Italian	Bleecker/6 Av
Da Silvano	Italian	6 Av/Houston
Dallas BBQ	Barbecue	University Pl./8 St
Dallas BBQ	Barbecue	6 Av/Bleecker
E J's	Diner	6 Av/9 St
Florent	French	Gansevoort/ Washington
Good	Pan-Latin	Greenwich/Bank
Gotham Bar and Grill ☆☆☆	New American	12 St/Univ Pl
Gradisca	Italian	13 St/6 Av
Grange Hall	American	Commerce/Barrow
Grano Trattoria	Italian	Greenwich Av/10 St
Gray's Papaya	Fast Food	6 Av/8 St

Note: Restaurants in ***boldface italics*** are Eric Asimov's choices for the best inexpensive restaurants in New York

Greenwich/West Village *(continued)*

		On / Near
Grove	Bistro/French	Bleecker/Grove
Hog Pit	Southern	9 Av/13 St
Il Mulino	Italian	3 St/Sullivan
'ino	*Italian/Sandwiches*	*Bedford/6 Av*
Inside	New American	Jones/Bleecker
Japonica	Japanese/Sushi	University/12 St
Jarnac	Bistro/French	12 St/Greenwich
John's Pizzeria	Italian/Pizza	Bleecker/6 Av
Junno's	Japanese/Korean	Downing/Bedford
Knickerbocker Bar & Grill	Steakhouse	University/9 St
La Metairie	French	10 St/4 St
La Nonna ☆	Italian	13 St/6 Av Greenwich
La Palapa	*Mexican*	*St. Marks/Greene*
Le Gigot	French	Cornelia/4 St
Lemongrass Grill	Thai	University/11 St
Lemongrass Grill	Thai	Barrow/7 Av S
Le Zoo	Bistro/French	11 St/Greenwich
Little Basil	*Thai*	*Greenwich/Charles*
Little Havana	Caribbean	Cornelia/Bleecker
Lupa	*Italian*	*Thompson/Bleecker*
Malatesta Trattoria	Italian	Washington/ Christopher
Marumi	Japanese/Sushi	LaGuardia/3 St
Merge	New American	10 St/Waverly
Mexicana Mama	*Mexican/Tex-Mex*	*Hudson/10 St*
Mi Cocina ☆☆	Mexican/Tex-Mex	Jane/Hudson
Midway	Brasserie	Charles/Washington
Miracle Bar & Grill	Southwestern	Bleecker/Bank
Mirchi	*Indian*	*7 Av/Morton*
Mona Lisa	Pizza	Bleecker/MacDougal
Moustache	*Middle Eastern*	*Bedford/Grove*
Noho Star	American	Lafayette/Bleecker
One If By Land, Two If ☆	French	Barrow/4 St
Panache	Bistro/French	6 Av/12 St
Papillon	Bistro	Hudson/Bank
Paris Commune	French	Bleecker/11 St
Pastis ☆	Bistro/French	9 Av/Little W 12 St
Patsy's Pizzeria	Pizza	University Pl./10 St
Pearl Oyster Bar	*Seafood*	*Cornelia/Bleecker*
Pepe Verde	Italian	Hudson/Perry
Pesce & Pasta	Italian/Seafood	Bleecker/6 Av
Philip Marie	New American	Hudson/11 St
Piadina	Italian	10 St/5 Av
Pico ☆☆☆	Portuguese	Greenwich/Harrison
Po	*Italian*	*Cornelia/Bleecker*
Rhone	Bistro/French	Gansevoort/ Greenwich
Rio Mar	Spanish	9 Av/12
Salam Café	Middle Eastern	13 St/6 Av
Sandwiches	American	Greenwich/7 Av S
Sazerac House	Cajun/American	Hudson/Charles
Sevilla	Spanish	Charles/4 St
Shopsin's General Store	New American	Bedford St/Morton
Stella	New American	Macdougal/Prince
Strip House	Steakhouse	12 St/5 Av
Sud	French	10 St/Bleecker
Surya ☆☆	Indian	Bleecker/7 Av S
Taka	Japanese/Sushi	Grove/7 Av S
Tanti Baci Caffe	Italian	10 St/7 Av S
Taqueria de Mexico	Mexican/Tex-Mex	Greenwich/12 St
Tea & Sympathy	English	Greenwich/12 St

Thali	Vegetarian	Greenwich/10 St
The Place	Mediterranean	4 St/Bank
Tibet on Houston	Tibetan	Houston/Sullivan
Time Cafe	New American	7 Av S./Barrow
Tomoe Sushi	Japanese/Sushi	Thompson/Bleecker
Tortilla Flats	Mexican/Tex-Mex	Washington/12 St
Trattoria Spaghetto	Italian	Bleecker/Carmine
Tsunami	Japanese/Sushi	3 St/Thompson
Velli	*Italian*	*Houston/Sullivan*
Village	9 St/5 Av	Bistro/French
Villa Mosconi	Italian	Macdougal/Bleecker

CHINATOWN

Big Wong	Chinese	Mott/Canal
Canton	Chinese	Division/Bowery
Dim Sum Go Go	Chinese	E. Bway/Chatham
Evergreen Shanghai	Chinese	Mott/Bayard
Excellent Dumpling House	Chinese	Lafayette/Canal
Funky Broome	*Chinese*	*Mott/Broome*
Golden Unicorn	Chinese	E. Bway/Catherine
Goody's ☆	Chinese	E. Bway/Chatham
Grand Sichuan ☆	*Chinese*	*Canal/Bowery*
Jing Fong	Chinese	Elizabeth/Bayard
Joe's Shanghai ☆☆	Chinese	Pell/Bowery
Lin's Dumpling House	Chinese	Pell/St. James
New Green Bo	*Chinese*	*Bayard/Mott*
Nha Trang	*Vietnamese*	*Baxter/White*
Nha Trang	*Chinese/Vietnamese*	*Centre/Walker*
Nyonya	Southeast Asian	Grand/Mulberry
Onieal's Grand Street ☆	New American	Grand/Centre
Ping's Seafood	Chinese/Seafood	Mott/Worth
Sweet 'n' Tart Cafe	Chinese	Mott/Canal
Triple Eight Palace	Chinese	E. Bway/Division
Shanghai Cuisine	Chinese	Bayard/Mulberry
Tai Hong Lau	Chinese	Mott/Canal

SOHO/TRIBECA

On/Near

Aggie's	New American	W. Houston/ Macdougal
Alison on Dominick ☆☆	French	Dominick St/Varick
Aquagrill ☆☆	Seafood	Spring/6 Av
Arqua ☆☆	Italian	Church/White
Arturo's Pizzeria	Italian/Pizza	Houston/W. Bway
Balthazar ☆☆	Brasserie/French	Spring/Lafayette
Baluchi's	Indian	Spring/Sullivan
Bistrot Margot	Bistro/French	Prince/Mott
Blue Ribbon	New American	Sullivan/Prince
Blue Ribbon Sushi ☆☆	Japanese/Sushi	Sullivan/Prince
Bouley Bakery ☆☆☆☆	French	W. Broadway/Duane
Cafe Colonial	New American	Houston/Elizabeth
Cafe Gitane	American	Mott/Houston
Cafe Habana	Latin American	Prince/Elizabeth
Cafe Juniper	New American	Duane/Greenwich
Canal House ☆☆	New American	W. Broadway/Canal
Canteen	New American	Mercer/Prince
Capsouto Frères	French	Washington/Watts
Caviarteria	East European	W. Broadway/Canal
Cendrillon ☆	Southeast Asian	Mercer/Broome
Chanterelle ☆☆☆	French	Harrison/Hudson

Note: Restaurants in ***boldface italics*** are Eric Asimov's choices for the best inexpensive restaurants in New York

SoHo/TriBeCa *(continued)*

		On / Near
City Hall ✪✪	New American	Duane/Church
Cupping Room	New American	W. Broadway/ Broome
Danube ✪✪✪	Viennese/German	Hudson/Duane
Downtown ✪	Italian	W. Broadway/ Broome
Ear Inn	Bar Snacks	Spring/Greenwich
Eight Mile Creek ✪✪	Australian	Mulberry/Prince
El Teddy's	Mexican/Tex-Mex	W. Broadway/White
Fanelli	Bar/Snacks	Prince/Mercer
F.illi Ponte ✪✪	Italian	Desbrosses/ Washington
Franklin Station	Southeast Asian	W. Broadway/ Franklin
Ghenet	African	Mulberry/Houston
Grace	New American	Franklin/Church
Gubbio ✪	Italian	W. Bway/White
Herban Kitchen	Vegetarian	Hudson/Spring
Honmura An ✪✪✪	Japanese/Noodles	Mercer/Houston
Il Giglio ✪	Italian	Warren/Greenwich
Isla	Pan-Latin/Cuban	Downing/Bedford
Island Grill	Caribbean	Lafayette/Centre
Jane	New American/Bistro	Houston/Thompson
Jean Claude	*Bistro/French*	*Sullivan/Prince*
Kana	Spanish	Spring/Greenwich
Kelley & Ping	Noodles/Thai	Greene/Houston
Kitchen Club	French/Japanese	Prince/Mott
Kitchenette	New American	W. Bway/Warren
Kori	*Korean*	*Church/Leonard*
Layla ✪✪	Middle Eastern/ Mediterranean	W. Broadway/ Franklin
L'ecole	French	Broadway/Grand
Le Gamin	French	Macdougal/Houston
Le Jardin Bistro	*French*	*Cleveland/Spring*
Le Zinc	Bistro	Duane/Church
The Little Place	Mexican	W. Bway/Warren
Lombardi's	*Pizza*	*Spring/Mulberry*
L'ulivo Focacceria	Italian/Pizza	Spring/Thompson
Match	New American	Mercer/Prince
Mekong	Vietnamese	Prince/Mulberry
Mercer Kitchen ✪✪	French	Prince/Mercer
Montrachet ✪✪✪	French	W. Broadway/White
Mottsu	Japanese/Sushi	Mott/Houston
Ñ Tapas Bar	Spanish/Tapas	Crosby/Broome
Nam Phuong	Vietnamese	Sixth Av/Walker
Next Door Nobu ✪✪✪	Japanese	Hudson/Franklin
NL	Dutch/Indonesian	Sullivan/Houston
Nobu ✪✪✪	Japanese	Hudson/Franklin
Odeon ✪✪	French/American	W. Broadway/ Thomas
Pacifica	Chinese	Lafayette/Howard
Palacinka	Crepes	Grand/6 Av
Pão	*Portuguese*	*Spring/Greenwich*
Peasant ✪	Italian	Elizabeth/Prince
Penang	Malaysian	Spring/Mercer
Pepolino	*Italian*	*W. Bway/Lispenard*
Pintxos	Spanish	Greenwich/Spring
Polanka	Polish	Warren/Church
Pravda	Russian	Lafayette/Prince
Provence ✪	French	MacDougal/Prince

Quilty's ☆☆	New American	Prince/Sullivan
Raoul's	Bistro/French	Prince/Sullivan
Rialto	New American	Elizabeth/Houston
Rice	PanAsian	Mott/Spring
Risa	Pizza/Italian	Houston/Mulberry
Ruben's Empanadas	Latin American	Bridge/White
Salaam Bombay ☆☆	Indian	Greenwich/Duane
Savore	Italian	Spring/Sullivan
Scalini Fedeli ☆	Italian	Duane/Hudson
Screening Room ☆☆	New American	Varick/Canal
Snack	*Greek*	***Thompson/Prince***
SoHo Kitchen & Bar	New American	Greene/Spring
Soho Steak	*Bistro/Steak*	***Thompson/Spring***
Sosa Borella	Latin American	Greenwich/ Desbrosses
Tennessee Mountain	Barbecue	Spring/Wooster
Tiffin	Indian/Veg.	Murray/Church
Tribeca Grill ☆☆	New American	Greenwich/Franklin
Va Tutto!	Italian	Cleveland/Kenmare
Walker's	Bar Snacks	N. Moore/Varick
Yaffa's T-Room	New American	Greenwich/Harrison
Zoë	New American	Prince/Bway

FINANCIAL DISTRICT   On / Near

American Park ☆	New American	Battery Park/State
Bayard's ☆☆	New American	Hanover Sq./Pearl
Delmonico's ☆	New American	Beaver/Williams
14 Wall Street ☆	French/New American	Wall/Bway
Grill Room ☆☆	American/Seafood	World Fin Ctr
Harry's	Continental	Hanover Sq./Stone
Hudson River Club ☆☆	New American	Vesey/World Fin Ctr
Ruben's Empanadas	Latin American	Fulton/Gold
Vine ☆	New American	Broad/Exchange
Wall Street Kitchen and Bar	New American	Broad/Beaver

THE BRONX

The Feeding Tree	*Carribean*

BROOKLYN

Bay Ridge
Lento's	Italian

Boerum Hill
Brawta Caribbean Cafe	*Caribbean*
Saul	New American
Smith Street Kitchen	*Seafood/New American*

Brooklyn Heights
Gage & Tollner	Seafood
La Bouillabaisse	French/Seafood
Queen	Italian
River Café ☆☆	New American
Tin Room Cafe	Italian
Tinto	Tapas

Carroll Gardens
Banania Cafe	Bistro/French
Ferdinando's Focacceria	*Italian*

Note: Restaurants in ***boldface italics*** are Eric Asimov's choices for the best inexpensive restaurants in New York

Carroll Gardens *(continued)*

Mignon	French
Patois	French
Sur	Latin American

Cobble Hill

Harvest	New American

Clinton Hill

Locanda Vini & Olii	*Italian*

Coney Island

Totonno Pizzeria	Pizza

East New York

Carolina Country Kitchen	Southern

Fort Greene

Cambodian Cuisine	Southeast Asian

Greenpoint

Thai Cafe	Thai

Park Slope

Al Di La	*Italian*
Bistro St. Mark's	*Bistro*
Blue Ribbon Brooklyn	
Coco Roco	*Latin American*
Lemongrass Grill	Thai
Lento's	Italian
Max & Moritz	French
Milan's	East European
Rose Water	New American/Mediterranean

Prospect Heights

Garden Café	*New American*

Sheepshead Bay

Lundy Bros.	Seafood

Sunset Park

Tequilita's	Mexican/Tex-Mex

Williamsburg

Bahia	Salvadoran
Fernicola Osteria	Italian
Diner	*Diner/Steakhouse*
Miss Williamsburg	*Diner*
Oznot's Dish	Mediterranean
Peter Luger ☆☆☆	Steakhouse
Plan-Eat Thailand	Thai

QUEENS

Astoria

Balkh Shish Kebab House	Middle Eastern
Christos Hasapo-Taverna	*Greek/Steakhouse*
Churrascaria Girassol	*Brazilian*
Elias Corner	Greek
Esperides	Greek
Mombar	Middle Eastern
Syros	Greek/Seafood
Ubol's Kitchen	*Thai*
Uncle George's	Greek

Corona
El Gauchito — Latin American
Green Field — Latin American
La Esquina Criolla — *South American*
Leo's Latticini — Italian/Sandwich

Elmhurst
Joe's Shanghai — Chinese

Flushing
East Buffet & Restaurant — *Chinese*
Joe's Shanghai — *Chinese*
K.B. Garden — Chinese
Kum Gang San — Korean
La Cascade — Chinese

Flushing (continued)
La Fusta — Latin American
La Perricholi — Latin American
Master Grill — Brazilian
Pachas — South American/Latin American
Penang — Malaysian
Shanghai Tang — Chinese
Sweet 'n'Tart Cafe — Chinese
Woo Chon — Korean

Jackson Heights
Afghan Kebab House — Afghan
Delhi Palace — Indian
Jackson Diner — Indian
Malaysian Rasa Sayang — Malaysian
Nostalgias — Latin American
Pearson's Texas Barbecue — *Barbecue*
Pio Pio — Latin American
Tibetan Yak — Tibetan
Tierras Colombianas — Latin American

Jamaica
Carmichael's Diner — American/Diner
Don Peppe's — Italian

Rego Park
Goody's — Chinese
Kazan Turkish Cuisine — Turkish

Sunnyside
La Lupe — Mexican/Tex-Mex

Woodside
La Flor — *Eclectic*
Rumi-Huasi — Latin American
Sapori d'Ischia — Italian

STATEN ISLAND
Aesop's Tables — French/New American

Note: Restaurants in **boldface italics** are Eric Asimov's choices for the best inexpensive restaurants in New York

A Guide to Restaurants by Cuisine

Afghani
Afghan Kebab House
Balkh Shish Kebab
Kabul Cafe

African
Africa No. 2
Chez Gnagna Koty's
Lotfi's Moroccan
Meskerem
Queen of Sheba
Tagine

American
The Algonquin
All State Cafe
An American Place ☆☆
Billy's
Carmichael's Diner
Fifty Seven Fifty Seven ☆☆☆
Good Enough to Eat
The Half King
Knickerbocker
Mickey Mantle's
Old Town Bar
Pete's Tavern
Popover Cafe
Prune
Red Bar Restaurant

See also: Barbecue, Bar Snacks, Diner, Hamburgers, New American, Southern, Southwestern, and Steakhouse

Argentine
Chimichurri Grill
Cooke's Corner
El Gauchito
La Fusta
Pampa
Sosa Borella
Sur

Australian
Eight Mile Creek ☆☆

Bar Snacks
All State Cafe
Chumley's
Corner Bistro
Ear Inn
Fanelli
McHale's
McSorley's
P.J. Clarke's
Walker's

Barbecue
Brother Jimmy's BBQ
Dallas BBQ
Pearson's Texas Barbecue
Tennessee Mountain
Virgil's Real BBQ

Belgian
Cafe de Bruxelles

Bistro
Abajour
Artisanal ☆☆
Banania Cafe
Barrio ☆
Bistro St. Mark's
Jarnac
La Tour
Le Zinc ☆
92
Orsay ☆☆
Panache
Papillon ☆
Pop ☆
Rhone
71 Clinton Fresh Food
Village
Vox ☆

Brasserie
Balthazar ☆☆
Brasserie ☆☆
Brasserie 8 $^1/_2$ ☆
Chinghalle ☆
Guastavino's ☆☆
L'Absinthe ☆
L'Actuel ☆☆
Les Halles
Midway
Pastis ☆

Brazilian
Cabana Carioca
Churrascaria Plataforma
Churrascaria Girassol
Master Grill
Rice 'n' Beans
Rio De Janeiro's
Riodizio ☆

Cajun/Creole
Acme Bar & Grill
Bayou
Sazerac House

Caribbean
Bambou ☆☆
Brawta
Casa Adela
El Presidente
The Feeding Tree
Island Grill
Island Spice
Little Havana
Maroons
Negril

Chinese
Big Wong
Canton
China Fun

Congee Village
Dim Sum Go Go ☆
East Buffet & Restaurant
Estihana
Evergreen Shanghai
Excellent Dumpling House
Funky Broome
Golden Unicorn
Grand Sichuan International
Henry's Evergreen
Jing Fong
Joe's Shanghai ☆☆
K.B. Garden
La Cascade
Lin's Dumpling House
Mee Noodle Shop
New Green Bo
Nha Trang
Ollie's Noodle Shop
Our Place Shanghai Tea Room
Pacifica Restaurant
Pig Heaven
Ping's ☆☆
Ping's Seafood
Shanghai Cuisine
Shanghai Tang
Shun Lee Palace ☆☆
Shun Lee West
Swee 'n' Tart Cafe
Tai Hong Lau
Triple Eight Palace
Tse Yang
Wu Liang Ye

Continental
Box Tree Inn
Cafe des Artistes
Cal's
Prune

Crepes
Palacinka
Rue des Crepes

Deli
Artie's New York Delicatessen
Barney Greengrass
Carnegie Deli
Katz's Deli
Pastrami Queen
Second Ave. Kosher Deli
Stage Deli

Diner
Barking Dog
Brooklyn Diner USA
Carmichael's Diner
Coffee Shop
Comfort Diner
Diner
E J's
Edison Cafe
Empire Diner
Leshko's

Mayrose
Miss Williamsburg
Viand

East European
Caviarteria
Milan's
Veselka

English
Lady Mendl's Tea Parlour
Nicole's ☆☆
Tea & Sympathy

Fast Food
F&B
Gray's Papaya
Knodel

French
Abajour
Adrienne
Alain Ducasse ☆☆☆
Alison on Dominick ☆☆
Alouette
Arabelle ☆
Avenue
Atlas ☆☆☆
Balthazar ☆☆
Banania Cafe
Bandol
Bayard's ☆☆
Bistro Le Steak
Bistrot Margot
Blue Hill ☆☆
Bouley Bakery ☆☆☆☆
Bouterin ☆
Brasserie ☆☆
Brasserie Centrale
Brasserie 8 ½ ☆
Café Boulud ☆☆☆
Cafe Centro ☆☆
Café Loup
Café Un Deux Trois
Capsouto Frères
Casimir
Cello ☆☆☆
Chanterelle ☆☆☆
Chelsea Bistro & Bar ☆☆
Chez Jacqueline
Chez Josephine ☆☆
Chez Laurence
Daniel ☆☆☆☆
D'Artagnan ☆
Destinée ☆☆
Florent
Fleur de Sel ☆☆
14 Wall Street ☆
French Roast Cafe
Guastavino's ☆☆
Jarnac
Jean Claude
Jean Georges ☆☆☆☆
Jubilee

Note: Restaurants in **boldface italics** are Eric Asimov's choices for the best inexpensive restaurants in New York

459

Jules
Kitchen Club
La Bouillabaisse
L'Absinthe ☆
L'Acajou
La Caravelle ☆☆☆
La Côte Basque ☆☆☆
L'Actuel ☆☆
La Goulue
La Grenouille ☆☆☆
La Metairie
L'Ardoise
La Tour
Le Bateau Ivre
Le Bernardin ☆☆☆☆
Le Bilboquet
Le Cirque 2000 ☆☆☆
L'ecole
Le Gamin
Le Gigot
Le Jardin Bistro
Le Madeleine
Le Max Restaurant
Le Perigord ☆☆
Le Petit Hulot
Le Quercy
Le Refuge
Les Halles
Le Singe Vert
Lespinasse ☆☆☆☆
Le Tableau
Le Taxi
Le Totof Bistro
Le Veau d'Or
L'Express
Le Zoo
Lucien
Lutèce ☆☆
Marika
Mercer Kitchen ☆☆
Metisse
Mignon
Montrachet ☆☆☆
Nicholson ☆
Odeon ☆☆
One If By Land ☆
Opaline
Panache
Paris Commune
Park Bistro ☆☆☆
Pascalou
Pastis ☆
Patois
Payard Pâtisserie ☆☆
Picholine ☆☆☆
Provence ☆
Quatorze Bis
Raoul's
René Pujol
Rhone
Savann
Sel et Poivre
Sud
Tocqueville ☆☆

Tout Va Bien
Triomphe ☆☆
Trois Canards
Trois Marches ☆
26 Seats
Union Pacific ☆☆☆
Village
Virot ☆☆

Fusion
Adrienne
AZ ☆☆☆
Hudson Cafeteria
Restaurant Above
Thali
Trois Marches ☆
Verbena ☆

German
Danube ☆☆☆
Hallo Berlin
Roetelle A.G.
Silver Swan
Zum Schneider

Greek
Artos
Avra ☆
Christos Hasapo-Taverna
Elias Corner
Esperides
Estiatorio Milos ☆☆
Meltemi
Metsovo
Molyvos ☆☆☆
Rafina
Snack
Syros
Uncle George's
Uncle Nick's

Hamburgers
All State Cafe
Island Burgers
Jackson Hole
McHale's
McSorley's
Mickey Mantle's
P.J. Clarke's
Prime Burger

Indian
Ada ☆☆
Baluchi's
Dakshin
Dawat ☆
Delhi Palace
Diwan Grill
Diwan's Curry House
Haveli
Jackson Diner
Mavalli Palace
Mirchi
Mughlai
Pongal

Raga
Royal Kebab
Salaam Bombay ☆☆
Sapphire
Shaan
Surya ☆☆
Tamarind ☆☆
Taprobane
Tiffin
Vatan

Indonesian
Bali Nusa Indah
NL

Italian
Al Bacio
Al Dente
Al Di La
Amarone
Antonio
Arqua ☆☆
Babbo ☆☆☆
Baldoria
Bar Pitti
Bar Veloce
Barbetta
Becco
Bellini
Beppe ☆☆
Bice ☆☆
Biricchino
Bonsignour
Borgo Antico
Bottino
Bricco
Brunetta's
Cafe La Grolla
Caffe Grazie
Carino
Carmine's
Ciao Europa
Cibo
Cinque Terre ☆☆
City Eatery ☆☆
Col Legno
Commune ☆
Cucina Stagionale
Da Antonio
Da Ciro
Da Mario
Da Nico
Da Silvano
Delmonico's
Don Peppe's
Elaine's
Emilio Ballato's
Erminia
Esca ☆☆
Felidia ☆☆☆
Ferdinando's
Fernicola Osteria ☆
F.Illi Ponte ☆☆

Frank
Gennaro
Gino
Gradisca
Gubbio ☆
Harry Cipriani
I Coppi ☆☆
I Trulli ☆☆
Il Bagatto
Il Covo dell'Est
Il Giglio ☆
Il Mulino
Il Postino
Il Posto Accanto
Il Valentino ☆☆
'ino
Isola
La Grolla ☆
La Locanda
La Nonna ☆
La Vineria
Le Madri
Lento's
Leo's Latticini
Le Zie
Limoncello
Locanda Vini & Olii
Luca
L'ulivo
Lupa
Lusardi's
Luxia
Mad.28
Malatesta
Maratti
Max
Meridiana
Miss Williamsburg
Naples 45
Nino's
Novitá ☆
Orologio
Orso
Osso Buco
Palio ☆☆
Paola's ☆☆
Patsy's
Peasant ☆
Pepe Verde
Pepolino
Pesce & Pasta
Piadina
Pietro's
Po
Primavera ☆
Puttanesca
Queen
Rainbow Grill
Rao's
Remi ☆☆
Ribollita
Sal Anthony's
San Domenico ☆☆☆

Note: Restaurants in **boldface italics** are Eric Asimov's choices for the best inexpensive restaurants in New York

San Pietro
Sant Ambroeus
Sapori d'Ischia
Savore
Scalini Fedeli ☆
Sistina
Supreme Macaroni Co.
Tanti Baci
Teodora
Three of Cups
Tin Room Cafe
Tony's Di Napoli
Trattoria dell'Arte ☆
Trattoria I Pagliacci
Trattoria Spaghetto
Trionfo Ristorante
Tuscan Square
Tuscan Steak
Va Tutto!
Velli
Vespa Cibobuono
Viceversa
Vico
Via Quadronno
Villa Berulia
Villa Mosconi
Vivolo

Japanese
Blue Ribbon Sushi ☆☆
Bond Street ☆☆
Choshi
Donguri
Esashi
Haru
Haru
Honmura An ☆☆☆
Inagiku ☆☆
Japonica
Junno's
Katsu-Hama
Kitchen Club
Kodama
Kuruma Zushi ☆☆☆
Maeda Sushi
Marumi
Menchanko-Tei
Mottsu
Nadaman Hakubai ☆☆
Next Door Nobu ☆☆☆
Nippon
Nobu ☆☆☆
Otabe ☆☆
Sandobe Sushi
Shabu-Tatsu
Shinbashi
Soba Nippon
Soba-Ya
Sushi Hatsu ☆☆☆
Sushi Masa
Sushi Of Gari
Sushi Rose
Sushi Zen
Sushiden
Sushisay

Sushi Yasuda ☆☆☆
Taka
Tea Box Café
Ten Kai
Tomoe
Toraya
Tsunami
Ya Bowl
Yakiniku JuJu

Korean
Cho Dang Gol ☆☆
Do Hwa
Dok Suni
Emo's
Han Bat
Hangawi ☆☆
Junno's
Korea Palace ☆
Kori
Kum Gang San
Mill Korean
Mandoo Bar
Woo Chon

Kosher
Caravan of Dreams
Estihana
Levana
Pongal
Sammy's
Second Ave. Kosher

Latin American
Asia de Cuba ☆
Bahia
Boca Chica
Bolo
Cabana Carioca
Cafe Con Leche
Cafe Habana
Chimichurri Grill
Churrascaria Plataforma ☆☆
Circus ☆☆
Cocina Cuzco
Coco Roco
El Gauchito
El Presidente
Flor's Kitchen
Havana NY
Ipanema
La Esquina Criolla
La Fonda Boricua
La Fusta
La Perricholi
La Taza De Oro
Margon
Mi Mexico
National Cafe
Nostalgias
Old San Juan
Pachas
Pampa
Patria ☆☆☆
Pio Pio
Rinconcito Peruano

Ruben's Empanadas
Rumi-Huasi
Sosa Borella
Sur
Tierras Colombianas
Victor's Cafe 52

Malaysian
Malaysian Rasa Sayang
Penang

Mediterranean
Acquario
Amaranth
Bar Six
Cucina & Co.
Gus's Figs
Il Buco ☆
Julian's
Lavagna
Layla ☆☆
Le Tableau
Medusa
Metrazur
Mezze
Nick and Toni's ☆☆
Niko's
Olives ☆
Ouest ☆☆
Oznot's Dish
Persepolis
Picholine ☆☆☆
Sharz Cafe & Wine Bar
Spazzia
The Place
Tappo ☆
Virage
Zanzibar

Mexican/Tex-Mex
Benny's Burritos
Café Frida
Casa Mexicana
El Teddy's
El Paso Taqueria
Fresco Tortilla Grill
Gabriela's
Hell's Kitchen
Komodo
La Cocina
La Lupe
La Palapa
The Little Place
Los Dos Rancheros
Manhattan Chili Co.
Maya ☆☆
Mexicana Mama
Mi Cocina ☆☆
Rinconcito Mexicano
Rocking Horse
Rosa Mexicano ☆☆
Samalita's Tortilla
Taco Taco
Taqueria de Mexico

Tequilita's
Tortilla Flats
Zarela ☆☆
Zocalo

Middle Eastern
Balkh
Bereket
Cookies and Couscous
Hoomoos Asli
Layla ☆☆
Mombar
Moustache
Salam Café
Turkuaz

New American
Aesop's Tables
Aggie's
Aleutia ☆
Alley's End
Alva ☆
American Park ☆
An American Place ☆☆
Anglers & Writers
Annie's
Annissa
Aureole ☆☆☆
Bayard's ☆☆
Blue Ribbon
Blue Ribbon Brooklyn
Bright Food Shop
Bryant Park Grill
Bull & Bear
Butterfield 81 ☆☆
Cafe Juniper
Canal House ☆☆
Candela Restaurant ☆
Canteen
Chat 'n Chew
City Hall ☆☆
The Commons
Commune ☆
Coup ☆
Craft ☆☆☆
Cupping Room
Danal
Della Femina ☆
Delmonico's ☆
The Dining Room ☆☆
District ☆
Druids
Eleven Madison Park ☆☆
Etats-Unis ☆☆
First
The Four Seasons ☆☆☆
44
14 Wall Street ☆
Fred's
Globe
Good
Gotham Bar and Grill ☆☆☆
Grace

Note: Restaurants in **boldface italics** are Eric Asimov's choices for the best inexpensive restaurants in New York

Gramercy Tavern ☆☆☆
The Grocery
Grove
Harvest
Heartbeat ☆☆
Herban Kitchen
Hourglass Tavern
Hudson River Club ☆☆
Icon ☆☆
Ilo ☆☆☆
Inside
Jack Rose
Jane ☆
Joe Allen
Josie's
Judson Grill ☆☆☆
Kitchenette
Le Cirque 2000 ☆☆☆
Levana
The Library
Lipstick Cafe
Lola
Lot 61
Mama's Food Shop
March ☆☆☆
Meli Melo
Merge
Metrazur
Michael's ☆☆
Morrell Wine Bar and Cafe
92
Odeon ☆☆
Onieal's Grand Street ☆
Palm Court
Panorama Cafe
Park Avalon
Park Avenue Cafe ☆☆
Park View ☆☆
Patroon ☆☆☆
Philip Marie
Pop ☆
Porters New York
Quilty's ☆☆
The Red Cat ☆
Redeye Grill ☆
Restaurant Above
Rialto
River Cafe ☆☆
Rose Water
The Saloon
Sarabeth's
Sardi's
Saul
Screening Room ☆☆
71 Clinton Fresh Food
SoHo Kitchen & Bar
Stella
The Tasting Room ☆
Tavern on the Green ☆
Time Cafe
Tonic Restaurant & Bar ☆☆
Top of the Tower
Town ☆☆☆

Tribeca Grill ☆☆
"21" Club ☆☆
27 Standard ☆☆
Union Square Cafe ☆☆☆
Verbena ☆☆
Veritas ☆☆☆
Vince & Eddie's
Vine ☆
Vinegar Factory
Vynl
Wall Street Kitchen
Water Club ☆☆
Willow
Wollensky's Grill
Yaffa's T-Room
Yura & Co.
Zoë

Noodles
Honmura An ☆☆☆
Kelley & Ping
Menchanko-Tei
Ollie's Noodle Shop
Republic
Soba-Ya

Pan Asian
Asia de Cuba ☆
AZ
Cafe Asean
Daily Chow
Komodo
Pop ☆
Rain
Republic
Rice
Ruby Foo's ☆☆
Tabla ☆☆☆

Pan-Latin
Boca Chica
Calle Ocho ☆
Chicama ☆☆
Cuba Libre
Esperanto
Good
Isla
Jimmy Armstrong's
Patria ☆☆☆
Vox ☆

Pizza
Arturo's
California Pizza
Candido
John's
La Pizza Fresca
Lombardi's
L'ulivo
Mona Lisa
Naples 45
Patsy's
Pintaile's

Polistina's
Risa
Sal's and Carmine's
Totonno

Polish
Polanka

Portuguese
Pao
Pico ☆☆☆

Russian
Caviar Russe
Firebird ☆☆
Moscow
Petrossian ☆☆
Pravda
Russian Tea Room

Scandinavian
Aquavit ☆☆☆
Christer's Restaurant ☆☆
Good World Bar and Grill
Knodel
Ulrika's

Seafood
Aquagrill ☆☆
Avra ☆
Blue Water Grill ☆
Bongo
Cello ☆☆☆
City Crab & Seafood
Dock's ☆
Elias Corner
Esca ☆☆
Estiatorio Milos ☆☆
Gage & Tollner
La Bouillabaisse
Le Bernardin ☆☆☆☆
Lundy Bros.
Manhattan Grille
Manhattan Ocean Club ☆☆
Maratti
Maritime ☆
Meltemi
Metro Fish
Ocean Grill ☆
Oceana ☆☆☆
Oyster Bar
Pearl Oyster Bar
Pesce & Pasta
Pisces
Rafina
Sea Grill ☆☆
Shaffer City Oyster Bar
Smith Street Kitchen
Syros
Tropica

Southeast Asian
Cafe Asean
Cambodian Cuisine

Cendrillon ☆
Elvie's Turo-Turo
Franklin Station Cafe
Nyonya
Penang

Southern
Acme Bar & Grill
Amy Ruth's
Bayou
Carolina Country Kitchen
Charles' Southern-Style Kitchen
Copeland's
Cowgirl Hall of Fame
Emily's
Hog Pit
Jezebel
Little Jezebel
Maroons
Miss Maude's Spoonbread Too
Old Devil Moon
Pan Pan
Shark Bar
Soul Cafe
Soul Fixins'
Sylvia's

Southwestern
Citrus Bar & Grill
Mesa Grill ☆☆
Miracle Bar & Grill
New World Grill
Penang

Spanish
Bolo ☆☆
Cafe Riazor
El Cid
Kāna
La Paella
Marichu
Ñ Tapas Bar
National Cafe
Pintxos
Rio Mar
Sevilla
Solera ☆☆
Xunta

Sri Lankan
Lakruwana
Taprobane

Steakhouse
Angelo & Maxie's ☆
Ben Benson's
Bistro Le Steak
Bobby Van's ☆
Christos Hasapo-Taverna
Churrascaria Plataforma ☆☆
Cité
Frank's ☆
Jack Rose

Note: Restaurants in ***boldface italics*** are Eric Asimov's choices for the best inexpensive restaurants in New York

Keens
Knickerbocker Bar
Maloney & Porcelli ☆
Manhattan Grille
Michael Jordan's ☆☆
Old Homestead
Palm
Palm Too
Peter Luger ☆☆☆
Pietro's
Post House
Ruth's Chris
Sammy's Roumanian
Smith & Wollensky ☆☆
Soho Steak
Sparks ☆
Strip House ☆
Tupelo Grill
West 63rd Street ☆
Wollensky's Grill

Sushi
Blue Ribbon Sushi ☆☆
Choshi
Donguri
Esashi
Estihana
Haru
Inagiku ☆☆
Japonica
Jewel Bako
Kodama
Maeda
Marumi
Mottsu
Nippon
Sandobe Sushi
Sushi Hatsu ☆☆☆
Sushi Masa
Sushi of Gari
Sushi Rose
Sushi Yasuda ☆☆☆
Sushi Zen
Sushiden
Sushisay
Taka
Ten Kai
Tomoe Sushi
Tsunami

Swiss
Roettele A.G.

Tapas
Dalia's
Ñ Tapas Bar
Sabor
Solera ☆☆
Tinto
Xunta

Thai
East Village Thai Restaurant
Holy Basil

Kelley & Ping
Lemongrass Grill
Little Basil
Pam Real Thai Food
Plan Eat Thailand
Royal Siam
Sa Woy
Seeda Thai 2
Thai Cafe
Thailand Cafe
Topaz Thai
Ubol's Kitchen
Vong

Theme
Hard Rock Cafe
Jekyll & Hyde Club
La Maison de Sade

Tibetan
Lhasa
Tibetan Yak
Tibet on Houston
Tsampa

Turkish
Hoomoos Asli
Kazan Turkish Cuisine
The Sultan
Turkish Kitchen
Turkuaz
Uskudar

Vegetarian
Candle Cafe
Caravan of Dreams
Hangawi ☆☆
Herban Kitchen
Mavalli Palace
Pongal
Tiffin
Zen Palate

Vietnamese
Blue Velvet 1929
Cyclo
Le Colonial ☆☆
Mekong
Miss Saigon
Monsoon
Nam Phuong
Nha Trang
River
Saigon Grill
Seeda Thai 2

Viennese
Danube ☆☆☆
Wallsé ☆☆

Restaurants with Special Features

Kid Friendly

Aggie's
Al Bacio
All State Cafe
Angelo & Maxie's
Anglers & Writers
Annie's
Arqua
Bali Nusa Indah
Balkh Shish Kebab
Barking Dog
Barney Greengrass
Benny's Burritos
Big Wong Restaurant
Billy's Restaurant
Blue Water Grill
Brooklyn Diner USA
Brother Jimmy's BBQ
Bryant Park Grill
Cabana Carioca
Cafe Centro
Café Con Leche
Cafe Habana
Cafe Luxembourg
Calle Ocho
Candido Pizza
Canton
Carnegie Deli
Casa Adela
Chat 'n Chew
China Fun
Churrascaria Plataforma
City Crab & Seafood Co
Coco Roco
Comfort Diner
Cosi Sandwich Bar
Cowgirl Hall of Fame
Cucina & Co.
Cyclo
Dallas BBQ
Diner
Dock's Oyster Bar
Don Peppe's
Edison Cafe
E.J.'s Luncheonette
Empire Diner
Evergreen Shanghai
Excellent Dumpling
Florent
Frank's
Fred's Restaurant
Fresco Tortilla Grill
Gabriela's
Golden Unicorn
Good Enough to Eat
Grand Sichuan
Hallo Berlin
Hard Rock Cafe
Island Burgers & Shakes
Jackson Hole
Jekyll & Hyde Club
Jezebel
Jing Fong
Joe's Shanghai
Katsu-Hama
Katz's Deli
Kelley & Ping
Knickerbocker Bar & Grill
La Cocina
La Fonda Boricua
La Fusta
La Lupe
Lombardi's
Manhattan Chili Co.
Mayrose
Mee Noodle Shop
Mi Cocina
Mickey Mantle's
Mill Korean
Miss Saigon
Mona Lisa Gourmet Pizza
Monsoon
Naples 45
Niko's Mediterranean Grill
Nostalgias
Ocean Grill
Old Devil Moon
Old San Juan
Ollie's Noodle Shop
Oyster Bar
Palacinka
Pan Pan Restaurant
Park View at the Boathouse
Pascalou
Pastrami Queen
Patsy's Pizzeria
Penang
Pepe Verde
Persepolis
Pig Heaven
Pintaile's Pizza
Pintxos
Polistina's
Popover Cafe
Prime Burger
Rafina
Rain
Redeye Grill
Republic
Rinconcito Peruano
Riodizio
River
Royal Kebab
Ruth's Chris
Saigon Grill
Sal's and Carmine's Pizza
Sarabeth's
Second Ave. Kosher Deli
Shabu-Tatsu
Shanghai Tang
Shopsin's General Store
Shun Lee West

Note: Restaurants in ***boldface italics*** are Eric Asimov's choices for the best inexpensive restaurants in New York

Silver Swan
Smith & Wollensky
Sosa Borella
Soup Kitchen Int'l
Spazzia
Stage Deli
Supreme Macaroni Co.
Sylvia's
Tai Hong Lau
Taka
Taqueria de Mexico
Tavern on the Green
Tennessee Mountain
The Saloon
Tortilla Flats Restaurant
Totonno Pizzeria
Tribeca Grill
Triple Eight Palace
Tuscan Square
Uncle George's
Vatan
Veselka
Vinegar Factory
Virgil's Real BBQ
Walker's
Wollensky's Grill
Wu Liang Ye
Ya Bowl
Yura & Co.
Zito's East

Outdoor Dining
Aesop's Tables
Al Dente
Amarone
American Park
Antonio Restaurant
Arturo's Pizzeria
Avenue
Bali Nusa Indah
Bar Pitti
Barking Dog
Ben Benson's
Benny's Burritos
Bice
Bistrot Margot
Blue Water Grill
Boat Basin Cafe
Bottino
Brasserie Centrale
Brunetta's
Bryant Park Grill
Butterfield 81
Cafe Asean
Cafe Centro
Cafe Colonial
Café Con Leche
Cafe Gitane
Candela Restaurant
Candido Pizza
Capsouto Frères
Caravan of Dreams
Chat 'n Chew
Chez Jacqueline
Choshi

Circus
Citrus Bar & Grill
Coffee Shop
Da Nico
Da Silvano
Danal
Downtown
Druids
El Teddy's
Elvie's Turo-Turo
Emily's
Empire Diner
F.illi Ponte
Fish
Florent
Fred's
French Roast Cafe
Fresco Tortilla Grill
Galaxy
Grano Trattoria
Hallo Berlin
Harvest
Herban Kitchen
Hourglass Tavern
I Coppi
I Trulli
Isola
Jackson Hole
Jean Claude
Jules
Julian's
Kana
La Goulue
La Pizza Fresca
Layla
Le Jardin Bistro
Le Madeleine
Le Madri
Le Max
Lemongrass Grill
Lento's
Le Petit Hulot
Le Refuge
Les Halles
Le Singe Vert
Le Tableau
Le Taxi
Lipstick Cafe
Lola
Lombardi's
Lundy Bros.
Luxia
Luzia's
Mad.28
Maloney & Porcelli
Marichu
Max & Moritz
Medusa
Mekong
Meli Melo
Meridiana
Mi Cocina
Mickey Mantle's
Miss Saigon
Moustache

Naples 45
New World Grill
Noho Star
Novitá
Ocean Grill
Old San Juan
Orologio
Pampa
Pao
Paola's
Park View
Patois
Persepolis
Pete's Tavern
Pisces
Pitchoune
Po
Pongal
Provence
Puttanesca
Quilty's
Radio Perfecto
Raoul's
Remi
Republic
Rialto
Riodizio
Roettele A.G.
Sal Anthony's
Salaam Café
The Saloon
San Pietro
Savore
Sel et Poivre
Sevilla
Shaffer City Oyster Bar
Silver Swan
Spazzia
St. Dymphna's
Stage Deli

Sushi Zen
Tai Hong Lau
Tanti Baci
Tavern on the Green
Three of Cups
Time Cafe
Tortilla Flats
Tribeca Grill
Trionfo Ristorante
Trois Canards
Tsunami
Uncle George's
Verbena
Veselka
Vespa Cibobuono
Vico
Vince & Eddie's
Vinegar Factory
Virage
Vong
Walker's
Water Club
Willow
Ya Bowl
Yaffa's T-Room
Zocalo

Good Views
14 Wall Street
American Park
Bali Nusa Indah
Boat Basin Cafe
Candela Restaurant
Hudson River Club
Park View at the Boathouse
Rainbow Grill
Restaurant Above
River Cafe
Top of the Tower
Water Club

Note: Restaurants in **boldface italics** are Eric Asimov's choices for the best inexpensive restaurants in New York

469